The Encyclopedia of
WOODWORKING

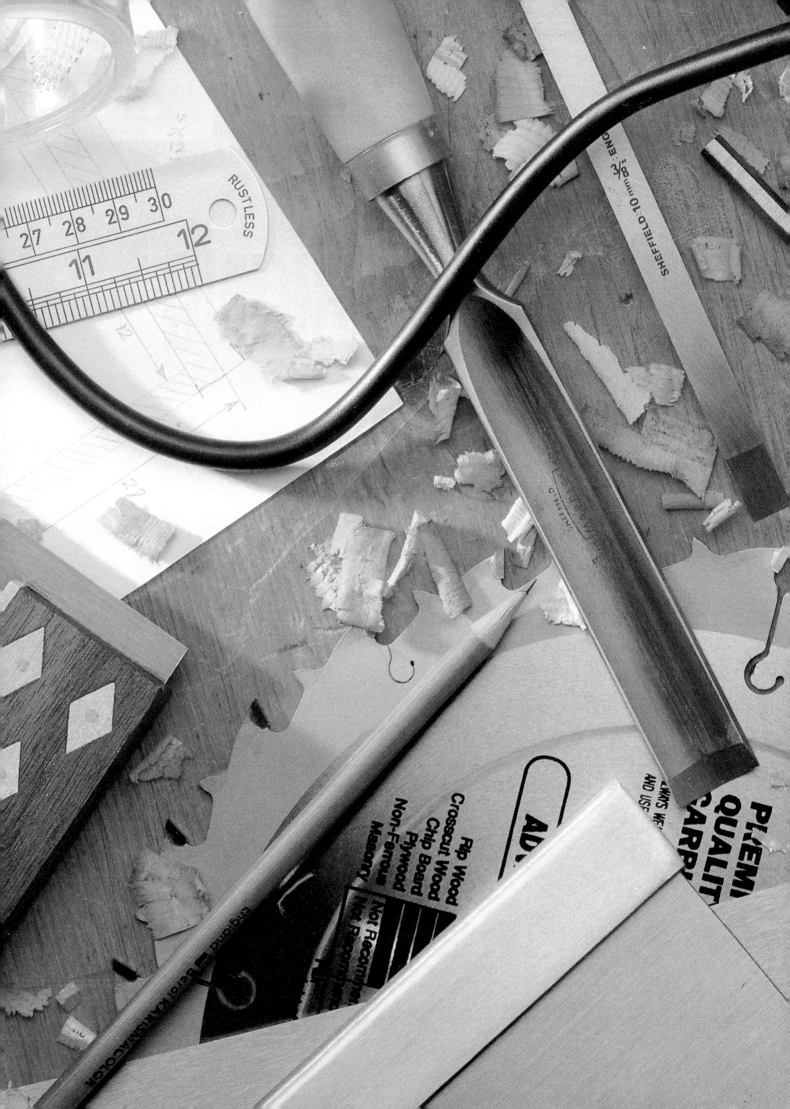

The Encyclopedia of
WOODWORKING

The essential reference guide for the home woodworker

**Consultant Editor
Mark Ramuz**

Oceana

AN OCEANA BOOK

This book is produced by
Oceana Books
6 Blundell Street
London
N7 9BH

Copyright © 2001 Quantum Publishing Ltd

This edition printed 2003

ISBN 0-681-78109-2

QUMCHOP

Designer: Peter Laws
Editor: Yvonne Worth
Project Editor: Maria Costantino
Editorial Manager: Julie Oughton

Manufactured in Singapore by
United Graphics Pte Ltd

Printed in China by
Leefung-Asco Printers Ltd.

PUBLISHER'S NOTE
Woodworking can be dangerous. Always read safety instructions
before using any hand or power tools, and exercise caution at all
times. As far as the methods and techniques mentioned in this
book are concerned, all statements, information, and advice
given are believed to be accurate. However, neither the
author, copyright holder, nor the publisher can
accept any legal liability for errors or
omissions.

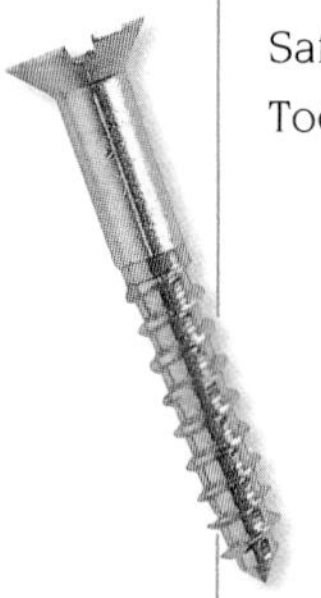

CONTENTS

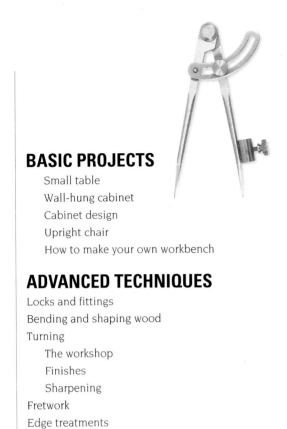

INTRODUCTION

The "Encyclopedia of Woodworking" is an essential reference guide for the home woodworker. Packed with step-by-step instructions, photographs, and illustrations, it provides the maximum practical help to those new to this absorbing craft. Naturally, any such guide can only summarize the basics of certain more specialist techniques, but you will find all you need to at least get you started in one of the most rewarding of hobbies.

Wood is a very versatile material—it can be painted, sanded and more. Added to this, when a piece of furniture breaks (even after years of use), or a favorite carving is chipped, it can usually be repaired.

To help the reader understand how to get the best out of this wonderful raw material, the encyclopedia begins with a section on the properties of the most common woodworking lumbers and describes how a living tree is converted into boards and blanks. Only hands-on experience will teach you how to deal with the demands of each new project, to recognize the different woods (what each looks like, how each behaves, and how much each is likely to cost), and to become familiar with the various types of boards on the market and their distinguishing characteristics.

As well as being able to choose the right lumber for the job, it is essential to understand the bewildering number of hand and power tools on offer in hardware stores and catalogs. Many of these will not be needed by the novice woodworker, but it is still important to understand what these tools can do and know what is available. The second section covers the tools, their uses, and setting up and organizing your own workshop.

Following on is a "Basic techniques" section, beginning with a guide to drawing up and reading plans—an essential first step in putting together even the most basic project. Step-by-step photography guides the reader through the techniques of sawing, planing, paring, and many other essential processes.

One of the biggest challenges for the new woodworker is making accurate joints. It is impossible to create an attractive piece of furniture without joining pieces of wood. The section entitled, "Making joints" guides the reader through the range of essential joints as well as explaining the uses for each one.

A poor woodworking project can never be improved with a good finish, but learning how to seal, protect, and decorate your latest project can be equally as important as the actual making itself. Traditional woodworking finishes such as French polishing and oil finishes are described in concise, easy-to-grasp terms. Advice on how to get the best from varnishes and waxes are given for working on more contemporary pieces.

Practice is, naturally, the best way to hone your new skills, and the five simple projects covered on pages 225-256 take you through every step of building a small table, a wall-hung cabinet, nursery furniture, an upright chair, and a workbench. Full cutting lists, combined with step-by-step pictures of each stage of construction, lead you through to completion.

The second half of this encyclopedia builds on the skills learned in the first half, giving suggestions for those wanting to take on more challenging techniques, such as veneering, fretwork, carving, laminating, and turning. Here, you are given the opportunity to develop your abilities and tackle more creative pieces. Just as in the earlier projects, the construction is accompanied by advanced finishing techniques, with a brief description of everything from gilding and distressing to liming and complex faux finishes—all backed up with plenty of helpful tips.

More advanced projects provide a challenge by combining many of the skills from both sections of the book. Remember, however, that even the most complex desk or cabinet is actually composed of a number of comparatively simple joints and subassemblies. The book covers troubleshooting guides to help you through the more demanding stages.

Many people turn to woodworking not to create new things, but to put right the old, and no book on woodwork would be complete

without a section on repairs and restoration. This encyclopedia is no exception, offering an essential guide to furniture repair, from gentle cleaning of a polished surface to full-scale rebuilds of large pieces of furniture. Tips from professionals show you how to use tricks of the trade to transform even the most dilapidated junkyard find.

Even the seasoned woodworker makes mistakes from time to time, and the final section, "Correcting mistakes" shows you the best ways to rectify or disguise your errors.

Safety

Remember, woodworking can be a dangerous activity. Even a hand tool can quickly sever a nerve or tendon, with disastrous results—a table saw or other power tool designed to cut wood can instantly remove a finger or worse.

Always exercise extreme caution when using any power tool. Read the instruction manuals provided by the manufacturer, paying particular attention to safety warnings. Use the guards and other safety devices designed for the tool. Do not work off balance or reach over a tool, and always keep your work area clean to minimize the chances of tripping over an electric cord or piece of scrap. Remove rings and other jewelry. If you have long hair, then tie it back and make sure cuffs and other pieces of clothing are fastened out of the way. Always wear eye protection and, when necessary, a dust mask. Wood and sheet material dust can be very harmful to your lungs—an efficient dust extraction system is an essential first step in establishing a safe workshop.

Take care of yourself, your tools, and your working environment and you'll enjoy many pleasurable hours exploring the fascinating craft of woodworking.

GETTING STARTED

THE NATURE OF WOOD

Wood is a natural material—its very character and feel provide ample encouragement to budding wood-workers to take up the craft. It is essential to have an understanding of the various types of wood and their different properties for effective and enjoyable working.

Tree growth

The tree is a living organism that performs functions essential to mankind —from oxygenating the planet to providing shelter and a variety of products. Water is drawn in through the roots and carbon dioxide is absorbed by the leaves, which then emit oxygen. Food is transmitted throughout the system.

heartwood

sapwood

Annual growth

The tree grows by adding to its girth each year, as well as to its height and breadth. At the center of the trunk is the pith, or medulla—the remains of the sapling from which the tree grew. Then follows a series of annual rings, each depicting the growth cycle— normally of one year. Horizontal rays radiate from the center. On the outside, the cambium layer forms new wood, and the bast and the bark ensure annual growth and protection.

Heartwood and sapwood

The wood near the center of the trunk, the heartwood, carries little food—it represents the structural support of the tree. The outer area transmits food and is called the sapwood. In some species, only the heartwood is used for woodwork since the sapwood is weak and prone to fungal and insect attack, while in others there is little difference, other than color, between the two.

Softwoods and hardwoods

These terms often cause confusion since they refer to the botanical characteristics of the tree. Some "hardwoods" are very soft—balsa wood, for example—while some "soft-woods" can be quite hard—yew is botanically a softwood.

Softwoods

Softwoods come from coniferous trees with needles instead of leaves, which tend to remain during winter. Softwoods are composed of tracheids—long cells where food and moisture are transmitted between the sides of adjacent cell walls. Softwoods may have vessels or pores, but these are generally channels for resin.

Hardwoods

Hardwoods come from deciduous trees—their leaves are shed in temperate climates each winter. The tree structure is made from long tubular vessels or pores that allow the tree to conduct moisture and food vertically. The horizontal rays carry food in a radial direction. Hardwood can be either ring porous or diffuse porous. Ring porous trees show clear annual rings marking the seasons, while diffuse porous trees live in areas where growth is year-round.

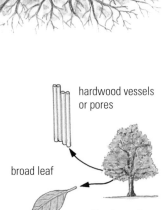

long grain

pith or medulla

rays

annual rings

cambium and bark

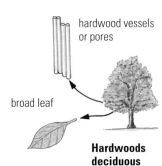

needles

tracheid cells

Softwoods coniferous

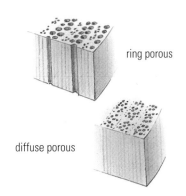

hardwood vessels or pores

broad leaf

Hardwoods deciduous

ring porous

diffuse porous

Conversion

Lumber is extracted from the forest as logs, mainly the trunk. Branch wood cannot usually be used, since its structure has stresses and strains present. The log is sawed into boards. Several different arrangements of cuts are used. The most common is where the trunk is simply cut into a series of planks. However, the plank cut at the top tends to bow as it dries, and the annual rings try to straighten. Lumber cut radially is very stable; therefore, logs are often cut radially or quartersawed.

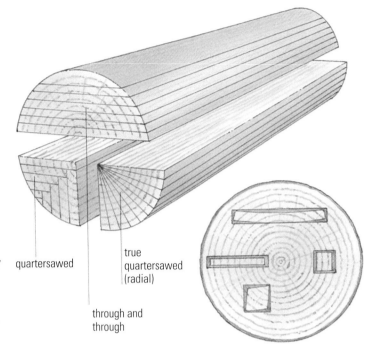

quartersawed

true quartersawed (radial)

through and through

Restacking the boards
When the planks have been cut, it is necessary to restack them in the order they were cut, with spacers between each board to allow air to circulate. These spacers, called sticks, are always placed vertically above one another (below).

Seasoning

Converted lumber still has moisture in the pores and cells, which must be removed before the wood can be used. The wood is therefore dried or seasoned and the moisture content reduced to an acceptable level. For lumber used in the open, moisture content of approximately 16 percent is suitable. However, if it is to be used indoors, it must be further reduced, down to 8 percent (or even less in some cases).

Air drying is the traditional method of seasoning. The cut log is placed in stick out in the open, with some form of cover over it. As a general rule, it takes one year for every 1in (25mm) of thickness of the converted planks. This method will not reduce moisture to less than approximately 16 percent, and for interior work the boards have to be mechanically dried.

The modern method of drying is by putting the lumber in kilns. The lumber in stick is placed on carts and put into the kiln—a large oven in which the temperature and humidity are precisely controlled. The kiln cycle starts with high humidity which is carefully changed to ensure that the lumber is dried at the correct rate. Lumber can be damaged if the wrong kiln schedule is used.

A recently-developed method, for small, valuable pieces of exotic wood, often used by wood turners, is to soak the wood in PEG (Polyethelene Glycol), which chemically converts the moisture.

Faults in wood

Some lumbers have a natural resistance to fungal and insect attack (i.e. teak), but others need treatment by preservatives to give the wood some resistance. Generally, do not use wood in damp conditions where it may be vulnerable to attack.

Faults may be found due to bad felling, poor seasoning, or erratic grain which causes trouble when wood is sawed. Lumber may have shakes, checking, splits, be bowed or twisted. When the board still has bark, it is called waney edged: it is advisable often with some lumber to remove the bark and sapwood since these attract pests—common in softwoods. Dead knots can be a problem because they will fall out, and such lumber should not be used in structural situations. In certain pieces of lumber live knots add to the unusual feature of the wood.

ABOVE: The various different ways in which boards can shrink and warp depending on the direction of the grain.

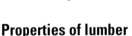

Properties of lumber

Grain in some lumbers is straight and even, but you will find cross-grain that crosses in spirals around the tree, or interlocked grain where the spirals go different ways. Cross- and interlocked grains are difficult to saw, plane and finish—hence the saying "against the grain"—but it can result in attractive, unusual features. Working "with the grain" is referred to frequently throughout this book.

"Figure" is when the grain runs in different directions, where the difference between early and late growth is marked, where color is present, where there are unusual features such as curl or burl—these all contribute to interesting figure in lumber.

Texture in lumber can range from fine, where the cells are small, to an open or coarse texture, where the cells are large.

Types of wood

There are many different species of wood, and their distribution throughout the world means that you will find certain woods in your area that will serve your purposes well. The following short selection of woods is common in furnituremaking areas.

Common softwoods

Generally, softwoods are used in construction and joinery, but good quality softwoods should not be considered as being inferior to hardwoods. They have their own uses. The nomenclature is confusing, however, since their common names do not always indicate their true botanical classification.

SCOTCH PINE (Pinus species)
also known as European Redwood
Reasonable to work and has a very interesting figure. Its color matures with age and it is one of the most attractive of the softwoods.

DOUGLAS FIR (Pseudotsuga species)
Used for construction.

SITKA SPRUCE (Picea species)
Straight grain and even texture. Good to work, with a wide range of uses.

CEDAR OF LEBANON (Cedrus species)
Good to work, but main attraction is its aroma, which is said to deter moths, so is often used for making drawers.

YEW (Taxus species)
Tough and hard. Difficult to work, but the most beautiful of softwoods. Very good for fine furniture.

Common hardwoods

The following selection is arranged without any consideration of location since color will direct choice.

OAK (Quercus species)
Coarse-textured and straight-grained, with distinct rays when quartersawed.

ASH (Fraxinus species)
Tough, straight-grained, and supple, a good wood for bending, with an attractive finish. Generally white, but with dark-stained heartwood.

MAPLE (Acer species)
Fine texture, hard- and straight-grained. Popular for furniture and flooring.

BEECH (Fagus species)
Straight-grained, even-textured, reasonable to work, good for steam bending. Often used in furniture—particularly chairs.

SYCAMORE (Platanus species US, Acer species, Europe)
Fine texture, generally straight-grained (except for fiddleback grain used in musical instruments). Light in color, good in taking stain.

CHERRY (Prunus species USA)
Hard, fine-textured and straight-grained; attractive coloring, good for furniture.

MAHOGANY (Swietenia species)

Medium texture, good to work, but many species. Varies from light color and weight, easy to work, to species which are darker, heavier, and hard.

WALNUT (Juglans species)

Good to work, the better boards have attractive color and grain. A beautiful wood for all fine work.

TEAK (Tectona species)

Substitutes—Iroko (*Chlorophora* species) and Afrormosia (*Pericopsis* species). Coarse texture, but oily feel. Good to work, but hard on tools, requiring constant sharpening. Often used in 1950s and 1960s Scandinavian furniture with a simple oil finish.

ROSEWOOD (Dalbergia species)

Hard and heavy. Medium to work, but now very expensive and usually used only for small, fine work, inlay, and veneer.

EBONY (Diospyros species)

Very hard and dense, difficult to work and one of the woods nearest to the color black.

Specialist woods

Some woods have become prized for specific uses.

BOXWOOD (Buxus species)

Fine-textured, dense, and heavy. Used for quality tool handles.

JELUTONG (Dyera species)

Soft and easy to work, a very good wood for pattern making and carving.

LIGNUM VITAE (Gualacum species)

Very hard and heavy. Close interlocked grain. Difficult to work. One of the heaviest and most resistant woods. Used for mallets and lumber pulleys and bearings.

Manufactured boards

Manufactured boards have been made possible by developments in adhesive and resin technology. These boards are generally inert, so that lumber movement is no longer a problem.

Plywood: Odd numbers of veneers are glued with the grain of each sheet at right angles to its neighbor. Plywood is normally available in sheets 4ft x 8ft (1.2m x 2.4m), often with a decorative face veneer on one or both sides, which saves you having to veneer large surfaces. Plywood is made using different grades of adhesive—interior grade uses UF adhesives, while marine ply uses phenolic or Resourcinol-based adhesives.

3-ply: Commonly used for drawer bottoms and cabinet backs; thicknesses can vary from (⅛in (3mm) to ¼in (6mm). Where the center veneer is thicker than the face veneers, this is called stout heart.

Multi-ply: Available in a range of different thicknesses, used to construct furniture.

Birch ply: Used for superior performance and quality, especially when making cabinet work. It looks good on its own with the surfaces finished.

Blockboards: These are similar to plywood, except that the inner core is made of strips of wood. There are three grades, referring to

the width of the center strips. Battenboard has the widest strips of all, in excess of 1in (25mm). Blockboard has strips of ¼in to 1in (6mm to 25mm).

Particle boards: Lumber is reduced to fibers and then glued back into sheets with synthetic resins. Chipboard is used in the furniture industry and is available in several qualities.

Fiberboards: The edges of fiberboards need treating, generally by applying a solid or veneer lipping. Medium Density Fiberboard (MDF) has been developed for furniture since its edge can be surfaced (by hand or machine) and it will take polish or finish directly.

Converting wood

The size, shape, and grain pattern of the lumber that the woodworker gets to use in his workshop is, to a great extent, determined by the way the tree is sliced up, or converted. There are many traditional ways of converting lumber: the log can be plain sawed to make a stack of planks, or cut radially into quarters, and so on. Sometimes a single large-diameter log is first quartered, and then each quarter is sawed in a different way. The diagrammatic illustration below shows four methods of converting a quartered log.

Radial sawing

Also called quartersawing, this is a method of sawing roughly parallel to the medullary rays with the result that the figure rays appear on the face of every board. Certainly the radial cut produces the best boards for overall dimensional stability, but the disadvantage is that there is a great deal of waste. This method is only used for high-quality work when a choice figure is desired.

Four different methods of quartering lumber

Medullary cut

Also called riftsawing, this method is a compromise between the more wasteful radial cut and the efficient thick plank cut. Though this is a good method for obtaining all-figured wood, it is more complicated and more expensive, and the dimensions of the resulting boards are necessarily smaller.

Thick plank cut

This method gives thick planks with the minimum of waste. It is primarily a way of obtaining a mix of choice boards and ordinary structural lumber.

Plain saw

Ordinary planks are described as being plain sawed, or you might say they are sawed through-and-through, or even slash-sawed. Though we show a quarter being sawed in this way, it is more usual to run the whole trunk through so as to produce 3in (75mm) or smaller planks, with the middle-of-stack planks being the full width of the trunk. Certainly, this is the easiest and the most economical way of converting lumber, and it is good for low-grade wood. Although it does produce the widest boards, some of the boards are unstable, depending upon the position of the planks in the stack. Thus there is a big difference in the handling characteristics and in the figure of the individual boards. When a whole log is plain sawed, the boards at the top and bottom of the stack are the narrowest with almost no figure, and then successive boards show more and more figure as they approach the halfway mark across the diameter. To put it another way, the majority of the boards show the minimum of figure, hence the term "plain."

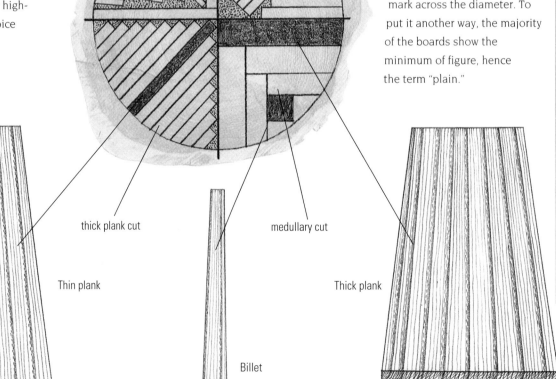

plain saw

radial sawing

thick plank cut

medullary cut

Thin plank

Billet

Thick plank

Defects to avoid

In the terms of this book, defects are classified as being either natural defects related to the tree's growth, such as disease and decay, and artificial defects that may relate to the way the wood has been cut and/or seasoned.

Decay

Although decay, such as rot and mold, does sometimes result in the wood being unusually colored or patterned, as in spalted wood, it is for the most part an indication that the wood is unusable. Best to avoid wood that in any way shows evidence of decay.

Insect attack

Insect pests can dramatically reduce the structural integrity of a piece of wood. Small, neat holes may indicate that the pest has come and gone, but for all that, a piece of wood that shows insect holes is best avoided.

Cup checking

Splits or checks that occur toward the middle of the tree around the pith are termed cup checks or shakes. The defect isn't serious in the sense that it is evidence of decay or whatever, but it does render the piece of wood less than perfect.

Star checking

Usually the result of rushed seasoning and consequent rapid shrinking, star-checked wood is best avoided if for no other reason than that the end that shows the checking has to be sawed off and wasted.

Heart checking

Heart checks are a really good indicator that the growing tree was old and shrinking from the heart. The end that shows the checks needs to be cut away; who knows how far the split runs up the wood?

Round checks

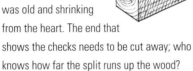

Round checks, or ring checks, at the pith of the tree seriously affect the value of the wood as they suggest that the growing tree was excessively old and/or that the growing tree was put under intense stress, such as heat, wind, or flooding. Such wood is best avoided.

Through checking

A check that extends from one surface through to another—caused by stress and/or old-age shrinkage—usually makes the wood useless.

Splits

Splits result when wood cells are torn apart. They are usually caused by careless seasoning, like too-rapid drying.

Loose knots

Loose, or unsound, knots suggest that some part of the wood is in an advanced state of decay. The problem is, of course, that loose knots are liable to fall out when the wood is used.

Waney edge

An edge of plank that shows bark is soft and generally unusable. Be aware that when you buy board widths that show bark on a waney edge, the bark will need to be cut away, resulting in narrower boards.

Tips box

Just as with solid wood, veneers will manifest many of the defects already described, including splits, holes, and decay. The best you can do is study the veneers available and then make decisions as to whether or not you can cut around the defects.

Movement in planks of wood. From left to right: springing, bowing, winding, and cupping.

Strength and qualities of wood

Woodworkers must take a natural material and cut and shape it to best effect. To this end, the woodworker must appreciate that woodworking is an equal partnership, a coming together of tools, techniques, and wood. It's no good trying to work wood with a dull tool, or to plane against the grain, or to run a chisel into end grain or in any way bully or force the wood into shape. The success of each and every procedure and technique hinges on the woodworker's understanding of how the inherent natural properties of the wood—its hardness, toughness, elasticity, durability, and so on—can be used to best effect.

Coarse-grained Honduras mahogany— not good for bending.

Hardness

Though hardwood comes from broad-leafed, deciduous trees, and softwood from evergreens, hardwood isn't necessarily harder or more difficult to work than softwood. When we describe a wood as being hard, we generally mean that the wood isn't easily dented or bruised on the end grain or face. So, for example, when a table design suggests that you build the surface from a wood that is hard, it means that you need to search out a wood that will resist surface impact. It could be a hard-surfaced softwood.

End-grain pine with clearly-defined annular rings—good for strength.

Quartersawed oak with characteristic medullary ray figure—strong and decorative.

Toughness

A tough wood is one that is difficult to split, a wood that has a lot of bending strength in relationship to its length. So, for example, English longbows were traditionally made from yew, golf club shafts from hickory, and ax handles from ash—all tough wood types that are wonderfully resistant to crushing and splitting.

Some woods are specifically chosen for their bending qualities.

Bending

Bending and toughness are in many ways similar. But while some tough woods will happily resist a long, slow bend, they might fail under what is termed a "shear impact." This being so, you must determine whether the item that you are building is going to be put under bending stress—as in a ladder—or if it is going to support a heavy weight, such as a house beam.

Splitting

Sometimes called cleavage, the splitting qualities of a piece of wood are of paramount importance. You need to know when you are cutting a joint, or designing a piece that has an area of short grain, just how much strength there is between the bundles of fibers. For example, a straight-grained softwood like pine will easily split down the length of the grain, whereas a piece of maple will resist splitting.

Durability

The qualities that make a wood last come under the heading of durability. For example, elm survives under water; larch pilings have survived for centuries; and cedar shingles seem to last forever. It is almost as if certain wood types enjoy being repeatedly wet, dried, and baked in the sun. Some woods will last for hundreds of years underground or under water, but have a short life when exposed to wind and weather.

Boxwood is extremely close, even, and dense in its grain—good for complex forms that show a lot of short grain.

Resistance

The total strength of a piece of wood when put under a load is termed the resistance. To a great extent, resistance brings together all the other qualities, including hardness, toughness, bending, and durability. The question you should ask yourself every time you select a piece of wood is "is it fit for its task?" The most reliable method of choosing wood for your window frame, or roof struts, is to determine what was used in the past.

A straight-grained wood will readily split along the grain.

DIRECTORY OF WOOD

From the many different species of trees in the world comes a huge variety of lumber of use to the woodworker for everything from delicate turnery to house construction. The following chapter describes the natural characteristics of some of the most widely-used lumbers.

Acacia melanoxylon
Family: Leguminosae
AUSTRALIAN BLACKWOOD

Where it grows
Of the hundreds of *Acacia* genus species of wattle found in India, South Africa, and South America, this is one of the most attractive. Australian blackwood, one of the largest, grows as an understory tree in forests of giant mountain ash in New South Wales, Queensland, southeastern Australia, Victoria, and Tasmania. It reaches a height of 80-100ft (25-30m), the diameter of the bole, or black wattle, is about 3ft (1m).

Appearance
The sapwood is straw-colored, the heartwood reddish-brown to almost black, with bands of golden- to dark-brown with a reddish tint. Dark-brown zones mark the growth rings. It is usually straight-grained, but with a fiddleback figure when the grain is interlocked or wavy. It is medium, even-textured, and lustrous in appearance.
Properties
Blackwood weighs about 41lb/ft³ (660kg/m³) when seasoned. A fairly heavy, dense wood with medium bending strength and stiffness, and a high crushing strength. It has good resistance to impact loads and a very good steam-bending classification. The wood dries fairly easily and is stable in service. It works satisfactorily with all tools, with a moderate blunting effect. Wattle takes nails and screws well, and absorbs stain and polish for an excellent finish. The heartwood is durable, but liable to attack by common furniture beetle and termites; the sapwood is vulnerable to powder post beetle. It is very resistant to preservative treatment.
Uses
This highly-decorative wood is used for fine furniture, cabinets, and paneling, shop fittings and interior joinery.

Acer pseudoplatanus
Family: Aceraceae
SYCAMORE

Where it grows
This tree is a native of central and southern Europe and western Asia. It grows to 105ft (35m) in height with a large, broad-domed crown, and a 5ft (1.5m) diameter bole. Known as sycamore plane, great maple (England) or plane (Scotland). Field maple (*A. campestre*) and Norway maple (*A. platanoides*) are similar; both grow in Europe.

Appearance
The sapwood and heartwood are similar; creamy-white in color with a natural luster. Slowly dried lumber changes to light tan and is known as "weathered." It is usually straight-grained, but curly or wavy grain produces a very attractive "fiddleback," or lace ray figure on quartered surfaces. The texture is fine and even.
Properties
Medium-density wood weighing about 38lb/ft³ (610kg/m³) when seasoned. It air dries rapidly, but is inclined to stain unless end stacked; it kiln dries well. There is medium movement in service. It has medium bending and crushing strength, low shock resistance, and very low stiffness, giving it very good steam-bending properties. It has a moderate blunting effect on tools and cutting edges, good nailing and gluing properties, and gives an excellent finish. Sycamore is perishable and the sapwood is liable to attack by the common furniture beetle and by *Ptilmus pectinicomis*, but it is permeable for preservation treatment.
Uses
Once used for ribs of lutes (1400s-1500s). "Fiddleback" sycamore is still used for violins. A good turnery wood (textile rollers, brush handles, domestic utensils, and food containers). It is dyed for marquetry and inlays.

Acer saccharum
Family: Aceraceae
ROCK MAPLE

Where it grows
A. saccharum and *A. nigrum*, jointly sold as rock maple, are known as hard maple (US, Canada, and UK); white maple, sapwood (US); and black maple. Rock maple is one of the most valuable wood growing east of the Rocky Mountains in Canada and in the northern and eastern states of America. Rock maple grows to 130ft (40m) tall with a diameter of 2-3ft (0.6-1m).

Appearance
The wood is creamy-white with a reddish tinge, sometimes with a dark-brown heart. It is usually straight-grained but often curly or wavy, with fine brown lines marking the growth rings on plain-sawed surfaces. The texture is even, fine, and lustrous. Pith flecks are sometimes present.
Properties
Rock maple weighs about 45lb/ft³ (720kg/m³) seasoned. It dries fairly slowly with little degrade, and there is medium movement in service. The wood is of medium density, has good bending and crushing strengths, with low stiffness, and shock resistance, and a good steam-bending classification. It has a moderate blunting effect on tools, with a tendency to create tooth vibration when sawing. Irregular grain tends to pick up when planing or molding on quartered surfaces: a reduced cutter angle is recommended. The wood has a tendency to ride on cutters and burn during endgrain working. Rock maple requires pre-boring for nailing, but glues well and polishes to an excellent finish. The wood is nondurable, liable to beetle attack, and subject to growth defects, known as pith flecks, caused by insects. The heartwood is resistant to preservation treatment but the sapwood is permeable.
Uses
Rock maple makes excellent heavy industrial flooring, for roller skating rinks, dance halls, squash courts, and bowling alleys. It is used for textile rollers, dairy and laundry equipment, butchers' blocks, piano actions, and musical instruments and sports goods. It is also a valuable turnery wood. Selected logs are peeled for "bird's-eye" figure, or sliced to produce fiddleback, curly, or blistered and mottled maple veneers for cabinets and architectural paneling.

Note: *Entries are listed alphabetically according to their Latin species name.   (S) denotes softwood.*

Araucaria angustifolia
Family: *Araucariaceae*
"BRAZILIAN PINE"(S)

Where it grows

The tree is not a true pine of the *Pinaceae* family. It grows mainly in the Brazilian state of Parana and is also found in Paraguay and northern Argentina. It is also known as "Parana pine" (UK) and is closely related to *A. araucana* "Chile pine" or Monkey puzzle tree (of no commercial importance). It grows to 131ft (40m) in height with a flat-topped crown and has a diameter of about 4ft (1.2m), with a clear, straight bole.

Appearances

The very close density of Brazilian pine, along with its almost total absence of growth rings and unusual coloring make it an attractive wood. It is mainly straight-grained and honey-colored, although dark-gray patches appear at the inner core of the heartwood, along with red streaks, which fade in time. The texture is fine and uniform.

Properties

The weight varies widely, between about 30-40lb/ft³ (480-640kg/m³) seasoned. The wood is not durable, with only medium bending and crushing strengths and very low resistance to shock loads. It is very difficult to dry, showing a marked tendency to split in the darker areas, and needs to be monitored constantly. If it is not well dried it can distort badly in service, particularly if wide boards are used. It works extremely well with all tools, and planes and molds cleanly to a very smooth finish. It glues and finishes nicely. The sapwood is liable to attack by the pinhole borer beetle and the common furniture beetle. The wood is nondurable and moderately resistant to preservation treatment, but the sapwood is permeable for preservation treatment.

Uses

This is Brazil's major export wood—only the higher grades are shipped. They are used for internal joinery, especially staircases, because of the sizes available and freedom from knots. It appears in cabinet framing, drawer sides, shop fittings, and vehicle building. Locally, it is used for joinery, furniture, turnery, sleepers, and construction work. The sizes and ease of working make Brazilian pine a good D.I.Y. wood, but the moisture needs checking carefully. It is also used for plywood manufacture and sliced for decorative veneers.

Buxus sempervirens
Family: *Buxaceae*
EUROPEAN BOXWOOD

Where it grows

This is one of the very few evergreen, broadleaved trees that occur in mild temperate climates. It grows in the UK, Europe, North Africa, the Middle East and western Asia. It is known as Abassian, Iranian, Persian, or Turkish boxwood, according to the country of origin. It is a small tree growing to a height of 20-30ft (6-9m). Imported billets are only 3-4ft (0.9-1.2m) long and only 4-8in (0.1-0.2m) in diameter.

Appearance

The wood is a pale, clear, orange-yellow color, occasionally straight-grained but often irregular, especially from small trees grown in Britain. It has a very compact, very fine and even texture.

Properties

The weight varies from 57lb/ft³ (830 to 1140kg/m³) when seasoned. Box dries very slowly, with a strong tendency to develop surface checks or split badly if dried in the round. The billets are usually soaked in a solution of common salt or urea before drying and end coatings applied: they should be converted into half-rounds and dried under covered storage conditions. It is a very dense, hard, durable wood with a high resistance to cutters, which should be kept sharp to prevent the wood from burning when boring or recessing. The irregular grain tends to tear when planing. It is an excellent turnery wood with a good steam-bending rating, high stiffness, good crushing strength, and resistance to shock loads. Pre-boring is required for nailing. It glues well, and when stained and polished gives an excellent finish. The sapwood is liable to attack by the common furniture beetle. The durable heartwood is resistant to preservative treatment.

Uses

Boxwood has an outstanding reputation for its fine, smooth texture and excellent turning properties, and is used for textile rollers, shuttles, pulley blocks, croquet mallets, and tool handles. It is also in demand for wood sculpture and carving. Specialized uses include measuring instruments, engraving blocks, parts of musical instruments, and chess pieces. It is also used for inlay lines and bandings in marquetry and reproduction and repair of period furniture.

Carpinus betulus
Family: *Betulaceae*
HORNBEAM

Where it grows

About 20 species of hornbeam grow in European northern temperate zones in rich soil on low ground. It occurs from southern Sweden to the Middle East, but the species of commercial interest grow in France, Turkey, and Iran. In Britain it is a woodland and hedgerow tree. It grows to a height of 50-80ft (15-25m), with a fluted bole that is seldom clear of branches. The trunk is usually elliptical instead of round. The diameter is 0.9-3-4ft (1.2m).

Appearance

There is no distinction between sapwood and heartwood—a dull white color marked with gray streaks and flecks caused by the broad ray structure, which produces a flecked figure on quartered surfaces. It is usually irregular or cross-grained, but has a fine, even texture.

Properties

The weight averages 47lb/ft³ (750kg/m³) when seasoned. Hornbeam dries fairly rapidly and well with little degrade, but with considerable movement in service. This heavy, dense wood has high bending and crushing strength, medium stiffness, and resistance to shock loads, and excellent shear strength and resistance to splitting. Similar to ash in toughness, it has a very good steam-bending classification. It is fairly difficult to work, as there is high resistance in cutting with a moderate blunting effect on tools. The wood finishes very smoothly, glues well, takes stain and polish easily, and can provide an excellent finish. The sapwood is liable to attack by the common furniture beetle and the heartwood is perishable but permeable for preservation treatment.

Uses

Hornbeam is an excellent turnery wood and is used especially for drumsticks, the shafts of billiard cues, and Indian clubs. It is also used for piano actions, clavichords, harpsichords, and other musical instrument parts such as violin bridges, wooden cog wheels, pulleys, millwright's work, dead-eyes, mallets, and wooden pegs. Its high resistance to wear makes it a flooring wood for light industrial use. Selected logs are sliced for decorative veneers.

Carya spp.
Family: Juglandaceae

HICKORY

Where it grows

Although more than 20 species of hickory grow in the large forests of eastern Canada and eastern states of the US, there are only four commercial species: *C. glabra* (Mill.) sweet hickory produces pignut hickory; *C. tomentosa*, mockernut hickory; *C .laciniosa*, shellbark hickory; and *C. ovata*, shagbark hickory. These four true hickories occur from Ontario in Canada to Minnesota, Florida, and Mexico in the deciduous forests. The trees vary according to species and grow from 60-120ft (18-36m) high. They have a straight, cylindrical bole, with a diameter of 2-3ft (0.6-0.9m). *C. illinoensis* is known as sweet pecan and pecan hickory; *C. aquatica* is sold as bitter pecan or water hickory.

Appearance

The very pale gray and wide sapwood, sold as "white hickory," is generally preferred to the heartwood, which is red to reddish-brown—"red hickory." It is usually straight-grained, but occasionally wavy or irregular, with a somewhat coarse texture.

Properties

The weight ranges from about 45-56lb/ft³ (700-900kg/m³) but averages 51lb/ft³ (820kg/m³) when seasoned. Hickory needs very careful drying, but is stable in service. It is very dense and has high toughness, bending, stiffness, and crushing strengths, with exceptional shock resistance. It has excellent steam-bending properties. The wood is difficult to machine, and has a moderate blunting effect on tools. It is also difficult to glue, but stains and polishes very well. Hickory is nondurable. The sapwood is susceptible to attack by the powder post beetle, and the heartwood is moderately resistant to preservation treatment.

Uses

Hickory is ideal for the handles of striking tools (such as hammer, pick, and ax handles), wheel spokes, chairs, and ladder rungs. It is a valuable sculpture and carving wood. It is used for sport equipment (golf clubs, lacrosse sticks, baseball bats, the backs of longbows, laminae in tennis rackets and skis), the tops of heavy sea-fishing rods, drumsticks, picking sticks in the textile industry, and vehicle building. It is rotary-cut for plywood faces and sliced for decorative veneers.

Castanea sativa
Family: Fagaceae

EUROPEAN CHESTNUT

Where it grows

This stately tree is a native of southwest Europe, and grows in Britain, France, Germany, North Africa, and western Asia. In favorable conditions of growth, it reaches a height of about 100ft (30m) or more, and has a diameter of 5ft (1.5m). In less favorable sites the short bole branches into several limbs. It is known as Spanish chestnut or European chestnut.

Appearance

The heartwood is a straw-to-brown color resembling oak, distinct from the narrow sapwood. The wood has prominent growth rings but finer rays, so it does not have the silver grain figure of oak on quartered surfaces. The grain is straight but often spiral, especially from mature trees, and has a coarse texture. Many logs are subject to cupping or ring shakes.

Properties

The weight of European chestnut averages about 34lb/ft³ (540kg/m³) when seasoned. It is quite difficult to air dry as it retains moisture in patches and tends to collapse or honeycomb; it does not respond well to kiln reconditioning. Its acidic character tends to corrode iron fastenings in damp conditions, and tannin in the wood causes blue-black stains to appear when it is in contact with iron or iron compounds. It is a medium-density wood, possessing low bending strength, very low stiffness, and shock resistance, and medium crushing strength. Air-dried wood has a good bending rating if free from knots. It works satisfactorily with both hand and machine tools, to which it offers only a slight blunting effect. It has good screw- and nail-holding properties, glues well, and stains and polishes to an excellent finish. The sapwood is susceptible to attack by the powder post beetle and the common furniture beetle. The heartwood is durable and extremely resistant to preservation treatment.

Uses

This is used as a substitute for oak in furniture, also for coffin boards, domestic woodware, kitchen utensils and turnery for walking sticks, umbrella handles, bowls, and so on. It is cleft for fencing and gates. Staves are used for casks for oils, fats, fruit juices, and wines. Selected logs are sliced for decorative veneers.

Cedrus spp.
Family: Pinaceae

CEDAR(S)

Where it grows

King Solomon built his temple with cedar from Mount Lebanon. The *Cedrus* species are the true cedars and should not be confused with other softwoods and hardwoods called "cedar" due to their fragrant scent. *C. atlanaca* (Endl.) Carr, Atlas cedar, Atlantic cedar occurs in Algeria and Morocco, *C. deodara* (Roxb.) G. Don produces deodar cedar from the western Himalayas, and is an important tree in India, *C. libani*, A. Rich produces cedar of Lebanon. The deodar grows to a height of about 200ft (61m) with a diameter of about 7ft (2.1m) while Atlantic and Lebanon cedars vary from 120-150ft (36.5-45.5m) tall, and up to 5ft (1.5m) in diameter. Parkland woods have a low, flattened crown with large, spreading branches near the ground.

Appearance

The resinous heartwood with its strong cedar odor, is light brown in color with a prominent growth-ring figure. Deodar cedar is straight-grained, but Atlantic and Lebanon cedars are usually knotty, with much grain disturbance. These also tend to produce pockets of ingrowing bark in the wood. The texture is fairly fine.

Properties

Weight averages about 35lb/ft³ (560kg/m³) when seasoned. The wood dries easily, with medium movement in use. It has medium bending strength, but is low in other strength properties, and has a poor steam-bending classification due to resin exudation. Cedar works easily with all tools, with only slight blunting effect on cutters. The large knots and ingrowing bark may cause problems in machining and cutters should be kept sharp. This durable wood has good holding properties, and stains, varnishes, paints, or polishes to a good finish. The sapwood is susceptible to attack by the pinhole borer and longhorn beetle, but the heartwood is resistant to preservative treatment. The sapwood varies from moderately resistant to permeable.

Uses

The best grades are used for furniture, interior joinery, and doors. Lower grades are used for sleepers, bridge, and house construction. Knotty material is used for garden furniture. Selected logs are used to make decorative veneers for cabinets and paneling.

Chlorophora excelsa
Family: Moraceae
IROKO

Where it grows
This species grows in the moist semi-deciduous forests of tropical Africa—from Sierra Leone in the west to Tanzania in the east. *C. regia*, A. Chév. grows in West Africa, and occurs from Senegal to Ghana. It is also known as mvule (East Africa), odum (Ghana and Ivory Coast), kambala (Congo-Kinshasa), tule or intule (Mozambique), and moreira (Angola). *C. excelsa* reaches 160ft (50m) in height, with a diameter of about 8-9ft (2.5m); the bole is clear and cylindrical up to 70ft (21m) or more. *C. regia* is not quite so tall.

Appearance
The pale sapwood is clearly defined from the yellow-brown colored heartwood, which matures to a deeper brown with lighter vessel lines. The grain is typically interlocked and sometimes irregular.
Properties
When seasoned, iroko weighs about 40lb/ft³ (640kg/m³). The wood dries well and fairly rapidly, with some degrade. This durable, medium-density wood is stable in use, has medium bending and crushing strengths, low stiffness, and shock resistance, and a moderate bending rating. Hard deposits of calcium carbonate known as "stone" are often hidden in the grain and only detectable from the darker surrounding wood. They can severely damage the cutting edges of tools, and tipped or hardened saw teeth are required. The fine machining dust can cause nasal and skin irritation. Nailing or screwing and gluing are satisfactory. When filled, it provides an excellent finish. It is susceptible to attack by the powder post beetle. The wood is very durable and extremely resistant to preservation treatment, but the sapwood is classed as permeable.
Uses
Iroko is used for similar purposes to, and instead of, teak, but lacks teak's greasy feel. It is valued for all high-class joinery, counters, and bench tops. It is ideal for sculpture, wood carving, and turnery. It is used in ship, boat, and vehicle building (but not for bent work), and as structural lumber for piling, marine work, and park benches. It is used for domestic parquet flooring where underfloor heating is used. Logs are rotary cut for plywood and sliced for decorative veneers.

Chloroxylon swietenia
Family: Rutaceae
SATINWOOD

Where it grows
This is a small- to medium-sized tree that reaches its best development in Sri Lanka, but also occurs in central and southern India. It is also known as East Indian satinwood (US, UK); burutu (Sri Lanka); and bhera, behra or mutirai (India). It grows to 45-50ft (14-15m) tall and has a diameter of about 1ft (0.3m) or more, with a cylindrical bole up to around 10ft (3m).

Appearance
There is very little distinction between the sapwood color and the heartwood, which is a beautiful golden yellow. The inner heartwood matures into a slightly darker golden brown. The grain is narrowly interlocked, sometimes wavy or variegated, producing roe or narrow ribbon-striped figure on quartered surfaces. It is often broken-striped, or with "bee's wing cross-mottled" figure. Gum rings can develop thin dark veins on flat-sawed surfaces. The wood is lustrous and fragrant; the texture is fine and very even.
Properties
The average weight is about 61lb/ft³ (980kg/m³) seasoned. The wood should be allowed to air dry slowly to avoid a tendency to surface cracking and distortion, but it kiln dries well with little degrade and is stable in service. This heavy, dense wood has high bending and crushing strengths, medium stiffness, and low shock resistance, but strength is of little importance for the end-uses of this lumber. It is fairly difficult to work with machinery and has a moderate blunting effect on cutting edges. Nailing requires pre-boring. It is a difficult wood to glue, but takes stain and polishes to an excellent finish when filled. The wood is durable, and extremely resistant to preservative treatment.
Uses
Ever since the "Golden Age of Satinwood" this wood has been highly valued for luxury cabinets, fine furnituremaking, and interior joinery. It is excellent for turnery, for the backs and handles of hairbrushes, and is also used for jute bobbins. It appears in paneling in shop fittings, and in the manufacture of traditional inlay motifs, lines, and bandings. Selected logs are sliced to produce extremely attractive decorative veneers with a range of ribbon-striped or mottled-surface figure.

Dalbergia spp.
Family: Leguminosae
ROSEWOOD (BRAZILIAN and HONDURAS)

Where it grows
Brazilian rosewood has been one of the world's most treasured woods for centuries. *Dalbergia nigra*, Fr., All. is sadly becoming rare. It is also known as Bahia rosewood or Rio rosewood in the US and UK, and as jacaranda in Brazil; it grows to a height of about 125ft (38m) and the bole is irregular. When the sapwood is removed, the heartwood is 1½ft (0.5m) in diameter. *Dalbergia stevensonii*, Standl. produces Honduras rosewood known as nogaed, and grows to 50-100ft (15-30m in height and 3ft (1m) in diameter.

Appearance
The heartwood of Brazilian rosewood is a rich brown color with variegated streaks of golden- to chocolate-brown and from violet to purple-black, sharply demarcated from the almost cream-colored sapwood. The grain is mostly straight to wavy, the texture coarse, oily, and gritty to the touch, and the wood has a mildly fragrant odor. Honduras rosewood has pinkish to purple-brown heartwood with irregular black markings; it is straight-grained and has a medium-to-fine texture.
Properties
Brazilian rosewood weighs 53lb/ft³ (850kg/m³) when seasoned, and Honduras rosewood weighs around 58-68lb/ft³ (930-1100kg/m³). Both woods air dry fairly slowly, with a marked tendency to check, but are stable in service. They possess high strength in all categories, but are low in stiffness, and have good steam-bending ratings. They are not unduly difficult to work, but have a severe blunting effect on cutting edges. Gluing is no problem if epoxy resin adhesives are used. A smooth, lustrous oil finish can be achieved. Both species are very durable, and the heartwood of both is extremely resistant to preservative treatment.
Uses
For more than 200 years, rosewoods (solid and veneer) have been prized for quality furniture- and cabinetmaking, for shop fittings, boardroom paneling, furniture, piano cases, and billiard tables. It is in demand for wood carving, sculpture, and turnery. Specialized uses include musical instrument fingerboards, percussion bars for xylophones, or marimba keys. Selected logs are sliced for highly-decorative veneers.

Dalbergia frutescens
Family: Leguminosae

BRAZILIAN TULIPWOOD

Where it grows

This small, often misshapen tree grows in northeast Brazil and around Bahia and Pernambuco. It is exported in small billets without sapwood 2-4ft (0.6-1.2m) long and 2-8in (0.06-0.2m) diameter. It is also known as pau rosa, jacaranda rosa, and pau de fuso (Brazil), pinkwood (US), and bois de rose (France). It is not to be confused with the tulip tree, *Liriomodendron tulipifera*.

Appearance

The very attractive pink-yellow heartwood has a pronounced striped, variegated figure in shades of violet-red, salmon pink, and rose red. In effect, the coloring of a red-and-yellow tulip blossom is reproduced by this beautiful wood. As it matures, it tends to lose its original vividness, but it remains a strikingly beautiful wood. The grain is usually interlocked and irregular because of its twisted growth, with a medium to fine texture and a pleasantly mild, fragrant scent.

Properties

The heartwood weighs about 60lb/ft³ (960kg/m³) when seasoned. It dries fairly easily and is stable in use. It is a very hard, dense, and compact wood and liable to split after conversion. It is somewhat wasteful in conversion as it is extremely hard to work, it is fissile and tends to splinter. There is severe blunting of cutting edges. It also requires pre-boring for screwing or nailing, but it glues well. The wood possesses a very high natural luster and provides an excellent finish. It is nondurable and resists insect and fungal attacks, but is highly resistant to preservative treatment.

Uses

This historical cabinet wood was known as bois de rose and used extensively in the furniture of the French kings Louis XV and XVI, and classical English furniture of the 1700s. The billets are usually saw-cut for decorative panel cross-bandings and marquetry inlay bandings in the restoration and repair of antiques. It is used in Brazil as a turnery wood for brushbacks, and for marimba keys, caskets, jewelry boxes, and fancy goods.

Diospyros spp.
Family: Ebenaceae

AFRICAN EBONY

Where it grows

The name ebony covers all species of *Diospyros* with predominantly black heartwood. African ebony includes *D. crassiflora*, Hiern, and *D. piscatoria*, Gurke, which occurs mostly in southern Nigeria, Ghana, Cameroon, and Congo-Kinshasa. It is named after its country or port of origin, e.g. Cameroon ebony, Knbi ebony, Gabon ebony, Madagascar ebony, or Nigerian ebony. "White ebony" refers to the sapwood. Small to medium in size, the tree grows to 50-60ft (15-18m) with a diameter of about 2ft (0.6m). It is exported as short billets.

Appearance

Since ancient Eygptian times, the black heartwood of ebony has been in great demand. *D. crassiflora* is considered to be the most jet-black. The other species have a very attractive black- and dark-brown-striped heartwood. It is usually straight-grained to slightly interlocked or curly, and the texture is fine and even.

Properties

This lumber weighs about 64lb/ft³ (1030kg/m³) when seasoned. The wood air dries fairly rapidly but is liable to surface checking, but kiln drying produces very little degrade. The wood is very stable in service. It is very dense, has very high strength properties in all categories, and a good steam-bending rating. Ebony is difficult to work with either hand or machine tools, as there is a severe blunting of edges. It is also inclined to be brittle, and needs a reduced cutting angle when planing the curly grain of quartered stock. It requires pre-boring for screwing or nailing. The heartwood requires care in gluing, but can be polished to a beautiful finish. The heartwood is very durable and extremely resistant to preservative treatment.

Uses

Ebony has always been used for sculpture and carving, and is an excellent turnery wood (tool handles, cutlery, pocket knives). It appears as door knobs, brushbacks, ends of billiard cues, and tee-square facings. Other uses include piano/organ keys, organ stops, violin fingerboards and pegs, bagpipe chanters, castanets, and guitar backs and sides. It is used for luxury cabinet work, marquetry, and inlay lines and bandings, and is saw-cut into veneers for antique repairs.

Dyera costulata
Family: Apocynaceae

JELUTONG

Where it grows

The tree is widely distributed throughout Malaysia and in the Indonesian islands of Sumatra and East Kalimantan. It grows to a substantial size, up to 200ft (60m) in height, with straight, cylindrical boles up to 90ft (27m) long with a diameter of 8ft (2.5m).

Appearance

Both the sapwood and heartwood are the same creamy-white color when first cut, maturing to a pale straw color on exposure, often stained by fungi after the tree has been tapped for latex. The wood is plain, almost straight-grained, with a fine and even texture.

Properties

This figureless wood is very lustrous, but contains slit-like radial latex passages on tangential surfaces, in clusters or rows about 3ft (1m) apart. These passages or canals, which appear lens-shaped on flat-sawed surfaces, about ¼in (6mm) wide and ½in (12mm) long, rule out the possibility of using jelutong where sizable pieces are required or where appearance is important. These defects are eliminated in conversion to relatively smaller dimensions. The weight is about 29lb/ft³ (460kg/m³) when seasoned. The wood dries fairly easily without degrade, but is difficult to dry in thick stock without staining. There is little shrinkage in service. This soft, weak, rather brittle wood is perish-able, with low strength in most categories and a poor steam-bending classification. The wood works easily with all tools with only a slight blunting effect, and provides a smooth surface, taking screws and nails without difficulty. It can be glued easily, takes stain well and can be polished or varnished to a good finish. It is nondurable, susceptible to attack by powder post beetle, but permeable for preservative treatment.

Uses

Ease of working makes jelutong an excellent wood for sculpture, carving, patternmaking, architectural models, drawing boards, clogs, and handicraft work. It has specialized uses for battery separators and match splints, lightweight partitions, and some interior joinery and fitment parts. Logs can be rotary cut for corestock for flush doors, plywood, and laminated boards. The latex is extracted for chewinggum manufacture.

Entandrophragma cylindricum
Family: Meliaceae
SAPELE

Where it grows
Sapele grows widely in the tropical rain forests of West, Central, and East Africa, from the Ivory Coast through Ghana and Nigeria to the Cameroons, and eastward to Uganda, Congo-Kinshasa, and Tanzania. It is known as aboudikro on the Ivory Coast. It grows to 150-200ft (45-60m) in height with a diameter of about 3ft (1m), and a clean bole for 100ft (30m).

Appearance
The narrow sapwood is pale yellow-white and the heartwood is salmon pink when freshly cut, maturing into reddish-brown. It has a closely-interlocked grain, resulting in a pronounced and regular pencil-striped or roe figure on quartered surfaces. Wavy grain yields a highly-decorative fiddleback or mottled figure with a fine and even texture.

Properties
Weight is 35-43lb/ft³ (560-690kg/m³), averaging about 39lb/ft³ (620kg/m³) when seasoned. The wood dries fairly rapidly, with a marked tendency to distort. There is medium movement in service. Sapele has medium density, bending, and shock resistance, high crushing strength and low stiffness, and a poor steam-bending rating. It works fairly well with both hand and machine tools, with moderate blunting of cutting edges caused by the interlocked grain. Nailing and gluing are satisfactory, and care is required when staining. When filled the surface can be brought to an excellent finish. The sapwood is susceptible to attack by powder post beetle and moderately resistant to impregnation. The heartwood is moderately durable but extremely resistant to preservative treatment.

Uses
Sapele enjoys a worldwide reputation as a handsome wood for high-quality furniture and cabinetmaking, interior and exterior joinery, window frames, shop, office, and bank fitting, countertops, and solid doors. It is widely used for boat and vehicle building, and for piano cases and sports goods. The wood is ideal for decorative flooring for domestic and public buildings. Logs are rotary cut for plywood and selected logs sliced for quartered ribbon-striped decorative veneers, used in cabinets and paneling.

Fagus spp.
Family: Fagaceae
BEECH

Where it grows
Beech grows in the northern temperate regions of Europe, Canada and the US, western Asia, Japan, and northern Africa. It is known as "the Mother of the Forest" because other hardwoods in mixed, broad-leaved forests would have a struggle to survive without it: its leaf drip kills weeds and leaf fall provides rich humus for the soil. *F. sylvatica*, L. produces European beech; *F. grandifolia*, Ehrh., American beech, *F. orientalis*, Lipsky, Turkish beech; and *F. crenata*, Bl., Japanese beech. Each is named after its country of origin. They grow to an average height of 150ft (45m), with a diameter of about 4ft (1.2m).

Appearance
The wood is very pale cream to pinkish-brown, and is often "weathered" to a deep reddish-bronze brown after steaming. It is typically straight-grained with broad rays, and has a fine, even texture.

Properties
Japanese beech, the lightest, weighs 39lb/ft³ (620kg/m³), Slavonian beech weighs about 42lb/ft³ (670kg/m³), European beech 45lb/ft³ (720kg/m³) and American beech 46lb/ft³ (740kg/m³) when seasoned. Special care is needed in drying as it dries fairly rapidly and well but is moderately refractory and shrinks in service. The wood has medium strength in bending, stiffness, and shock resistance, and high crushing strength, with a high steam-bending rating. It works readily with all tools and has good holding properties, glues easily, and can be brought to an excellent finish. The heartwood is perishable and susceptible to attack by the common furniture beetle and death watch beetle. The sapwood is affected by the longhorn beetle. Beech is classified as permeable for preservative treatment.

Uses
Beech is perhaps the most popular general purpose wood—furniture, interior, and (when treated) exterior joinery. It is a turnery wood for tool handles, brush-backs, domestic woodware, sports goods, musical instrument parts, domestic flooring. It is used for bent work and cooperage, rotary cut for utility plywood and corestock, and sliced for some decorative veneers.

Fraxinus spp.
Family: Oleaceae
ASH

Where it grows
Ash thrives throughout North America, Europe, and Japan. *F. americana*, L. is known as white ash (Canada), *F. Pennsylvania*, Marsh., American ash, is known as green ash (US) or red ash (Canada), *F. exclesior*, L., European ash, is named after the country of origin as English, French, Polish, Slavonian, and so on in the UK. The tree grows to a height of 80-120ft (25-36m), with a diameter of 2-5ft (0.6-1.5m).

Appearance
American ash is gray-brown in color with a reddish tinge. European ash is cream white to light brown, sometimes with a sound dark-brown to black heart which is sold separately as "olive ash." It is straight-grained and coarse-textured, and the growth rings produce a decorative figure on plain-sawed surfaces.

Properties
Weight varies as follows: *F. americana*, 41lb/ft³ (660kg/m³), *F. Pennsylvania*, 43lb/ft³ (690kg/m³) and *F. exclesior*, 36lb/ft³ (580kg/m³) when seasoned. The wood dries fairly rapidly, with little degrade and medium shrinkage in use. It has medium bending and crushing strength and shock resistance, low stiffness, and an excellent steam-bending classification. It works satisfactorily with both hand and machine tools. Pre-boring is advised for nailing. It glues with ease and takes stains and polishes well to provide a good finish. Ash is nondurable and perishable. It is susceptible to attack by the powder post beetle and the furniture beetle. The heartwood is moderately resistant to preservative treatment, but the black heartwood is resistant.

Uses
Ash, one of the very best woods for bending, is used extensively for chairmaking and in cabinetmaking, furniture, and interior joinery. Specialist uses include bent handles for umbrellas, shop fittings, vehicle building, wheelwrighting, and agricultural implements. It is used in boat building for bent parts for frames for canoes and canvas boats, also for sports goods, tennis rackets, hockey sticks, baseball bats, billiard cues, and gymnasium equipment. It is an excellent turnery wood for tool handles, shovels, and pick axes. It is sliced for decorative furniture and paneling veneers.

Guaiacum spp.
Family: Zygophyllaceae
LIGNUM VITAE

Where it grows
This wood, known as "The Wood of Life" in the 1500s because its resin was believed to cure diseases, is one of the hardest and heaviest woods in commerce. It is produced from three species: *G. officinale*, L., known as guayacan (Spain), bois de gaiac (France), guayacan negro, and palo santo (Cuba) and ironwood (US); *G. sanctum*, L., known as guayacan blanco, gaiac femelle, or guayacancillo; and *G. guatemalense*, Planch, which occurs in Nicaragua. All three types are exported as lignum vitae. They occur from southern Florida and the Bahamas through Jamaica, Cuba, and the West Indies, and from Mexico down through Central America to Colombia and Venezuela. It is a small, slow-growing tree about 30ft (9m) in height, with a 10-18in (0.25-0.45m) diameter.

Appearance
The wood is dark greenish-brown or nearly black, with a closely-interlocked grain and a fine, even texture.
Properties
The wood weighs on average about 77lb/ft³ (1230kg/m³) when seasoned. It dries very slowly, is refractory and liable to check. There is medium movement in use. The wood has outstanding strength properties in all categories, particularly hardness, and has a very high crushing strength. Unsuitable for bending, it is a very difficult wood to machine, with its very high resistance to cutting. Gluing can be somewhat difficult, but the wood polishes well. It is extremely durable and resistant to preservation treatment.
Uses
The self-lubricating properties of lignum vitae, from its high oil content, make it ideal for marine equipment such as bushing blocks and bearings for ships' propeller shafts, pulley sheaves and dead-eyes, and as a replacement for metal thrust bearings in steel and tube works. It is used anywhere where lubrication is impractical or unreliable, such as in wheels, guides, rollers, and blocks; and in the textile industry for cotton gins, polishing sticks, and rollers. It is also used in die cutting. Lignum vitae has long been a favorite for wood sculpture and carving as well as an excellent turnery wood for mallet heads, and for bowling "woods."

Ilex spp.
Family: Aquifoliaceae
HOLLY

Where it grows
There are about 175 different species of holly, possibly the whitest-known wood. In the UK, *I. aquifolum* has become a hedgerow small tree, about 30ft (9m) tall, with a bole of 10ft (3m) and a diameter of 18in (0.5m). The tree occurs in Europe from Norway, Denmark, and Germany down to the Mediterranean and west Asia. It reaches a height of 80ft (25m), with a diameter of about 2ft (0.6m). *I. opaca* produces holly in the US.

Appearance
The heartwood is white to gray-white, sometimes with a slight greenish-gray cast, with little or no figure. The sapwood is not distinct from the heartwood. The grain tends to be irregular, with a very fine, even texture.
Properties
The weight averages about 49lb/ft³ (780kg/m³) when seasoned. Holly is fairly difficult to dry, and it is best to cut the stock into small dimensions, then slowly air dry under a weighted-down pile. It is stable in use when dry. This heavy, dense wood is tough in all strength categories, but not suitable for steam bending. It has a high resistance to cutting and sawing and a moderate blunting effect on tools, which should be kept very sharp, especially when working with the irregular grain. The wood turns well, requires pre-boring for screwing or nailing, glues easily, and can be brought to an excellent, smooth finish. In the round, logs are susceptible to attack by forest longhorn or Buprestid beetles. The heartwood is perishable and the sapwood is susceptible to attack by the common furniture beetle, but is permeable for preservation treatment.
Uses
Holly is available in limited quantities, in small dimensions and narrow veneers. It is mainly used as a substitute for boxwood; when dyed black, it is a substitute for ebony for marquetry inlay motifs, lines, bandings, and stringings in antique repair and restoration and reproduction furniture. It is excellent for fancy turnery and engraving blocks. It is used for musical instrument parts, piano and organ keys, parts of harpsichords and clavichords, and billiard cue butts.

Juglans nigra
Family: Juglandaceae
AMERICAN WALNUT

Where it grows
This is one of the true walnut trees, widely distributed throughout North America from southern Ontario in Canada down to Texas, and in the east from Maine to Florida. It is also known as black American walnut, Virginia walnut (UK), walnut, canaletto, black hickory nut, or walnut tree (US), and Canadian walnut (Canada and US). In favorable conditions, the trees reach a height of 100-150ft (30-45m), with a diameter of about 4-6ft (1.2-1.8m).

Appearance
The attractive heartwood matures into a rich dark-brown to purplish-black color. It is usually straight-grained, but sometimes wavy or curly. Texture is somewhat coarse, but uniform.
Properties
The weight is about 40lb/ft³ (640kg/m³) when seasoned. The wood requires care in drying to avoid checking and degradation. There is small movement in service. Walnut is of medium density, bending, and crushing strength, with low stiffness, and shock resistance, it has a good steam-bending rating. The wood works well with all tools, with a moderate blunting effect on cutting edges. It holds nails and screws well, and can be glued satisfactorily, works well, takes stain and polish with ease, and can be brought to an excellent finish. Walnut is very durable. The sapwood is somewhat to attack by powder post beetle. The heartwood is resistant to preservative treatment and biodegradation, but the sapwood is permeable.
Uses
All species are extensively used for rifle butts and gunstocks, high-class cabinets and furniture, interior joinery, boat building, musical instruments, clockcases, turnery, carving, and wood sculpture. It is a major lumber for plywood manufacture, and selected logs are sliced for decorative veneers of all kinds for cabinets and paneling. Related species *J. neotropica*, *J. columbiensis*, and *J. australis* produce South American walnut in Peru, Colombia, Ecuador, Venezuela, Argentina, and Mexico (called Peruvian walnut in the US and UK). *J. sieboldiana* produces Japanese walnut.

EUROPEAN WALNUT

Juglans regia
Family: Juglandaceae

Where it grows

The walnut tree originated in the Himalayas, Iran, Lebanon and the Middle East, but today commercial supplies come from France, Italy, Turkey, Yugoslavia and southwest Asia. It is known as Ancona walnut, Black Sea, Circassian, English, French, Italian, or Persian walnut, according to the country of origin. In favorable conditions, it attains an average height of 80-100ft (25-30m), a diameter of 2-5ft (0.6-1.5m), with a rugged bole about 20ft (6m) long.

Appearance

The heartwood is usually gray-brown, with irregular dark-brown streaks accentuated by a natural wavy grain. This highly-figured wood often forms a central core, sharply defined from the remaining plain heart-wood; this is more pronounced in Italian than in English walnut, and French is paler and grayer than English. Its grain is straight to wavy. It has a somewhat coarse texture.

Properties

The weight averages about 40!b/ft³ (640kg/m³) when seasoned. Blue-black stains occur if the wood is in contact with iron compounds in damp conditions. Walnut dries well, but with a tendency for checks to occur in thicker material. There is medium shrinkage in service. It has medium bending strength and resistance to shock loads, with a high crushing strength and low stiffness. It has a very good steam-bending rating. The wood works easily and well with hand and machine tools, glues satisfactorily, and can be brought to an excellent finish. The heartwood is moderately durable. The sapwood is susceptible to attack by powder post beetle and the common furniture beetle. The heartwood is resistant to preservative treatment, but the sapwood is permeable.

Uses

Ever since the "Age of Walnut," this beautiful wood has been used for high-class cabinets and furniture; interior joinery, bank, office, and shop fittings. It is also popular for attractive rifle butts and gunstocks, sports goods, carving, sculpture, turnery, and fascias and expensive car cappings. Highly decorative figured veneers of stumpwood, crotches, and burrs (burls) are used for plywood, doors, and paneling.

"AFRICAN MAHOGANY"

Khaya spp.
Family: Meliaceae

Where it grows

The name "African mahogany" covers all trees of the Khaya species. The bulk of commercial lumber is produced by *K. ivorensis*, A. Chév, which occurs in the coastal rain forests of West Africa from the Ivory Coast to Cameroon and Gabon, and is known as Benin, Degema, Lagos, or Nigerian mahogany. *K. anthotheca* (Welw.) C.DC. is not found in the coastal belt of West Africa and grows in areas of lower rainfall. It occurs in Uganda and Tanzania and is known as krala (Ivory Coast), mangona (Cameroon), munyama (Uganda), mbaua (Mozambique), mbawa (Malawi), and mkangazi (Tanzania). *K. nyasica*, Stapf. ex Bakerf. occurs in Uganda and Tanzania. African mahogany reaches a height of 180-200ft (55-60m) and a diameter of 4-6ft (1.2-1.8m)

Appearance

The tree has a typically reddish-brown heartwood. The grain can be straight, but is usually interlocked, producing a striped or roe figure on quartered surfaces.

Properties

The weight of *K. ivorensis* averages about 33lb/ft³ (530kg/m), *K. anthotheca*, 34lb/ft³ (540kg/m³), and *K. nyasica*, 37lb/ft³ (590kg/m³) when seasoned. The wood dries fairly rapidly with little degrade and is stable in use. It is of medium density and crushing strength, has a low bending strength, very low stiffness, and resistance to shock loads, and has a very poor steam-bending rating. Mahogany works easily with both hand and machine tools. Nailing is satisfac-tory, the wood glues well, and can be stained and polished to an excellent finish. The heartwood is mod-erately durable and the sapwood, susceptible to attack by powder post beetle, is resistant to impregnation.

Uses

This is a very important lumber for furniture, office desks, cabinetmaking, shop and bank fittings, and for high-quality joinery for staircases, banisters, handrails, and paneling, also for domestic flooring, boat building, and vehicle bodies. Logs are rotary cut for plywood and selected logs sliced for decorative veneers for cabinets and paneling.

TULIP TREE

Liriodendron tulipifera
Family: Magnoliaceoe

Where it grows

This large "yellow poplar" tree, not a true poplar (*Populus*), occurs in the eastern US and Canada, where it is called canary wood. In the UK it is canary white-wood; tulip tree in the UK and US; poplar and yellow poplar in the US. The magnificent burr (burl) from this tree is marketed as "green cypress burr" in the UK. It grows to a height of 100-150ft (30-50m), with a long, clear, cylindrical bole of 6-8ft (1.8-2.5m) in diameter.

Appearance

The wide sapwood is creamy-white, the heartwood varies from yellow-brown to pale olive-brown, streaked with olive-green, dark gray, black, pinkish-brown, red, and sometimes mineral stains of steel blue. A wide band of parenchyma shows as pale veins on flat-sawed surfaces. It is straight-grained, with a fine, even texture.

Properties

The weight is 28-32lb/ft³4 (50-510kg/m³) when seasoned. The wood kiln dries easily and well, and air dries easily with little degrade. There is little movement in service. The lumber has medium crushing strength, low bending strength, stiffness, and resistance to shock loads, and a medium steam-bending rating. It works easily by hand and machine, has good nailing properties, glued joints hold well, and it can be stained, painted, or polished to a good finish. The heartwood is nondurable, and the sapwood is susceptible to attack by the common furniture beetle. It is moderately resistant to preservative treatment, but the sapwood is permeable.

Uses

American whitewood is a favorite wood for pattern-making, sculpture, and wood carving. It is used for interior parts of furniture, joinery, and doors, for dry cooperage, packaging, and pallets, and interior trim for boats. It is extensively used for plywood manufacture and corestock for laminated boards. Sliced for decorative veneers, it appears in cabinets, marquetry, and paneling. When treated, it is used for external joinery not in contact with the ground; it is also used for wood pulp and wood flour.

Lovoa trichilioides
Family: Meliaceae
"AFRICAN WALNUT"

Where it grows
This tall tree, not a true walnut (*Jugians spp.*), occurs in Nigeria, Ghana, Cameroon, Congo-Kinshasa, and Gabon. It is also known as "Benin walnut," "Nigerian golden walnut," "Nigerian walnut," and "Ghana walnut" (UK), apopo, and sida (Nigeria), bibolo (Cameroon), dibetou, noyer d'Afrique, and noyer de Gabon (Ivory Coast), eyan (Gabon), nvero, and embero (Spanish Guinea), alona wood, congowood, lovoa wood, and tigerwood (US), bombolu (Congo-Kinshasa), and dilolo (France). It grows to a height of 150ft (45m) and 4ft (1.2m) in diameter, with a clear, cylindrical bole of 60ft (18m).

Appearance
The sapwood is pale brown to buff, clearly demarcated from the golden brown-bronze heartwood, which is marked with black streaks caused by "gum lines." The grain is interlocked, sometimes spiral, producing a beautiful ribbon-striped figure on quartered surfaces. The texture is moderately fine and lustrous.
Properties
The weight averages 35lb/ft³ (560kg/m³) when seasoned. The wood dries fairly well. Existing shakes may extend slightly and some distortion may occur, but the degrade is not serious. There is small movement in service. The lumber has low bending strength and resistance to shock loads, very low stiffness, medium crushing strength, and a moderate steam-bending classification. It works well with hand or machine tools. The wood tends to split when nailed and needs pre-boring. By sanding and scraping before filling, the surface can be brought to an excellent finish. African walnut is fairly durable, and the sapwood is susceptible to attack by powder post beetle and dry wood termites in Africa. It is extremely resistant to preservative treatment, but the sapwood is moderately resistant.
Uses
African walnut is a decorative wood used extensively for furniture and cabinetmaking, edge lippings, and facings, billiard tables, and chairs. It appears in flush doors, decorative interior joinery, paneling, and domestic flooring. It is an ideal turnery wood for bowls and lamp-standards, it is used for gun stocks, car window and door cappings, and sliced for decorative veneers.

Millettia laurentii
Family: Leguminosae
WENGE and PANGA-PANGA

Where it grows
Wenge occurs mainly in Congo-Kinshasa, Cameroon, and Gabon. A very closely-related species, *Millettia stuhlmamii* Taub., producing panga-panga, occurs in Mozambique. They are also known as palissandre du Congo (Congo); dikela, mibotu, bokonge, and tshika-lakala (Congo-Kinshasa); awong (Cameroon); nson-so (Gabon); and panga-panga (Mozambique). Trees reach about 60ft (18m) with a diameter of 2ft (0.6m).

Appearance
The sapwood is whitish, clearly defined from the heartwood; this is dark brown, with close black veining and alternate closely-spaced whitish bands of light and dark parenchyma tissue, which produces a very decorative figure. The wood is straight-grained and has an irregular, coarse texture.
Properties
Wenge weighs 52-62lb/ft³ (830-1000kg/m³), and panga-panga weighs 50lb/ft³ (800kg/m³) when seasoned. Both dry very slowly and require care to avoid surface checking, but generally the degrade is minimal. The wood is stable in service. Wenge has high bending strength and resistance to shock loads, and is especially noted for its shock resistance and medium stiffness. It has a poor steam-bending rating, but high resistance to abrasion. This durable wood works readily with both hand and machine tools, but cutters should be kept very sharp. It requires pre-boring for nailing. Resin cells in the wood structure can interfere with gluing and polishing, but filling is the answer for a very good finish. The wood is durable and extremely resistant to preservative treatment.
Uses
Wenge has a high natural resistance to abrasion, and is thus excellent for flooring for public buildings, or where there is heavy pedestrian traffic. The dark chocolate-brown makes for a dark floor, but this is not a disadvantage for certain types of hotel, showroom, and boardroom. It is also used for all forms of interior and exterior joinery and general construction work. It makes a very good turnery wood and is ideal for wood sculpture. Selected logs are sliced for decorative veneers for cabinets and architectural paneling.

Olea hochstetteri
Family: Oleaceae
OLIVEWOOD

Where it grows
The olive tree *O. europaea* is grown in the Mediterranean for its edible fruit and olive oil, and is usually small and misshapen. Commercial lumber comes from Kenya, Tanzania, and Uganda. *O. hochstetteri* produces East African olive, also known as musheragi in Kenya, *O. welwitschii* (Knobl.). Gilg. & Schellenb. produces loliondo in Tanzania, and "Elgon olive" in Kenya. Olivewood grows to about 80ft (25m) in height, is heavily fluted and crooked, with a diameter of 1½-2½ft (0.45-0.75m).

Appearance
The sapwood is pale creamy-yellow and quite plain, but the heartwood has a pale-brown background with very attractive irregular markings of mid- to dark-brown and blackish streaks. The grain is straight to shallowly interlocked and the texture very even.
Properties
O. hochstetteri weighs on average 55lb/ft³ (880kg/m³), and *O. welwitschii* weighs about 50lb/ft³ (800kg/m³) when seasoned. The wood is somewhat refractory and needs to be air dried slowly, especially as internal checking or honeycombing may occur in thicker pieces. It can be kiln dried successfully. There is considerable movement in service. The wood has excellent strength in every category. The sapwood may be bent to a small radius, but because of resin exudation, olivewood has only a moderate steam-bending classification. The wood is quite difficult to work as the interlocked grain affects machining. There is high resistance in cutting with a moderate blunting effect on tools. It requires pre-boring for nailing. The wood glues well, and can be brought to an excellent finish. The heartwood is moderately durable and resistant to preservative treatment, but the sapwood is permeable.
Uses
This very attractive wood has a good resistance to abrasion and makes an excellent decorative flooring for public buildings. It is used for furniture, cabinets, and paneling, and is ideal for turnery, for tool and fancy handles and bowls. Olivewood is popular for sculpture and carving, and logs are sliced for decorative veneers.

Peltogyne spp.
Family: Leguminosae
PURPLEHEART

Where it grows

Purpleheart is widely distributed in tropical America from Mexico down to southern Brazil. Those of commercial importance in the Caribbean are *P. pubescens*. Bench., *P. porphyrocardia*, Gnseb., and *P. venosa* (Vahl) Benth, var. *densiflora* (Spruce) Amsh. They are known as amaranth or violetwood in the US. *P. venosa* from the Guianas is also important in the Amazonas of Brazil, and other areas of South America; it is known as koroboreli, saka, or sakavalli (Guyana), purperhart (Surinam), pau roxo, nazareno, or morado (Venezuela), tananeo (Colombia), and amarante (Brazil). The semi-deciduous trees reach a height of 125-150ft (38-45m), with a diameter of 2-4ft (0.6-1.2m).

Appearance

The lumber has a white-to-cream sapwood. The heartwood turns bright purple on exposure to light, then matures into a dark purplish-brown. It is generally straight-grained, but sometimes wavy or interlocked with a moderate-to-fine, uniform texture.

Properties

The weight averages about 54lb/ft^3 (860kg/m^3) when seasoned. The wood dries fairly rapidly with little de-grade. There is little movement in service. The wood has high bending and crushing strength and stiffness, with medium resistance to shock loads. It has a moderate steam-bending rating. It is somewhat difficult to work, with a moderate-to-severe blunting effect on tools. It requires pre-boring for nailing, but glues well, and polishes easily. Spirit finishes tend to remove the purple color. The sapwood is susceptible to insect attack. The heartwood is very durable, and extremely resistant to preservative treatment, but the sapwood is permeable.

Uses

Purpleheart is used locally as a cabinet and furniture wood, but also for heavy outdoor constructional work—bridges, freshwater piling, dock, and harbor work. It makes an attractive flooring. It is used for sculpture, carving, and turnery for tool handles and small fancy items. Specialized uses include boat building, gymnasium apparatus, diving boards, skis, wheelwrighting, billiard cue butts, vats for chemicals and filter presses. It is also sliced for decorative veneers.

Pericopsis elata
Family: Leguminosae
AFRORMOSIA

Where it grows

This tree occurs in the Ivory Coast, Ghana, Congo-Kinshasa, and Nigeria. It is also known as assamela (Ivory Coast), kokrodua (Ghana and Ivory Coast), ayin or egbi (Nigeria), and andejen (Cameroon). It reaches a height of 150ft (45m) and a diameter of about 3ft (1m).

Appearance

The creamy-buff sapwood is well defined from the heartwood, which is golden-brown when freshly felled and darkens on exposure. The grain varies from straight to interlocked, which produces a rope-striped figure on quartered surfaces. The texture is moderately fine but without the oiliness of teak. The wood is liable to blue mineral stains if in contact with iron or iron compounds in damp conditions because of its high tannin content.

Properties

The wood weighs about 43lb/ft^3 (690kg/m^3) when seasoned, and dries slowly but well, with little degrade. There is exceptionally small movement in service. It has medium stiffness, high crushing strength, and medium shock resistance with a moderate steam-bending rating. The interlocked grain can affect machining. Tipped saws should be used as there is a moderate blunting effect of tools. Pre-boring is required for nailing and screwing. Afrormosia glues well and takes a good finish. It is very durable, resistant to both fungi and termites, and extremely resistant to preservative treatment.

Uses

Afrormosia was originally used as a substitute for teak in the furniture industry for framing and fittings, edge lipping, and facings for panels. Today it is used extensively in its own right where a very attractive, strong, stable, and durable wood is required. It appears in high-class furniture and cabinetmaking, chairs, interior joinery, stairs, shop, and office fitting, and agricultural implements. It makes an attractive floor, and is also used for exterior joinery, boat building, and marine piling. Selected logs are sliced for decorative veneers for furniture, flush doors, and wall paneling.

Picea abies
Family: Pinaceae
SPRUCE, EUROPEAN, or WHITEWOOD(S)

Where it grows

This wood occurs throughout Europe, with the exception of Denmark and the Netherlands, into western Russia. The tree reaches an average height of 120ft (36.6m) and a diameter of 2½-4ft (0.76-1.2m). In the mountains of Rumania it reaches a height of 200ft (61m) with a 5-6ft (1.5-1.8m) diameter. It is also known as white deal, common spruce, or Norway spruce, and Baltic, Finnish, or Russian whitewood according to the country of origin.

Appearance

The color varies from almost white to pale yellow-brown and has a natural luster. The annual rings are clearly defined. The wood is straight-grained and has a fine texture.

Properties

Weight averages 29lb/ft^3 (470kg/m^3) when seasoned. This wood dries rapidly and well with some risk of distortion. It has low stiffness, and resistance to shock loads, medium bending and crushing strength, and a very poor steam-bending rating. There is medium movement in service. It works easily with all tools, holds screws and nails well, glues satisfactorily, and takes stain, paint, and varnishes for a good finish. The sapwood is susceptible to attack by the common furniture beetle; the nondurable heartwood is resistant to preservative treatment.

Uses

Norway spruce provides a traditional Christmas tree from its thinnings. The best-quality spruce comes from the most northerly regions, but trees grown at the same latitude will produce different qualities according to the altitude. It is used for interior building work, carcasing, domestic flooring, general carpentry, boxes, and crates. Small logs are used in the round for masts, pit props, and ladder stringers. Spruce from central and eastern Europe and from Alpine areas of North America produce excellent quality "tone-woods" for piano and keyboard soundboards and the bellies of violins, lutes, and guitars, because of its unsurpassed resonance qualities. It is used in the manufacture of pulp and paper, and in Germany the bark is stripped and used for tannin extraction. It is also used for plywood.

Picea sitchensis
Family: Pinaceae

SITKA SPRUCE(S)

Where it grows

Sitka spruce occurs on the Pacific coast of North America and western Canada down to California. It grows to 125-175ft (38-53.4m), with a diameter of 3-6ft (0.9-1.8m); it occasionally reaches 250ft (76.3m) in height and 8-12ft (2.4-3.7m) in diameter.

Appearance

The pale pink sapwood blends into the light pinkish-brown heartwood, which is mostly straight-grained, sometimes spiral. It has a fairly coarse but uniform texture and is odorless, non-resinous, and non-tainting.

Properties

The wood weighs about 27lb/ft³ (430kg/m³) when seasoned. Care is needed in drying large sizes as it dries fairly rapidly, and tends to twist and cup. There is medium movement in service. It has medium bending and crushing strengths, stiffness, and shock resistance. Its strength-to-weight ratio is high, and it has a very good steam-bending rating. Sitka spruce works easily with both hand and machine tools, finishes cleanly, takes screws and nails without difficulty, and gives good results with various finishes when care is taken to prevent raising the grain. The heartwood is nondurable, and resistant to preservative treatment.

Uses

Strength varies considerably according to the location and growth conditions, and selective grading is necessary for joists, rafters, and studding for building. Split poles are used for ladder sides. In Canada, sitka spruce is used for interior joinery, cooperage, and boxmaking; specialized uses include boat building, oars, and masts. Special grades are selected for their resonance to make soundboards for pianos, and guitar and violin fronts. Logs are rotary cut as corestock for birch and Douglas fir plywood, but sitka is seldom used for plywood faces. It is sliced for special laminates for aircraft and glider construction, sail planes, and racing sculls; it is also used for boxmaking, and is the world's most important pulp for newsprint because of its whiteness.

Pinus monticola
Family: Pinaceae

WESTERN WHITE PINE(S)

Where it grows

This tree grows in the mountain forests of western Canada and the western US, from sea level up to over 9750ft (3000m). It occurs south down to the Kern River in California and east into northern Montana; it is most abundant in northern Idaho. It reaches 75-120ft (23-37m) with a diameter of about 3ft (1m) or more. It is also called Idaho white pine. Closely related species include *P. contorta* Dougl., producing lodgepole pine known as contorta pine (UK); and *P. banksiana*, Lamb. produces jack pine known as princess pine and Banksian pine in Canada and the US.

Appearance

The sapwood is white, the heartwood is only slightly darker and varies from a pale straw color to shades of reddish-brown. Fine brown lines caused by resin ducts appear on longitudinal surfaces. It is straight-grained with an even, uniform texture. Yellow pine is always called "white pine" in Canada and the US, though there are differences in weight and marking.

Properties

The wood weighs about 28lb/ft³ (450kg/m³) when seasoned. It dries readily and well, with little checking or warping, and has a slightly higher shrinkage rating than yellow pine. There is little movement in service. This low-density lumber has rather low strength properties, and is not suitable for steam-bending. The material works easily with both hand and machine tools, takes screws and nails without difficulty, glues well, and takes paint and varnish well. The wood is nondurable, susceptible to beetle attack and moderately resistant to preservative treatment, but the sapwood is permeable.

Uses

Western white pine is chiefly used for interior joinery for doors and windows, interior trim, fitments, shelving, light, and medium building construction. Specialized uses include furniture and cabinets, boat and ship building, patternmaking, drawing boards, domestic wooden ware, and match splints. It is rotary cut for plywood and corestock, and selected logs are sliced for decorative paneling veneers.

Pinus palustris
Family: Pinaceae

AMERICAN PITCH PINE(S)

Where it grows

Pitch pine is the heaviest commercial softwood. *P. palustris* and *P. elliottii* grow through the southern US in a curve from Virginia through Florida to the Gulf. The heaviest lumber is shipped as pitch pine, the lighter wood as southern pine. They grow to a height of 100ft (30.5m) and a diameter of 2-3ft (0.6-0.9m). Other names: *P. palustris*, longleaf pine, Florida long-leaf, yellow pine, or Georgia yellow pine; *P. elliottii*, slash pine, longleaf yellow pine, or longleaf (US); and Gulf coast pitch pine or longleaf pitch pine (UK).

Appearance

The creamy-pink sapwood is quite narrow, and contrasts with the heartwood, which is a yellowish-red to reddish-brown, with a wide, conspicuous growth ring figure, especially in fast-grown lumber. It is very resinous and has a coarse texture.

Properties

The weight for seasoned lumber varies from about 41-43lb/ft³ (660-690kg/m³). The wood dries well with little degrade and is stable in service. It has high bending and crushing strengths and high stiffness, with medium resistance to shock loads. It is not suitable for steam-bending because of the resin content. Pitch pine can be worked readily, with both hand and machine tools, but resin can be troublesome in clogging cutters and saw teeth. It holds screws and nails firmly, glues without difficulty, and takes paint and other finishes satisfactorily. The lumber is moderately durable; sometimes beetle damage is present. It is resistant to preservative treatment, but the sapwood is permeable.

Uses

The lumber is used for heavy construction work, truck and railway wagons, ship building, exterior joinery, piling, dock work, bridge building, decking, and chemical vats. Lower grades are used for interior joinery, general building, domestic flooring, crates, and pallets. The wood is rich in resinous secretions and also produces the largest percentage of the world's resin and turpentine.

Pinus ponderosa
Family: Pinaceae
PONDEROSA PINE(S)

Where it grows
Ponderosa pine occurs in the drier regions of southern British Columbia and from Montana, western Nebraska, and Texas into Mexico and west to the Pacific coast. The tree reaches an average height of 100ft (30.5m) with a diameter of about 2ft (0.6m), but can get up to 170ft (51.9m) with a 4ft (1.2m) diameter. It is also known as western yellow pine (US and Australia); bird's eye pine, knotty pine, British Columbia soft pine (Canada); and Californian white pine (US).

Appearance
Mature trees have a very thick pale yellow sapwood, which is soft, non-resinous, and uniform in texture. The heartwood is orange to reddish-brown, with prominent dark-brown resin duct lines on longitudinal surfaces. It is considerably heavier than the sapwood.
Properties
Weight is about 32lb/ft³ (510kg/m³) when seasoned. Ponderosa pine dries easily and well with little degrade, but the wide sapwood is liable to fungal and blue staining if the wood is not carefully piled during air drying. There is very little movement in service. It has medium bending and crushing strength, low stiffness, and shock resistance, and a poor steam-bending rating. The wood works easily with both hand and machine tools, but resin exudation tends to clog cutters and saws. The wood can be glued satisfactorily, takes screws and nails without difficulty, and, if it is treated to remove the surface gumminess, gives good results in painting and varnishing. It is nondurable and moderately resistant to preservative treatment, but the sapwood is permeable.
Uses
The valuable sapwood is used in the US for pattern-making. The heartwood is used for kitchen furniture, building construction, window frames, doors, general carpentry, and for packing cases, crates, and pallets. When treated, it is used for sleepers, poles, and posts. Logs are rotary cut for veneers and sliced for knotty pine paneling.

Pinus strobus
Family: Pinaceae
YELLOW PINE(S)

Where it grows
This species occurs from Newfoundland to the Manitoba border and south to north Georgia. It can reach a height of 150ft (45.7m) and a diameter of about 5ft (1.5m), but averages about 100ft (30.5m) high and 2-3ft (0.6-0.9m) in diameter. It is also known as white pine, eastern white, cork, and soft pine (Canada and US), northern white, northern pine (US), Quebec yellow, Quebec pine, and Weymouth pine (UK).

Appearance
The sapwood is white and the heartwood varies from a light straw brown to a light reddish brown. It is not particularly resinous. The ducts appear as thin brown lines on longitudinal surfaces, but the growth rings are inconspicuous. It is straight-grained and the texture is very fine and even.
Properties
Seasoned weight varies from 24-26lb/ft³ (390-420kg/m³). The wood dries fairly rapidly and well, but sap stain should be avoided when air drying. Yellow pine has extremely low shrinkage and is very stable in service. The lumber is weak in all strength properties, and is not suitable for steam bending. It works very easily with both hand and machine tools, has good screw and nail-holding properties, glues well, and can be brought to an excellent finish. It is liable to attack by the common furniture beetle. The heartwood is nondurable and resistant to preservative treatment, but the sapwood is permeable for treatment.
Uses
Yellow pine, with its low shrinkage and extreme stability in use, is particularly suited for engineers' patternmaking for very fine detail, and drawing boards, doors, and similar high-class work. It is also used for sculpture and carving, and high-class interior joinery, cabinet- and furnituremaking, shelving, and interior trim. Specialized uses include parts for stringed instruments such as guitars, organ parts, ship and boat building, and light construction. Second growth lumber is coarser in texture and is usually knotty. It is used for match splints, packaging containers, and wood flour.

Pinus sylvestris
Family: Pinaceae
SCOTCH PINE(S)

Where it grows
This common commercial softwood occurs from the Sierra Nevada in Andalusia and the mountains of western Spain, through the Maritime Alps and Pyrenees, the Caucasus and Transylvanian Alps, up into western Siberia. In good conditions, the tree reaches 130-140ft (39.6-42.7m), with a diameter of 2-3ft (0.6-0.9m).

Appearance
The knotty wood has a mildly resinous pale red brown heartwood, distinct from the paler creamy-white to yellow sapwood, with clearly marked annual rings. Texture varies from the slowly-grown fine wood of northern Russia to the coarser and denser wood of northern Europe.
Properties
The weight of seasoned lumber is about 32lb/ft³ (510kg/m³) and it dries very rapidly and well, with a tendency to blue sap stain. There is medium movement in service and the wood is stable in use. The wood has low stiffness, and resistance to shock loads, low to medium bending and crushing strength, and a very poor steam-bending rating. It works easily with both hand and machine tools. It holds nails and screws well, but gluing can be troublesome because of the resin. The wood can be stained, painted, or varnished to a good finish. It is susceptible to attack by the common furniture beetle. It is nondurable and moderately resistant to preservative treatment, but the sapwood is permeable.
Uses
The best grades are used for furniture, interior joinery, turnery, and vehicle bodies. Other grades go for building construction and carcasing. When treated, redwood is extensively used for railway sleepers, telegraph poles, piles, and pit props. Logs are cut for plywood and sliced for decorative veneers. It is also used in the chemical wood pulp industry for craft paper.

Prunus spp.
Family: Rosaceae
CHERRY

Where it grows
P. avium, L. syn. *Cerosus avium*, Moench. produces European cherry, also known as gean, mazzard, cherry, or wild cherry (UK). It is native to Europe, and occurs in the mountains of north Africa. *P. serotina*, Ehrh. produces American cherry, also known as black cherry (Canada and US) and cabinet cherry (US), and occurs from Ontario to Florida and from the Dakotas to Texas. The tree grows to a height of 60-80ft (18-25m), with a diameter of about 2ft (0.6m). American black cherry reaches a height of 100ft (30.5m).

Appearance
The creamy-pink sapwood of *P. avium* is clearly defined from the heartwood (pale pinkish-brown maturing to red-brown). *P. serotina* is a darker red-brown, with narrow brown pith flecks and small gum pockets. Both have straight grain and a fairly fine, even texture.

Properties
The weight of *P. avium* is 38lb/ft³ (610kg/m³) and *P. serotina* is 36lb/ft³ (580kg/m³) when seasoned. The wood dries fairly rapidly, with a strong tendency to warp and shrink and with medium movement in service. It has medium bending and crushing strengths and resistance to shock loads, low stiffness, and a very good steam-bending rating. It works well with both hand and machine tools, with a moderate blunting effect on cutting edges, but cross-grained lumber tends to tear in planing. The wood holds screws and nails well, glues easily, and takes stain and polishes to an excellent finish. It is moderately durable; the sapwood is susceptible to attack by the common furniture beetle, but is almost immune to attack by powder post beetle. The heartwood is moderately durable and resistant to preservative treatment.

Uses
This wood has a most attractive figure and color and is used for cabinets and furnituremaking, carving and sculpture, and decorative turnery for domestic ware, toys and musical instrument parts. American cherry is used for patternmaking, tobacco pipes, boat interiors, and backing blocks for printing plates. Both types are rotary cut for plywood and sliced for decorative veneers for cabinets and panels.

Pseudotsuga menziesii
Family: Pinaceae
DOUGLAS FIR(S)

Where it grows
This softwood, not a true fir, is known as "British Columbia pine," or "Columbian pine" in the UK, and "Oregon pine" in the US. It occurs in abundance in British Columbia, Washington, and Oregon, through Wyoming to southern New Mexico and west to the Pacific coast. It has been introduced to the UK, Australia, and New Zealand. In Canada and the US, trees reach a height of 300ft (91.5m), averaging 150-200ft (457-61m), and 3-6ft (0.9-1.8m) in diameter. The bole is clear of branches for about two-thirds of its height, yielding a very high percentage of lumber free of knots and other defects.

Appearance
The sapwood is slightly lighter in color than the heartwood, which is a light reddish-brown. There is a prominent growth ring figure on plain-sawed surfaces or rotary cut veneers. Grain is mostly straight but often wavy or spiral. Texture is medium and uniform.

Properties
Weight is 33lb/ft³ (530kg/m³) when seasoned. The wood dries fairly rapidly and well without much warping, but knots tend to split and loosen. Resin canals also tend to exude and show as fine brown lines on longitudinal surfaces. Douglas fir is stable in service, has high bending strength, stiffness, and crushing strength, medium resistance to shock loads and a poor steam-bending rating. The wood works readily with both hand and machine tools. Cutters should be kept very sharp as there is a moderate blunting effect on tools. It is subject to beetle attack, is moderately durable and resistant to preservative treatment.

Uses
This is the world's most important source of plywood. The solid, large baulks are used for heavy construction work, laminated arches, roof trusses, beams, interior and exterior joinery, dock and harbor work, marine piling, ship building, mining lumber, railway sleepers, cooperage for vats and tanks for chemical plants, breweries, and distilleries. Selected logs are sliced for decorative veneers for paneling.

Pterocarpus soyauxii
Family: Leguminosae
AFRICAN PADAUK

Where it grows
This tree occurs in central and tropical West Africa. It grows to a height of about 100ft (30.5m) and a diameter of 2-3ft (0.6-1m), with wide buttresses and a divided bole.

Appearance
When freshly cut, the heartwood is a very distinctive, vivid blood-red maturing to dark purple-brown with red streaks. It is sharply demarcated from the straw-colored sapwood. The grain is straight to interlocked and the texture varies from moderate-to-very coarse.

Properties
Padauk weighs 40-50lb/ft³ (640-800kg/m³) when seasoned and dries very well with the minimum of degrade. The wood is very dense, with high bending and crushing strengths and medium stiffness, and resistance to shock loads, but it is not suitable for steam-bending. It is exceptionally stable in service. The wood works well, with both hand and machine tools, with only a slight blunting effect on cutting edges. It holds nails and screws without difficulty, glues easily and well, and can be polished to an excellent finish. The wood is very durable and renowned for its resistance to decay. It is also moderately resistant to preservative treatment.

Uses
Padauk is world-famous as a dye wood, but it is also extensively used for high-class cabinets, furniture, and interior joinery. As an excellent turnery wood it is used for knife and tool handles and fancy turnery. It is very good for carving and sculpture; other specialized uses include electrical fittings and levels. It is an ideal boat-building wood. In Africa, it is used for making paddles, oars, and agricultural implements. Its abrasive qualities make it a good heavy-duty flooring of very attractive appearance, suitable for heavy pedestrian traffic—especially where under-floor heating is installed, as it has such good dimensional stability. Selected logs are sliced for decorative veneers for cabinets and paneling.

Quercus spp.
Family: Fagaceae
RED OAK

Where it grows
The red oak, growing in eastern Canada and North America, is also found in Iran as Persian oak, but is not as important commercially as the white oak. The principal species are *Q. rubra*, northern red oak (Canada and US) and *Q. falcata* var. *falcata*, southern red oak, Spanish oak (US). In Canada, the red oak is more abundant than in the US, and grows to a height of 60-70ft (18-21.5m), with a diameter of 3ft (1m).

Appearance
The tree outwardly resembles the white oak, except that the heartwood varies from biscuit-pink to reddish-brown. The grain is usually straight; southern red oak is coarser textured than northern. Both species produce a less attractive figure than white oak because of the larger rays. There is a considerable variation in the quality of red oak; northern red oak grows comparatively slowly and compares favorably with northern white oak, while red oak from the southern states grows faster and produces a harder, heavier wood.
Properties
The average weight of both types is 48lb/ft³ (770kg/m³) seasoned. It dries slowly, and care is needed in air and kiln drying to prevent degrade. There is medium movement in service. This dense wood has medium bending strength and stiffness, high shock resistance and crushing strength, and a very good steam-bending classification. It usually offers a moderate blunting effect on cutters, which should be kept sharp. It requires pre-boring; gluing results are variable, but red oak takes stain well and polishes to a good finish. The wood is nondurable, moderately resistant to preservative treatment, and unsuited for exterior work.
Uses
Red oak is too porous for tight cooperage purposes and its lack of durability and drying problems limit its use. However it is good for domestic flooring, furniture fitments, interior joinery, and vehicle construction. Logs are rotary cut for plywood manufacture and sliced for decorative veneers. Persian red oak (*Q. castaneaefolia*) is impermeable and used for barrel staves.

Quercus spp.
Family: Fagaceae
OAK

Where it grows
The genus *Quercus* produces the true oaks and has more than 200 different species. Most white oaks occur in the temperate regions of the northern hemisphere; in warmer climates they grow in the montane forests. The white oaks occur in Europe, the Middle East, North Africa, the eastern US, southeastern Canada and Japan. The principal species producing European oak are: *Q. petraea* (sessile oak, durmast oak in the UK, and English/French/Polish/ Slavonian oak according to origin); also *Q. robur* producing pedunculate oak (UK). American white oaks are *Q. alba* (white oak, US), *Q. prinus* (chestnut oak), *Q. lyrata* (overcup oak), and *Q. michauxii* (swamp chestnut oak). Japanese oak is from *Q. mongoiica*. White oaks are all similar in character and grow to 60-100ft (18-30m) in height and 4-6ft (1.2-1.8m) in diameter.

Appearance
The sapwood is lighter than the heartwood, which is light tan or yellow-brown, usually straight-grained, but often irregular or cross-grained. It has a characteristic silver-grained figure on quartered surfaces because of broad rays and a moderately coarse texture.
Properties
Weight is 45-47lb/ft³ (720-750kg/m³). Volhynian, Slavonian and Japanese oak weighs 41-42lb/ft³ (660-672kg/m³) when seasoned. The wood air dries very slowly with a tendency to split and check. These dense woods have high strength, low stiffness, and resistance to shock loads, and a very good steam-bending rating. They are corrosive to metals, and liable to blue stain in damp conditions. Machining is satisfactory and they take an excellent finish. The wood is durable but liable to beetle attack, but it is highly resistant to preservative treatment, though the sapwood is permeable.
Uses
One of the world's most popular woods, light oaks are ideal for furniture, and cabinetmaking. English oak is used for boat building, dock and harbor work, vehicle bodywork, high-class interior and exterior joinery, and flooring. It is excellent for ecclesiastical sculpture and carving, and also tight cooperage for whiskey, sherry, and brandy casks. It is sliced for decorative veneers.

Shorea spp.
Family; Dipterocarpaceae
LIGHT/DARK RED MERANTI/SERAYA/LAUAN

Where it grows
A large number of species of the genus *Shorea* occur in southeast Asia, which produce meranti, seraya, or lauan. Meranti is from Malaya, Sarawak and Indonesia, seraya from Sabah, and lauan from the Philippines. These woods vary in color and density and are grouped as follows: light red meranti, light red seraya and white lauan, dark red meranti, dark red seraya and red lauan. These trees reach 200-225ft (60-70m) in height and 3-5ft (1-1.5m) in diameter.

Appearance
Due to the number of species, these details are very general, in the first group the color is pale pink to red, and in the second it is medium to dark red-brown with white resin streaks. Both have interlocked grain and a somewhat coarse texture.
Properties
The light red woods of the first group have an average weight of 34lb/ft³ (550kg/m³), and the dark red woods weigh about 42lb/ft³ (670kg/m³) on average when seasoned. Drying is usually fairly rapid, without serious degrade. Both woods are stable in use, but the first light red group is much weaker than the darker woods. Both types have medium bending and crushing strengths, low stiffness, and shock resistance, and a poor steam-bending rating. They work well with both hand and machine tools, hold screws and nails satisfactorily, can be glued easily, and produce a good finish when filled. The light red woods are nondurable, and the dark red group are moderately durable and resistant to impregnation.
Uses
The light red woods are used for interior joinery, light structural work, domestic flooring, cheap furniture, and interior framing. The dark red second group is used for similar purposes, plus exterior joinery, cladding, shop fitting, and boatbuilding. Logs of both groups are used for plywood manufacture and sliced for decorative veneers for cabinets and paneling.

Taxus baccata
Family: Taxaceae

YEW(S)

Where it grows

The common yew is widely distributed through Algeria, the Middle East, the Caucasus, northern Iran, the Himalayas, and Myanmar, and throughout Europe. It grows to a height of 40-50ft (12-15m) with a short twisted or fluted bole, and often consists of several vertical shoots that are fused together to form multiple

stems.

Appearance

The heartwood varies from orange-brown streaked with darker purple, to purplish-brown with darker mauve or brown patches, and clusters of in-growing bark. The irregular growth pattern produces wood of varying ring widths, which combine with narrow widths of dense latewood to give a highly-decorative appearance.

Properties

Yew is among the heaviest and most durable of softwood lumber, and weighs 42lb/ft³ (670kg/m³) when seasoned. The wood dries fairly rapidly and well, with little degrade if care is taken to avoid shakes developing or existing shakes from opening. Distortion is negligible and it is stable in use. This hard, compact, and elastic wood has medium bending and crushing strength, with low stiffness, and resistance to shock loads. Straight-grained, air-dried yew is one of the best softwoods for steam bending, even though it is inclined to check during drying. It works well in most hand and machine operations, but when irregular, curly, or cross grain is present, it tears easily. Nailing requires pre-boring and the oiliness of the wood sometimes interferes with gluing, but it stains satisfactorily and provides an excellent finish. Yew is durable, but not immune from attack by the common furniture beetle; it is resistant to preservative treatment.

Uses

For many centuries, yew was prized for the English archer's longbow. It is an excellent turnery and carving wood, and is used for reproduction furnituremaking, interior and exterior joinery, garden furniture, fences, and gate posts. It is the traditional wood for Windsor chair bentwood parts. It is sliced for highly decorative veneers and burrs (burls).

Tectona grandis
Family: Verbenaceae

TEAK

Where it grows

Teak is indigenous to Myanmar and grows extensively throughout India and in Thailand, Indonesia, and Java. It has been introduced into Malaysia, Borneo, and the Philippines, tropical Africa and Central America. In favorable locations, it grows to 130-150ft (40-45m), with a diameter of 6-8ft (1.8-2.4m), but averages 30-35ft (9-11m) with a diameter of about 3-5ft (0.9-1.5m).

Appearance

True Burma teak has a narrow, pale yellow-brown sapwood and a dark golden-brown heartwood, darkening on exposure to mid- or dark-brown. Other types have a rich brown background color with dark chocolate-brown markings. The grain is mostly straight in Burma teak, and wavy in Indian teak from Malabar. The texture is coarse and uneven and it feels oily to the touch.

Properties

Weight is 38-43lb/ft³ (610-690kg/m³), averaging 40lb/ft³ (640kg/m³) when seasoned. The wood dries rather slowly, and there is small movement in service. Teak has medium bending strength, low stiffness, and shock resistance, high crushing strength, and a moderate steam-bending classification. It works reasonably well with both hand and machine tools and has a moderately severe blunting effect on cutting edges, which must be kept sharp. Machine dust can be a severe irritant. Pre-boring is required for nailing, and it glues well and can be brought to an excellent finish. The wood is very durable.

Uses

Teak enjoys a well-deserved reputation for its strength and durability, stability in fluctuating atmospheres, and its excellent decorative appearance. Its vast number of uses include furniture, and cabinetmaking, decking for ship and boat building, deck houses, handrails, bulwarks, hatches, hulls, planking, oars, and masts. It is also used for high-class joinery for doors, staircases, and paneling, and externally for dock and harbor work, bridges, sea defences, and garden furniture. It makes a very attractive flooring. Good chemical resistance enables it to be used for laboratory benches, fume ducts, and vats. It is cut for all grades of plywood and decorative veneers.

Thuja plicata
Family: Cupressaceae

GIANT ARBORVITAE(S)

Where it grows

The tree is known as British Columbia red cedar in the UK, giant arbor vitae in the US and red cedar in Canada. It occurs from Alaska south to California, and east from British Columbia to Washington, Idaho, Montana, and the northern Rockies. It has been planted in the UK and New Zealand. It grows to a height of 150-250ft (46-76m) with a diameter of 3-8ft (0.9-2.5m). It is not a true cedar.

Appearance

The sapwood is white, in contrast with the heartwood, which varies from dark chocolate-brown in the center to a salmon pink outer zone that matures to a uniform reddish-brown. Once dry and exposed, the wood weathers to silver gray, which makes it a particularly attractive prospect for shingles, weatherboard, and lumber buildings. The wood is non-resinous, straight-grained, and with a prominent growth-ring figure. It has coarse texture and is somewhat brittle.

Properties

Weight is about 23lb/ft³ (370kg/m³) when seasoned. Thin sizes dry readily with little degrade, but thicker stock requires careful drying. There is very small shrinkage in changing atmospheres, and stability in service. The wood has low strength in all categories and a very poor steam-bending classification. It works easily with both hand and machine tools, with little dulling effect on tools. Cutters should be kept very sharp. It has fairly good nailing properties but galvanized or copper nails should be used, as its acidic properties cause corrosion of metals and black stains in the wood in damp conditions. The wood can be glued easily and nailed satisfactorily, and takes stains of the finest tint without fading. It can be polished to an excellent finish. Sapwood is susceptible to attack by powder post beetle; the heartwood is durable and resistant to preservative treatment.

Uses

This softwood is used in the solid extensively for greenhouses and sheds, shingles, exterior weather-boarding, and vertical cladding. It is also used for beehives, and in the round for poles, and fences.

Triplochiton scleroxylon
Family: *Triplochitanaceae*

OBECHE (WAWA)

Ulmus spp.
Family: *Ulmaceae*

EUROPEAN ELM

Ulmus americana
Family: *Ulmaceae*

AMERICAN ELM

Where it grows

The tree occurs throughout West Africa. In Nigeria, it is also known as arere, in Ghana as wawa, in the Ivory Coast as samba, and in Cameroon and Congo-Kinshasa as ayous. It attains a height of 150-180ft (45-55m), with a diameter of 3-5ft (0.9-1.5m), and a clean cylindrical bole free from branches up to 80ft (25m).

Appearance

There is little distinction between the sapwood and heartwood, which is creamy-yellow to pale straw. The grain is interlocked, producing a striped appearance on quartered stock, and the texture is moderately coarse but even. The wood has a natural luster.

Properties

Obeche weighs 24lb/ft³ (380kg/m³) when dry. It dries very rapidly and easily with no tendency to split or for shakes to extend, but slight distortion may occur. There is small movement in service. The wood has low bending and crushing strength, very low stiffness, and shock resistance, and a moderate-to-poor steam-bending classification. It works easily with both hand and machine tools with only a slight blunting effect. Sharp cutters with a reduced sharpness angle are recommended. The wood nails easily but has poor holding qualities. It glues well, but requires a light filling to obtain a good finish. This nondurable wood tends to stain blue if in contact with iron compounds in moist conditions. The sapwood is susceptible to attack by the powder post beetle. The heartwood is perishable and resistant to preservative treatment, and the sapwood is permeable.

Uses

Where durability and strength are relatively unimportant, obeche is used for whitewood furniture and fitments, interior rails, drawer slides and linings, cabinet framing, interior pinery, moldings, sliderless soundboards for organs, and in modelmaking. It is rotary cut for constructional veneer for corestock and backing veneer for plywood, and it is sliced for decorative-striped veneers. The blue-stained obeche is particularly sought after by marquetry craftsmen.

Where it grows

Trees of the *Ulmus* genus occur widely throughout the temperate climes of Europe, western Asia, North America, and Japan. English elm (*U. procera*) is known as red elm and nave elm; smooth-leaved elm (*U. carpinifolia*) is the common elm of Europe, known as French elm or Flemish elm; there is Dutch elm (*U. hollandica*); and wych elm (*U. glabra*) or Scotch elm, mountain elm or white elm. European elms reach an average height of 120-150ft (38-45m), with a diameter usually of 3-5ft (1-1.5m); wych elm grows to 100-125ft (30-38m) tall and up to 5ft (1.5m) in diameter.

Appearance

The heartwood is usually a dull brown, often with a reddish tint, and is clearly defined from the paler sapwood. The heartwood has distinct and irregular growth rings, giving the wood a rather coarse texture. It is cross-grained and of irregular growth, which provides a very attractive figure. Wych elm has a greenish tinge. Continental elms are usually more straight-grained.

Properties

European and Japanese elms (*U. laciniata*) weigh about 34lb/ft³ (550kg/m³); wych elm 42lb/ft³ (670kg/m³) when seasoned. The wood dries fairly rapidly, with a strong tendency to distort. The wood has low bending and crushing strength, with very low stiffness, and resistance to shock loads. All elms have a very good steam-bending rating. It can be difficult to work, tending to pick up in planing and bind on the saw, but it takes nails well, glues satisfactorily, and provides a good finish. The sapwood is susceptible to attack by powder post beetle and common furniture beetle. Elm is nondurable, moderately resistant to preservative treatment, and the sapwood is permeable.

Uses

The Rialto in Venice stands on elm piles. Elm is used for boat and ship building, dock and harbor work, weatherboards, gymnasium equipment, agricultural implements, vehicle bodywork, ladder rungs, coffins, and Windsor chair seats. It makes attractive flooring. It is used for meat chopping blocks, and as a turnery wood for bowls. It is sliced for decorative veneers, and elm burrs (burls) go for cabinets and paneling.

Where it grows

The *Ulmus* genus has five species growing in eastern Canada and the US. *U. americana*, L. produces white elm in eastern Canada as far west as Saskatchewan, and in eastern and central parts of the US; it is also known as water elm, and swamp elm. *U. fulva*, Michx. produces slippery elm, also known as soft elm, red elm, and slippery barked elm, which occurs in the St. Lawrence River valley; and *U. thomasii*, Sarg. produces rock elm, also known as cork elm, hickory elm, and cork bark elm, which occurs in southern Quebec and Ontario, extending into the US. Elms average 50-80ft (15-25m) in height, with a diameter of 1-4ft (0.3-1.2m).

Appearance

The heartwood is medium to light reddish-brown, with a paler sapwood. Rock elm is straight-grained with a moderately fine texture. White elm is sometimes interlocked and the texture is coarse and quite woolly.

Properties

White elm weighs 36lb/ft³ (580kg/m³); slippery elm is a little heavier. Rock elm weighs 39-49lb/ft³ (620-780kg/m³) when seasoned. The wood dries readily with minimum shrinkage. American elms have medium bending and crushing strength and very low stiffness. White elm has high resistance and rock elm has very high resistance to shock loads. All have very good steam-bending ratings. The lumber works fairly easily with only moderate blunting effect on tools. They take nails without splitting, glue easily, and provide an excellent finish. The sapwood is susceptible to attack by powder post beetle but is resistant to fungus. Elm is nondurable and moderately resistant to preservative treatment.

Uses

American elm is used in boat and ship building for stern posts, ribs, general framing, gunwales, bilge stringers, keels, rubbing strips, and other, underwater, components; also for parts in dock and harbor work. Other uses are wheel hubs, blades of ice hockey sticks, agricultural implements, chair rockers, gymnasium equipment, bent work for vehicle bodies, and ladder rungs. The wood is excellent for turnery, and is sliced for decorative veneers and burrs (burls).

WORKSHOP AND TOOLS

Wherever you begin woodworking, you will want to develop a workshop dedicated to the task of making furniture. You need to consider environmental factors such as heat, ventilation, and light—as well as the layout of the bench and machines, and how easy it will be to get materials in, and completed items out. A small workshop cannot have space dedicated to each activity. Each space must be used for several tasks.

BELOW: Choosing and using the right tools for the job is essential for successful project-making.

Workshop layout

Planning your workshop

Draw a scale plan of your workshop, and make cardboard cutouts of the bench and machines. Mark the locations of doors, windows, and power outlets, and experiment to find the best situation for each item.

Manmade board and wood are heavy, and take up a lot of space. Tools and other materials should be within easy reach. Each machine needs space around it: materials must be able to pass through saws and planers unobstructed, and on most other machines, the material projects to one side or another. Also, make sure that one machine does not interfere with another.

Incoming material

Wood can be up to 15ft (5m) long, and manmade boards are typically 4ft x 8ft (1220mm x 2440mm). Full-sized sheets may have to be cut in the garden or by the supplier. These materials must be kept in the workshop so that they remain dry—with even temperature and humidity—while they are being made up.

Storage

Finish, hardware, glue, and other supplies can be stored in well-planned shelves, drawers, and cupboards. It is worth spending time in planning and making them. If you do not hold large stocks, bring them into the workshop, but try to put them in a secure, possibly fireproof, cupboard.

Workbench

A sturdy bench is essential. Position it, if possible, in natural light, near a window. If this is not possible, good artificial light will be necessary.

Hard floor surfaces get very uncomfortable if you are working for long periods. Lay industrial rubber matting around the work area in front of the bench.

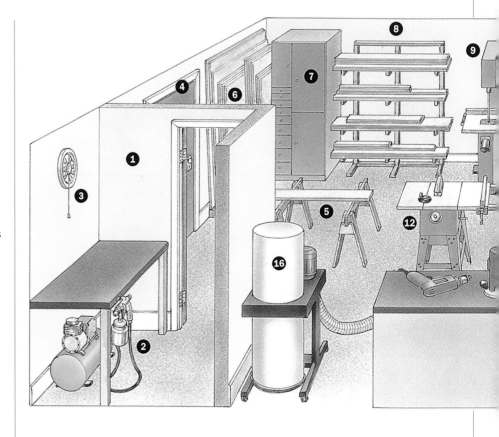

Cutting and assembling

To facilitate larger projects, leave space for a couple of sawhorses—so that wood can be laid down for chalking and rough cutting, and for assembling cabinets. Consider height as well as ground area for large items like sideboards, dressers, and tables.

Finishing

Your choice of finish may have to be influenced by your working environment. If you are using varnish, you must have some means of air extraction— necessary if you are using a brush, but absolutely vital if you are spraying. When using oils, always unfold the cloths, and, preferably, put them outside to dry. Oily cloths, left in a bundle, can self-ignite.

Dust extraction

When spraying, the air must be free of dust. Machining and sanding generate a lot of dust. If possible, make sure that all machines are connected to a dust extractor. Wear a face mask when spraying, or doing dusty jobs.

Light

One of the most important considerations is light. A good source of natural light is best, backed up with carefully, placed sources of artificial light. Tungsten light is preferable to fluorescent, with individual spotlights over the workbench and some of the machines.

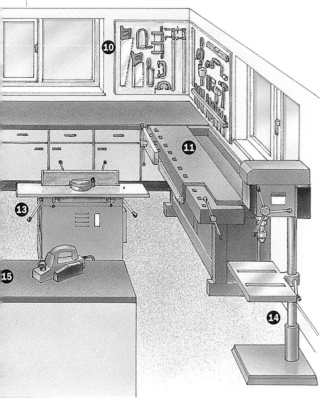

Anatomy of a workshop

1 Finishing room
2 Compressor and spray gun
3 Exhaust fan
4 Main entrance
5 Sawhorses
6 Manmade boards
7 Small fittings and consumables
8 Lumber storage
9 Handsaw
10 Hand tool storage
11 Workbenches
12 Table saw
13 Thickness planer
14 Pillar drill
15 Power hand tools
16 Dust extractor

Workshop environment

- Keep the workshop well ventilated at all times.

- Always use a dust mask or face shield in a dusty atmosphere.

- Be tidy, this saves time and prevents accidents.

- Always store flammable chemicals, lacquers, varnish, etc., in a cool, safe place.

Heat

Your workshop should be heated to just below the temperature of the place where the piece of furniture will finally be situated. Furnituremakers working in cold and damp workshops have had work ruined by wood movement when a completed piece of furniture has been taken into a heated environment.

Scrap and waste

You will often have small pieces of wood and other materials that can come in handy for subsequent jobs. Anything of a respectable size is worth putting in a special place where you can reach it easily.

What is not usable scrap—shavings, sawdust, etc.—is waste. Sweep up daily, since any waste left lying on the floor is a potential hazard.

Safety

Keep the work space tidy. Have a fire extinguisher and first aid box attached to a wall where they are in plain view of anyone coming into the workshop. Install a smoke alarm.

Delivery

Make sure you can get finished furniture out of the workshop, into the car, trailer, or van, and into its final location. Large pieces may need to be made in sections for final construction or delivery.

Health and safety

No subject has come to public attention in recent years more than health and safety. The popularity of woodworking and the consequent increase in the numbers of people involved in the activity have inevitably led to more accidents. Although legislation has been introduced to cover industrial and educational establishments, home woodworkers—who are usually working alone—are left to exercise their own discretion.

Health and safety should primarily be a matter of common sense, and no amount of legislation or safety guards on machines can prevent someone from cutting off a finger on a saw or severing a nerve by allowing a chisel to slip. Manufacturers invariably provide clear and comprehensive instructions for the safe operation of the tools and equipment they produce, and you should always read these carefully before any item is used.

Safe workshop setup

Floor space

Machines must be located so that there is room to maneuver. There needs to be plenty of all-round space, so that a workpiece can be freely fed into the machine at one side and extracted at the other. The amount of space should relate to the size and type of work produced. For example, the space needed to make small toys will obviously be less than that needed to make furniture. As lumber always comes in lengths, and as the procedures necessarily involve walking from one machine to another (and all kinds of bending, stretching, and lifting activities besides) it is best to aim for as much space as possible.

Tips box

A considerable number of workshop accidents are caused by slippery floors. If you are at all worried about slipping—say in front of a hazardous machine like a lathe—you might consider creating anti-slip surfaces. A swift money-saver is to paint selected areas with a rubber-type adhesive, sprinkle sharp, dry sand over the adhesive, wait for it to cure, then sweep up the excess sand. Remember, always keep the floor space as clear as possible, to avoid tripping or slipping. Never leave waste or garbage lying around, and always clean up any accidental spillages immediately.

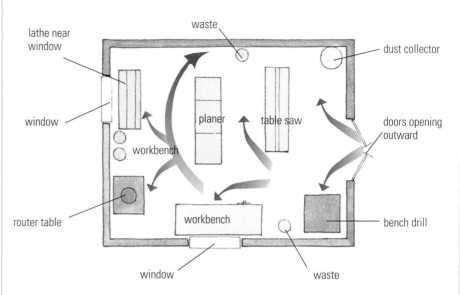

ABOVE: Arrange the work tables and machines so that you are able to move freely from one to another.

ABOVE: A rubber mat provides an anti-fatigue surface and has the added benefit of doubling as an anti-slip surface.

Floor surfaces

The floor surface should be stable, dry, hard-wearing, fireproof, easy to clean, pleasing to they eye, and non trip-and-slip. Most woodworkers favor a solid concrete slab, with selected areas covered with various secondary finishes. Depending upon your personal likes and needs—and, of course, the size of your bank balance—a concrete floor might be painted, or covered with industrial-grade sheeting, rubber/cork/vinyl-tiled, or even finished with strip hardwood. If you work for extended periods of time standing in one place—such as at a workbench or lathe, you may want to put down a rubber anti-fatigue mat.

Floor coverings

Cushion-backed vinyl (top); untreated cork tile (center); rubber tile (bottom).

Wall surfaces

Clean, bright walls make for a safe working environment. Though your workshop might be built of anything from concrete block to wood framing, the actual interior wall surfaces need to be smooth, light in color, fire resistant, dry, and generally easy to clean and maintain. Most woodworkers favor white-painted plasterboard or plywood for the walls and ceilings. Fiber or cork bulletin boards are useful for displaying designs, telephone numbers, timetables, and the like—and battened areas are good for shelving. Some woodworkers find sections of Pegboard useful for hanging up tools, but make sure peg hooks are secure so that they do not come out when you pull down a tool.

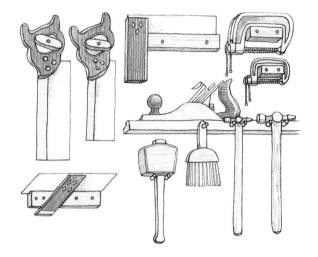

LEFT: Organize your tool board with pegs and brackets so that everything is in full view and easy to reach.

RIGHT: Store all your heavy items on shelves and in pigeon holes.

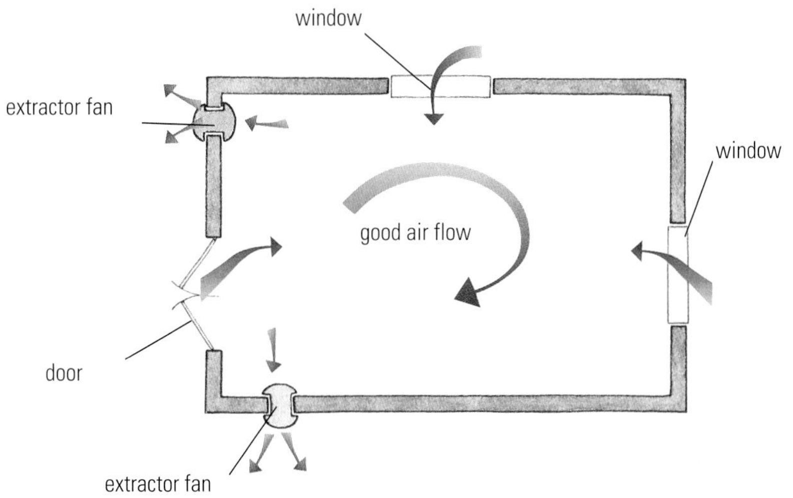

Air needs to be flowing in through the doors and windows, and out through extractor fans. The air should be dry and live.

Air and windows

For health and safety's sake, clean air is a must. Your workshop must be ventilated by opening windows and an air-filter system. Planning regulations generally recommend that the area of opening windows must equal 20 percent of the total floor area. If you need to remove fumes and stale air, you will require a positive-pressure ventilation system (PPV). A good, swift money-saver, is to set a fan outside the workshop in such a way that fast-moving air flows directly into the workshop, and out through windows and vents. Alternatively, on a summer's day, you can throw the doors open, and work with plenty of sunshine and fresh air. In winter, you will save on heating bills by keeping windows closed and using a ceiling-mounted recirculating air filter.

window

extractor fan

window

good air flow

door

extractor fan

A first floor workshop.
An enclosed woodburning stove
with a boiler and radiators is an
allround winner—it gets rid of your
waste, and keeps you warm. Plan
the layout so that there is an
adequate fuel storage area.

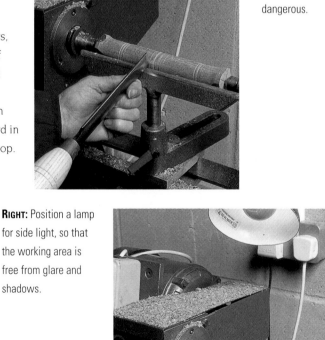

waste radiator window

low iron-bar gate

sawdust

waste

window

offcuts

woodfired boiler fireproof wall radiator

Heating

Cold fingers and toes equal slow
response times—your workshop needs
adequate heating. Oil-fired, electric, and
wood heat systems similar to those used
in homes are all workshop options. Bear
in mind that, whatever system you use,
the object of the heating is two-fold—
to keep you warm and to eliminate the
condensation that does so much
damage to tools and machines.

If you must use
temporary space
heaters, always
avoid gas and
kerosene heaters,
as these give off
water vapor and
also present a
potential carbon
monoxide hazard in
a closed workshop.

LEFT: A poorly-lit
lathe can be
dangerous.

RIGHT: Position a lamp
for side light, so that
the working area is
free from glare and
shadows.

Lighting

Ideally, all machines and work surfaces
need to be positioned so that there is a
well-balanced mix of natural and
artificial light. In windowless workshops,
take extra care to provide adequate
lighting without shadows. Specific tasks,
and left- and right-handedness, might
call for additional lighting options. The
overall goal is a lighting level that
eliminates glare and hard shadows. For
example, with a lathe positioned in front
of a window, and with ceiling lights at
top-center, you might also require
additional flexiblearmed lamps to your
right, to throw light directly into the
point of cut.

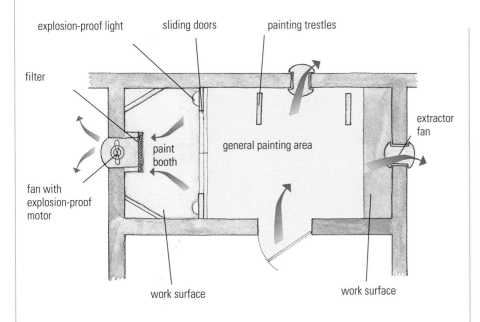

explosion-proof light   sliding doors   painting trestles

filter

paint booth

general painting area

extractor fan

fan with explosion-proof motor

work surface   work surface

Set an area aside for brush and spray painting.

Painting area

If you plan to do a lot of woodwork, then you should have a small, clean, dust-free area set aside for finishing. You could either screen off some part of the workshop, and provide it with positive ventilation—so that air flows from the painting area to the outside—or you could set up a totally separate room. Any fan used in a spray finishing area should be of the explosion-proof variety.

A spray gun needs to be used with great care and caution.

Electrical safety

Wiring

All electrical wiring must be in good condition and properly insulated. If the installation is old—say about 25-30 years—then it really needs replacing with modern insulated cable. It is best to check local building and electrical-code requirements, and have the system wired by a qualified electrician. Work with the electrician to locate wiring and outlets convenient to work areas with adequate provisions for both 110-volt and 220-volt circuits as needed. You may even wish to consider locating cables in surface-mounted raceways. Then, not only can you swiftly and safely modify the system to meet your changing needs, but, better yet, you will not have problems when you want to mount shelves and machines on the walls. You may also consider ceiling-mounted wiring for some machines.

Bad electrical layout

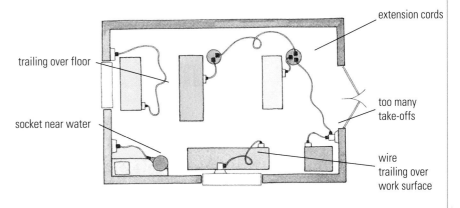

extension cords

trailing over floor

socket near water

too many take-offs

wire trailing over work surface

Assess your electrical needs, then plan the wiring layout so that there is plenty of room for expansion.

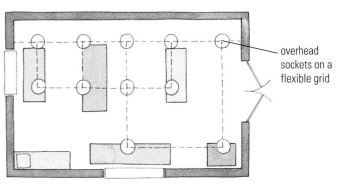

overhead sockets on a flexible grid

Good electrical layout

Circuit breakers

You do not need to understand how circuit breakers work. Suffice it to say they are the primary way of protecting you and your machines from electrical damage. In use, the circuit breaker literally breaks the circuit when the system is overloaded, or when an accident occurs such as a severed power cable. Have your electrician make sure your circuit breakers and electrical service are adequate for your needs.

Unplug for safety

One of the most common causes of accidents is not taking the little extra time to do something the safe way. This is particularly true when it comes to electricity and machine setups. When you need to change a bit or blade, unplug the machine first. Do not take a chance on it accidentally getting switched on with your hand in the works. Whenever you work on a machine, unplug it and keep the power cord end in plain view, so you that know it is unplugged.

For optimum safety, pull out the plug and keep it in full view.

Personal protection

Health and safety includes taking precautions against the dangers that can arise through dust and debris, and through noise pollution. Eye and ear protectors are essential and should always be worn. In addition, not only should you wear a respirator, but you should also use equipment that extracts dust at its source. Noise pollution can be minimized by insulating individual pieces of equipment, and, of course, the workshop itself.

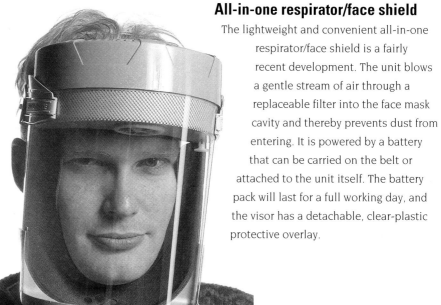

All-in-one respirator/face shield

All-in-one respirator/face shield

The lightweight and convenient all-in-one respirator/face shield is a fairly recent development. The unit blows a gentle stream of air through a replaceable filter into the face mask cavity and thereby prevents dust from entering. It is powered by a battery that can be carried on the belt or attached to the unit itself. The battery pack will last for a full working day, and the visor has a detachable, clear-plastic protective overlay.

Goggles

Goggles

Putting on a pair of goggles or a visor before you start work should become second nature. Eye injuries are the most commonly reported injuries among woodworkers, so you should always wear some form of protection.

Dust mask

Dust mask

It is always worth buying the best possible quality dust mask. Some brands are less effective than others, especially if they do not fit snugly around the contour of your nose. Make sure that you choose masks that have a nose clip as an integral part of their design.

Be disciplined about wearing your dust mask. It is not much use to you if you buy one and simply leave it lying in a drawer somewhere. You may find it a nuisance to wear at first, but it is an essential form of protection and an important piece of equipment for you to get used to using.

Earmuffs

You should wear earplugs or earmuffs to protect your hearing from long-term damage whenever you use power tools such as saws and routers. These soft, padded protectors are inexpensive, and it should soon become a matter of habit to put them on.

Earmuffs

Toxic wood

Some woods are toxic—to the touch, to breathe in as dust, when they are in contact with some foods, when they are in contact with eye and nose membranes, and so on.

- Always use a respirator, checking first that it is approved for use with wood dust, and wear goggles or a face shield.
- If you are working indoors, or in any kind of enclosed space, make sure that there is adequate ventilation.
- If you are at all uncertain about the toxicity of the wood you are working with, check it first before starting work. It is not worth the risk.

Tips box

Never allow chemicals and adhesives to come directly into contact with your skin or eyes. Always wear protective gloves and goggles when working with them. If you do accidentally splash any toxic substance on your skin, or get any in your eyes, wash off immediately with plenty of cold water and seek medical assistance if necessary.

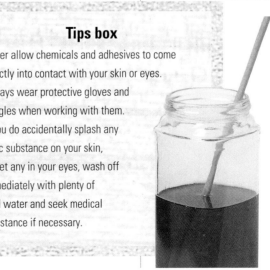

Working with tools

Bending and lifting

When you come to lifting a heavy chunk of wood—like a big turning blank or a small log—from floor level, squat down, with your knees together, throw your arms around its middle, then slowly straighten your legs.

Be warned—if you stoop over a heavy item, and try to lift it with a loose, belly-sagging, knees-apart, curved-back action, then you are asking for trouble. If your work requires lots of lifting or bending, consider wearing a back-support belt for extra protection against injury.

Lifting boards

When you are lifting heavy manmade boards up from the floor to the bench—say a ¼in (6mm) thick sheet of plywood, particleboard, or MDF—you most certainly put yourself at risk if you try to do it on your own. If you work alone, strap it with a flat webbing to make a handle, stand in a well-braced upright position, and use a controlled lift-and-slide action to ease it up onto the bench.

Adjust the straps so that the point-of-lift is at a comfortable height.

Reaching

It does not matter how tall or short you are, if you are stretching and reaching to do something, then you are doing it wrong. Not only is there the potential for falling, or hurting your back, but, if machines are involved, the hazards increase. Stretching to control a workpiece on a table saw, for example, could very quickly bring you into contact with the saw blade. If you repeatedly find yourself stretching or reaching, then ask yourself why. Is the shelf too high? Is the bench too wide? Is the walk-around space restricted? Then solve the problem by getting a pair of steps, or lowering the shelf, or whatever seems appropriate.

Working with hand tools

Always keep your hand tools sharp, as they will then be easier to control, and therefore safer. Working practices have evolved so that cuts are made away from the body. Remember this rule and never take risks.

Chisels

Of all your hand tools, the chisels are the most widely used, the most open to abuse, and the most vulnerable. If you have a choice and are buying new, go for hand-forged, laminated-steel blades, with fully-honed, ready-to-use cutting edges. The laminated steel will hold an edge longer. The guards that are usually supplied with the tools are designed to protect both you and the cutting edges—so do not lose them. Store chisels at a low level—never high up on a shelf where they are hard to reach and might fall, possibly damaging both you and their fine cutting edges.

Work with a safe two-handed cut—one hand pushing, and the other holding and guiding.

When the job is done, protect the razorsharp bevel edge with a plastic guard.

Working with power tools

Most modern power tools are now equipped with a variety of guards to help protect the operator. Do not ignore them. Use them as much as possible. If you find a guard difficult to use, do not just take it off and run the machine unprotected. Call the manufacturer's customer service representative to see if additional help is available. Maybe you have not installed the guard properly, or maybe it is defective. If you still do not like the guard, check out the various devices available. You will see several models demonstrated at most tool shows.

straight cutting edge

circular cutting edge

Never work with the guard in the "up" position (above left). Adjust the guard height shields so that they fit the size of the work piece (above right). Guards and other safety devices will never replace care and common sense, but they can be very valuable.

Power tool safety checklist

- Always follow the manufacturer's instructions.

- When working with machinery, never wear loose clothing, and tie back long hair.

- Keep hands well away from moving or cutting edges.

- Wear ear protectors and goggles, especially when working a spindle molder or power planer.

- Beware of trailing cables when using hand-held machinery.

- Always turn off the main power supply before adjusting machinery.

- If in doubt, read or get some instruction before using any unfamiliar tools.

- Be sure all power tools and machines are correctly wired and insulated before use.

- Never work unprotected. One of the undeniable laws in woodworking is that something can always go wrong.

Always follow the manufacturer's instructions when using power tools.

Scrap collection and cleanliness

Possibly the greatest risk in the home workshop is from fire. Always sweep up dust and chippings at the end of the day and dispose of them carefully.

Scrap collection

Woodshop scraps, in the form of shavings and offcuts scattered around the floor, are a dangerous nuisance. On the one hand, the shavings will polish the floor to the extent that it becomes slippery, and, on the other hand, loose offcuts can easily be tripped over. It is good woodshop practice to make a point of sorting the scraps into stuff that can be used for small projects, bits that might be recycled into, say, dowels, and pieces that need to be thrown away.

Oily rags

Oily rags—meaning rags soaked in motor oil, solvents, French polish, oil-based varnish, linseed oil, brush cleaner, and the like—are dangerous. Under certain warm, enclosed conditions, the rags can smolder and spontaneously combust. Remove the rags from your workshop as soon as you have finished with them. Wet them and put them into a metal trash can. Never drop the rags into a plastic wastebasket—or seal them up in a plastic bag—as this can increase the risk of fume build-up and fire. Special air-tight metal cans are available for temporary rag disposal.

Organize your scraps collection for maximum efficiency—bags for dirt, garbage cans for fragments, and racks and boxes for offcuts.

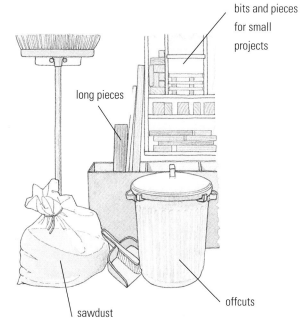

bits and pieces for small projects

long pieces

sawdust

offcuts

Make sure that all your small power tools are fitted with dust bags.

Use a portable dust-vacuum system to service individual machines.

Dust collection

According to health and safety regulations, you should limit your exposure to fine wood dust. In very broad terms, they suggest that if you were to puff a heaped teaspoon of dust into the average garage-sized woodshop and then spend more than fifteen minutes a day in this atmosphere, you would be exceeding the safety limits. For safety's sake, you need to adhere to the following rules of thumb:

- Cut down on the amount of dust at source by using filtered machines, and/or by producing shavings rather than dust.

- Capture as much dust as possible by using a vacuum system.

- Wear a dust mask/respirator.

What to do in an emergency

Phone

The phone is a double-edged tool. On the one hand, its noisy interruption can in itself be a hazard—especially when you are working on a fast-moving machine—but on the other, it can quickly put you in touch with the emergency services. Put the phone in a convenient position—but away from machines—and have a list of emergency numbers handy.

Work program

You do not want to be caught alone for hours—bleeding, trapped under a heavy object, or with your finger caught in some machinery—without anyone wondering where you are. That is why it is a good idea always to tell friends and family what you are doing, and how long you intend to be in the workshop.

Eye injuries

If you get something in your eye, do not rub the eye, or the eyelid, or poke around with a toothpick or use an eye bath. Simply hold a sterile dressing over the closed eye with surgical tape, and immediately go to a doctor or to the emergency room. DO NOT DRIVE — get a friend or helper to do the driving.

Cuts and splinters

If you have a workshop, it is only a matter of time before you scrape a knuckle, cut your finger on a chisel, run a splinter up your fingernail or incur any of a number of such injuries. It is a good idea to be ready with a well-stocked first aid kit. You need bandages, gauze, a pair of scissors, a pair of tweezers, a sterilized needle, and a tube or bottle of antiseptic to rub on the wound.

First aid kit

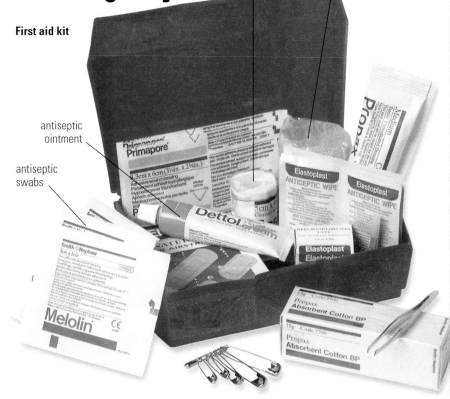

gauze   bandages

antiseptic ointment

antiseptic swabs

First aid chart

Accidents and injuries are not uncommon in the workshop, so you should display a basic first aid chart on the wall, familiarize yourself with recommended first aid practices, and list the numbers of your nearest doctor or emergency room.

Fire extinguishers

Every workshop should have at least one fire extinguisher (dry powder type), a bucket of water, a bucket of sand, and a fire blanket. In an emergency, like, for example, an electrical glue pot bursting into flames, you should first turn off the power, and then control the fire with the sand and/or extinguisher. On no account should you start throwing the water around onto live machinery. For even more protection, position extinguishers at different points around the workshop.

Make sure that your fire extinguishers are in good condition and easy to reach.

Water   Sand

Always keep your smoke alarm clean, in order for it to be fully effective.

Smoke alarms

Smoke alarms are a must, especially if you are anxious about fire risks—and this is perhaps more of a problem if your workshop is an integral part of your home. They are a swift, sure, and inexpensive means of detecting smoke. The average, large-garage-sized workshop should have three alarms—one at the center of the room, one as far away from the door as possible, and one next to the door.

The workbench

A woodworking bench is one of the first things you will need when you start woodworking. The bench must be sturdily made and heavy enough not to vibrate as you plane or saw. It is often useful to attach it to the floor or a wall.

The bench vise is an essential part of the bench. You will need one of the following types. The integral vise has wooden jaws, tightened by rotating a screw. It is often supplied mounted on the front of the bench, with another mounted on the end.

The metal vise is larger, and you need one of a good size, with minimum 9in (230mm) jaws with an opening width of up to 12in (305mm), preferably with a quick-release handle. You must fit hardwood vise "cheeks" to this vise, to protect your work.

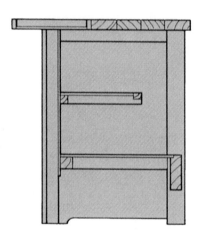

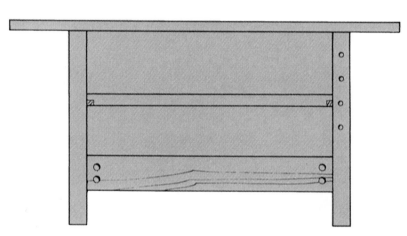

Plans for bench (above, left, and right) are not dimensioned; dimensions will depend on the space available and the preferred working height.

Square mortises are cut in the top to accept a bench dog (right), while the holes in the right-hand leg accept a peg, which supports the far end of any long piece gripped in the front vise at the left-hand side (above right).

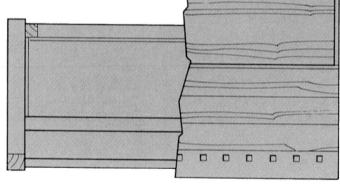

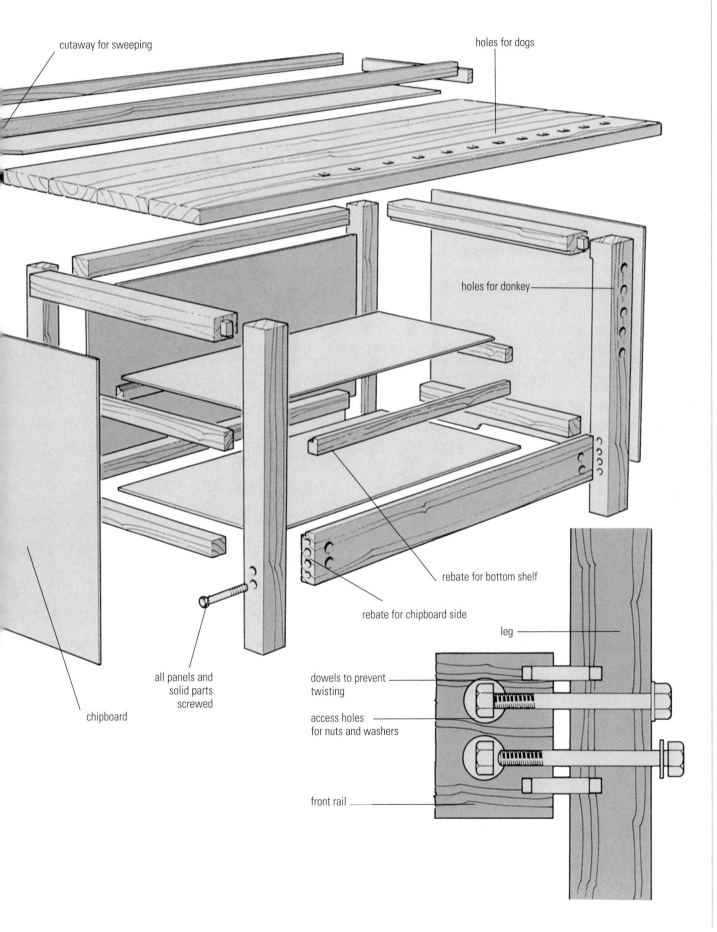

cutaway for sweeping

holes for dogs

holes for donkey

chipboard

all panels and
solid parts
screwed

rebate for bottom shelf

rebate for chipboard side

leg

dowels to prevent
twisting

access holes
for nuts and washers

front rail

Portable folding bench or "workmate"

The workmate is a superbly-designed device, which takes up little room when it is not needed, but which can grip or support awkwardly-shaped work in its vise jaw top and plastic "dogs"—small blocks which grip the work flat on the workmate. Extra support can be achieved when planing if you place one foot on the "step." The bench's versatility extends to gripping circular sections of wood of large and small diameters. However, its lightweight construction means that it is not designed to take a pounding from a mallet.

RIGHT: This workbench has a slot along the back edge in which to store tools, and a shelf to hold pieces of wood and large equipment. The sturdy worktop is made of beech.

ABOVE: A lightweight, low-cost vise.

TOOLS

The tools in this section provide a basic kit to start the projects in this book. Woodworking tools are precision instruments and their purchase, storage, and use all need care if they are to last. Always buy the best tools you can afford—it is usually false economy to buy cheap ones. Price can be a guide but, more importantly, look closely at the tools and you will see the difference in quality.

BELOW: Even a basic tool kit is a substantial investment, but if you look after your tools, they will last a lifetime.

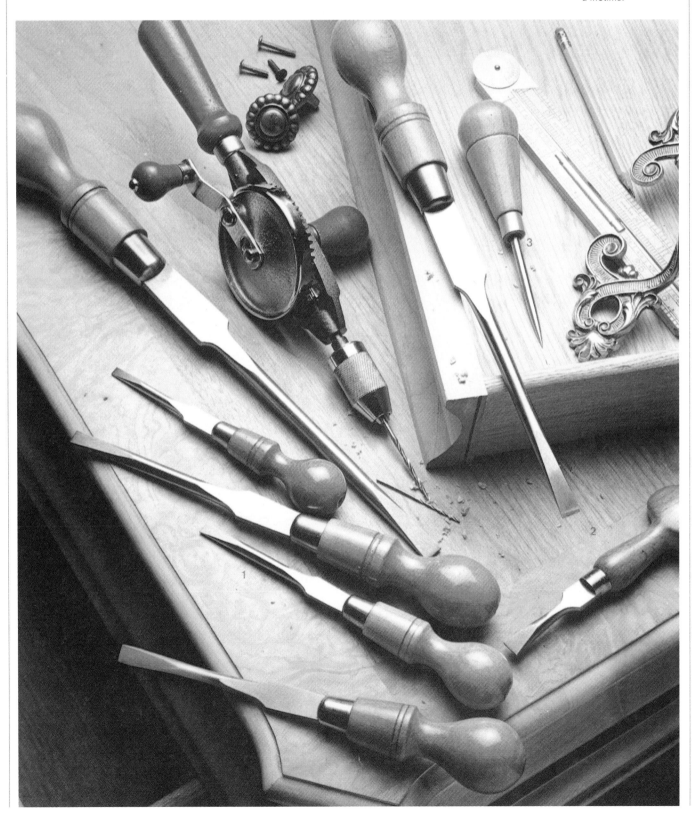

Hand tools

Most woodworking tools are hand held—indeed, woodworking is itself a manual activity. However, tools that are operated by the muscles rather than an external power source are defined as "hand tools." When time is pressing, you may prefer to use a powered tool, but there are occasions when it is both quicker and more efficient to use a hand tool—when machines have to be set up, for example. Hand tools are vital in measuring and marking out, for no power tool (aside from a robot) can perform these tasks.

Some woodworkers prefer to use hand tools and to "feel" the wood they are using with their fingers.

Hand tools are, in any case, an essential part of the kit of all woodworkers, and one of the great pleasures in woodworking is building up a collection of personal tools.

The try square is a vital piece of equipment. It is used for marking and checking lines at 90 degrees and is available in a variety of sizes.

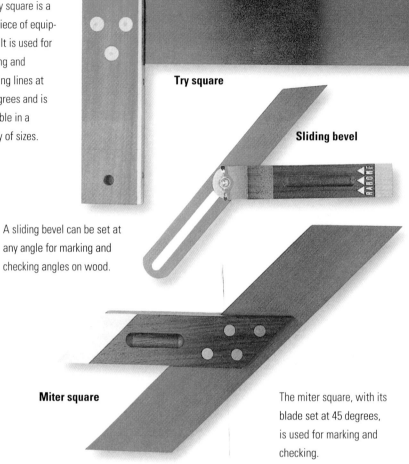

Try square

Sliding bevel

A sliding bevel can be set at any angle for marking and checking angles on wood.

Miter square

The miter square, with its blade set at 45 degrees, is used for marking and checking.

Marking knife

A marking knife, the most accurate scoring tool, is generally used against a straight-edge.

Coping saws are used for cutting curves or decorative patterns. The blade may have up to 30 teeth per 1in (25mm).

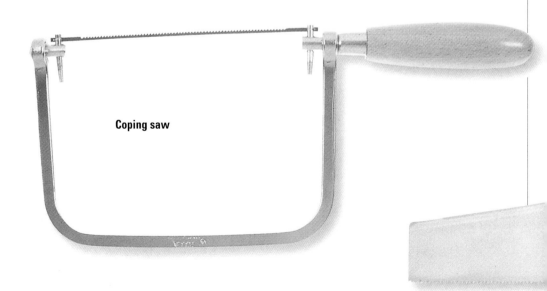

Coping saw

A beech marking gauge is used to mark parallel lines. The stock is held firm against the edge of the wood, while the spur is trailed across the surface.

A mortise gauge, or combined mortise and marking gauge, as it is sometimes known, has a single spur and two movable spurs, which can be set to the width of a mortise chisel. The stock is then held in position with its locking screw.

A tenon saw is the best general-purpose saw for cutting straight lines. They are usually 12in (30cm) long and have 13-15 teeth per 1in (25mm). A dovetail saw (right) is a miniature tenon saw for finer work. They are about 8in (20cm) long and have 16-22 teeth per 1in (25mm).

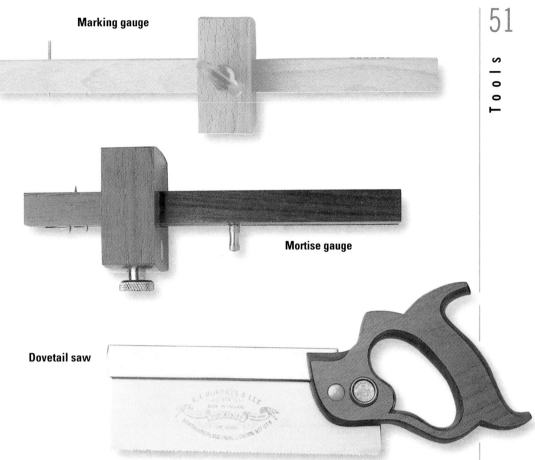

Marking gauge

Mortise gauge

Dovetail saw

Handsaws are either rip, crosscut or general purpose for cutting straight lines down or across the grain. They are approximately 650mm (25in) long and have 6-8 teeth per 25mm (1in).

Tenon saw

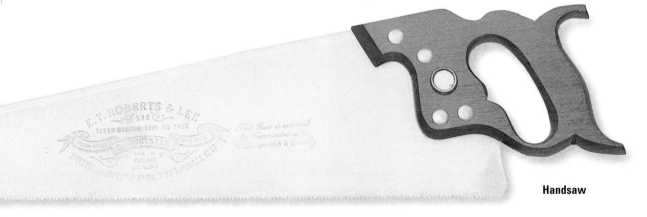

Handsaw

Bevel-edged chisels, available in sizes from 1⁄8in (3mm) to 1½in (38mm), are lightweight, versatile tools, but they should not be used with a mallet.

Available in the same size range, firmer chisels are more robust than bevel-edged chisels.

Cutting deep slots or mortises requires a stout tool and mortise chisels range in size from 1⁄4in to 1⁄2in (6mm to12mm).

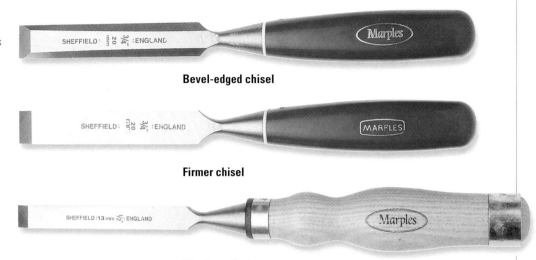

Bevel-edged chisel

Firmer chisel

Mortise chisel

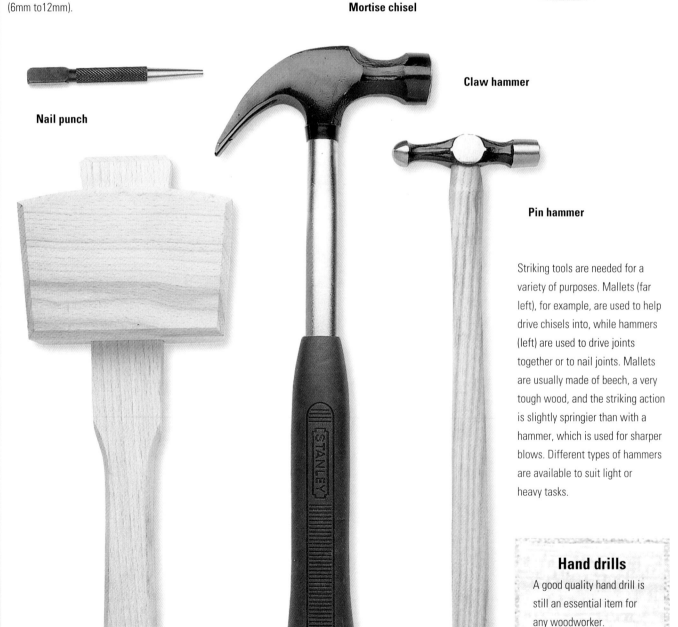

Nail punch

Claw hammer

Pin hammer

Striking tools are needed for a variety of purposes. Mallets (far left), for example, are used to help drive chisels into, while hammers (left) are used to drive joints together or to nail joints. Mallets are usually made of beech, a very tough wood, and the striking action is slightly springier than with a hammer, which is used for sharper blows. Different types of hammers are available to suit light or heavy tasks.

Hand drills

A good quality hand drill is still an essential item for any woodworker.
See "Drilling" section pages 137-144.

Spokeshave

For accurate shaping, there is little to beat the spokeshave, which can have a flat or a rounded sole.

Smoothing plane

About 9in (22.5cm) long, the steel smoothing plane, with its fine blade adjustments, is a vital tool for flat and shaped skimming.

Block plane

The smaller block plane, which has a shallower blade angle, is used for delicate work.

The jack plane, which can be 13¾-15¼in (345-388mm) long, makes long pieces truer, and the extra weight gives more control.

Jack plane

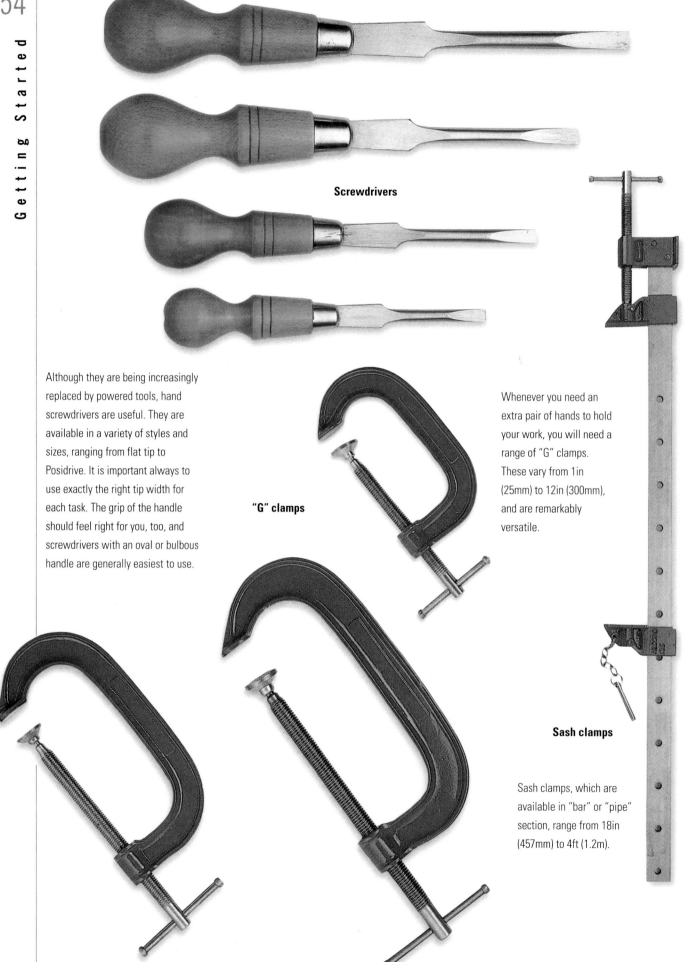

Screwdrivers

Although they are being increasingly replaced by powered tools, hand screwdrivers are useful. They are available in a variety of styles and sizes, ranging from flat tip to Posidrive. It is important always to use exactly the right tip width for each task. The grip of the handle should feel right for you, too, and screwdrivers with an oval or bulbous handle are generally easiest to use.

"G" clamps

Whenever you need an extra pair of hands to hold your work, you will need a range of "G" clamps. These vary from 1in (25mm) to 12in (300mm), and are remarkably versatile.

Sash clamps

Sash clamps, which are available in "bar" or "pipe" section, range from 18in (457mm) to 4ft (1.2m).

Power tools

In the past few decades, the development of power tools has changed the face of woodworking. Not only do these tools remove the drudgery from such arduous tasks as drilling and planing, but the technology offers new ways in which wood can be fashioned—by the router, for instance. The development of aluminum casting, plastics molding and silicon chip technology has brought the power tool a long way from the simple portable drill or drill attachment. Improvements in the electric motor and advances in cutting technology—tungsten-carbide tipped (TCT) blades, for example—have also been significant. Most recently, cordless tools have provided the woodworker with a new range of convenient and compact tools.

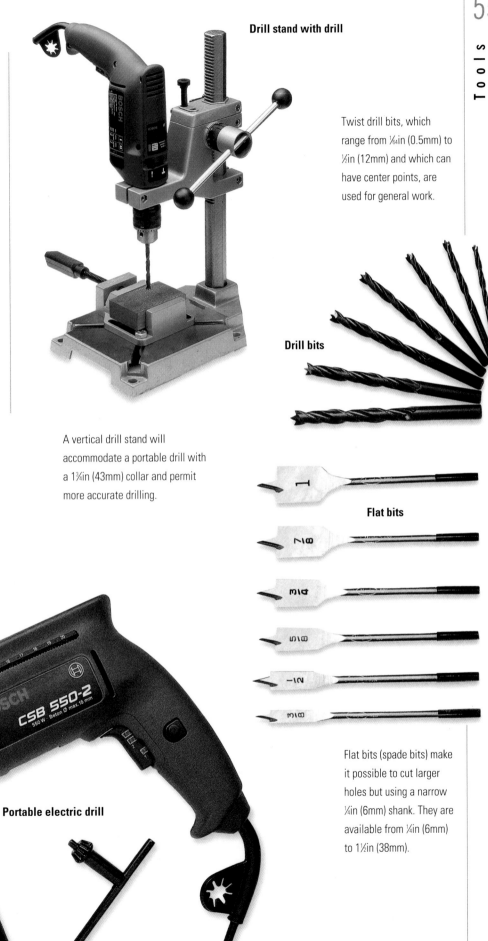

Drill stand with drill

A vertical drill stand will accommodate a portable drill with a 1¾in (43mm) collar and permit more accurate drilling.

Twist drill bits, which range from ⅟₆₄in (0.5mm) to ½in (12mm) and which can have center points, are used for general work.

Drill bits

Flat bits

The portable electric drill is the original power tool, and there can be few home workshops without one. With a keyed or fast-action chuck, a mains-powered drill should have around 550 watts of a ½in (13mm) chuck.

Portable electric drill

Flat bits (spade bits) make it possible to cut larger holes but using a narrow ¼in (6mm) shank. They are available from ¼in (6mm) to 1½in (38mm).

Cordless drill and bits

Recent advances in technology have seen the rates at which battery chargers operate fall from 16 hours to 5 minutes, and some chargers can even diagnose the state of the battery, drain it completely if necessary, and recharge all the cells evenly. Some chargers take batteries from a variety of tools.

Available in voltages from 3.6 to 24, the cordless drill with keyless chuck can never be as powerful as its electrical counterpart, but it is safer and more convenient.

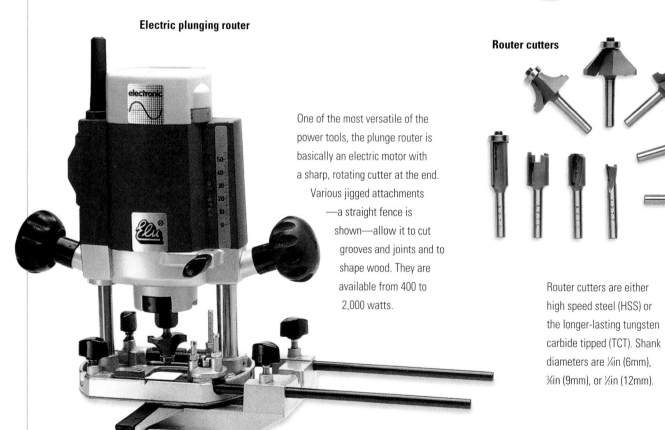

Electric plunging router

One of the most versatile of the power tools, the plunge router is basically an electric motor with a sharp, rotating cutter at the end. Various jigged attachments —a straight fence is shown—allow it to cut grooves and joints and to shape wood. They are available from 400 to 2,000 watts.

Router cutters

Router cutters are either high speed steel (HSS) or the longer-lasting tungsten carbide tipped (TCT). Shank diameters are ¼in (6mm), ⅜in (9mm), or ½in (12mm).

The jigsaw is a versatile hand-held tool for making straight, curved, or angled cuts. The blade moves up and down and the cut is more efficient when the action is "orbital." Different blades are available for use with different materials.

Jigsaw

Jigsaw blades

Oilstone

The combination oilstone (left) has coarse/medium or medium/fine grade surfaces. It is lubricated with oil and used to sharpen chisels and plane blades. The diamond stone has a grid of durable diamond particles set in plastic.

Portable circular saw

The portable circular saw is used to cut solid wood or manufactured board material. A straight fence can be attached for parallel cuts. The blade can be set to different depths for grooving, and the sole plate tilted for angled cuts along and across the grain. Blades are 5in (130mm) to 9in (225mm) in diameter.

Random orbital sander

The random orbit sander has a self-gripping, backed abrasive disk, which moves eccentrically while it rotates to create a random abrading effect. It is used for flat and curved work.

Orbital sander

The orbital sander uses ½ or ⅓ size abrasive sheets, which are clamped to a padded baseplate. The action is elliptical, and the tool should be used under its own weight.

A belt sander uses a 3in (75mm) or 4in (100mm) continuous belt for heavy-duty abrading.

Belt sander

Biscuit joiner

A biscuit joiner offers a versatile method of connecting solid board or sheet wood. The blade of a small circular saw is plunged to form elliptical recesses into which compressed wood "biscuits" are glued.

TOOL MAINTENANCE

Saw sharpening is always done in three sequential stages: jointing, fitting, and setting.

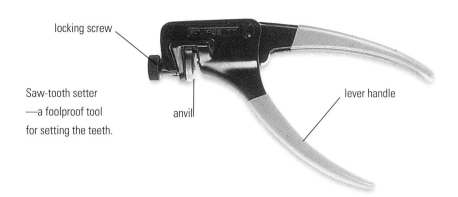

locking screw

lever handle

Saw-tooth setter
—a foolproof tool
for setting the teeth.

anvil

Sharpening saws

1 Jointing ensures the teeth are the same height. Sandwich the saw between two pieces of wood held in the vise, then use a flat file to cut all the teeth down to the same level. The jointing procedure takes no more than a few strokes of the file.

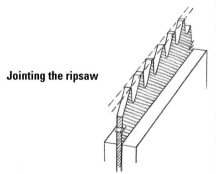

Jointing the ripsaw

2 Setting adjusts the teeth for proper cutting clearance. Use a plier-like tool called a 'saw set' to splay the teeth. The jaws of the set are opened, the tool is located on the tooth, and then the handles are clenched to bend the tooth over at an angle. The teeth need to be set alternately left and right down the length of the blade. The angle of set determines the width of the kerf and amount of cutting clearance. Use a generous set for cutting greenwood and a small set for cutting well-seasoned hardwood.

Setting the ripsaw

3 Fitting makes sure that all teeth are at the correct angle. Use a triangular-section, 60-degree file to cut the leading edge of each tooth to the correct angle. The angle that the file is held in its approach to the saw blade varies according to the type of saw being sharpened. Ripsaw teeth are filed at an approach angle of 90 degrees, meaning the file is held at right angles to the saw blade. Crosscut teeth are filed at an approach angle of about 45 degrees. Alternate teeth are worked from one side of the blade, and then the whole procedure is rerun from the other side. With crosscut saws, the leading edge of each tooth is canted back by about 12 degrees.

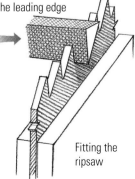

Fitting the ripsaw

Sharpening chisels

Grinding to remove chips

If the cutting edge of a chisel is nicked, the edge will need to be squared. If the nicks are small, they can usually be touched up with a file or on a coarse benchstone, but if they are deep, the edge will need regrinding on a wheel. Wheel grinding is done in three steps —squaring off to take out the nicks, polishing the back, and grinding the primary bevel. To square off the leading edge, set the rest so that it is horizontal (180 degrees) to the surface of the wheel. Lay the chisel on the rest with the bevel uppermost, and grind the chisel on the wheel, moving it from side to side until you have ground back the leading edge to the depth of the deepest nick. When done, lay the blade flat on a benchstone, again with the bevel uppermost, and make a few circular strokes to polish the back of the blade. Finally, adjust the tool rest to an angle of about 25 degrees to the wheel, lay the chisel with the bevel flat against the wheel, and grind it against the wheel, moving from side to side, just enough to establish the bevel angle. When using a bench grinder, don't grind off too much metal, don't allow the blade to overheat, and always wear goggles.

Honing with a gauge

Once grinding on the wheel is done, hone the bevel on a benchstone to polish it. If you are a novice, use a honing guide or gauge. Position the chisel in the guide bevel down, and set the angle to place the bevel flat against the stone. Dribble a few drops of light oil on the stone, and then hone the chisel backward and forward. With experience, you can dispense with the guide—many woodworkers say it develops better hand-eye coordination without.

Hold the guide firm and square so that the movement is even and controlled.

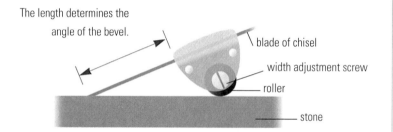

The length determines the angle of the bevel.

blade of chisel

width adjustment screw

roller

stone

ABOVE: Side view of a sharpening guide. The guide is helpful in that it maintains a square edge. It is crucial that you follow the instructions that come with it—they will tell you how far the blade should protrude for the different bevels.

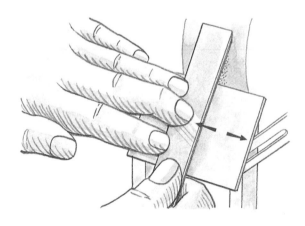

Lay the chisel bevel side down on the stone and rub it from side to side. Be careful not to overheat the steel.

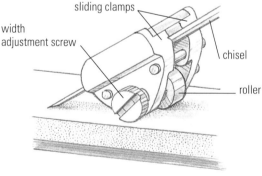

sliding clamps

width adjustment screw

chisel

roller

Lay the chisel bevel side down in the gauge, tighten up the adjustment screw slightly so that the blade is captured, make fine adjustments until you have the correct bevel-to-stone angle, and then tighten the screw.

Honing on a diamond stone

Many woodworkers advocate using a diamond stone. The manufacturers claim that such stones will cut up to 95 percent faster than conventional oil and water stones. Diamond stones are graded from extra coarse to extra fine, and can be used for everything from grinding to fine honing.

A manmade combination oilstone

A diamond stone— the blue indicates that it is a fine grade.

1 Many woodworkers feel that polishing the back of a chisel blade—after the leading edge has been ground square, and before honing the primary bevel—is at the heart of successful chisel sharpening. The object is to flatten the back of the chisel so that all traces of the burr (burl) have been removed. A diamond stone is perfect for this because it is exceptionally flat.

Tips box

Many chisels may appear smooth on the back when taken out of the packaging, but most will have diagonal machine marks across the steel. Rub the back of the tool across a diamond hone or use fine-grade abrasive paper taped to a piece of thick glass to form a perfectly flat surface. Hold a tape measure at around 90 degrees to the finished surface— you should be able to see the numbers reflected in the polished steel.

2 Place the chisel flat on the stone, apply pressure with your fingertips, and work with a firm circular action. With precision and the right pressure, a few strokes are all that is needed (above).

3 After the primary bevel is ground comes the much-maligned polishing of the secondary bevel. I say maligned, because this stage has been variously described as a waste of time, difficult to achieve, and fussy. What you do is sprinkle a few drops of water on the stone, set the chisel bevel face-down so that the whole bevel is in full contact with the stone, and then raise the handle slightly so that a bead of water pushes out in front of the blade. Then draw the chisel toward you with a careful dragging action. If you then hold the bevel up to a light, you will see that a secondary bevel, or microbevel, can be seen as a thin line of light running along the cutting edge (left).

Maintaining planes

Stripping down

The bench plane, a tool at the very heart of woodwork, is one of the most abused tools in the workshop. The success of the cutting action depends not only on the cutter iron being sharp, but also on all the parts being properly adjusted. The challenge is to achieve a balance of all the settings.

First, strip the plane down to its component parts.

1 Lift the cap lock and pull up and remove the lever cap. Draw the cap iron and cutter up toward the handle and ease it forward and up, so that it clears the location screw.

2 Undo the cap iron screw, and separate the cap iron and cutter by turning the cap around and down—so that it is at right angles to the cutter iron—and then slide it down toward the cutting edge until the screw head is clear of the slot.

3 Undo and remove the screw at the back of the frog and the two screws at the front of the frog, and lift the frog clear.

4 Turn the adjusting nut clockwise so that it clears the 'Y'-shaped adjusting lever.

5 Finally, unscrew the single screw that attaches the front knob to the toe and the two screws that attach the back handle to the heel.

Lapping the iron and iron cap

Lapping is the procedure of flattening, removing rust and polishing. It is done on a lapping board, which is a sheet of flat material – a board, a sheet of plate glass or whatever – on which is mounted a sheet of fine-grade abrasive paper with the abrasive side facing up. Something like silicon carbide, garnet or aluminium oxide works well. I usually mount the paper with double-sided sticky tape. If you choose to mount the paper on a sheet of glass, support it on a piece of board so the glass does not break.

1 Dribble a few drops of oil on the lapping board, lay the plane cap iron on it, top up, and lap the underside edge to a perfectly smooth finish. The idea is to flatten the underside edge, so that it meets the cutter iron absolutely flush, leaving no room for shavings to push up between the two pieces.

2 Lap both sides of the cutter iron until the metal is free from high spots and polished smooth. The cutter must be pressed flat throughout the whole operation.

Lapping the sole

Just like the cutter iron, the body of the plane should be lapped to flatten the sole (bottom). The frog, knob, and handle should be attached to the body. Use a pad of fine-grade steel wool and mineral spirit to clean off all traces of rust and resin. Color the sole and the sides of the plane with a felt-tipped marker. Dribble a few drops of light oil on the lapping board, and begin stroking the sole of the plane backward and forward. Continue until the whole sole is bright and gleaming. Repeat for the sides.

Clearing the frog

Start by brushing the dust and scraps out of the various nooks and crannies. Pay particular attention to the area behind the lateral adjusting lever. Lightly oil it and the "Y"-shaped adjusting lever so that both move freely. Set the frog back in place so that it is very slightly back from the mouth, and tighten up the three screws. Replace the adjusting nut, making sure it fits into the "Y" lever. Make sure that the leading edge of the frog is square with the mouth.

If the lateral adjusting lever is stiff, chances are there is a mix of wood dust and oil packed between the lever and the body of the frog. Clean it out with a small brush.

Honing the cutter iron

Just like a chisel, the cutter iron has two bevels—a primary bevel and a secondary microbevel. The honing procedure is much the same as for the chisel.

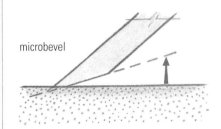

microbevel

The microbevel is honed by laying the primary bevel flat on the stone, lifting the blade slightly, and fine-honing just the front edge of the bevel.

1 First, hone the primary bevel to an angle of about 25 degrees, and then cock the cutter iron up at an angle that is slightly greater than that of the primary bevel and hone the microbevel. Use a honing guide if you want to take the guesswork out of setting the angles.

2 Re-assemble the plane, and adjust the nut for depth of cut. Push the lateral adjusting lever left or right to set the cutting edge of the cutting iron parallel with the plane mouth.

Sharpening a scraper

The important thing about the scraper is not so much how it is used—easily learned by trial and error—but how it is sharpened. If you have a close look at a scraper in action, you will see that it is the minute, turned-up edge of the burr (burl) that does the cutting. When the burr gets to be rounded, then the scraper fails to cut. To sharpen the scraper, set it in the vise and use a file to cut the edge down square. Next, hold the scraper edge-down on an oilstone, keeping it upright and at right angles to the stone, and run it straight backward and forward until the filed edge is square, crisp, and clean. Now, set the scraper flat-down on the stone and polish the slight burr (burl) left by the honing. Lastly, set the scraper in the vise so that the edge is standing proud, then take a burnisher or any hardened, round-section tool, like the back of a round gouge, and run it repeatedly at an angle along the corner-edge to raise the burr (burl). Repeat this procedure on both edges. If you have done it right, the edge will be "burnished and burred" or turned up at the corners.

1 Use a flat file to bring the edge of the scraper to a level, clean-cut finish. Repeat this procedure for both cutting edges.

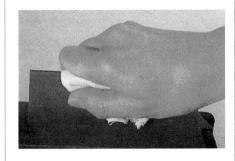

2 Hold the scraper with a piece of cloth so that you don't cut your hands. Hone the filed edge on a medium stone. Aim for a square-cut polished edge.

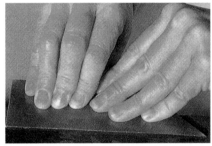

3 Burnish and remove the slight burr (burl).

4 Run a hardened round-section tool, such as a burnisher, along the edge to bring up the burr (burl). Do this on both edges.

5 A well-tuned scraper will produce the best of all surfaces—many times smoother than a plane or sandpaper.

Routers

General everyday cleaning

Routers soon get dirty. Wood dust gets in the air intake and in the springs, resin builds up on the base and the posts, and so on. A little dust and dirt can make a sensitive tool like a router stop working well. You should routinely clean out all the dust and dirt, just as you might clean out the car after a trip. Start by vacuuming it well. Then spend time with a small brush getting the dust out of all the little nooks and crannies. Polish the poles and generally keep all the brightwork gleaming. After cleaning, spray a small amount of very light oil on the various moving parts, and wipe the whole works with a lint-free cloth.

Clean away all the dust and resin and burnish the brightwork.

Spray a small amount of light oil over mating surfaces so the various parts are able to move freely.

Use a mild solvent to clean off all traces of resin. DO NOT USE ABRASIVES.

Checking the collets

Router collets must be painstakingly disassembled, inspected, and then reassembled at regular intervals. The reason is that you can't see if the collet splines are free from cracks just by looking. A damaged chuck collet is an accident waiting to happen. Always err on the side of safety and replace anything that looks suspect.

A suspect collet must be replaced immediately.

Checking for a build-up of resin and dirt

Have a good look at your bits and check them out for a build-up of resin. Resin is the sticky substance that oozes out of some woods. When it builds up on the bits, it forms a black, glazelike coating, which causes the bit to overheat. Once this starts to happen, a whole sequence of events occurs—the bit is difficult to fit, it tends to run off-balance, the glaze burns the wood being

worked, and so on. This all sounds bad, but the whole problem can be quickly corrected by using oven cleaner to remove the resin. Protect the clean bit with a smear of light engine oil. WARNING—never use an abrasive to scrape the shank, or to clean out the collets.

Sharpening

If on close inspection you see that the bit edge is dull—maybe, because you have used it to work a manmade material that contains bit-blunting resin glue—then it is possible to sharpen the cutting edges slightly by careful honing. The key word here is "slightly." First, establish whether your bit is made from high-speed steel or carbide steel. If it is carbide, then take a small diamond hone and work around the bit, just stroking each cutting face in turn. If it is high-speed steel, then use a diamond hone as before, only this time use it much more cautiously. Stay away from pilots and bearings, and make sure to hone each of the cutters evenly. If in using the router you find that, however careful you were, the bit is off-balance and causing a vibration, then for safety's sake send it out to be professionally honed.

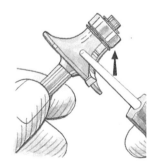

Hone the cutting edges to a bright finish. Treat both cutters equally.

BASIC TECHNIQUES

DESIGN, LAYOUT, AND FITTING

Story sticks and rods

A story stick or pole is a clean piece of wood that is laid out with all the full-size dimensions and details that go to make up the design of a piece of furniture. The system dates back to the time before paper was commonplace and when cabinetmakers were possibly illiterate. Joiners, chairmakers, and framers still use poles to transfer measurements. The pole is either set out from a working drawing, or directly from a piece of furniture that you want to duplicate. Though rods are in many ways the same as story sticks, the term has come to mean full-size mockups that are made in flat sheet material—more like a working model or prototype. So, for example, a chair might be mocked up in plywood so that you can test out its proportions.

Using story sticks

The wonderful thing about story sticks and rods is that the whole system works without the need for measurements and calculators. Let's say then, that you want to copy a hope chest in a museum. All you do is sketch the chest, and then set the story sticks against the piece (ask permission from the museum curator first!) and pencil off the various widths and heights directly. Ideally, you need three sticks, one for the vertical height, one for the width across the front, and one for the depth. And, of course, if there are unusual joints, or fancy details or whatever, then these are all written down on the stick. All necessary details and notes are written down. When you get back to the workshop, you then set the sticks down alongside your chosen wood and either copy the measurements off directly, or step them off with a pair of dividers.

Set the story stick directly against the piece and transfer the measurements of the various component parts.

Working drawing showing the back of a chair

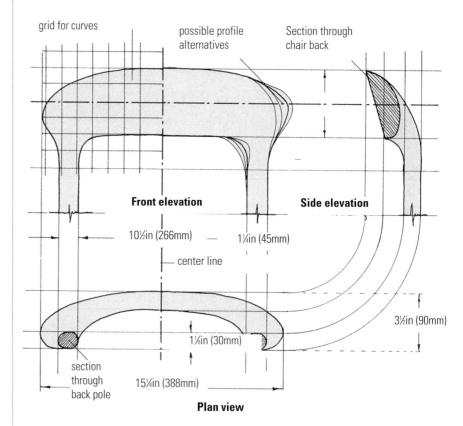

grid for curves

possible profile alternatives

Section through chair back

Front elevation

Side elevation

10½in (266mm) — 1¾in (45mm)

center line

3½in (90mm)

1⅛in (30mm)

section through back pole

15¼in (388mm)

Plan view

Calculating dimensions

The very first thing to do when you are presented with a working drawing is to look for dimensions. These are stated either in imperial measurements (fractions of inches, inches, and feet), or in metric form (millimeters, centimeters, and meters), and written on the drawing between arrowheads. Some drawings are done to scale, meaning that, for example, ½in (1cm) on the drawing equals 3ft (1m), and you must measure the dimensions and translate them to full size. Or, the drawing may be done on a grid, with a scale that reads "one grid

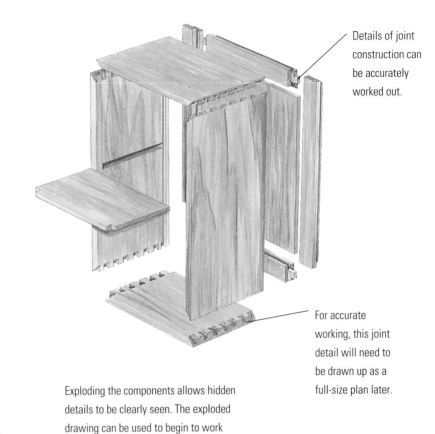

square is ½in² (1cm²)." Again, you must translate the grid to dimensions of each part so that you will know how to measure and cut.

Reading drawings

All but the simplest projects require an accurate scale drawing to be completed before making any piece of furniture. The drawing allows you to check proportions, measurements, and construction details.

There are basic drawing conventions followed by designers of all kinds, including furniture designers. These conventions, once you understand them, speed up the drawing process and remove any possibility of misunderstanding between designer and maker.

As an example, a wall-hung cabinet is used here to demonstrate various drawing techniques and conventions.

Sketch drawings and 3-D projections

Nearly all designers will begin with rough sketches, working them up to progressively more detailed and accurate drawings. Even if you have no drawing skills, you can still follow the same process using the drawing conventions and the basic projections.

Projections allow a 3-dimensional object to be represented on a flat piece of paper. This exploded 3-dimensional view of the wall-hung cabinet is a sophisticated illustration of an isometric projection, but it still keeps to certain basic conventions which anyone can follow with the help of a "T" square and a 30/60 degree try square. All vertical lines are drawn vertically, and all other lines are drawn at 30 degrees to the horizontal.

Details of joint construction can be accurately worked out.

For accurate working, this joint detail will need to be drawn up as a full-size plan later.

Exploding the components allows hidden details to be clearly seen. The exploded drawing can be used to begin to work out proportions.

Scale drawings

Most drawings need to be reproduced to scale if they are to be a manageable size. The scale chosen should suit the size of the object being drawn and will always be indicated on the drawing.

Again, there are conventions in the choice of scale which most designers will follow. For individual pieces of furniture, a scale of 1:4 in imperial measurements is common. This means that on the drawing ¼in or 3in equals 3in or 1ft on the piece of furniture. In metric measurements, the convention is to use a scale of 1:5 meaning 1cm=5cm or 10mm=50mm on the piece of furniture.

For larger pieces of furniture or room layouts, scale of 1:24 imperial and 1:20 metric and are common.

Small items or details may be drawn full size or even larger, and joints, moldings. and other details are often drawn alongside scale drawings of the whole piece of furniture. It is quite

common for drawings to include several items at different scales.

In recording dimensions, the convention is to write all measurements between extension lines for clarity. All dimensions should be placed so that they are readable from the bottom right-hand corner of the drawing.

Dimensions should be complete enough for full cutting lists to be worked out from them.

The first-angle projection and the third-angle projection are commonly used for accurate scale drawings. Both make use of the front view (front elevation), placing side views on the left or right, and a plan view at the top or bottom.

European projection

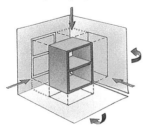

A first-angle projection imagines the object suspended in a square corner and being projected back onto the three surfaces.

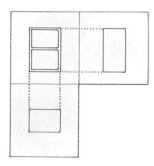

In a first-angle projection, the corner is cut along the red line, and opened out flat to produce the drawing.

Anglo-Saxon projection

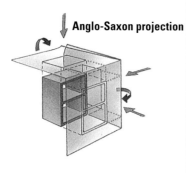

A third-angle projection imagines each face of the object projected forward onto a glass corner.

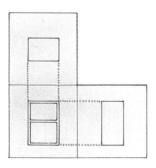

The glass corner is cut and opened out flat to produce the drawing.

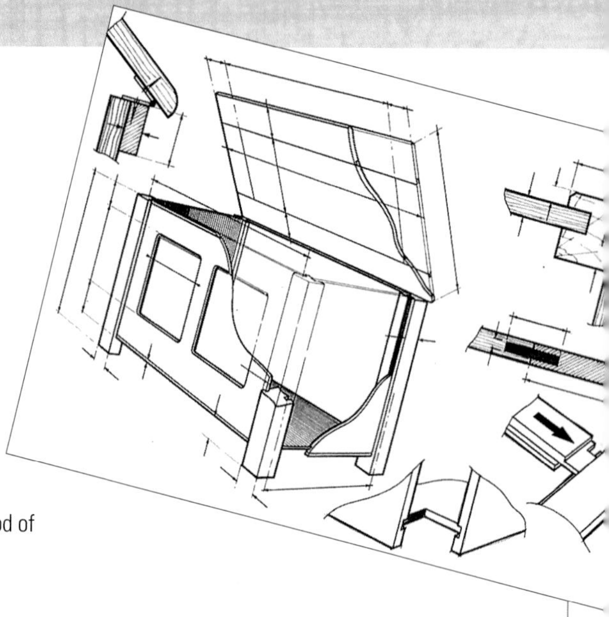

RIGHT: The 3-D cutaway drawing with detail annotations shows how intricate or shaped components fit together.

Third angle projection

The third angle projection is one method of laying out a drawing.

Sectional views are slices through the work to show internal construction details. This sectional side elevation has been taken through the centre line or A-A.

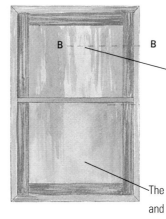

B-B, indicated here, relates to the further internal details that are included on the plan view.

The front elevation enables accurate internal and external dimensions to be shown.

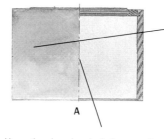

'Grain' lines are an accepted convention to represent sections through solid timber.

Here, the plan view includes a sectional half plan taken through B-B (below).

A detail clarifies the way in which the back components fit together and the way the cabinet attaches to the wall batten.

Broken lines indicate where the full-size drawing has been "compressed" to exclude parts that do not require this detailed treatment.

Getting ideas down on paper

1 With a little practice, quick freehand-perspective sketching comes easily. You may prefer to use a felt-tipped pen or a soft-leaded pencil such as a 2B.

2 The hand naturally draws lines in a clean sweep (the wrist serves as a pivot point), so constantly turn the paper to draw each line with ease.

3 A series of light lines can build up the picture quickly. Then go over with a bolder line for the outline. Leading edges are usually thickened. (In most drawings, there are three types of lines: a feint projection line, the outline, and the dimension line.)

Drawing circles

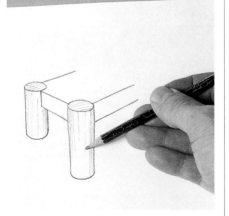

1 Perspective circles or curves can be drawn within a grid, which can be very helpful! Try drawing the circle first within a quartered box, then draw the same box at an angle and fill in the curves. Remember to rotate the paper and use your hand naturally.

After a while, you will be able to draw perspective circles freehand. Remember that it is an ellipse which has its long arc perpendicular to the walls of the cylindrical object to be drawn.

2 Circular solids can be shaded to give depth. Imagine a series of equidistant points marked around the circle with lines extended vertically.

Choice of marker

What is crucial to accurate laying out, whether you use a measuring stick, steel rule, or other aids, is the choice of marker. Effective laying out is bold and precise, and the areas to be cut away as "waste" are shaded clearly.

Traditionally, woodworkers use a pencil or marking knife; increasingly, ballpoint pens are used. A pencil tends to blunt as it draws, which makes a wider and less accurate line (unless it is a hard pencil and then it can be difficult to see the mark). A marking knife gives the most accurate results, but leaves an incised mark, difficult to remove afterward, and allows no margin of error for beginners.

The most fundamental rule of all in measuring and marking is to check, check, and check again.

Squaring lines

1 A marking knife and try square are used to square the lines across. The marking knife is more accurate although a pencil can be used.

2 When using a try square (which is fixed at exactly 90 degrees), always squeeze the stock against the edge of the wood using all fingers. Carefully score a line with the knife tight against the steel blade of the square.

3 Extend the line all the way around the wood, using the try square against the face side and face edge with their respective reference marks.

Measuring to length

When cutting boards to length (see Squaring wood page 78) it is always best to start off with a fresh "squared" edge. Measure in with the rule about ¼in (6mm) to square the first line across. (This is the minimum distance for sawing without the fibers disintegrating, and when this happens control of the saw is very difficult.) Set the zero at the ¼in (6mm) mark and measure off the required dimension, spreading the fingers again to keep the steel rule steady.

Measuring and marking parallel lines

1 There are various ways to measure and mark parallel lines. The easiest is to use a tape measure stepping off two marks at either end of the board. But you can also use a steel rule or measuring sticks.

2 A steel straight-edge or steel rule can be used to mark a line across the two measured points. Spread your fingers along the straight-edge to ensure it does not slip. Mark the line up to the edge of the ruler.

Measuring and marking

All woodworking starts with measurements. From the very outset of a project, you will need to use measuring and marking techniques, not only for preparing the materials and establishing dimensions, but also for laying out cutting lines and for testing that faces and edges are true. Once the wood has arrived, then comes the critical stage of using a whole range of tools and techniques for transferring the measurements from the working drawings to the wood. The fact that accuracy is crucial for good woodworking is very neatly summed up by the traditional adage, "Measure twice and cut once."

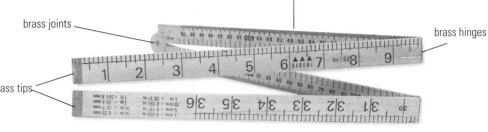

imperial and metric graduations

brass joints

brass hinges

brass tips

Measuring rules

The traditional 2ft (61cm), four-fold boxwood and brass rule has long been considered the best all-around tool for measuring in woodwork. Of course, there are alternatives—folding extension rules, two-fold rules, tape measures and many more besides. But nevertheless the four-fold rule is still the most economical, the easiest-to-use, and the most versatile measuring tool for woodworking.

A good traditional method of using a rule to divide a board into a number of equal widths is as follows. Suppose a board is 6in (15.25cm) wide, and you want to divide it into seven equal widths. Set the rule across the board at an angle—so that 0 and 7in (17.8cm) are aligned with opposite edges of the board. Draw a line across the board and mark it off at 1in (2.5cm) intervals. Now use a marking gauge or a long straight-edge to run parallel lines down the length of the board so that they intersect with the step-offs. Then the board will be divided into seven equal widths. If you use this technique, it doesn't matter if the board is an indeterminate width of anything less than 6in (15.25cm); the board will still be divided into seven equal parts.

Traditional four-fold boxwood and brass rule

Stainless steel rules

The traditional boxwood rule is still a top-quality tool. Place rule on edge for accurate markings.

Make sure that the 0 and 7in (17.8cm) marks are perfectly aligned with the edges of the board.

metric and imperial graduations on one side only

engraved graduations

imperial graduations on one side and both edges, metric on the other

Tips box

Measurements often vary from one rule to another, so it's important that you stay with the same rule for the full run of a project. Be warned: if you are working on a week-long project, and you use a steel rule on one day and a boxwood rule on another day, and so on, then the chances are you will finish up with mismatched component parts.

Measuring sticks

One of the easiest and most traditional ways of transferring a measurement from the working drawing to the wood, or from one piece of wood to another, is to use a measuring stick, sometimes called a story pole (see page 66). So, if you want to make a copy of an existing item such as a chair rung, all you need do is set a stick alongside the rung, make a notch with a knife, and from then on in all the other lengths can be marked off from the stick directly. And of course, if, at the end of the project, you label the stick with all the details and hang it on the wall with a loop of string, then next time around, you can relate to the stick without the need for a rule or the rung. If the sticks are well-labeled, then this system will save you a good deal of time and effort. In many ways, this method of measuring is more accurate than working with a couple of rules that might differ slightly.

Tapes

One of the most commonly used measuring tools is the flexible tape—known usually as simply a "tape" or a "tape measure." In use, the end of the tape is hooked on the edge of the workpiece and then the hand-size body of the tape is drawn out in such a way that the sprung ribbon is pulled straight and stays rigid.

thumb-operated blade lock

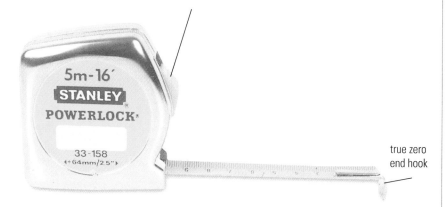

true zero end hook

Power lock measuring tape.
The tape measure is an indispensable tool.

Marking knives

The line of cut – meaning the line that will eventually need to be cut with a saw or chisel – should be marked out with a knife. Certainly the initial layout can be done with a hard-point pencil, but when the pencil lines are in place and you have identified the cutting line, then the pencil lines will need to be reworked with the knife. If you use the knife the scored line will not only more positively establish the position of the line of cut, but, better yet, the severed fibres of the wood will provide a

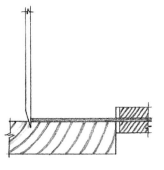

Make sure that the flat face is hard up against the straight-edge.

Use the fingers of the left hand to pull the bevel hard up against the workpiece.

blade

rosewood handle

scratch awl

The classic western combination marking knife and awl

hand-forged laminated steel   European-style angle for right-handed use

The Japanese marking knife

starting point for the saw or chisel, reducing the potential for chipping.

Although marking knives come in all shapes and sizes, the very best type has a bevel on one side only, so that the flat face of the blade can be run hard up against the straight edge.

Many woodworkers worldwide are now coming around to the idea that the Japanese marking knife is the best tool for the job. These knives—designed for left-, right-, or double-handed use—are razor sharp with a hollow-ground bevel. In use, the square or metal straight-edge is positioned on the line to be marked, the flat side of the marking knife is held hard against the edge, and then the line is struck—or scored—by the knife drawn toward you in a single, uninterrupted stroke.

Tips box

- You can make up your precision marking knife from a piece of hacksaw blade or a broken craft knife blade. Form a handle from two sections of a hardwood such as oak and bolt together with small nuts and bolts, countersunk into the wood on each side.
- You can buy Japanese adjustable twin-bladed marking knives which can make exact parallel lines in one stroke. These are ideal for adding stringing or inlay to a veneered surface.

Square-bladed "birdcage" awl

The scratch awl is the perfect tool to spike pilot holes in softwood to start nails and screws.

across grain

When you are using the "twist" technique with the bradawl, it is important to start the twist with the chisel point set across the run of the grain.

Scribes and awls

Known variously as marking awls, striking awls, scratch awls, or simply as awls, these pointed tools are used to scratch lines and spike holes. The most basic form—called a scratch awl—has a 5in (12.7cm), needle-like spike and a ball-shaped handle. In use, the handle is cupped in the palm of the hand with the index finger extended along the spike. Then the tool is either drawn to make a line, or swiveled on the spot to make a hole, usually for starting a screw or nail in exactly the right position.

A slight variation is a chisel-pointed version called a bradawl, which is used for spiking holes in heavily, grained hardwood. The nd must be placed across the grain ore starting to twist the handle. This severs the wood fibers instead of splitting them along the grain direction. Awls are becoming less common in many workshops as the power drill/driver and self-starting screw is so easy and quick to use. However, the awl is still an essential tool for more delicate work such as boxmaking.

Carpenter's steel square

engraved graduations for permanence

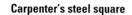

imperial graduation on one side, metric on the other

heavy gauge-tempered steel

Try square

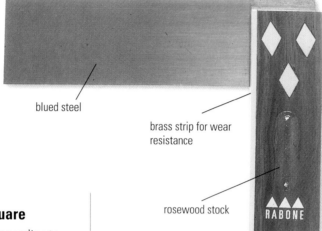

blued steel

brass strip for wear resistance

rosewood stock

RABONE

Carpenter's steel square

The woodworker is forever needing to use one or other of a whole range of squares to variously test that lines, edges, and faces are at right angles to each other. The simplest square, known as a carpenter's square, is simply a single piece of "L"-shaped steel that is marked out with various measurements and tables. The carpenter's square is designed primarily to be used for large work—tabletops, cabinet frames, doors and so on. The short arm is known as the "tongue," while the long arm is known as the "blade." Being made from a single piece of steel, a square of this character is just about as strong, precise, and foolproof as a square can get. Better yet, the large size of the square—the tongue is 16in (40.65cm) long and the blade is 24in (60.95cm) long—ensures a high degree of accuracy. If you are new to woodwork, and if you are looking to get yourself a square, and if you have in mind to build large items, then remember that the longer the arms of the square, the longer the contact with the workpiece, and so consequently the greater the accuracy.

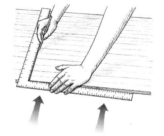

Butt the long arm hard up against the side of the wood.

Hold the square so that the wooden handle—sometimes known as a "stock"—is hard up against the workpiece.

Try square

The familiar try square with its steel blade and rosewood handle—the handle is called a "stock"—all fitted and fixed with fancy brass inlay and rivets, is designed primarily for bench work. If you want to mark lines that run at right angles to edges and faces, then this is the tool for the job. To use the try square, first plane and mark the true face and edge of the wood. Then press the try square's stock hard up against the true face, striking lines off against the steel blade. The superior try square has an "L"-shaped blade, one arm of which is encased in the wood. Lesser models have a strip of metal that is top-mounted to the wood. You can appreciate that if the poor grade square is dropped, then the chances are that the blade will be knocked out of line.

"T" bevel or bevel gauge

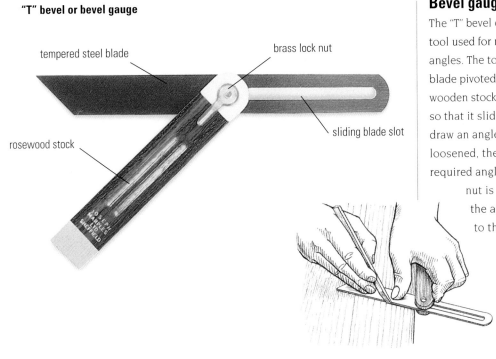

tempered steel blade

brass lock nut

rosewood stock

sliding blade slot

Bevel gauge

The "T" bevel or bevel gauge, is another tool used for marking and laying out angles. The tool comes either with the blade pivoted to the middle of the wooden stock, or with the blade slotted so that it slides along the pivot. To draw an angle, the wing nut or screw is loosened, the blade is set to the required angle against a protractor, the nut is retightened, and then the angle can be transferred to the workpiece.

It is important to make sure that the wooden stock of the bevel is held hard up against the edge of the workpiece.

Gauges

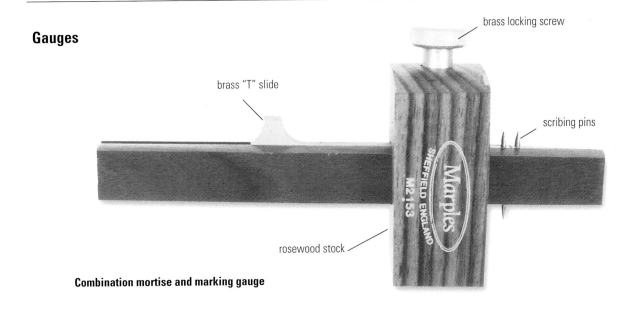

brass locking screw

brass "T" slide

scribing pins

rosewood stock

Combination mortise and marking gauge

Setting the single-pin marking gauge

There are two primary ways of setting a marking gauge: you can either set the distance by taking a direct reading from the edge of a rule, or better still, you can make a mark on scrapwood, and then set the gauge to the mark. Let's say then that you want to go for the latter technique, and you want to run a line 1in (25.5mm) in from the edge of the wood.

The procedure is simple: first use a square ruler and pencil to make a mark 1in (25.5mm) in from the edge of the wood. Then loosen the thumbscrew, spike the pin on the mark, slide the fence hard up against the edge of the wood, tighten the screw, and finally have a trial run on a piece of scrap to test the setting.

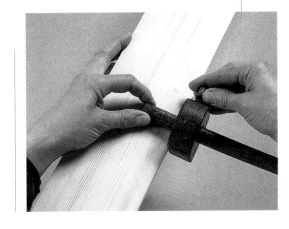

Setting and using the mortise gauge

The mortise gauge has two pins—one fixed and the other movable. To use the tool, set the distance between the two pins to the width of your chisel. Adjust the fence so that the pins are centered on the middle of the workpiece. When you are happy with the adjustment, butt the mortise fence hard up against the face side of the wood, and then draw the gauge away from you with an even dragging stroke. It's important that the pin is dragged rather than pushed.

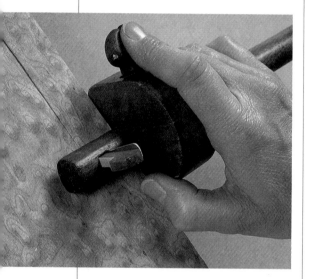

Using the cutting gauge

Let's say you want to cut a 1in (25.5mm) wide strip from a ⅛in (32mm) thick piece of stock or from a piece of veneer. Having first of all honed the cutter to a razor sharp edge, refit it in the stem and set the fence so that it is 1in (25.5mm) away from the cutter. This done, support the veneer so that the true edge is flush with the cutting board, butt the fence hard up against the board, and then drag it away from you—in much the same way as when using the marking gauge. Repeat the procedure until the strip is free.

Using clear symbols

Some projects are made up of dozens of parts, so it is vital that your symbols are clear and unambiguous. Use face-edge marks to identify the true face and edge, and triangle markings to show how groups of parts relate to each other. If mating parts are placed in the same order as they are when assembled, you can assume that the triangle always points up or away. If the parts are mixed up, simply rebuild the triangle for the correct order.

It is important that each part of a piece carries two lines of the triangle —in this instance each board that makes up the slab.

Dividers

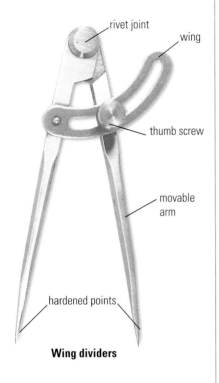

- rivet joint
- wing
- thumb screw
- movable arm
- hardened points

Wing dividers

- bow spring joint
- adjusting nut
- threaded rod

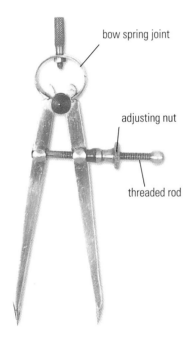

Spring dividers

Laying out a hexagon

Dividers are used primarily for reading measurements off a rule, for transferring measurements, and for scribing out circles and arcs. If you are thinking of getting a pair of dividers, get the type that have a screw-thread adjustment and a locking nut.

1 Set the legs or points of the dividers to the desired radius measurement.

2 Spike the dividers down on the workpiece and scribe out the circle.

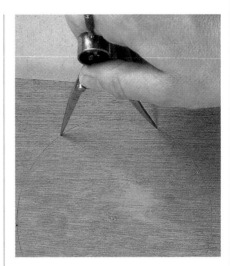

3 Spike the dividers down on the scribed circle, then step the radius off around the circumference to make six equal intersections.

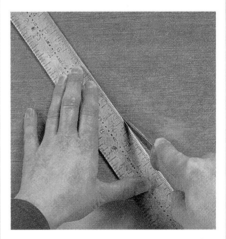

4 Use a straight-edge to link up adjoining step-offs to make a hexagon.

Tips box

- Don't buy small, cheap dividers without a locking mechanism. If they are knocked off the bench, you have lost the set-up you need.
- Work on the side of the workpiece that will be hidden to avoid spike marks ruining the exposed wood surface.
- Keep divider points sharp with abrasive paper or a small hone but be careful to maintain the relative positions of the points.

Dressing rough lumber

After logs are sawed into boards, dried, and sent to lumber yards for sale, the lumber isn't yet ready for use. The rough boards from the mill saw need to be surfaced, or smoothed and flattened. Their edges have to be jointed, or straightened. Sometimes the mill or lumber yard machine planes each side of the board until it reaches a certain thickness. The techniques they use, or drying, storage, and weather conditions, result in lumber defects that have to be corrected before joinery begins.

Pictured here, the basic defects in lumber are cupping, bowing, crooking, and twisting. They all result from problems in the drying process that cause the board to warp out of a straight or flat plane.

Defects that aren't obvious to the eye are detected by placing a long, steel straight-edge across or along the board and sighting for a gap. The straight-edge also checks the progress of surfacing and jointing once they're begun. Winding sticks are used to check for twisting. The perfectly straight and parallel sticks are placed at each end of a board and sighted across. They show whether a board is in winding (twisted) or out of winding (flat).

Dressing lumber is a process that removes material until the wood is smooth, flat, straight, and of the desired thickness. There are two choices for correcting defects to yield usable material. Which correction is used depends on the severity of the defect.

Mild defects are corrected by planing down high spots until the board is straight, flat, and to thickness. More severe defects require sawing the wood into shorter lengths or narrower widths before planing or jointing to minimize the defect so less material is wasted.

The process of dressing lumber is basically the same whether done by hand tools or by machine. The first step, which flattens the face, is the most critical, whether hand- or power-planed,

because the remaining steps reference from this face. Once the face is flattened, it should be marked as shown, and the first straightened edge also marked. These original surfaces are used to guide further processes like cutting or laying out joints.

Squaring wood

Because woodworking depends on accuracy—which usually means working to a line—it is important to make sure the wood is accurately prepared to size beforehand. This technique is called "preparation of lumber" or "squaring."

When lumber has been bought rough-sawed or even pre-planed it requires squaring, not least of all because there are likely to be twists or bows, especially in softwoods which are not fully seasoned.

A piece of lumber has been squared when all surfaces are flat, adjacent surfaces are 90 degrees to each other and opposite surfaces are parallel. You may find it necessary, when making a table for example, to prepare accurately four identical pieces for the legs and a series of identical pieces to edge-joint the top together. Hence the need for a standard squaring procedure.

The full procedure is achieved by either hand or power tools, the latter being far quicker. You will find it is an advantage to practice the hand process first, however painstaking, as such difficulty leads to a full appreciation of the need for skill and accuracy.

A board is cupped when it is not flat across its width, so the high edges have to be planed level with the center.

A bowed board isn't flat along the length of its face and the two high ends have to be planed down to the center.

Common faults in lumber

Rough lumber that hasn't been surface planed or edge jointed isn't smooth, flat, or straight and ready for building, which is often true even if it's dressed by the lumber yard.

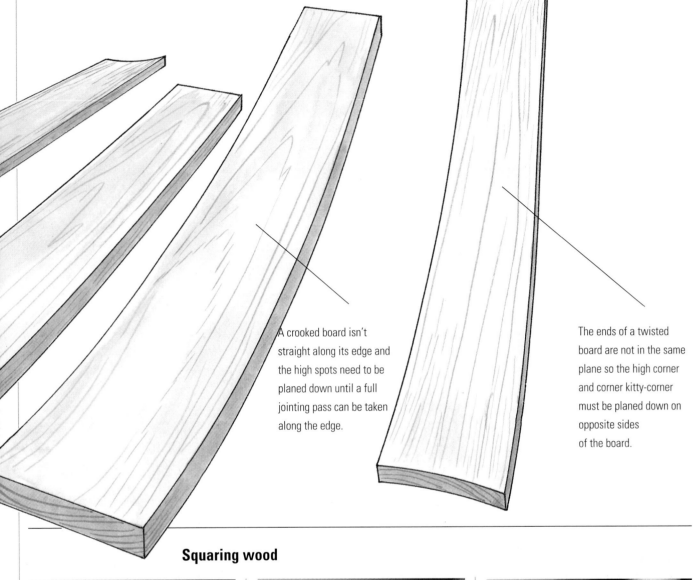

A crooked board isn't straight along its edge and the high spots need to be planed down until a full jointing pass can be taken along the edge.

The ends of a twisted board are not in the same plane so the high corner and corner kitty-corner must be planed down on opposite sides of the board.

Squaring wood

1 Select the best side (face side) and plane it flat and smooth (see Planing section pages 97-112). Hold the work on the benchtop using dogs or stops, checking with a straight-edge or rule. Now mark the first side with a face side mark that extends to the best edge (face edge). Face marks are important when gauging or using a square, the stock is normally placed against the face side or face edge.

2 Mount the wood low in the vise and plane the face edge square (90 degrees) to the face side. Check the accuracy with a try square and steel rule. Mark the face edge mark so it adjoins the face side mark.

3 A marking gauge is set to gauge to width. Use it vertically with the spur touching the appropriate calibration on the steel ruler. Now mount the wood at an angle in the vise and carefully gauge to width, trailing the spur at a shallow angle and ensuring the stock is kept firmly against the face edge. Mark a line all the way around the wood.

Squaring wood (continued)

4 Shade the waste portion and then mount the wood in the vise and plane to width. As you approach the line, adjust the plane to cut a fine shaving. Almost as the marking gauge line is reached, a fine sliver of wood can be easily rubbed away at each edge, indicating that only a few fine plane strokes are required to reach the line. In theory, the edge should be perfectly square.

5 Check the minimum thickness of the wood and set the marking gauge, this time to gauge the thickness. Now gauge to thickness a line all the way around the wood. With a little practice, you can quickly gauge holding the lumber freehand. Plane to thickness, making sure to constantly check the line after a few plane strokes.

6 Square to length using a try square, steel rule, and marking knife. First set the zero of the steel rule against one end of the lumber and measure in about ¼in (6mm). This is the minimum amount of wood which can be easily cut off with a tenon saw. Now move the steel rule so that the zero lines up with the ¼in (6mm) mark and measure off the required length (leaving at least ¼in/6mm).

7 You should use the try square with its stock against the face edge. Locate the marking knife in the first mark, slide the try square up to it, and mark a line carefully across. Locating the knife in the previous cut line, square the line all the way around the lumber, keeping the stock of the try square against either face side or face edge. This is important to ensure the lines will meet up.

8 Shade in the waste with a pencil or ballpoint pen ready for cutting the ends off. Using a bench hook mounted in your bench vise, saw off the ends with a tenon saw on the waste side of the line. Work steadily through the lumber with even strokes and make sure the cut is through to the bench hook before trying to separate the waste wood.

9 Finally, if necessary, trim the end grain with a plane. Make sure to avoid splitting the end grain, by using a waste piece. Clamp the waste block of lumber firmly against the rear face of the work and gently plane across both surfaces in a continuous motion. Keep the work low down in the vise to give plenty of support and reduce vibration.

SAWING

Before wood can be planed, laid out with the design, jointed, fretted and otherwise shaped, it first has to be sawed from the rough board. There are all kinds of saws, each designed for a specific task. Because sawing is pivotal to all the other woodworking procedures, it is critical that you build up a good collection of quality handsaws and spend time perfecting the various sawing techniques.

BELOW: If possible, always try a saw before buying to ensure the handle, weight, and balance of the saw feels right.

Handsaws

There is a woodworking saw to cope with almost every cutting task you will encounter. Generally, the blades of handsaws are taper-ground. This means that the blade is narrow at the tip and the metal is of a uniform thickness above the teeth, so the saw does not bind.

Ripsaws

The ripsaw is designed specifically for cutting along the length of the grain. The teeth are filed at 90 degrees across the blade so that each tooth is square-cut, in other words, without a bevel on the side face. In use, the teeth act just like a series of chisels, with each tooth cutting directly into the grain, and removing the waste as shavings or strands of fiber, in much the same way as a paring chisel. If you intend to cut parallel with the fibers of the wood—down a plank, or down a block—then a ripsaw is the tool for the job.

Crosscut saws

The crosscut saw is designed to cut across the grain. The teeth are filed at an angle of about 65 degrees across the blade. In use, the crosscut teeth first sever the fibers by scoring each side of the cut, and then remove the waste by reducing it to fine particles. Most woodworkers will require a selection of crosscut saws to handle different-sized jobs.

Using a ripsaw

A ripsaw is ideal for efficiently cutting wood along its length. If you need to cut wood in the direction of the grain, then look for a ripsaw that has the following features: teeth that are filed at right angles across the saw blade, a well-detailed, good-to-hold wooden handle, a good number of shoulder bolts that fix the handle to the blade, and a ground, tapered blade that is straight and flexible.

It is important when using the ripsaw to support the workpiece at a comfortable height. In most instances, you need to have the board supported on a pair of sawhorses, at a height that prevents the toe of the blade from touching the ground. Set the work at an angle and height that lets you look directly down on the line to be cut, while at the same time enabling you to get your shoulder behind the thrust.

When you are ready to start the cut, having marked a cutting line on your piece of lumber, position the saw blade well to the waste side of the drawn line, holding the blade at a low angle and pointing your index finger along the blade. Make a few initial dragging strokes to establish the cut, and then proceed to make increasingly larger strokes until you are using the full length of the blade.

When you are about two-thirds of the way along the length of the board, reverse the board on the horses, set the saw on the waste side of the drawn line, and repeat the procedure as already described—until you meet the first cut.

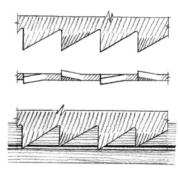

ABOVE: The shape and profile of the ripsaw blade results in a chisel-paring cut.

back

nickel chrome and steel blade

5 brass fixing screws

E.T. ROBERTS & LEE
DORCHESTER
NORTHUMBERLAND PARK, TOTTENHAM, N17

walnut handle

toe

ABOVE: A classic ripsaw

heel

Ripping in a vise

When ripping a short plank, set the wood to one side of the vise screw with a piece of waste the other side, to balance it. Start the cut in much the same way as described opposite. Don't force the pace of the "thrust" stroke, as this will leave the exit side of the wood looking ragged and torn and you may pull the blade out of the kerf completely and risk damaging the work. Let the weight of the saw do the work (right). Regularly reposition the work so that the cutting point is always close to the vise jaws. Keep your index finger along the blade edge to guide you and to keep the cut as vertical as possible.

Overhand ripping on the bench

Overhand ripping is a technique that traditional woodworkers claim is "easy on the back." The wood is first clamped flat-side-down to the bench so that the end to be cut is facing toward you (above). A few low-angle starter cuts are made with the toe of the saw pointing away, the saw is reversed so that the teeth are pointing away from your body, and then both hands are clenched around the handle to supply the thrust.

Overhand ripping on the horse

Overhand ripping on the sawhorse is a technique of making precise and accurate short-distance cuts along the grain when you want to be ready to receive the piece that is being cut. Support and position the wood on the horse so that you can look directly down on the line of cut. Keep your knee directly behind the saw blade, but at least 4in (100mm) from the cutting edge. Start the cut from a kneeling-on-the-floor position, then stand up, reverse the saw so that the teeth are facing away from you and along the drawn line, and proceed to cut toward the mark.

Tips box

• If the wood starts to chatter (vibrate), then reposition it in the vise or on the horse. There should be only a short distance between the support and the point of cut.

• Alternatively, you can adjust your stance so as to correct the alignment of the saw. If the saw binds in the wood, use a small wedge to open up the kerf, and/or burnish the saw blade with a wax candle.

BELOW: A classic crosscut saw

5 brass fixing screws

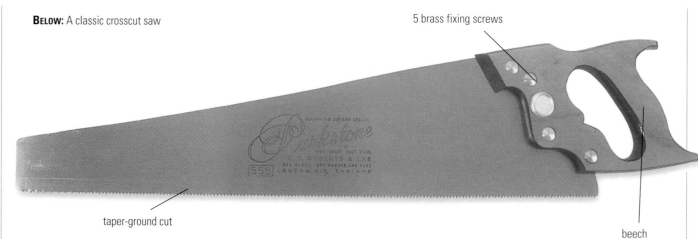

taper-ground cut

beech
handle

Using a crosscut saw

Crosscut saws are designed specifically
for cutting wood across the grain. If you
look closely at one side of the blade, you
will see that every other tooth has been
filed at an angle so that it has a bevel on
both edges. And, of course, you will see
a reverse of this on the other side of the
blade. Though there are all manner of
crosscut saws, everything from huge two-
man saws with a handle at both ends, to
miniature saws, they all share certain
features: all have the same tooth
formation and all are designed primarily
to cut across the grain. A typical crosscut
saw is a large, general-purpose, straight-
backed saw about 22-26in (56-66cm)
long with five points to 1in (2.55cm).

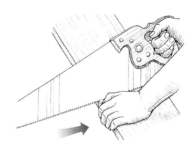

ABOVE: Starting the cut

Stance when using a horse

Let us say that you are trimming the ends off a
board. Bridge the wood across the horses so
that the line of cut is to the right-hand side of
the right-hand horse. Stand between the horses,
and rest your knee on the wood so that your
weight holds it securely.

Starting the cut

Set the saw down to the waste side of the
drawn line. Grip the wood with your left hand
and steady the blade with your thumb nail.
Make a few careful dragging strokes with the
middle-to-heel of the saw to establish the line
of cut, and then finally use the full length of the
saw to make the stroke.

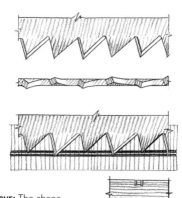

ABOVE: The shape
and profile of the
crosscut saw results
in a scoring-and-
slicing cut.

Completing the cut

When you come to within approximately 2in
(5cm) of finishing the cut—when the waste end
looks as if it is ready to fall away—then,
simultaneously hook your left hand around the
waste piece to support it, and make a series of
increasingly lighter strokes until the wood is
sawed through.

Panel saws

A panel saw is best thought of as a refined version of the general purpose crosscut. Designed for cabinet work, the smaller teeth leave a finer kerf. A popular size of panel saw is 20-24in (51-61cm) long with about seven points to 1in (2.55cm). A panel saw is a choice tool for cutting large joints at the bench.

Cutting a panel with a skewed saw

1 Many traditional woodworkers favor the use of a skewed panel saw. The term "skewed" refers to the back edge of the blade being dipped or curved along its length. The combined characteristics of a seven-point cut and a skewed back add up to an exceptionally easy-to-maneuver tool. Generally, a skewed panel saw is lighter in weight than a straight-back (right).

2 The skewed feature of the panel saw reduces the softness of the blade so that it can be used to cut relatively full curves. The wood is supported on a pair of horses. The blade enters to the waste side of the drawn line, and then the blade is twisted and maneuvered along the way so that it follows the curve (left).

Tips box

Don't throw away an old wooden-handled saw just because the handle is split or broken. Use the parts you have to shape a cardboard template and produce a new version from scrap beech or other hardwood that you have around the workshop. Cut the rough profile on a band saw or with a jigsaw and file to the finished shape. Coat with an exterior varnish to protect the wood from dirt.

A cure for binding

If your saw binds in the lumber, try rubbing a candle in a zigzag pattern over the blade to reduce friction.

heavy brass back

2 brass fixing screws

handle

ABOVE: A classic medium length tenon saw.

1 Having marked out the lines that go to make up the joint, set the wood in the vise at an angle of about 45 degrees and saw down to the shoulder mark. Turn the workpiece around in the vise and repeat the procedure for the other side of the joint. This technique ensures you can control the accuracy of the cut line around the joint—it's easy for a saw blade to wander when cutting along the grain as the blade will tend to follow the grain pattern. The two 45-degree kerfs leave only a small amount of cutting at the base of the joint to complete the rip sawing.

Backsaws

Backsaws can be recognized by their brass or iron backs, the closed handle and the 12-16in (30.5-40.65cm) long blades with 12-14 points to 1in (2.55cm). These are choice saws for cutting joints and for general joint work. Always take the chance to try out a tenon saw for weight and balance before buying. This will be one of the most used tools in your toolbox, so it pays to find the most comfortable tool available. Plastic handles often have sharp molding lines and the hard "feel" is not as comfortable for prolonged use as wood. A heavy brass back is essential in keeping the small blade in the kerf and working efficiently. Finally, check the handle is firmly fixed with good-quality brassware.

2 When you have run a 45-degree angle kerf down to the shoulder line on both sides of the joint, reposition the workpiece so that it is upright in the vise, and complete the cut.

3 Finally, butt the workpiece hard up against a bench stop and make the shoulder cut to remove the waste.

Using a back saw with a bench hook

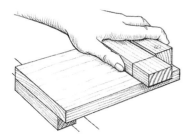

Secure the bench hook in the vice. With the workpiece being pushed hard up to the stop with your left hand, set the saw to the waste side of the drawn line and use the toe of the blade to make a few light dragging strokes. When you have established the cut, use the full length of the blade to complete. If the saw is in good condition, and the workpiece is held tight, then the cut will only require the minimum of clean-up.

Using a backsaw with a miter block

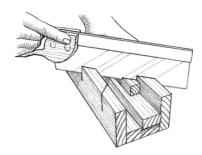

Having first made sure that your backsaw and miter block are compatible—meaning the saw blade is the same thickness as the slot—clamp the block securely in the vise so that the top of the base is standing proud. Protect the base of the block with a piece of flat waste, then set the workpiece down and butt it hard up against the stop. Hold the whole work firm with your left hand, then ease the saw into the slot and proceed with the cut.

Using a backsaw with a sizing board

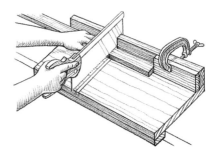

Using a backsaw in conjunction with a sizing board is the best technique for cutting short, repeat lengths. The board is clamped in the vise, and the stop is adjusted to the required length. The workpiece is pushed against the back of the hook and slid to the right so that the end butts hard up against the stop. Finally, the saw is eased into the slot to make the cut.

Gent's saws

The term 'Gent's' refers to the nineteenth century, when smaller 'more refined' tools were designed specifically for gentlemen. Although you can often use a small tenon saw in place of gent's saw, this delicate little tool is still useful to add to your collection of hand tools. This type of saw, with its turned handle, brass back and fine blade at about 25.5cm (10in) long with 15-20 teeth to 2.55cm (1in), is a good tool for cutting fine kerfs, especially on mitres and end-grain joints. The handle is held in one hand and the toe is sometimes gripped in the other, in much the same way as when using a large rasp or plane. Guide the cut as you would other larger saws, with the index finger along the back of the blade.

brass back or rib

brass ferrule

walnut handle

blade

ABOVE: Some gent's saws are so delicate that they need to be used with two hands.

ABOVE: Extend the finger along the back of the saw to help guide the cut.

Tips box

If you find the in-line handle awkward to use, there are offset-handle gent's saws available. Some makers also produce an interchangeable blade version for working on plastics and metal, as well as wood.

Tenon and dovetail saws

Small backsaws, known variously as tenon saws and dovetail saws, are in fact small ripsaws. With a blade length of 12-16in (30.5-40.65cm) and a tooth size of 12-14 points to 1in (2.55cm), they are designed for cutting with the grain; for instance, when cutting tenon and dovetail joints.

BELOW: A classic dovetail saw with rip teeth, designed for use on softer woods.

brass back

traditional-shaped handle

rip cut

Cutting a tenon

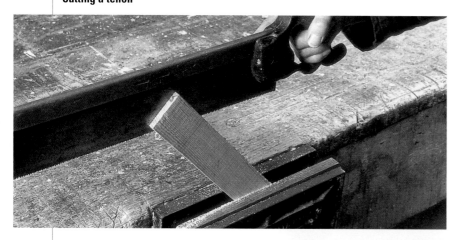

1 Secure the workpiece at a 45-degree angle in the vise. With one hand holding the saw, and the other holding the workpiece and steadying the saw blade, run the line of cut down to the shoulder line. Repeat the procedure for both cuts on both sides of the joint. Then secure the wood upright in the vise, set the saw in the kerf, and cut the remaining peak down to the shoulder line. Do this for both kerfs.

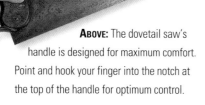

ABOVE: The dovetail saw's handle is designed for maximum comfort. Point and hook your finger into the notch at the top of the handle for optimum control.

2 Finally, butt the workpiece hard up against the bench hook, align the saw to the waste side of the scored shoulder line so that the teeth just skim the line, and cut down to the cheek.

Sawing dovetails

1 Having used the gauge and bevel to carefully mark in the shape of the dovetails on the tail board, use a pencil to shade in the areas of waste that need to be cut away.

2 Secure the workpiece in the vise and use the dovetail saw to cut down to the shoulder line. Be sure to cut to the waste side of the drawn line.

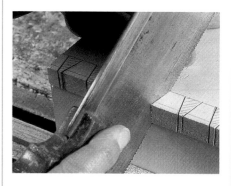

3 Secure the other board—the board that has the pins and sockets—in the vise. Set the sawed dovetails in place and at right angles on the end-grain face. Use the dovetail saw to transfer the lines through to the end face of the pin board. Finally, use a square to run lines down to the shoulder line.

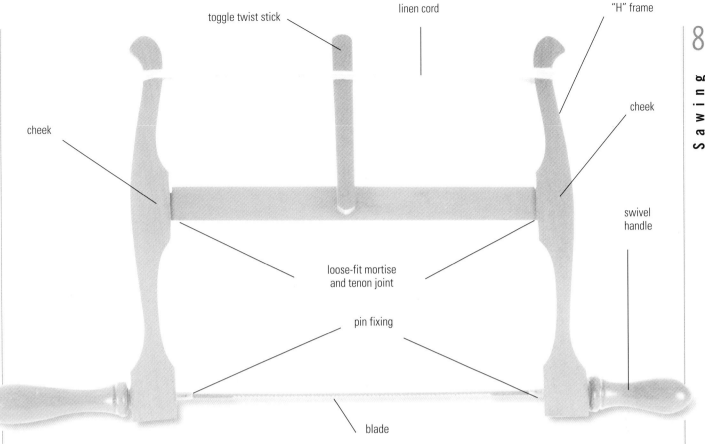

toggle twist stick

linen cord

"H" frame

cheek

cheek

swivel
handle

loose-fit mortise
and tenon joint

pin fixing

blade

Bow saws

The bow or frame saw, with its traditional wooden "H" frame and flexible
blade sporting about eight points to
1in (2.55cm), is probably one of the
most versatile of all the curve-cutting
saws, although much of its work can
now be done with a powerful jigsaw
fitted with a long blade or, of course,
the band saw. The design is such that
the handles can be pivoted within the
frame so the saw can be set to work
in any direction. The twisted cord with
the toggle adjustment not only makes
for quick blade replacement, it also
allows the woodworker to keep the
blade at the correct tension.

Cutting out a chair seat

1 First, twist the toggle stick to give
tension to the the bow-saw blade.
Continue until the blade "pings."

2 Hold the saw upright so that it is at
right angles to the face of the wood.
Run a starter cut straight in toward the drawn
line (above).

3 Maneuver the saw with both hands,
bracing your body against the workpiece and turning the frame of the saw around
so that it is out to the waste side of the line.

4 Since the drawn line necessarily runs
both with and across the grain, be
ready for the rate of cut to change as you saw
around the curve.

5 If you find it difficult when you come
to saw directly into the end grain, you
could change your approach so that you cut only
with the grain.

Tips box

Once you have finished cutting, release
the tension on the frame and blade by
untwisting the central toggle stick.
Regularly inspect the cord for any signs
of fraying and replace if necessary.

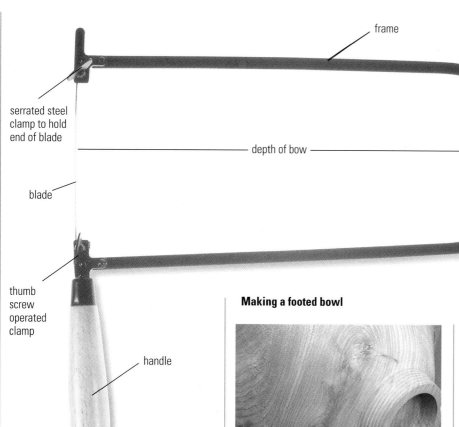

frame

serrated steel
clamp to hold
end of blade

depth of bow

blade

ECLIPSE

Left: The traditional,
wooden-handled, deep
bow fretsaw.

thumb
screw
operated
clamp

handle

Fretsaws

The fretsaw's bow-shaped frame and thin
blade make it perfect for cutting out
intricate curved designs in thin wood. If
you wish to cut out pierced holes, make
a jigsaw puzzle, or build small tabletop
toys, then this is the tool for you.

The blade is fitted in the frame using
a couple of thumb screws, with the frame
itself having enough spring to keep the
blade under tension. To install a new
blade, use your body to push the frame
against the side of the bench until the
old blade goes slack and drops out. Then
set the ends of the new blade in the little
clamps, tighten up the thumbscrews and
let the frame spring back.

In use, set the workpiece in the vise,
or clamp it face-down so that it overhangs the bench, and then work with a
delicate push-and-pull action. Most
woodworkers prefer to mount the blade
so the teeth point toward the handle.
That way they cut on the pull stroke,
offering better control for cutting
thin wood.

Making a footed bowl

1 The spigot of this bowl has been
turned so that it is long enough to
create three feet that are in proportion with the
rest of the bowl. The recess in the center must be
of a depth to follow the curvature of the
bowl when the waste is cut away.

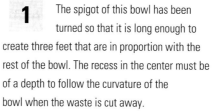

2 Using a fretsaw, carefully cut away
the waste between each foot. Sight
the saw blade through an imaginary point at the
center so that the cut faces are all aligned to
the center.

3 Remove any excess waste left by the
saw and refine the spaces between
the feet with a rasp. You can now see why it is
important for the recess to follow the curve of
the bowl.

Coping saws

The coping saw is designed for quick tight curves in wood up to about ½in (1.25cm) thick. If you want to cut out an intricate shape or maybe an enclosed "window", then this is the tool for the job. The thin flexible blades can be replaced quickly by simply unscrewing the handle to release the tension. The idea is that you use the blades until they become dull or slack and then throw them away. If you plan to make small fancy items like toys, then this is a great tool.

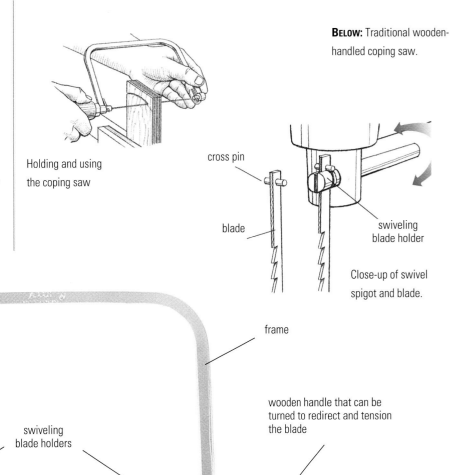

Holding and using the coping saw

BELOW: Traditional wooden-handled coping saw.

cross pin

blade

swiveling blade holder

Close-up of swivel spigot and blade.

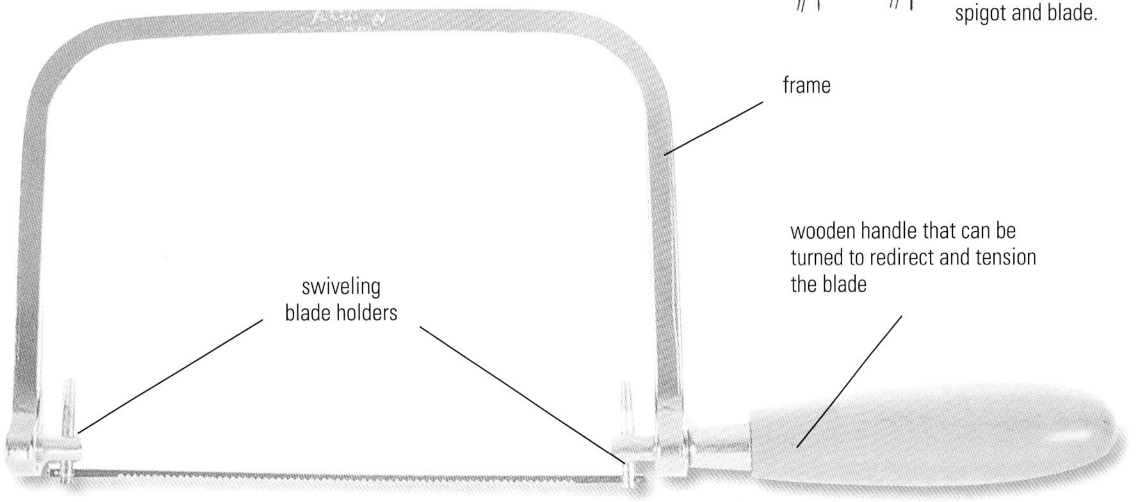

frame

swiveling blade holders

wooden handle that can be turned to redirect and tension the blade

Cutting dovetails with a coping saw

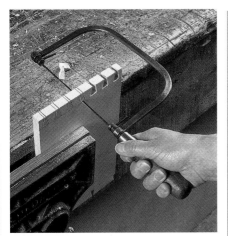

1 Used as a follow-up to the dovetail saw, the coping saw is an efficient and easy-to-use tool for clearing the waste in and around the dovetails and pins. But first, use the dovetail saw to establish all the straight primary cuts.

2 Take the coping saw, making sure that the blade is fitted with the teeth pointing away from the handle, and slowly tighten the blade tension until the blade "pings" when plucked. It is preferable to cut on the "push" stroke when cutting a dovetail in a vise.

3 Slide the blade down to the bottom of one or other of the primary straight cuts made by the dovetail saw, then work with a steady stroke to cut across the neck of waste. Be sure to keep well to the waste side of the drawn line.

Electric saws

Some sort of power saw is an essential first purchase for the home woodworker. A small- to medium-sized table saw is compact enough to be used in a garage and provides an accurate means of sizing boards and sheet materials.

Portable saws

Although table saws can handle most of the woodworker's demands, it is also extremely useful to have a powered saw in your collection of tools, which can be taken on site or used outside the workshop.

Portable saws fall into two categories, circular saws and jigsaws. You will need a jigsaw for curved cuts—choose a model with a pendulum action for efficient cutting, and a powerful motor (at least 300W) for use on lumber up to about 2in (50mm) thick. Before buying, check that the base plate is rigid—a thick alloy plate is much better than the cheaper pressed-steel variety.

Using a power jigsaw

The electric jigsaw has a short reciprocating blade with teeth facing upward. It is a versatile tool for sawing straight and curved work usually to a line. It is easy to operate once you learn to keep the pressure constantly against the surface of the wood to counteract the upward snatching of the blade. The jigsaw is capable of removing stock in tight areas such as curves and narrow slits (the band saw has a similar capacity).

ABOVE: The jigsaw is a versatile hand-held tool for making straight, curved, or angled cuts. Different blades are available for use with different materials.

Using a portable circular saw

Circular saws are used for straight cuts across or along the grain and can be set to full or part depth by lowering or raising the blade. The blade can also be adjusted to cut at an angle. You can use the saw to cut "freehand" along a marked line by positioning the tool at the appropriate mark. Start the motor before the blade engages with the wood, and hold the handles firmly with both hands to control the saw.

The standard straight fence can be adjusted to make parallel cuts similar to a router.

A clamped batten can serve as a guide for making straight cuts through the wood at any desired position or angle.

Right: The portable circular saw is used to cut solid wood or manufactured board material.

Table saws

The table saw is one of the most valuable tools in the workshop—and one of the most dangerous. It is fast, powerful, and can do a wide variety of cuts with great accuracy. But it must always be treated with respect. Consult the owner's manual and always pay special attention to the safety precautions.

A table saw is used for straight cuts along and across the grain. You can raise, lower, and tilt the blade. The sliding miter fence is set to 90 degrees for cutting wood across the grain. You should use both hands to grip the wood against and operate the sliding fence. The clamped block on the rip fence is used for repeat cuts.

Note: Guards removed for photography only (above and right).

The table saw is used for single or repeat cuts along the grain (ripping), and the rip fence is first adjusted and tightened to position before the power is switched on. The riving knife is there to prevent the wood closing in and jamming the saw cut as the wood passes through. Use push sticks (easily cut on a band saw) to guide the wood along and against the fence.

The blade can be tilted to cut wood to any angle up to 45 degrees. The sliding fence is used, and, if set to 45 degrees, will facilitate compound miter cuts.

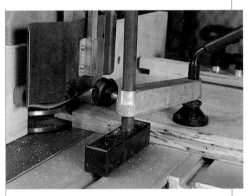

The circular saw blade can be lowered to cut grooves using the rip fence as a guide. Grooves can be widened by adjusting the fence after each cut, and this is particularly useful for cutting the cheeks of tenons. Sometimes a jig is used to secure the wood as it is passed over the blade. Grooved or rebated cuts can be achieved by using the miter fence with the wood lying the other way around.

Tips box

There are two types of stationary power circular saws: the table or bench saw on which the workpiece is moved over the table, and the radial arm saw, which is pulled over the stationary workpiece. Although both saws can be used for ripping and crosscutting, the table saw is best for ripping, while the radial arm saw excels in crosscut work.

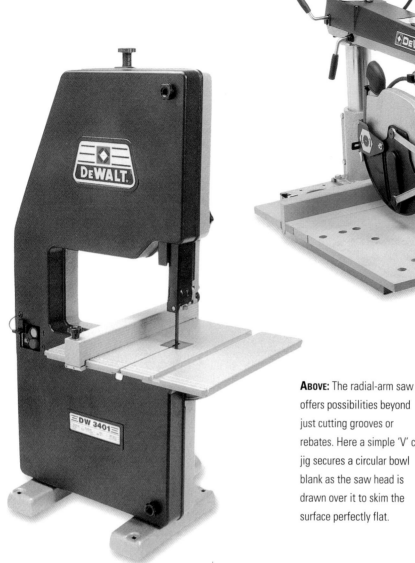

ABOVE: The radial-arm saw offers possibilities beyond just cutting grooves or rebates. Here a simple 'V' cut jig secures a circular bowl blank as the saw head is drawn over it to skim the surface perfectly flat.

Being truly versatile, the band saw can cut circles or other curves to a marked line. Make sure your fingers are always away from the blade when supporting and feeding the workpiece.

Band saws

ABOVE: The bandsaw is an extremely useful machine. It can cut both straight and curved lines with the table fixed at 90 degrees or tilted up to 45 degrees. The continuous loop blade cuts quietly and efficiently, creating less noise, less waste and less dust than a circular saw.

A bandsaw is a quiet, efficient machine for cutting both straight and curved work. Its continuous loop blade passes over two large diameter wheels. The 'throat' of the bandsaw refers to the distance between the blade and the nearest part of the machine when measured across the table. This determines the length of the piece it can cut across the grain. The wood is supported on the saw's table.

The band saw is capable of cutting thick pieces of wood. This should, however, be done slowly, both because a band saw blade is quite fragile and because the waste or sawdust in the cut needs time to clear to avoid overheating. The straight fence on the band saw can be used for repeat parallel cuts or for jigging square pieces.

Radial arm saws

The radial arm saw is an overhead circular saw; the wood is mounted stationary on the table and the saw head drawn across it. It is primarily used for crosscutting, but can also be used for rip, miter, and compound cuts. It has a facility for raising or lowering the saw head for grooves and rebates. The wood is held against the fence and lined up to the saw blade at the marked position for the cut. The saw head can be positioned at any angle to make a cut in the crosscut or fixed-head mode by simply adjusting knobs.

The radial arm saw should not be used for ripping boards down their length, as this can be dangerous. In some countries it's forbidden by legislation. This is because the wood may lift off the table. It's advisable to use a circular table saw instead.

Electric scroll saws

The electric scroll saw is without a doubt one of the easiest machines to use—and this very fact all too often results in its being taken for granted and treated like a toy. Fledgling woodworkers simply set their new scroll saw on the bench, switch it on, and start sawing. The result is that it bounces around and ruins their work. The best arrangement is to bolt the saw onto its own table. This cuts out all vibration. Some woodworkers favor a long bench seat, so that they can sit at one end, with the machine bolted down at the other. Choose the correct blade and fit it so that it is loose-pivoted at top and bottom. Adjust the tension so that the blade pings when it's plucked.

ABOVE: The fretsaw is a fine-toothed reciprocating saw with an inexpensive, disposable blade. It is used for cutting fine, tight corners in materials up to 1in (25mm).

Cutting tight angles

A common problem that beginner woodworkers have when using the scroll saw is cutting tight angles correctly. They either tend to go too slowly and burn the wood, or they change direction too rapidly, which twists and breaks the blade. The guidelines below describe the best method.

- If you want to keep the wood on both sides of the outline, slow down at the angles and mark time so that the blade clears space around itself, then change direction.
- If the wood within the angle is waste, run the blade straight through the middle of it to the angle, then back the blade out and make cuts from each side that follow the line and finish at the angle.
- The finer the blade teeth and the tighter the tension, the easier it is to turn an angle.
- Never try to turn an angle with an old blade.

Sandwich cutting

Many woodworkers use the scroll saw for making small wooden items like toys with lots of identical parts. Let's say, for example, that you want to cut seven identical number shapes out of wood ⅛in (3mm) thick, with each number standing about 3in (76mm) high and 2in (51mm) wide.

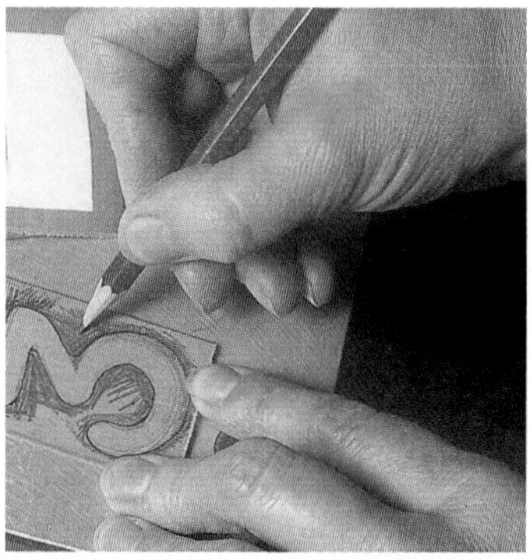

1 Cut seven wooden mats—one for each cutout that you want to make. Transfer the image to one mat and shade in the waste areas. Sandwich the mats together with double-sided tape so that the image is on top of the stack.

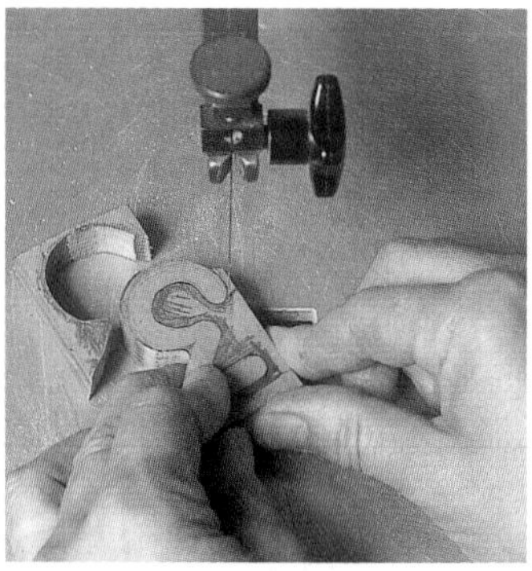

2 Fit the saw with a new fine-toothed blade so that the teeth point down, and adjust the tension until the blade pings. Wipe the worktable with a cloth, and make sure that the saw is in good order. Hold the stack firmly down on the table and push it into the saw at a steady pace. Guide and maneuver the stack so that the moving blade is always presented with the next outline. Don't force the pace and don't slacken the downward pressure of your hands.

3 When you have sawed around the image, ease the layers apart and remove the tape. If you have followed the instructions as described, the sawed edge will be so smooth that it hardly needs sanding.

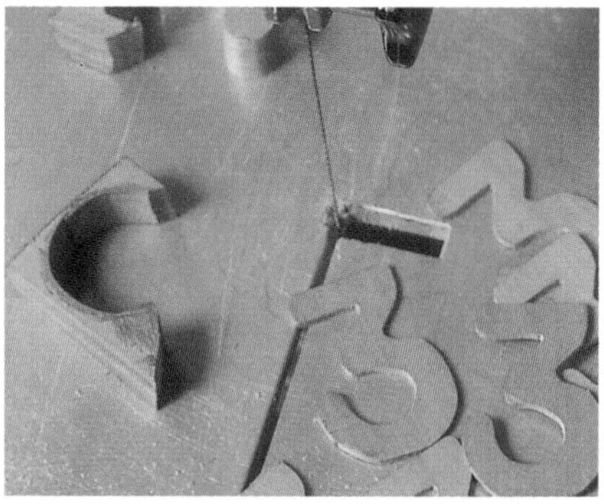

Sawing jig

Making a sawing sizing board

The sizing board illustrated here is a simple but reliable and efficient way of ensuring that a length of wood is cut in completely equal sizes. The base is made from ½in (12mm) blockboard, with a renewable hardwood insert to protect the base. The upright section is made from beech or any other hardwood ⅝in x 1¾in (16mm x 45mm). It has a sliding hardwood stop which can be fastened with a coach bolt and wing nut.

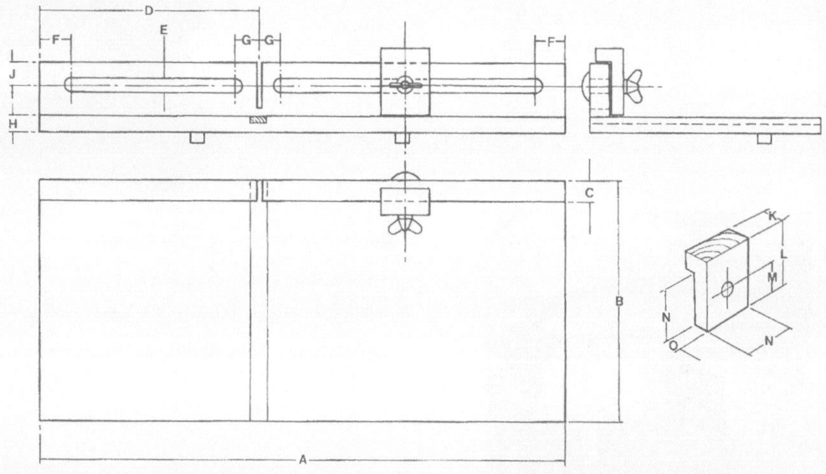

Sliding stop half full-size

Dimensions

A 18in (450mm)	H ½in (12mm)
B 8in (200mm)	J 13/16in (21mm)
C ⅝in (16mm)	K ¾in (18mm)
D 7⅜in (187mm)	L 2¼in (58mm)
E ⅜in (10mm)	M 1in (24mm)
F 1in (25mm)	N 1¾in (45mm)
G ¾in (19mm)	O ⅜in (10mm)

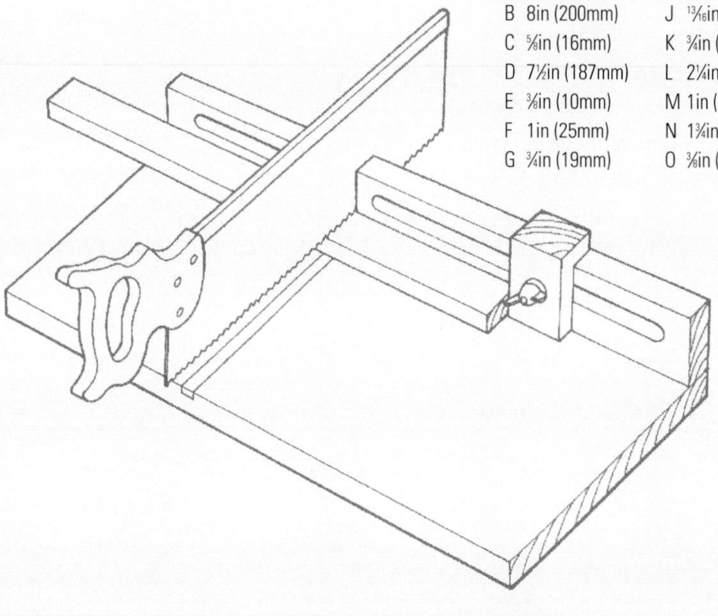

PLANING

Planing prepares the wood for the accurate marking and cutting out of joints, and smooths the wood ready for the finishing steps. The plane blade must be razorsharp and carefully adjusted to take shavings of the depth required. Planing is a skill that takes practice to acquire—be prepared to spend quite a lot of time getting used to the tool, and to learning the techniques needed to sharpen, adjust, and use it accurately.

BELOW: Although most woodworking planes are now made of metal, the shape and design has changed little in the last two hundred years.

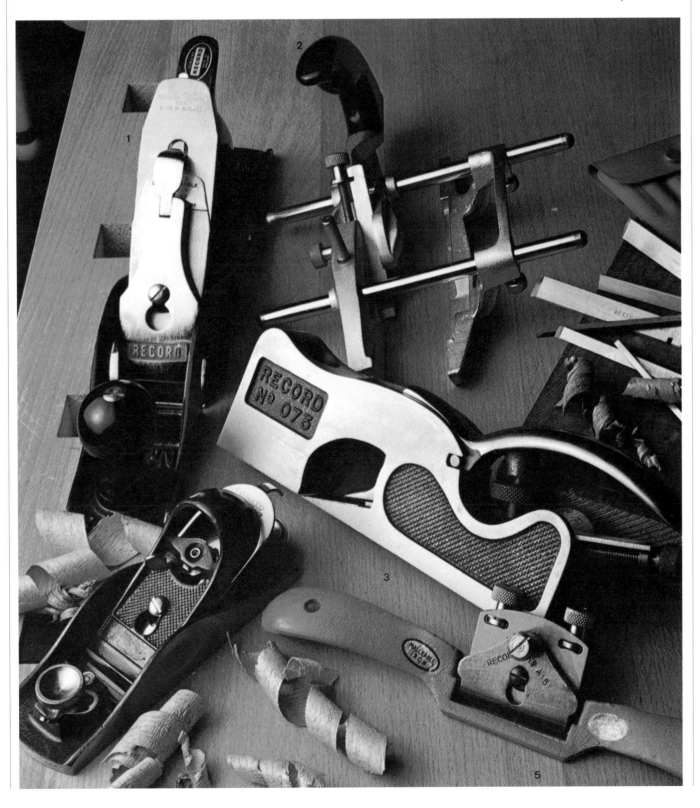

Planing sequence

There is a sequence to planing that should be followed at all times. Plane the face side, then the face edge. Then gauge and plane to width, and finally plane to thickness. Sawing a component exactly to length is left until later.

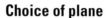

Choice of plane

A long plane gives a more accurate result. It rides over high spots on the wood, gradually removing them until the wood is even and a single long shaving can be taken off. A smaller plane follows the contours of the surface. A smoothing plane or small jack plane makes a good choice for a first buy.

Set the plane to take a fine cut at first until you are used to the action. There is less resistance and more control than if you set the blade to take a thicker cut. As you plane, adjust the blade until you are taking a good shaving from the surface.

Tips box

- The best way of finding out about your new plane is to strip it down to its component parts and then see how they all fit and work in relation to each other.

- As with chisels, planes fresh from the factory are liable to have rough casting marks and machine grinding lines on the body and blade. A little time removing these on abrasive paper taped to a flat surface will make the tool more efficient and a joy to handle.

How to plane

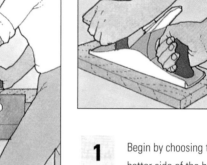

1 Begin by choosing the better side of the board, which will become the face side. Hold the board on a firm horizontal surface, against a bench stop—or in a vise for small pieces. Stand with shoulder, hip, and plane in line for full control, feet slightly apart.

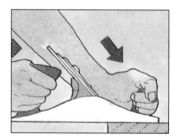

2 Aim to work with a smooth motion, applying even pressure. As you pass the plane over the wood at the beginning of the stroke, pressure is on the front handle.

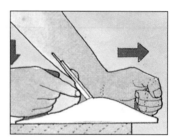

3 In mid-stroke, press evenly, and as you reach the end of the stroke, transfer pressure to the rear handle. Do not lift the plane up until the plane blade is beyond the end of the board.

Squaring the wood: planing face side, face edge, width, and thickness

Think of planing and checking for straightness and squareness as one skill—one is of little use without the other. Stop frequently to check the wood. Always lay the plane on its side when you put it down, to prevent the blade from being damaged.

4 As you plane the face, stop and check the wood carefully for flatness across the width; and sight along the wood to check it for straightness.

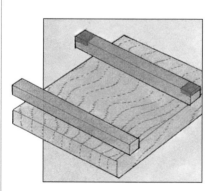

5 To check for "winding" or twisting, place two wooden strips at each end and sight across the tops to see if they are parallel.

6 Place a steel ruler or straight-edge along the grain at intervals to check that the surface is flat along its whole length. Alternatively, tilt the plane on its side and use that as a straight-edge.

Planing the edge

7 To plane the face edge, put the wood against a bench stop or in a vise. To keep the plane centered on a narrow edge, put your thumb on top of the sole near the handle, and run your fingers along under the side to guide the plane.

8 Use a square to check that the edge is square, with the face along its whole length. Be sure to push the stock of the square tight up against the face side of the wood. Hold the wood up to the light, if possible.

Marking and planing the other sides

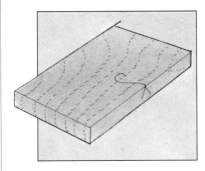

9 Once you have a face and edge that are perfectly straight and at right angles to one another, mark them with the face and edge mark. With these surfaces true, it is relatively easy to make the wood the width and thickness you need for your project.

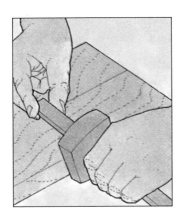

10 Use a marking gauge to mark the width of the board from the face edge. Set the gauge to the width, hold the fence against the face edge and gauge a line. Turn the board over to mark the width on the sawed, unplaned side. Again, run the fence of the gauge against the face edge. Plane, or saw and plane, the board to this width, checking frequently.

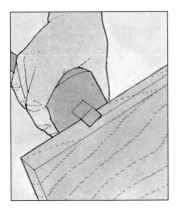

11 To mark the thickness required, run the fence of the marking gauge against the face side, marking a line on the face edge and one on the far edge. Then plane the board down to these marks. Stop and check the work often for squareness.

Planing wide boards

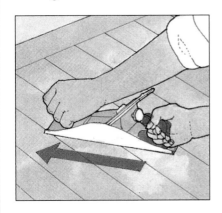

12 Plane wide boards, or boards that have been joined together, working diagonally, with and across the grain in overlapping strokes to cover the whole surface. Finish by taking fine shavings in parallel strokes in the direction of the grain.

Tips box

Before using a smoothing plane to take any machining marks out of a board's surface, make sure the corners of the blade have been rounded over so that they don't make tramlines on the surface.

Hand planes

Bench planes

RIGHT: The metal bench plane in disassembled view showing the component parts.

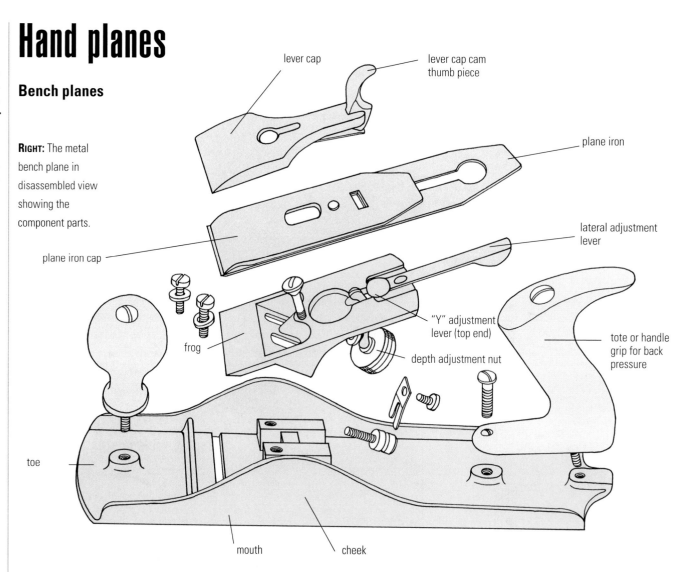

lever cap

lever cap cam thumb piece

plane iron

plane iron cap

lateral adjustment lever

frog

"Y" adjustment lever (top end)

depth adjustment nut

tote or handle grip for back pressure

toe

mouth

cheek

Adjustment techniques

Although the modern bench plane is a delight to use and a joy to hold and handle, it is also the most abused and misused tool in the workshop. Part of the problem has to do with the fact that there are so many moving parts and possible adjustments.

Adjusting the size of mouth

In simple terms, a big mouth equals big, greedy shavings from softwood, while a small mouth equals fine, petite shavings from hardwood. To adjust the size of the mouth, set the frog in place with the three screws, then try out the adjustment screw. You will see that a clockwise turn pushes the frog forward and makes the mouth smaller. When you have achieved a setting to suit you, tighten up the two frog screws.

Adjusting the cap and cutter irons

If you could take a close-up, wood-worm's-eye-view and watch the plane at work, you would see that the lower "cutter" iron—the one with the bevel—does the cutting, while the top "cap" iron breaks the shavings and directs them away from the throat. You would also see that the two irons need to be clamped together, so as to stop the whole works from shaking and chattering. To adjust the irons, simply undo the screw, slide the cap iron backward or forward and then tighten up. Allow a bigger distance between the leading edges for rough work and a smaller distance for fine work. If there is a gap between the underside of the leading edge of the cap and the cutter, then it is important that you grind the underside edge of the cap iron to a flush fit.

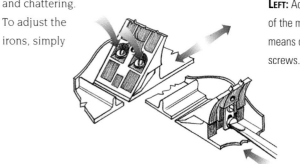

LEFT: Adjust the size of the mouth by means of the three screws.

RIGHT: The classic metal bench plane in side view cross section, showing how the whole tool is assembled.

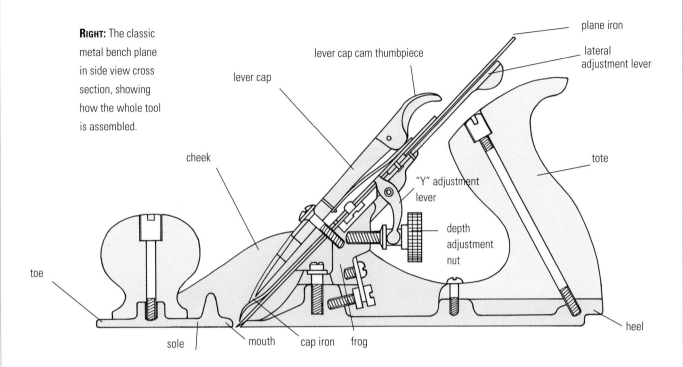

plane iron

lever cap cam thumbpiece

lever cap

lateral adjustment lever

cheek

"Y" adjustment lever

tote

depth adjustment nut

toe

heel

sole · mouth · cap iron · frog

RIGHT: Move the lateral lever left or right to set the iron square in the mouth.

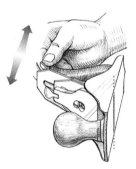

Adjusting the lateral movement

When you have adjusted the frog and the two cutters, set the cutter assembly in place. Then push the lateral lever either left or right to set the cutting iron square or parallel with the mouth.

RIGHT: Adjust the depth of the cut by advancing or retracting the blade.

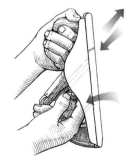

Adjusting the depth of cut

With the irons in place and set square to the mouth, slide the lever cap on its screw and secure the whole works with the cap lock. It needs to be tight, but not so tight that you cannot make adjustments with the lateral lever and the depth wheel. The depth of cut is adjusted simply by turning the large brass wheel—clockwise for a deeper, heavier cut, and counter-clockwise for a shallow, skimming cut.

General bench plane techniques

The bench plane is designed to be held in both hands, one hand holding and bearing down on the front knob, and the other hand gripping the back handle or tote. The workpiece is secured to the bench, and the plane is set down with the left hand gripping the front knob and the right hand gripping the tote. The weight of the right shoulder is then used to push the plane forward. The plane

should be well tuned and adjusted—with the cutter honed, all the moving parts lightly oiled and the sole burnished with a wax candle—and the wood should be carefully chosen.

With that done, only three important factors in the planing procedure remain to be considered: the height of the bench, the depth of the cut, and the amount of pressure that you put down on the front of the plane. The height of the bench is something you will have to decide to suit your own needs, but the other two considerations can be learned by trial and error. Most woodworkers start with the cutting iron set well up so that it does not cut, then repeatedly tweak the wheel very slightly clockwise and take a stroke until they are achieving the thinnest of paper-thin shavings. As to the question of how hard you should bear down on the front knob, the best way of finding this out is to make a series of test runs so that you can make a positive judgment.

Jointer planes

extra-long sole

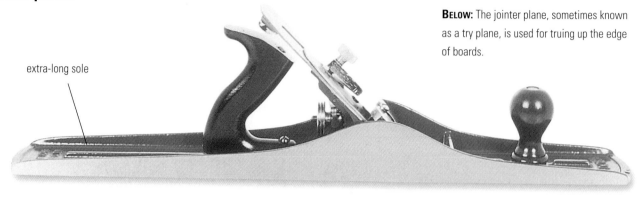

BELOW: The jointer plane, sometimes known as a try plane, is used for truing up the edge of boards.

The jointer plane—sometimes also called the long plane—is designed specifically to prepare the edges of boards that are to be glued or other-ways butted and joined together. The obvious difference between the jointer and other large planes is that the sole of the jointer is impressively long at 22in to 36in (50cm to 80cm). The not-so-obvious difference is that the jointer cutter iron is ground square. The cutters of the other large planes are variously ground with a slight crown or camber, or rounded at the corners so that they can be used to face large boards without worrying about the corners of the cutter scoring the wood. Certainly you can use the other large planes for jointing, and vice versa, but only if the cutters are correctly ground.

Jointing defined

The technique of planing the edges of boards true, straight and square is termed "jointing". The object of the exercise is to create a wide board by joining one or more narrow boards edge to edge. One might ask why the woodworker should not just select a wide board.

The answer is beautifully simple: wide boards are expensive and difficult to obtain, and they tend to shrink excessively across their width, while narrow boards are relatively inexpensive, easy to obtain, and offer minimal shrinkage and warping. The jointing procedure involves planing away all the high spots down to the level of the low spots and then truing up edges so that the boards can be perfectly mated edge-to-edge along their length.

Jointing a single board

To joint a single board, set the board on the bench so that one end is placed at eye level and sight down the edge. Mark the high spots, or peaks, with a pencil. Next, secure the board in the vise, and plane off the pencil markings. Repeat this procedure until you have what you consider is a fairly true edge. When you have cleared the obvious peaks, secure the board in the vise, and use the jointer plane to plane the edge. If you work at it slowly and carefully, the joiter plane will ride very nicely on the remaining peaks, so that you only skim away the remaining high spots. Finally, test the edge with straight-edge and square.

LEFT: Plane down the high spots. You may want to make light pencil crosses over the raised areas so you can easily see which parts to plane.

LEFT: Use both hands to achieve a well-balanced stroke. The jointer plane's exceptionally long sole means it will take the tops of high spots and form a level surface if used with smooth, even strokes.

Jointing boards

The "book" technique of jointing is used when you need to butt two boards edge to edge to make a larger board or panel. If, after jointing, the board edges are less than square—and they nearly always are—then the "book" procedure resolves the problem.

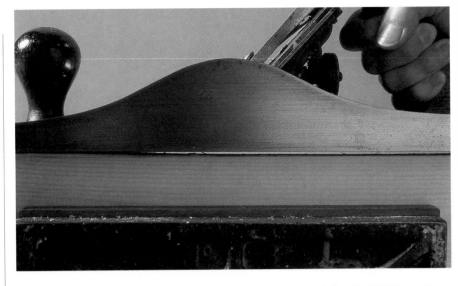

1 Secure the two boards side by side in the vise, with the mating edges uppermost and the best faces turned outward. Then use the plane to estimate how much wood needs to be removed (top right).

2 Run the plane along the wood, first removing the peaks of waste, then cutting down to a true square finish (right). Make sure to keep the plane's sole at right angles to the lumber face and transfer pressure to the rear handle at the end of a stroke.

3 Remove the boards, fold them out so that the mating edges are together and the best faces are uppermost, like pages or the cover of a book (above).

4 Once the two boards are completely opened and the edges butted together, you will see how the technique compensates for edges that are somewhat less than true (right). The joint produced by this technique can be reinforced with biscuits, a loose tongue, or dowels, but the exact fit of the boards should mean that glue alone will form a very strong bond. Make sure there is a thin, even layer of adhesive along the entire length of the boards.

Tips box

Avoid boards with knots running through a face and into the edge. These will often break out when planed.

Smoothing planes

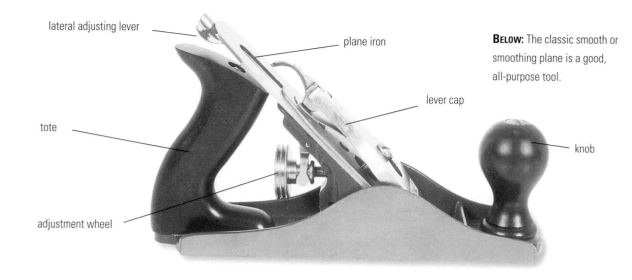

lateral adjusting lever

plane iron

BELOW: The classic smooth or smoothing plane is a good, all-purpose tool.

lever cap

tote

knob

adjustment wheel

The smoothing, or smooth, plane has been described variously as a good starter plane, a good all-purpose plane, and the plane to buy if you plan to get just one large plane. Although the smooth plane will not finish an edge as well as a jointer plane, and will not handle end grain as well as a block plane, it is still more versatile than any other single plane. The smooth plane has a sole 9in to 10in (23cm to 25.5cm) long and a cutter that is ground square. However, there is some dispute about how precisely a smoothing plane iron should be ground and honed. Some woodworkers prefer the edge to be straight with the corners sharp and at right angles, while others opt for having the edge straight but the corners slightly rounded. They maintain that the round corners avoid making scratches and ridges in the workpiece. If you are a beginner, the best approach is to start out with the straight-edge, and then, if you run into problems, try rounding the corners. The one sure-fire rule about using a smoothing plane is that the lateral lever must be perfectly set, so that the cutting edge is parallel to the mouth.

Smoothing defined

The technique of using a plane to take the surface of a board to a level, flat finish, is termed "smoothing". The aim of the operation is to prepare the surface for the final scraping.

Holding the workpiece

The first thing that you have to figure out before you start smoothing is how to hold and secure the wood. Though this will, to a large extent, depend on the size of the board, most woodworkers go for having the end butted against one or more bench stops, and the sides contained by nailed battens. But no matter how you do it, the board must be completely flat—and arranged so that you are working with the grain—and the stops must be set lower than the surface to be planed.

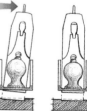

Using the plane

Once you have the work properly secured, set the plane's cutter and blade depth for the merest skimming cut, then start work. Test that the shavings are paper thin—this is very important—then start at the far

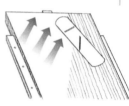

ABOVE: Direction of cut.

end of the board, and skim off the high spots. Work with a skewed, drifting stroke, all the while backing up along the length of the board. When you think that the surface is nearly smooth, set a straight-edge across the width and take a sighting to see if light shines through.

If you still see light, repeat the procedure.

LEFT: Check that the blade isn't skewed, which would result in an uneven surface.

Smoothing

1 Spend time tuning and setting up the plane. Make sure that the cutting edge of the blade is parallel to the mouth.

2 With the workpiece well secured, start at the end farthest away from you and make a series of slightly skewed shearing strokes.

Tips box

A modern power planer is great for achieving a quick finish, but its design is such that the blades soon become nicked, resulting in thin ridges running in the direction of the wood grain. The best solution is to take out these ridges with a smoothing plane.

3 Use a try square to check that the face and the edge of the lumber are true and square to each other.

4 If you are after a super-smooth finish—and if the length of wood allows—then avoid running the plane off the end of the wood. The best procedure when you come to the end of the stroke is to relax the pressure on the front knob, so that the plane ceases to cut. In this way, you will avoid rounding the wood over or marking the wood with the back end of the plar

Remember, never leave wood shavings and other waste lying on the floor. Get into the habit of regularly sweeping up any waste and disposing of it as soon as possible.

Block planes

BELOW: Low-angle block plane for use on laminates and end grain.

lateral adjustment lever

guide knob

depth adjustment lever

mouth adjustment lever

Designed originally for trimming the end-grain surface of butcher blocks, block planes are different from the large bench planes in just about every respect. For example, a block plane has a single blade instead of a paired-up cutter and cap iron, and the block plane cutter is reversed so that the bevel is facing up and set at a low angle. The most obvious difference of all is that the block plane, at about 5½in to 6in (14cm to 15.25cm) long, is small enough to fit into the hand. All this adds up to a precision tool that is designed specifically to plane end grain. Though the beginner might be confused by the number and types of block planes on the market, the main differences between models has to do with ease of adjustment rather than function. Certainly a screw adjustment for blade advancement is a good idea, and a lever for lateral control makes it that much easier to set the blade. The only difference that affects function, however, is the angle of the blade. There are two angles to choose from: the 20-degree angle for general tasks, and the extra-low 12-degree angle for very hard wood or troublesome grain. If you want

to buy a block plane secondhand, look out for the choice double-ended bullnose block plane, which is now out of production. It is the perfect block plane for general work and for planing into tight corners.

Pulling

This is a simple technique in which the user holds the block plane backward and in both hands, and then pulls the plane instead of pushing it. This is particularly useful when you want to work end grain from side-to-center— when you cannot get the plane to push easily from the other side, for instance. It is very easy to splinter the edges of the wood if the plane is dragged too far. You must have a well-sharpened blade for the technique to work successfully.

Shearing

This technique is perfect for planing tough end-grain wood. The plane is held firmly in one hand so that you can put all the power of your shoulder behind the stroke. Then you run the plane with a sideways sliding or shearing cut. If the cutter is well honed and you catch the grain right, you will achieve a silky smooth surface that will not need sanding. As only a small amount of the plane's blade is presented to the wood surface at the beginning of the cut, there is less chance the plane will chatter and tear the wood fibers. The shaving is sliced off with a clean, slicing action. Work from several different angles to find the best way of dealing with wild grain patterns.

bevel uppermost

RIGHT: Cross section showing the bevel and mouth.

Shearing

1 Set the workpiece in the vise so that the end grain face is uppermost, and clamp strips of waste at both the end and the start of the run. Make sure that the wasters are perfectly aligned with the edges to be planed (above).

2 Turn the plane over so that you can sight down the length of the sole, then advance the blade and make a trial cut. Repeat this procedure until you achieve the finest possible cut (above center).

4 If the plane is correctly tuned and your technique is good, the resulting surface will be perfectly smooth and almost polished (above).

3 If need be, adjust the plane's lateral control (above).

5 If the wasters are correctly placed and clamped, they will take any splitting damage rather than the workpiece (above).

Glue repair

If you accidentally split an end grain when planing across it, don't worry, it is very easy to correct. Simply ease some glue into the split with a slip of paper and then clamp or wrap it with masking tape. If the workpiece is special—a prestigious project or an irreplaceable piece of wood—then use a quick-setting glue to speed up the procedure. Glue the split as soon as it occurs, while the torn faces will fit back together well. If a piece of wood has completely broken away or the wood is to be sanded, use a glue that is not gummy.

Bench rebate planes

A bench rebate plane is designed specifically to cut a step—or rebate—along the edge of a board. The feature that enables it to do what it does is the open throat, allowing the cutter iron to extend to the outside face or cheeks of the plane body. This feature allows the plane to make a right-angled rebate that is as wide as the sole of the plane. In use, the plane is handled in much the same way as any large bench plane; the

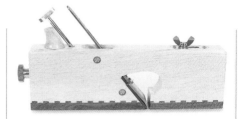

ABOVE: The bench rebate plane—with the characteristic open cheeks.

only difference being that it is mostly used in conjunction with a wood strip or fence clamped against the lumber to guide the plane.

Rebate filister planes

When a rebate plane is fitted with its own fence, it becomes the rebate filister. With its adjustable fence, depth gauge and side body spurs, this beautiful plane is designed to cut rebates up to 1½in (38mm) wide and 2¼in (64mm) deep. The features that make this plane so special are the spurs that enable it to cut across the end grain, and the bull nose that allows the blade to be relocated so that it can cut into tight corners. To correctly

use the rebate filister plane, first secure the workpiece in the vise, and adjust the fence to the width of the rebate. Then position the depth guide to the desired depth, set the plane down on the farthest end of the board, clench the fence hard up against the side of the board, and run the rebate. This procedure allows you to gradually back up as the rebate is cut.

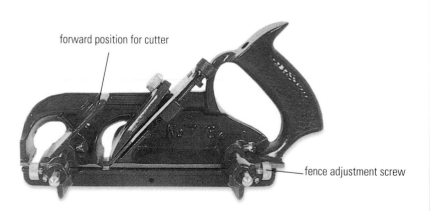

forward position for cutter

fence adjustment screw

ABOVE: The rebate filister is also known simply as a filister. The cutter can be used in the forward position for bullnose work.

Bullnose planes

Bullnose, or bullnosed, planes are perfect for skimming, trimming, and cleaning up tasks. With the cutting iron running the full width of the sole—like a rebate plane—and with some planes having a removable nose, they are designed specifically to trim rebates and wide housings.

Though there are many types of bullnose planes to choose from, some with many add-ons and embellishments, the main differences between models have to do with ease of adjustment rather than actual function. As with all low-pitch planes, the blade is always set bevel-side up.

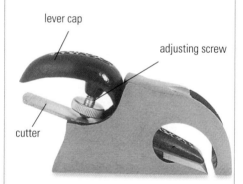

lever cap

adjusting screw

cutter

ABOVE: Cleaning up end grain with a bullnose plane.

Shoulder planes

The shoulder plane might almost be described as a small rebate plane, since it also has the mouth open at the sides or cheeks and a blade that is the full width of the sole. With the blade set bevel up and at a low angle of about 20 degrees, this plane is designed specifically to clean up end grain shoulders, as well as the end grain presented in various other elaborate cabinet joints.

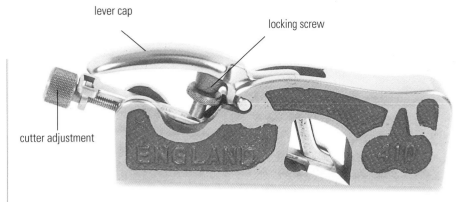

lever cap

locking screw

cutter adjustment

ABOVE: The classic shoulder plane—the perfect tool for shooting shoulders and trimming up dovetails.

end nose

middle nose and shins

LEFT: The 3-in-1 plane is a combined shoulder, bullnose and chisel plane—a fully-adjustable tool.

chisel plane

Compass planes

The compass plane—also known variously as the circular plane and the wheelwright's plane—is designed to plane concave and convex curves.

When to use a compass plane

The compass plane is an indispensable tool for woodworkers who want to produce curved work. It is the perfect tool for such projects as round-top tables, curved windowsills, curved cabinet construction, arched door tops, bow-fronted chests, and all the other tasks that cannot be done with a flat-soled plane. Of course, you could use a drawknife to shape large convex curves on traditional farmhouse pieces, such as Windsor chairs and round-top chests,

that benefit by having "free" curves, but for pieces of formal furniture that are going to be worked with molding planes, or possibly veneered, there is no choice but to use a compass plane.

ABOVE: The flexible sole of the circular or compass plane can be easily adjusted for either concave or convex work. Always work in the direction of the grain to avoid cutting directly into the end grain.

Shooting boards

A useful addition to the plane kit is the shooting board, consisting of two boards—usually beech—fixed together to form a rebate.

Two types are available—one for cutting at 90 degrees, and the other for angles of 45 degrees. The wood that is to be planed is laid across the top board and rests against the stop. The end grain is smoothed with either a jack or a jointing plane, which is held on its side against the board.

Many woodworkers like to make their own shooting boards, and details for 90-degree and 45-degree boards. The measurements can be adjusted to suit individual requirements.

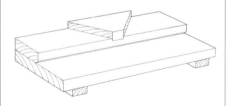

Miters can be planed by either modifying the standard board by placing a 45-degree wedge against the stop or, better, by making a purpose-built miter shooting board. The stop is placed in the middle of the upper board with its edges cut at 45 degrees; this enables both sides of the stop to be used.

Electric planes

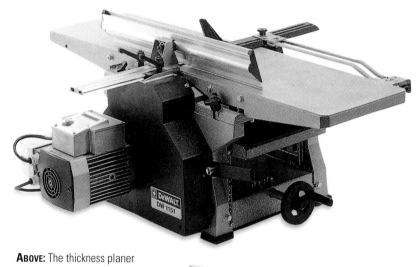

ABOVE: The thickness planer can be used to plane the wood to create a flat surface and then, using the fence, to square the edges ...

Thickness planer

A thickness planer can surface the side and edges of wood (on the top of the machine), in which mode it is hand-fed by the operator. It can also make the opposite sides and edges parallel and flat in the thickness planer (underneath). For this operation, it is equipped with automatic feed. It is well worth running a piece of lumber back through the machine after it has been planed and thicknessed on both sides entirely on automatic feed to eliminate any small ripples. It is in areas such as this that power tools score so heavily over hand methods.

... As a thicknesser, it enables the wood to be machined parallel to the already dressed surfaces by means of an automatic feed.

In some models, the surfacing table swings clear when the thicknesser action is in use. Before buying one of these machines, check how easy it is to switch from planing to thicknessing mode. Some machines have an extraction hood built into the underside of the table that doesn't have to be removed when changing working modes.

Planing wood using an electric planer-thicknesser

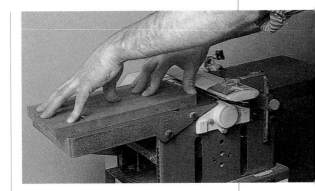

1 First stand toward or astride the machine within easy reach of the start/stop switch and set the feed table height to make a fine cut. Adjust the bridge guard so that the wood can pass underneath it. This is a vital safety precaution, because your fingers should never be exposed to the rapidly-rotating cutter block.

3 As the wood is fed into the cutter, apply firm downward pressure all the time. "Walk" the fingers across the bridge guard to maintain the momentum. Some woodworkers prefer to use the palms of their hands for maximum friction grip and ease of operation as the hand passes over the bridge guard. The important factor is safety and keeping fingers far away from the cutter.

4 Pass the board straight through to the end of the surfacing table. Your stance astride the machine gives equal reach for infeed and outfeed, especially on larger machines. On a smaller machine, such as the one shown here—the kind that home woodworkers are most likely to own—this is not necessary. Smaller boards require the use of a push stick to make sure that fingers are kept away from the cutters.

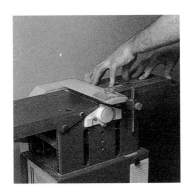

2 Switch on the machine and pass the wood over the cutter, holding the wood down at both ends. Keep your fingers on top of the wood, except for a minimal finger grip to pull the wood through.

Edge planing with an electric planer

1 Set the fence in position and check that it is square to the surfacing table. Position the guard so that it covers the cutter up to the board. Feed the lumber against the fence. Making sure to avoid the unguarded portion of the cutter block, make a series of light cuts. Check with a square for accuracy and re-adjust the fence angle if necessary. Always disconnect the power supply before making any adjustments to the machine. Use a scrap off-cut to check any adjustment before feeding the real workpiece through the machine.

2 To plane an angled edge, set the adjustable fence to the desired angle using a sliding bevel and operate as for Step 1. Ensure strict contact is made between the wood and the machine surfaces. Don't trust the fence calibration marks if you need an accurate bevel, say for a chair component. Use a protractor or other measuring device to check the fence angle.

Tips box

Look for a sturdy fence before buying one of these machines. Ideally, it should have positive locking in two places to provide rigid support for the workpiece.

Using a thickness planer to make perfectly parallel cuts

1 Check the thickness of the wood and set the thicknessing table to the height of the cut—no more than approximately ⅟₁₆in (1.5mm). Feed in the wood into the thicknessing table. The automatic feed rollers will engage with the wood and plane the piece. On aluminum-cast machines, there is more natural friction between the metal and the wood, so use a little lubricant such as talcum powder to keep the wood moving.

2 Make a series of cuts to the desired dimension, turning the handle a few degrees for each pass. After a while, you will learn to judge how much to turn each time. The final finish is achieved by turning the wheel a fraction. Machines with a simple handle mechanism instead of screw adjusters are generally easier to set and use. Make several light passes instead of one larger cut and regularly check the wood thickness as you work.

Portable electric planers

This is a versatile tool for quick stock removal and finishing lumber. It also has the advantage of being able to deal with particularly long and heavy boards, which would be cumbersome to feed through a planer-thicknesser. Instead, the board is stationary, and the tool is taken to it. Hold the planer firmly, because, when it is switched on, its rotary cutter tends to pull it forward quite sharply as it engages with the wood.

The portable planer can be up-ended and fixed in a purpose-built table, making an inexpensive mini-surface planer. With its fence attached, you can square up lumber easily.

BELOW: Portable planers are light enough to be used around the home or in the workshop.

Using a portable electric planer

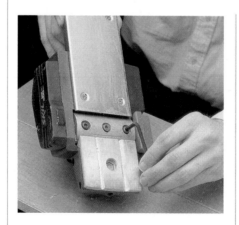

1 The portable planer is particularly useful for removing stock quickly across the grain. The fibers are weak in this direction and break up easily. Give the piece a final finish working with the grain.

2 You will find it best to use both hands and "skate" the planer along the surface of the wood to maintain even flatness. The depth of cut is set by an adjusting knob, which lowers or raises the front part of the planer's soleplate or base. Replace cutters by loosening the Allen-key fixings on the cutter block.

ROUTING

Routers are the most versatile of portable power tools. The tool is simply a powerful motor driving a profiled cutter at high speed. The result is a tool that can be used to cut grooves, form joints, shape decorative edges, and even create relief carving. Once the depth of cut and guide fence or batten have been set up, you can make any number of precise joints. Always make a test cut in scrap wood before cutting the joint.

BELOW: Portable power routers are perfect for neat jointmaking and edge decoration.

Electric routers

The electric plunging router is almost unprecedented as a modern woodworking tool, because of its enormous creative potential. It is probably the most creative tool in the workshop, limited only by your imagination.

LEFT: The most basic jigging device is the adjustable straight fence which is attached to the router. It is used for straight grooves and rebates parallel to the edge of the wood.

The electric router is basically an electric motor with a sharp-edged rotating cutter at the end of its spindle, and its most simple function is in converting a hole into a groove by simply plunging the cutter into the wood and drawing the tool via its adjustable fence across the lumber—like a marking gauge. When you extend the range of cutters to include profiled shapes of different size and variety, and then expand the function of the fence, which serves as a guiding jig by using other types of jigging device, the router does not stop at just cutting grooves and rebates.

It can profile edges, cut through wood to any shape, cut joints, trim wood flat, make screw threads, and much more. Despite its simplicity of concept, the router is a very sophisticated shaping tool. The three main elements of routing are: the size of the router, the variety of cutters, and the types of jigging devices.

Router sizes

There are primarily three main sizes of router, specified by their collet (chuck/cutter shank) diameter and power rating: small ¼in (6mm) collet routers are rated from about 400 watts to 750 watts (approximately 1 horsepower); ⅜in (9mm) collet routers range from about 750 watts to 1,300 watts; and ½in (12mm) collet routers range up to about 2,000 watts.

Cutter size

Cutters are available in ¼in (6mm), ⅜in (9mm) and ½in (12mm) shank diameters.

Collet sleeves allow smaller diameter cutters to be used in larger collet routers.

The range of cutters is greater in the larger and stronger shank size, but it is deceptive to consider that routing creativity relies on numerous cutters: a handful of basic profiles can be used for a variety of purposes.

Cutters are made of high-speed steel (HSS) or tungsten-carbide-tipped steel (TCT). The latter is more expensive, but lasts much longer.

Setting up

Cutters are fragile and expensive. Most new cutters are protected in an oiled plastic coating that you need to peel off. The plunging router usually requires two wrenches to tighten the collet chuck once the cutter has been inserted, although, increasingly, routers have a spindle lock and just one wrench.

There is a knack to tightening and loosening the collet chuck when you use two wrenches. Wrap your hand around both wrenches and squeeze. When loosening, it is very easy to slip and graze your knuckles.

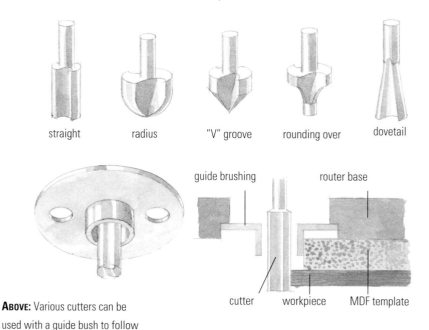

straight   radius   "V" groove   rounding over   dovetail

guide brushing   router base

cutter   workpiece   MDF template

ABOVE: Various cutters can be used with a guide bush to follow the shape of a template. This method is well proven and very accurate.

Fitting cutters

1 Use a wrench to tighten the collet so that it grips the cutter firmly. Some machines have a spindle lock, others need a pin through the spindle to immobilize it while you tighten the collet nut.

2 If your router does not have a collet nut, use two wrenches, one to grip the spindle and one to tighten the collet nut. Arrange the wrenches in a "V" formation so that you can squeeze them in one hand.

Jigging devices

- The most basic jigging device is the adjustable straight fence, which is attached to the router. It is used for straight grooves and rebates parallel to the edge of the wood. The fence can also be used for cutting mortises and tenons.

- Other jigs include the roller guide—which allows parallel cuts to be made to a concave or convex edge—and a variety of guide bushes which are used against shaped templates.

First steps in freehand routing

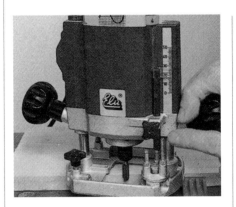

1 To get the "feel" of a router, try freehand routing shallow grooves (a simple name plaque is a good first exercise). First set the cutter to depth using the depth-stop. A golden rule is to cut to a depth of no more than half the diameter of the cutter in one pass (stroke). Most modern routers have what is known as a turret depth stop —a swiveling disc with three protruding screws of different sizes. Use these to set progressively deeper grooves with each pass of the router. Stick to a straight cutter until you have mastered the technique.

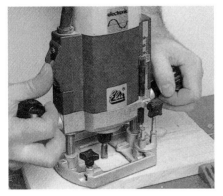

2 It is important that the power switch is within finger reach. With the router switched off, position the cutter where you want to plunge the first cut. Now switch the router on, and firmly but slowly plunge the cutter into the wood to the depth-stop. As you do this, start the horizontal movement, passing the router freehand over the marked line. Keep the cutter moving. The router cutter should always be cutting against the direction of movement—you can feel the steady resistance of the wood as you move the router. Apply even pressure to both handles and try to keep the whole of the base in contact with the wood at all times.

3 At the end of the stroke, release the plunge lock (either untwist the hand grip or use the plunge-locking lever) and the cutter will spring back up. You can see that in this simple freehand exercise keeping to the line is not crucial but it offers excellent practice in controlling the tool. Try to avoid burn marks. These are one of the most common problems faced by the novice user and are often caused by a slowing down of the router as you switch positions or when a curve or corner is being worked. There is a natural tendency to slow down the router movement at these points, but this increases the chance of burning because the cutter is in contact with the same section of wood for longer.

Using a router

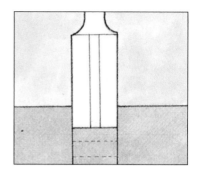

1 To prevent the wood from burning, and to lengthen the life of your cutters, make a series of shallow cuts, instead of attempting to make one deep cut. As a general rule, only cut to a depth equal to half the cutter diameter with any one cut. There are specialist spiral cutters available that reduce edge tear-out and are excellent at removing waste dust quickly—ideal for deep grooving.

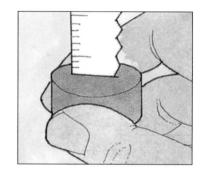

2 Most routers have rotating multi-depth stops so that you can set the range of cuts for the job. The router illustrated here has three threaded stops in a revolving holder to give a sequence of cutting depths. Some routers also come fitted with a micro-adjustable depth stop. This sort of accuracy is rarely needed for freehand work, but is a useful feature for a table-mounted router used to make complex profiles or joints.

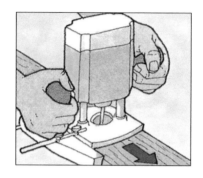

3 Router cutters rotate in a clockwise direction, so, as the machine is pushed forward, it has a tendency to pull to the left. In cutting a groove with the fence on the right-hand side, the router's leftward pull holds the fence firmly against the work. Always make sure all the locking nuts on the depth adjuster and fence are tightened before you start work. The high speed of a router motor can easily loosen items that are not tightly secured.

4 To operate the plunging router, make sure that the cutter is locked in a raised position above the work. Position the router where you want to begin the cut. Switch on the router. The plunging mechanism is either controlled by rotating one of the handles of the tool or flipping a cam-operated lever at the base of the motor. Check the tool plunges smoothly—it may need dust cleaning from the pillars.

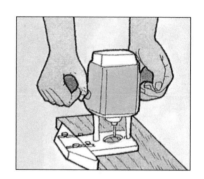

5 Loosen the plunge handle to plunge the cutter into the wood as far as the depth stop. Move the router forward to make the cut. Keep the router moving steadily. Moving too fast may overload the motor, moving it too slowly may burn the work and damage the cutter. With experience, the sound of the motor is your best guide.

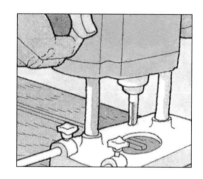

6 At the end of the cut, loosen the plunge handle and let the bit retract from the work. Then switch off. This is the basic freehand process. Always let the router cutter come to a complete stop before moving on to the next cut or unplugging the tool from the power socket. You may also need to use a workshop vacuum to remove dirt that has built up in the groove. Regularly check that the cutter has not slipped down in the collet and adjust if necessary.

Using the straight fence

The straight fence is supplied with the router as standard, and it can be adjusted to width to rout grooves, rebates, and edge profiles such as chamfers (using a "V" cutter). You will need to attach a wooden facing strip to the fence, because for this and other operations a cutaway is required in the fence. It is common practice for woodworkers to make up their own wooden fences for routers—and also for other tools—such as circular saws.

To cut a simple chamfer, set the cutter to depth, lock the plunge mechanism, and draw the router along the wood, keeping the fence in contact with the edge, like a marking gauge. Two screws on the router adjust the fence for cutting grooves. This stopped groove is simply marked first and the groove is cut in steps by a series of "passes." This maximizes the life of the cutter and does not overload a small router. It is always good practice to make several shallow cuts instead of one large one.

Batten routing

It is possible to make a versatile jig by securing a batten onto the workpiece using clamps. First, measure the distance between the edge of the router base and the cutter, then place the batten the same distance from the desired cut. When working, press the router base firmly against the batten. Straight, "V"-grooved or radiused cutters can be used to make different profiled cuts.

Template routing using a guide bush

 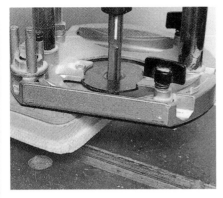

1 Creative routing can be achieved using a guide bush as a spacer between the cutter and a template for grooving and edge trimming. A guide bush is a lipped collar, which is screwed into the router base. You can get a variety of diameter lips to accommodate different cutter diameters. The general rule is to coordinate a measurement of ⅛in (2-3mm) between cutter edge and lip edge.

2 The guide bush rides along the outer edge of your template and copies the profile to the edge of your lumber. Use double-sided tape to fix the template onto the slightly oversized workpiece (clamps can be used, but they have to be moved around to allow the router to pass). A long, straight cutter is used here to finish a rough-sawed edge perfectly smooth and square. Do not try to cut the full depth of the wood in one pass, because this will strain the router. Instead, make a series of cuts until you reach full depth. For such long cutters, a large capacity router is usually needed.

Using a router head in the drill stand

1 Simple drilling or milling (horizontal grooves) can be achieved with some routers, using a standard 1⅝in (43mm) collar. Release the router from its plunging/base assembly and insert it into the matching 1⅝in (43mm) collar of a drill stand, tightened.

2 The router can be used for drilling much cleaner holes than a normal twist-bit or flat-bit, but you have to be careful to avoid burning the wood as the debris has to escape. Using a drill stand with a tilting head makes the router even more versatile, allowing it to be used for special jigged operations, including dowelling at an angle.

Using a router table

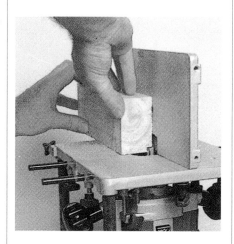

1 Most routers fix into a proprietary table, converting the tool into a mini-spindle molder. The position and height of the cutter are fixed, and the wood passed over the table surface against the appropriate jig. Press the wood firmly into the base/fence as it passes over the cutter, keeping your fingers clear.

2 The router table is set up with a wheel guide for profiling convex and concave work. The wheel serves the same function as the router fence, guiding the lumber into the cutter at a fixed angle. Once this is finished, the work should be sanded.

Routing rebates, chamfers, and profiles on edges

1 Molding and edging cutters have a guide pin, or a ballbearing guide, which runs along the edge of the wood below the rotating cutter, so the cutter can be used without a guide fence.

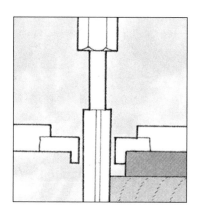

3 To cut shapes and edges, use a template and a guide bush. The guide bush is screwed into the router base. It allows the router to follow the edge of a template. The size of the guide bush relates to the cutter diameter. There should be a ⅛in (3mm) gap between the cutter and the guide.

2 If the work is straight, and not too wide, shape the edge by running the guide fence along the opposite side.

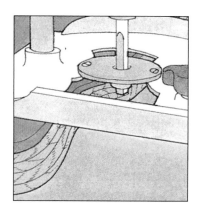

4 Make the template from MDF or plywood. Roughly cut the workpiece oversized and secure the template to it with double-sided tape. Run the guide bush along the edge of the template, taking a series of cuts, if necessary, to shape the edge of the work.

Tips box

Some boxed router sets have a number of bearing guided cutters included, with interchangeable bearings of different sizes. This allows you to mix and match bearings to suit a particular job. Always remove the bearing when you hone a router cutter so that the rounded edge isn't accidentally damaged. With more experience of routers, one of the most versatile accessories you can make is your own router table. You can make up a carcase of 1¼in (18mm) plywood and the top form melamine-faced board to reduce friction as you pass the work across the cutter. Fit your inverted router to a central removable section. You must add a sturdy back fence and fittings to allow a dust extraction pipe to be fitted as close to the cutter as possible.

Cutting a tenon using the router

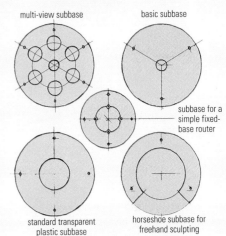

1 To cut a tenon with a router, you will need to use a straight fence and straight cutter. Make two marks on the wood to indicate the settings of the straight fence and the depth of cutter. To set the fence to the correct width, set the router in position, with its cutter lowered to just above the wood surface. Set the depth-stop to the vertical mark.

2 Work the router along the edge of the wood by first setting it to half the depth of the waste wood depth, and working the cutter back and forth to the shoulder line (up to the fence). Set the depth-stop to full depth-of-cut and work the router across the wood, making sure to keep the router sole flat against the wood and not tilt it so the cutter cuts below the intended path. Now reverse the wood and cut the other tenon cheek.

Burn marks

Burn marks are a common problem for woodworkers using a router. They can be caused by a number of different things—blunt cutters, resin build-up on your cutters, changes in the rate of feed, or trying to make too deep a cut. Whatever the cause, the first thing that you have to understand is that a router burn is almost invariably glazed, and as a result it is almost impossible to sand away. The best way of removing a burn is to cut it away with another pass. You can redesign the project slightly, and then saw the edge off and re-run the router around it. If this is impossible, you might make a slightly deeper cut that runs over and removes the burn. If this is also impossible, then you might fit a slightly larger cutter and make a second run over the first.

While cutting away the burn will solve the immediate problem, you should also ascertain the reason for the burn, so that you can prevent it from happening again. If your cutter's edges are blunt—perhaps because you have used it to work a manmade material that contains cutter-blunting resin glue—you will need to sharpen them slightly by careful honing. The key word here is slightly. First establish whether your cutter is made from high-speed steel or carbide steel. If it is carbide, then take a small diamond hone and work around the cutter, just stroking each cutting face in turn. If it is high-speed steel, then use a diamond hone as before, only this time use it much more cautiously. Stay away from pilots and bearings, and make sure to hone each of the cutters evenly. If when using the router you find that, however careful you were, the bit is off-balance and causing a vibration, then for safety's sake send it out to be professionally honed.

Building a subbase

multi-view subbase

basic subbase

subbase for a simple fixed-base router

standard transparent plastic subbase

horseshoe subbase for freehand sculpting

A subbase is a thin sheet of super-smooth plastic, or compound, fitted onto the base of the router, on which the router travels. Subbases come in all shapes and designs—round, rectangular, with circular holes cut out, and so on. One problem with some routers is the fact that the subbase supplied may block your view of your work—either it is made of an opaque material, or the bit hole is so small that you can't see what is going on. This is a particular problem when you are trying to work freehand, and, if this is the case, you will need to build or buy an auxiliary subbase to replace the one supplied with the machine.

The advantage of replacing the router subbase with one of your own is that, while manufacturers tend to give you the minimum, you will be able to design a subbase customized to fit your specific needs. You can make one of see-through acrylic, or one with large openings, or whatever. However you choose to make your subbase, you will find it easier if you can see where you are going. If your router's subbase is attached with screws, then you have no problem—you just copy the pattern of its screw holes, unscrew it, and replace it with your custom one. If it is cemented on, however, it is better to leave it in place and attach your customized subbase to it with double-sided tape—the type used to hold down carpets.

A sliding rod is held at this point on the body of the router.

The "stops" are three height-adjustable screws of different lengths.

Subbases are screwed to the base of the router. Do not over-tighten these, otherwise you will strip the threads.

The screws are mounted in this revolving turret. Select one of three pre-set cutting depths by turning the turret to a new position.

Locking nuts ensure the screws do not move after they are set.

ABOVE: Always switch off the power and unplug the tool before making adjustments.

You may find, on checking your cutters, that there is a build-up of resin on them. Resin is the sticky substance that oozes out of some woods. When it builds up on cutters, it forms a black glazelike coating, which causes the cutter to overheat. Once this starts to happen, a whole sequence of events occurs—the cutter becomes difficult to fit, it tends to run off-balance, the glaze burns the wood being worked, and so on. This all sounds bad, but the problem can be quickly corrected by using oven cleaner to remove the resin. Protect the clean bit with a smear of light engine oil. WARNING—never use an abrasive to scrape the shank, or to clean out the collets.

In many instances, burns are caused by changes in the rate of feed. If you slow down or come to a stop, or your progress is hesitant, then the cutter whirs away on the spot, heats up the resins in the wood, and burns the wood. It is not easy to say what particular rate of feed is best, as so many different factors enter into deciding the optimum rate—for example: the state of the wood you are working (hard, soft, sticky, damp, or whatever), the run of the grain in relation to the direction of the cut, the size and

power of your router, the shape and design of your cutter, the depth and width of the cut, whether you are running a straight edge, an outside corner, an inside corner, or a complex curve, and so on. Given all that, the general rule is: the faster the better. Of course, your set-up has to be safe, but, overall, a fast feed causes fewer problems than a slow one. If you have any doubts about this, then it's a good idea to have a trial run with a scrap piece of the same wood and the same cutter you intend to use for the project. Working in this way, you will build up your confidence and generally be able to judge when everything is going well. As to direction, you should always feed against the cutter rotation—meaning that when you are moving forward, the edge being worked is to the left of the cutter.

Finally, the reason for burns may simply be that you are trying to make too deep a cut. The best advice here is to make the cut with two or three passes instead of one. This is easily done by setting the mechanism known as a rotating stop block, or a rotating turret. All this is, in effect, is a small cluster of

screws—usually three—which are mounted on the top side of the router base. If you look closely, you will see that the screws are set at three different heights, with each screw having its own micro adjustment. In use, the stop rod is lowered and set to the depth of the cut. The distance between the bottom of the rod and the top of the screw equals the depth of the cut. When you come to make the three-stage cut, you make the first pass until the rod comes to rest on the first screw, then you turn the turret around for the next deeper setting, and so on. The turret stop allows you to plan the sequence of depths in advance.

Routing a cover up groove

One of the best ways to conceal a bad butt joint is to route a decorative bead over the joint. Of course, it doesn't do too much for structural integrity, but at least you have boards looking as if they had been done that way on purpose. The bead can be as simple or as fancy as you like—from a straightforward "V"-section groove, to a full "V"-and-bead section. The procedure is as follows:

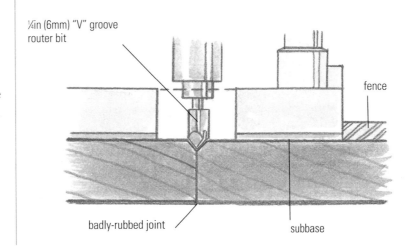

¼in (6mm) "V" groove router bit

fence

badly-rubbed joint

subbase

1 Choose a suitable bit, then clamp the workpiece securely to the bench. Clamp a batten to the workpiece so that it is parallel to the seam, and the distance between the straight-edge and the seam matches the base of your router. Spend time with a square and measure, making sure that the set-up is right. When this is done, set your router on the guide and touch down—just to make absolutely sure that the center of the bit is right on target. You can buy purpose-made straight-edge guides with cam-action clamping jaws on each end. These are perfect for accurate groovemaking in the middle of a board. Snap the guide over the board edges, parallel with the groove position and adjust as described. As these guides don't need a separate clamp at either end, they are easier to fix in awkward positions where clamp handles may interfere with the path of the router.

2 Finally, when you have checked and double-checked that the guide is precisely where it needs to be, set the depth stop to fit the cutter, switch on the power, and begin. You will not go too wrong as you are cutting if you make sure that the flat edge of the router base is always firmly up against the guide edge.

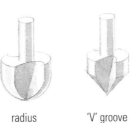

radius   'V' groove

ABOVE: A typical plunge router, complete with a three-screw turret stop. Retighten the locking nuts each time you use the router—they can become loose and fall out with heavy use.

Routing a channel

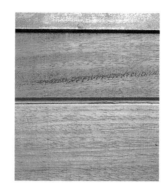

1 First find a suitable inlay band. Then select a router bit of the appropriate width, and cut a trial slot in a piece of waste wood to establish the depth of the cut. The channel should be fractionally shallower than the thickness of the band so that it stands slightly above the surface. It also should be a reasonably tight fit in the slot. Once you have worked this out, fit a batten guide to the joined boards and cut the channel.

2 Remove the router and the guide set-up, and clear away all the dust and scraps. Try the fit of the inlay band. If everything fits together well, the strip will stand slightly above the surface. When you are happy with the fit of the band, pull it out, spread glue on it, and push it back into place.

3 Use the back of a hammer to press the inlay band firmly down into the channel.

4 Wipe up any excess glue with a slightly dampened cloth.

5 Finally, take a well-sharpened scraper and cut the inlay band down to the level of the surface, then scrape the whole surface to remove all traces of glue. Aim for a surface that is burnished to a sheen.

Tips box

• Some router cutter makers sell sets of small diameter straight cutters for hobby and dollhouse work. The narrow blades are easily snapped so be careful not to knock them.

• Use sanding sealer or a pale polish to protect the new inlay as you stain the surrounding woodwork. Mask each side with tape and apply the sealer with a small artist's brush.

Alternative method for cutting accurate mortises

1 Attach a fence to the router, and screw a piece of wood to the fence. The piece should be at least 1in (25mm) wider than the length of bit, so that it contacts the stock before the bit does. With the fence tight against the work and the bit over the mortise location, plunge the spinning cutter into the wood and cut backward and forward until the desired depth is reached. Keep the fence pressed squarely against the wood at all times to control the cutter's path. The bit diameter sets the width of the mortise. The stops on the plunge router control the depth of cut. Only remove a small amount of waste wood with each pass and stop if the sound of the motor changes or the wood begins to burn—you are cutting too deeply and straining the tool and cutter. Rout the whole mortise, then stop the tool before removing the bit (right). Vacuum out any dust left in the bottom of the mortise.

2 If the mortise piece is too narrow to work with the fence on your router, sandwich the workpiece between two pieces of squared-up scrap. You can rout the width of the mortise by hand, or you could mount stops on the assembly to prevent the cut from extending beyond the layout lines (right).

3 Since the router bit leaves a mortise with round walls at the ends, you either have to square up the corners with a chisel or round over the corners of the tenon to make the joint fit together. Many woodworkers find it easier to round over the tenon edges. Just turn over the edge with a rasp or file, then refine the corner with a piece of sandpaper, using the same motion as you would to shine shoes with a cloth (above). However, chopping the mortise corners gives more mechanical strength to the joint. Whatever you choose, spread an even layer of glue on the mating surfaces and clamp together as normal.

Tips box

- It's very easy to accidentally tilt the router slightly when working on narrow sections, so work carefully and support the base of the tool as much as possible.

- You can also use two side fences on a single pair of rods to support the router from both sides as you cut the mortise.

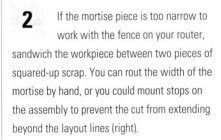

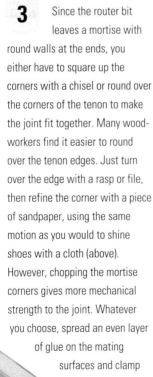

Half lap using a router

The half-lap is just what its name implies—you remove half the thickness of each component, then lap the two pieces together, so that the resulting joint is the same thickness as one of the original components.

   The joint has a great deal of glue surface, but it is not as strong as a mortise and tenon, which it resembles. Generally, lap joints are used for cabinet work, doors, and other non-structural work. A half lap joint can also be used as a design accent, since it contrasts end grain against side grain, as on this vividly-figured Southern Pine piece (right).

   You can cut the joint with any of the methods used to cut dadoes or tenons. Basically, all that is involved is removing the waste, then paring to fit.

   You can also cut the joint with a router, or use the router to clean up the surface after roughly sawing away the waste.

1   To rout out the lap joint, you will need a straight bit and a guide fence.

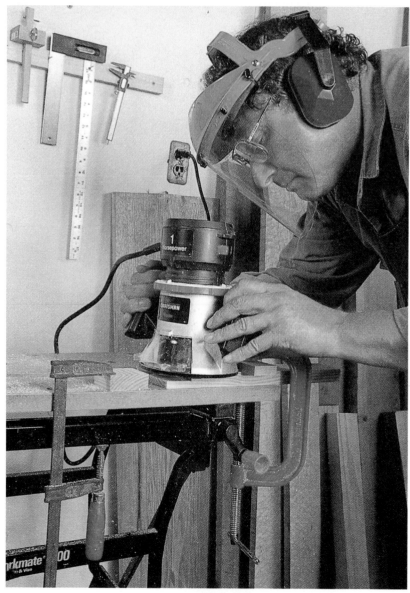

2 To locate the fence, determine the distance between the cutting edge of the router bit and the edge of the router base. This distance will vary according to the diameter of router bit being used, so it is a good idea to check your measurement before each job, unless you always use the same router and bit set-up. After marking out the shoulders of the joint, locate the fence to guide the router. To do this, measure off a space back from the shoulder that equals the distance between the router base edge and the bit. Draw a straight, perpendicular line across the board as a guide for setting the fence. It is important that the fence be mounted exactly perpendicular to the edge of the workpiece.

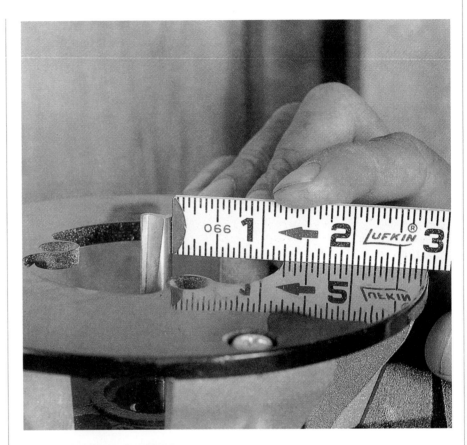

3 If you are working on the end of the board, it is very hard to support the router on the edge, so mount an auxiliary board in front of the workpiece to support the router at the beginning of the cut.

Tips box

• If you need a batch of tenons for the same project, cut them all at the same time. Mark out all the tenons and lay all the components side by side on the bench. Place a batten across the work, spaced so that the router cutter will trim the shoulder of the tenon. Cut straight across all the pieces to form the shoulders and then remove the rest of the waste.

• You can make up a variety of MDF templates to use with a router and guide bush to make door hinge recesses and other common tasks.

• To stop the router from tilting, make up an extension plate to fit on the base of your router using the two screw holes as fixing points. Make the plate in a teardrop shape and add a wooden handle on the narrow end to steady the router as you work.

4 Remove the waste in stages, starting on the end of the board and moving toward the fence. Work slowly, always moving the router so that the bit is rotating toward the surface being cut. If you move with the rotation, the router could pull itself away with a dangerous lurch. The same method can be used to remove waste in the middle of a board; just mount a fence on each side of the joint.

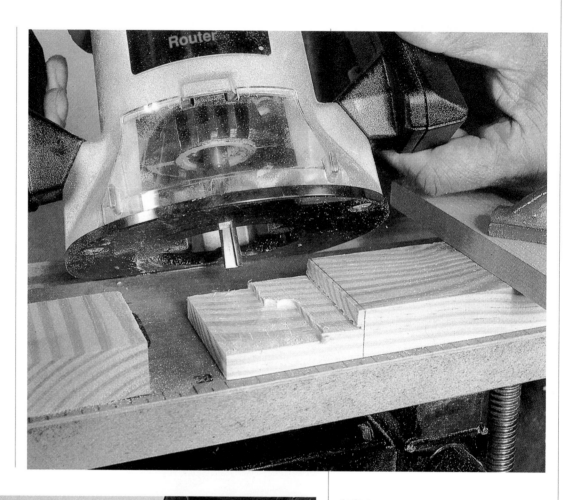

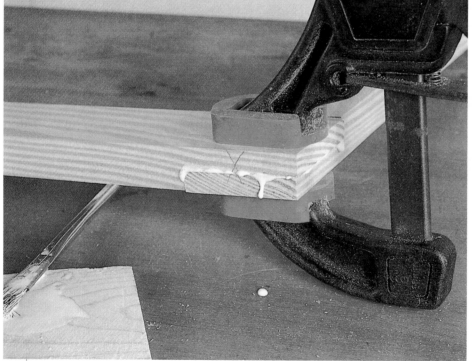

5 When you assemble the joint, you must clamp the two laps together to ensure a tight joint.

Alternative method

- A router table is a good way to clear away waste or trim tenons and half-laps. You can hold the piece flat on the table or rig some type of clamp to hold it down.

- Always work from right to left on a router table so that you are cutting against the direction of rotation of the cutter. If not, the work could be pulled out of your hands. Press the work firmly against the fence as it passes over the cutter.

Making a dovetailed stopped housing or dado joint with an electric router

1 The dovetailed housing is cut in stages, first using a straight cutter and then a dovetail cutter to prolong the life of both. First set up a plunging router with a small straight cutter. Then clamp a batten to the wood to serve as a guide. The router is placed on the wood with the cutter in line with the groove, and the batten is clamped tight against the side of the router. With a pencil, mark where the groove stops. Now rout a series of shallow, stepped cuts down to almost full depth.

2 Replace the straight cutter with the appropriately-sized dovetail cutter, setting the depth-stop so that the cutter achieves the full profiled cut in one pass.

3 Carefully rout out the dovetailed housing in one pass, being sure to keep the router pressed tight against the batten. Do not be tempted to release the plunge mechanism at the end of the cut. Instead, withdraw the cutter back along its own path.

4 Set the router upside down in a router table, using the same cutter.

5 With a tenon saw, remove the stopped portion—first sawing down the grain, and then across it. The stopped portion, remember, has to be cut away, because, in this case, the groove on the other piece did not go right across the full width of the wood.

6 Use a sharp chisel to round off the end of the joint, to match the curved end of the dovetailed housing.

7 Carefully slide the two pieces together, ready for gluing. There is a tendency for wide panels to warp, making it difficult to withdraw dry joints, so gluing should commence as soon as possible.

Router planes

The router plane comes in various sizes and is designed specifically to smooth the bottom of channels and grooves, such as stopped housings and recesses for locks and hinges. To use a router plane, first define the width of the channel with saw cuts, and set the footlike cranked cutter to make the shallowest possible cut. Next, make decisions as to whether or not you want to have the mouth open or closed and set the depth gauge. Finally, take the tool in both hands and work with an even, pushing stroke.

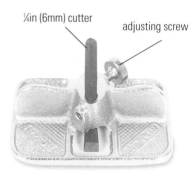

¼in (6mm) cutter

adjusting screw

ABOVE: Miniature router for delicate work such as carved work, lettering, veneers, and inlays.

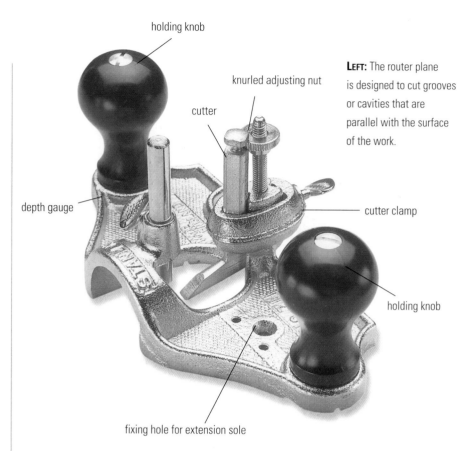

holding knob

knurled adjusting nut

cutter

depth gauge

cutter clamp

holding knob

LEFT: The router plane is designed to cut grooves or cavities that are parallel with the surface of the work.

fixing hole for extension sole

Tips box

Though many experienced hand tool woodworkers would claim that a task like preparing grooves for miniature inlay banding can only be managed with a small router plane or maybe with a scratch tool, there are now one or two power tools that can do the job. For example, some well-known "multi miniature power tools"—sometimes called moto-tools—can rout grooves to a width of less than ⅟₁₆in (1.5mm).

1 Adjust the foot blade so that it makes the finest cut, and set the depth gauge to the required depth. The blades of these tools should be kept as sharp as possible or the wood fibers will tear instead of coming away as shavings, and the result will be a ragged groove.

2 Hold the tool firmly in both hands, and make a series of advancing cuts, pressing down on both sides as you move the tool forward. Be careful not to run off course and damage the sides of the trench. Regularly check the depth of the trench.

PARING

Beginners tend to take the chisel for granted. What they fail to understand is that there are many different kinds of chisels, each designed for a specific range of operations. If you are making unsatisfactory joints, the chances are that you are making inappropriate cuts with a poorly chosen chisel. The following solutions will put more power into your elbow.

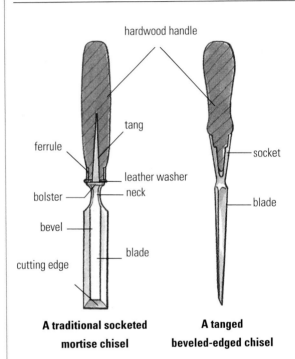

hardwood handle

tang

ferrule

socket

leather washer

bolster — neck

bevel

blade

cutting edge

blade

A traditional socketed mortise chisel

A tanged beveled-edged chisel

Anatomy of a chisel

You need top-quality chisels. The generic chisel is a flat-bladed tool made up of a long, straight blade that has a cutting edge on one end and a handle on the other. While there are many families of chisels, there are only three basic types—the tanged chisel that has a tang running from the bolster into a wooden handle, the modern chisel with a stub shaft running into a molded plastic handle, and the socket chisel with a wooden handle fitting into a socket. The length and structure of the blade and the way the blade fits into the handle equates with the quality and the life expectancy of the tool.

Common chisel types

While there are dozens of chisel types—each designed for a specific task—there are only three types of chisels in common use: the firmer chisel, the beveled-edged chisel, and the mortise chisel.

SHEFFIELD: 20 mm 3/4" : ENGLAND

Firmer chisel

Firmer chisels: The firmer chisel with its rectangular, straight-sided blade is strong enough to be driven with a mallet. It is designed for general-purpose, everyday work.

SHEFFIELD: 20 mm 3/4" : ENGLAND

Bevelled-edged chisel

Bevelled-edged chisels: The beveled-edged chisel, sometimes called a paring chisel, has a blade beveled on both sides. It is designed for paring and joinery. The beveled edges allow you to chisel into tight corners without the blade binding.

SHEFFIELD :13 mm : ENGLAND

Mortise chisel

Mortise chisels: The mortise chisel is characterized by having a heavy, straight-sided blade tapered from front to back along its length. There are two kinds—a heavy-duty type for cutting deep mortises and for house framing, and a lighter version used for general joinery.

Using a chisel

There are three primary chisel cuts: vertical paring, horizontal paring, and mallet-driven cutting.

Vertical paring: Clamp the workpiece flat down on the workbench. Grip the beveled-edged chisel with your right hand, so that it is at right angles to your forearm. Place your left hand, knuckles down, on the workpiece so that your forefinger is behind the mark. Back the cutting edge of the chisel up to the mark, and then control the cut by hooking your right thumb around the chisel blade. Push the chisel down with your right shoulder.

Use the thumb and fingers of one hand to set the chisel on the mark, and the grip of the other hand to power the thrust.

Horizontal paring: Secure the workpiece in a vise—or hold it down with a clamp. Take the chisel in your right hand so that the handle butts into your palm, and your forefinger points down the length of the blade. Put the knuckles of your left hand down so that the length of your forefinger is resting against the side of the workpiece, and lay the back of the chisel blade on the pads of your fingers. Nip the blade with your left-hand thumb and forefinger, place the cutting edge to the mark, and push to cut. Put your shoulder into the stroke.

Place the blade on the mark and use the mallet to strike a careful blow.

Use one hand to set the blade on the mark, and the other hand and shoulder to power the thrust.

Mallet cuts: Clamp the workpiece flat down on the workbench. Take the chisel in your left hand with your fingers wrapped around the handle in a comfortable grip. Use your right hand to position the blade edge on the mark. Take the mallet in your right hand and strike the top of the handle with a well-aimed blow. The important part of this procedure is taking care to position the blade precisely on the mark.

Working across the grain

1 The chisel can be used efficiently to sever fibers across the grain—a little help with a mallet is needed here. A general rule is that when cutting a mortise, or similar square recess, the fibers are cut across the grain first to avoid splitting.

2 After the fibers have been severed across the grain you can then chisel down the grain without the fibers splitting. A series of cuts to loosen the fibers precedes the final cut to the line.

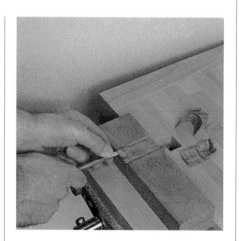

3 With both hands behind the chisel's cutting edge, one hand is used to deliver the power and the other to guide the chisel. The guiding hand is crucial for control and here the fingers squeeze tightly around the chisel blade and the forefinger rests against the edge of the work, acting as a depth-stop.

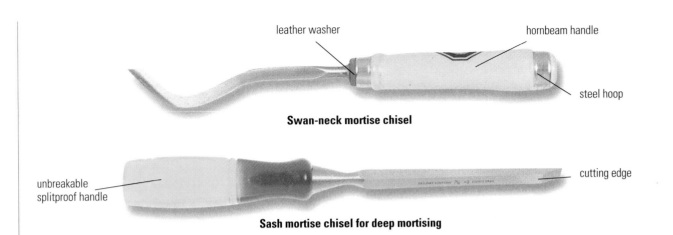

leather washer

hornbeam handle

steel hoop

Swan-neck mortise chisel

unbreakable
splitproof handle

cutting edge

Sash mortise chisel for deep mortising

Mortise chisels

Mortise chisels are, as the name suggests, used primarily for chopping mortises and holes. With a heavy blade, solid wooden handle, a leather washer between the handle, and shoulder and/or between the tang, or socket, and sometimes also with an iron ferrule around the end of the handle, they are designed for heavy work. The handle can take repeated blows of the mallet, the leather washer deadens the blows like a shock absorber, and the heavy section of the blade means that the tool can be wrenched and levered without a problem. There are four main types of mortise chisels: the joiner's, the sash, the registered, and the swan neck.

Joiner's mortise chisel

With a thick blade and a heavy wooden handle, this chisel is designed primarily for chopping wide and deep mortises. It is very good for cutting large holes in hardwood.

Sash mortise chisel

With its narrow blade and relatively delicate wooden handle, this chisel is designed for light work such as small holes in easy-to-cut softwood.

Registered mortise chisel

With a flat blade and a wooden handle that has a ferrule on the butt end, this chisel—sometimes also called an "extra heavy mortise chisel"—is designed specifically for cutting hardwood.

Swan-neck mortise chisel

With a thick, socketed blade, a hooked swan neck and a wooden handle, this chisel is designed for chopping lock mortises in the edge of heavy security doors, cutting a deep hole into which the lock is fitted. The swan neck is designed to cut and scoop out the end grain of the cross rail tenon.

Powered chiseling (mortising)

A hollow chisel mortiser is easy to use once the work-piece has been aligned and cramped. Be sure to spend time in getting this right, it is a very important part of the job.

Cutting a mortise

1 First use a pencil, ruler, square and gauge to mark out the mortise, and then clamp the workpiece so that it is flat-down on the work surface. Take the mallet and chisel and start by cutting a small "V"-shaped notch at the center of the mortise.

2 Stand to one end of the workpiece, set the chisel at the center so that the bevel is looking away from you and then back up with the chisel. Make sure along the way that the cuts are progressively deeper and at about ¼in (6.5mm) intervals. Work to within about ⅟₁₆in (1.6mm) of the end, and then reverse the chisel and repeat the procedure for the other end.

3 Finally, when you have worked down to the required depth for a blind mortise, or turned the workpiece over and repeated the procedure from the other side for a through mortise, put down the mallet and clean up the ends with a few crisp paring strokes. The final paring cuts will clean up the rough ends left by the levering.

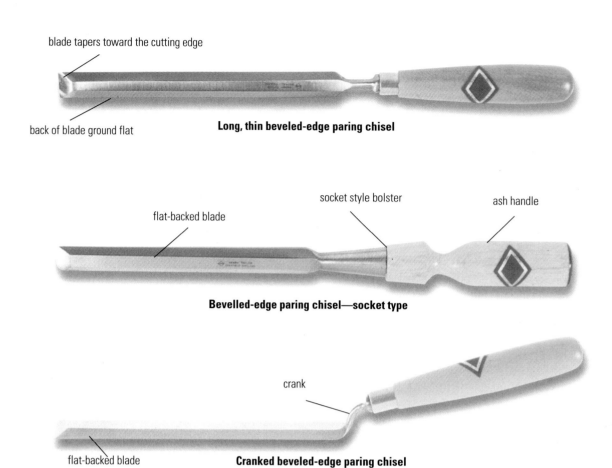

blade tapers toward the cutting edge

back of blade ground flat

Long, thin beveled-edge paring chisel

flat-backed blade

socket style bolster

ash handle

Bevelled-edge paring chisel—socket type

crank

flat-backed blade

Cranked beveled-edge paring chisel

Bevelled-edge chisels

The beveled-edge chisel, sometimes also called the beveled-edge firmer and the paring chisel, is much the same as the straight-sided, general purpose chisel, except that the top face of the blade is beveled along both sides. In use, it is designed to be held in one hand and pushed with the other. The beveled edges allow the chisel to be used to pare out difficult-to-reach angles, as in undercut joints like sliding dovetails and housings.

If you are a beginner looking to get a good all-around chisel, one that you are certainly going to use, then the beveled-edge chisel is a good bet. There are many choices of design—ones with plastic handles, ones with the handle set in a socket,

Japanese types with beveled blades that are triangular in section, and many more. If you are looking for a great tool and one made in the western tradition, then you can't go wrong with a chisel that has an octagonal boxwood "London Pattern" handle, a long blade, and a leather washer between the bolster and the handle. Though the beveled-edge chisel will stand up to a small amount of light mallet tapping, it is primarily a two-handed

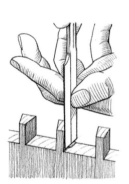

The shape of the beveled-edge chisel allows you to clean out an under cut—such as this dovetail housing.

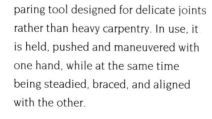

Making a delicate paring stroke with a beveled-edge chisel.

paring tool designed for delicate joints rather than heavy carpentry. In use, it is held, pushed and maneuvered with one hand, while at the same time being steadied, braced, and aligned with the other.

English

Spokeshaves

The spokeshave is essentially a short-soled plane with a winged handle at each side. It is designed primarily to shave and shape the edges of thin-section wood. If you need to shave the edge of a tabletop or sculpt the edge of a fancy curved shelf or bracket, then this is the tool for the job. The key words are "shave" and "thin wood." There are four basic forms: the traditional wooden version with a beech stock and a straight-tanged cutter; an all-metal version with a straight blade that might or might not have a screw adjustment; an all-metal version designed to shave a convex section; and an all-metal version designed to shave a concave or hollow section. The basic working procedure is to hold the spokeshave in both hands, set it across the thickness of the wood at a right angle and then push like a plane. However, in some situations, it is an advantage to skew the spokeshave across the wood so as to make a shearing or slicing cut and/or reverse the tool and pull it like a drawknife. No matter how the spokeshave is held, or what type you are using, the one constant is that you always work with the grain, or you might say, downhill.

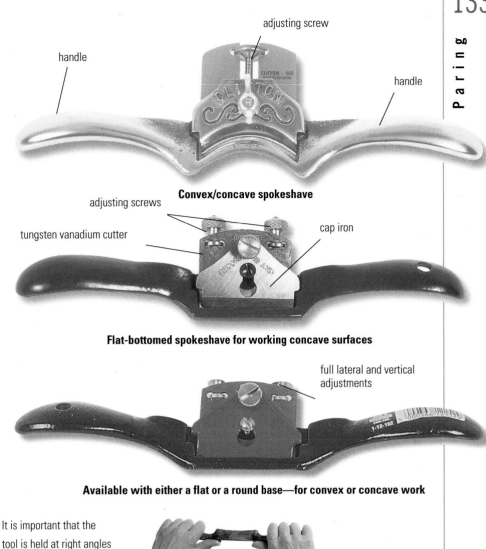

handle · adjusting screw · handle

Convex/concave spokeshave

adjusting screws · cap iron · tungsten vanadium cutter

Flat-bottomed spokeshave for working concave surfaces

full lateral and vertical adjustments

Available with either a flat or a round base—for convex or concave work

It is important that the tool is held at right angles to the wood.

Shaping a chair arm

First, make sure that the blade is razor sharp. Adjust the setting until the blade edge is parallel with the body of the stock or the throat. Secure the workpiece in the vise with the edge to be worked uppermost. Take the spokeshave firmly in both hands, and brace your thumbs in the little depressions or curves in the frame at each side of the blade. Stand to one end of the workpiece so that the tool bridges the wood. Set the tool down on the wood and draw your elbows back and tuck them into your waist. Begin moving the spokeshave forward until you feel the blade begin to bite, then straighten your arms to complete the stroke.

1 Start by cutting the rough-sawed faces to the level of the drawn line. Adjust your approach/the wood so that you always cut downhill in the direction of the grain. Be careful not to split off the relatively short grain at the curved hand-hold end of the arm. Use a wooden spokeshave to round over the edges of the arm.

2 Continue by redrawing the guide lines, removing the waste with one or other of the shaves, and reworking the lines until you have the correct shape.

sharpened on both sides

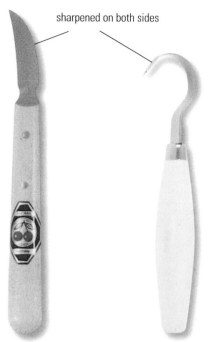

**Chip-carving knife—
with a straight blade
and skew edge**

**Chip-carving knife—
with a skew edge**

**Chip-carving knife—
with a double-sided
curved blade**

Double-edge hook knife

Single-edge hook knife

Knives

The knife is one of the oldest tools known to man. Whoever it was that first discovered that a flake of flint could cut wood made one of the biggest technological breakthroughs ever!

There are about four basic knife-holds: the grasp with the blade facing away from the body for big slicing strokes; the elbows hard into your body with both hands braced by your chest for more controlled slicing strokes; the thumb-braced levering stroke when you are cutting toward your thumb; and a thumb-push stroke for tight control when you are detailing. But which knife to use? The following directory will help you understand your options.

Chip carving knives

Chip carving is a patternmaking technique that involves using knives to cut triangular-shaped pockets in the surface of wood. There are three basic knife forms: the "sheepsfoot," which is characterised by its short blade and long handle, and is used with a pushing action; the "skew-blade," which is

designed to be used like a pushing or paring chisel; and the "off-set," which is designed to make a dragging stroke.

Crooked knife

The crooked or hooked knife, as used traditionally by the Northwest Coast Native Americans, is the choice tool for carving and whittling hollows in bowls and dishes. It is a long hook-bladed knife with a curved handle. It is gripped like a dagger so that the thumb is looking toward the end of the handle and then it is rocked and levered by the action of the thumb so that it removes waste with a scooping and hooking action.

A crooked knife in action

Sheath knife

The sheath or hunting knife with its long, single-edged blade is, in many ways, a jack-of-all-trades, or you might say it is anything that you want it to be! It is good for whittling and for splitting wood. It will sharpen dowels and tackle all the other cutting, scraping, splitting, and spiking tasks that crop up in the workshop. It wins over many other knives in that the fixed, through-handle blade makes for a strong, trustworthy tool.

Hacking knife

The traditional hacking knife, sometimes called a chipping knife, has a heavy, thick-backed through-blade and a rivetted hide handle. The tool is something more than a knife

Hack knife

but less than an ax. In use, the blade is set down on the end grain, and the back of the blade is struck with a hammer. The thick hide handle cushions the blows. It is a good tool for all the rough tasks.

Jack knife

If you are one of those woodworkers who is always on the lookout for driftwood, special sticks in the hedges, little sticks or crutches from the mountains and woods, then you may be looking for a good traditional fold-up pocket knife, a knife that can be used for a wide range of tasks. This is the one to choose.

Sloyd knife

A genuine Swedish sloyd knife is a must. Made from the famous laminated Mora steel,

the blade can easily be sharpened to a razor edge. Many woodworkers, especially those who like to whittle figures, spoons, bowls, and so on, claim that this knife is the best of the best.

Pocketknife

A small pocketknife is a joy to own and use. Small enough to slip into a side pocket, it is a wonderful tool for all the small, delicate marking, skimming, whittling, and trimming tasks that crop up in most workshops. Search the markets for a little two-bladed, bone-handled English knife about 4in (10cm) long—one made before the age of stainless steel.

Whittling a pan slice

All you need for this project is a good sharp knife and a piece of smooth-grained, easy-to-carve wood like basswood, cherry, or plum. Before you start the project, experiment with some scrap wood. If the blade cuts up rough, then either the wood is ragged and unsuitable, and/or your knife is blunt. And just in case you are a little bit nervous—say a parent showing a child how to whittle, or a teacher with a student—then you can derive comfort from the old adage, "a dull knife is a dangerous friend." You are more likely to have an accident with a blunt knife that needs to be bullied into action, than with a sharp one that does the job efficiently. As to how sharp is sharp, you should be able to shave the hairs on your arms with a good knife.

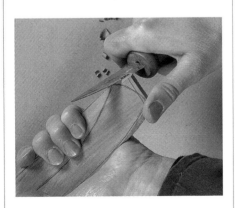

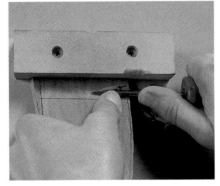

1 Brace the workpiece against the work surface and use big, controlled stokes to clear the bulk of the waste.

2 When you have established the overall shape of the form, use more restrained, thumb-braced paring strokes to define the details.

3 Use the two-handed stroke for a stroke-controlled cut. Link the thumbs for maximum efficiency.

4 Butt the business end of the slice hard up against the bench hook stop and use the sharpened knife of your choice to cut the bevel. Finally, use a little of your favorite cooking oil to burnish the finished slice to a high sheen.

Tips box

A small diamond sharpening stone is an ideal tool for sharpening the blade of a carving or pocketknife. However, these stones remove a lot of metal in a short time, so use a fine grade stone and only use a few strokes per side.

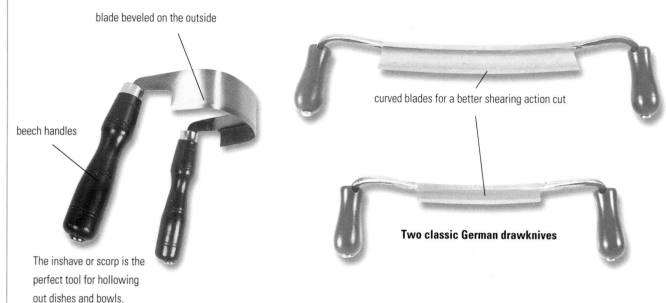

blade beveled on the outside

beech handles

The inshave or scorp is the perfect tool for hollowing out dishes and bowls.

curved blades for a better shearing action cut

Two classic German drawknives

Drawknives

Drawknives in all their many guises are simply single-bevel blades that are fitted with a handle at each end. There are straight knives for general work, slightly curved knives that are used to skim a surface to a flat finish and the "U"-shaped knife—called an inshave—that is used for hollowing. The very best knives have good-to-grip, slightly splayed wooden handles that are fitted by having the tangs running through the handle and clenched over at the ends. The drawknife is a wonderfully efficient and safe tool to use.

The two-handed pulling action not only allows you to put the whole weight of your body behind the stroke but, better still, the stance with both arms held straight out from the elbows makes it almost impossible to cut yourself. If you want to make items like Windsor chairs, boat spars, and large carved bowls, then you need a couple of drawknives.

Drawknife technique

With the workpiece held securely in the vise or with a holdfast, take the drawknife in both hands so that the bevel is set down on the workpiece. Brace your feet in readiness, cock the knife at a slightly skewed angle, and then draw the knife toward your body to make a shearing or slicing cut. You will soon find that by adjusting the angle and/or putting more weight behind the cut, it is possible to achieve anything from the lightest paring cut through to a deep-splitting rough cut. As for the question of which way to have the bevel facing, don't worry about the "experts" who claim that there is only one way. The general rule is: bevel down for maximum control and skimming cuts, and bevel up when you are aiming to remove great slices of waste. The inshave is used in much the same way as the straight-bladed drawknife. The only real difference is that the strokes always need to be short and slicing rather than long and deep. When you are working dished forms, you always have to work from side-to-center into end grain.

Hold the drawknife with well-braced arms, and clear the waste with a series of short, shallow, slicing strokes.

For full and safer control, always hold the drawknife with two hands.

Making a green wood chair leg

All you need for this try-out project is a length of green wood, a good sharp drawknife and a way of holding the wood while it is being worked. To start with you will find that the bench vise is adequate. The term "green wood" should be taken to mean wood from a fresh-cut log at about 10in to 14in (25cm to 35cm) in diameter. The best way of getting at the wood is to use a wedge and sledge hammer to split the log down its center, then to split the halves into quarters and so on until you have cake-wedge sections about 3in to 4in (7.5cm to l0cm) wide across the span of the circumference arc.

1 Set the roughed-out billet in the vise so that the end to be worked is set up at a comfortable work angle. Take the drawknife firmly in two hands. Set it at a skewed angle so that the bevel is looking toward the wood, and then draw it toward your body. It is best to shave a little, and then turn the wood slightly, shave a little more, and turn the wood, and so on.

2 When you have shaved one end to a round cross-section, then all you do is repeat the procedure for the other end.

DRILLING

The woodworker is forever needing to make holes in wood for screws, dowels, nails, bolts, and for many other reasons besides. The traditional hand brace has, to some extent, been dropped in favor of the portable power drill, and, indeed, the electric drill press is good for boring large-diameter holes. Whatever you use, choosing the correct bit for the job is essential for a crisp, accurate result.

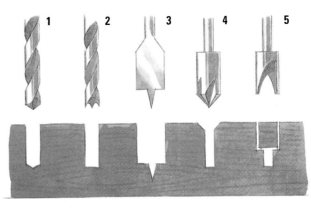

Selection of twist-drills and flat bits

1 Twist-bit for making small holes; also useful for waste clearance and starting screws.
2 Doweling bit for setting wooden dowels needing a square-bottomed hold.
3 Flat-bit works with a scraping action, cuts large holes very rapidly.
4 The countersink bit allows a wood screw head to lie flush with the work's surface.
5 The plug cutter removes waste in one piece to allow it to be replaced later.

Jennings pattern screw bit (right), center-pattern screw bit (center) and solid-center bit (far right) can all be used in a traditional brace.

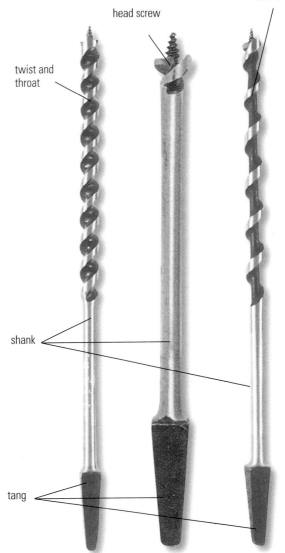

twist and throat

head screw

twist and throat

shank

tang

Hand drills

swivel handle
and bit storage

drive handle

screw chuck

Archimedean drill,
also called a fret drill,
is used for boring small-
diameter holes in
thin-section wood.

Putting the bit in
the chuck.

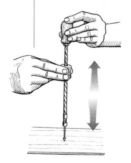

Archimedean drill in
action.

Twist bits

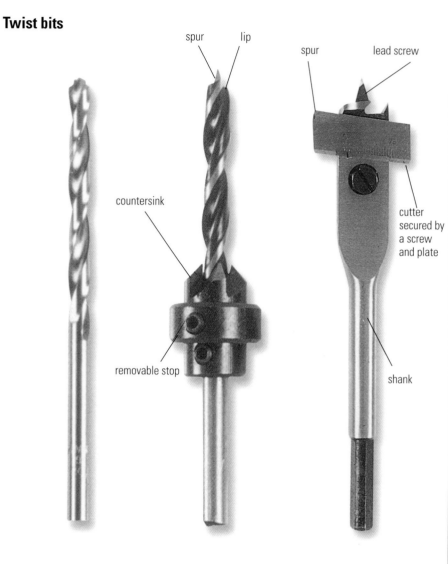

spur   lip

spur   lead screw

countersink

cutter
secured by
a screw
and plate

removable stop

shank

Twist drill bit (above)
Combined lip and spur drill bit
with countersink—good for
countersinking and boring at
the same time.

The expanding bit
Expanding bit with patented
non-slip cutter.

**Reamers, rimmers, rinders,
and hollow-taper bit**

flute

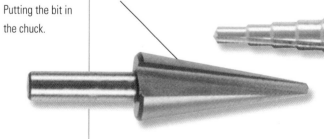

Step drill—designed to drill and
de-burr at the same time.

Conical drill

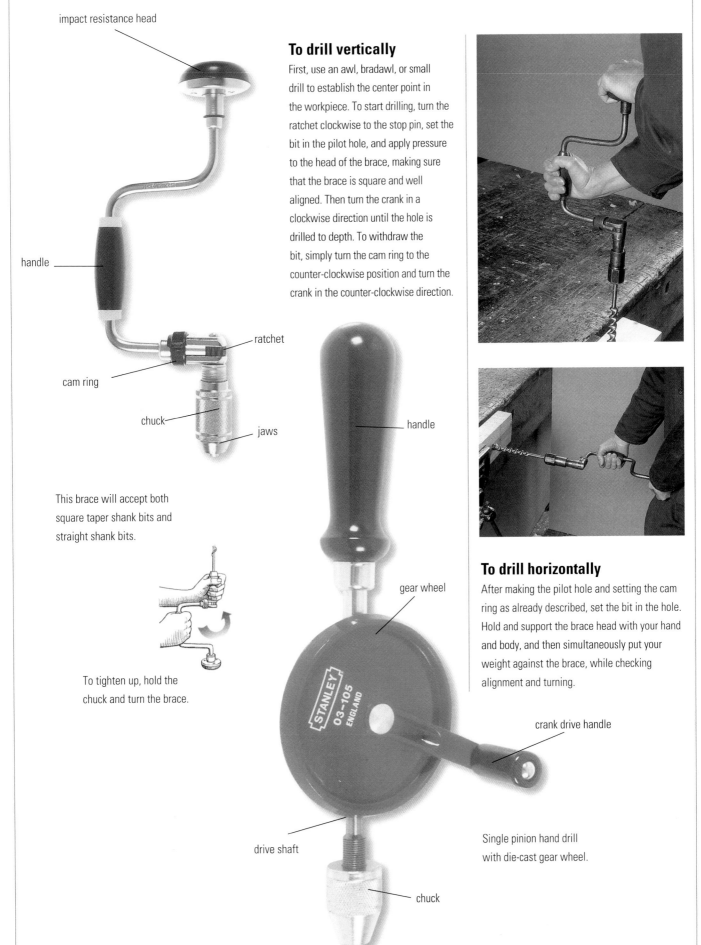

impact resistance head

handle

cam ring

ratchet

chuck

jaws

This brace will accept both
square taper shank bits and
straight shank bits.

To tighten up, hold the
chuck and turn the brace.

handle

gear wheel

STANLEY
03-105
ENGLAND

crank drive handle

drive shaft

chuck

Single pinion hand drill
with die-cast gear wheel.

To drill vertically

First, use an awl, bradawl, or small
drill to establish the center point in
the workpiece. To start drilling, turn the
ratchet clockwise to the stop pin, set the
bit in the pilot hole, and apply pressure
to the head of the brace, making sure
that the brace is square and well
aligned. Then turn the crank in a
clockwise direction until the hole is
drilled to depth. To withdraw the
bit, simply turn the cam ring to the
counter-clockwise position and turn the
crank in the counter-clockwise direction.

To drill horizontally

After making the pilot hole and setting the cam
ring as already described, set the bit in the hole.
Hold and support the brace head with your hand
and body, and then simultaneously put your
weight against the brace, while checking
alignment and turning.

Anatomy of a brace

Braces are available with sweeps of
6in to 12in (150mm to 300mm), and with or
without a ratchet. The sweep is the diameter
of the circle described by the grip. The ratchet
mechanism, as on this brace, allows drilling
in the spaces where there is insufficient
room to turn the grip a full circle.

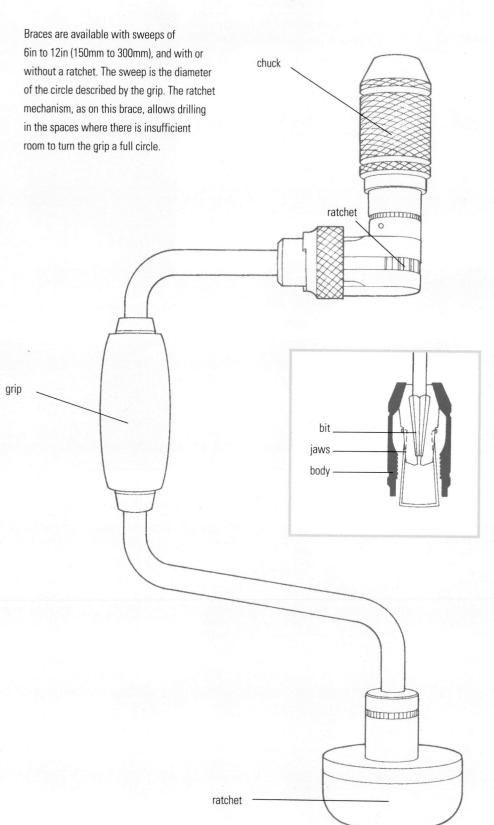

chuck

ratchet

grip

bit

jaws

body

Cross section of a
chuck showing how
the square shank of
the bit locks into
the jaws.

ratchet

Making and using a depth stop

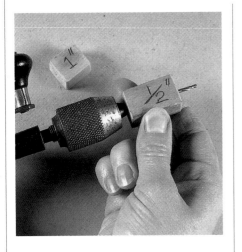

1 Take your depth stop block—marked ½in (12mm)—and set the drill bit down in the chuck so that a ½in (12mm) length of bit sticks out from the end of the block.

2 In use, the block will ensure that the hole runs no deeper than ½in (12mm).

Tips box

Another quick way of making a depth stop for drilling is to wrap a few turns of masking tape around the bit at the correct depth. You can also buy small depth stop rings that slide onto the bit and are fixed in place with a small grub screw. However, these can be difficult to fix accurately.

1 Set the workpiece in the vise so that the hole to be drilled is at a comfortable height, and make a few turns until the screw point begins to bite. Even at this early stage it's important to keep the drill as straight as possible. A sharp screw thread should only need gentle pressure to bore into even hardwood.

2 Check the alignment by eye and use a try square to keep the bit horizontal. Hold the square with the stock firmly against the workpiece and the blade in line with the auger bit. Check the side of the bit at the same time. Repeat after every few twists. You may need to remove the auger completely to re-align a skewed hole.

3 Use a ruler and/or a marked dowel to check the depth of the hole. Clean out any debris in the end of the hole to obtain a precise measurement. If you are boring all the way through the lumber, remove the auger as soon as you see the lead screw protrude through the rear of the wood and start drilling from the other side.

Using the Archimedean drill

1 After transferring the design to the wood, use the Archimedean drill to run a small pilot hole through the area of waste. Hold the drill upright and work with an easy constant stroke.

2 Pass the end of the fret saw blade through the pilot hole and hitch up. Make sure that the teeth are pointing down toward the handle.

3 You need to use both hands, one holding and positioning the workpiece so that the blade is presented with the line of the next cut, and the other hand operating the saw.

Power drills

Portable electric drill

BOSCH CSB 550-2

Choose a power drill with a reverse action (for taking out screws) and variable speeds to cope with all types of bit, and materials to be drilled.

Use a drill stand for consistent, accurate boring. Pre-set the depth stop and fix the stand to the bench before starting work.

How to use a hand-held power drill

1 Insert the required drill bit into the chuck, making sure it is tightened with the key in all three holes.

2 When marking positions for drilling holes, a cross is generally used to denote the center. For end grain drilling it is preferable to use a drill bit that has a clearly-defined center point.

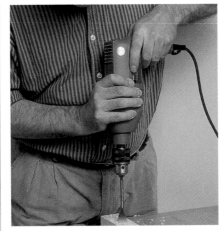

3 Clasp your hands around the drill comfortably, positioning yourself above the workpiece, and locate the drill bit and commence drilling. Occasionally withdraw the drill bit in order to clear the chippings, which have a tendency to clog and overheat.

4 When drilling straight-through holes it is important to stop drilling when the point of the flat bit appears through the wood, then turn the workpiece around and drill from the other side; this is to prevent splitting or what is known as "breakout."

Using a drill stand

1 Install the drill into the drill stand making sure it is secure, and insert the correct bit, using the chuck key to secure it.

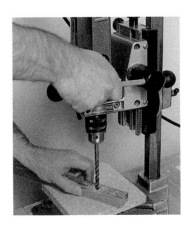

2 Place scrapwood underneath the workpiece for straight-through holes. For blind holes (holes which do not go all the way through) you will need to set the depth-stop on the drill stand. Carefully hold down the workpiece with one hand, anticipating the rotary snatching of the drill bit (especially wide-diameter flat bits). Switch on the power with your other hand and gently lower the bit into the wood.

3 Countersunk holes (for sinking the screw head level with the surface of the wood, or deeper) can be achieved by setting the depth-stop.

Countersinks

cone-shaped cutting end

Three rose countersinks in various sizes and designs

A countersink is a tool much like a reamer, which is designed to cut a beveled or conical recess. There are two basic types: the hand-held countersink that is used with a quick rotating or reciprocating action, and the countersink bit that is used in a brace. Of the drill bit types, there is the conical rosehead and the much older flat "V" head. As a general rule, the greater the number of cutting edges and the faster the action, the smoother the resultant countersink.

Spoon bits

The spoon bit is gouge shaped along its length and enclosed like a spoon at the leading end. It is one of the oldest of all the drill bit types. There are special spoon bits for traditional uses, such as the brushmaker's spoon bit, chairmaker's spoon bit, and cooper's spoon bit. Other names describe the form, for example the duck-bill spoon bit and shell spoon bit. The spoon bit is unusual in that the cutting edge isn't dragged into the wood—as with the auger bit—but instead it is simply the downward pressure that produces the cut. This action makes the spoon bit particularly suitable for woodworkers who need simultaneously to drill holes at a low angle and to be in total control of the rate of cut on entry and exit—like Windsor chairmakers.

Using a hand countersink

1 Give the hand countersink several quick swivel-turns.

2 If all is well, the top face of the screw will be a clean fit, but fractionally lower than the surface of the wood.

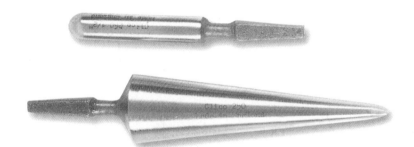

ABOVE: The spoon bit wins over most other bits in that it can be used either vertically or at an angle.

SANDING AND SCRAPING

The general term applied to smoothing wood flat prior to applying a finish is abrading. The same term is used to describe shaping wood using hand or power tools. Although much abrading does consist of sanding for a fine finish, it would be limiting to confine the term to this function only, since abrading is also a very important shaping technique. There are many instances, which you will no doubt come across, when other tools cannot easily fashion the wood. For example, in instances when chisels or planes might split the grain, or when a saw is used to cut out the desired profile roughly and the general shaping and finishing is done by abrading.

Abrading chart

grade	grit		applications
very coarse	50 60	1 1/2	heavy shaping
coarse	80 100	0 2/0	shaping—belt, disc, orbital and hand
medium	120 150 180	3/0 4/0 5/0	shaping and finishing —belt, disc, orbital and hand abrading
fine	220 240 280	6/0 7/0 8/0	finishing—power and hand abrading
very fine	320 360 400 500 600	9/0	final finishing, taking off sharp edges, sand sanding in between coats of varnish— hand abrading

Abrading involves the wearing away of wood fibers by the multiple sharp-toothed action of an abrasive material such as glasspaper. It also refers to the action of files or rasps and specific power tools and their accessories.

In some instances, both hand- and power-tool abrading methods can be used, although the latter is generally quicker and more efficient. At the heart of most abrading is abrasive paper—usually a sheet or roll onto which the abrasive particles are bonded. The particle sizes are graded as a "grit" and these are numbered. Generally you work through the grades, starting with a coarser grit, and working through to the finer ones—until the wood is smooth, and there are no visible sanding marks.

A selection of sanding blocks

dual foam block—the soft side is for curved surfaces

hard foam

cork

velcro-backed abrasives

Hand sanding—shaping with an abrasive stick

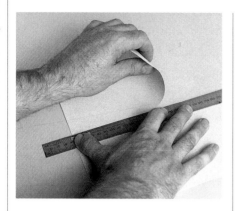

1 Use an aluminum oxide paper for this method—the particles are firmly bonded to the backing paper and can be wrapped around even tightly curved shapes without shedding too much grit. Traditional "sandpaper" will soon lose its cutting ability.

2 Wrap the abrasive paper around a workshop-made wood forming block, creasing the edges back on themselves to form a sharp edge which clings to the block. If you regularly sand a lot of awkward shapes, make up several such custom blocks at one time so you don't waste the remains of the torn abrasive paper.

3 Hold the workpiece in the vise and use the abrasive block or stick like a file, preferably with both hands, cutting across the fibers. Change the sanding strips when they begin to lose their bite, and clog up with waste (especially when sanding resinous woods). Keep the block flat to the surface so that as much of the abrasive is in contact with the fibers as possible. Try to avoid rounding over the corners of the work.

4 Work a thin strip of coarse sanding paper "bath-towel" fashion to form circular sections accurately. It is very easy to sand too deeply across one section and produce bands or ridges. Always keep the abrasive paper moving up and down the wood to achieve a smooth, even finish. Even with narrow sections, it's vital to still work through the grades of abrasive from coarse paper to fine to reduce the risk of sanding marks.

Making a mini drum sander for the drill press

If you enjoy woodturning, make yourself a shaped drum sander – a cylindrical sanding block—used in conjunction with a drill press.

1

Mount a block of easy-to-work wood in your lathe chuck, and turn it down to a cylinder. Turn a hollow in the middle that matches the edge that needs sanding. Turn a spigot at one end so that it can be mounted in the drill chuck.

2

Use masking tape and double-sided tape to cover the drum with sandpaper. Do not worry about wrinkles. Check for a good fit.

3

Finally, drill a hole through the drum, and rig up a pivot jig to support the bottom of the drum. To sand, pass the spinning drum over the workpiece.

For more precise straight-edge work, you may want to invest in a bobbin sander. This consists of a powerful motor attached to small table. The motor spindle protrudes through the table. Abrasive paper is wrapped around the bobbins and the workpiece is moved around the spinning bobbin.

Using a hand block

1 A cork hand block is normally used for flat work. Mount the paper on the block, secure the workpiece in the vise or on the bench, and apply firm pressure, working along the grain. More pressure and control can be achieved with both hands on the block. Use 120- to 180-grit paper.

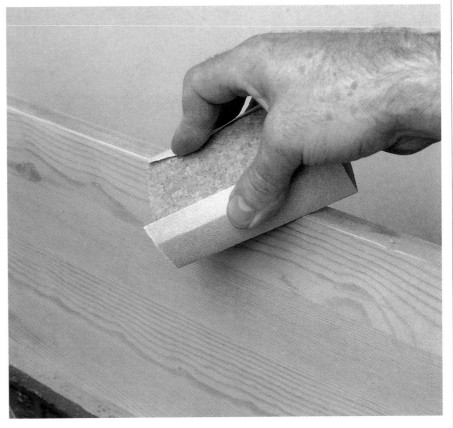

2 Always try to sand with the grain, otherwise scratch marks will show.

3 Generally speaking, wooden objects should not be left with sharp edges. A final finishing procedure is to soften all edges with a fine (400-grit) sandpaper. Try to work evenly along each edge to produce a tiny bevel. This will reduce the risks of fine splinters catching. For some projects, a small block plane may be used to remove the sharp edge, but never use a power sander, as this is too aggressive for this kind of work.

Tips box

You can buy rubber sanding blocks with a detachable foot and hidden spikes that hold the abrasive paper firmly at each end. These are less abrasive on the hands for prolonged use, as the paper does not wrap around the sides of the block, which are gripped.

Making a disc pivot jig

Suppose that you want to make a small round plywood tabletop about 24in (610mm) in diameter, and you want to sand the edge to a fine finish before covering the edge with a strip of veneer. The edge needs to be perfectly smooth.

Take the square sheet of plywood and establish the center by drawing crossed diagonals, and then draw and cut out the circle. Then take a 1in (25mm) thick block of wood about 6in (150mm) square, drill a ¼in (6mm) diameter hole through the center, and mount it on the underside of the tabletop at the center.

Set a piece of ¼in (6mm) diameter rod in your lathe's tool rest, and mount the whole works on the rod. Fit a sanding disc to the faceplate, and clamp a block to the bed so that the tabletop is level and the edge meets the sanding disc at right angles.

You should be able to rotate the tabletop against the disc. All you do now is switch on the lathe and slowly pivot the top until the edge is sanded to your satisfaction.

Surforms®

solid molded plastic handle

replacement blades

die-cast alloy body

Surform® tools have replaced the more traditional rasps and files for some woodworkers. In form, they appear to be a combination of files and planes. Though the open-toothed structure of the surform allows the user to easily cut and shape the wood without worrying about the teeth clogging, this means that the surform needs to be used with care and caution.

ABOVE: Standard file (top), planer file (middle), and flat file (bottom).

Rasps

The rasp is best thought of as the big brother to the file. Files and rasps look much the same—they are both bars of steel of various shapes, lengths, and cross sections, with patterns of teeth cut into their surface. However, the file will cut both metal and wood, while the rasp is dedicated to cutting wood. The rasp should be held in both hands—one hand gripping the wooden handle, the other hand holding the point at the far end— and then it is variously drawn, stroked, twisted, or skew-planed across the workpiece. As with the other cutting tools, best results are achieved when the stroke is made either with, or at a slight angle to, the grain. Rasps are particularly useful in woodcarving.

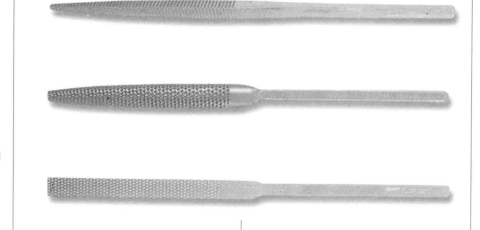

ABOVE: Three carver's rasps—each forged from one piece to create an integral handle.

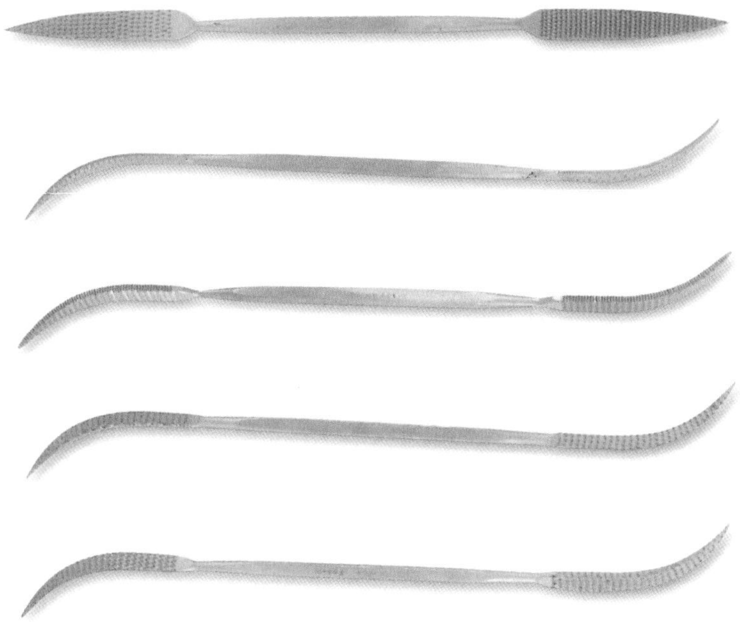

Rifflers

Rifflers are small, double-ended rasps. At about 7in to 8in (180mm to 205mm) long—with both ends being the same shape, section, and cut—they are perfect for woodcarving. The hooked and pointed shape of the end allows you to work in small, tight, otherwise inaccessible areas. They are particularly useful in relief woodcarving, for cutting the lowered ground down to a uniform texture. They should be held at the middle, with the index finger running down the length of the blade, and used in much the same way as you might use the back of a spoon for burnishing. By using the different-shaped rifflers—round, oval, square, triangular, and knife-edge—and by judiciously varying the direction of the stroke, it is possible to achieve a whole range of textural effects.

ABOVE: Rifflers files, with shaped blades and rasp teeth – good for cleaning out difficult-to-reach spots.

Scratchstock

The scratchstock—sometimes also called a scratch tool or a scratch gauge—is usually a homemade tool used for shaping small-section headings, profiles and grooves. It consists of two identical "L"-shaped pieces of wood that are screwed together to sandwich a steel cutter. The cutter is filed and ground to the reverse section of the desired molding or groove. Many woodworkers make scratch stocks from old marking gauges. To use the tool, butt the wooden stock hard up against the workpiece, and run the cutter backward and forward with a scraping action. It is perfect for cutting grooves for inlay banding, and for shaping short lengths of small-section moldings.

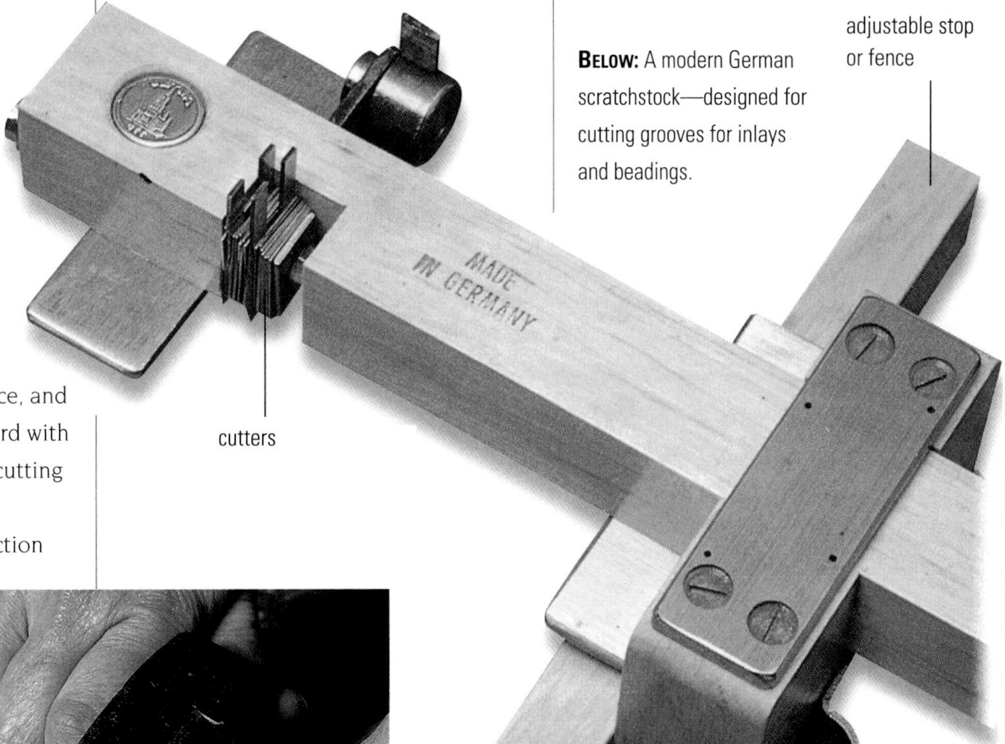

RIGHT: Drag the scratchstock along the edge of the workpiece so that the blade scratches a reverse profile.

BELOW: A modern German scratchstock—designed for cutting grooves for inlays and beadings.

adjustable stop or fence

cutters

Beading tool

The beading tool is a sort of cross between a marking gauge and a scratchstock. There is a central post, a head or fence that slides along the post, and a selection of profile cutters that can be fitted to the post. To use the tool, first select a cutter, and clamp it in the center post at roughly the distance to be worked. Set the fence to the correct position, and butt it hard up against the edge of the workpiece. Push and drag the tool alternately backward and forward across the workpiece.

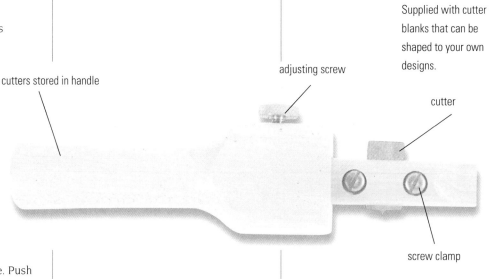

cutters stored in handle

adjusting screw

cutter

screw clamp

BELOW: Beading tool for fine detail work. Supplied with cutter blanks that can be shaped to your own designs.

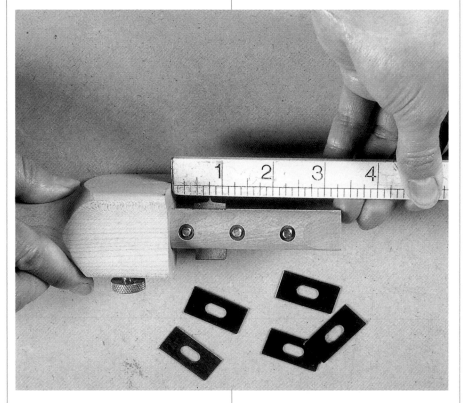

1 Fit the desired cutter blade, making sure that it is perfectly aligned and at the correct depth. Then measure, set the fence and tighten up. Test the profile made on a scrap piece of lumber.

Note: These tools can usually be bought with a pack of various profile blades or blanks which can be shaped to the profile you require. Make up extra cutters from broken pieces of hacksaw blade.

2 Set the tool down on the workpiece, adjusting the dragging angle until the blade begins to bite, then make successive passes until the blade ceases to cut. This technique needs to be practiced on a length of scrap wood to form an even cut. The stock must be pressed firmly against the edge of the lumber all the way along the cut—otherwise the grain may drag the cutter off course.

Beading tools

Beading tools are some of the most under-valued tools available to the woodworker. Often it is much quicker and easier to form a small molding on a cabinet door frame or jewelry box lid with one of these simple devices than it is to set up a power router.

RIGHT: Curved scrapers are used for shaped work. The cutting edge extends all the way around, so any section can be used.

all-around cutting edge

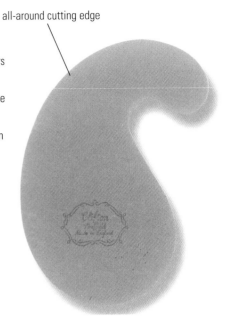

Scrapers

Made from spring steel—like saw blades—scrapers are used for cleaning up the surface of wood prior to the final finishing. There are two basic forms: the rectangular type at about 6in (150mm) long and 3in (75mm) wide, which is used for finishing flat surfaces, and a goose-neck or kidney shape, which comes in various sizes and is used for finishing concave hollows. There are also smaller rectangular scrapers available for getting into awkward corners. The scraper is held in both hands, flexed slightly with the thumbs and then either pushed or dragged along the grain, sometimes at a skewed angle. The tiny burr (burl) on the back of the scraper acts like a plane and should produce wafer-thin ribbons of wood as the metal passes over the workpiece. Unfortunately, these tools do need frequent sharpening to work efficiently. Scrapers are much favoured by cabinetmakers and carvers who are looking to achieve a smooth finish without going through the chore of using sandpaper. They are ideal for smoothing areas of wild grain.

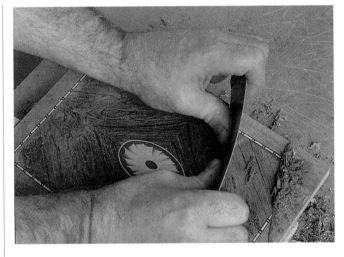

LEFT: A well-tuned scraper will produce the best of all surfaces—many times smoother than a plane or sandpaper.

LEFT: The double-handed scraper is used in the same way as the cabinet scraper but is more comfortable to hold, relieving the strain on the thumb. Since the blade is held at an angle, altering its curvature controls the shaving depth.

The scraper plane in action.

Power sanders

Using an orbital sander

An orbital sander is ideal for sanding large panels flat. Sanding sheets are attached to the cushioned oscillating baseplate. Let the weight of the tool do most of the work, and keep it moving up and down and across the workpiece in gentle sweeping actions.

LEFT: An orbital sander uses ½ or ⅓ size abrasive sheets, which are clamped to a padded baseplate. The action is elliptical, and the tool should be used under its own weight.

1 A belt sander has a continuous 3in or 4in (75mm or 100mm) wide belt passing over a flat bed via two rollers. It abrades faster than other power sanders and the tool has to be held firmly to prevent it from snatching and taking off.

2 The belt is changed quickly by releasing a lever that slackens the tension. Tracking is adjusted with a knob.

3 A belt sander can be inverted for flat and curved sanding. Ensure it is clamped to the bench and the workpiece held firmly as it is fed into the sander.

BELOW: A belt sander uses 3in (75mm) or 4in (100mm) continuous belt for heavy-duty abrading.

RIGHT: This narrow-belt power abrading tool can fashion wood fast and furiously. First, secure the workpiece in the vise. The tool needs firm control directed at its tip where it does the work.

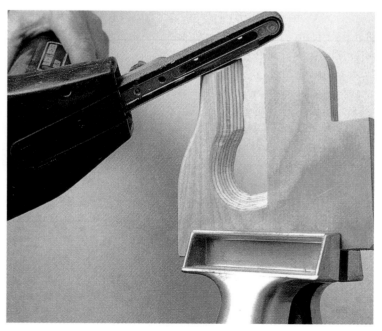

GLUING AND FIXING

Although the need to hold, secure, and otherwise stabilize a piece of woodwork is crucial to woodworking success, it is surprising how many projects catastrophically fail at the assembly stage. What usually happens is that the woodworker takes the various assembly and fastening techniques for granted—the nailing, gluing or whatever—to the extent that the workpiece splits, warps, stains, or is otherwise less than perfect. At a time when there are many more sophisticated assembly techniques than ever before, it is very important that you keep up with current techniques.

Gluing

Most woodwork needs to be glued. There are all types of dry joints that rely on nails, screws, dowels, and various patent hardware, but modern glues are so fast, easy to use, reliable, and strong that gluing is a technique that needs to be mastered. But what glue to use?

Dry run gluing

Having chosen your glue, and generally made sure you know all there is to know about mixing, setting time, precautions, and all the rest, you need to do a dry run before the actual glue-up. This procedure involves doing everything except actually brushing on the glue. Start by choosing a clean, dust-free area in the workshop, somewhere that you can work without interruption. Make sure that the mating faces to be glued are clean and free from dust, then put them together. If you need a mallet, then have it ready. Prepare scraps of clean wood to protect the workpiece from the clamps, and clamp up. Make decisions along the way as to whether or not you want throw-away containers, clothes, or protective gloves and lay them out accordingly. Continue through the procedure from first to last, until the workpiece is clamped and complete. Finally, when you have run through the whole checklist, and are happy with the order of work, remove the clamps, set out the various elements of the workpiece, and start gluing-up for real.

Types of glues

There is a wide variety of glues (adhesives) available. The glue you use will depend on what you want to achieve. Do you want a user-friendly glue that allows you the option of disassembling the workpiece at some time in the future? Or do you want a fix that is forever—a bond that is stronger than the wood itself? The following selection guide will help you match your needs to the available choices.

Hide glue (hot)

An animal-protein glue, hot hide glue requires a glue pot. It has fast tack, is transparent, not water resistant, non-toxic, can be sanded, and is good for restoring antique furniture.

Hide glue (cold)

Also an animal-protein glue, cold hide glue used straight from the tube or can is a glue with slow tack. It is transparent, non-toxic, can be sanded, and is slow setting and good for difficult assemblies.

Casein glue

Made from milk, this glue must be mixed with cold water. It is opaque, non-toxic, and good for cool working conditions and oily, exotic woods.

White glue

A PVA glue, this adhesive is made from petrochemicals. Used straight from the squeezy container, it is transparent, non-toxic, and good for interior woodwork. White glue goes rubbery when sanded, but it is good for general do-it-yourself woodwork.

Aliphatic resin glue

Also a PVA glue, this glue is similar to white glue. You can use it straight from the squeezable container. It offers fast tack, is almost transparent, non-toxic, can be sanded, and is good for both indoor and outdoor use.

Resin glue

A mix-with-water powder glue, this adhesive is brown in color. Be warned that it is toxic in its powder form. Resin glue tends to be brittle, but it sands well and is good for general use.

Gluing a dovetail joint

1 A dovetail joint has an extended gluing contact area, so it is best to use a glue—such as urea-formaldehyde – with a longer pot life. First check that the joint fits "dry."

2 Mix up the glue with the powder, then add small amounts of water— never the other way round. Allow four parts glue to one part water.

3 To avoid lumps, mix a thick paste, and gradually thin it with water.

4 When the glue runs off like honey, it is correctly mixed. Leave it to stand for a few minutes. The pot life of urea-formaldehyde is about 10 to 20 minutes, after which it thickens and becomes unusable.

5 Using a wooden spatula, thinly apply the glue to both surfaces.

6 Tap the joint together, using a hammer and scrapwood along the shoulder line.

BELOW: To remove a dribble of glue, wait for the glue to become rubbery, then cut off the dribble with a sharp chisel.

7 Place the scrapwood between the joint "fingers," and gently hammer down to make good shoulder-line contact.

8 A cut-away clamping block should be used to allow for the slight joint protrusion. Check for squareness with a try square, and leave the whole assembly to cure for at least eight hours.

Steam and disassembling

The wonderful thing about using hot hide glue is the fact that it is so user-friendly. Admittedly, it smells a bit, but once you get to know its positive attributes, the smell will not matter. It is easy to prepare, it keeps well, it is sandable, it fills gaps, it bonds to oily wood, it can be cleaned up with water, it is cheap, it is non-toxic, and—best of all – it is totally reversible. If you do not like the glue-up, you simply soften the glue with steam, and start again.

1 Take your steamer and get to work softening the glue. A wallpaper steamer fitted with a fine-point nozzle works best. Direct the full force of the steam on and into the joints. When you feel the joints begin to move, use a rubber-headed mallet to knock and ease the structure apart. Be warned: if you try to twist and bend the chair apart before the glue has softened, you risk breaking the wood. Be patient, and be generous with the steam.

2 Before disassembly, label the component parts with a pencil, so that you know precisely what goes where—and how. Spend time scraping off all the glue from the mortises and the ends of the rails. Finally, do a dry run to make sure that you know the right order of reassembly.

Tips box

After doing a trial dry assembly—so that you know precisely what goes where and how—use low-tack masking tape to cover all the areas outside the joint that you want free from glue.

Use a small fine-point brush to apply glue carefully to all mating surfaces. Put the piece together, checking for alignment and squareness, and clamp. Wait until the glue is set, then peel away the tape and scrape the surfaces to a fine finish.

Using a rope clamp

One of the best ways of clamping up a chair—or any other irregular structure—is to use a rope-and-stick clamp. This consists of a stick, and a length of strong rope or webbing 2in (51mm) wide, with a metal clamp at one end, through which the other end threads.

If one is not available, you can use the following emergency procedure.

Wrap the rope or webbing several times from leg to leg across the diagonal, knot off, pass the stick through the loop, and wind up until the twisting takes up the slack and begins to pull everything together. Compare diagonals until they more or less match up, then tie the stick so that it stays put (see below). The rope-and-stick method is great for pulling the legs onto the stretchers. Just about the only thing that you have to watch out for is that you do not overdo the winding, and break the chair. Having said that, be careful that the stick does not unwind all of a sudden, and hit you. It is a good idea to wear goggles.

ABOVE: Hold the boards together so that you can glue both edges at the same time.

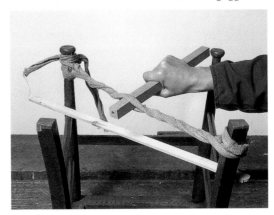

LEFT: The rope clamp or "Spanish windlass" is ideal for pulling together a chair frame.

Fixing

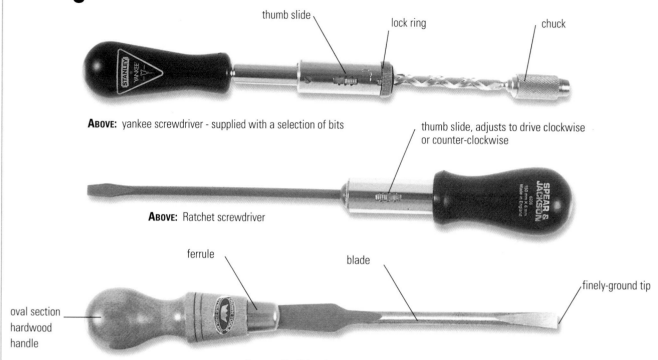

thumb slide

lock ring

chuck

ABOVE: yankee screwdriver - supplied with a selection of bits

thumb slide, adjusts to drive clockwise or counter-clockwise

ABOVE: Ratchet screwdriver

ferrule

blade

finely-ground tip

oval section hardwood handle

ABOVE: Traditional cabinet screwdriver

Screwdrivers

Though the screwdriver is one of those tools that gets to be used for just about everything from stirring paint to chiseling out mortises, it is nevertheless a tool that crucially affects the quality of the finish. Use the wrong screwdriver, and the chances are that you will damage the screw or scratch your work or both.

The screwdriver blade needs to fit fair and square in the slot.

Screwdriver type

For a screwdriver to successfully perform its task, the tip needs to fit the head of the screw, and the handle needs to fit your hand. Most woodworkers agree that you cannot do better than the traditional "cabinet" pattern, with its oval-section wooden handle. However, there are currently so many screw types on the market—Phillips, Pozidrive, clutch, and Torx, to name a few—that a good option is to have a selection of cabinet-pattern screwdrivers for the traditional slotted screws, and a spiral-type "yankee" screwdriver or cordless screwdriver with slug bits, to do the rest. When you come to choose a screwdriver head to match the screw, make sure that it fits snugly into the slot. It should not be so wide that it projects from either side of the screw and scratches the workpiece, nor so narrow that it twists around on the spot and strips the head of the screw.

LEFT: The yankee-type screwdriver—with its chuck and selection of bits—is a great all-around tool.

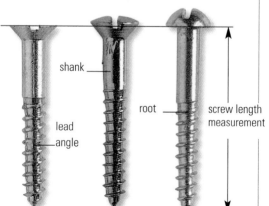

shank

root

screw length measurement

lead angle

Screws for woodwork

Wood-screw heads sit either flush or proud, the shanks are long and bare, threads climb the root at a low angle, and the root tapers to the tip.

Fixing a dovetail joint

1 Drill a small diameter pilot hole into the wood.

2 Drill into the pilot hole with a bit the same size as the screw you intend to use.

3 Use a countersink bit to sink a cone-shaped hole big enough to take the screw head. Dip brass screws in beeswax polish to prevent them from snapping, and drive them home.

Hammers and nailing

Woodworkers need at least three hammers: a claw hammer, a small cross-peen pin hammer, and a Warrington cross-peen hammer. As with planes, there is a hammer for every task—and of course, there are good hammers and bad hammers. Though the hammer is one of those tools that is often abused – or simply taken for granted—a good hammer can make the difference between a job well done, and a job less than perfect.

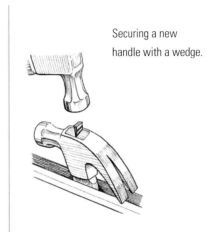

Securing a new handle with a wedge.

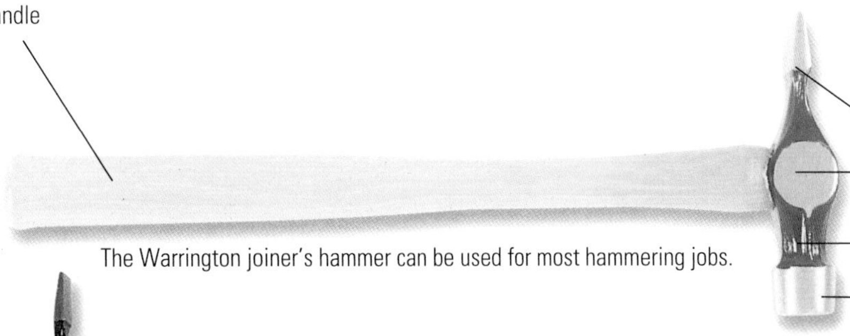

ash handle

peen

cheek

neck

bell

The Warrington joiner's hammer can be used for most hammering jobs.

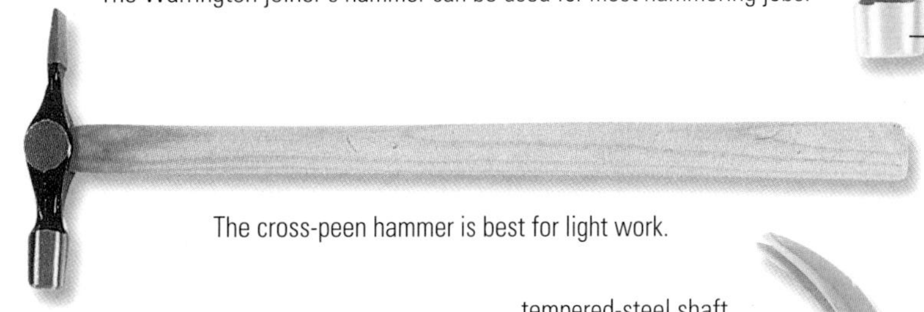

The cross-peen hammer is best for light work.

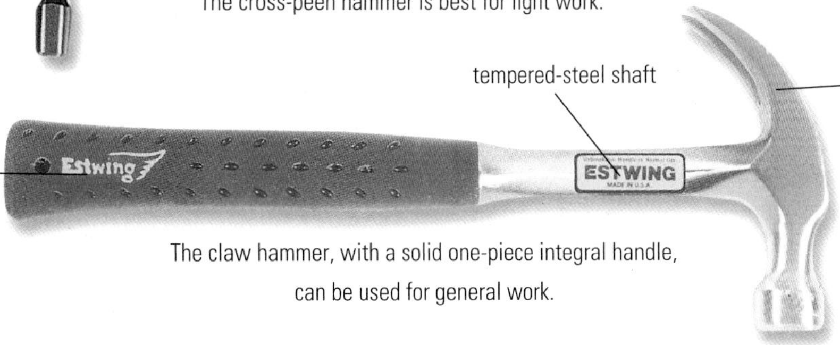

tempered-steel shaft

claw

blue vinyl grip

The claw hammer, with a solid one-piece integral handle, can be used for general work.

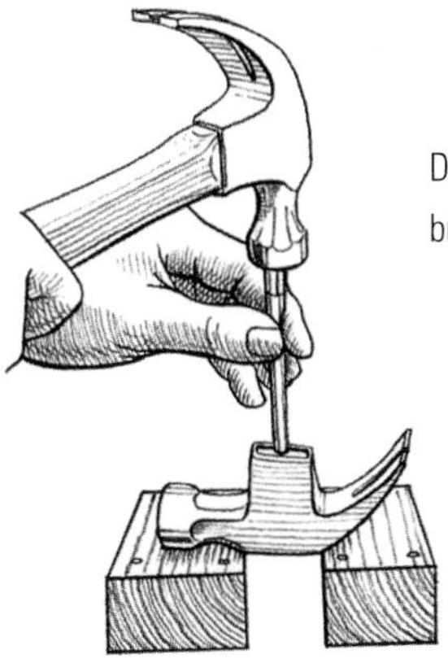

Driving out the remains of a broken handle

Claw hammer

The claw hammer—usually called a carpenter's or joiner's hammer—is the hammer to use for driving large nails. Usually these hammers come in three weight sizes: a 16oz (450g), a 20oz (600g) and a 24oz (750g). These hammers are characterized by having a striking face that is both hardened and polished, a head that is softer than the face and a claw shape that enables the woodworker to draw out even the most awkward nails. If you have a choice, choose the socket-head type. As for handles, they are available in wood, steel, fiberglass, and other hybrids—though most woodworkers prefer a hickory handle, as they claim that wood absorbs shock without being too springy.

Hold the hammer by the end of the handle to achieve maximum leverage.

Warrington cross-peen

The cross-peen Warrington-pattern hammer has long been thought of as being the best tool for the cabinetmaker. Coming in six weight sizes—ranging from 6oz (170g) to 16oz (450g), the Warrington hammer has a slender, flat-ground peen for starting off the nails, and a flat-forged, polished face for accurate driving.

Warrington cross-peen pin hammer

At 100g (3½oz), the pin hammer is simply a lightweight version of the Warrington-pattern, with a much longer, more slender handle. If you plan to do many small, delicate tasks – such as picture framing, or maybe making small desktop toys – then this is the tool you want.

Using a pin hammer

A pin hammer is also a useful tool for some DIY jobs around the home that might need a more delicate touch. For example, attaching narrow beading to window frames. When using a pin hammer to tap a pin into a delicate bead, first of all locate the pin, then tap it into place using the tad (or peen) of the hammer. This can be quite difficult and needs just a few carefully placed blows, which drive the pin into the desired location. Once the pin is securely in place and you are happy with its location, turn the hammer over. Using the face (or bell) of the hammer you can then very easily drive the pin home with a few more well-placed blows.

Pulling out nails with a claw hammer

1 To remove the nail, ease the first 1in (25mm) or so out with the claw.

2 For extra leverage, use a block of waste to raise the head of the hammer well clear of the surface, then arc the hammer over to lever out the nail.

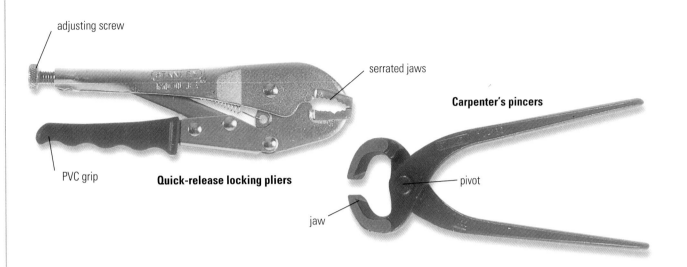

adjusting screw

serrated jaws

Carpenter's pincers

PVC grip

Quick-release locking pliers

pivot

jaw

Pliers and grips

Woodworkers are forever needing to use pliers and grips for pulling out tacks, for holding tacks, for shaping wire, for making running repairs to tools, for straightening this, and for bending that. You cannot always know what type of pliers or grips you will need the next time around, but the following will give some idea of the options.

Pliers

A couple of pairs of well-made pliers are a must. Best get a large, general-purpose pair for all the heavy gripping, twisting, bending, and cutting, and then get a pair of long-nosed pliers for working in tight corners, and extracting broken screws. As for quality, always go for the type described as "made from high-quality carbon steel."

Pincers

Carpenter's pincers are one of those much used and abused tools that seem to have been around forever. They come in a variety of shapes and sizes, with names like Tower pincers, French-pattern pincers, boxed pincers—and one or two other curious names besides—and are perfect for easing out bent and battered nails. To use the tool, first grip the nail in the jaws, then roll and pivot the whole tool on the outside of the jaw, so that the tool becomes a very efficient lever. As to the purpose of some of the outlandish knobs that some of these traditional pincers have at the end of the handles—who knows?

Tips box

- If you want to use pliers on a shaft without making marks, protect or pad the shaft with several winds of masking tape.

- Grind the face of pincer jaws flat so they can grip as far as possible on the protruding nail.

- Pincers are ideal for removing old nails from a piece of old furniture, but if you plan to re-upholster a chair or sofa, it is worth investing in a tack lever. This is a simple wooden-handled tool shaped like a screwdriver but with a notch in the tip for levering out small upholstery tacks.

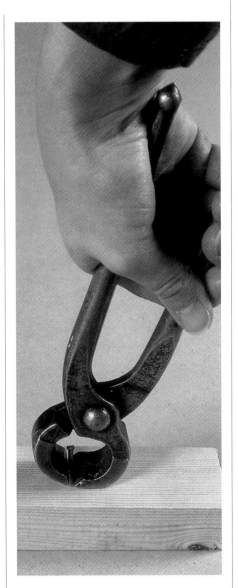

Grip the nail so that the rounded jaws of the pincers are in contact with the workpiece.

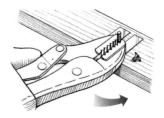

The split end of the handle is designed to be used as a tack extractor.

Using a pair of grips to extract a broken screw.

Locking pliers

Wrenches of this type are so familiar that they hardly need describing. Perhaps it is enough to say that the clamping mechanism makes this tool extremely useful for all types of gripping and twisting tasks. They are especially useful for gripping and holding circular objects like bolts and rods, and for extracting broken screws.

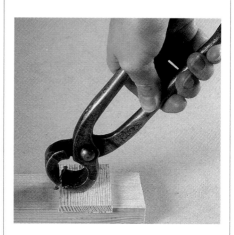

Lever pincers down and over so the rounded jaws act as a fulcrum.

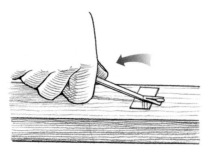

Using a nail extractor.

Nail extractor

Nail extractors come in many shapes and sizes—some have wooden handles and look a bit like a screwdriver, while others are made of black iron and look for all the world like a chicken's foot. Either way they are useful when you want to ease out a nail without using the claw hammer.

Screw extractor

Though there are all kinds of extractors, the simplest is a bit like a plug cutter. In use, the tooth-ended tube is placed over the screw and given a couple of turns so that the stump of the screw is revealed. The screw is then gripped with a pair of long-nose pliers and extracted.

Adjustable wrench

A good quality adjustable wrench is the perfect tool for the woodworker who needs to deal with the occasional large nut and bolt, but does not want to go to the expense of purchasing a whole set of large open-ended wrenches. For example, a large wrench is needed on older style lathes to grip the drive shaft when the four-jaw chuck is unscrewed. Then again, it is sometimes necessary to crawl under the workbench and get a pair of pliers on the coach bolts that secure the vise. All this adds up to the fact that a good-quality wrench is a good idea.

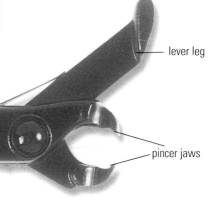

ABOVE: A patented nail puller, designed to pull everything from the small, headless tack to a 5in (125mm) nail.

lever leg

pincer jaws

hammer claw location bolt

MAKING JOINTS

Designing joints

ABOVE: A lap joint in the "T" orientation is a simple combination of two basic elements.

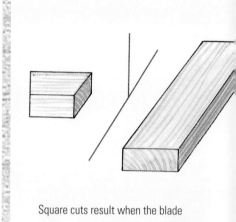

Square cuts result when the blade angle is 90 degrees to the wood surface and the blade path runs 90 degrees to the entrance end or edge of the wood.

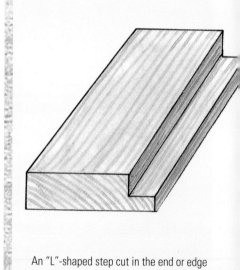

An "L"-shaped step cut in the end or edge of the wood is called a rebate. The depth and width of a rebate can be as varied as needed.

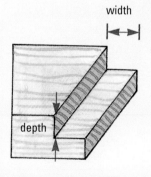

The basic elements of joinery

Each woodworking joint is a combination of at least two basic joinery elements. Two of these elements are mated and mechanically interlock—or create glue surfaces that "join" two parts. As joinery gets more complex, the basic elements are modified and enhanced to improve joint strength or design, but these basic components will always form the building blocks of a joint.

Elements, or cuts, fall roughly into two categories. Sawed elements can be completed by one cut on the wood's end or edge by a hand or power saw. Shaped elements are part of a step-by-step process. It begins with sizing the part, then removing material to leave a shape cut into the wood.

A sawed element, either square, angled or compound angled, is butted to its complementary cut to make width joints, mitered corners, six-sided boxes, or cone shapes, to name some examples. Sawing is the quickest and most common method for giving the wood

ends or edges these shapes, but it is not the only method. Hand planing, power jointing, or routing are alternative techniques.

Shaped elements come in a variety of forms—the "L"-shaped rebate, variously shaped pockets or sockets, and the "U"-shaped groove, dado, and edge dado or notch. These flat-bottomed "U"-shaped cuts are distinguished by whether they are parallel to the grain (groove), cross the grain (dado), or cut into the board's edge (notch). Different joint families combine these elements with other cuts to form joints suited to any particular design. A square cut and a pocket yield a mortise-and-tenon joint for joining aprons to legs. A dado and a square cut give us the housing joint for shelves. A rebate and a dado create a lap joint for "T"-joining wood parts, and so on.

Sawed elements

In an angled cut, either the blade angle is not 90 degrees to the wood surface or the blade path does not run 90 degrees to the entrance end.

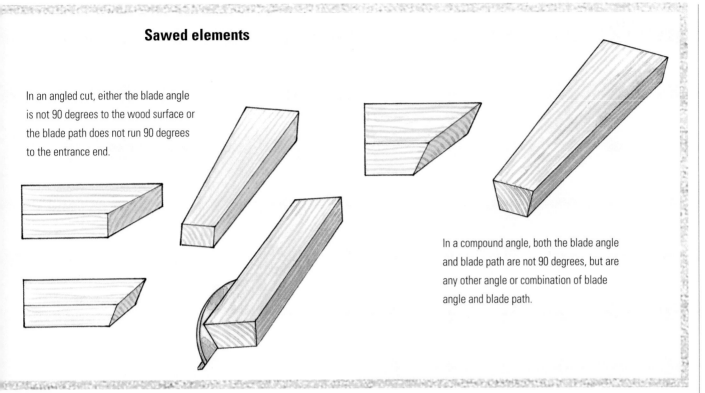

In a compound angle, both the blade angle and blade path are not 90 degrees, but are any other angle or combination of blade angle and blade path.

Milled elements

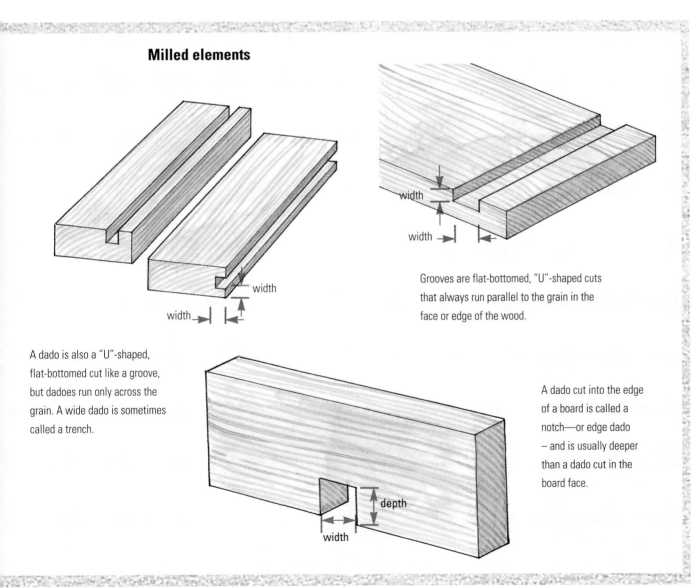

width

width

Grooves are flat-bottomed, "U"-shaped cuts that always run parallel to the grain in the face or edge of the wood.

width

width

A dado is also a "U"-shaped, flat-bottomed cut like a groove, but dadoes run only across the grain. A wide dado is sometimes called a trench.

depth

width

A dado cut into the edge of a board is called a notch—or edge dado — and is usually deeper than a dado cut in the board face.

The knack of making tight joints

1 Tight joints rely on care and accuracy in initial marking out. Your choice of marking instrument is vital. For precision cabinet work, a marking knife makes the most accurate line.

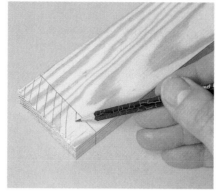

2 Clearly shade the waste areas (those to be cut away) with a medium/soft-leaded pencil. Diagonal shading is the most effective, as it is easy to see.

3 Many woodworkers use a pencil for marking out. A hard-leaded pencil gives the most accurate line, but is difficult to see. A soft-leaded one is bolder but blunts as it draws, which affects accuracy. An effective modern marking tool is a ballpoint pen —this leaves a bold and consistent line.

4 A steel rule gives the best accuracy, and, in fine woodworking, you need to be able to measure in approximately 1/64in (half millimeters). Mark with a marking knife instead of a pencil as the latter will not be precise enough.

5 A tight joint relies on the springiness, or "give," of the wood, so you need to make the joint slightly tight—though it is hard to say exactly how tight, as this depends on the size of the joint and the character and hardness of the wood. As a guide, in a medium-density hardwood, the joint might be about 1/64in (approximately 0.5mm) oversize.

6 A crucial factor is where on the line to make the saw cut. This is where the "half millimeter" rule makes sense because you do not actually measure it, but instead you place the saw on the line, or just off it, so that the line is left after sawing. This is the knack of cutting a tight joint. The line therefore serves as a cutting reference point.

7 This rule applies to lines marked and cut down the grain, in which the springiness of the wood is a factor. For lines marked across the grain—for example shoulder lines on joints—the cutaway portion is usually made right on the line as wood doesn't deflect as much across the grain (right). This is why shoulder lines are generally marked with a marking knife.

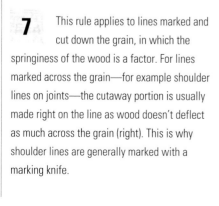

Wood material and joint design

The most important fact to keep in mind when designing wood joinery is that the exact dimensions of solid wood are not fixed. The cell structure of wood can be likened simplistically to a bundle of straws, which adsorbs and exudes water vapor in response to changes in the relative humidity to maintain moisture equilibrium with the environment. This constant fluctuation of the wood's moisture content results in expansion and contraction across the width of the grain, and a negligible change in length. Unless this phenomenon is addressed at the design stage, wood movement may destroy a joint or the material itself.

Wood material also has strengths and weaknesses of grain that affect joinery design. With effort, wood can be broken across the grain, but the likelier breakage is along the grain—when wood is left too thin, or when weak "short grain" created by milling cannot hold the material together. Conscientious design can reduce or eliminate all these problems.

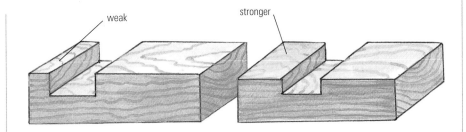

weak   stronger

Choosing a joint

One school of thought says a crafts-person should design around the construction; another says the construction should be based around the design. In reality, both methods interact. The design dictates the possible joints, or is modified so joints that will overcome the structure's weaknesses can be used.

Before the basic orientations of wood are joined and put into service in a structure, the forces the joints have to resist in any design need to be analyzed. This does not require an engineering degree, simply an awareness of the mechanical stresses on joints and some joinery solutions to them. As with problems with dimensional conflict, potential problems from stresses on an

The depth of the cut should not be more than the width at the remaining end.

assembly in use are easy to predict and solve—with an appropriate joint.

Utility, economy and the work's aesthetic priorities all influence the choice of joinery for a design. Certain styles seem to exist just to showcase well-crafted joinery, while in others an overall look predominates and assembly techniques are hidden. Elaborate joinery is time consuming and not always necessary for structure, nor economically justifiable for function. The wide range of visible and invisible joints can accommodate every taste.

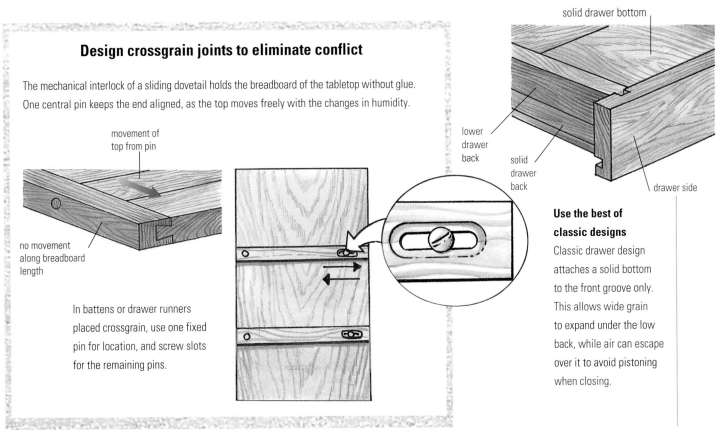

Design crossgrain joints to eliminate conflict

The mechanical interlock of a sliding dovetail holds the breadboard of the tabletop without glue. One central pin keeps the end aligned, as the top moves freely with the changes in humidity.

movement of top from pin

no movement along breadboard length

In battens or drawer runners placed crossgrain, use one fixed pin for location, and screw slots for the remaining pins.

solid drawer bottom

lower drawer back

solid drawer back

drawer side

Use the best of classic designs

Classic drawer design attaches a solid bottom to the front groove only. This allows wide grain to expand under the low back, while air can escape over it to avoid pistoning when closing.

Stresses on joints

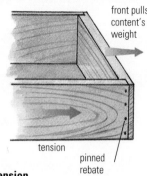

front pulls content's weight

tension

pinned rebate

Tension

Tension is best overcome by mechanical resistance to the force pulling the joint apart. This can be either as an inherent feature of the joint, or one added by wedging or pinning.

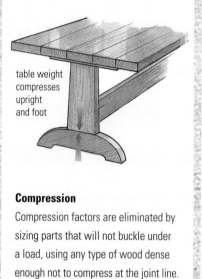

table weight compresses upright and foot

Compression

Compression factors are eliminated by sizing parts that will not buckle under a load, using any type of wood dense enough not to compress at the joint line.

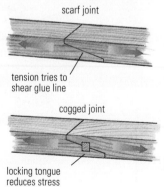

scarf joint

tension tries to shear glue line

cogged joint

locking tongue reduces stress

Shear

Shear forces can be a factor when there is insufficient material for loading, but usually shear refers to push/pull stress on a glue line. Such stress can be relieved mechanically by joinery pins or reinforcing screws.

Edge and scarf joints

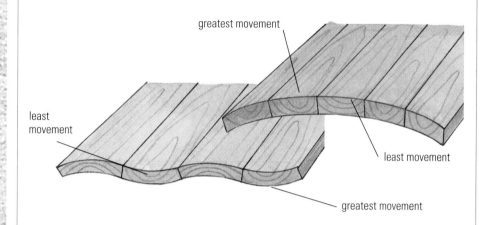

greatest movement

least movement

least movement

greatest movement

About edge joints

Unfortunately, edge joints are not entirely free from problems of wood movement. However, these problems relate more to the elements of the whole than to the joints themselves. For example, there are a number of considerations for gluing up panels or slabs. When gluing up a slab, whether to place all boards heartwood face up or alternate them up and down is a matter of preference, and a cause of much debate among woodworkers. Greater moisture loss at the ends of the boards can cause shrinking, splitting, or joint failure, and is overcome by the finish or a "sprung" joint. An assembled panel's ends is automatically hidden in frame-and-panel construction, but on a table or other top, adding an aesthetic or stabilizing lipping at the ends requires careful thought, as it introduces crossgrain construction.

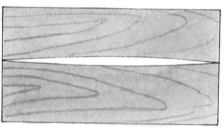

ABOVE: Placing the hollow of a sprung joint under clamps, anticipating moisture loss, results in end shrinkage, relieving tension on the wood and glue instead of creating it.

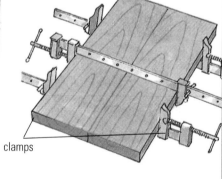

clamps

ABOVE: Clamps top and bottom equalize pressure on the edges.

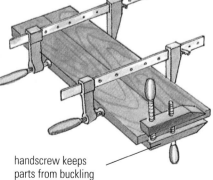

handscrew keeps parts from buckling

Wood movement and edge-joint gluing

Edge-joined boards with heartwood sides up move as a unit, but boards alternating heartwood up and down will buckle in opposite directions, creating a washboard effect that is harder to hold down.

Clamps can provide a solution here, as, under clamps, the ½in (1mm) hollow of a sprung joint presses ends tightly, anticipating moisture loss, so end shrinkage relieves tension on the wood and glue instead of creating it.

Clamping width joints

Edge clamping does not require expensive clamps, but cross clamping requires measures to keep the panel flat—such as alternating clamps top and bottom, or using a handscrew or temporary battens at the ends.

Plain butt glue joint

A butted edge joint is strong enough for the majority of glue-ups for width. It is one of the few edge joints that can be "sprung," or pre-tensioned, so later end-grain shrinkage does not pull the joint apart. All this joint requires is flat, straight lumber, so the key to success is knowing how to accurately surface and dimension lumber by hand or with power tools.

Cross-tongue joint

Using a cross tongue is a quick and easy way to reinforce a width joint. If referenced from the marked face, it takes little calculation or layout for an accurate joint with a perfect alignment of the faces. Cross-tonguing also helps hold the boards in place until the glue has dried. Double tongues in thick lumber are equally simple to reference from both faces.

Plain butt glue joint

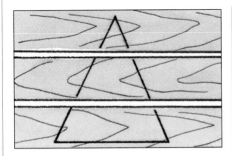

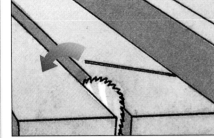

1 Rip stock to within ¼in (6mm) of the final width, then cut it to length, or leave enough for trimming after glue-up. Arrange for grain pattern, and mark for position.

2 Once rough ripping reduces the stock for better control, trim each edge to its final dimension, alternating mating boards up and down to cancel any out-of-square in the blade setting which may be caused by boards being tapered along their length.

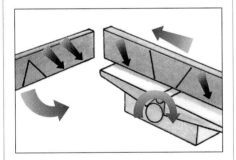

3 For final dimensioning on the planer, always feed the stock onto the saw so that you are cutting with the grain, thus avoiding tearing the wood. Do not alternate faces to cancel out-of-square; set a precise fence to allow jointing for best grain direction.

4 Clamp mated edges together and take a light shaving—just to remove mill marks—or use a short sole to plane in a ½in (1mm) hollow for a sprung joint. Set out the clamps on a flat surface and assemble the boards, checking for fit, then stand the boards on edge, spread the glue, and clamp with battens protecting the edges.

Test a tongue for fit. If it is too wide it will prevent the joint from closing; if it is tight, it may put pressure on the grooves when it is swollen by glue moisture. To fix the joint, spread glue on the lips and in the grooves, assemble, and clamp.

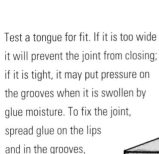

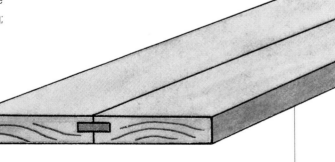

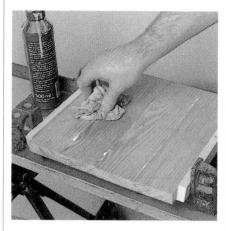

ABOVE: Always wipe off excess glue with a damp cloth, before it dries.

Manmade materials work well for tongues. Exactly-sized hardboard is the easiest to match to standard cutter widths. Less-accurate plywood might require two grooving passes with an undersized cutter for a good fit. Make the thickness of the solid-wood tongues to match the cutter, or widen the groove to fit available tongue stock within the limits of joint proportions.

Tongue-and-groove

The integral tongue acts like a loose tongue that reinforces and aligns the joint, but takes a little more calculation to machine. Boards must be ripped wider to provide material for the tongue. Even without special groovers or a dado head, the table saw makes an acceptable joint with a combination or rip blade that has a raker—a square tooth that leaves the bottom of the kerf flat. Bowed lumber will misalign the groove or make the tongue uneven unless hold-downs and fingerboards (splined safety devices that push the wood against the fence, as in step 2 below) are used to keep the lumber against the fence. Add a high wood fence for stability, or to prevent cutters from contacting the metal fence.

The tongue-and-groove as a width joint is worth the extra trouble in production. You should also use a tongue-and-groove if the look at the end grain is preferred, in a dry assembly with a detailed edge like flooring, in a cabinet back, or in wainscotting, where the matching tongue is likely to become exposed when the wood shrinks. You can also use it as a corner joint, to assist carcase assembly—though the tongue is often offset.

Hand-planed rubbed joint

Edge joints can be hand-planed, and then glued without clamps by rubbing the tacky glue surfaces together. However, rubbed joints cannot be sprung, as, without clamping, edge contact will not occur. Rubbing is suited to lengths of wood less than 3ft (92cm), so a shooting board can be used for edge jointing. It requires glues that quickly develop tack such as animal glues or cross-linked aliphatics.

Tongue-and-bead

Adding a bead to the edge of a tongue-and-groove joint is a detail common to architectural finish work. Applied to assembled panels in furniture, such detailing of a tongue-and-groove adds visual interest and enables a dry-fitting option for handling wood movement over an expanse.

Tongue-and-groove

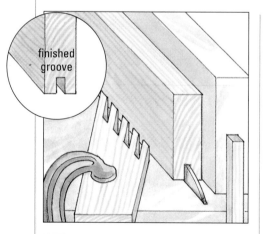

finished groove

1 Raise a raker-toothed blade to half the stock thickness, set the fence to a third of the thickness from the blade, make one grooving pass, then reverse the board and make a second pass to widen the groove.

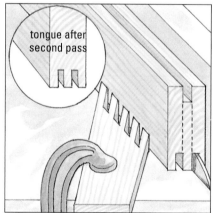

tongue after second pass

2 Lower the blade a fraction so the tongue is not too long, move the fence in to shave the tongue just outside the width of the groove, reverse for the second pass.

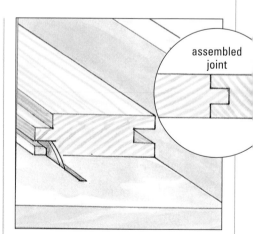

assembled joint

3 First test that the tongue fits the groove, then lower the blade and set the fence to cut the waste from the shoulders at the tongue's depth. Fit the joint as shown.

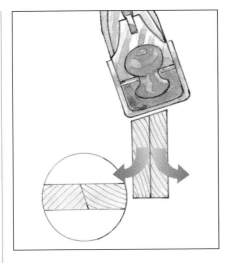

Hand-planed rubbed joint

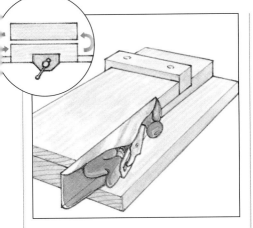

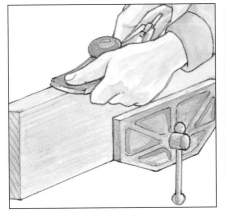

1 Plane the edges of both boards and test straightness, rotating one board against the other in the vise to find crowning that will rock the board, or hollowing that causes the ends to scrape.

2 Check the edges for squareness, and correct any deviation by steadying the plane with a knuckle against the board and then planing the high spot until a full shaving can be taken.

3 Alternatively, plane both edges together in the vise. In this way, if you plane the edges to anything other than 90 degrees, the angles of the two edges will cancel each other out when joined together, allowing the boards to align flat.

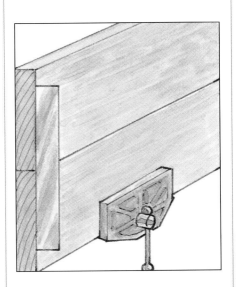

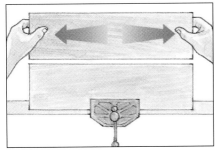

4 Lay thin stock flat for rubbing, or clamp thicker stock in the vise—holding the top board low down to slide back and forth in the glue until suction grabs it.

5 Joints in thin wood should not be disturbed until completely dry. Thicker boards, however, should be removed from the vise once it is safe to do so, and leaned against a support to dry thoroughly.

Tips box

• After checking that all the boards are flush (flat and level)—persuading them with hammer and scrapwood, if necessary—wipe away any excess glue with a damp cloth. This is very important and saves unnecessary work afterward.

• Keep the joint clamped together until the glue is completely cured. This may mean waiting overnight, especially during cold, damp weather when the adhesive takes longer to harden.

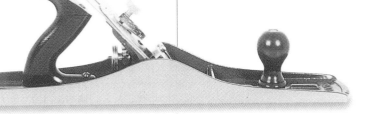

Scarf joints

The shallow angle of the basic glued scarf (also called a splice) exposes long-grain surfaces for a good glue joint. Simple gluing at the slope ratio of 1:8 bonds the parts into a unit that—theory says—is as strong as a single board. As with edge joints, there is no perfect solution to orienting the growth rings of solid-wood scarfed parts—either to cup opposite to each other or to cup in the same direction. Worked scarfs that are more than simple glue joints also expose long grain for gluing, but, in imitation of their lumber-framing ancestors, begin to employ fitted joinery, locking and pinning to hold the joint together. When scarfs are used structurally, another member should give direct or nearby support, and, if needed, provide a place to hide a less than decorative joint. Used visually as a design element, elaborate scarf joints that defy machining are the most challenging and awe-inspiring of all woodworking joints.

ABOVE: A simple but effective scarf joint. Scarf joints were often used in lumber-framed buildings as a way of joining long sections of lumber. The joint is not as obvious as some joints as the cut line is diagonal instead of at right angles to the grain.

End-to-end scarf

Glue-scarfing boards end to end does not make a pretty joint, but it can be a useful way of creating a joint. For extreme strength in a glue-only joint, use epoxy. With any glue, first spread a priming coat that will be absorbed into the grain, filling the hollow cells so the next coat stays at the gluing surface.

This scarf can be made angled, as it is used to angle a guitar's peg head back from the neck. In this application, both parts are aligned bevel side up, and one bevel is glued to the back of the other bevel, creating the angle. Draw the parts of a desired angle full-size in profile, to find the angle setting for the sliding bevel to use in laying out the parts.

Edge-to-edge scarf

Scarfing edges oblique to the grain is also a way of creating a utilitarian joint that joins lumber for length. It can be used to stretch a too-short board by first ripping it diagonally, then sliding the halves a little along the cutting angle, gluing, and finally trimming to width when dry. A double tongue can reduce the extreme angle required for a glue-only joint by introducing mechanical reinforcement and another gluing surface. Gluing is best preceded by a priming coat to prevent a glue-starved joint.

Tips box

- Use a bevel gauge to accurately mark an 8:1 angle on the pieces of an edge-to-edge joint.

- Scarf joints must have an even coating of glue over the mating surfaces to form a strong bond. Use a glue roller to spread the adhesive.

End-to-end scarf

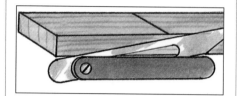

1 Measure from each board end eight times its thickness, square a line across the face, set the sliding bevel to the 1:8 angle and mark the angle clearly on both edges.

2 If material size prevents wasting the acute bevel with any saw and planing smooth, start at the top corner and plane the entire bevel back to the squared line.

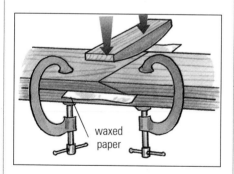

waxed paper

3 Using waxed paper where glue may ooze, immobilize the parts against slipping and clamp the joint or, on a wide joint, use a crowned batten to provide pressure in the center.

Edge-to-edge scarf

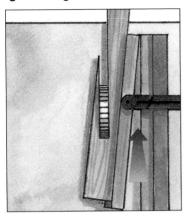

1 For a strong glue joint, mark a taper eight times the board's width—or set the jig to cut any angle under 20 degrees for non-structural work, if the wood glues well.

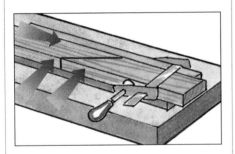

2 Apply glue, and clamp one part to the fence of a non-stick gluing sled (a holding jig to support the work as it dries), press the mate in against it, and clamp both to the fence until the joint dries.

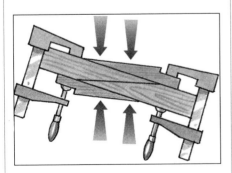

3 Alternatively, clamp the notched cut-offs to the parts (cut at an angle from the workpiece), creating a parallel purchase for clamping the joint. Prevent slipping by using a dowel, biscuit, or headless brad, pressed between the parts.

The halving cuts that form lap joints are basically dadoes or rebates—although wide dadoes are sometimes called trenches and deep dadoes are often termed notches. A halving cut in the board face results in a frame lap, used in supporting frameworks, or, more literally, to frame panels. Edge laps notch into board edges to half the part's width, and appear in crossed stretchers, sash moldings, shoji, chair back, or window lattice, and egg-crated dividers. The large gluing area of a frame lap is long-grain for a strong gluing, but always with dimensional conflict. The edge lap has little long-grain contact, and the wood is weakened by deep notching into the width—so it is liable to split without reinforcement.

That is why edge laps are light-duty joints, or worked in plywood, whose alternated grains strengthen the material. Frame laps come in two basic versions: end laps are halving rebates cut at the board's end; center laps are halving dadoes cut somewhere in the board's length (except at the very end or it loses a shoulder and becomes a rebate). End laps and center laps (rebates and dadoes) in various combinations form all the basic corner "L," "T," and crossed-frame lap orientations.

Lap-joint components

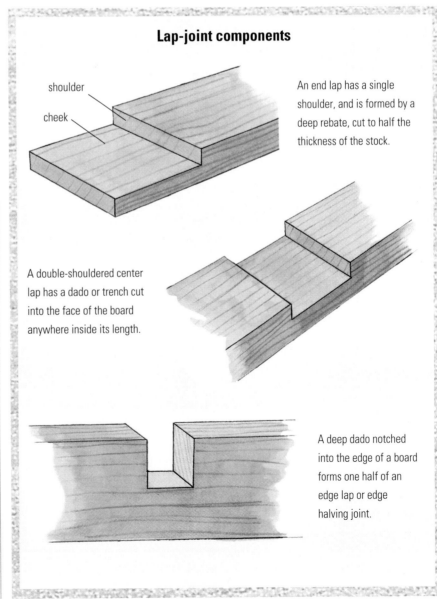

shoulder

cheek

An end lap has a single shoulder, and is formed by a deep rebate, cut to half the thickness of the stock.

A double-shouldered center lap has a dado or trench cut into the face of the board anywhere inside its length.

A deep dado notched into the edge of a board forms one half of an edge lap or edge halving joint.

Types of lap joint

Halvings cut into the face of the board and assembled in "L," "T," or crossed configurations are called frame laps, with excellent gluing strength, and shoulders that resist bending.

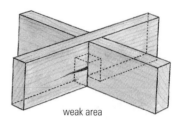

weak area

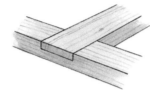

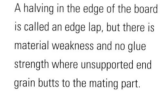

A halving in the edge of the board is called an edge lap, but there is material weakness and no glue strength where unsupported end grain butts to the mating part.

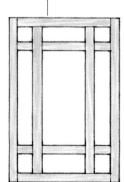

Using lap joints

Straight and angled laps are good joints for decorative lattice work windows, doors, outdoor furniture, and structures like gazebos.

Routing methods

A shop-made square fence guides a router base to make an end lap, while excess end material helps to support the router and is cut off later.

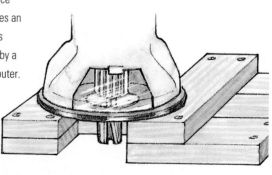

To rout multiples, the workpiece slides under a fence that guides an overbearing straight bit, and is stopped at the shoulder mark by a block that also supports the router.

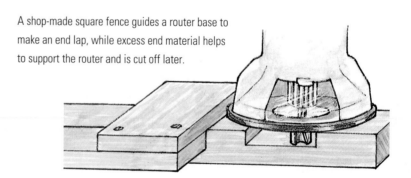

Cutting an "X" halving joint by hand

1 After preparing the lumber to size, trace the width of each piece on the corresponding piece with a pencil or ballpoint pen.

2 Using a try square—held with the stock against the face side of the lumber – extend the marks both across the wood and to halfway down the edges.

3 With a marking gauge set to exactly half the thickness of the wood, gauge the depth lines, using the stock of the gauge against the face side. Shade in the waste.

4 Fix the wood firmly in the vise, and saw carefully on the waste side of the line with a tenon saw to the halfway mark.

5 After sawing the other line— checking it carefully against the width of the other piece—chisel away the waste wood. Work into the center, then turn the wood around and repeat the action to avoid splitting the end fibers. A mallet greatly helps to control the chiseling action.

6 Carefully chisel a slight leading edge where the joint will fit together. This will prevent too much pressure having to be applied, and will gradually ease the two halves into position.

Tips box

Whenever you cut joints by hand, make sure you have the right tools for the job ready on the bench or at hand. Hone the correct size of chisel of the job and make sure your saw is sharp. You can also buy small try squares or engineers' squares which are useful for marking out small, intricate joints.

7 Squeeze the joint together using a vise. If it is too tight, plane a fraction off the side edges in preference to chiseling back the saw line (chiseling is difficult to do accurately, as the error is likely to be very fine, and you would be chiseling across the grain in small bites). Then clean up the surfaces using a smoothing plane.

Center lap

There are many methods for removing the waste between the shoulders of a center lap. The easiest method is to saw repetitive kerfs to half the piece's thickness, either by hand or machine. This weakens the material so it can be broken out, and the cheek cleaned up by chiseling, hand planing or routing.

Possibly no other joint requires so much material removal as a halving joint. A dado head cutter removes material fairly effectively, but some types of dado heads do not leave an entirely flat bottom, or the outer teeth leave deeper scribe marks with each cut that will show at the glue line. With heads like this, wasting cuts have to be held short of the centerline and cleaned up by hand tools or a router.

End laps

One end lap can combine with another end lap to form an "L"-corner lap, or it can be set into a center lap to make a "T"-lap joint.

Cheeks and shoulders can be cut by router – whether most of the material is wasted by sawing, or wasted completely by routing. A router table is a handy assistant, but routing the parts handheld is also a good solution. If many pieces are needed, set up a jig to assist in repetitive cutting—this also avoids tedious clamping and unclamping of fences.

Angled "T" lap

It is very easy to cut the angle of the center lap tilted in the wrong direction if careful attention is not paid to laying it out for final assembly. The radial arm saw is only one method for milling this joint. It is simple to rout hand-held, using an angled fence.

House joints

The housing joint—or dado joint, as it is often called—is a strong, simple joint, whereby a groove is cut across the grain of one piece of wood into which another piece is fitted. The joint is usually found in cabinet construction—for shelves and dividers in furniture such as dressers or bookcases.

In its simplest form, the housing joint consists of a shallow-bottomed groove running the full width of the lumber into which the square-edged piece sits. Variations of the joint include stopped shoulders—where the groove does not run the full width of the lumber, so the joint is not visible from the front—and dovetailed sectioned grooves for maximum mechanical strength, which, nowadays, are usually cut with a router.

Cutting an "L" halving joint on the radial arm saw

This example is for the "L" configuration of the halving joint, but it could be used for any other. The radial arm saw is predominantly for use in cutting across the grain, where, by taking a series of very closely-spaced cuts across the grain of the joint, the need to chisel down the grain for cleaning away the waste is eliminated.

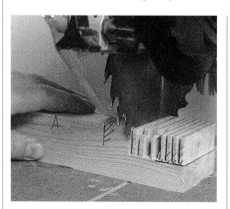

1 After you have marked the wood for width and depth of cut, and adjusted the blade height (checking that the cut is centered), draw the saw head across the piece in a series of narrow cuts.

2 Remove the narrow strips of short grain by knocking the wood against a benchtop, then level the surface using the radial arm saw.

3 It should be possible to achieve a perfectly flush joint, even if the contact surfaces have to be reworked fractionally on the radial arm saw.

Full housing

A full housing has little resistance to racking and less to tension, so the overall structure has to be considered before this joint is chosen. A tapped-home fit makes the joint work both mechanically and aesthetically, but it is a fit that is easily lost if the housed piece is sanded. With no shoulder to cover any deviations along the dado edge, accuracy and the flatness of the housed piece are both in sharp focus.

A housing deeper than half the thickness of the piece will weaken it. A depth one third the thickness is all that is necessary. If housing drawer runners in solid wood so crossgrain construction is introduced, screw the runners at the front of the carcase and slot-screw them at the back, without glue to allow for wood movement. Make runners or drawer frames a little short of the back, or shrinkage of the sides will cause these long-grained parts to push on it. Runners or drawer frames in plywood housings can be glued.

Center lap by hand

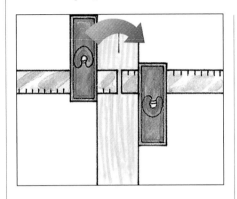

1 Scribe a line near the end grain's center, flip the square and scribe again, split the marks and set the blade to the exact center, then scribe the end and joint's edge.

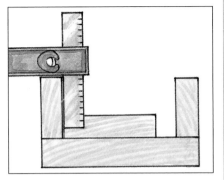

2 Put the stock – blocked up if necessary—in a miter box and extend and lock the square's blade just shy of the center mark on the end of the stock.

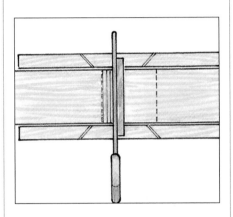

3 Lay out the shoulders as far apart as the width of the stock to be joined, and square them across to make a series of saw cuts between them in the waste.

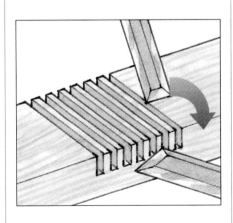

4 Break away the waste with a chisel, and carefully pare the ridges left at the bottom of the joint, plus any saw marks on the shoulders.

Making a band-sawed and routed end lap

Fit the router table with a straight bit, and bump-cut the edge of some scrap stock, then flip and cut again, raising the bit until the cuts center. Clean the joint by feeding the piece back and forth across the bit, fitted in a router table.

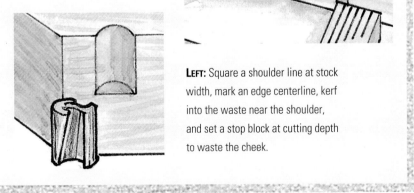

LEFT: Square a shoulder line at stock width, mark an edge centerline, kerf into the waste near the shoulder, and set a stop block at cutting depth to waste the cheek.

Making a through housing or dado joint by hand

1 Cut the wood accurately to size. Mark out the position of the joint on the piece by tracing thickness marks onto it, using a marking knife, pencil, or ballpoint pen.

2 Extend the lines across the wood using a large try square—or by extending the reach of a standard one by placing a straight-edge next to it.

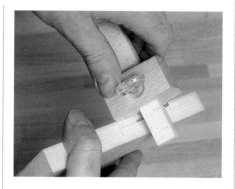

3 With the try square, extend lines to about one third (as a general rule) of the thickness of the wood on the other face, to give you the depth of the groove to be cut. Set a marking gauge, and mark the line on both ends of the piece. Shade in the waste to show clearly which part has to be removed.

4 Secure the workpiece to the bench with one or two clamps, and use a tenon saw to cut the walls of the housing joint to the line. For extra control, you can use both hands on the saw handle. Try it each way and see which suits you best.

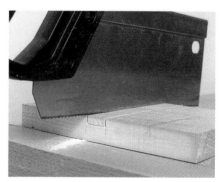

5 Saw just on the waste side of the line, leaving the thickness of the line intact. This will give you a nice, snug fit.

6 Remove the waste with a chisel and mallet. The fibers should break away quite easily as they are weak across the grain, where they have been severed lengthwise by the saw. By using the bevel of the chisel tip, you can cut in more without the handle fouling the wood, but this takes a little more skill. This is because there is less of the tool in contact with the wood, which makes it harder to control.

7 Plane a fractional bevel on the end of the other piece to create a "leading edge" for ease of entry, and "persuade" the two pieces together, using a hammer and piece of scrapwood to avoid any bruising. Make sure the ends are flush.

MORTISE AND TENON JOINTS

About the mortise-and-tenon

There are two basic tenon types that mate with two basic mortise types. A through tenon fits into a through mortise, a hole right through the mortised piece. A stub, or blind, tenon fits into a blind mortise, one which bottoms in the material of the mortised piece, instead of passing through it. Mortise shapes are mostly rectilinear, round, or a long slot with rounded ends.

The shoulders that are added to the tenon serve several purposes. They increase rack resistance to stabilize the joint. They move the tenon (and with it the mortise) away from the weaker ends or edges of mortised pieces. They cover the joint's edges and create a depth stop. Both tenon shoulders and mortises can be angled to modify the basic "T" or "L" square orientation of the mortise and tenon.

LEFT: The open slot mortise is a relative of the mortise and tenon joint.

Mortise and tenon terminology

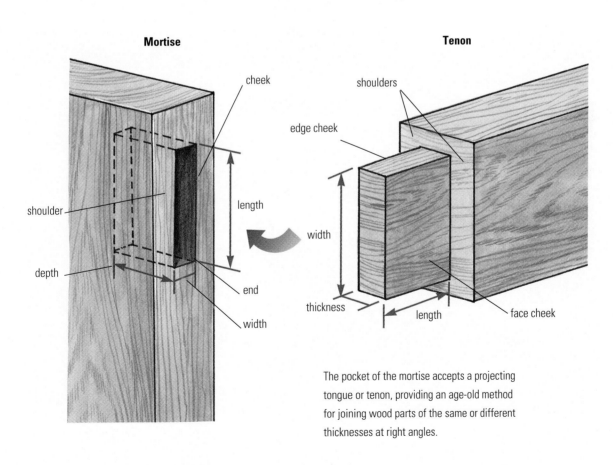

Mortise — cheek, shoulder, depth, length, end, width

Tenon — shoulders, edge cheek, width, thickness, length, face cheek

The pocket of the mortise accepts a projecting tongue or tenon, providing an age-old method for joining wood parts of the same or different thicknesses at right angles.

Mortises

Blind mortising

The standard width of a mortise in edge grain is about one third the stock thickness. This proportion varies, since the mortise is usually matched to the mortising chisel closest to one third the stock thickness. However, creating too wide a mortise will cause the cheeks to be too weak and narrow, and the tenon to be too weak—so this proportion is a general guide.

Chopping an accurate mortise entirely by hand takes practice. Scribing the layout lines deeper once they are placed lets the first chisel cuts remove the waste cleanly, leaving a good guiding shoulder for the chisel. Chiseling tiny bevels in the mortise waste also helps to guide a good chop.

The length of the tenon must be just short of the depth of the blind mortise, usually about three quarters of the way through the material. A piece of tape on the mortising chisel will provide enough of a depth gauge. A mortise made by hand will not be perfectly flat at the bottom, but this is is not important, since it gives the glue somewhere to escape to, and the tenon end grain is not a useful bond, as the glue on the end of the tenon does not add any strength to the joint. Cut all mortises you need first, then fit tenons to them, as it is much easier to shave a little off a tenon cheek than off a mortise cheek. Any blind tenons that are too loose can be shimmed with a piece of veneer. Mortise and tenon joints are the bread and butter joints used in furnituremaking and provide an exceptionally strong joint that can be used in all sorts of cabinet, and chair-making projects. Don't rush the marking out process—even a basic joint for a piece of rustic garden furniture must be set out with care for a tight fit.

The basic types of mortise

A blind mortise has a flat bottom that stops short of the opposite face, and the tenon end is enclosed by the wood.

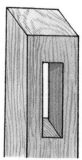

A through mortise makes a hole through the material, and, once the joint is assembled, the tenon end can be seen on the other side.

The specialized slot mortise is nothing more than a deep dado cut in the end of the part and is used in slip or bridle joints—mortise and tenon relatives.

Making a blind mortise by hand

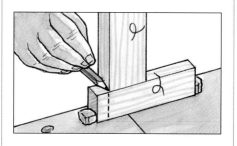

1 With trued faces and edges aligned, outline the tenon piece onto the mortise piece, leaving a temporary horn to prevent splitting if the mortise falls at a corner.

2 Locate the mortise length within the outline of the tenon part—insetting for any shoulders—and scribe each mortise end square across from the trued face with a knife.

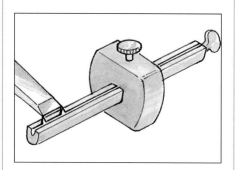

3 Set the spurs of the mortise marking gauge to the chisel width nearest a third the stock thickness; leave at least a quarter of the stock for each mortise cheek.

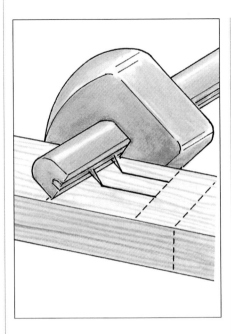

4 Referencing from the marked face, adjust the gauge fence to position the mortise width on the stock thickness and scribe it between the squared end lines.

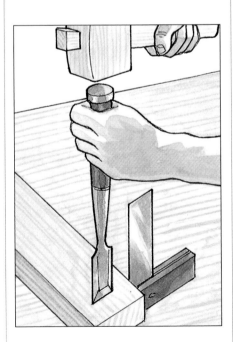

5 Clamp the mortise piece over a bench leg, and hold the mortise chisel on the wood so that the back is at 90 degrees to the direction you are going to work. Stand a square nearby to help you check that you have the angle right.

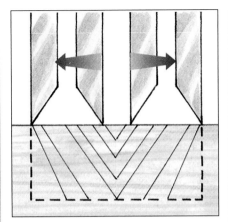

6 Start by cutting a small groove at the center of the marked mortise. Gradually lengthen and deepen this groove until you have reached the ends and depth of the mortise. Then pare out the remaining waste to square off the shape.

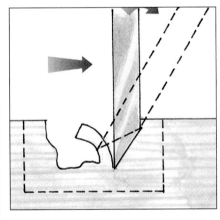

7 Alternatively, lever out slivers of wood the length of the mortise. Continue until you reach the required depth, then pare out the remaining waste to square off.

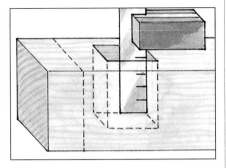

8 Clean up the bottom by leveraging out the waste with the chisel, and extend a square to check that cheeks are flat and square to the face and the depth is correct.

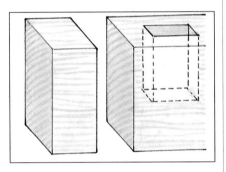

9 Trim the ends to their mark with a last paring cut to clean up any edges marred by leveraging, glue the joint, then saw off the horn.

Other methods for blind mortising

Guide a plunge router along the mortise part while it is clamped in the bench vise and raised flush with another board for clearance and extra router support.

Set up the mortiser with the appropriate bit, and set the depth guide using the lumber marks for alignment. Adjust the fence so that the bit aligns perfectly to the gauged lines, and position the top clamp so that the wood can slide comfortably underneath.

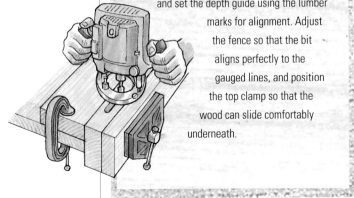

Tenons

Making a basic tenon

Opinions differ on the best sequence for sawing tenons. One school of thought holds that first sawing the shoulders risks weakening the tenon by severing long grain if sawing goes too deep. By sawing the cheeks first, the worst consequence of over-sawing is a small, visible saw kerf on the wood's edge after assembly.

On the other hand, sawing the shoulders first is preferred when a piece is tenoned at both ends, as the shoulders establish the length of it. There is no repair for a shoulder that is cut too short—as there is for shimming a cheek—so the crucial cut is made first before too much work is invested.

The length of a tenon should be slightly less than the depth of the mortise to leave a little space for glue at the bottom. A tenon swollen with glue acts like a piston in a blind mortise, compressing glue that can split the wood under clamping, if it has nowhere to escape.

Break the leading edges of a tenon with sandpaper or a file to make it easier to insert into the mortise. If the tenon runs through, leave a little extra length so that the broken edges do not sink in around the shoulders of the mortise on the through side. Plane or sand the extra length flush after glue-up—unless you want it to stand proud for decorative reasons.

Cut multiple pieces to length and clamp them together to scribe the shoulders square across all the pieces at once. This is especially important for parts that will be in the same frame, on opposite sides of a table or between opposite pairs of legs, because it ensures an accurate structure.

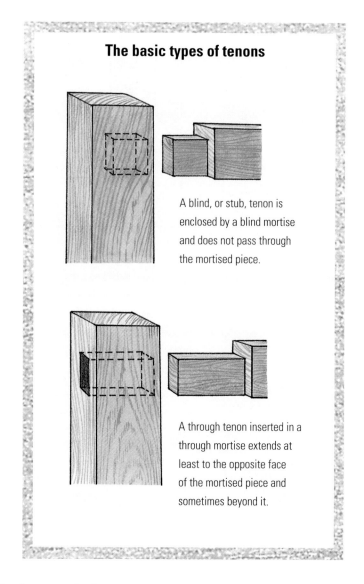

The basic types of tenons

A blind, or stub, tenon is enclosed by a blind mortise and does not pass through the mortised piece.

A through tenon inserted in a through mortise extends at least to the opposite face of the mortised piece and sometimes beyond it.

Basic tenon by hand

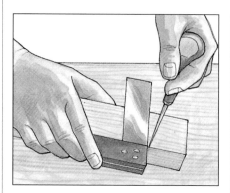

1 From the trued edge, scribe a shoulder square across the piece's face, then square the line around, marking all the shoulders and the tenon length to fit the mortise depth.

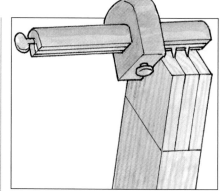

2 Set the mortise marking gouge slightly over the mortise width, and adjust the fence, then score the position and shape of the tenon.

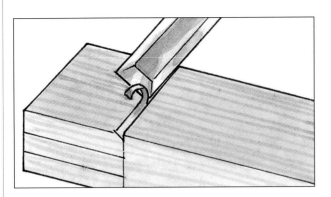

3 Score the shoulder lines deeper, and use a chisel to pare a small bevel along the waste of the face shoulders—to guide the saw.

4 Hold the piece and cleat of a bench hook between thumb and fingers, using the index finger to steady the saw, then saw the shoulder to the tenon line.

5 Clamp the tenon upright and tilted away from you. Saw along the lines you scored with the mortise marking gauge, starting at the top corner of the clamped tenon. Keep the saw steady with your thumb, to keep the kerf in the waste side of the material.

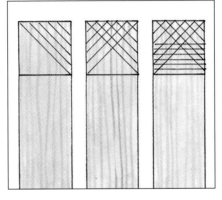

6 Once you have sawed down to the shoulders of the tenon from one corner, flip the piece around, and repeat the process from the other. Use the kerf of the first cuts as guides for your second cuts. Then clamp the piece vertically, and saw to remove the remaining waste.

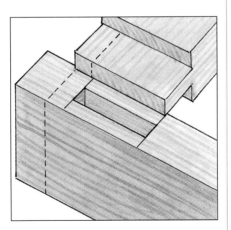

7 Align the tenon to the mortise layout, and mark the cutting line for the third shoulder, gauging each successive part from its own mortise. For this and other forms of tenon joint, it is worth marking the waste area with pencil shading so that you don't accidentally extend a mortise to the shoulder line.

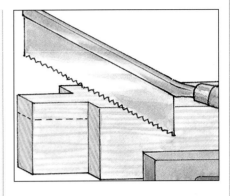

8 Cut the third shoulder down to the marked line, being careful not to saw into the face shoulders. Then saw along the tenon grain and remove the waste.

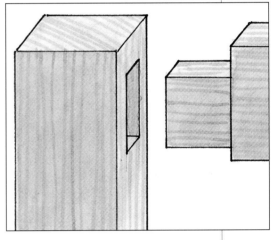

9 Pare the tenon with bench chisels— or plane it with a rebate plane—until it will slide into the mortise.

Tips box

- A router is ideal for machining batches of identical tenons. You can make up an MDF jig to support the router over the area to be cut and incorporating a fence that can be set to the exact width to be cut.
- You should be able to fit a tenon straight from the saw. Don't be tempted to use abrasive paper to smooth a rough tenon—you may round over the corners and spoil the fit.

Reinforcing tenons against tension

When the load on a structure puts the mortise and tenon in tension, the glue bond is the only thing that keeps the joint together—unless the joint is reinforced. Pinning, wedging, and wedging with a key or tusk are the basic methods for increasing resistance to tension on the joint.

Splaying the exiting side of a through mortise, and kerfing the tenon for one or more wedges is a sure sign of durable hand joinery. Run wedges of a contrasting wood across the grain of the mortise to keep it from splitting. Make the wedge no wider than the tenon thickness. Wedges that are too wide will bite irreparably into the cheek of the mortise and forever draw attention to the error. For thicker wedges, do not use a saw kerf. Instead, remove small sections of the tenon in a shallow "V" shape. Another method leaves the tenon unkerfed, and places the wedges on either side of it at the mortise ends.

Through wedged tenon

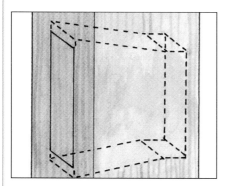

1 Add about ⅟₁₆in (2mm) to each end of the mortise length and taper the end cheeks toward the front, leaving a flat where the tenon enters.

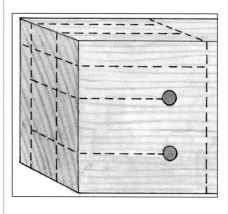

2 Lay out tenon cheeks, shoulders, and wedge locations, then drill a small hole about a quarter of the tenon length from the shoulder to locate the bottom of each wedge slot.

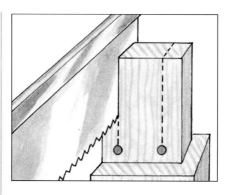

3 First saw the tenon cheeks and shoulders, then saw down the cheek to the small holes, which will prevent splitting when the wedges are inserted.

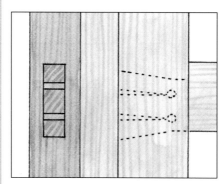

4 Glue the joint and clamp the shoulders home temporarily, until the cheeks are clamped. Then tap the glued wedges in, alternating taps so they penetrate to equal depth. When the glue is dry, remove the clamp from the cheeks, and saw off any existing wedges. Then sand, or plane, the joint flush.

Draw-bored tenon

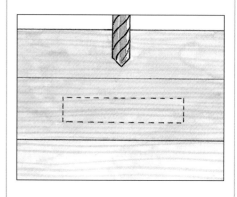

1 To drill a hole at the center of the mortise length, lay out the mortise and back it up with scrap, about a quarter of the stock width from the edge.

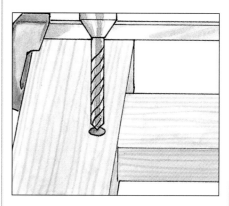

2 After cutting the mortise and tenon as usual, assemble and clamp the joint, then insert the drill bit into the hole, just to mark its location on the tenon.

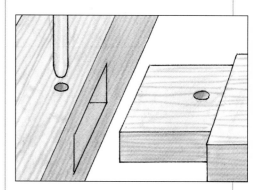

3 Drill a hole in the tenon slightly closer to the shoulder than the bit mark. Then assemble the joint, driving a tapered peg into the hole to pull the pieces home.

Stabilizing tenons

Edge and face shoulders on a tenon increase its mechanical resistance to racking. But each shoulder reduces the material in the tenon and replaces it with the shoulder's end grain, which lacks gluing strength. Deep-edge shoulders subtract gluing area from the tenon's cheek and make a wide piece vulnerable to twisting, which easily breaks the shoulder's end-grain bond. Wood movement and shrinking in the joint also stress the glue bond. Haunches and multiple tenons help to overcome these difficulties.

The square profile of a haunch neatly fills the panel groove that runs through the stiles, ensuring that there is no gap on the top edge of the panel end in frame-and-panel construction. More importantly, the second shallow mortise that houses the haunch lets the edge shoulder into the wood without weakening the end of the piece when the tenon falls there.

Haunched tenons are seen in door frames, windows, and many other pieces of domestic joinery. Professionals often use a heavy-duty piece of machinery called a tenoner to make this part of a mortise and tenon joint. This uses high-speed cutters to chop away the waste in a few seconds, even in hardwood. For the home workshop, a router

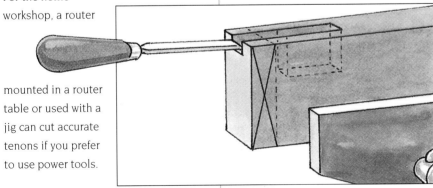

mounted in a router table or used with a jig can cut accurate tenons if you prefer to use power tools.

Haunched tenon

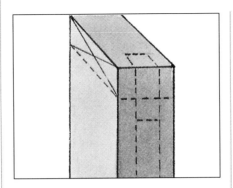

1 Gauge the mortise width on the edge and horn end, marking a depth there equal to the mortise width, and start the mortise its width away from the horn cut-off line.

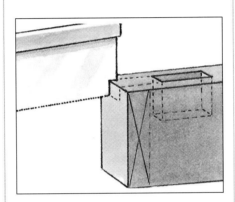

2 After chopping the mortise, saw along the lines—extending from it on the horn edge and down the horn end to the depth marked.

3 Tap a chisel lightly into the end grain between the sawed lines to chip out the waste down to the depth mark, paring the bottom parallel to the face.

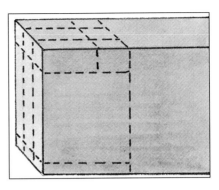

4 Lay out the tenon to fit the mortise and scribe the haunch line across the outside edge at a distance from the face shoulders equal to the thickness of the tenon.

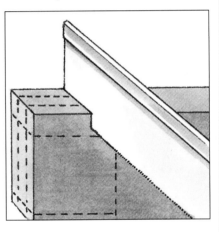

5 Do not saw an edge shoulder on the haunched edge, just saw down the haunch line to the tenon, then saw the face and bottom edge shoulders and the tenon cheeks.

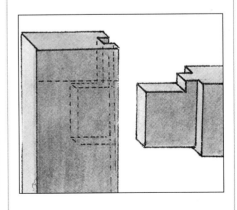

6 Test fit the tenon, making sure neither the haunch nor the tenon length prevent the shoulders from seating, then glue the joint and cut off the horn.

Sloped haunch tenon

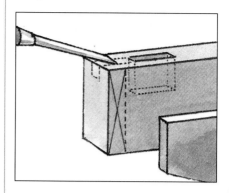

1 Lay out and chop the mortise as for a haunched tenon, then chisel from inside the horn cut-off line, angling down toward the mortise, to reach a depth equal to mortise width.

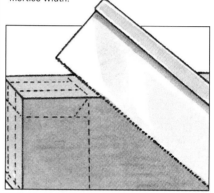

2 Lay out the tenon, and make the first saw cut across the top edge, angling from the face shoulder line to a measurement from it equal to the tenon thickness.

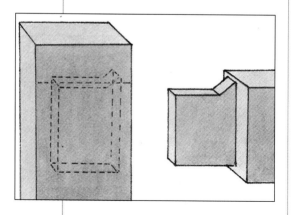

3 Pare the slope slightly down from the top edge (matching its socket started inside the layout), so that removing material to flush up the pieces after gluing will not expose the slope.

Special framing tenons

The basic joint between a frame and panel is a groove housing or a rebate housing with a stop holding in the panel. The important thing to know is how frame mortise and tenon accommodate them.

A groove runs centered on the inside edges of the frame, right over the mortises. The groove width is about one third the stock thickness, with its depth about the same as its width—to keep the material strong. The mortise width and tenon thickness match the groove width. Decide this width first and lay out the mortise and tenon cheeks to it. Then mark the groove depth on the end of the tenon stock, allotting the remainder to the tenon and haunch. This determines the length and placement of the mortise on its stock. Mark the frame rebate on the end of the tenon stock to find the tenon width, and so the mortise length and placement. The rebate should remove about two thirds of the material thickness—to house the panel and stop—and cut into the width of the stock about one third the thickness or more. The tenon shoulder on the face side of the frame is set back to house the lip formed by rebating.

Some frames have a molded detail on the inside edge that is continued around, or returned, by mitering. After mortising, run a rebate to a depth equal to the molding width. However, instead of cutting the tenon's face shoulder back to house the lip left on the mortise piece, remove the molded detail flush with the mortise and rebate, then miter it to match the tenon.

Mortise and tenon with a panel groove

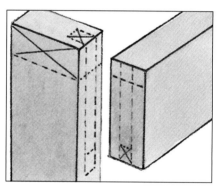

1 Choose a panel groove width, lay out the mortise and tenon cheeks to it, mark its depth under the tenon to find the tenon width, and place the mortise.

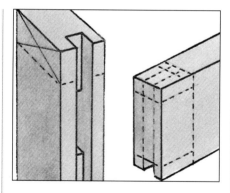

2 Chop the mortise on the inside groove of the parts, and run the panel groove over it on the inside edges of all pieces. Then lay out the tenon so that the haunch length fills the groove.

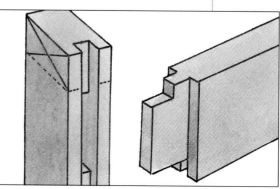

3 Saw the haunch shoulder first, then the face shoulders and tenon cheeks, glue the joint and saw off the horn.

Mortise and tenon with a panel-molded edge

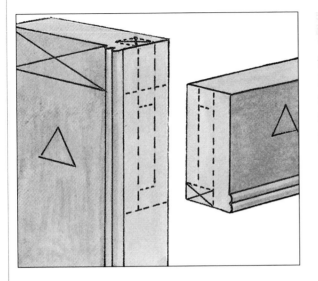

1 Run the molding detail on the inside face edge of the stock, then lay out the rebate and haunched tenon mortise so that they stop in line with the molding detail.

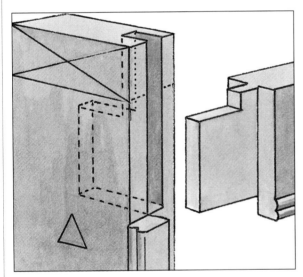

2 Chop the mortise, run the rebate to the line of the molding detail, finish the tenon layout and saw it. Then saw the molding detail away flush with the mortise.

3 Use a 45-degree chisel guide on the edge of the stock to miter the molding detail away from the tenon shoulder and mortise, then fit the joint together.

Tips box

- Always leave around 1in (25mm) of horn on the end of a workpiece. This protects the corner of the frame from damage before it is installed and also gives a wider purchase for the sash clamps during assembly. Use a tenon saw to remove the horns.
- Try to use lumber and set out the joint based on the size of your straight cutter.

More framing tenons

Frames for divided panels have tenoned center rails or muntins whose molded detail will run on both edges. Whether the frame is grooved or rebated, to return a molding around each separate panel the width of the molding is cut away at the mortise and mitered to match the tenon. Increase the length between tenon shoulders by the width of moldings cut away. Also increase the length by the amount that mitered tenon shoulders are let into mortise pieces to prevent weak short grain on arched rails.

A molded detail on a frame for several panels is run on both edges of the center rail or muntin like the groove, and the detail is returned by mitering.

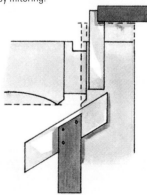

To prevent weak short grain on an arched rail, a small miter is cut on the shoulder of the tenon and housed in the shoulder of the mortise.

MITERS AND BEVELS

Miters and bevels are cuts made at angles other than 90 degrees. Aesthetically, miters or bevels can unify a shape visually by continuing the line of grain around it. Structurally, miters add softening facets and bridge the gap between squares and circles.

The terms "miter" and "bevel" sometimes interchange. An important distinction is that a bevel cut is not perpendicular to the face of the wood, whereas a miter is either an exact 45-degree cut (even if it is a bevel) or a general term for an angled cut.

About miters and bevels

There are three basic types of miters—and they create a fourth type when used in combination. Frame miters angle the blade path across the with of the wood, but the blade tilt is perpendicular to the face. Cross and length miters angle the blade tilt to the face and are really just bevel cuts. The cross-miter path is perpendicular to the wood edge, while the length-miter path is parallel to it. The fourth type is a compound miter. It combines a bevel tilt with an angled path either across or along the grain.

The glue surface of a length miter is all long grain, but other miters are weak because the glue surface is on the end grain. Consequently, miters need to be reinforced, and even though the gluing orientation is strong, clamp pressure causes miters to slip out of gluing position, unless loose tongues or other mechanical restraints are used in combination with special clamping techniques.

Inaccurate miter joints are hard to get away with, and difficult to correct. It is a good idea to spend time adjusting machines, and making tests on waste before committing to the actual cut. The angle gauges on stationary machines are often imprecise, so miter joints have spawned a business in precision gauges and jigs plus an endless array of shop-made devices and set-up methods that aid accurate work.

Cutting miters and bevels by machine generates extra force that pulls or pushes the wood, encouraging it to slip out of position during cutting. Sharp blades, hold-downs, stops on the miter gauge, and sandpaper on its face all reduce slipping and unnecessary accidents.

Types of miters

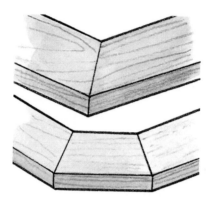

The angle of a frame miter will vary with the number of sides, but the cut is always across the width of the board face.

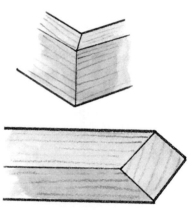

Cross miters are really bevels on the end of the board, so it is not unusual to hear them called bevels.

The bevel angle of a length miter (also called an edge bevel) will vary, as all miters do, with the number of sides in the structure.

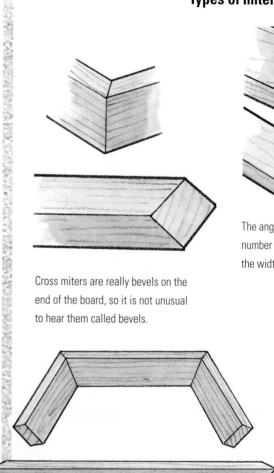

Compound miters combine a bevel with a frame miter or a taper cut to make shadow boxes, or other slope-sided shapes.

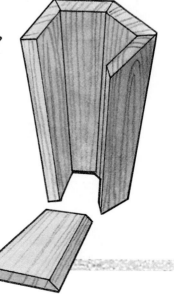

Figuring miters and bevels

The cutting angle for frame miters and bevel joints is calculated by dividing the number of sides into a circle's 360 degrees to find the miter angle, and then dividing the result by two. Depending on the angle, or the machine's calibrations, the gauge, blade, or radial arm is set either directly to the cutting angle or to its complement (the remainder when the cutting angle is subtracted from 90 degrees).

To improve on the miter gauge's accuracy, lay out permanent settings for common angles on the table saw top, using a framing square and a little geometry. First make sure the table saw blade sits parallel to the miter gauge slots. This can be checked by measuring from the miter gauge slot to the same tooth positioned at the front and rotated to the back of the blade. Once the gauge is checked or adjusted according to the manual, use the method shown to draw in common angles that you will need.

Extend the miter fence with a batten to a point marked on the bisecting line, lock the setting, and test the cut for accuracy with layout tools or against a careful drawing. The farther out the testing point is placed along the bisecting line, the finer the adjustments to tune the gauge setting. Punch a permanent small dent in the tabletop when the right setting is found.

Applying geometry to machine set-ups

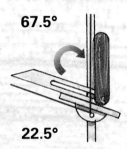

67.5°

22.5°

To find a 45-degree angle on the table saw, erect a perpendicular to the miter slot and bisect the angle, then punch a dent on the line you are going to use to set the miter fence with a batten.

Bisecting the 45-degree angle below yields an accurate 22.5 degrees; transfer any of the marked angles or complementary angles to a sliding bevel to set tilt of the blade.

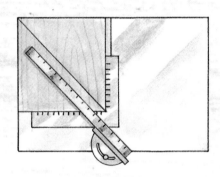

Miters and math

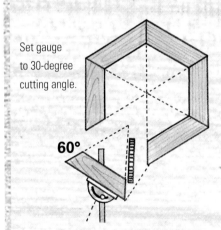

Set gauge to 30-degree cutting angle.

60°

The formula for finding miter or bevel cutting angles is: 360 degrees divided by the number of segments (n) divided by two equals the cutting angle.

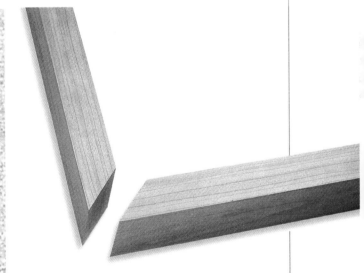

ABOVE: A mitered corner continues the wood grain visually to harmonize with the design.

Frame miters

A simple frame miter is an end grain butt joint whose only strength comes from the glue holding it together. A very light frame glued with epoxy might survive a low-stress application, but most frame miters need reinforcement to last.

Frame miter reinforcements are either an integral part of the joint or enhance an assembly after glue-up. Loose tongues—or joinery that creates long-grain glue surfaces, like the lap miter—are the common integral reinforcements.

Dadoes for loose tongues are run in the mitered ends prior to glue-up by whatever method is most convenient, given the length of the pieces. Short pieces can run firmly supported upright over the table saw blade or over a straight bit on a router table. Longer pieces are more convenient to work face down with a router tongue-and-groove cutter or on a radial arm saw.

Alternatively, after a butt-glued assembly dries, the mitered frame can be carefully reinforced by nails, feathers, gussets, or butterfly keys (wing-shaped blocks of wood). When frames are built around a plywood panel, or field, like a tabletop which has no risk of seasonal movement, gluing the frame parts to the panel groove or rebate will reinforce the glued miters.

Similar to the radial arm technique shown here, a decorative hand technique for feathering frame corners is to handsaw two or three kerfs, and glue contrasting veneer into them. If nails are used, drive them into the miter through the frame sides, so that the weight of the frame does not pull them out.

Frame miter by hand

1 Mark 45 degrees with a layout tool—or scribe the diagonal of a square whose sides equal the wood width—and clamp a block there to guide the saw.

Lap miter

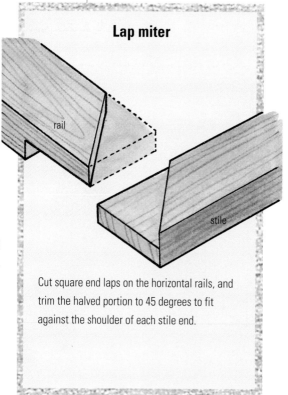

rail

stile

Cut square end laps on the horizontal rails, and trim the halved portion to 45 degrees to fit against the shoulder of each stile end.

Professional framers saw miters close to length, and use expensive guillotine devices to pare the joint smooth. In the home shop, skilled use of handplanes and miter shooting boards are the best alternative.

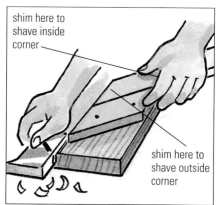

shim here to shave inside corner

shim here to shave outside corner

2 Place the piece on a miter shooting board, and lightly shave off any saw marks with a rebate or other plane, shimming a playing card between the fence and piece to correct misfits.

3 Heavily coat the end grain with glue, then clamp the frame, using a tool like this adjustable shop-made device (frame clamp) that keeps the parts from sliding out of position when clamp force is applied.

Tips box

Before you invest in a miter saw, check that it is easily adjustable. The cutting angle indicator should be movable, so that it can can be recalibrated if necessary. The powerful motor and sweeping movement of the blade mean that these machines are often knocked out of exact alignment and need to be checked before each use.

Cross miters

Feathered miter on a radial arm saw

1 Set the arm to the miter angle, and cut one end of each piece. Then clamp a stop block on the fence to gauge the final cut to length.

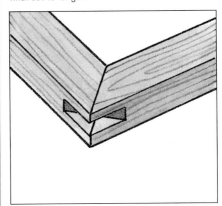

2 Turn the saw horizontal, extending the blade into about a third of the miter's length, and kerf through the frame's glued corners by sliding them into the blade on a height table.

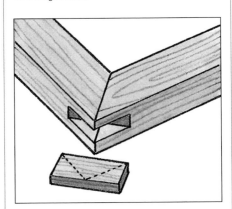

3 Thickness a strip of key material to fit the kerf, cut lengths, and glue them in. Then trim with a saw and sand flush after drying.

Cross miters made by bevel cuts across the grain are, like frame miters, inherently weak joints because of their end-grain glue surface. So, also like frame miters, they are usually used in a supplemental, rather than structural, capacity. Most of the reinforcing techniques that are used on frame miters also apply to cross miters, but the decorative butterfly key is eliminated and replaced by the dovetail key (with only one "wing"), which makes mock dovetails of the cross miter.

With end grain to end grain in an "L" orientation, a cross miter is hard to modify for long-grain contact, except by combining it with a finger or pin joint. Not even internal tongues make long-grain contact, unless the joint is part of a six- or eight-sided structure—where the joint angle is greater than 120 degrees. Feathering through the corners does bring long-grain strength to cross miters.

The table-sawed lock-miter joint automatically interlocks the joint, so that it depends less on glue strength, but it is only effective when it is correctly oriented to resist tension. Lock miters are a common joint for drawers, as they have the strength to resist the tensions exerted by pulling on the drawer front, and show no end grain on the front or side.

The house rebate miter adds no long-grain glue surface to a cross miter joint. Its slight shoulder adds a little glue shearing strength and some assistance.

Housed rebate miter

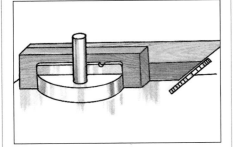

1 Using material that is the same thickness as its mating corner (or thinner, like this drawer side), bevel the end to 45 degrees.

2 Cut the drawer front to length, and kerf across its inside face within an outline of the side's thickness, and just to the height of its bevel.

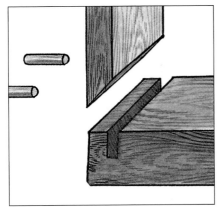

3 Tilt the blade to 45 degrees, to remove the waste inside the front, and glue the joint together. When it is dry, drive pins through the side for reinforcement.

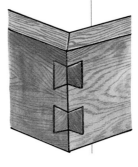

RIGHT: Mock dovetails are a decorative way to reinforce cross miters.

Locked miter

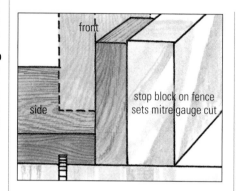

1 Set the blade in line with the thickness of the front and kerf on the inside face of the side with the blade height about a third of the side's thickness.

against racking, but the real strength comes from pins driven through the joint from the outside, or from making the joint long-grain. The pinned housed rebate miter is a common drawer joint in Japan; it is simple, strong, and decorative if contrasting pins are used. The advantage of the housed rebate miter is that it can join different thicknesses of wood.

The width of tongues in cross and other miters should be about twice the wood thickness, and kept inside the centerline of the joint. To cut dadoes for the tongues, hold the wood face flat on the table saw and use the same tilt angle that cut the bevel. If an angled fence tilts the bevel flat against the table, the cutter is upright at 90 degrees. Stopped tongues are most easily made by a router. The diagrams may look complex but this is a relatively simple joint to make and assemble. You can buy router cutters to make the miter as well as the grooving needed for cross miters. Make sure the router is mounted in a router table for this type of joint and check the workpiece is fully supported as it passes over the cutter.

2 Using the table saw (or a molding machine) cut a groove in the front to a height corresponding to the thickness of the side, while leaving a narrow tongue to fit the kerf already made in the side.

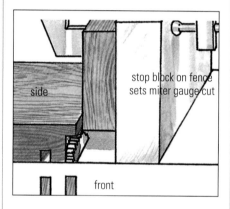

3 Set a stop block on the fence, lower the dado blade to two thirds of the thickness, then cut a rebate that leaves a tongue to fit the dado in the front.

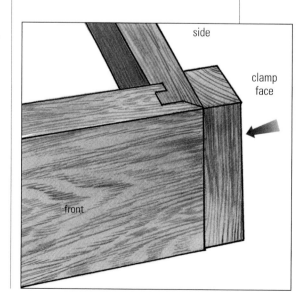

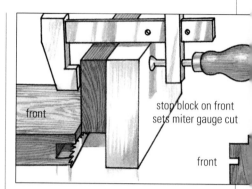

4 Use a normal blade, lowered to cut only the narrow tongue in the front, trimming it to the depth of the dado kerfed one third into the side thickness.

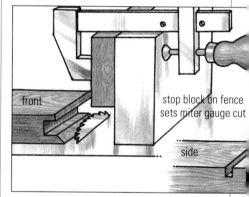

5 Tilt the blade to 45 degrees and use a stop block on the fence to control the beveling of projecting tongues on the front and side.

6 Unlike most miters, a lock miter needs clamp force to be applied in only one direction, but a block should distribute the pressure on the miter itself.

Length miters

A plain bevel joint along the grain brings a certain air of harmony to joinery, probably because the joint line blends so well with the material, that the parts merge into a single unit. Length miters (or bevel joints) also bring with them the new world of segmented joinery populated by umbrella stands, planters, and kaleidoscopes. Length miters have a grain orientation that is strong for gluing, once the parts are persuaded to cooperate with clamping.

A self-squaring joint like the rebate miter—with its inside step to butt the miters and keep the joint in position—is a helpful choice for square structures. Still, the outside corner of the miter benefits from corner clamping blocks to press it tight. This joint is possible on a router table with a straight bit and a chamfering bit, but to be made on the radial arm saw, it requires the dangerous ripping position.

The waterfall joint capitalizes on a miter's ability to carry the grain around a turn. It is particularly good in custom-veneered plywood cabinets where the back is seen. The back is taken from the center of the sheet, the ends joined to it by a waterfall and the face frame attached.

Waterfall joint

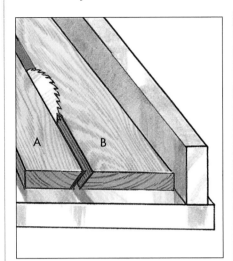

1 Tilt the blade to 45 degrees, and rip a bevel with the outer face up for a tilt toward the fence or the inside face up for an outward tilt.

2 Flip the piece that is against the fence end for end, and rip again to remove a triangular waste strip from the wood's edge.

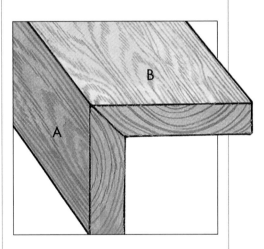

3 Flip the fence piece back again and join the first piece for a near-perfect grain match.

Coopering

Coopering uses bevel-modified width joints to join segments of a circle's arc into a single unit that is planed smooth of facets after the glue dries.

Bad surface preparation

Fresh and cleanly-shaven mating surfaces must make contact for a good glue bond to form. High spots inside the joint prevent full contact, as do low spots that allow the glue to "pool". The "hairiness" of rough-sawed surfaces breaks the glue film and makes joints harder to pull up tight for an invisible glue line. Dull planer knives produce a glazed surface that doesn't glue well, and exotic woods have surface chemicals that require special glues or wiping down with acetone for a good bond.

Rebate miter

1 Kerf the inside face with the distance between the fence and the outside of the blade equal to the wood thickness, and the blade height set to half the thickness.

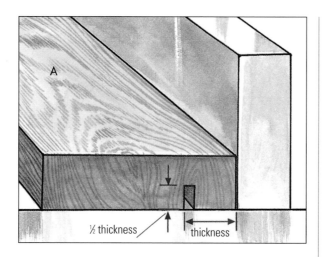

½ thickness

thickness

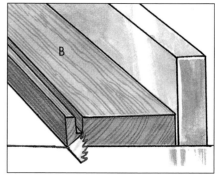

B

4 Flip the second part end to end so that the inside is facing upward, and tilt the blade to remove the waste to the kerf at a 45-degree angle.

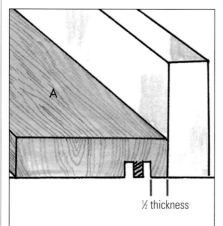

A

½ thickness

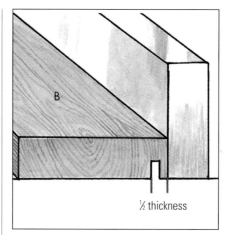

B

½ thickness

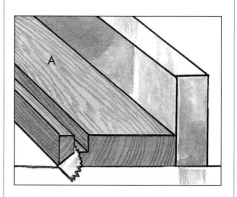

A

2 Move the fence so that the distance to the blade's inside is half the wood thickness, and kerf again, then move the fence to cut out the waste material between the kerfs.

3 Without changing the blade height, move the fence back so that the distance to the blade outside is half the thickness, and kerf the inside face of the second part.

5 Flip the first piece inside up, and bevel its edge at the same 45-degree bevel angle, cutting to the groove left by kerfing out the waste.

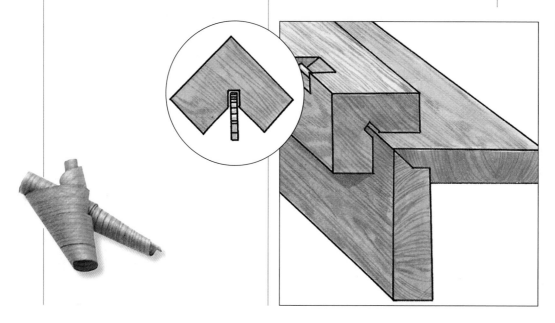

6 To aid gluing, make two cuts in a long wood square to waste out a corner and kerf inside the clamping block's angle to stop excess glue from sticking it to the miter.

DOVETAILS

Often considered the hallmark of fine workmanship in wood, dovetails are interlocking joints with a great deal of mechanical strength. A dovetail joint is constructed with an angled male part—shaped like the joint's name—which fits into a similarly-shaped female socket. In its best-known configuration at an end-to-face corner, a dovetail joint is a series of tails fitted into a series of sockets. The parts between sockets are called pins. They fit like interlocking tenons into the spaces between the tails. The widening tail braces the joint against tension, adding great mechanical strength to the long-grain glue surface between the tails and pins.

Using a template

Using a dovetail template and pencil, mark out the positions of the dovetails on one piece. Always shade in the waste. The pitch angle is usually around 1:7, and can be marked alternatively with a sliding bevel. Pitch is the term used to denote the angle of the slope.

Making through pins

When developing a corner-dovetail layout, make the pins about half the wood's thickness or more at their widest, and evenly-spaced tails two or three times the pin width. Variable spacing uses wide tails at the center and narrower tails toward the joint's ends, setting out more pin gluing surface there, but not necessarily proportioning the pins to either tail. This places strong construction where it's needed and helps restrain cupping if the wood dries. Layout should orient the heartwood side facing outward to compensate for drying—drawers will stick if the sides cup outward.

The half pins at each end of a corner dovetail joint are not necessarily half the width of a whole pin. They are called half pins because only one side has the dovetail angle. Often, they are made as wide at their widest end as a whole pin, or wider. Proper corner dovetails end with half pins to provide a gluing surface for the tail.

The higher the ratio for the pin and tail angle the less chance there is of damage to the corners. A ratio of less than 1:5 makes the dovetail corners fragile, especially in coarse woods. The higher angle ratios flatten the wedge shape, and so are used for hardwoods

less likely to shrink, or softwoods under little tension. Some pins on fine work narrow almost to points, but the width of the pin doesn't threaten joint strength like a tail that is too thin and weak at its narrowest part.

It is possible to saw pins on the table saw holding the piece vertical against a scrap fence attached to a miter gauge to angle the lumber relative to the blade (i.e. 1:5 angle on the saw). Angle the gauge until the blade cuts through the piece at the pin angle, lowering the blade to the gauged line. Make all the cuts on one side of the pins in the waste, then turn the opposite face to make the other cuts.

On the scroll or band saw, the piece is placed face down on the table and the end where the pins are marked is presented to the blade. The tilting saw table or a tilting auxiliary table aligns the pin angle to the blade.

2 Design the layout on paper to develop the dovetail sizes; tilting a rule diagonally is an easy way to set equal increments for the pin centerlines and the spaces for mating tails (right).

Through pins

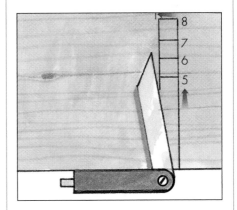

1 Considering the type and species of wood, butt a sliding bevel to the bench edge and set the dovetail angle to a ratio of between 1:5 and 1:8 (above).

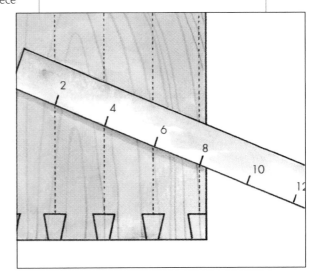

3 Dress and sand the wood, set the marking gauge just over the tail part's thickness, and scribe around the end of the pin piece to mark its faces and edges.

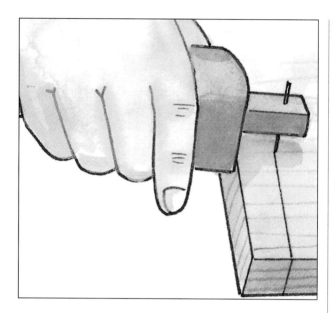

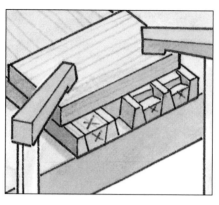

8 Flip the piece and chop away the remaining waste with small steps that move back toward the gauged line and down into the waste until all the waste is removed.

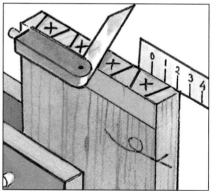

4 Facing the board's inside, lay out the pin centerlines, mark half the pin's widest end on each side of the centerline, scribe the angles with a knife, and mark the waste.

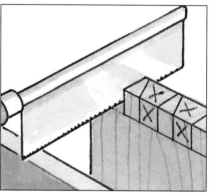

6 Starting at the front corner, on the waste side of the pin lines, saw part way on the face and end, then level out to saw to the gauged line.

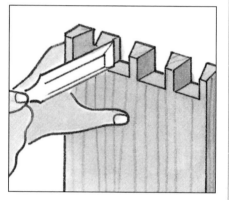

9 Clean up inside the pins, making sure to keep the cheeks flat and perpendicular, and pare the end grain flat, or undercut to a slight "V" indent.

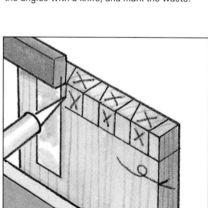

5 Square the pin angles down each face of the board to the gauged line with a knife, and clearly mark the waste.

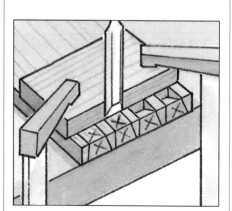

7 Clamp the piece over a bench leg with a guide block on the gauged line, chop down at the line with a chisel and pare away half the waste, angling down from the end grain.

Basic types of mortise

 A **blind mortise** has a flat bottom that stops short of the opposite face, and the tenon end is enclosed by the wood.

 A **through mortise** makes a hole through the material and the tenon end is visible on the other side.

 The **specialized slot mortise** is a deep dado cut used in slip or bridle joints—mortise and tenon relatives.

To mark the tails from the pins, gauge the pin-stock thickness around the end of the tail board, and butt the pin board to the line in the assembled position, clamping if necessary. Scribe the sides of the pins onto the inside face of the tail board from the inside face of the pins, so the knife does not follow the grain away.

As with any handsawing, small bevels can be chiseled into the waste of the end grain layout, or a shallow kerf can be made along the line to guide the saw. Tilt the board to make the cuts vertical if it gives better control. An initial light cut at the back corner is another technique to keep the saw aligned.

To saw tails on the table saw, tilt the blade to the tail angle, and hold the piece vertical against a squared miter gauge. First cut the same side of each tail, then reverse the board faces to cut the other side. Alternatively, carefully band saw the cuts, with the board face flat on the table.

Setting the marking gauge slightly wider than the thickness makes the joint ends proud, so they can be sanded flush after glue-up. Many woodworkers prefer this option to gauging slightly under the thickness, which leaves the ends recessed in their sockets, so that the whole face of the board needs to be planed or sanded down. In the case of a fitted drawer, the final width is the critical issue. It is a matter of preference whether the drawer face is cut overlong to compensate for sanding down proud ends to fit, or cut to exact size and the sides planed down to the recessed ends to fit.

Choosing to leave the ends proud complicates clamping. The proud ends prevent clamps from pushing the dovetails into the sockets by direct pressure, unless comblike clamping blocks are used to press between the ends. However, since the glue surface is between the tails and pins, the important force should be against the width of the joint after other clamps seat the pieces. Some woodworkers feel that tight dovetails do not need to be clamped at all, just left until the glue dries.

Using a layout tool

Another homemade layout tool for dovetails can set the angle for the tails and pins, as well as square the lines across the end grain, and down the face.

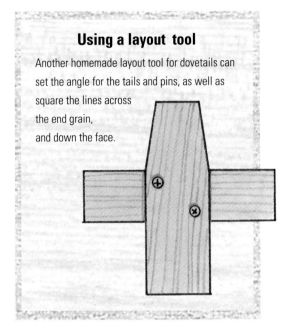

Through tails

1 Set the marking gauge slightly over the thickness of the pin stock, and scribe around the end of the tail stock after it has been dressed, squared, and sanded.

2 Hold or clamp the widest side of the cut pins to the gauged line on the tails, scribing inside the sockets to mark the pin positions inside the tail stock.

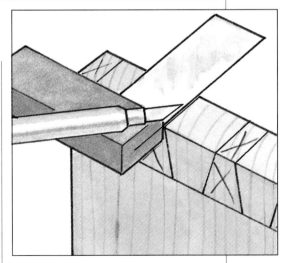

3 Square the scribed pin angle lines across the end of the board, and mark the pin positions as waste.

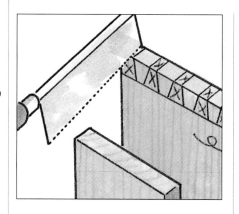

4 Saw on the waste side of the pin angles, starting on the front corner to saw face and end simultaneously, tilting the board to make the cuts vertical, if preferred. Try to use only enough pressure to guide the saw through the work and regularly check that you are cutting just clear of the joint pencil line.

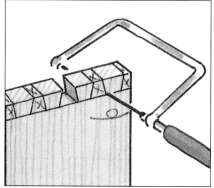

6 Alternatively, remove the waste by sawing near the line with a fine-bladed coping saw, then paring the end grain flush to the gauged line. Support the work upright in your bench vise. Regularly check that the saw blade isn't wandering over the marked line by leaning over and inspecting the rear side of the work.

8 Protect the joint with a block, and tap it together—making sure that the pins and tails align with their sockets, and that their wide ends are not so tight that they risk splitting the wood. This is a critical stage, so don't try to rush the assembly and risk damaging the tails or pins. Use a pencil to shade any protruding areas that may need a little more trimming.

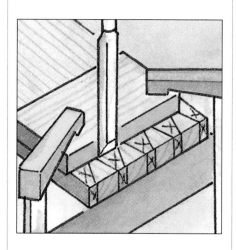

5 Chop out the waste with a narrow chisel, using the same process as with the pins, tilting the chisel slightly if undercut end grain is desired. As with any jointmaking, always work with a razorsharp blade to reduce the risk of tearing the wood fibers and creating a ragged edge to the tails.

7 Clean up the sockets between the tails, using, if necessary, special skew or dovetail chisels with angled edges that can reach under the overhang of the tail. To stop the wood from tearing out at the back as you work, lay the work flat on the bench with a waste board behind it.

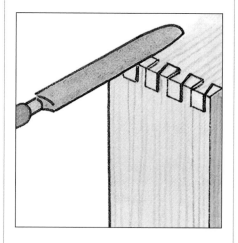

9 After gluing, the pins and tails will be slightly raised because the line was gauged a little over the thickness of the stock. File or use a sanding block to make them flush with the board's surface. Make sure to work parallel with the surrounding surface so that you do not round over the crisp new corner joint.

Making lapped dovetails

The biggest difference between lapped dovetails and through dovetails is that lapped dovetails help to hide all or part of the joint. The three basic lapped dovetails are half-blind, blind mitered, and full-blind.

A dovetailing preference that is brought into focus by the lap family is whether the pins or the tails should be made first. The method shown for through dovetails makes the pins first and scribes the tails from them. Some woodworkers prefer to work the other way around. In practice, the length of the parts decides the order, because one is easier to align to the other for scribing. Dovetails in the lap family can be made either way, but blind mitered and full-blinds with the lap on the tails cannot be made tails first because scribing is awkward or impossible .

Half-blind dovetails use two gauge settings for layout regardless of the thickness of the parts, while through dovetails can use the same setting for all gauging, unless the part thickness differs. When laying out half-blinds, the scribe on the end grain not only sets the length of the tails, but establishes the joint's strength, based on glue surface and mechanical resistance. Never under-scribe this dimension onto the tails piece or misalign the tails to it for scribing, or the joint will not fit tight.

Initially, the tail and pin parts of blind mitered dovetails are laid out the same. Equally thick pieces are rebated from the inside face about two thirds of the thickness toward the opposite face, and about one third of the distance down to the inside scribed line. The rebate width and depth should intersect at a point along the 45-degree shoulder line scribed on the

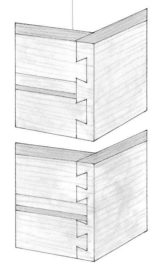

piece's edge. Then the pins are laid out on the rebate like a mitered corner dovetail, and the tails are scribed from them.

Full-blind dovetails let the pins or tails carry the lap so the joint can be oriented against tension and still hidden. The layout determines whether the end grain section shows on the side or top.

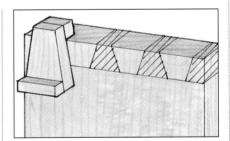

LEFT: When using half-blind dovetails, lay out the runner groove of side-hung drawers so it uses the drawer front as a stop.

Half-blind dovetails

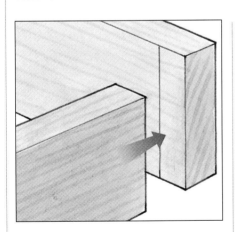

1 Using a drawer as the example, square and sand the stock, set the marking gauge to the side's thickness, and then make a scribe on the inside face of the front piece of wood.

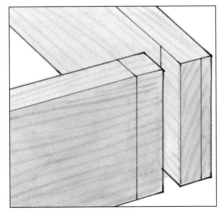

2 Reset the gauge to scribe about two thirds of the thickness of the front piece on its end grain, and also around the end of the side on both the faces and edges.

3 Determine the layout spacing and sizes, and use a template or sliding bevel to scribe angles for the tails on the side's outside face, then square the lines across the end.

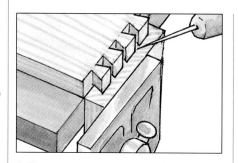

4 After sawing and chiseling the tails, hold the parts in assembly position with the tails exactly on the front's end grain scribe line in order to scribe them onto the front's end.

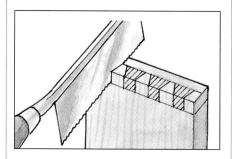

5 Mark the tails scribed on the front's end as waste, and saw tilted from the front corner until the kerf reaches both scribed lines but does not go past them.

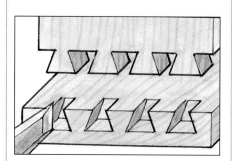

6 Chop down into the waste wood, and chip it out from the end grain. Carefully guide the chisel against the pin side to reach the unsawed inside corners, then test-fit the joint, tapping together with a mallet and scrap piece of lumber. This is one of the most common woodworking joints to be found on antique furniture and is well worth mastering if you intend to tackle any restoration projects, as well as for your own projects.

Blind mitered dovetails

1 Scribe the exact thickness of the wood inside each piece, connect a 45-degree scribe from each edge, then rebate about one third toward the face scribe, but not past the angled line.

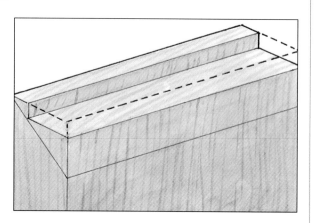

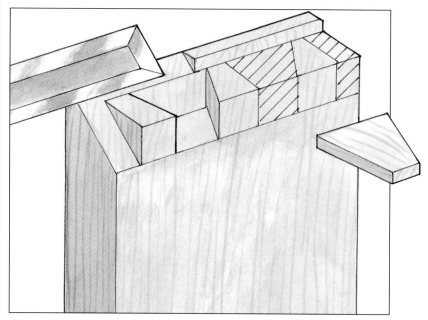

2 Lay out the pins with a template, leaving material past the half pin as in mitered corner dovetails, clear the sockets with a narrow chisel, then saw the edge's mitered shoulder. Finish off the pin side of the joint by using a razorsharp chisel to slice along the square end lip— be careful not to dig into the edges of the new pins. This should be an exact 45-degree miter when complete. Use a shoulder plane to give a smooth finish.

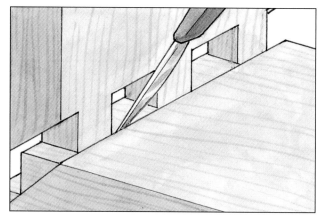

3 Place the pin piece in position on the tail piece against the scribed line. Use a knife to mark off the shape of the pins. Square the lines onto the wood end and remove the socket waste. Cut the mitered shoulder and mitered end as for the pins.

Dovetail keys, slip feather tongues and butterflies

The dovetail shape in the form of keys, tongues, and butterfly keys is popular and effective as a decorative reinforcement. The butterfly key has even become the signature reinforcement of certain craft movements and craft builders.

For strength, dovetail keys are cut with the grain. One use creates mock dovetails that reinforce corner miter joints. Keys can be of a contrasting wood, but even using woods of the same species yields a color change, because the trimmed key shows all end grain.

The sliding dovetail batten is a utilitarian key, made wide and fitted un-glued into a dovetail housing on one side of slab glue-ups such as tabletops or doors. These battens allow the wood to move but keep the assembly flat.

The least common dovetail tongue is just as easy (or difficult) to fit as a machined sliding dovetail. The housings are simple, but fitting the dovetail to it requires a lot of testing in scrap. Once the machine set-up of the router or table saw is fine tuned, running the tongues is easy. As with other tongues, the grain runs across the width of dovetail tongues for strength.

Dovetail keys

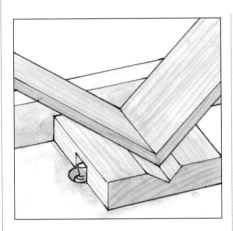

1 Rout dovetail housings in mitered corners using a "V" block with a through dado for bit passage and turning the frame to cut each corner (i.e. placing each corner of the frame in the jig to work each one in turn).

LEFT: Dark wood butterfly keys.

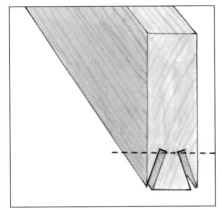

2 Set the table saw blade to the dovetail angle, take a piece of batten, and make two kerfs in the edge with the grain, in order to create a dovetail shape matching the routed housings, then rip off the key.

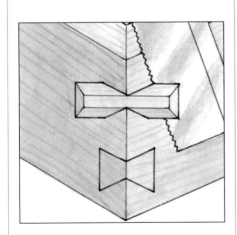

3 Tap short lengths of key material into the dovetail housings with glue, trim off the ends with a saw once dry, and sand them flush with the corners.

RIGHT: Rout dovetail housings or even tongues in edges and ends by clamping on extra material to support the router and by aligning the cut with the router edge guide.

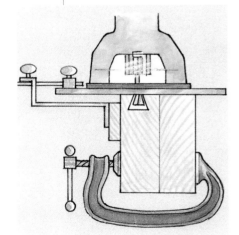

Tips box

Specialist woodwork catalogs and stores should be able to supply a flush-cutting saw with a thin, flexible blade and no back. This makes neat trimming of butterfly keys relatively easy.

Dovetail slip feather tongues

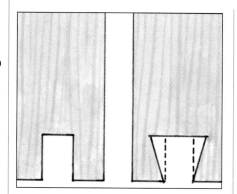

1 On a router table or table saw, make a groove to waste some of the material, removing as much wood as possible inside the dovetail shape (above left), then rout with a dovetail bit to form the dovetail housing (above right).

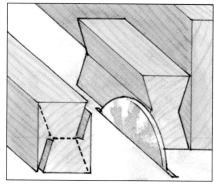

2 On the edge of a board, design dovetails to match the housing. Adjust the angle and depth of the table saw blade, and cut the first two angles, then rotate the board end for end, and cut the rest.

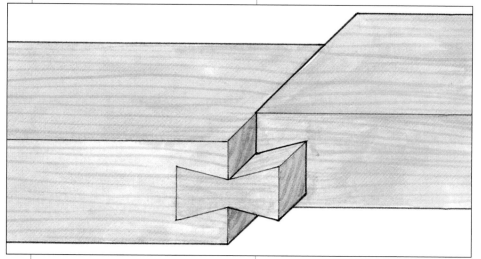

3 Test the tongue's fit—thinning it slightly with a rebate plane or sanding block if it's too tight—then either tap the parts together, or pull them together with the aid of a clamp. It's very easy to misalign the parts and damage the key, so work slowly and keep the parts flat on your bench as you assemble the joint. A router fitted under a table is the easiest way of making the parts for this joint.

Tips box

It is much easier to cut the exact bevels of a butterfly key if you choose a hard wood such as oak or rock maple.

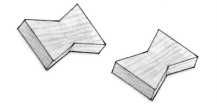

Butterfly keys

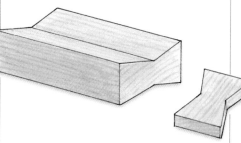

1 Make a length of dovetail tongue, then cut "slices" about one third the stock thickness being inlaid, plus extra to plane flush after gluing.

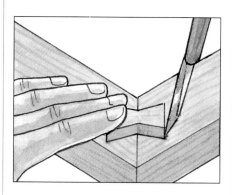

2 Hold or clamp the reinforcing inlay in place across the joint, and scribe around it, tilting the knife handle away from the inlay so that the tip bevels in toward it.

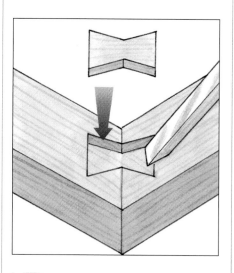

3 Chop the outline deeper, and prise out the waste with the chisel's bevel side down. Glue in the inlay—beveling its entry edge if necessary—and plane it flush with the corner when dry.

DOWELS AND BISCUITS

Modernized versions of common joints have developed over time to speed up manufacturing or accommodate new materials. Dowel joints and biscuit joinery are both by-products of industry. They make quick work of joinery by eliminating time-consuming fitting of joined elements, and are alternatives that should find an appropriate place in every woodworker's repertoire.

Dowel joints

The dowel joint is quick and simple to make, because it involves using small wooden pegs (dowels) instead of hand-cut lumber. It offers a strong, versatile system for joining wood, requiring limited equipment. The joint can form any configuration of pieces—"L"-shaped, "T"-shaped, "X"-shaped etc.—and is often used instead of the mortise and tenon joint. To ensure that the joint is strong, several dowels are used instead of the single tenon.

The joint comprises two pieces butted or mitered together, with a series of carefully-aligned drill holes to accommodate the wood dowel. Normally, dowels are made of a stout wood, such as beech or ash, manufactured in short lengths of three main diameters— ¼in, ⁵⁄₁₆in and ⅜in (6mm, 8mm and 10mm)—with flutings or grooves along their lengths, to allow the glue to disperse evenly. Without these, the dowel can sometimes act as a piston and compress the glue in the bottom of the hole. The quickest and most accurate method of dowel jointing is to use proprietary dowel center points (or barrels) or a locating/drilling jig, both of which are readily available from good tool shops.

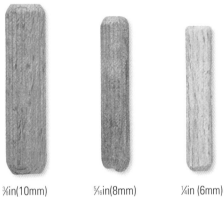

BELOW: Commercial dowels matched to standard drill sizes.

⅜in(10mm)   ⁵⁄₁₆in(8mm)   ¼in (6mm)

ABOVE: Commercial spiral-fluted dowels allow excess glue and air to escape from the hole, avoiding hydraulic pressure as the joint is assembled. Straight-fluted commercial dowels don't scrape all the glue off the sides of the hole and are easy to insert, but they are not as readily available.

ABOVE: Doweling is a simple and economical way to reinforce a light-duty butted corner joint.

A dowel-locating device

A simple alternative to dowel center points is to use a panel pin as a dowel-locating device. Drive the pin in, and take off the head with a pair of cutters or pliers. Locate the matching hole, and, after the pieces have been pressed together, withdraw the pin with the cutters or pliers.

Making a dowel joint with dowel center points

1 After the lumber has been accurately prepared to size, mark out the center lines on the end of the wood, using a try square, steel rule, and marking gauge. Select the appropriate diameter dowel center point, and, with the same diameter drill bit, drill the holes. To ensure that you do not drill in too far, use tape or a proprietary depth-stop attached to the drill bit.

2 When making this type of dowel joint, it is particularly important to use a special dowel bit with a center point. This will ensure that you will be able to locate the marked position accurately.

4 Use the pointed ends of the center points to mark off the corresponding drill hole positions. For a "T"-shaped joint, you can square a guide line across the second piece of wood, and align the first piece with it. Then either press or drive the pieces together.

3 To mark off the positions on the corresponding piece of wood, insert the proprietary dowel center points into the holes.

5 Drill the corresponding holes, being careful to drill straight and square. This can be tricky, so be careful. Apply glue to the dowel rod, the dowel holes, and the edges of the boards, and clamp the work together.

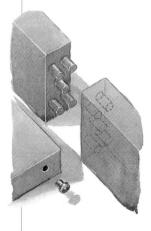

ABOVE: Using several dowels instead of one is the modern equivalent of the mortise and tenon joint. Small brass centering points help to secure the joint.

Using a doweling jig

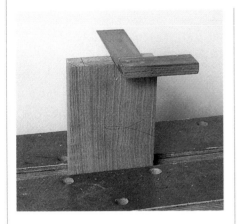

1 Mark the positions of the dowel joints by squaring a line across the wood. No matter how good the tool you are using, the initial marking out is critical. The golden rule in all woodwork is measure twice and cut once. Clamp the dowel jig to the bench, then clamp the wood—with the marked line visible—in the center of the jig drilling hole.

2 Using the appropriate dowel bit, and with the depth-stop attached, carefully drill through the guide hole in the jig, straight into the wood. Move the wood along to drill subsequent holes in the same manner.

4 Drill out the holes in turn. The jig clamps will need to be re-arranged to drill all the holes.

3 Now insert the other piece of wood into the jig using the clamps in the adjacent position. Align the marked positions with the jig drilling hole.

5 The dowel joint should align perfectly, ready for gluing.

Tips box

• You can make up your own lengths of dowel if you want to use a particular wood or diameter. Grip a piece of strong steel plate in your vise and drill a hole the exact diameter of the dowel required. Cut a strip of the wood to approximately the same diameter and hammer this through the plate to form the rounded shape. Trim to exact length.

• For items where the ends of the dowels will be visible on the surface of the finished piece, an attractive option can be to choose a wood for your doweling that is in a contrasting color to the wood used for the piece itself.

Marking out

Never underestimate the importance of marking out your piece of lumber with clear and accurate measurements before starting drilling. It is well worth taking your time with this vital stage and checking your measurements carefully to avoid wasting any wood unnecessarily.

Reinforced width miter

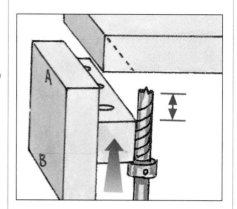

1 Cut the parts to the length you require, make a jig for drilling inside the miter, set the stop to drill the chosen depth, and tap on the jig with brads (temporarily fixing the jig in place with panel pins).

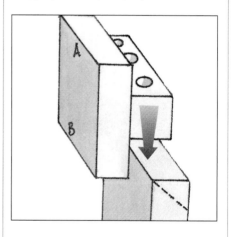

2 Drill matching holes in the second piece of wood from the opposite side of the jig, then saw the miter across all the parts, without removing any length.

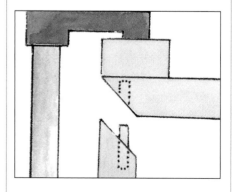

3 Brush glue in the holes and on the dowels, and insert them in one of the parts. Then use a block and clamp to press the other part onto the dowels.

Biscuit joints

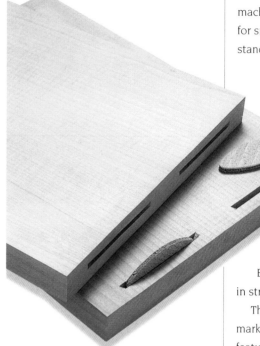

ABOVE: A biscuit joint can be made quickly using a devoted hand power tool.

Biscuit—or plate—joining is a relatively new method of joining wood. It was developed to join manmade materials like plywood and particle board, but it has also become popular for joining solid wood, too.

Biscuits are thin, soccerball-shaped pieces of compressed beech that join parts like loose tenons, dowels, or tongues. Most biscuit joints are made by a portable electric tool called a biscuit or plate joiner which looks like a small right-angle grinder with a carbide-toothed saw blade. The machine's main function is to plunge its blade to a calibrated depth into the ends of mating parts. Each semicircular kerf left in the parts by the blade encloses half the biscuit.

Biscuits themselves are made from compressed beech, cut so the grain runs diagonally across them for strength. There are three standard sizes (0, 10, 20),

used by all machines, and certain machines can use larger biscuits or kerf for smaller, thinner biscuits using a non-standard blade. Tongue-and-groove cutters—used in routers or laminate trimmers— can rout kerfs for special round biscuits.

Biscuits require water-based glues, like aliphatic resins. By design, the moisture swells the slightly compressed biscuit, tightening it in the kerf. Biscuit joints perform extremely well in strength tests.

The number of plate joiners on the market offers woodworkers a choice of features over an extended price range. Important considerations are the ease and range of fence adjustment, the range of fence angles, and the miter indexing method.

Most biscuit joinery references the machine's fence against the wood's face or end to position the kerf. The distance between the blade and the fence can be adjusted slightly. The most versatile blade height adjustment uses a rack and pinion to move the fence up and down in relation to the blade, although in practice an infinite number of positions are not often needed, given common wood thicknesses.

On all machines, the fence references at 90 degrees to the surface being kerfed, to make most parallel, "T"- or "L"-joints, and at 45 degrees for end or edge miters. Some fences also reference at any angle in between, a handy feature for joining beveled work. The machine also references off its flat base.

About biscuit joiners

The retractable spring-loaded base of the plate joiner encloses a small circular saw blade that can be plunged into the end of a piece of wood to various depth settings, making arced kerfs that fit the biscuits.

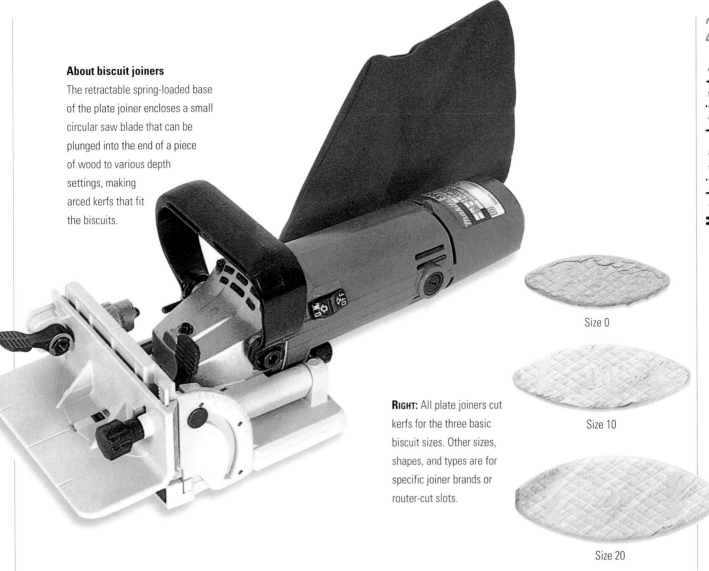

RIGHT: All plate joiners cut kerfs for the three basic biscuit sizes. Other sizes, shapes, and types are for specific joiner brands or router-cut slots.

Size 0

Size 10

Size 20

Flush framing joint

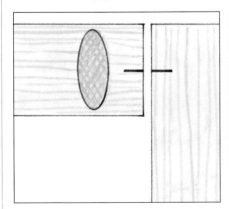

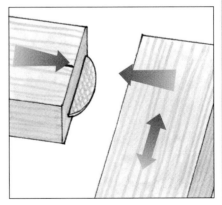

1 Cut the pieces to length and place them in assembly position, then choose the largest biscuit that fits the stock and mark its center across the parts with a soft-leaded pencil.

2 Adjust the 90-degree fence up or down to center the blade in the stock, set the machine for the biscuit size, index on the marks, and plunge in the blade.

3 Spread glue in the kerfs and surrounding wood, but not on the biscuit. Insert a biscuit and assemble the joint using the play in the kerfs to align the pieces.

Biscuited "T" orientation

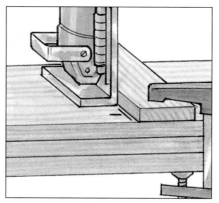

1 Clamp a guide across one piece. Use this guide to line up the other in position so that a row of biscuits can be laid out and marked on both pieces.

2 Set the joiner's fence (or remove it altogether) so that the machine's nose is at right angles to its base. Align the base vertically against the straight guide, and kerf to the marks keeping within the joining piece's edges.

3 Clamp down the second piece and use the benchtop to make sure all the slots align. Then spread glue, insert biscuits, assemble, and clamp.

Offset "L" joint

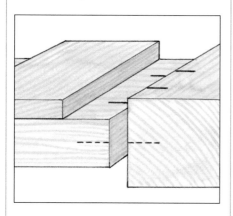

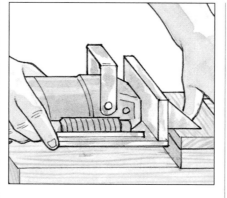

1 Mark for biscuits and stack a shim the same thickness as the offset on the thin part, using the stack to set the fence to cut at the thin stock's center.

2 Place the shim on the thin stock under the fence, to cut mating kerfs at the index marks.

3 Without changing the blade height setting, kerf the thicker piece at the index marks, then spread glue, assemble, and clamp as usual.

Spacing biscuit joints

The spacing of biscuit joints is not critical, every 2-3in (50-80mm) is adequate. In thick-sectioned frameworks, the biscuits can be double inserted across the thickness of the stock, but the joint should be used for center rails and not as a replacement for a mortise-and-tenon on corners of frameworks.

The biscuit jointer can also be used to run grooves along the wood as a housing or locating point for other joints.

Wood knockdown joints

Making miter cuts

1 For maximum-strength miter cuts, the fence has to be set so that the biscuit center is slightly closer to the inner face of the panel. Secure the panel in the vise, and carefully plunge the tool at the marked positions on both pieces.

2 Alternatively, the biscuit jointer's miter fence can be used in conjunction with the mitered edge of the other panel clamped securely and squarely to the workpiece. When cutting mitered joints to the miter fence, fine horizontal blade adjustment can be made. Note that there are numerous alignment marks on the baseplate.

3 Glue the joint together with PVA glue, using a thin wood strip to coat every surface. Remember that particle board absorbs glue, so be generous and work quickly. Drive the joint home with a hammer and scrapwood block, using bar clamps. If there is a lot of gluing to be done, instead of PVA use a synthetic glue.

LEFT: The tusked tenon joint has been used in knockdown furniture for hundreds of years.

Furniture that breaks down into its components is part of a tradition that includes Roman military campaign furniture and "traveling" medieval trestle tables that were designed to be moved on a daily basis. The design of any large piece has to consider its bulk, weight, and maneuverability, if only to move it from the shop into the house. Woodworkers who enjoy the challenge of building all-wood structures that break down into smaller and lighter components will find the glueless knockdown joinery of old still useful today.

The through-keyed, or tusked tenon, is a strong, visible joint that resists racking (movement), but has to be integrated with the overall design. The sliding dovetail, on the other hand, is invisible, and allows furniture to be broken down and reassembled easily—especially when the joint is waxed. However, the effect of solid wood movement in the dovetail cannot be compensated for by tightening or loosening a tenon key, so sliding dovetails work best in short lengths—or as a plywood tongue that stays stable.

The key mortises in tenons can be square, or drilled round, with double-wedged dowels inserted from each side as the key. After the tenon is scribed along its face to mark its exit, it is critical during layout that the key mortise be set back from this line. Otherwise the key will not bear on the upright to pull the joint tight, especially if the wood shrinks. The key mortise has to leave at least a finger's width of material in the short-grain section at the tenon's end or the grain will break out from the wedge's pressure on it, resulting in the wood splitting. Sometimes the end of the key mortise is angled slightly to match the key.

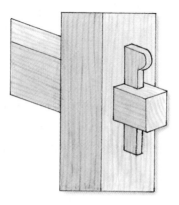

When rails are thick enough, tusk a tenon with a vertical wedge, following the same procedure outlined for a keyed tenon.

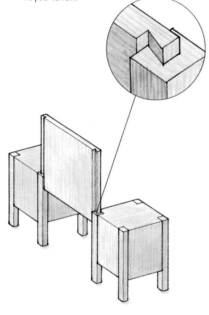

To make moving or shipping easier, use un-glued sliding dovetails to allow bulky furniture to break into components—for example, allowing a desk to separate into its modesty panel, end cabinets, and top.

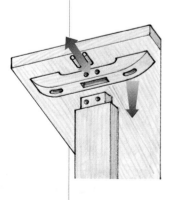

Removable pins in a blind tenon hold it tight, but allow the furniture to be broken down for handling.

Keyed tenon

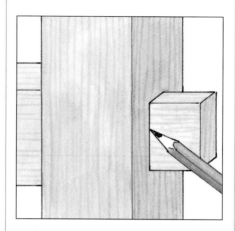

1 Make an overlong through tenon, so that it has some extending material that can be mortised, insert the tenon through, and mark its face where it exits its mortise.

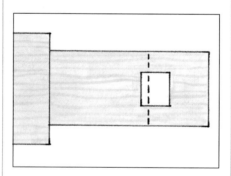

2 Lay out a mortise on the tenon, starting it just inside the line on the tenon face, and leaving enough material to prevent short grain when the mortise is cut.

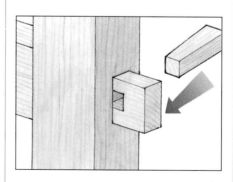

3 Make a key whose outside face tapers slightly, and insert it through the mortise in the tenon so that it bears against the upright and pulls the tenon tight.

Half-dovetail tenon

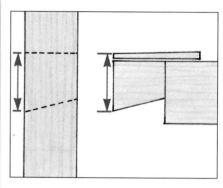

1 Lay out the through mortise for a half-dovetail tenon, so that its bottom end angles to the dovetail and the exiting side is long enough to include a wedge's thickness.

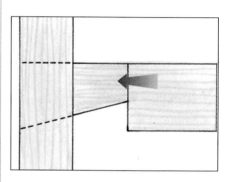

2 Make sure that the tenon can enter the mortise when its top edge is aligned with the top end of the mortise.

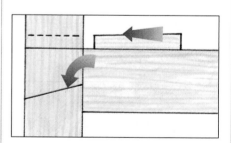

3 Insert the tenon, and drop it down to fit the angles together, then slide in the tapered wedge, shaving it thinner until it stops flush with the tenon end.

BASIC FINISHING

Preparation

No finish is better than its preparation. A smooth, clean surface is essential, as any blemish will be exaggerated by the finish. Use your fingers and eyes to check for faults very carefully—though you will soon be able to judge instinctively whether a surface has been adequately prepared.

Brushes for finishing

Brushes are an important part of any finisher's equipment, and most suppliers offer a variety of designs for specialist applications. They are made of different bristles and hairs, both synthetic and natural, and there are many names given to these brushes. Generally, the higher the price, the better the quality of bristle and brush. In the long run, it is worth purchasing quality brushes. The finest hair commands the highest price, with badger, horse, sable, camel and hog providing the raw materials

Natural-hair brushes give a fine finish and have a spring in them, which allows the material being coated to cling to the hair. Brush manufacturers use a mixture of bristles to suit requirements. Sable artists' and round brushes are the most expensive, but create the best results.

Care of brushes

- Keep mops and brushes in a polythylene bag.

- Suspend brushes in solvent to soak them clean.

- Think of brushes as tools. Take good care of them, and they will last for years and pay for themselves.

Mottler

These are used to mottle glazes and scumbles when marbling or graining. They are made from hog hair.

Badger or softener

These are for "softening in" grain or marble effects. They are made from badger hair.

Wire brush

Useful for opening up the grain when applying a limed finish, and for stripping moldings and carvings.

Pencil brush

These are used for touching up and for graining and grain simulation. They are sold in sizes 2 to 10, and are made from camel, sable, or synthetic hair.

Swan or quill

These are small brushes for touching up.

Mop

These are used for applying stains, color or polish. They are available in sizes 2 to 20, and are made from hog, or sable.

Flat or paintbrush

These can be used to apply stains, varnish, undercoats, and glazes. They are made from hog or horse hair.

Stippling brush

Made from coarse hog-hair bristles and used to produce a decorative stippled effect on wood and other substrates.

Grass brush

These are made from vegetable fibers. They are ideal for bleaching, since ordinary decorating brushes are not resistant to acid and tend to shed their bristles when used with bleach.

Stencil brush

These are specifically designed for stencilling. They are shaped like shaving brushes and are used with a dabbing action.

Flitch

These are for work on moldings and edges. They are made from hog hair.

Dulling brush

These brushes, made from short hog hair, are used for dulling down finishes.

Flogger

These are for use in the graining process, and are made from hog hair.

Bruises, dents, and scratches

Indentations in the surface are caused either by the compression of fibers (in the case of bruises and dents) or by the fibers being broken by scratches. These faults must be removed before you begin sanding. If the bruises or scratches are deep, it is best to raise them, instead of attempting to sand them out. Heavy sanding is likely to result in an uneven surface, and on a veneered piece it may even cause further problems by breaking through the veneer.

The way to raise bruises is to swell the fibers of the wood using a combination of heat and steam. The expansion of the fibers levels the surface. However, this may not work effectively when the fibers are badly broken—especially with particularly deep scratches across the grain—but swelling will at least reduce the amount of filling or sanding needed to provide you with a surface fit for finishing.

Ironing out a bruise

1 Before ironing out the bruises, make sure that any previous finish is thoroughly cleaned off the piece.

2 Dampen the surface around the bruise with a cloth soaked in water. Always check that the water and cloth are clean—it is easy to discolor the wood. Use a clean, white cloth— not one that has been used for staining.

After steaming out the bruise, leave the surface to dry and then sand with fine sandpaper.

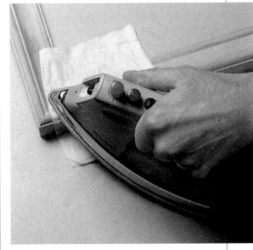

3 Lay a damp piece of white cloth over the bruise. Press an iron on the damp cloth. Make sure the iron is very hot —the steam should not be allowed to disperse before it has entered the wood. Press down with the iron until the steam stops. Remove the iron and cloth to inspect the bruise. If the bruise is still there, repeat the operation, soaking the cloth in water each time.

Staining wood

Stains consist of dyes dissolved in a medium and are used for coloring wood. They soak into the grain of the wood, giving it a tint—unlike the pigments used for coloring paint, which lie on top of the surface as solid matter.

The medium carrying the dye determines the characteristics of the stain—such as drying time, compatibility, and spread. A stain should enhance the grain and improve the appearance of the wood. It needs to be easy to apply, has to be compatible with the finish, and should dry within a reasonable time. It should also maintain its color without fading. Stains are particularly good at upgrading wood, and making unattractive surfaces more interesting.

Water stains

Water stains are supplied in a dry-powder or crystal form, which can be dissolved in water. They have been used for hundreds of years, and were originally made with vegetable dyes obtained from trees and plants. They are now the cheapest of all stains, and can be bought by mail order from finishing suppliers. Although the original natural dyes are no longer available, the manmade alternatives are useful to have around the workshop.

The most useful dyes are Van Dyck crystals (brown), mahogany crystals (warm brown), and nigrosine (black). You can mix these dyes in order to produce different colors. By changing the ratio of water to powder, you can adjust the depth of color. Always test water stains on a piece of waste wood before applying them. Also check the effect of adding a finish.

Working with water stains

Apply the stain with a cloth or brush. You will find that a brush is best for moldings, corners, and carvings, and that a cloth holds the most stain. Wet the wood before applying the first coat of stain, to aid an even spread. Rub the stain into the grain, keeping a wet edge all the time.

For a tabletop, you will need about a cupful of stain, but make sure you have enough for the whole piece. Use plenty of stain, but do not actually pour it onto the surface. Water stains dry slowly, so you will have time to wipe off the excess with a cloth or paper towel. Once the stain has dried, go over any light areas with another coat.

Hints for staining

- Although stains dry lighter, they are darkened by subsequent finishes—so test the effect on a piece of waste wood or hidden area first.

- Remember, you can always make a surface darker with more stain, but it is impossible to lighten the color without resorting to bleach.

- A dark stain has a stronger effect on a light wood than on a dark one.

- Always keep a wet edge when applying stain, to avoid patchy color.

- Plan your staining pattern before starting, so that you maintain a uniform color.

- If the workpiece is dampened very slightly with water, that will give some idea of the color effects of applying a clear finish before or after staining.

- When trying to match colors, do so gradually. Do not attempt to mix the perfect combination of dyes straight off—instead, use progressive coats of individual dyes.

Using water stains

1 Water stains are supplied in powder form. Make up the stain by adding the powder to water in different proportions—depending on the color required. Add more stain to make it darker, and more water to make it lighter.

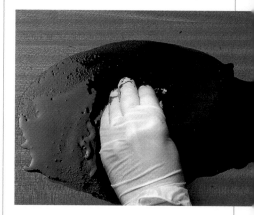

2 Apply the stain with a rag. Use plenty of stain, keeping it wet on the surface all the time, to produce an even spread. Rub it in with a circular motion. Use a brush for staining moldings, corners, and carvings, but, as with a flat surface, always keep a wet edge.

Oil dyes

These dyes are supplied both ready-mixed and in powder form. They are mineral spirits, dissolved in naphtha or a similar hydrocarbon solvent. They are classified by wood color, with names like "dark mahogany" or "light oak." However, all these dyes can be used on any wood, and the names are no more than general guides.

Working with oil dyes

Oil dyes do not raise the grain, but they do bite into deep and uneven grain (as occurs in beech), which may show up as dark patches. It is therefore important to prepare rough areas especially carefully. Wood dyes are convenient to use and penetrate deeply into the wood.

Alcohol stains

These stains are oil-based stains dissolved in denatured alcohol. Professional woodworkers prefer to use them because of the wide range of colors available.

Dyes are named by their color (for example, yellow and green), except for Bismarck brown, which, confusingly, is nearer to red. They can be applied by brush, cloth, or spray gun and are also used for dipping work. Because of the alcohol base, they can be mixed with shellac polish for color-matching and touching up during the polishing process.

Alcohol stains dry very fast. As a result, they are ideal for spraying. Also, the wood is ready for coating almost immediately. However, the fact that they dry so quickly makes them difficult to apply successfully, and can result in a patchy finish. Use alcohol stains for items such as toys that are small enough to be dipped in a small dipping tank or container. One disadvantage of an

Sealing inlay before staining

1 The contrast in color between different inlays may be lost when a piece is stained. To prevent this, apply white or blond polish to seal an inlay before staining.

2 Using a No. 6 artist's brush, carefully pick out the inlay, making sure that no part of it is missed. Leave to dry for at least 15 minutes.

3 Once the sealer is dry, apply the stain over the whole panel. Use a water or oil dye, but not an alcohol stain. Denatured alcohol would dissolve the polish and ruin the seal. Rub in the stain evenly, applying it wet in circular motions and then straightening up along the grain. Leave to dry.

4 Once the stain has dried fully, the unsealed parts of the piece will have changed color, but the sealed parts will have retained their natural color.

alcohol base is that, if coats of shellac are applied later, they are likely to lift the stain and affect the color.

Working with alcohol stains

Alcohol stains are sold in powder form, as aniline dyes, and mixed to the desired color—more powder being used to provide a darker shade. The dyes can be mixed together for a wider range of colors. Apply the stain sparingly, or the dye will be removed by the polish. When dipping, leave the item in the tank for about five minutes. It is a good idea to add a small quantity of transparent French polish to the formulation to "fix" the alcohol stain on the wood.

Pigment stains

This range of finishes is made from finely-ground pigments, suspended in a medium. The pigments do not dissolve, as dyes do. Pigment stains give a semi-opaque color to wood. They are useful for improving low-grade wood—producing greater tone and making the piece more attractive.

Working with pigment stains

Pigment stains are available in a ready-mixed range of colors. Apply them generously with a brush or cloth. Be sure to remove surplus stain, otherwise the color may look patchy and opaque.

Wax stains

Wax stains are supplied in soft-wax form—ready-made in various colors—and are used directly on the wood, or over existing stain. Wax stains cannot be used under finishes such as poly-urethane or varnishes because they stop the top layer from drying fully.

Working with wax stains

Apply wax stains with a cloth, like a wax polish, rubbing the wax into the wood. Leave the surface to dry, preferably overnight, before buffing.

Bleaching wood

Bleaches are used to lighten the color of wood. This may be desirable for purely aesthetic reasons, as a matter of taste, on new materials or older, darkened wood. Bleaches can also be used to remove blemishes and stains, or make darker components compatible with other parts of a piece. Bleaching may be needed to tone down the color of stripped wood, or to remove ink or water marks.

There are many different types of bleaches, and the household variety can be used on wood—though the best approach is either to mix your own, using oxalic acid with water, or to buy a special wood-bleach (sold in a two-part pack) that generates a stronger reaction with the surface. For the latter product, a neutralizer is essential—in order to halt the chemical reaction, and ensure that any residue of bleach does not further harm finishes. A 50-percent solution of white vinegar in water is the traditional way to neutralize two-part bleach, with plenty of water to clean the surface.

Since bleaches are likely to react with metal (they are used to reverse the effects of iron filings on wood), always use glass, plastic, or earthenware containers when working with these chemicals. They are dangerous substances, so read the manufacturer's instructions carefully, and follow the safety advice given. Always keep bleaches away from children; and never store or use in food containers—in case they are mistakenly eaten or drunk.

Using two-part bleaches

1 Apply the contents of pack "A" (or "1") with a brush, keeping both the container and brush clearly marked to avoid confusion between this and pack "B" (or "2"). Always wear heavy protective gloves, and apply the chemical thoroughly so that the piece has an even coat.

2 Five minutes after coating the surface with the first application, apply the contents of pack "B" (or "2"), also with a brush, and also wearing gloves. The surface will look darker at this stage. The reaction of the two chemicals lightens the wood, and will sometimes produce a foam. Leave the piece until the desired effect is achieved.

3 Once the required color has been achieved, the reaction must be neutralized. Use a 50-percent solution of vinegar and water, applied with a clean brush.

4 Once it has dried, the bleached item will have an even, paler color than it had originally.

Grain fillers

Some woods, such as oak, have an open grain structure that makes the perfectly smooth finish characteristic of French polishing hard to achieve. With these woods, the open pores need to be filled with a fine powder, applied as a paste or liquid. This choking of the grain also makes polishing quicker, as the grain does not have to be filled with polish, which is the alternative more time-consuming solution.

Originally, grain fillers were made of plaster of Paris mixed with water and a pigment, but these plaster fillers tended to turn white and show up in the grain. Modern grain fillers are therefore made from a mixture of filling powder, binder, pigment, and solvent. There are many variations on this theme, each

recommended for specific tasks—the distinguishing feature being the type of binder used.

Fillers are sold in a variety of colors. A selection of mahogany, walnut, and light oak is sufficient to start with. Oil dyes or pigment colors can be mixed with neutral filler to make any color you want.

Use burlap or a coarse cloth to apply grain fillers, rubbing them into the grain in a circular motion. Do not work the filler in the direction of the grain, or the filler may not hold in the pores. Wipe off excess filler across the grain with a piece of burlap.

Applying grain filler

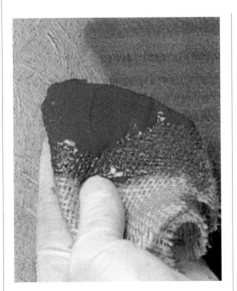

1 Prepare the surface to be filled by sanding and staining if required. Make sure the surface is clean of dust and dirt so that the grain filler clings effectively to the wood. Use burlap to apply the thick grain filler. Take a hand-sized piece of burlap and bunch it into a swab, before dipping it into the grain filler. The swab must be well-charged with filler.

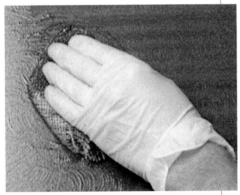

2 Rub the swab over the surface using a circular motion, keeping it wet at all times and sliding across the surface, to push the filler gently into the pores. Apply more grain filler as required and keep rubbing until the whole surface has been covered. Wipe off surplus filler with a clean piece of burlap, working across the grain (for fillers that can be thinned with mineral spirit, use a rag dampened with mineral spirit). The filled surface loses some of its grain pattern. Very lightly sand the surface to remove any remaining surplus filler.

BASIC FINISHING TECHNIQUES

Most woodworkers are introduced to finishing by the varnishing of their own projects. Varnish can be the perfect finish for specific tasks, but there are times when French polishing, oiling, and waxing are more suitable—and they are surprisingly easy to accomplish.

French polishing

The simple principle of French polishing is to build up a lustrous finish with thin coats of transparent or colored polish. The joy of this finish is that it is worked into the surface, rather than laid on top like a paint, varnish, or sprayed lacquer.

French polish in its many guises is possibly most highly regarded on mahogany, as the close grain of the wood is admirably suited to the finish, and its attractive figure is enhanced by the "depth" of the polish. Woods such as walnut, rosewood, sycamore, and stained pine are equally suitable. Oak is less so, and is usually given a wax finish.

Building up

Once a sealing coat has been applied, and the surface has been lightly sanded (to remove dust nibs) and dusted, you can start applying the polish to build up the finish. Start with straight strokes following the grain, then across the grain. Maintain a slight pressure. The pressure is equivalent to that needed to plaster walls or spread butter on toast. Having covered the surface two or three times, continue with circular movements, which help to smooth out the polish. Try to maintain even pressure throughout each circle; there is a tendency to press harder as your hand moves toward your body on the inward strokes. Use 5in to 6in (125mm to 150mm) circles, making sure the pad covers the circle. Larger pieces, such as tabletops, need larger polishing pads; and smaller items require smaller pads.

Making a French polishing pad

1 The polishing pad is used to apply French polish. Start by folding a 6in² (150mm²) piece of batting in half (cotton can be used but the result will not be as good).

Maintain the flow of polish with increased pressure whenever the pad seems to stick or drag. The surface is likely to soak up polish fast at this stage, so you will have to add polish to the pad frequently as the flow dries up. Continue to work the polish in with a combination of circular and figure-eight movements, keeping the pad constantly on the move.

Try to keep the pad away from soft areas of polish. Test to see if the finish is still tacky, and, if it is, leave it to harden for a few minutes. When the finish develops an overall sheen, finish off with straight strokes, following the grain, and then leave to dry.

2 Fold over the ends of the batting to make a point. At this stage, it will look a little like a pointed hat.

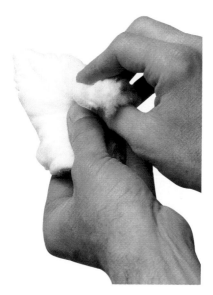

3 Fold the long ends toward the center, and tuck them in.

4 Work the batting into a pear shape. It is important that the sole is flat when held between the fingers. The idea is to produce a firm core to the polishing pad.

5 Place the batting core diagonally on the corner of a piece of 9in² (230mm²) white-cotton cloth, with the sole of the batting facing down. The cloth must not be starched or colored.

7 Make another fold, and turn the ends together under the core, folding the cloth and forming a point.

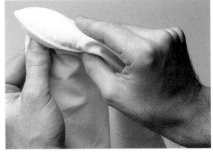

8 Pull the excess cloth across and start to twist together to tighten.

6 Turn the cloth over and hold the core between the index finger and the thumb, to let the folds of the cotton cloth drop down to the sides. Make a fold to form the point.

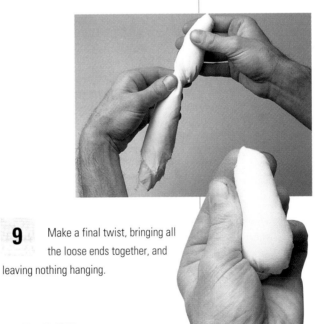

9 Make a final twist, bringing all the loose ends together, and leaving nothing hanging.

Tips box

When adding polish to the pad, the polish must soak through the core, but must not then drip through the outer cloth. You need to be able to produce a small trickle of polish by cupping the pad in your hand (with your forefinger running along the point) and gently squeezing.

10 When polishing, hold the pad between the thumb and fingers. When not in use, the pad must be stored in a sealed container to prevent it from drying out.

Sealing the surface

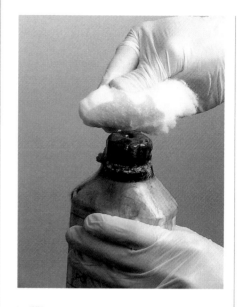

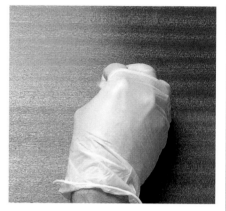

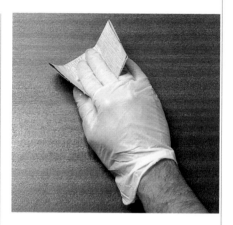

1 Coating the surface with an initial coat of shellac is known as sealing. Use a piece of batting that has previously been used in a pad (a new piece will leave fluff on the surface). Load it with polish from an unbreakable container of polish, with a small hole or slot in the lid to let the finish out slowly. Add about two teaspoons of polish into the batting. Squeeze the batting to remove any excess polish. The batting must feel damp, but not soaking wet.

2 Wipe the batting across the surface following the grain. Use no pressure at all for the first two or three passes. Continue to apply the polish in tight circles, and, as the batting dries out, increase the pressure, reloading when it dries out completely. Continue to work the surface until it becomes too sticky to apply more polish. Leave to dry.

3 When the shellac coat has dried, the surface will feel rough. Lightly sand (a process known as denibbing) using fine 320 silicon-carbide, self-lubricating sandpaper.

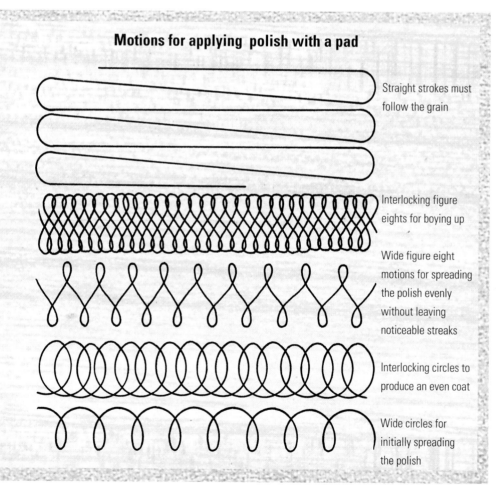

Motions for applying polish with a pad

Straight strokes must follow the grain

Interlocking figure eights for boying up

Wide figure eight motions for spreading the polish evenly without leaving noticeable streaks

Interlocking circles to produce an even coat

Wide circles for initially spreading the polish

Color matching

Any discrepancies in the color will show up once the polish has dried. Wooden pins in chair joints may be too light, and there may be shading around joints in veneer. Stand back and look at the piece to get an overview of the finish. Color irregularities will need to be touched up and disguised. Look carefully at the surface to judge which colors are visible, or lacking, in the wood.

Use alcohol stains for matching colors, and mix them in with the polish. Go easy with these stains, as the colors are strong, and are only required in a much diluted form to produce a tint. Remember, it is easier to make a surface darker than lighter (as extra coats can be easily added, but not removed), so mix colors gradually. Apply the color with a cloth or brush.

Defects such as knots, glue marks, and wood filler must be touched up and hidden using pigments. Make sure that the pigment does not show up as a blob of solid color, and, if necessary, use an artist's brush to add flecks of color to imitate the grain.

Tips for French polishing

- Always keep plenty of polish on the pad—but never too much.

- Use linseed oil sparingly—little and often is best.

- Try to maintain an even pressure when using the pad.

- Work in a dust-free environment.

- To clear excess polish from a pad, simply press it down onto a clean surface.

- Try to keep the workshop at about 65°F (18°C) for polishing.

Building up the surface

1 Once the surface has been sealed and lightly sanded, it is time to start applying polish using a polishing pad. This is known as building up. First load the pad with polish by opening up the outer layer of cloth and pouring polish into the core until it is saturated. Squeeze out the excess by pressing onto paper or a spare piece of wood.

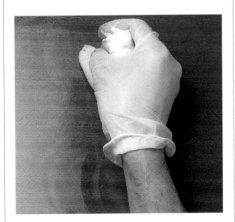

2 Build up the polish with straight strokes along the grain, making four or five passes. Then move the pad in circles. Increase the pressure as the pad dries out, and then load again. Use figure eight patterns, as well as circles.

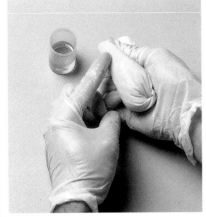

3 After the surface has been worked with four or five applications, it will become sticky, and the pad will need to be lubricated with linseed oil. Dip your finger in the oil, and rub it onto the sole of the pad. Do not use too much oil. Continue working the pad in circular motions.

4 The building up will have created a finish by now, but continue to work the pad around the piece in circles, figure eight movements, and straight up and down. Load the pad when it starts to dry out—doing so little but often.

Finishing off

You are now ready to finish off the surface, using the pad—which should be ready for use in its airtight container. Apply polish, and start working on the surface. If the pad starts to drag, put a touch of boiled linseed oil on the sole for lubrication. This will leave a smear on the surface. As an even coat of polish appears, start working the pad "dry" adding only denatured alcohol, to level the surface.

Finally, add polish to the pad, and, using straight strokes, work along the grain from end to end. Leave to dry once a gloss finish has been achieved.

Removing the oil

For a really high gloss finish, add only denatured alcohol to the pad, and work over the surface with circular and straight movements. The polishing pad must feel cold to the touch and not moist. The alcohol will take off the last of the remaining oil, and give the surface a high-gloss finish.

Dulling

A satin or flat finish is popular, as it provides a more natural-looking finish. Instead of polishing with a pad and denatured alcohol, dull the piece when dry with pumice powder or fine steel wool and wax. The pumice powder can be applied straight onto the surface, and worked with a shoe brush. Follow the grain using a mop or brush for dulling moldings, and corners.

When dulling with steel wool and wax be careful not to use too much wax. Once the surface is dry, wipe off the excess with a clean, soft cloth to produce a satin finish.

The steel wool needs to be fine—either 000 or 0000. However, test the steel wool on a practice piece before dulling to find out which is suitable. Sometimes 0000 steel wool is so fine that it actually glosses the surface.

Polishes

The technique is called French polishing, but the polishes used have different names, and different applications.

French polish

French polish is orange, and is used mainly on mahogany.

Button polish

Button polish is a golden-brown color.

Garnet polish

This is dark brown, and is recommended for the renovation of old surfaces.

White polish

White polish is made from shellac that has been bleached, and is a milky-white color. It is used for light woods such as sycamore and ash.

Transparent polish

Transparent polish is made from shellac that has been bleached and dewaxed.

Dulling with pumice powder

1 Pour the pumice powder into a shallow tray. Pour carefully, making sure the powder does not spill around the work.

2 Work the pumice powder against the piece by following the grain, making sure that all areas are covered and treated evenly. Pumice powder should be kept clean, and stored in a dry place.

Working with colors

Wood can be colored with either pigments or dyes. The difference between the two is that dyes are dissolved in a solvent, and penetrate into the grain of the wood, whereas pigments are used in suspension, and lie on top of the grain. This is why pigments fall to the bottom of a can, having been mixed with a liquid. They are used for disguising or hiding a defect or knot, or for touching up a polished surface. Dyes are the coloring agents of stains, and can be dissolved in alcohol (in the case of aniline dyes) or other solvents, such as water or oil.

Dyes and stains

Dyes become part of the wood, and are used for matching woods. Their translucence allows the grain to show through. The idea is to use colors to bring out the color inherent in the wood. This might mean adding warmth with a red dye, or even cutting back red hues by using green. Sometimes the whole piece will need coloring, sometimes only small parts—especially during restoration, or when components do not match within a new piece. It is very common for the legs or rails of a table to have been milled from a different batch of lumber from that of the top. As a result, the colors may vary slightly, but this can be rectified using dyes.

Mixing colors for matching

1 To camouflage new or restored sections of a piece with matched colors, mix alcohol stains with French polish and denatured alcohol to produce a translucent color that does not mask the grain. A paper "boat" is the traditional container for mixing colors, but any non-food container can be used.

2 Mix a shade by adding a small quantity of color at a time. Use a No. 6 artist's brush to mix the colors with a 50:50 combination of denatured alcohol and French polish. Make sure the color is thoroughly blended into the polish and denatured alcohol.

Oil finishes

Oiling is one of the oldest treatments for preserving and finishing wood. Originally, linseed oil—which is derived from flax and dries by oxidation—was used. Today, oil finishes are becoming increasingly popular, as they can be restored and maintained easily—and, unlike varnishes and sprayed finishes, they do not conceal the wood's tactile qualities.

It is true that oils do not have the resistance of more-modern finishes, and oiled surfaces are likely to become marked. However, they are not as vulnerable as French-polished surfaces. Teak and Danish oils dry faster than linseed, and they represent the easiest method of finishing wood.

If you want to stain the wood, do so before oiling. Use a water stain—avoid oil dyes, as they react with the finish, resulting in patchy coloring.

Linseed oil

A linseed oil finish is simple to produce. However, it takes time to dry, and new wood will need a number of coats, especially if it is porous. During the complex process of oxidation, raw linseed oil actually gains weight as it dries, but it does not dry as fast as the boiled variety. Boiled linseed is partially oxidized and takes a day to dry—compared with three days for pure linseed, which is more resistant to external conditions. However, neither linseed oil nor boiled linseed oil are suitable for oiling exterior woodwork.

Apply the oil with a cloth and rub it into the wood. Leave it to dry for at least 24 hours. You can try mixing linseed oil equally with mineral spirits for the first

The use of an oiled finish on this box has brought out the natural, rich patina of the wood.

few coats to encourage the finish to penetrate the wood and dry faster. Next, apply coats of oil until a surface film is achieved. Warming linseed oil lowers its viscosity, and aids penetration. However, it combusts easily, so the safest way to warm it is to pour the oil into a container and stand it in a pot of very hot water. Check if the oil has dried by wiping your hand across the surface and looking for oil marks before applying the next coat. Once you are satisfied with the finish, buff the surface with a soft cloth.

Teak and Danish oils

Teak and Danish oils dry faster than linseed, and provide a more resistant film on the surface. Teak oil produces a slight sheen; Danish oil leaves a more natural, low luster and is therefore better for new pieces; use linseed on older ones. Some of these oils are tinted with color. They all include driers, and sometimes tung oil to enhance their protective nature. You can buy pure tung oil, which comes from the seeds of the Chinese tung tree. It is used in a similar manner to Danish or teak oils. Tung produces a durable finish for exterior hardwood joinery.

Oil finishes

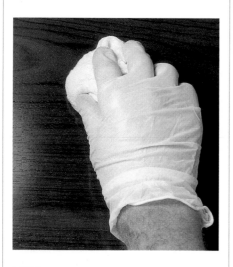

1 Load a soft cloth with enough oil to apply a wet, uniform coat to the surface, then rub the oil evenly into the whole surface. It is important to check that the grain is completely wetted, otherwise the finish will turn out patchy. Use circular strokes at first, then straighten up and follow the grain to finish.

2 Leave the oil to dry overnight. Some deep-grained woods will soak up most of the oil, leaving little on the surface. Lightly sand the rough surface with fine 320 self-lubricating sandpaper. Apply further coats until the required finish is achieved, leaving each coat to dry overnight and lightly sanding between applications—three or four coats of oil are usually enough.

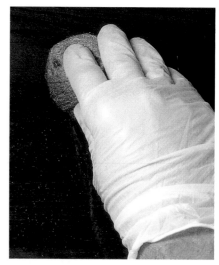

3 When dry, take a palm-sized piece of fine 0000 steel wool, and give the surface a final sheen. Rub in the direction of the grain, maintaining an even pressure, and stroke over the whole piece to produce a satin finish. Finally, burnish the surface with a clean, soft cloth to remove any dust.

Waxed finishes

Waxing is a traditional way of protecting and enhancing wood—beeswax was used by the ancient Egyptians, and wax finishes have been found on Jacobean furniture—and to this day wax remains the most popular finish for oak in England. Only the introduction of French polishing diminished the popularity and general use of wax. Waxing produces a natural finish. Like an oiled surface, it is never complete, and the constant rubbing by hands continues to improve the finish, deepening its patina, over the years.

Beeswax and carnauba wax have been the most consistent ingredients of furniture wax. The two are often mixed together with turpentine, by warming, to produce hard but compliant waxes.

As with any finish, it is important to prepare the workpiece carefully. Apply two thin coats of shellac sanding sealer before waxing, to protect the wood and fill the pores. Sand with fine silicon carbide between, and after, the coats of sealer.

Tips for waxing

- Seal with shellac sanding sealer before waxing.

- Make sure the wax is dry before further applications.

- Use small quantities of wax.

- Apply the wax evenly.

- The final finish depends on the burnishing, rather than the build-up of wax.

Waxing

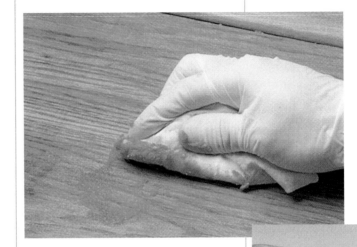

1 Apply the wax with a soft cloth folded into layers. Pick up the wax on the cloth, and rub it liberally into the grain, using a circular motion. Level off, following the grain. Make sure the surface is covered evenly and thoroughly.

2 Leave the piece to dry for 15 minutes, and then apply further coats of wax with fine 000 steel wool, rubbing with the grain. Build up the finish gradually, leaving each coat to dry overnight. Four or five coats should be enough.

3 For a more lustrous finish, buff the waxed surface with a soft cloth. Do not press too hard—it is possible to break up the even coat of wax.

4 After waxing, the natural beauty of the piece will show up clearly.

Varnishing

Varnish is a protective finish favored by joiners and carpenters. It is suitable for pieces that will be exposed to continual wear and tear, such as staircases, windows, and doors. Varnishes come in a variety of forms, with different properties and a range of applications. Unlike polishes, they sit on the surface of the wood as a coat. Some have good waterproofing qualities, others are fast-drying. Today they are known by their resin ingredients, polyurethane being the most common. They are applied with a brush, and are available in gloss, matt, and satin finishes. The matt and satin varnishes contain a flatting agent to produce an irregular surface that does not reflect light with the same directness as gloss. A matt finish shows the nature of the wood better than gloss, on which reflections tend to hide the figure.

Tips for varnishing

- Decant varnish into a can, and attach a wire across the top of the can—so that you can wipe off excess varnish from the brush.

- Make sure there is no dust in the workshop. Sprinkle the floor with water, and check that your clothes are free from hairs and dust.

- Use a good-quality brush for varnishing. A cheap paintbrush will give a very poor varnished finish.

- Press with a thumbnail to test varnish for hardness.

Producing a flat finish

1 A better flat finish is obtained by working with gloss varnish than by applying proprietary flat varnishes. First, apply gloss varnish, as usual. Then abrade the dry surface with fine 000 steel wool. This creates very fine scratches on the surface of the piece, reducing its ability to reflect light. Always work with the grain, rubbing gently.

2 Having rubbed the piece with steel wool, apply wax with a soft cloth, following the grain. Do not use too much wax, otherwise it will be difficult to buff later.

Applying varnish

Special brushes are made for varnishing, and these are worth the extra cost. Apply the varnish across the grain first, to spread it evenly over the surface. Then, applying very little pressure, draw the brush diagonally across the surface. Finish off by spreading with the grain, exerting a very light pressure. This method will leave the fewest brushmarks.

3 Leave the waxed piece to dry for an hour or so. Then burnish the waxed surface with a clean, soft cloth. Rub along the grain. This will produce a lustrous flat finish, full of color.

Small table

The techniques and processes used in making this small table can be applied to many other designs that use a frame construction. The finished table is a classic, timeless design. Its construction covers many of the processes that will form the basis of further projects: wood selection and sawing, measuring and marking, cutting joints, making a mitered frame, and finishing.

In later projects, and as your tool kit increases, you may consider using power hand tools or machinery. However, at this stage, "bite the bullet" and master these basic processes by hand. The feel of the hand tool is basic to an understanding of the material.

Choosing wood

Your choice will be based on color, workability, availability, and cost. Hardwood is preferable to softwood when beginning furnituremaking. Softwoods are not recommended, as they do not saw or chisel crisply. For this project, buy wood with a straight grain. You will not need to maximize grain pattern or avoid defects, so laying out will be simplified.

Color

Choose a wood that will best suit the place where the table is to be used. Lighter woods could be English oak, American white oak or beech, maple, or sycamore. Medium woods could be mahogany, teak, or American red oak, and dark woods could be American black walnut, French walnut, or rosewood.

Workability

Choose a wood that works well, is not so soft that it is difficult to achieve crisp saw and chisel cuts, nor so hard that it is brittle. The wood should have a close grain and good working properties.

LEFT: A table may seem too complicated a project for a beginner, but the joints used are ones that are likely to be familiar to woodworkers of all levels.

Cutting list

No.	Sawed	Planed
4	LEGS 1ft 10in x 1½in x 1½in (560mm x 40mm x 40mm)	1ft 7in x 1¼in x 1¼in (480mm x 30mm x 30mm)
4	TOP RAILS 12in x 2in x 1in (305mm x 50mm x 25mm)	9½in x 1¾in x ¾in (240mm x 45mm x 20mm)
4	BOTTOM RAILS 12in x 1½in x 1in (305mm x 40mm x 25mm)	9½in x 1¼in x ¾in (240mm x 30mm x 20mm)
4	TOP FRAME SIDES 1ft 4in x 3¼in x 1in (406mm x 80mm x 25mm)	1ft 2in x 3in x ¾in (350mm x 75mm x 20mm)

+ masking tape, finishing, adhesive, dowels, screws and sheet material for inset top measuring 9in x 9in x ¼in (230mm x 230mm x 6mm)

Exploded diagram

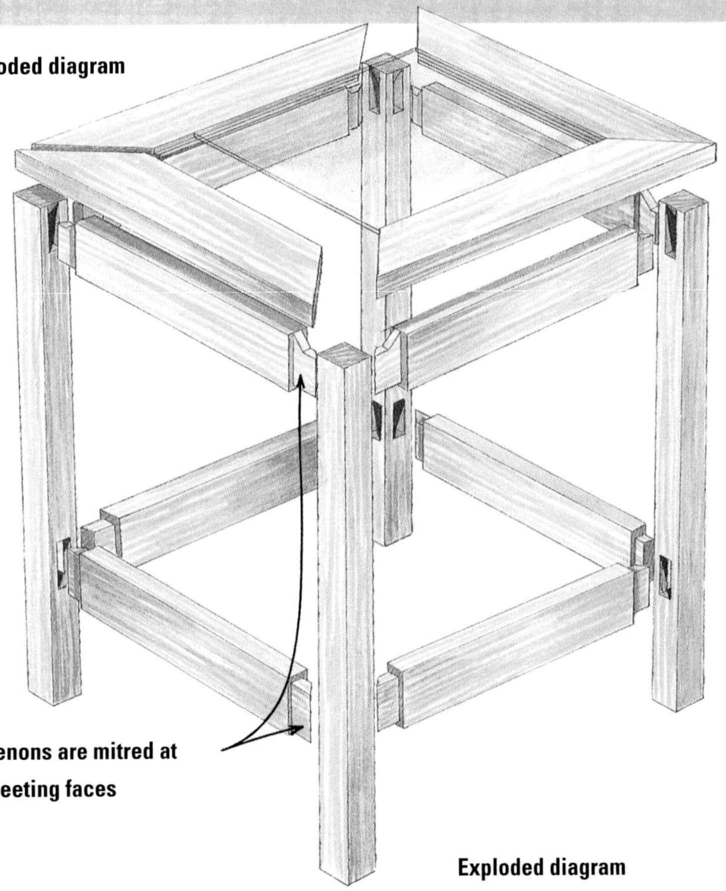

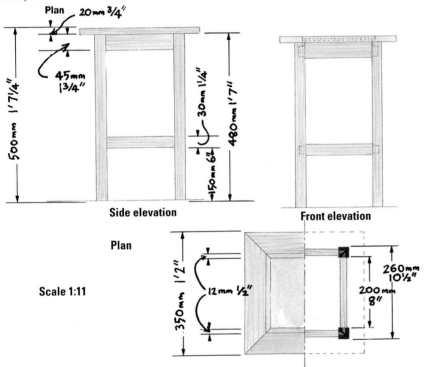

Tenons are mitred at meeting faces

Plans

The drawings on this page show the elevations and sections, together with an exploded perspective view of the finished piece.

Plan 20mm ³/₄″

45mm 1³/₄″

500mm 1′7¼″

30mm 1¼″

150mm 6″

480mm 1′7″

Side elevation

Front elevation

Exploded diagram

Sectional end elevation

Plan

Scale 1:11

350mm 1′2″

12mm ½″

260mm 10½″

200mm 8″

3 Cut the components from the marked board, using a panel saw.

4 Plane all components, and mark them with face and edge marks.

Timber purchase

1 Buy wood as a sawn board. You must make an allowance for waste in converting it from its sawn state to planed size. The length of 240mm (9½in) for the rails allows 200mm (8in) between shoulders, plus 20mm (¾in) each end for tenons. Two thicknesses of board are needed, 40mm (1½in) and 25mm (1in). Buy one board of each thickness from which to cut the components.

Mark and cut components

2 Mark the components onto the sawn board with chalk, making an allowance for the saw cuts (right).

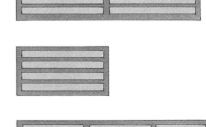

Mark out legs of table underframe

5 Mark the four legs together. Set the legs with the face sides uppermost, and the face edge toward you. Hold them together with a clamp (above).

6 Using a pencil, mark the length of the legs and the position where the rails will be fitted. Then mark the length of the mortises. The lower rails have a small ⅛in (3mm) shoulder on the top and bottom. The top rails have a shoulder on the bottom, and a sloping haunch at the top. A haunch is a shortened portion on the tenon. It helps lock the joint, to prevent the frame from twisting out of line.

7 Pencil in the mortise waste. Then, at the top and bottom of the legs—at the mortise positions—scribe a line with a craft knife ⅛in (3mm) inside the pencil marks, indicating the rail positions at the ends of the mortises.

Transfer marks to the face edge

8 Unclamp the four legs, and, with a try square, transfer all the pencil marks from the face side to the face edge. Then transfer the scribe lines on the ends and at the ends of the mortises, and pencil in the waste. This will give you four legs, with joints marked on the eight inside faces. Complete the top and bottom cut lines all around the legs.

Gauge mortises

9 Set the mortise gauge pins to the width of the mortise chisel at the pin points. Then set the gauge so that the mortise marks are central on the legs. Do this by marking the points from one side, then turning and marking from the other side, adjusting to correct any discrepancy. Make the marks from the face side and edge (below).

10 Mark the eight rails of the table underframe—four top and four bottom. Clamp the upper set together, and mark the lengths on the four face edges with a craft knife (above). Mark the length of 8in (200mm) between the shoulders, plus an extra ¾in (20mm) on each end for the tenons, giving a total length of 9½in (240mm). Take off the clamp.

11 Now repeat this procedure with the lower set of rails clamped together. Use the cut lines on one of the top rails to mark the precise position on this set, and to ensure both are exactly the same.

12 Check the marking and transfer these lines to the other three faces of each rail (right). Always use the square from the face side or the face edge.

13 Cut the rails exactly to length. Then, with the pins of the mortise gauge as already set to the mortise chisel, adjust the stock to center on the rails and mark the tenons around the end of the rails. Now mark the shoulders and haunches on the tenon sides, using a marking gauge. Pencil the waste that will be removed. Recheck all marking.

Tips box

- Hardwoods soon blunt chisels. Regularly resharpen to avoid tearing the wood fibers.

- Place a try square on the face of the rail to use as a guide for drilling vertically.

Cut mortises in legs

14 There are 16 mortises to cut in the legs. Remember to cut to the shoulder line, not the penciled position of the rail (above).

15 Hold the work in the vise, and chop out the waste up to the lines.

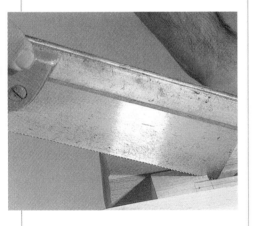

16 In the eight mortises for the top rails, make the entry for the haunch, saw down at the ends of the mortise (above).

17 Chop out the waste to accept the haunch (above).

Saw tenons on rails

18 There are eight tenons with haunch and shoulder, and eight with two shoulders. Saw down to the shoulders on all tenon pieces in the same way. Then cut the sloping line of the haunch (above).

19 Lay each piece flat, to cut the main tenon shoulder (above).

Drilling for the pocket screws

20 Mark two drill holes in the underside of each top rail for the pocket screws to hold the top frame. With a small table like this, it would be difficult to drill the top rails to accept pocket screws after the frame is glued up.

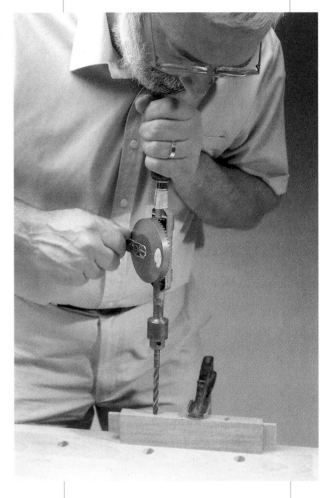

21 Countersunk screws are needed when a deep rail is to have a top attached by screws. To simply drill a clearance hole for the screw with the screw head at the bottom face of the rail would require very long screws. Therefore, drill a hole larger than the screw head only part way through the rail, from the underside. The screw then sits in a hole at a pre-determined depth, allowing a shorter screw to be used. Mark carefully, drill the clearance hole for the screw, then countersink the screw head to the required depth (above).

Number and fit all joints

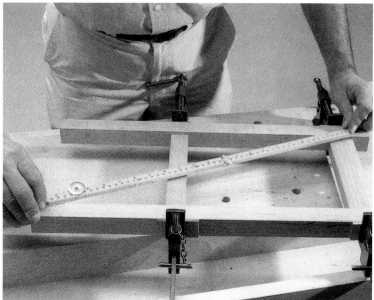

22 Number or letter each joint and carefully fit each tenon into its mortise. With practice, it will be possible to make the mortise and tenon so that they fit accurately from the saw, but it is likely that for some time you will have to pare with a chisel to fit the joints (above).

23 It is standard practice, as in this design, for the rails on all four sides to reach the same level. Therefore, the tenons at each corner will meet, and it is necessary to cut a miter on the end of each tenon, so that they fit in the mortise together. Check, and re-check, that you have marked this correctly before you cut.

Finish inside faces

24 You will soon be ready to prepare for assembly, but, with this design, it is best to finish all the internal faces first. Scrape and sand the four faces of each rail, and the two faces of each leg. Then, mask all of the joint faces so that the chosen finish will not prevent gluing, and apply the finish.

Clamp two sides

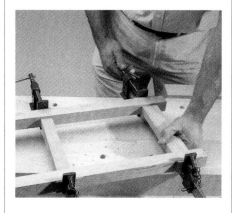

25 Remove the masking tape. Assemble the two side frames dry, without glue, and test that all joints close (above).

26 Check that the frame is square and flat. Check internal angles with a try square (above).

27 Measure the diagonals to check that they are identical. If all is well, apply adhesive and clamp with bar clamps, using small blocks of wood between the outside of the legs and the clamp faces to prevent damage (above).

Checking for square

28 It is vital at this stage to check again to ensure that the frame is square and out of winding. If the frame is out of square, this can be remedied by adjusting the position of the clamps, but the dry assembly should already have shown up any problems.

Remove excess glue

29 When clamping is complete, remove the excess glue. Either do this when the glue is wet, using a damp cloth and water, or wait until the glue has cured to a gel, and remove it with a chisel. If you wait until the glue is hard, damage can be caused to the surface around the joints. Also check the mortises, and clean out any glue that may prevent the final assembly.

30 Clamp the whole frame dry again, check that all joints fit, and that the structure is square in all directions (above).

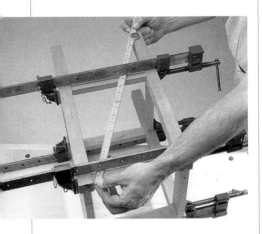

31 This process is slightly more complex than assembling the individual frames, but, if you arrange the clamps as shown, there should be no problems (above).

32 Once all is sufficiently dry, disassemble, apply the glue, and clamp the frame. Use small clamping blocks of softwood to prevent damage to the wood and make sure the metal parts of the clamps do not touch the wood, as these can cause stains. Wipe all the excess glue from the joints with a damp cloth to reduce the chances of adhesive staining the lumber.

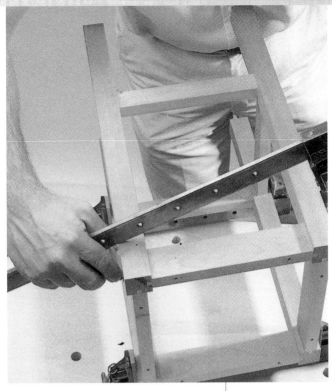

33 When the glue has cured, remove the clamps, carefully saw off the waste at the top and bottom ends of the legs, and plane these end-grain surfaces flat (above).

34 Scrape and sand the outside of the frame (above). Always sand in the direction of the grain to avoid obvious scratches ruining the finish. Work through the grit sizes of abrasive paper and use a sanding block. This will stop the edges from being rounded over.

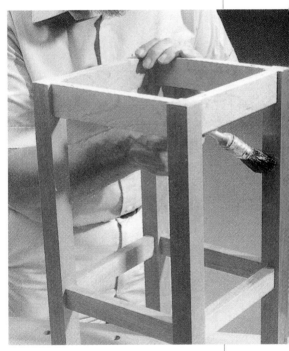

35 Check all the pre-finished surfaces and apply an overall coat of finish to the structure (above). If you wish to use a hardwearing varnish finish, dilute the varnish with about ten percent mineral spirit, and apply at least two thin coats to keep the finish from sagging as it dries. Lightly sand between each coat. Alternatively, use a sanding sealer, followed by a clear wax polish applied with a nylon pad and buffed with a soft cloth.

Mark out the top frame

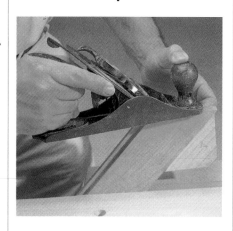

36 The four pieces for the top frame have already been planed square. Mark the miters at the corners and saw accurately to this line. Glue triangular scraps to the corners to aid assembly. Then plane the miters so that all faces fit. You will need to place the frame together and carefully trim the miters to achieve a perfect fit (above).

Cut the rebate to hold the center insert

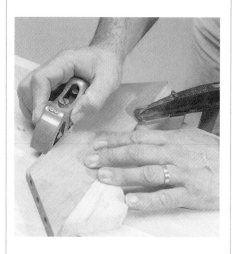

37 This can be done before or after the above process, but must be completed before the frame is assembled and glued. The rebate is to be ¼in (6mm) deep, so that it can accept a veneered plywood insert, or a sheet of glass or mirror. Use either a rebate or a shoulder plane for the job (above).

Mark the dowel positions

38 The top frame could be assembled using tongues or biscuits. Dowels are the safest method, since the joint cannot slip when it is being clamped up.

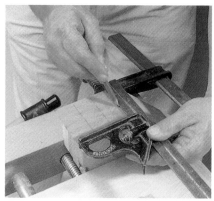

39 Gauge a centerline along each miter face. Then carefully align the four frame pieces in the vise. Mark the centers of the dowel holes, making a cut line across the four ends to intersect with the gauged centerline on each piece (above).

40 Mark location joints for the dowel drilling using a nail punch (above).

41 Drill the holes for the dowels. Ensure that the drill is upright (above).

42 Cut the dowels to length. Fit them loose in the holes and clamp the joints dry. You may need to make final adjustments to the miter faces at this stage.

Assembly

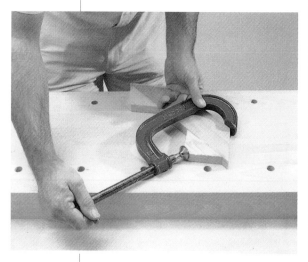

43 It is possible to use four bar clamps to clamp this frame, and this method works with dowels better than with tongues or biscuits where the joint can slip out of place. A preferable method is to glue triangular off-cuts to the outside corners of the joints (above).

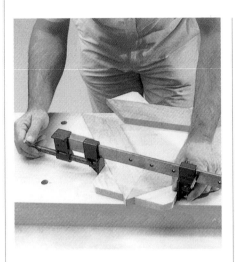

44 When the whole frame is assembled, the blocks enable clamping pressure to be applied at right angles to the joint face (above).

45 If the joint is tight when clamped dry, apply glue and finally clamp.

46 When the glue has cured, remove the clamps and chisel or saw off the triangular blocks.

47 Plane all outside surfaces (above).

48 Screw the underframe to the top frame (above).

49 Scrape, sand, and finish the frame (above).

Top insert

50 If you choose glass or mirror, give the glazier a precise cardboard template, as it is very difficult to fit glass that is even slightly oversized.

51 If you decide that you would like an insert with a wood finish, cut a piece of ¼in (6mm) ply, with veneer applied to one face (above).

52 The finished table (above)— a pleasing addition to any setting.

Wall-hung cabinet

The finished appearance of this small, wall-hung cabinet is deceptively simple. The cabinet sides are joined to the top and bottom with secret miter dovetails. The dovetail joint is completely hidden by the mitered shoulders, and its construction is a real test of accurate laying out and cutting. The back consists of a panel fitted into a grooved mortise, and tenon frame.

A rebate cut around its outside edge allows the back frame to slot neatly into a matching groove in the cabinet. The shelf is tongued into blind dadoes cut in the sides. Finally, the completed cabinet

RIGHT: This project is perfect for introducing secret miter dovetail joints and blind dado joints into your work. If you are new to woodworking, allow plenty of time for this project—at least three or four weekends.

is cleverly and neatly suspended from the top rail, which is beveled to rest on a wall-mounted batten.

Choosing wood

It is possible to use almost any of the quality furniture hardwoods for this project. Choose a wood that is neither too hard nor too soft. Maple, ash, or beech would be appropriate from among the light-colored wood; mahogany would be a suitable red wood, and walnut a darker choice. Softwood is not recommended because precise, clean cuts are essential for well-fitting joints.

Buying lumber

1 Most of the wood for this job could be prepared from 1in (25mm) thick, rough-sawed board.

2 Using a piece of chalk, mark out all the components on the board. Then carefully saw them.

Cutting list

No.	Sawed	Planed
2	SIDES	
	2ft x 11in x 1in	1ft 10in x 10 in x ⅞in
	(610mm x 280mm x 25mm)	(560mm x 250mm x 20mm)
1	TOP	
	1ft 5in x 11in x 1in	1ft 3in x 10in x ⅞in
	(432mm x 250mm x 25mm)	(380mm x 250mm x 20mm)
1	BOTTOM	
	1ft 5in x 10in x 1in	1ft 3in x 9¼in x ¾in
	(305mm x 40mm x 25mm)	(380mm x 235mm x 20mm)
1	SHELF	
	1ft 3in x 10in x ¾in	1ft 2in x 9in x ½in
	(380mm x 250mm 20mm)	(356mm x 230mm x 12mm)
2	FOR FRAMED BACK STILES (UPRIGHTS)	
	2ft x 1¾ in x 1in	1ft 10¼in x 1½in x ¾ in
	(610mm x 45mm x 25mm)	(565mm x 38mm x 20mm)
2	RAILS	
	1ft 4in x 2½ in x 1in	1ft 2in x 2in x ⅞in
	(406mm x 60mm x 25mm)	(356mm x 50mm x 22mm)
1	WALL BATTEN	
	1ft x 1¾ in x ½in	11in x 1⅜ in x ⅜in
	(305mm x 45mm x 12mm)	(280mm x 35mm x 10mm)
1	BACK PANEL manmade board approx.	
	1ft 7in x 12in x ¼in	
	(480mm x 305mm x 6mm)	

+ masking tape, finishing, adhesive, 2 screws for cabinet back, wall fittings for batten

Plans

The drawings on this page show the elevations and sections, together with an exploded perspective view of the finished piece.

Exploded diagram

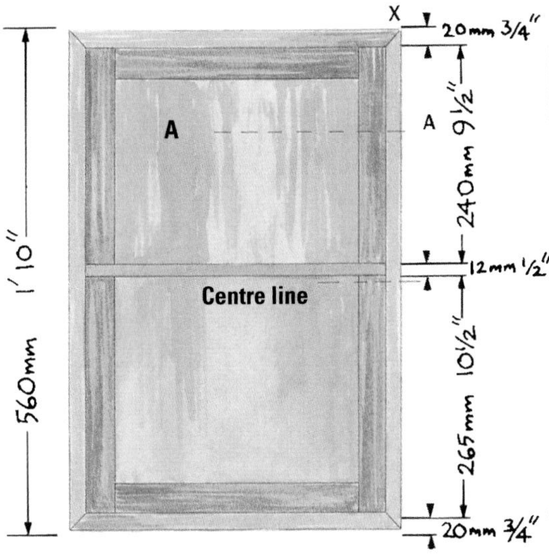

Back slides up from bottom in grooves on sides and top

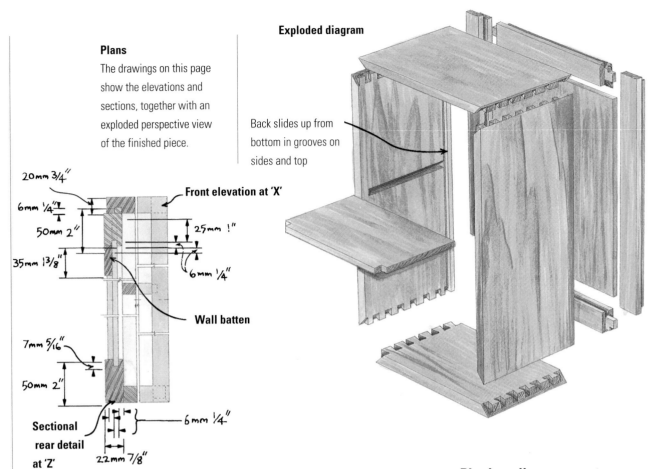

20mm 3/4"

6mm 1/4"

50mm 2"

35mm 1 3/8"

25mm 1"

6mm 1/4"

Front elevation at 'X'

Wall batten

7mm 5/16"

50mm 2"

Sectional rear detail at 'Z'

6mm 1/4"

22mm 7/8"

X   20mm 3/4"   Z

240mm 9 1/2"

12mm 1/2"

265mm 10 1/2"

20mm 3/4"

A ---- A

Centre line

560mm 1' 10"

250mm 10"

Sectional side elevation through centre line

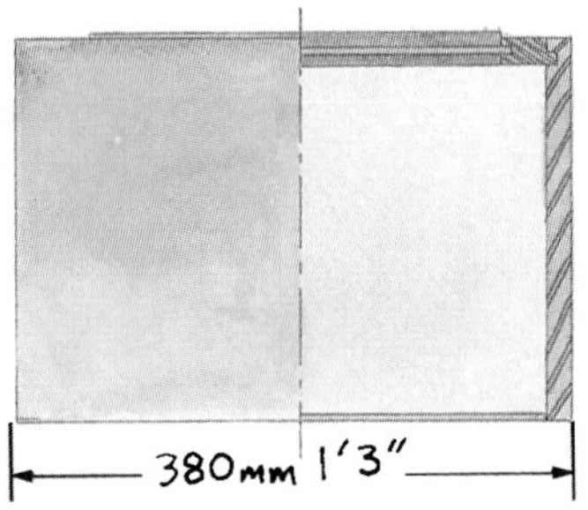

Front elevation

380mm 1' 3"

Sectional half plan through A-A

Scale 1:9

Planing all components

3 Plane the face sides and face edges. Apply face and edge markings. Gauge and plane to width, then gauge and plane the thickness.

Mark out the cabinet

4 Mark out the main cabinet parts, the two sides, the top and the bottom. You will see from the drawing that the bottom is slightly narrower than the other three components, since the back will slide up in a groove from the bottom of the cabinet.

5 Mark overall and shoulder lengths in pencil. Mark the shelf position. Check all marking before you begin any cutting.

6 Cut the grooves in the sides and top, to accommodate the back panel. This will be an easy job if you have a router, or use a plow plane (above).

Corner joints

7 The joints on this cabinet could be either miters using dowels, tongues or biscuits, or dovetails using through dovetails, half-blind, full-blind or secret miter. For this project, bite the bullet and make a secret miter dovetail. It is essential that you practice this joint on scrap wood before doing it on the main carcase.

8 Pay particular attention when laying out to the junction between the two sides and the bottom at the back, because, instead of a miter in this position, the sides must be kept square.

9 Mark the shoulders on the inside faces. Mark the miter on the edges. You must remove wood from both parts of the joint in the form of a rebate across the end. The wood that is left represents the dovetail pins and tails. As is normal practice, the dovetails will be on the sides and the pins on the top and bottom.

10 Mark and cut the pins first. Mark the dovetail pins on the two components—at the ends of the top and the bottom (above).

11 Cut the pins, and remove the waste by a series of saw cuts, and by paring with a chisel (above).

12 Mark the tails onto the sides, but before doing so, letter or number each joint clearly. Working on one joint at a time, mark the precise position of the tails from the pins. Be sure to pencil in the waste that you wish to remove (above).

13 Remove the waste from between the tails, using a dovetail saw and chisel.

14 The lap dovetails on the bottom corners can now be tapped together, the dovetails on the secret miter will only fit partially together, but you can check and adjust at this stage (above).

15 The secret miter joints will not come tightly together until you have cut the miter on the front faces, on the rear faces, and across the corner. When this miter is cut, you should be able to tap the dovetail home (above).

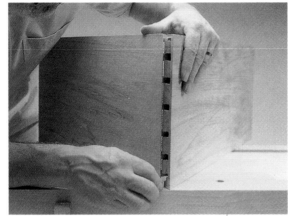

16 Assemble the cabinet dry at this stage and check that the joints fit (above).

Shelf

17 The total length of the shelf includes the housing depth. Mark in pencil a ¼in (6mm) shoulder all around both ends of the shelf. Check that the shoulder lines are precisely the width of the shoulders on top and bottom (right).

18 Now saw the shoulders, and finish with the shoulder plane (above).

19 Disassemble the cabinet, and mark the dadoes—first in pencil, then with scribe lines. It is advisable to have a shoulder all around, even though dadoes can be made barefaced, or with a dovetail on one edge.

20 Cut the housings in the sides. Check the shoulder length, and mark and cut the tongues to fit the housings (above). Here, a straight lumber batten has been clamped across the work, parallel with the housing position to guide the router base. Use a straight cutter and make sure the shank is firmly gripped in the collet and the depth pre-set before switching on. Form the housing in several passes across the board and remove the debris.

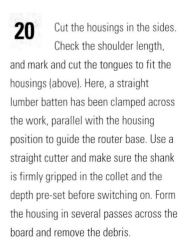

Back frame

21 Again, reassemble the whole carcase dry, and check it for square at the corners and diagonally—both front and back (above).

22 Apply bar clamps to determine the best sequence for assembly. Generally, with this type of cabinet joint, you should only need to clamp the tails into the pins from side to side.

24 Remove the masking tape from the joints, apply the glue and clamp the carcase, remembering to check again for square.

26 Lay out the back components. This is a simple frame with mortise-and-tenon joints at the four corners. Since the frame is grooved to hold the ply panel, the haunches on the tenons are square, so that they fill the groove (above).

23 Disassemble the pieces, clean up the insides of the cabinet, and all around the shelf. Mask the joint surfaces where they will be glued, and apply finish to the inside.

25 When the glue has cured, sand the outside of the carcase and apply the required finish (above).

27 Cut the groove for the ply panel on the inside of the frame components, using a router. Notice that the top rail is thicker than the two stiles. This is so that the cabinet carcase will be held away from the wall when the top rail is located on the wall-mounted batten (above).

Tips box

- To simplify the making, you could use a plain piece of plywood as the back piece.
- Use a recessed brass strip and banjo clips if you want to add adjustable shelving to a cabinet, although this is only applicable to larger units.

28 Mark and plain the bevel on the top rail where the support batten will fit. When marking, remember that the extra thickness is on the outside of the back frame, refer to the full-size detail drawing for clarity, and double check all marking out before cutting.

29 Cut the mortises and haunched tenons, having first checked your marking yet again.

30 Mark the back panel out on the plysheet. Check your marking, and cut and fit the panel into the back frame. Assemble the frame and panel dry, clamp, and check for square.

31 The back frame has a rebate cut around the outer edge, which enables it to slide into the back of the cabinet. Work this rebate now (above).

32 If all is well, glue up the back, checking it for square and wind. Remove the clamps when the glue has cured. Then check that the back slides into the cabinet (above).

33 Finish all components on both cabinet and back. Slide the back into place from the bottom upward. Remember to have the beveled rail at the top of the cabinet. Fix the back into the cabinet with two screws at the bottom (above).

34 Make the wall batten, and plane the bevel to fit the top rail. Fit the batten to the wall (above).

35 The finished cabinet brings together a number of classic cabinetmaking techniques (left).

Cabinet design

Shape and size

Cabinets can be made in a variety of different shapes and sizes depending on what they will hold, and the space available. Large cabinets stand on the floor to become bookcases or cupboards. A wall-hung cabinet must be securely fixed. For extra support, screw a batten to the wall for the cabinet to rest on.

Floor-standing cabinet

Wall-hung cabinet

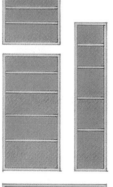

Above: Make a scale drawing of the front elevation to consider variations in the proportion of your cabinet designs. A long design may need extra support in the middle. A tall design may not be stable, and may need fixing to the wall, even if it is floor-standing.

Left: This room divider is made in painted MDF and ash. It cleverly incorporates shelving into the design for an added dimension.

Display cabinet (below right)—the shelves form an important part of the design.

Right: A cabinet interior can be arranged in many different ways. Shelves can be varied in number and proportion, or they can be combined with drawers.

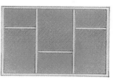

Shelves can be fixed or adjustable (right).

Types of doors

A single door opening on a simple hinge is the most basic form of the door (right). Double-hinged doors (below) are hinged in the same way, but the central break down the front of the cabinet creates a very different look.

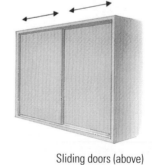

Sliding doors (above) are useful in a restricted space, but only half the cabinet is accessible at any one time. Fold and slide doors (left) allow access to the whole of the cabinet interior. The doors must be mounted on a proprietary roller-guide system.

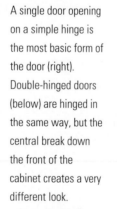

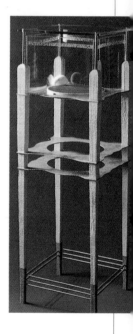

Above: This elegant museum display case was commissioned by a museum. The tapering legs are made from bleached and sandblasted oak and the shelves are in patinated copper.

Upright chair

Traditional chairmaking demands a high level of skill. The main challenge is that in order to fit the curves and angles of the human body, the components rarely meet at right angles. Modern chair designers tend to tackle this problem by combining straight sections with pre-curved components—as this design does.

This is the first project to introduce wood curving techniques. Curved seat and back pieces are attached to a straight-sectioned frame joined by mortise and tenon joints.

Choosing wood

Beech, ash, and oak are often used in chairmaking, because a slightly flexible wood is needed. Beech is used specifically in upholstered chairs because it takes tacks and staples well without splitting. Your choice of wood for a single chair will depend on availability, and how and where you wish to use it. For a later project, you could make a set of these chairs.

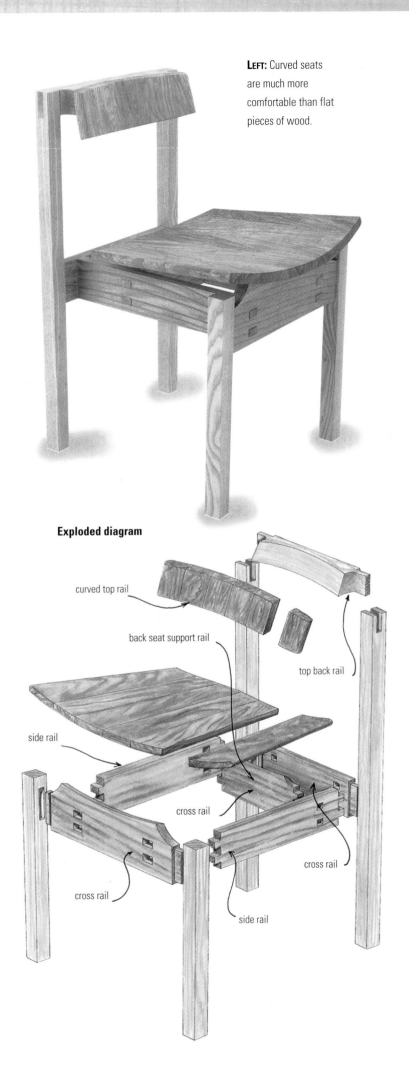

LEFT: Curved seats are much more comfortable than flat pieces of wood.

Exploded diagram

curved top rail

back seat support rail

top back rail

side rail

cross rail

cross rail

cross rail

side rail

RIGHT: An exploded perspective view of the finished chair. The frame of the chair is simply mortised and tenoned together.

Buying wood

1 The lumber is in two sizes, the legs being out of 1½in (38mm) material and the rails out of 1in (25mm) material. The seat and back barrel forms are out of 1in (25mm) thickness, but the top rail that holds the back is out of 1½in (38mm) thickness.

Plane all components

2 Saw the components from the board, plane them all face side, face edge, width and thickness, and leave slightly over length.

Mark out components

3 Mark out all the components, working from the face side and face edge and marking in pencil.

Making the underframe

4 Start with the frame before proceeding to work on the seat and back. Mark and cut the underframe components.

Tips box

- With this kind of project involving curves, it pays to make a mock-up of the finished seat in cardboard or plywood to check that the proportions look and feel right.

- Try to ensure that the grain and color of each set of components are closely matched—one darker-colored leg will upset the symmetry of the chair.

Cutting list

No.	Sawed	Planed
2	BACK LEGS 2ft 4in x 1½in x 1½in (711mm x 38mm x 38mm)	2ft 3in x 1¼in x 1¼in (686mm x 30mm x 30mm)
2	FRONT LEGS 1ft 5in x 1½in x 1½in (432mm x 38mm x 38mm)	1ft 3in x 1¼in x 1¼in (380mm x 30mm x 30mm)
2	SIDE RAILS 1ft 6in x 3⅓in x 1in (457mm x 85mm x 25mm)	1ft 5in x 3in x ⅞in (432mm x 75mm x 22mm)
3	CROSS RAILS 1ft 6in x 5in x 1in (457mm x 130mm x 25mm)	1ft 4in x 4½in x ⅞in (2 at 406mm x 115mm x 22mm) 11in x 4½in x ⅞in (1 at 280mm x 115mm x 22mm)

TO MAKE SEAT

No.	Sawed	Planed
6	1ft 4in x 3in x 1in (406mm x 75mm x 25mm)	1ft 3in x 3in x ¾in (380mm x 75mm x 20mm)
1	TOP BACK RAIL 1ft 3in x 1½in x 1½in (380mm x 38mm x 38mm)	1ft 2½in x 1¼in x 1¼in (368mm x 30mm x 30mm)

6 VERTICAL SLATS SAWED FROM SOLID

	1ft 6in x 3in x 1¾in (457mm x 75mm x 45mm)	Several can be sawed from 1 piece
1	CURVED TOP RAIL 1ft 3in x 3in x 1¾in (380mm x 75mm x 45mm)	

+ adhesive, screws, masking tape, finishing

5 The two side rails and the back seat support rail are joined into an "H" frame. The back seat support rail is wider than the side rails since it has to have the curve to support the seat cut into it. Mark the curve and the decorative curves at the side, and cut outside the line. True the main surface later when the underframe is glued, but smooth the curves with a spokeshave and scraper (right).

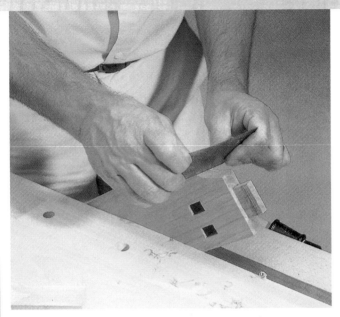

6 The back seat support rail is joined to the side rails with twin through mortises and tenons. The twin tenon is a decorative feature and forms a stronger joint than a single large mortise and tenon. Mark them in pencil, check that they are correct, mark with a scribe line, then saw and chisel the mortises and tenons.

7 Scrape all flat surfaces (above). The picture shows a cabinet scraper held in a special holding jig to make it easier to adjust the angle. It is more comfortable to hold than working freehand.

Plans

The drawings below show the elevations and sections. Note how the chair uses variations of the simple mortise and tenon joint to achieve strength in the rails beneath the seat. Halving joints are used on the back to fix the top back rail to the upper ends of the back legs. The slats of the seat are from solid wood, but a plywood seat could be used instead.

Sectional side elevation through centerline

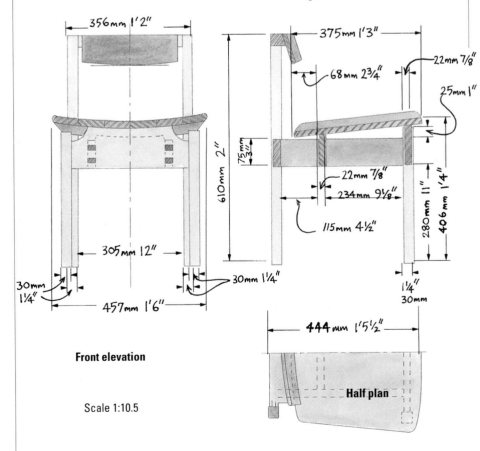

356mm 1'2"

375mm 1'3"

22mm 7⁄8"

68mm 2¾"

25mm 1"

75mm 3"

610mm 2"

22mm 7⁄8"

234mm 9⅛"

280mm 11"

406mm 1'4"

115mm 4½"

305mm 12"

30mm 1¼"

1¼" 30mm

30mm 1¼"

457mm 1'6"

444mm 1'5½"

Front elevation

Scale 1:10.5

Half plan

8 Assemble the "H" frame dry (right). A small scrap of softwood is placed between the frame assembly and the mallet to reduce the chances of denting the wood fibers and to spread the force along the joint.

9 It is convenient at this stage to drill holes in the back and front seat support rails for the countersunk screws that will later hold the seat in place (above).

10 The front rail and back rail are also joined by twin through-mortise and tenon joints to the two side rails of the "H" frame. Twin tenons are ideal for this kind of construction, providing a larger gluing surface area than a single mortise and tenon. The mechanical strength is also greater.

11 The front rail has to have the curve formed for the seat. Mark the curve and cut outside the line as before. Leave precise finishing until later. Mark and cut the tenons that will fit into the legs on both the front rail and the back rail. Note that the shoulder lengths are not the same on the two rails.

12 Mark four sets of twin tenons on the side rails and their mortises on the front and back rails.

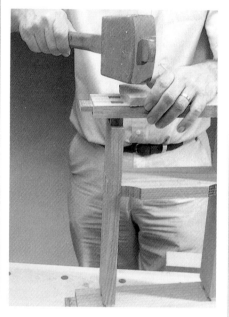

13 Assemble the "H" frame and front and back rails dry (above).

The legs

14 Mark out the front legs and mark and cut the mortises (above). To ensure that the mortise edges are crisp, hone your chisel until it is razorsharp before cutting the mortises.

15 Dry fit the legs to the front rail. Repeat the process with the two back legs and back rail (right). Be careful not to soften the edges of the joints with repeated dry runs. Test the joint and shave off just enough excess material, if any, to provide a tight fit.

16 Mark and cut the front legs and the bottoms of the back legs to length. Assemble all these components dry; you should now have an underframe that is together, but the back legs have nothing in between them at the top (right).

Curving the seat supports

17 Take a rule, place it across the front rail and the back seat support rail, and mark the angle that you will need to spokeshave on the curved position of those two rails (above).

Assembling the frame

18 Even though the legs are now fitted to the frame, do not glue them at this stage. Sand the seat frame and glue this underframe assembly of five pieces together, starting with the initial "H" frame and then adding the front and back rails (above).

Making the seat

19 The seat is composed of six slats glued together into a curved form. Prepare these pieces and mark the angles on the edges that will make the series of slats that form the curve.

20 Cut some scrap pieces of wood to the curve of the seat, then lay the slats on these and check that the angles when you plane are correct to form the required curve. It can help assembly if you make four of these curved pieces—two male and two female. A pair at the front and back help during clamping. The curved pieces must be in contact with the whole width of the seat assembly during clamping or the pressure will be uneven across the wood and may distort the shape.

21 When the slats fit together dry, glue them. Put masking tape on the underside of the curve that holds the bottom edges together and run the glue on the two faces, allowing the masking tape to hinge them open. When you later rest the seat assembly on the female curve, all the joints close up.

22 Clamp across the barrel curve of the seat, and it is here that the male and female support curves are handy. "G" clamp these lightly to the back and front of the seat and fit small bar clamps across the seat. You should get enough pressure to just squeeze those angled faces together.

24 Mark the taper on the seat from front to back, and the slight curves on the front and on the back and saw to these lines (above). Plane the edges and work the radii on the two sides. Sand the seat all over.

23 Remove the glue before it dries. It is much easier to wipe away PVA glue with a dampened cloth at this stage than trying to scrape it away later. Wiping away the glue also stops it from staining the surrounding wood. When the glue has cured, take the seat curve out of the clamps and work the seat shape. You can use a plane on the outside of the curve, but you will have to use a spokeshave on the inside (above).

Tips box

Spokeshaves can be difficult to work across the grain smoothly. Try to work in diagonal strokes across the grain to shear away the surface fibers. Keep the blade sharp and only take off fine shavings with each pass.

25 Place the seat on the underframe sub-assembly. If necessary, adjust the curve on the front and back seat support rails (above). This is probably the trickiest part of the assembly stage, so take your time and be careful not to take off too much from the curve. Regularly check the fit.

26 It is useful at this stage to locate the seat and screw it into place. You may have to remove it before finally finishing the chair, but it is more manageable this way (above).

27 The back legs are attached to the seat frame dry with a clamp holding them. Mark the top back rail with the lap joints that connect it to the top of the back legs, and mark the curve that will hold the slats that make up the back (above).

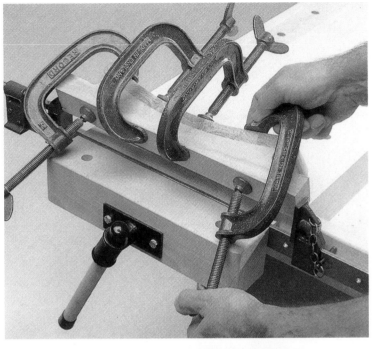

28 Cut and fit the halving joints, but do not glue in position yet. Cut the curve in the top back rail. Mark and cut the slats for the curved top rail. Since these slats will be glued into position, you do not have to make the barrel first, but can glue the slats to the curve of the top back rail. Fix the center slat in position first and then place and glue the remaining slats (above).

Tips box

The individual slats that make up the curved top rail are small and are easily damaged. Spread an even layer of glue on the back of each piece and make sure that the glue is completely dry before final shaping. It is best to let the parts stand overnight to ensure that they have cured fully.

29 Mark and work the shapes on the bottom of the back rail and the radii on the sides of the back rest (above). The back rail will be a part of the chair that is handled frequently. Make sure the pieces are exactly flush to form a continuous, smooth curve. The radius can be worked over the sides of the rail with a rasp and files and smoothed with abrasive paper.

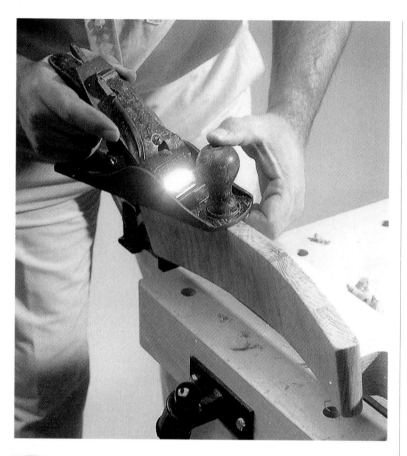

Final assembly

31 Sand down all the components. Glue the front legs to the front rail, the back legs to the back rail, and the back assembly to the top of the back legs (above). Make sure that the back rail is exactly horizontal by standing the chair on a flat, horizontal surface.

30 Plane the bottom of the slats and the top level with the top back rail (above). Guide your plane across the end grain with your fingers directly under the front of the tool to act as a fence. Aim to take off fine shaving with each pass.

32 If you wish, for a later project you could make a complete set of these chairs (left). If you do decide to make up a set of chairs, it's worth using batch production techniques and making all the same parts (i.e. the legs) in one operation so that the sizes are exactly the same for each piece.

Tips box

- If you don't feel confident enough to make a solid wood seat, you could use a piece of shaped plywood instead.

- Try using contrasting, colored woods for the seat and back rest to add visual impact to the project.

Upright chair design

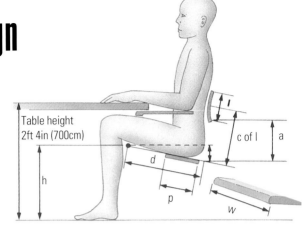

Table height 2ft 4in (700cm)

Center of gravity
The best position for accomplishing tasks, whether eating, writing, or typing, is one where the spine is upright with the center of gravity running down the spine from the skull to the pelvis.

Upright chair seats may be made from cane, rush, fabric, wood, leather or any other material that can be shaped. Before making your project, it may be worth constructing a plywood or cardboard mock-up to check the proportions.

Chair sizes These basic measurements are the starting point for a range of design adaptations and must be adapted to suit anyone who is not of an average height or build. If you are design-ing a chair to match a table, make sure that that chair will be able to be pulled up to the table.
h=seat height 15½-17in (392-430mm). Always start working from this measurement.
p=pelvic support 6in (150mm). This area supports the weight of the body.
d=seat depth 13½-15in (343-380mm)
r=seat rake approx. 1in (25mm) or 5-8 degrees.
c of l=center of lumbar 8in (200mm). The distance from the seat rear to the center of the lumbar region is where back support is needed.
l=lumbar region 4in (100mm). This should be shaped to follow the lumbar curve.
a=arm height from rear of seat 9½in (237mm)
w=width of seat 19-20in (475-500mm) between arms.

RIGHT: This dramatic Phoenix chair from the John Makepeace workshops is made with a laminated holly bark with burr elm, bleached and scorched oak.

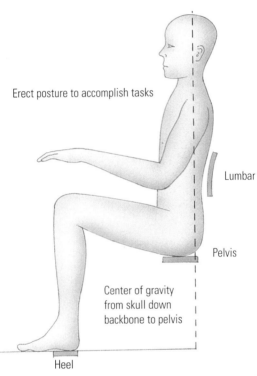

Erect posture to accomplish tasks

Lumbar

Pelvis

Center of gravity from skull down backbone to pelvis

Heel

Cross-legged

Balans

ABOVE: Hans Wegner has been one of the most prolific and consistent of the Scandinavian designers. Throughout his career he has produced classic, timeless pieces (e.g. China chair, above), that are still fresh today, 50 years after they were designed.

| # How to make your own workbench

This bench is fitted with two woodworking vises—you can make your choice from the wide variety of vises currently available.

A workbench must be sturdy and stable. It should also be sized to accommodate the individual worker (especially in terms of height) and the work that will be done on it. It should include as much storage and as many clamping facilities as possible. Another common feature is a "well" at the rear, in which tools can be placed so that they do not protrude above the level of the work surface; some benches, however, are designed so that you can work from both sides.

Traditionally, benches are made from hardwoods like beech, and many such excellent models can be bought. But they are expensive, and a homemade version can be detailed to your exact requirements. This one is made from plywood and ordinary softwood. The plywood provides the weight and rigidity of the classic pattern at a much lower cost.

A particularly useful feature is the absence of framing underneath the front of the work surface. This means items can be clamped to it easily.

The cabinetmaker's bench is excellent for handwork and dealing with smaller components, but once you start using power tools and larger pieces of sheet material, more space and support is often essential. This bench has been designed specifically to meet these needs. It offers a large work surface with an adaptable clamping system, and space below to build storage to hold all your power tools and cutters safely. The frame is assembled with mortise and tenon joints for strength, and layers of plywood are used for the top. It is simple to make, especially if you are equipped with a set of modern power tools.

First steps

Begin by cutting the frame components to length and marking out the joints. The tenons are 1½in (40mm) in length and the mortises are ½in (12.5mm) wide. The mortise for the top rail must stop at least ½in (12.5mm) from the top of the leg.

Finishing touches

The vises chosen for this project are Record 52ED quick-release models. The jaws were made from 1⅛in (30mm) oak bonded together and then bored to take standard Workmate pegs. You could use custom-made dowel dogs instead.

As a final touch, give the top several coats of Danish oil and maybe a coat of wax, which makes it look good and also allows any future glue spills to be easily removed.

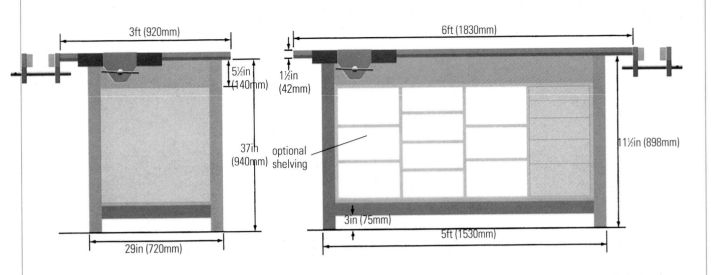

3ft (920mm)

6ft (1830mm)

5½in (140mm)

1½in (42mm)

37in (940mm)

optional shelving

11½in (898mm)

3in (75mm)

29in (720mm)

5ft (1530mm)

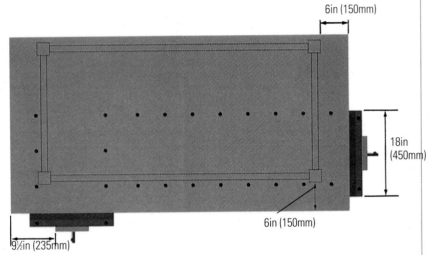

6in (150mm)

18in (450mm)

6in (150mm)

9½in (235mm)

Plans

Plans for bench (above and left) are not dimensioned; precise dimensions will depend on the space available and the preferred working height.

Power tool list

½in (12mm) router
¼in (6mm) router
Trimsaw
Guide rail kit
Cordless drill/driver
Planer
Palm sander

Cutting list

2 sheets ¼in (6mm) ply
6 x 1½in (38mm) PAR lumber 15ft (4.5m)
3 x 1½in (38mm) PAR lumber 15ft (4.5m)
3 x 3in (75mm) PAR lumber 13ft (4m)
No. 12 x 3in (75mm) screws
No. 8 x 1½in (38mm) screws
Panel pins
Adhesive
Vises
1 set Workmate pegs

1 To cut the mortises, use a powerful ½in (12.5mm) router fitted with a long reach straight bit. Use a pair of side fences to sandwich the leg. An offcut of the same material is needed to support the router as it runs off the end of the leg. Take several shallow passes until the required depth is reached. Square the ends with a chisel. If you don't have a ½in (12mm) router, you can use a long reach bit in a smaller ¼in (6mm) machine, but don't try to remove more than around ⅛in (3mm) of wood in each pass to avoid straining the bit and the motor. Whichever router you use, always use the dust extraction facility to remove the fine dust produced.

2 A router is again used for the tenons. Here a smaller ¼in (6mm) model will do the job, and is a little lighter to handle. No special jigs are needed, use any straight cutter and the parallel side fence. Set it to cut to your marked line. Plunge the router to full depth and work across the joint from the end, taking narrow passes until the line is reached. Be careful not to let the router tip at the edges and keep the base pressed firmly against the side fence for the final cut. You could add a router base extension to keep the machine steady as you work. Miter the ends with a block plane or sander. This miter allows the tenon to be made to its maximum length to add strength to the joint. The mitered ends of the tenons will meet in the center of each leg, so make sure they are cut accurately.

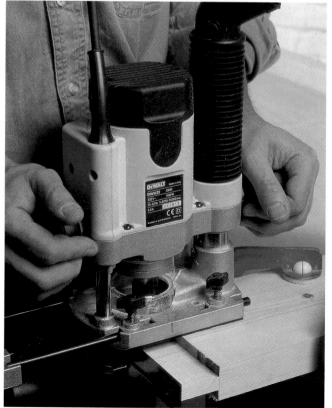

3 Mark the positions of the vises on the rails. Because the top overlaps the frame by 6in (150mm) at the front and ends, only the vise bars will extend through the rails. Cut these pieces out using a bandsaw or jigsaw (right). Do not cut the recess over-size as it will weaken the rail. Here, quick-release vises are used, but you could use an engineer's version, if needed. These vises are heavy, so you may find it easier to work with the bench on its side as you fit the metalwork. Lubricate the screw thread so that the vise action will be smooth.

4 Dry assemble the frame and check all the joints. Dismantle and make any necessary adjustments. Webbing clamps are fine for pulling together the bottom sections. You could mark and bore peg holes for extra strength to the joints at this stage. You can use a shop-bought dowel to make the pegs to push through the leg joints. Apply plenty of glue and use a fine-toothed saw to trim off the excess.

5 It is easy to glue up the frame in two stages. First, assemble the end sections and allow them to set fully before inserting the long rails and completing the job. Measure the diagonals as you work. The two measurements should be exactly the same to ensure that the workbench is square. Leave overnight for the adhesive to fully cure. The photo shows the mitered mortise, used for extra rigidity (above). The frame is now complete and ready to accept the bottom shelf.

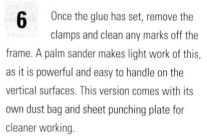

6 Once the glue has set, remove the clamps and clean any marks off the frame. A palm sander makes light work of this, as it is powerful and easy to handle on the vertical surfaces. This version comes with its own dust bag and sheet punching plate for cleaner working.

7 The shelf is made from ¾in (18mm) ply. A cordless trimsaw combined with a guide-rail kit makes cutting up large sheets an easy task, and is light enough to use with one hand. The guide rail also supports the saw at the beginning and end of the cut. All the sheets are cut using this method.

8 The shelf is screwed to the bottom rails and finishes flush with the edge. Cut out the corners with a jigsaw. If there is an overlap, it is easy to clean up using a router fitted with a bearing-guided trimming cutter. The ends where the router cannot reach may be finished off with a sharp, wide-bladed chisel. You can adapt this bench design to incorporate three or four extra shelf or drawer units between this shelf and the underside of the bench top. Make the parts from ¾in (18mm) MDF and seal with an MDF primer sealer or clear varnish to protect against dirt. Use to store your power tools and accessories.

9 Next, cut the top two pieces of plywood to size. The top is made from two layers of ¾in (18mm) ply, which must be bonded together using a good-quality adhesive. Again set aside, laid flat, to dry fully.

10 The top is screwed through into the rails with 2in (50mm) long No. 12 screws. These must be driven down hard and countersunk into the top. A cordless screwdriver is a great help here. The back panel is made from ¼in (6mm) ply and is simply screwed to both the top and bottom rails. Make it as tight a fit as possible.

11 Clean up the edges with a power planer and make sure they are square. It is worth using the side fence for accuracy. The vises may be fitted now. Use M10 bolts and sink the heads below the surface. Cut a recess to allow the backplate to finish flush with the bench edge.

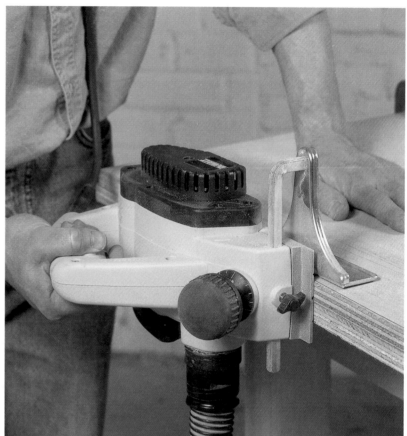

12 The bench top is finished with a layer of ¼in (6mm) ply, which is pinned on to cover all the fixing screws and vise bolts. It can easily be replaced if the bench top gets damaged. To accommodate the Workmate pegs, ¾in (20mm) pegs, ¾in (20mm) holes are drilled a regular intervals. A cordless drill and flat bit will do this, but be sure that the holes are vertical, or angled slightly toward the vises.

13 The completed bench is large enough to use as a power tool workstation.

LOCKS AND FITTINGS

Some advanced woodworkers devise ingenious ways of opening cabinet doors or locking the lids on trinket boxes, etc., without resorting to proprietary metal hinges, locks, or catches. A poor-quality, mass-produced hinge, or crudely-designed handle will certainly let down an otherwise finely-crafted cabinet.

Most woodworkers, however, whether beginners or highly skilled, will resort to standardized fastening hardware, of which there is now considerable choice for most applications. Choose hardware to suit the job. For example, if you are building a wardrobe door, a pressed steel or brass-plated hinge which can be simply screwed onto the surface might be enough. But, if you are making a delicate trinket box, a precision-made cast-brass hinge would be called for.

Visual appeal, strength, durability, size, and specific function are important factors to consider when choosing the right hinge, lock, or catch.

Once the choice has been made, you should select the best tools and woodworking techniques to attach the hardware accurately. As you develop your woodworking skills, you will find that being able to hang a door correctly or to fit a lock that engages properly is both satisfying and extremely useful.

Cabinet locks

There are three traditional types of cabinet locks: the straight lock, which is screwed to the rear face of the door; the cut-in lock, which is recessed into that face and the edge; and the mortise lock, which is recessed wholly into the edge. Other locks are made for insertion into circular holes, for drawers, for lids, for flaps, and for sliding doors—especially glass ones.

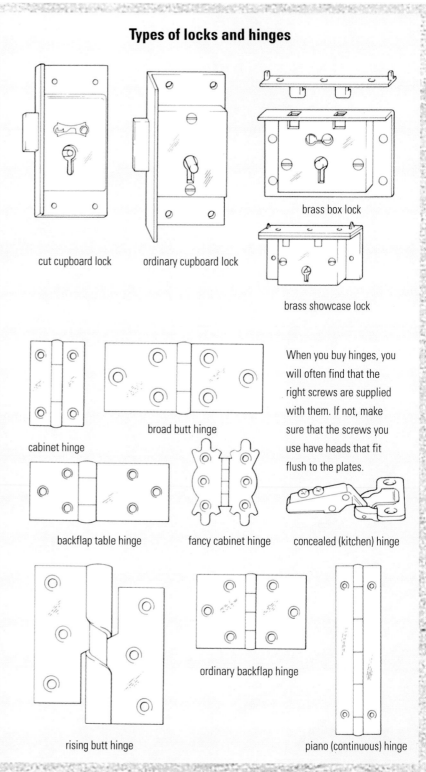

Types of locks and hinges

cut cupboard lock

ordinary cupboard lock

brass box lock

brass showcase lock

cabinet hinge

broad butt hinge

backflap table hinge

fancy cabinet hinge

concealed (kitchen) hinge

When you buy hinges, you will often find that the right screws are supplied with them. If not, make sure that the screws you use have heads that fit flush to the plates.

rising butt hinge

ordinary backflap hinge

piano (continuous) hinge

Fittings

Delicate boxes require small precision castings: sometimes it is best to custom-make parts from brass strip.

Specialist mail-order suppliers can provide iron and steel finishes.

Sinking a brass hinge into a small casket

1 Mount the casket firmly on the bench. A bar clamp held in the vise with an appropriate packing piece is convenient. The block between the clamp head and the casket is to prevent bruising or marking when the clamp is tightened. Mark out the hinge lengths on the wood with a sharp marking knife. Their positions can be guessed—each one should be closer to the end of the casket than the middle—but make sure they are both the same.

2 Using a try square, lightly square the lines across the wood to the approximate hinge width and down the edge to the approximate hinge thickness.

3 Set a marking gauge to the width of the hinge (use the hinge itself). Note that the spur (or point of the gauge) is set to the center of the pivot of the hinge. This action is repeated for gauging the depth of the hinge recess. This is very important and ensures that the lid and box faces meet exactly.

4 Gauge the width of the hinge recess using the locating points that you marked originally, to prevent over-run of the gauge. Reset the gauge to mark the depth of the hinge recess and repeat the process. Now deepen the squared cut lines to where the marking gauge lines intersect and shade in the waste.

5 Mark the opposing hinge lengths on the lid by carefully extending the lines so that the hinges will align perfectly. Then repeat the marking out operations. For larger boxes, it's worth putting a "G" clamp at each end of the hinge join to keep the lid and box tightly together and exactly aligned as you mark across with the craft knife. Try not to extend the line beyond the exact size of the hinge so that there are no marks left on the finished box.

6 With a mallet and chisel, carefully sever the waste fibers across the grain with a series of fine parallel cuts, say ⅒in (2mm) apart. Work from the center moving outward in each direction, carefully locating the chisel for each cut.

7 Now work the chisel horizontally to lift out the severed fibers. After the fibers have been severed across the grain, carefully pare the fibers back to the line along the grain.

8 Finally, trim the ends of the recess across the grain to the line.

Using a router to cut a hinge recess

1 An alternative method to cutting a hinge recess is to use a router and a straight cutter. The same marking techniques can still be applied, or the hinge can be held against the router bit to establish the depth of the recess. Making a trial cut in a piece of waste wood is another way of establishing the depth for the recess. One drawback with using a router is that the recess will always finish with curved ends. Finish with a chisel.

2 When using a router, the curve left by the bit has to be removed with the chisel. The final step is to trim the ends of the recess across the grain to the line. You will only need a small ¼in (6mm) wide blade for most box hinges. Make sure the edge is razorsharp so that you do not tear off any of the delicate areas around the recess. Use only light pressure and keep the box firmly supported so that it can't move as you work.

Inserting hinges

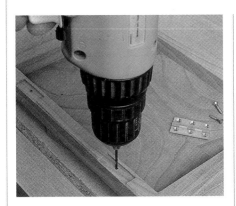

1 Insert a hinge and mark off the center hole with a pencil. Then drill a pilot hole fractionally nearer the shoulder (where the long edge of the hinge will butt against) to ensure a tight fit.

2 After cutting all four hinge recesses, run a finely-set plane along the edge to produce a slight bevel. This enables the lid to clear the edge of the box each time it is opened and closed. You only need a tiny bevel to allow the box to open freely. You can now fit the hinges.

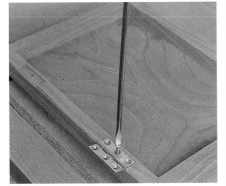

3 Now screw the hinges in position, using the correct width screwdriver to avoid scratching them. In tough woods, use a steel screw as a primer. This means a steel screw is inserted first to widen the pilot hole. Brass screws are much softer and would be likely to break when driven into hardwoods.

4 Drill the pilot holes for the remaining screws (left). Now insert the remaining screws. It looks much neater if all the slots are in line or on the same diagonal (above).

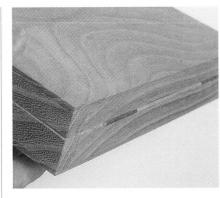

5 When the box closes, the faces should meet with no more than the clearance of a thin piece of paper to allow for the thickness of a coating of varnish at the finishing stage. If the hinge recesses have been accurately marked out to start with—and then cut out with care—perfect alignment should result. Note that the hinge knuckles protrude slightly.

6 Rub down any fractional misalignment with an abrasive block on the front and side edges, to bring them level, although this should only be used for fractional misalignments—don't try to correct a badly offset lid using this technique. Instead, remove the fixing screws and refit.

Locks

Advanced Techniques

Inserting locks

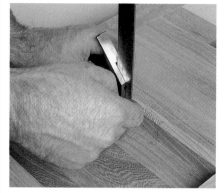

1 The various recessed parts of the lock need to be marked and cut in stages. First, place the lock onto the wood to mark out its overall outline.

3 Use the adjustable-depth try square facility of the combination square to extend the lines downward.

5 Mark the various features of the lock by holding it against the wood.

4 Use a tenon or dovetail saw to cut across the grain to the line on the side and edge.

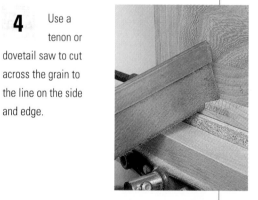

2 Square the marks across with a combination square and marking knife, in a similar way to marking out for the hinges. Apply only gentle, controlled pressure to score through the surface fibers. It's worth investing in a small 3in or 4in (75mm or 100mm) engineer's try square if you are going to be working regularly on smaller-scale items that need fittings.

6 For the shallow recess, chisel out the waste horizontally across the grain (above). In such a confined space, the trickiest part is to cut an accurate line along the grain at the bottom of the lock. Here, the bevel of the chisel is used to make a vertical cut (left).

Keyhole location

1 Mark out the keyhole position using a marking gauge and try square to transfer the information from the lock.

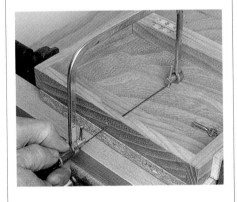

2 Drill a slightly oversized hole for the keyhole. Using a coping saw, insert the blade into the hole, then carefully cut the keyhole verticals, before trimming with a narrow chisel.

3 Now insert the lock into its recess and check that everything is flush. In this confined space, use a nail with its tip flattened as a screw pilot hole.

4 Fix the lock with fine screws, and check the key for operation when the catch plate has been attached.

5 The catch has to be very accurately recessed into the lid, so that the key operates smoothly. Mark out its profile with a try square and marking gauge.

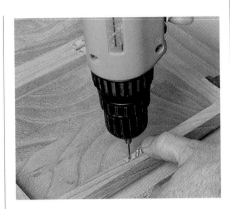

6 Recess the catch using the same methods for sinking the hinges.

7 Drill pilot holes, and fix with fine screws, ensuring that everything is flush. A fine bevel can be run along the edge with a smoothing plane as a continuation of the hinge bevel for visual effect.

BENDING AND SHAPING WOOD

Most woodworking projects use straight sections of lumber because it is readily available and easy to measure and joint. However, curves add interest and a more ergonomic shape to pieces such as chairs. Curves may be added by cutting and shaping, or by bending the wood to shape.

Much furniture today is, however, "flat panel" work made from composite board such as chipboard, with curves "introduced," minimizing the waste of this valuable resource.

It takes time, often several hundred years, for the shapes and curves of a tree to form, and it takes time to produce curves in the process of working wood. Shapes and curves add a lot of interest to a piece of furniture, and history is full of examples of the extravagant and skilful shaping of wood. The styles vary greatly from individuals such as the eighteenth-century woodcarver Grinling Gibbons to the present-day designer John Makepeace.

Curved and shaped work is also characteristic of specific craft traditions such as boat building and musical-instrument making. Entire cultures express the "bendiness" of the natural tree in furniture traditions such as the wood laminating and steam bending practiced in Scandinavia.

Wood can also be shaped or curved by coopering, bricking, stack laminating, saw kerfing, or simply cutting to shape from solid lumber. The age-old practice of searching for the right piece of wood which presents the natural structural curve is still in our consciousness, despite the evolution of shaping techniques, especially those whereby the curve is imposed on the grain of the wood.

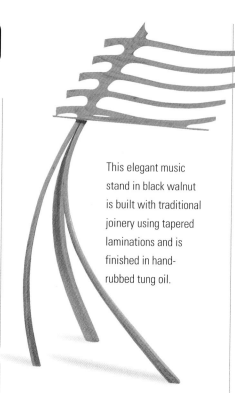

This elegant music stand in black walnut is built with traditional joinery using tapered laminations and is finished in hand-rubbed tung oil.

The lectern, designed to bear weights of up to 22lb (10kg) is made of solid African wenge. It is laminated from sawed-cut veneers and glued together with epoxy resin.

The top and back of this low table are of English oak, inlaid with sycamore. The under-structure is made of thin, laminated sheets of oak.

Imposing curves or shapes onto the grain

Most curves in woodwork are imposed onto the grain as opposed to following it, but you still have to observe the nature of the grain to obtain adequate strength. Here, the piece will be weak at the top where the grain is very short.

In this hoop, with the grain running vertically, the ticks indicate adequate grain strength and the crosses indicate weak or "short" grain. When introducing curves in a piece of woodwork try to avoid short grain because the wood is likely to break along it.

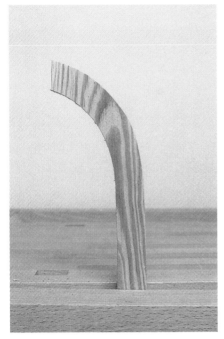

A simple and economical way to introduce a curve at the end of a straight piece is to glue on an extra piece of wood, making sure that the grain matches. In the illustration above, the shaded portion and cutaway section show the intended shape.

Tips box

- Lumbers with a dense interlocking grain will provide the strongest material for making a curve.

- To strengthen the joint between a straight section and an extra piece of lumber, use dowels or biscuits. Be careful with your marking out and check that the ends of the dowels or biscuits will not protrude through the other side of the small extra piece.

Shaping with a spokeshave

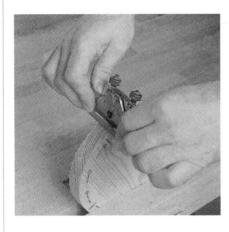

1 Imposed curves can be easily marked out and cut with a variety of saws. Finish with a flat-bottomed spokeshave, working in the direction of the arrows to cut with the grain, and holding the spokeshave between fingers and thumbs. Rotate the workpiece in the vise to make sure that you are always cutting more or less horizontally.

2 A convex-bottomed spokeshave can be used to cut concave shapes. You can also achieve a fine finish by abrading. Note the arrows indicate the change of cutting direction to go with the grain.

Shaping three-dimensionally from a solid piece of wood

1 This curved stool—or table—leg can be easily sawed to a rough shape, once the lines have been marked on two adjacent surfaces. The band saw is ideal for

2 Hold the leg in a vise, or clamp it to the bench, then shape with a spokeshave or carving gouge. Hold the gouge like a chisel and pare away the fibers working with the grain. Always keep the gouge razorsharp.

Brick and stack laminated constructions

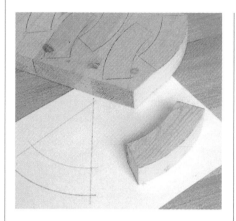

1 Brick construction has numerous applications. Traditionally, it is used to create curves for bowed drawer fronts, which are veneered afterward. The technique involves marking out the required curved segment, then tracing or transferring the data onto a piece of wood, which acts as a template for marking all the bricked pieces.

3 Stack laminating involves the vertical gluing of any identically-shaped pieces of wood. It can include plywood, in which case the ply is also a decorative feature.

2 The pieces can be cut on the band saw and then glued together using a rubbed joint (applying a thin, even layer of glue to one surface and pushing the mating surface across it to squeeze out the air and excess glue), or by clamping if you feel this is necessary. The more accurate you are in sawing to the line, the less trimming you will need to do to finish the curve evenly.

Tips box

- Always stagger the vertical joint lines when building up a laminated curve.
- Try to avoid blocks of wood with large or dead knots on the surface that will be on show because they will be difficult to smooth the surface flush.

Making a coopered shape

1 Coopered work involves the segmenting of identical pieces to form a part or whole circle. First, mark out the segments by scribing two concentric circles, dividing them into the required number of segments, and converting the curved sides into two flat sides. Then transfer the relevant data to a length of wood with a steel rule and sliding bevel.

2 The wood is then planed and sawed. The angles are obviously critical in the marking out and cutting. Glue the segments together. A rubbed joint should be enough; i.e. it is not necessary to clamp them. However, the joining surfaces must be smooth—saw to the approximate shape and use a plane to finish to the exact angle. Leave the segments to dry on a flat papered surface to prevent the assembly from sticking to the bench.

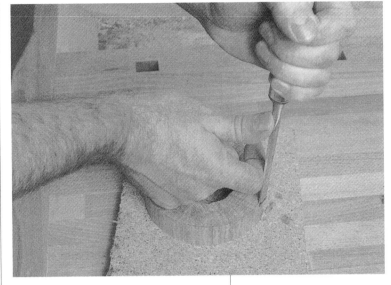

3 When the joints are dry, mark on a line and you can then trim the outer edge in a variety of ways. Here, a chisel is used with the grain, but you can also abrade the curve.

4 Alternatively, a plane can be used. In this method, the end grain is showing, so you will be planing across the grain and so the fibers will cut willingly. For ease of working, rotate the wood in the vise, keeping the plane more or less horizontal. You could use a bench disc sander instead, as long as the curve is kept at a constant distance from the abrasive disc.

5 The inner curve can be finished off by abrading or using a firmer gouge. Work along the grain, but only take shallow cuts with the gouge, or it may dig in and spoil the finish. You will find that a good way to finish the inside is to wrap some coarse abrasive paper around a shaped stick, and work horizontally. You can also buy a selection of shaped rasps and files that can all provide a smooth finish to your project. Seal and protect the finished shape in the normal way and make sure the polish or varnish is applied to the inner and outer surfaces so that moisture does not penetrate and expand the wood.

Bending

It is not always possible to produce shaped components by cutting shapes from solid lumber, because short grain can make a component prone to failure.

Bending and laminating in a home workshop are generally confined to making a shape in one plane. It is possible to make steam bends in several planes, and it is possible to make panels with double curvature, but this needs very advanced industrial machinery. There are, however, several ways to create simple one-plane shapes.

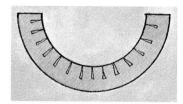

Saw kerfing

This is a method of bending a flat sheet of either solid wood or manmade board. The principle is based on the removal of a series of saw cuts or kerfs to a standard depth through the wood where the remaining material is capable of bending. Bending the material brings the tips of the saw kerfs together.

Tips box

- Portable trim saws are supplied with thinner blades than conventional circular saws and can be used for kerfing on site as well as in the workshop.

- You can straighten a cupped length of skirting or other board by cutting a kerf lengthwise on the rear of the board. This may give enough movement to ease the board flat.

Saw kerfing

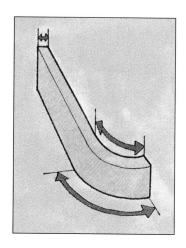

1 This method needs very careful calculation and a full-sized drawing. You must make sure that you know the precise width of the saw kerf and calculate the distance between kerfs to give the required bend.

2 To calculate the spacing of the kerfs, mark the point at which the bending will start, and saw a kerf here, leaving at least ⅛in (3mm). Measure and mark the radius of the curve from this first kerf. Make sure the kerfs are all made to the same depth and, more importantly, cut parallel with each other so that the curve produced is even and doesn't twist.

3 Clamp one end of the wood firmly, then lift the free end until the kerf closes. Wedge the free end in position at this point, and measure the distance between the bench and the underside of the board. This is the distance between kerfs.

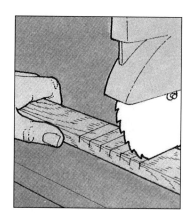

4 Sawing the kerfs with a radial arm saw is accurate but creates a fairly wide kerf—unless you use a thin blade. Mark the distance between kerfs in pencil on the guide fence. Radial arm saws are excellent for this type of repetitive cross-cut work. The work must be held firmly against the back fence as you cut.

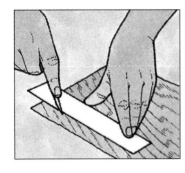

5 Other methods of sawing kerfs require a batten clamped to the work as a guide. Hand sawing is very labor-intensive. A power circular saw requires a thin blade if you are not going to cut wide kerfs.

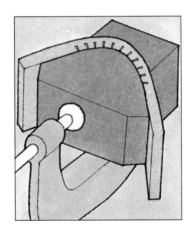

6 You will need formers around which to make the bend. By its very nature this method is not very strong since only the tips of the kerfs are glued. The cavities between them need a gap-filling glue or filler. The bend can be strengthened by applying thin ply to the kerfed face.

Laminating

Wood cut into thin strips is glued and pressed into shape between male and female forms.

Special, thick veneers, usually made from poplar, are often used for the laminate. The grain follows a longitudinal direction in all the pieces, instead of being set at alternate right angles like plywood.

You can make your own veneers from solid wood, but this method is quite wasteful since the thickness of the saw means you waste as much as you use. Be very careful to follow all safety procedures if you do cut your own strips. You will also need a thicknesser planer to smooth the laminate strips.

Laminating is not difficult, but it is essential to draw the full-size shape accurately; and when producing laminates with several curves, careful planning for clamping procedures is necessary, as forms must sometimes be made in more than two parts to accommodate the curves.

1 Make forms from manmade board such as particle board or MDF. Mark out the shape carefully, allowing for the thickness of the laminates. Make sure the shapes are precise, and finish the internal faces of the forms exactly. It is important to make sure that the entire length of the laminate is in contact with the former edge when the pieces are clamped together.

2 Make the mold and the laminates wider than the laminated component, to allow for cleaning up. Cut the laminates along the grain, using a knife and straight-edge. A decorative facing veneer may also be included in the laminate.

3 Always make a trial run—bending and clamping the laminates without glue—to check the position of clamps, and ensure that everything comes together tightly.

4 Use synthetic glue, preferably urea-formaldehyde. Wrap the laminates in waxed paper to prevent the package from sticking to the forms. Place it in the forms, tighten the clamps—working from the center out—and leave to cure. To finish, trim the face edge, gauge, and plane to width.

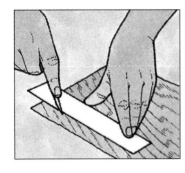

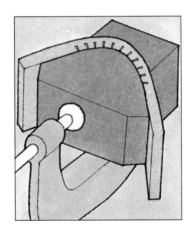

Steam bending

1 Build a form using plywood or chipboard to the desired shape and thickness. You can cut large holes to accommodate "G" clamps. Make a bending strap from thin steel sheet and anchor it into the handles with bolts and screws.

3 Make wooden plugs for the ends of the steam chamber. Mount the chamber at a slight downward slant, so that condensed water can escape from one end into a bucket.

5 After the wood has been steamed, quickly transfer it to the bending jig, strap it in, and make the bend in one go. Some trial and error is required to get this right. The steel strap helps prevent fiber break out.

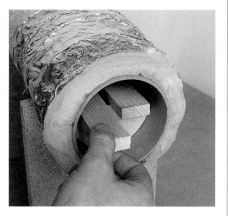

2 For steaming the lumber you will need a steam generator—such as the pressure cooker shown here—and a steam chamber—for example, a plywood box, or piece of plastic drain-piping plugged at either end with wooden discs. Into one end, insert a tube to carry a constant source of steam. It is important to insulate the steam chamber in order to keep the temperature as high as possible. Insulate the drain-piping with tinfoil and fiberglass roof insulation. For a budget steam bending kit, you could buy a wallpaper steam stripper and use this to produce the steam.

4 Remove the top plug (with the hose in it), and stack the wood on spacers inside the chamber. Replace the plug and switch on the steam generator, controlling the heat setting so that a constant supply of steam passes through the chamber (escaping from the drainhole at the other end). As a rule of thumb, three quarters of an hour is needed for every 1in (25mm) thickness of wood to be bent. Bending wood can be hit and miss. You should experiment with an off-cut of the wood you plan to use for the project to see exactly how it reacts under the steaming process.

6 Now secure the jig with "G" and bar clamps, and allow it to dry for several days. Don't rush this final part of the bending process because clamps taken off too early can ruin the result. Set the piece to one side of the workshop and forget about it.

Laminating using veneers

1 Usually, beech constructional veneer is used with a more decorative facing veneer. Constructional veneers are thicker than normal veneers. The bends can be fairly tight because the veneer is pliable. In this simple form, a thin protective plastic sheet is used to keep glue from sticking to the former. Apply a thin coating of glue onto one side of the veneers.

2 Now clamp the veneers in the form with "G" clamps, making sure to align the male and female parts of the form perfectly. The laminated veneers are left to cure overnight in a warm environment.

Tips box

You can make up your own thin veneer laminate pieces by using a band saw to cut thin strips from a solid board. Check that your fence is set up square to the blade so the strips are of even thickness.

Microwave bending

1 A domestic microwave can be used to heat small sections of wood sufficiently for subsequent bending and forming in male and female molds. This method requires some experimenting.

2 Keep the wood moist by wrapping it in a stout, sealed polythylene bag with a little water in it, or wrap it in a saturated cloth. Set the microwave to its "high" position and allow 3-5 minutes for a bend about ⅛in (3mm) thick. After microwaving, quickly place the wood in the former and clamp together. Leave it for a few hours to fully dry out.

Twisting wood to form shapes

Twisting wood is a novel way of shaping wood using lateral pressure at either end of the workpiece to twist the wood instead of imposing a bend in the shape; experiment using thin, solid lumber or plywood. Here, a few layers of thin plywood have been clamped and turned to demonstrate the simplicity of the method. A simple jig can be improvized to hold the clamps in the desired position (for example, a length of wood in the vise can be clamped to the upper clamp). The twist maintains adequate pressure if a fairly liberal coating of synthetic glue is used. Such decorative twists can be veneered either before or afterward to give the appearance of a solid piece. Again, it's essential to keep the clamps on the work until it is completely cured. Clean up the edge using a spokeshave or abrading stick.

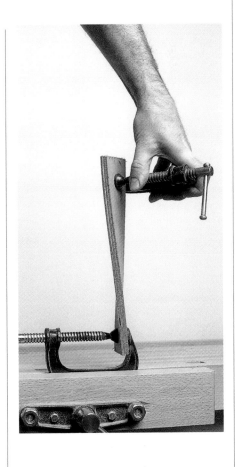

Bent wood chairs

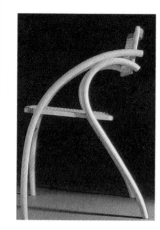

RIGHT: The frame of this dining chair is available in natural or black lacquer with either matching or contrasting upholstery.

RIGHT: The laminated construction of this elegant ash chair uses bending techniques.

ABOVE: The radical shape of this classic nineteenth-century-design chair relies entirely on steam bending. The plywood seat is formed in one continuous bend.

LEFT: This practical chair is made from beech veneer and has both Eastern and Western influences in its design.

ABOVE: The Windsor chair is possibly the best-known English chair, and its origins probably lie in the mid-eighteenth century. "Windsor" is a term now used to describe chairs of stick construction, but the distinctive style employs bending by steaming ash and yew. The technique of turning is used for the legs and back members, which are dowel-jointed into the seat.

TURNING

The attraction of wood turning as a hobby is that the results are almost instant: with a few basic tools and a lathe, simple items can be produced very quickly. A chunk of wood can be shaped with a chisel in a matter of minutes on a lathe, whereas with other wood-orientated crafts such as carving, progress is much slower.

There are three distinct parts to wood turning: sharpening, turning, and finishing. To achieve good results, all three have to be blended together, and equal amounts of time need to be devoted to each one. The fun part is making shavings and creating shapes, but without sharp tools you can't cut the wood cleanly to produce those shavings. And having created your shape, a well-chosen and carefully-applied finish will not only enhance your work, but will also protect it from the vagaries of climate and storage.

Hollow forms: Sometimes different wood colors can be introduced to emphasize the natural figure of pale wood, as with the front and center two pieces here.

More than anything else, wood turning is one of the few manual occupations that can engage your hands and head, and also capture your imagination at the same time—the combination of hands-on work with the need for a sharp eye and the satisfaction of creating a useful object from a blank of whirling raw material is hard to beat.

ABOVE: An ideal starter project is a cord pull with "V"-cut decoration.

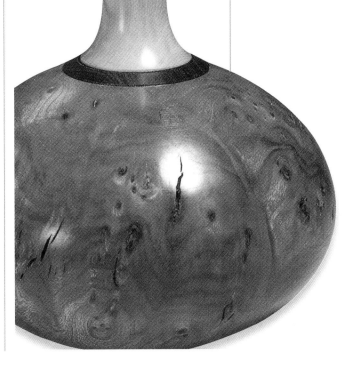

ABOVE: Lidded boxes provide an excellent opportunity to improve your tool control skills.

ABOVE: Many kitchen utensils were traditionally made of wood. This spatula is a simple between-centers project.

The workshop

Where you work is a subject to which entire books have been devoted, and the various options covered range from a fully-equipped professional space allotted solely to woodworking, to a kitchen work surface used for turning small bowls.

This dedicated workshop combines plenty of natural and artificial light with lots of work and storage space.

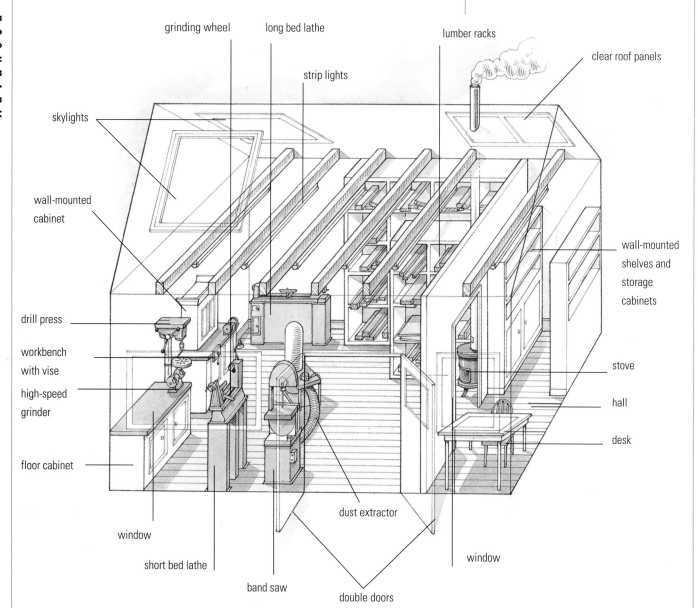

grinding wheel · long bed lathe · lumber racks · clear roof panels · strip lights · skylights · wall-mounted cabinet · wall-mounted shelves and storage cabinets · drill press · stove · workbench with vise · hall · high-speed grinder · desk · floor cabinet · window · short bed lathe · dust extractor · window · band saw · double doors

For many amateur woodturners, the garage doubles as a workshop, with the lathe mounted on a bench at one end and any other equipment having to share space with the car and all the paraphernalia normally associated with a garage. This does encourage you to clean up frequently and use the space wisely, but it is hardly ideal. The illustration above shows one way of setting up a dedicated workshop; you can use graph paper and cut-out paper shapes to find the best way of using the space available to you. The following points should be considered, wherever you end up establishing your working space.

• If possible, the lathe should be situated near natural light—usually a window or skylight. An adjustable lamp can be placed near or on the lathe. Make sure that the rest of the workshop space is adequately lit.

• There should be plenty of space available to move around the lathe, and to swing tool handles without any obstruction. Because the correct stance when turning is essential (see p. 276),

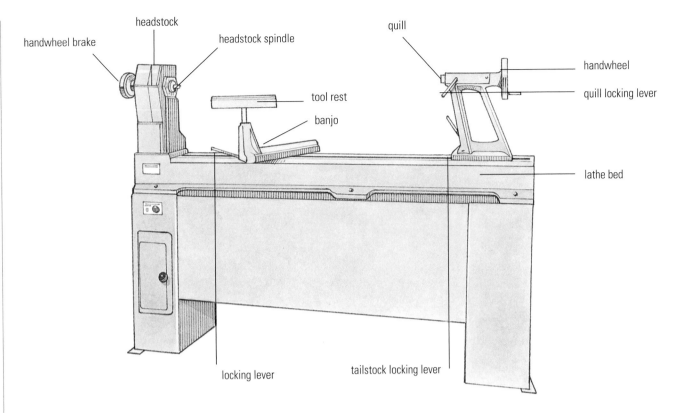

handwheel brake · headstock · headstock spindle · quill · handwheel · quill locking lever · tool rest · banjo · lathe bed · locking lever · tailstock locking lever

if you are cramped or cannot move freely, you should rethink your workshop space.

- You can never have too many electrical outlets for stationary and other power tools, but make sure that they are installed by a qualified electrician, and never be tempted to overload sockets or power circuits.
- If you are planning to do a lot of turning, especially in or adjoining living areas, some form of sound insulation should be considered.
- Wood turning in a cold environment is not only unpleasant, but can be dangerous, because your reflexes and alertness become dulled. Insulation and heat should be a priority, and if you have the space or are putting together a custom-built workshop, a shaving burner is worth thinking about; this will provide the necessary heating and will also get rid of your wood waste.
- Old kitchen cabinets make excellent storage; some can be cut in half along their depth and be made into two.
- If you have invested in quality tools, it would be foolish to leave them lying around where they can be damaged. Make tool storage a priority.

Choosing a lathe

Before buying a lathe, test as many as possible: try out a friend's lathe, join a club, or wood turning association and try all the lathes that they have, take a course with a reputable instructor and ask advice and opinions of the different models available, or visit woodworking shows to check out what's available.

Once you have seen what there is, you have to decide just what kind of turning you want to do and how much space you have to work in—if you want to turn miniatures exclusively, you obviously won't need a huge floor-mounted lathe, and, if you plan to make bowls and nothing else, a lathe that will only swing 6in (150mm) will not prove to be of any use at all.

Most woodturners compromise and end up going for a swivel-head lathe that allows them to do both of these extremes and everything in between; if you decide to go this route, your lathe needs to have a good range of speeds that will cope equally with out-of-balance bowl blanks (which need a slow speed) and spindle work (which

ABOVE: An illustration of a good-quality, floor-standing, heavy-duty, variable-speed lathe with all the key features labeled.

Selecting tools

There are literally hundreds of turning tools available today, and trying to select which ones to start with can be difficult. An all-around set for beginners only need consist of six tools (see p. 276). These will allow you to complete all the projects in this book.

There is also the choice of whether to buy carbon-steel or slightly more expensive high-speed steel (HSS) tools, although some manufacturers only produce turning tools in HSS. Carbon-steel tools can be sharpened to a much finer edge, but will lose that edge fairly quickly, whereas HSS doesn't take quite as fine an edge but is claimed to hold the edge up to six times longer. The benefits of buying HSS tools are that they hold their edge longer, so they need less sharpening, you are not grinding as often, so the tools last longer, and the risk of bluing or taking the hardness out of the tool is reduced.

As you progress and become more adventurous you will probably decide that you need a larger selection of tools, most of which are designed for specific jobs.

Working practice
Good lighting and a comfortable stance are essential for safe wood turning.

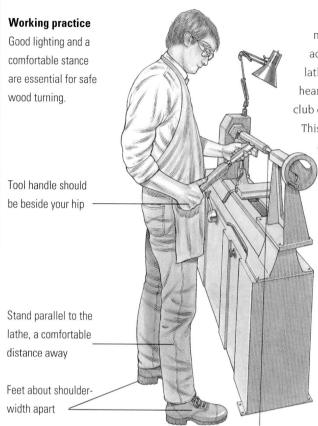

Tool handle should be beside your hip

Stand parallel to the lathe, a comfortable distance away

Feet about shoulder-width apart

requires a high speed). A good range for this type of lathe is 300-370rpm, increasing in five or six steps.

When deciding whether to go for a free-standing or bench lathe, the most important things to remember are that a free-standing lathe should be as stable and as heavy as possible (so it might well not be suitable for a wooden floor without reinforcement), and that bench-mounted lathes are only as good as the bench to which they are fixed. Here, the ideal solution is to build a sturdy bench to the correct height for you—the spindle centers should be at elbow height once the lathe has been bolted securely to the bench.

As with any woodworking purchase, it is always advisable to go for the best that you can afford; the quality is almost invariably reflected in the price. This is not to say that all less-expensive lathes are useless—some are surprisingly well-made and are very suitable for learning on—but you do tend to get what you pay for.

Woodworking magazines and local

newspapers often advertise secondhand lathes for sale, or you may hear of one from your local club or by word of mouth. This is certainly an excellent way to look for a lathe with a good reputation that may no longer be made, but if you are interested, make out a checklist before viewing. This should include the general condition of the lathe, and also the details—if the visible electrical wiring is in bad condition, for example, what will the rest be like?
Always ask to see the lathe running, and don't be afraid to set the different speeds or test the chuck yourself. And, if it's a free-standing model, who is going to transport it to your workshop, and is this included in the price?

Stance

How you stand at the lathe is important. The wrong stance can cause tiredness

Starter tool kit: You only need a handful of turning tools to get started. Also add a scraper (see p. 283) to improve the finish of a piece.

and lead to other problems with your back and neck. When turning between centers you should stand parallel to the lathe, a comfortable distance away, with your feet about shoulder-width apart, so that as you traverse the tool you can sway your body instead of moving your feet. This is not always possible, but the tool handle should be beside your hip, instead of in front of your body. The tools should be thought of as an integral part of your body, like a pair of snow skis, so giving you greater control of the tool. A big part of being comfortable at the lathe is its height, or the height of the centers from the floor. This should be at, or slightly above, elbow height when your forearm is held in a relaxed position across the front of your body. If your lathe is bench-mounted, it should be fixed as close to the front edge as possible, instead of towards the middle, so that you can stand at the lathe instead of having to reach to it.

Having said all this, the main priority is to feel comfortable and relaxed, instead of being cramped or having to reach too much.

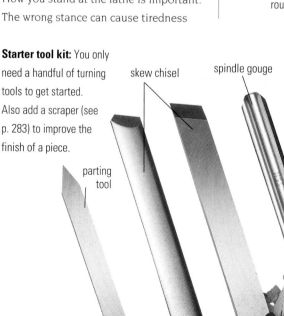

bowl gouge

roughing gouge

spindle gouge

skew chisel

parting tool

Center finding

Finding and marking accurate centers for turning blanks is vital to good wood turning for several reasons. The first, and probably the most important, is that it means the blank is properly balanced, and therefore is less likely to fly off the lathe; and the second is that if a square section is included in the design of the turned piece, it must be central to the axis.

1 There are all kinds of gadgets to find the centers of turning blanks, but the simplest method is to lay a straight-edge or ruler from corner to corner and draw a pencil line, and do that same from the opposite corners on both ends of the blank. Where the lines intersect, make a small indentation with an awl.

Mounting between centers

Turning between centers means that the workpiece is held between two points, a drive center which grips the wood, and a tail center which supports and provides enough pressure for the drive center to grip. Basically, there are three types of drive center: two-prong, four-prong, and friction drives, available in a variety of sizes.

1 Two- and four-prong drives need to be driven into the wood for the drive dogs to locate firmly. After finding the centers, stand the blank on a solid surface, locate the point on the center mark, and give it several sharp taps with a wooden mallet; this should be enough to locate the drive dogs. Insert the center into the Morse taper of the headstock before relocating the blank onto the drive dogs.

2 You do not need to drive a friction-drive center into the workpiece in the same way as a pronged drive; instead, locate the point in the awl-mark in the center of the blank.

3 When the blank has been located on the drive center, slide the tailstock into position so that the tail center is just short of the blank, then locate the tail center in the other awl-mark by winding the tailstock handle. With a pronged drive, you need only apply enough pressure with the tailstock to ensure that there is no movement between the drive dogs and the wood. Using a friction/ring drive, you can vary the amount of pressure the ring has seated by backing the hand wheel off a bit. The benefits for a novice are that if the tool cuts too deeply or digs in, the workpiece stops revolving. In production turning, the work can be loaded and unloaded without switching the lathe off.

4 When the blank has been successfully mounted, position the tool rest parallel to the workpiece and about level with the height of the centers. The workpiece must be rotated by hand to check that it clears the rest by at least ¼in (6mm).

5 Before turning on the lathe, check that everything is securely in position and won't move during turning.

Mounting on a screw chuck

Bowl blanks can be mounted in a variety of ways: screwed directly to a faceplate, glued to a waste block which is then screwed to a faceplate, a faceplate ring screwed to the blank then fixed onto the chuck, and so on. One of the simplest and quickest methods is to use a screw center or screw chuck to hold the blank while the outside of the bowl is turned.

1 Screw centers and chucks come in various sizes and lengths. If the screw center is too long for a shallow bowl, a spacing washer can be made to reduce its length. With modern deep-grooved parallel-thread screws, a 2in to 3in (50mm to 75mm) thick bowl blank only needs about 1in (25mm) of screw thread to hold. The face of the washer needs to be slightly concave to allow for the fibers that pull out around the thread.

Tips box

- The jaws of the chuck must make firm contact with the sides of the recess so make sure you cut exactly to the scribed line.

- Clean away all dust before fitting the chuck and double check that all the adjusting screws are tightened firmly before starting on the workpiece.

2 A recommended hole size is usually supplied with the chuck. Mark the required depth of hold on the drill bit with a piece of tape, and make sure that the hole is at right angles to the face of the blank.

3 Screw the blank firmly onto the chuck until the faces of the washer and blank meet squarely. You can use a try square to act as a guide as you drill into the turning blank. Check from the side that your drill bit is at right angles to the lumber surface. It is essential that the turning blank is square to the check and fitted firmly onto the screw chuck. Any misalignment could cause vibration and loosen the workpiece.

Chuck mounting expansion mode

There are two ways of holding a bowl to hollow out the inside: a recess into which the chuck jaws expand, or a spigot that the jaws grip. Both of them need to be cut accurately for maximum grip and stability.

1 The optimum grip of a chuck is achieved when the jaws are slightly opened forming a complete circle; this is the point at which the whole rim of each jaw is in contact with the recess.

2 Transfer this measurement with the dividers to the underside of the blank, being careful not to let the outer come into contact with the upward rotation of the blank.

3 Cut the dovetail out to the scribed line with the long point of a skew chisel. The depth of the recess for a bowl of this size doesn't need to be more than ¼in (6mm).

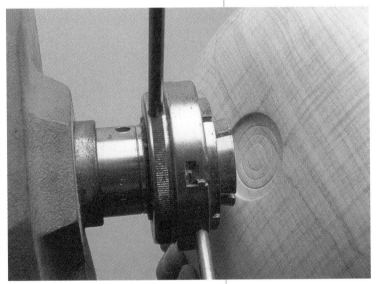

4 As long as it doesn't interfere with the seating of the jaws, the recess can be decorated with small beads to disguise it. Before locating the recess onto the jaws, check that it is clean, with no dust or shavings that might impair the positioning of the jaws.

Tips box

- If you want to turn items regularly, it is worth investing in a band saw to cut wood to length and make your own bowl blanks.

- Don't tackle faceplate turning until you have mastered the techniques of spindle work. The stresses on the tool are a lot greater in faceplate work.

Faceplates

A 4in (100mm) faceplate is all that you will need for most work; these faceplates are normally supplied with most lathes. They provide a very secure hold for larger pieces of cross-grain work, provided that the appropriate size of screw is used.

1 Position the faceplate over the center mark, which you should be able to see through the thread aperture. Pre-drill the screw holes before fastening with the screws, especially when using very dense or heavy hardwoods.

2 When using faceplates on end-grain work, use slightly longer and thicker screws because the smaller ones do not grip as well. You may need to drill a few more holes in your faceplate in order to provide a more secure hold for larger pieces of wood.

Roughing gouge

The roughing gouge is primarily used to rough out a blank, that is, to take it from square section to round, when working between centers. It is normally the first tool used in any spindle-turning application and should only be used on spindles, never on faceplate work. Roughing gouges have a wide, deep "U"-shaped flute with a fairly thick wall section; they are usually ground square across the end at an angle of about 45 degrees. For the beginner, a ¾in (19mm) width is recommended; other commonly available widths are 1¼in (32mm) and 1½in (38mm).

3 When you reach this point you must reverse the direction of the cuts. It is safer to cut away from the end of the workpiece than to cut into it, because there is less chance of the tool digging it. Practice roughing out a cylinder on a number of pieces—they won't go to waste, because just about everything you make between centers needs to be roughed out first.

1 If the workpiece is longer than the tool rest, position the rest so that the gouge can't fall off it before the cut is finished; it should be parallel to the work and about center height. To get used to the movement, do a dry run first: put the gouge on the rest about 2in (50mm) from the end of the blank, with the handle held low down beside your body. Roll the flute over slightly and point the gouge in the direction of the cut toward the tailstock. Keeping the gouge on the tool rest, raise the handle and at the same time slide the tool along the rest toward the tailstock.

2 Check that the workpiece rotates freely and everything is locked up tight, then start the lathe and begin the movement again. Gently raise the handle until you hear a knocking sound, which is the heel of the bevel touching the corners of the blank. Raise the handle until the gouge starts to cut and shavings appear, then traverse it along the rest at the same angle; keep the shavings flowing until the gouge is clear of the rotating wood, then push the handle down again (above top). Continue making the cuts until you have a cylindrical surface with no flat area on it. Start each cut a little further toward the headstock, and when you reach about 2in (50mm) from that end, stop cutting (above).

4 You can also use a roughing gouge to make planing cuts. Here the flute faces slightly toward the workpiece, instead of away from it, and the angle at which the gouge is presented to the wood is much greater, so that a slicing cut is made. This should produce a nearly polished surface.

Parting tool

In addition to their primary function, parting finished items from their waste blocks, parting tools can be used to perform a variety of other tasks. There are six types of parting tools, all of which are useful in their own right: standard-section, available in ⅛in (3mm) or ¼in (6mm) widths—the ⅛in (3mm) type is the most suitable for a beginner; diamond-section, which is ³⁄₁₆in (5mm) wide at the center or waste line; fluted, ³⁄₁₆in (5mm) wide at the flute, which runs down the underside of the tool; beading and parting, which has a ⅜in (10mm) wide square section; bedan, which has a single bevel and is rhombus-shaped in a ⅜in (10mm) wide section; and super-thin, which is ³⁄₃₂in (2mm) thick.

1 The standard, parallel-shanked parting tool should nearly always be used with the bevel rubbing and be held at right angles to the workpiece. Start the cut with the heel at right angles to the workpiece and with the heel of the bevel rubbing, then gently raise the handle vertically until you reach the desired depth of cut. To remove the tool from the cut, lower the handle.

2 To make sizing cuts, the parting tool is used in conjunction with a set of Vernier calipers or adjustable measuring calipers.

Spindle gouge

There are two types of spindle gouges: one is ground from a solid round bar, and the other is forged from a flat strip of metal. The ground type has an uneven wall thickness due to the way it is manufactured, and needs to be ground with a fingernail profile with an angle of about 40 degrees to compensate for this. The forged, or continental, type has an even wall thickness throughout its section, and is usually ground with a slightly radiused profile at the cutting edge, with an angle of about 45 degrees. Although they are more expensive, these gouges are worth buying because they are easier to use. For the most part, spindle gouges are used to cut coves and hollows, but in experienced hands can be used to produce a wide range of shapes on spindles.

Spindle gouges are commonly available in widths from ⅛in (3mm) to ¾in (19mm), in increments of ⅛in (3mm); a ½in (12mm) continental type is recommended as a starter tool. They come in such a variety of sizes because a gouge will not easily cut a cove less than its own width.

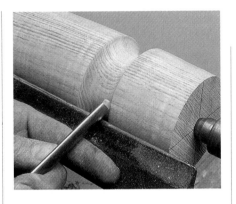

1 Coves are produced by making scooping cuts to either side of a hollow. The edge is unsupported when starting a cut, so lay the tool over on its side, with the handle down and the flute facing the center of the intended hollow. Raise the handle and start the cut with the tip of the cutting edge; once the bevel has support, roll back the gouge as the cut progresses, until the bottom of the hollow is reached.

2 As the cut reaches the bottom of the hollow, the flute should be almost flat. Push the handle down to bring the edge away from the wood.

3 Continue the procedure, cutting either side until you have the width of cove that you require.

Skew chisel

The skew chisel is to turners what the hand plane is to cabinetmakers: it should produce fine shavings and a smooth, clean surface that needs little or no finishing. Although it is one of the more difficult tools for the beginner to use, once mastered it is efficient and rewarding. For descriptive purposes, the cutting edge of a skew is divided into three sections: the long point or toe, the center, and the heel or short point. If the back of a skew is referred to, it means the edge of the blade that forms the long point.

Skews come in two sections, oval and standard. The oval skew has no sharp corners to it that can catch in any nicks on the tool rest, and slides smoothly along the rest. It has a thinner section than a standard skew and is fine for small, delicate work, but for general turning a standard ¾in (19mm) skew is more suitable for beginners. Both types are available in sizes of ½in (12mm), ¾in (19mm), 1in (25mm) and 1¼in (32mm), and are ground to an angle of 30 degrees.

1 The most basic cut made with a skew is a planing cut, where you want a smooth, flat surface. Present the chisel to the workpiece at an angle of about 45 degrees, with the tool rest slightly above center. With the bevel rubbing, cuts are made with the center section of the edge as you move the chisel along the tool rest.

2 When you make a planing cut from left to right toward the end of the workpiece, the shavings will be produced from the center section of the cutting edge.

3 The long point, or toe, is used when cutting "V" grooves. Lay the tool on its back at 90 degrees, so that the long point is closest to the work. Hold the handle low while lining up the tool.

Bowl gouge

Since bowl gouges are supplied ground square across the end, you need to grind back the wings so that they don't catch. The compound angles that are now being used on swept-back gouges overcome this problem with a steep bevel angle at the point; as the bevel sweeps around to the wings, this angle becomes a lot more acute. On the outside of a bowl, these gouges are drawn across the face, instead of being pushed as with a conventionally, ground gouge; on the inside of a bowl they are used in much the same way as the standard grind. The problem here for a beginner is that a lot of practice or costly jigs are required to replicate the grind each time the tool needs sharpening.

Depending on the amount of bowl turning you do, you will probably need more than one gouge, ground at different angles to cope with different depths and shapes. Bowl gouges are ground out of a solid round bar, with a deep flute and a long, strong shank, to cope with the distance by which they sometimes have to overhang the tool rest. They are available in sizes of ¼in (6mm), ⅜in (10mm), ½in (12mm), and ¾in (19mm); ⅜in (10mm) is recommended for beginners.

1 When using a bowl gouge, it is more important for the bevel to rub than when using a gouge between centers. If possible, the handle should be held down by your hip, and any movement of the tool should be made with your body.

2 Keep the tool rest as close to the work as possible, to minimize the amount of tool overhanging the rest. This does, however, make it difficult to effect a single cut from the base to the rim to finish off.

3 Before making the final finishing cut, it is a good idea to resharpen the gouge to get the best possible surface, so reducing the amount of scraping and sanding needed later.

Scraper

On the whole, scrapers are a fairly inefficient way of removing a lot of material when working on cross-grain work, such as bowls, and between centers, for example, spindles. However, they can also be very effective when hollowing end-grain or working with very hard, dense hardwoods as long as the lathe speed is high and the edge is kept sharp. For the beginner, the RS 200KT Multi-tip shear scraper from Robert Sorby is a very versatile tool for all kinds of applications, and is probably the only scraper you will need.

When working cross-grain, scrapers should only be used to produce the best possible finish with a tool before sanding begins. Shear-scraping, or shear-cutting as it should be called, is where the tool is presented to the face at an angle of about 45 degrees, creating a slicing action that cuts very cleanly and is a lot safer than conventional scraping.

1 Use a narrow, dome-ended scraper with the tool rest positioned above center. Make sweeping cuts from the center outward.

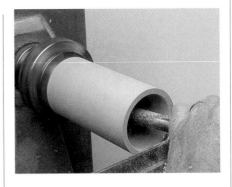

2 The best way to refine the interior shape is to make a light cut by pulling the tool toward you from the base to the lip, following the profile.

3 For working the outside of a bowl, set a straight edge of the head at an angle to the shank, with the tool working at about center height from the smallest diameter to the largest one.

4 The inside of the bowl is treated in the same way, except that the tool is now working from the largest to the smallest diameter, so that the fibers being cut are supported by those beneath or around them.

Hollowing

No matter what size they are, or whether they are done end grain or cross grain, hollow forms have to be tackled in a set sequence. The interior has to be treated differently than the interior of a bowl. With a bowl, cuts are made from the rim through to the center in one pass, but this is not possible in a hollow form, because most of the time, it is impossible to see what the tool is doing. The following steps allow you to keep track of the tool even though you cannot see it.

1 Once you have established the shape of the vessel, establish the depth by drilling a hole down the center of the workpiece.

2 Cranked hollowing tools are designed so that the tip is in line with the straight part of the shank, and so the tool rest has to be positioned far enough away from the opening for only the straight part of the shank to sit on the tool rest. The hand acts as a pivot, gripping both the tool and the rest.

3 Deal first with the area just inside the opening, making small, sweeping cuts from the center outward. The final wall thickness must be established and finished at this stage, because it will become too fragile to return to later.

4 When the neck area has been dealt with, remove a central core of waste in the next section to allow room to maneuver the tool, again making small sweeping cuts. Clear the debris frequently; if allowed to build up, it can cause the tool to grab or dig in, resulting in a broken pot.

5 Finish the walls in each section before you move on to the next. The wall thickness should be constantly checked with calipers to avoid the possibility of going through them.

6 Continue hollowing in the same manner, and when the sides start narrowing in, pull the cuts toward you, following the sweep of the outside curve (above and right).

Drilling on the lathe

There are two main ways of drilling on the lathe. In the first, the drill is fixed in a Jacobs chuck on a Morse taper mounted in the rotating headstock spindle, and the workpiece is advanced onto the drill. This method is used in projects that require drilling before they are turned, such as tool handles. In the second, the workpiece is held in a chuck and the Jacobs chuck is mounted in the tailstock, which is advanced into the workpiece.

1 Find and mark the centers of your blank with an awl. Fix the drill bit into the chuck, and the chuck into the lathe spindle. Place the blank between the drill and tail center, locating the drill in the hole made by the awl. At this stage, apply only enough pressure with the tailstock to hold the blank in place. Position the tool rest so that one face of the blank just rests on it.

2 Steady the workpiece with one hand before switching the lathe on with the other, then advance the tailstock until you have achieved the required depth.

3 Flat-bottomed, saw-toothed bits are the best type to use in this type of drilling operation; the lathe speed should be relatively slow when using them, about 500rpm.

4 Slide the tailstock up and lock it into position, then steadily advance the drill into the revolving workpiece until it reaches the marked depth. Clear the shavings by backing the drill out frequently before they pack up around the shank and make it difficult to remove the drill. Slide the tailstock up and lock it into position, then steadily advance the drill into the revolving workpiece until it reaches the marked depth. Make sure the drill bit is firmly fixed in the chuck jaws before you turn on the lathe. Always put the chuck key into all the locking holes and tighten them. You can use a small piece of tape wrapped around the shaft of the drill bit to show the required drilling depth.

Tips box

- You can buy long hole-boring kits, consisting of a 4-prong drive and a long auger bit.

- Always make sure the workpiece is well supported as you drill into the center. Vibration can snap the drill bit or cause the bit to wander off course.

- You can use small metal files to sharpen the tip of the drill bit if the hole edges appear rough.

Finishes

The type of finish should be appropriate for the use of the article. For example, items that are to come into contact with foods or to be used by small children need a non-toxic finish; liquid paraffin is ideal because it is non-toxic and colorless, and does not go rancid. Try out different finishes until you find what is best for you—but remember that no finish can cover up hasty surface preparation.

Friction polish

Friction polish should only be used for small decorative items, because it can be quite difficult to achieve an even finish on larger surfaces.

1 With the lathe stationary, wipe or brush on an even coat of polish, making sure to get it into any corners.

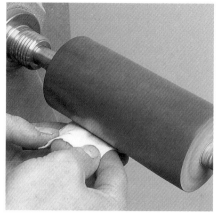

2 Start the lathe and gradually build up pressure with the towel until you have the desired luster, without streaks or lines. If the finish is too shiny, apply a coat of wax with 0000-grade steel wool to soften it.

Oils

Most woodfinishing oils are based on tung oil, a natural oil that penetrates the wood. They also contain resins and driers to give heat- and water-resistance, so that the dry surface will not scratch or chip. Two or three coats are needed to build up a nice, soft sheen without obscuring the wood's tactile qualities, and the workpiece can be easily re-coated at a later date if necessary.

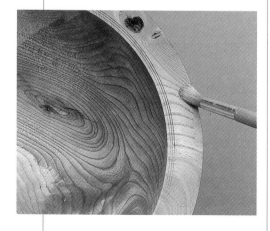

The easiest way to apply oils is with a brush. Apply a liberal coating to the whole object and leave it to soak in for a while; the actual time will vary according to the manufacturer's recommendations and the weather conditions.

Liquid paraffin

This is a non-toxic finish readily available from hardware stores and is ideal for use on anything that will come into contact with children or food.

1 Sand the workpiece normally, running through the different grits until you reach the final grit, then brush on a coat of liquid paraffin over the whole surface. Do this with the lathe stopped, otherwise you may end up covered in the finish yourself.

2 Restart the lathe and use your final grit—320 or 400 grit—to sand the liquid paraffin into the surface. One of the benefits of using this method is that it reduces the amount of dust that you have to cope with; another is that the item can be easily maintained.

Scorching

Burning the surface of a bowl that you have spent some time turning might seem a bit drastic, but it can be a very effective means of decoration. Open-grained or coarse-grained wood, like oak, ash, or sweet chestnut, is more suitable than fine, close-grained wood, and burrs (burls) take on a crumbled appearance.

1 In scorching, the surface of the object is burned with a blowtorch to blacken it and give it an aged and weathered appearance. This type of decoration is not good for thin-walled bowls and things which would probably burst into flames.

2 When the surface is burned to a dark color, the softer summer growth burning away quicker than the winter growth, it leaves a layer of soot that is removed with a fine wire brush to reveal the true surface.

3 Sometimes you can cut a series of grooves to define certain features—in this piece the band below the rim.

5 Scorching is only really suitable for coarse, open-grained woods such as oak, where there is a distinct difference between the summer and winter growths.

4 You can leave parts of the object natural. Here, the chuck recess was left because the accuracy could be affected by the scorching, and it provides a nice contrast and leaves you somewhere to sign, date, and identify the wood.

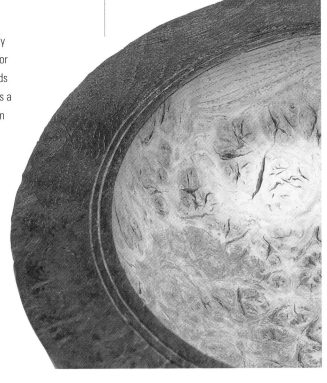

Sharpening

Because they are quickly blunted by the amount of wood that they remove, turning tools need sharpening a lot more often than other hand tools. The difficulty for beginners is achieving a single-faceted bevel with the correct angle without bluing or changing the temper of the steel. Three different techniques are shown here, ranging from the simple and inexpensive to using a professional-quality machine.

Wet-stone grinding

Although wet-stone grinding is quite slow, it eliminates the risk of overheating the tool; and the slow-running wheels are made of fine material, which produces a far more superior edge than any other form of grinding. The various jigs available give you total control over whatever tool you are sharpening.

1 Skew chisels are difficult tools to sharpen without overheating or changing the bevel angle. On the wet-stone grinder, the large diameter of the wheel and the slow speed, combined with the simple jig, make the task a fairly easy one.

2 You can hone the bevel to remove the burr (burl) raised by the grinding, and polish the bevel to give an even finer edge.

Lathe-mounted sharpening

The beauty of this system is that your line of sight is parallel with the face of the disc, which makes it very easy to line up the bevel. Modern turning tools are produced with a flat bevel instead of concave one, because manufacturers grind the bevels on flat belts.

1 The simplest system can be made in your own workshop or bought as an inexpensive kit. It consists of two ⅜in (10mm) thick x 5½in (140mm) diameter MDF discs with self-adhesive abrasive discs in three different grits (80, 150, and 320), and a leather disc, which are all mounted on a central screw or directly onto your screw chuck.

You can make an arbor that fits the jaws of your chuck to facilitate quick changing of the discs, without tying up your screw chuck. This will also ensure that the discs always run true if you should make the face slightly concave.

2 Stick the leather on one face of a disc, using contact adhesive, and the 320 grit on the other; these are the faces that will be used most often. Just before screwing it onto the arbor, run some thin superglue into the hole, to create a more permanent thread.

3 Position the tool rest at 90 degrees to the disc and as low as possible. Lay the tool to be sharpened—here a ¾in (19mm) roughing gouge—on the rest at an angle so that the bevel is parallel to the face. Try to use the bottom of the disc so that the direction of rotation is away from you. Set the lathe on a medium speed.

FRETWORK

Powered fretwork using thin wood

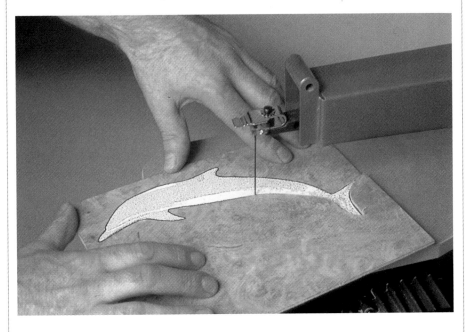

Draw, trace, or paste the desired shape onto a piece of thin plywood, such as ⅛in (3mm) veneered plywood. It is easier at first to use thin wood with a fine-toothed blade that can cut tight corners. Sometimes, if the corner is too tight, it's a good idea to back the blade out of the cut and to start another cut from a different angle. Look at the ventral (bottom) fin of the shark and you can see how difficult it would be to turn in such a tight spot. If you started another cut in line with the top edge of the fin, you could come right up to the body and cut away the waste quite easily.

Insert the blade with its teeth pointing downward. The wood will want to snatch up, so hold it down firmly while you are cutting. Keep your fingers clear of the blade and blow away the dust as you cut. Many fretsaws nowadays are fitted with blowers that clear away the sawdust while you are working. These normally consist of a small plastic tube fixed near the blade and connected to bellows operated by the up-and-down movement of the saw arm.

Working enclosed cuts

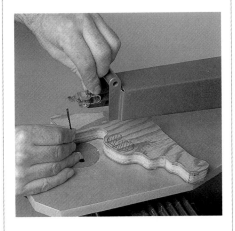

1 When making an enclosed cut, for example, one that does not come to the edge of the workpiece, there is obviously a problem in getting the blade to initially pass through the wood. This is done by first drilling a hole in the part of the wood to be removed, disconnecting the blade at one end in the saw, threading the blade through the hole, and reconnecting it. As always, you should shade in the part to be cut out to avoid mistakes. It is remarkably easy to cut away the wrong bit, especially when working on complicated patterns.

Powered fretwork using stout wood

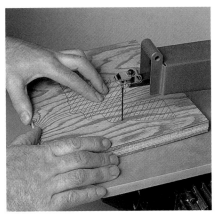

1 To fret stout wood such as ¾in (18mm) plywood you should use a medium-toothed blade. This is because it has a more robust cutting job to do and is therefore less likely to break in thicker lumber. Holding the wood firmly down, slowly feed the wood into the blade. You can sense the speed of cut by the sound and feel. Never try to force the rate of feed into the blade. At best, the blade will overheat and, at worst, it will break.

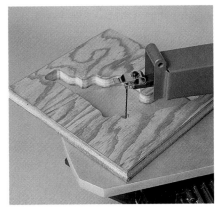

2 Cut tight curves slowly; again this is to prevent overheating and blade breakage. The finish left from the fretsaw blade is remarkably smooth, which is a great advantage in toy making where tiny fingers will be handling the finished article.

The fretsaw

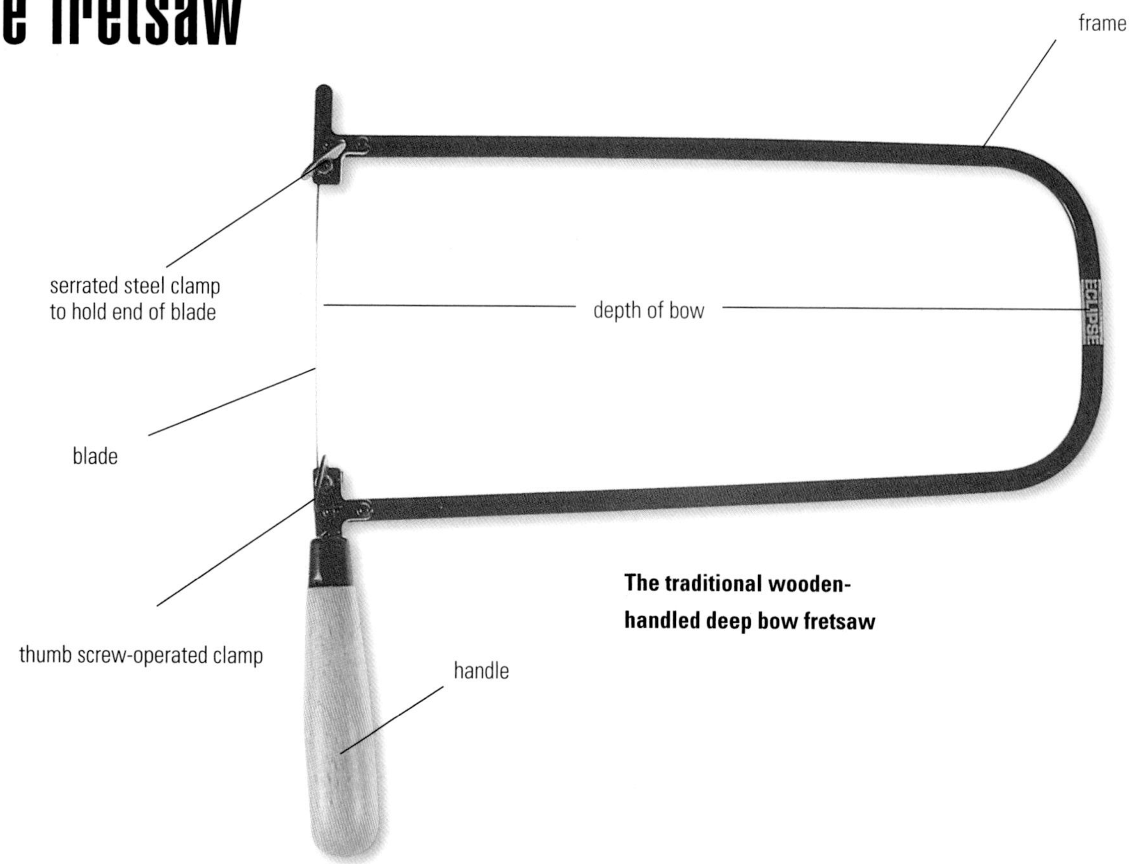

frame

serrated steel clamp
to hold end of blade

depth of bow

blade

thumb screw-operated clamp

handle

**The traditional wooden-
handled deep bow fretsaw**

The fretsaw's bow-shaped frame and thin blade make it just perfect for cutting out intricate curved designs in thin wood. If you want to cut out pierced holes, make a jigsaw puzzle, or build small tabletop toys, then this is the tool for you.

Using a fretsaw

The blade is fitted in the frame with a couple of thumb screws, with the frame itself having enough spring to keep the blade under tension. To install a new blade, use your body to push the frame against the side of the bench until the old blade goes slack and drops out. Then set the ends of the new blade in the little clamps, tighten up the thumb screws, and let the frame spring back.

In use, you set the workpiece in the vise, or clamp it face down so that it overhangs the bench, and then you work with a delicate push-and-pull action. Most woodworkers prefer to mount the blade so that the teeth will be pointing toward the handle. That way, they cut on the pull stroke, offering better control for cutting thin wood.

Fretting a chair splat

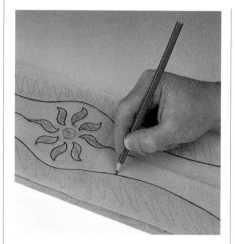

1 Having drawn up the profile and established the "windows" of the design, take a tracing and pencil-press transfer the traced lines through to the wood.

2 Drill ⅛in (3mm) diameter pilot holes through each of the enclosed windows. Use either the power saw or the handsaw to cut out the overall profile.

EDGE TREATMENTS

In much period furniture the edges of wood panels (for example, carcases, shelves, tabletops) were seldom left plain or "square" but were profiled in some way to add visual interest. These sometimes ornate profiles are called moldings and they serve also to soften the edges for more comfortable handling. Moldings are also often put on to other wood artefacts solely for aesthetic reasons, such as in the case of picture or window frames.

Today there is a practical need for treating the edges of furniture for both tactile and visual reasons, especially as much of it is made of veneered chipboard. The brittle edges of this cheap substitute for solid wood need reinforcing with solid wood strips called "lippings." This can be done before the panel is veneered, so that the edges blend in discreetly with the face veneer, using the same material for the lipping. Lippings are usually at least ¼in (6mm) wide, offering scope for molded profiles similar to those used in solid wood construction.

Traditional moldings used to be cut with differently-profiled handplanes, and there is an interesting vocabulary of profiles such as carvetto, ogee, cove, reed, and astragal. Many of these planes are now collectors' items and woodworkers of all ages are eager to acquire them for largely sentimental reasons.

Present-day routing technology has, to a large extent, replaced the old molding planes, and a huge range of profiled router cutters for shaping edges is used instead (see Routing pages 113-28).

3 Finally, having secured the workpiece in the vise, take the fretsaw, disconnect one end of the blade, pass the blade end through one of the pilot holes, re-attach the blade, and then get to work fretting out the enclosed area of waste. Repeat this procedure for all the pierced areas of the design.

The bow-back chair with the splat in place.

Tips box

The secret of using the fretsaw has to do with being able to change the direction of the cut at tight angles without breaking the blade or friction-burning the wood. The correct procedure is to run the line of cut up to the angle and then at the same time increase the rate of the stroke while re-aligning the frame so that the blade is following the new route.

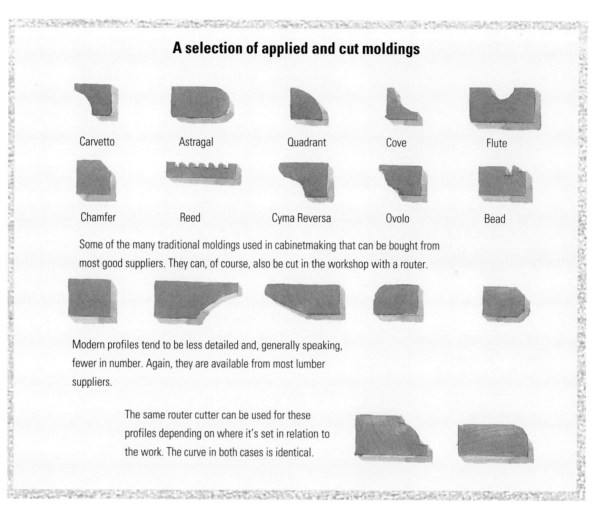

A selection of applied and cut moldings

| Carvetto | Astragal | Quadrant | Cove | Flute |

| Chamfer | Reed | Cyma Reversa | Ovolo | Bead |

Some of the many traditional moldings used in cabinetmaking that can be bought from most good suppliers. They can, of course, also be cut in the workshop with a router.

Modern profiles tend to be less detailed and, generally speaking, fewer in number. Again, they are available from most lumber suppliers.

The same router cutter can be used for these profiles depending on where it's set in relation to the work. The curve in both cases is identical.

Types of edges

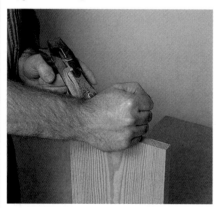

1 The simplest edge is a "square" edge and this can be achieved with a handplane or by machine planing.

2 If you want to make a thicker board look thinner or more delicate, plane a chamfer (or slope) along the bottom edge, first use a marking gauge, and then plane to the line.

3 All edges of furniture should be slightly softened with very fine abrasive paper. This removes the sharp edge, which is known as an "arris," and creates an edge that is soft on both the eye and the hand.

Applying lippings to a veneered panel

1 Make sure the edges of the manufactured board are true and square. This is very simply done with a try square but, make sure that the stock of the square rests firmly against the surface of the board.

2 Prepare to size some ¼in (6mm) wide lippings, which should be fractionally thicker than the chipboard. Miter the corners and then glue and tape the lippings in position on the edges.

3 With a handplane, trim the lippings flush, ready for veneering. Work inward to avoid splitting the grain. After the panel has been veneered, the edges can be profiled as though they are solid wood, provided that the lipping is wide enough.

Edge treatments

2 The set-up can also be used for plowing grooves and other shapes in the middle of the board. Make sure to use a fence and push sticks (right).

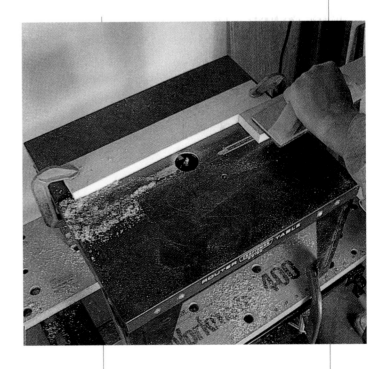

1 A simple router table set-up is perfect for rounding over the edges of a board or cutting a variety of shapes in wood. The rounding over bit shown above has a pilot bearing to guide the wood as it is being cut. Just feed the board into the direction of the cutter rotation and the bit will do the rest. For the smoothest cut, make at least two passes. You can remove most of the material in the first pass, then make another pass, just taking off a tiny bit to polish up the edge.

VENEERS

Veneers are thin slices of wood, used for decorative or constructional purposes. Wood is converted into decorative veneer because some species are too rare or expensive to be used as solid wood, or their structure makes them unsuitable to be used in solid form. When glued to a stable substrate, they produce fine colors, shapes, patterns, and textures that may be impossible to achieve using solid wood. Do not think of veneer as a substitute, or as giving a lower-quality result. Veneer is a viable and respectable alternative to solid wood. Decorative veneers are usually very thin ¼in to ½2in (0.6mm to 1mm) thick. Constructional veneers are used in the production of plywood or laminated shapes and are generally much thicker, from ¾2in to ⅛in (2.5mm to 3.5mm).

Veneer production

The specialized veneer manufacturer must be able to gauge the likelihood of valuable or interesting veneer that will result from cutting by looking at the uncut log. The expertise of the veneer cutter lies in knowing how to cut the log to produce the greatest quantity of valuable veneer. It is possible to cut large sheets from some wood, but in wood with unusual features, the veneer sheets will be quite small. There are three main methods of cutting veneer: rotary cut, sliced, and sawed.

Saw cutting

Before the development of veneer slicing machines in the 1700s, all veneers were cut by sawing. Now sawing is only used for particular species or logs that are difficult to peel or slice, or where a specific grain feature can be obtained only by sawing.

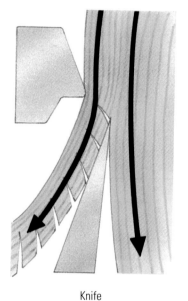

Knife

The knife is set forward of the pressure bar by the required thickness of the veneer.

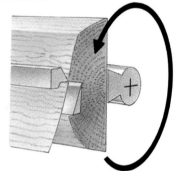

Veneer cut from a half-round log is narrower, but has a similar figure to veneer produced by off-center cutting.

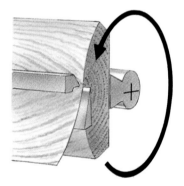

In back cutting the log is mounted with the heartwood facing outward to produce decorative figures, such as burrs (burls) and curls.

Rotary cutting

The log is first softened by soaking it in water or steaming. A large knife is set to cut the veneer to the required thickness, assisted by a pressure-bar that helps the veneer part evenly.

The log is held between centers, and rotated against the knife to produce a continuous sheet of veneer.

This is an efficient method for producing large sheets for plywood and laminates; it is also used for some

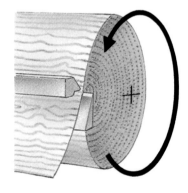

Mounting the log off-center produces a wide veneer, but with a decorative grain figure.

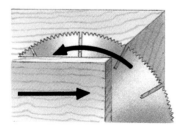

Saw cutting is very wasteful. Up to 50 percent of the log may be lost in the saw cut.

decorative veneers, particularly to produce the bird's-eye effect in maple.

Rotary cutting produces a veneer with a distinctive pattern, produced by the tangential cut through the growth rings.

Slicing

This method produces decorative hardwood veneers. The log is first cut lengthwise, and its grain is assessed to determine how more cuts can produce very interesting and valuable veneers. The log is then cut into "flitches," which are mounted on a sliding frame. As the frame moves down, it pushes the wood against the knife blade and pressure bar to slice off a sheet of veneer.

The flitch can be mounted in several different ways to produce various grain patterns.

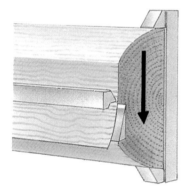

Flat slicing Is the most common method, and produces traditional crown-cut veneer with bold curves and ovals.

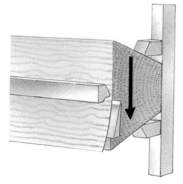

Flat-sliced veneer may also be cut tangentially from a quartered log; this produces narrow but attractive veneers.

Types of veneer

Decorative veneers are always cut to maximize the attractive features of the wood species.

Veneers are stacked in sequence from the slicer so that patterns can be matched, and they are then sold in sequence. To match veneers, always take them consecutively from the pack.

Veneer can be commercially colored, subtly or in vivid hues, lines, bandings, and readymade patterns are also available.

Stringing lines are fine strips used to divide different areas of veneer. Decorative bandings are made from side grain sections glued together, then sliced into strips. Always buy enough of each pattern to complete a project because you may not be able to obtain the exact color and pattern again.

Inlay motifs are bought readymade to inset in a veneer surface or for use in marquetry. If possible, the inlay should be the same thickness as the veneer for even pressure during gluing. Traditionally, other materials like mother-of-pearl and brass have also been used for veneer inlay.

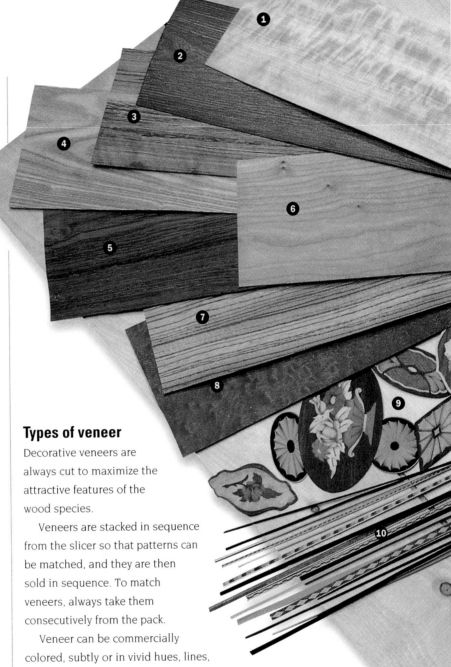

Veneers, inlays, and bandings

1 Aspen
2 Colored pine
3 Tropical olive
4 Olive ash
5 Brazilian rosewood
6 Cherry
7 Zebrano
8 Pomelle
9 A selection of different inlay motifs
10 Patterned bandings and stringings

Laying veneer

One of the thrills of woodworking is to use solid wood. However, some wood is too expensive or has grain that is unsuitable to work in solid form. Many exotic woods are available only as veneer.

In industry, veneers are applied in a hydraulic press with heated platens. Traditional woodworkers make a hand press or "caul" to do a similar job. The technique described here shows how to apply and press veneer with a simple handmade caul.

Veneer can also be applied by hand using animal glue, pressing the veneer with a special veneer hammer. This is a very skilled technique and is usually limited to restoration or reproduction.

Laying and pressing

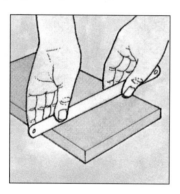

1 Careful preparation is necessary. The ground or face on which the veneer is going to be laid should be flat and clean. You can roughen the surface slightly with a saw blade to provide a key for the adhesive.

Tips box

If you are working with buckled sheets of burr (burl) veneer, there will often be areas that have small holes or cracks. Apply the veneer in the usual way and fill these areas with a filler, colored to match the surrounding veneer. Sand smooth and protect the veneered surface with your chosen polish or other finish.

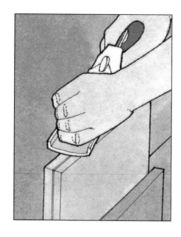

2 If jointing is needed to make the sheets of veneer wide enough, the joint must be precise. Clamp the veneer between two boards and plane the edges straight.

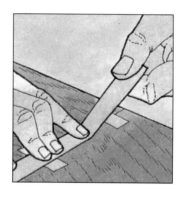

3 Use paper tape to hold joints together. Masking tape is too thick, and transparent tape, while it is useful because of its transparency, can lift the grain when it is removed (unless it is a special low-tack type).

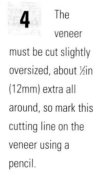

4 The veneer must be cut slightly oversized, about ½in (12mm) extra all around, so mark this cutting line on the veneer using a pencil.

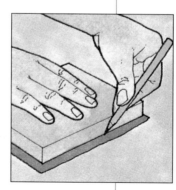

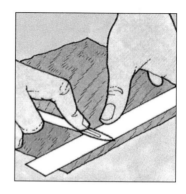

5 Cut veneer with a sharp marking knife against a steel straight-edge. Cut about ⅛in (3mm) outside the pencil line, and cut across the grain first as this is most likely to split.

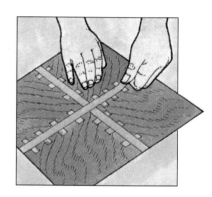

6 If pieces of veneer must be cut and jointed, do this first, then lay them on the ground in one piece. It is essential to make a clean cut along each mating edge—use a sharp craft knife or scalpel and a metal straight-edge. Put the pieces together and hold flat as you apply strips of tape across the joint line. Complete the jointing by adding a continuous strip of tape along the joint. The tape shrinks slightly as it dries, so drawing the parts together for an exact fit.

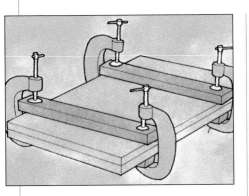

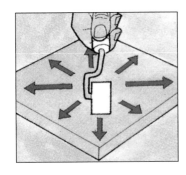

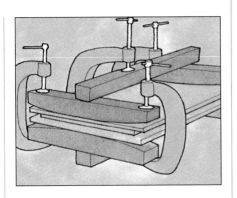

7 Make the caul or press from two substantial boards or sheets of blockboard, or chipboard at least 1in (25mm) thick and larger than the panel to be veneered. Do not use jointed boards for the caul.

10 Lay the veneer, smoothing it down by hand. Then, with a clean roller, press it down, working from the center to the edges. The principle with veneer laying is always to squeeze adhesive from the center out and ensure that no air is trapped.

12 On a larger job, use battens, cut to a slight curve, on the outside of the caul. Then, when the clamps are tightened, pressure is applied first to the center of the caul.

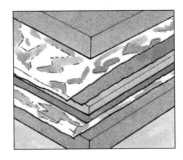

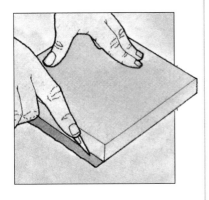

8 It is a good idea to finish and wax the inside surfaces of the caul. With some veneers, the adhesive can weep through and may stick to the caul. For the same reason always place paper or clean polythylene sheet between the caul and the veneer.

13 Allow enough time for the adhesive to have thoroughly cured before opening the press.

The time will depend on the type of glue used, but overnight is always preferable, except if you are using hardeners or accelerators to part-cure the glue. Keep the workshop at a reasonable temperature, 60-70°F (15.5-21°C).

Trim the veneer with a sharp craft knife, remove any paper tape with a little warm water and then sand lightly before applying a finish.

9 The choice of adhesive is important. Use either PVA or UF. It is not generally advisable to use contact adhesive for natural lumber. Only use this when laying surfaces like plastic laminates or linoleum. Metal surfaces, tiles, and mosaics need special adhesives.

Apply adhesive to the ground only and not to the veneer. It is worth spreading the adhesive with a roller to obtain a film of consistent thickness (right).

11 Large "G" clamps will give enough pressure on a small job. But because of the depth of throat on most, there will not be enough pressure on the center of the caul (above). Traditional thread action "G" clamps are ideal for this kind of work because they exert a large amount of force and can be precisely controlled. Quick-action clamps are fine for holding carcases together as the glue sets, but don't usually exert enough pressure to hold the veneer surface flat. Tighten each clamp by the same amount.

Veneering a lipped panel

1 Select a piece of veneer slightly larger than the lipped groundwork (see Edge treatments pages 291-2). Use veneer tape to bind any splits in the veneer by taping the outer side. Place the lipped panel over the veneer mounted on a backing board and mark the perimeter.

2 Using a steel straight-edge and a sharp marking knife, carefully cut the veneer about ⅛in (3mm) outside the marked line. It is important to cut across the grain first because this is most likely to split. By using the marking knife at a shallow angle, with the forefinger applying firm pressure the action is firm and slow, especially at the end of the cut where the grain is likely to break out. The blade at this point is almost horizontal. Only the tip of the knife is used to sever the wood fibers of a thin veneer sheet and this area can blunt quickly. Have plenty of replacement blades ready and change blades as soon as the edge seems to drag, or if the veneer edge breaks.

3 Now prepare a flat clamping caul: get some "G" clamps ready, and place paper under the groundwork; apply PVA glue with a spatula. Sometimes groundwork is "keyed" (roughened up) with a toothing plane or saw edge, but it is not necessary with modern glues. The spatula here is serrated to help spread the glue evenly.

4 The PVA glue is left to dry for a few minutes, to allow water to evaporate before the veneer is placed over the groundwork. This is to avoid glue stains coming through the veneer, or excessive water buckling the veneer, which is still possible even when it is under pressure in the clamped caul. Even though the veneer may look solid, the thinness of the sheet means that adhesive can easily seep through from one side to the other. Always lightly sand the completed panel to smooth the veneer surface, and remove any dried glue and dirt marks before the finishing stage.

5 Mount the veneered panel against one or two flat cauls and clamp up so that the pressure is even. Allow to dry overnight, or for at least two hours under pressure at 60°F (15°C).

6 When the veneered panel is dry the oversized veneer is carefully trimmed with the marking knife against a backing board. Tilt the panel with a spacer to transfer pressure at the knife cut. The veneered panel is now ready for sanding or scraping.

Tips box

When choosing a decorative veneer that is to be used for a box lid or other area that will always be on display, take time to source the most interesting piece of figure—do not make do with a design that you are not completely happy with.

Applying veneers, motifs, and bandings to a flat panel

1 Interesting effects can be achieved by laying veneers. Here, a small panel is quarter-matched and bandings added. Cut the veneer using a marking knife and backing board and use the veneer sheet as a marker for the other pieces required.

2 Very carefully join and trim the four matching pieces using veneer tape. Also, tape any splits in the veneer. Replace any severed pieces with veneer tape. Veneer tape is dampened (you can lick it) and is removed easily by dampening it more after the panel has been glued.

3 Decorative motifs can be purchased in a variety of shapes, sizes, and patterns. This oval motif is laid onto the center of the quarter-veneered panel with its paper backing up.

4 Carefully cut through the veneer by tracing with the marking knife on a backing board. The motif is fitted inside the opening, taped down, and glued with the panel using paper, cauls, and clamps. The groundwork is cut large to accommodate a banding strip.

5 To border the veneered panel, a cross-banding is cut with the grain running shortwise for decorative effect. Cut strips of veneer for the cross-banding, joining with tape where necessary to achieve the desired length. First, trim the edges of the veneered panel to form a parallel border around the panel. The miters can be cut by laying the bandings in situ and carefully cutting through both together. Glue cross bandings separately using veneer tape and flat cauls.

6 Narrow strips in varying patterns of short-grained lumber sections can add enormous visual interest to a veneered panel. After the cross bandings have been glued and dried, the veneered panel is ready for inlaying the stringing. Using the straight fence, a router can be used to rout a very fine groove around the panel (see Routing page 122). Take great care with narrow cutters because they are very fragile. The depth of the groove is just under ½in (2mm).

7 The radiused corners of the routed grooves are straightened up with a chisel (see Chiseling pages 129-144). Carefully cut the string by marking the mitered joins with a chisel. Then cut the stringings to the marked line against a backing board.

Use a veneer spatula to apply a little PVA glue into the grooves and carefully inset the stringings. A pin hammer can be used to press the stringings into place.

8 After gluing, the panel is ready for the satisfying part—the cleaning up. This is best done with a cabinet scraper. First, the veneer tape is moistened with a damp cloth and then scraped away to reveal the beauty of the wood underneath. The scraper is used in all directions, but be sure to work with the grain or diagonally to maintain a smooth cut. Although veneer is very thin, it is amazing how it stands up to being scraped. The panel is now ready for finishing.

Marquetry

Marquetry is the name given to the art of producing recognizable pictures using the distinctive colors and grain patterns of different veneers. There are many different ways of producing a marquetry picture—the "window" method, demonstrated here, is just one of them. Make a tracing of your picture, reverse it, and tape the top edge to a flat cutting board. In the "window" method, the background is made by tracing through the essential elements onto the veneer and jointing them to produce a complete panel into which the other elements are cut. The remaining elements are set into the background. The whole operation is done in reverse because when you cut the windows, and then the pieces to fit into them, the way the blade cuts into the veneer produces a tighter fit at the bottom of the cut because the blade is tapered. This means that you will have much cleaner, tighter joints on the underneath of the picture.

Marquetry requires a lot of patience and accurate cutting, but the results can be stunning. This brightly-colored picture is very much a beginner's project. Experienced craftsmen can produce anything from elaborate rural scenes to copies of photographs and oil paintings, using the full range of wood tones to produce almost a sepia effect.

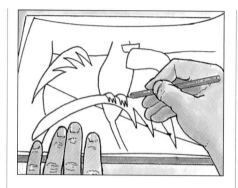

1 Draw the design, or your version of it, or draw a completely different design if you prefer, and trace this on good-quality tracing paper. If you are new to the technique, try to keep the design fairly simple.

2 Reverse the tracing and tape the top edge to the top of a cutting board. Remember that the operation is carried out in reverse, with the elements being set into the background. You will also need to be able to lift the tracing paper, so secure it along the top edge only.

Making the background

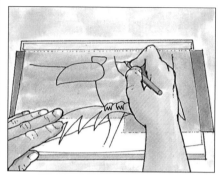

3 Place a piece of light blue veneer, large enough for the sky, under the tracing and trace through the skyline onto it. In this particular picture, this is a fairly narrow strip.

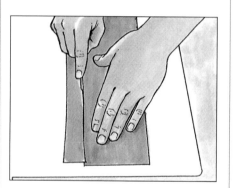

4 Cut this line by hand with a craft knife, keeping the angle of cut low. The line does not need to be perfectly straight and should have a natural look.

5 Now place this over a piece of dark blue veneer, large enough for the sea, and cut along the edge, making sure to hold the blade firmly against the edge of the sky.

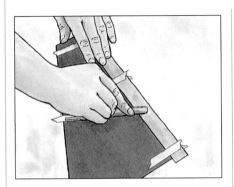

6 Check the fit and rub glue along the edge of one piece and tape them together. Tape "stitches" to pull them together on both sides and pieces along the length where necessary. Rub the joint with the handle of a scalpel or similar tool to ensure that it is flush.

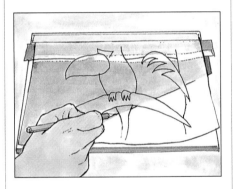

7 Place the sky/sea assembly back under the tracing paper and trace the "shoreline" through. Work in the same way as before and again not too formally, but aim to give it a natural feel.

8 Cut this line and place a piece of yellow veneer for the sand under it. Hold this firmly in place, cut along the line, and join as before with glue and tape.

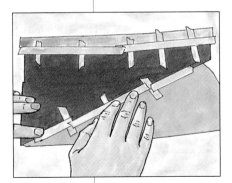

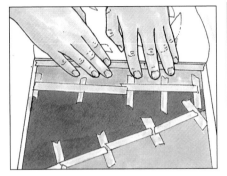

9 When dry, trim the edges square but leave the whole slightly oversized. Tape the top edge of the assembled background in place between the tracing and the cutting board. Both the tracing and background must be able to be folded up and down easily.

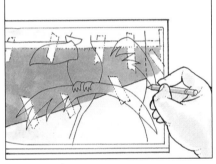

10 Because the palm trunk does not fit into a "window", it is treated as part of the background. Trace its profile onto the background—follow the dotted lines shown above. Cut this out and cut a piece from your chosen veneer to fit. Glue and tape in position to complete the background.

Fitting the features

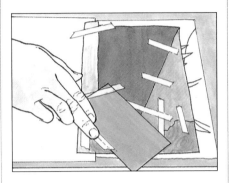

11 Trace the top small branch onto the background and carefully cut out this shape, using a fresh scalpel blade. Tape a piece of green veneer to the underneath, "right" side to cover this "window."

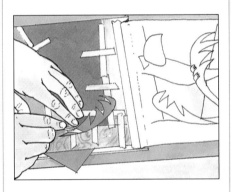

12 Now cut through the window slowly and carefully until you have cut all the way around. Remove the piece of veneer and carefully complete any cuts that have not gone right through.

Tips box

Marquetry can be a way of introducing a decorative motif to a flat surface—from a jewelry box lid to the front of a chest. Use a pale polish or clear sanding sealer to protect the finished motif—a dark polish will tint the veneers and lessen the effect.

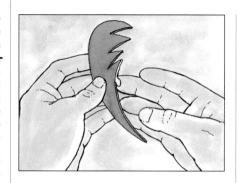

13 Test the piece in place by pushing through from behind. Apply glue to the edges and push it into place. Tape and rub the edges. Repeat steps 11 and 12 for the bird's body—two pieces meeting under main branch; main branch; bird's feet; dark glasses.

Fitting the beak

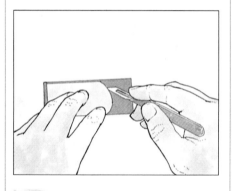

14 Make a template from ⅟₁₆in (1.5mm) birch ply, or something similar, to mirror the shape where the beak joins the bird's head. Leaving enough for the back end of the beak, cut the shape of the template out of a piece of orange veneer.

Tips box

Marquetry is an intricate process. You will need a good source of natural light or a lamp that you can direct on to the work. Because the pieces are only small and there is no machinery involved, it can easily be made up on a kitchen table in the evening, instead of in the workshop.

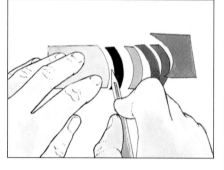

15 Using the template, cut a series of narrow segments out of a selection of colored veneers. Finally, cut another piece of orange for the other end of the beak.

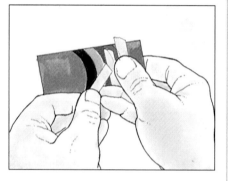

16 Glue these pieces together by rubbing a little glue on the edges and taping them together. When dry, remove the tape. Cut out the window for the beak and tape the prepared piece behind the window and cut out and glue in place as before.

17 Remove all the tape and veneer the completed picture to a slightly oversized board. Remember to veneer the "right" side up.

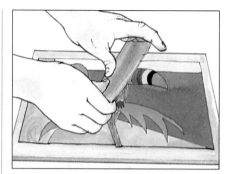

18 When it is dry, use a cabinet scraper to scrape the surface absolutely flat, noting the grain direction of the pieces. You can scrape across the grain, but do not work absolutely square because this can pull up the fibers. Do not sand, to avoid colored dust in the grain.

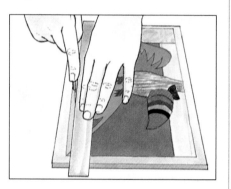

19 Trim the edges square and form a border as required. Now mount as a picture or use the design as the lid for a box. Some very delicate designs can be made with this technique and great levels of skill can be reached.

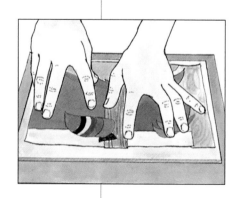

Tunbridgeware

This is a seemingly complex way of decorating boxes and other small items, but it is actually very straightforward. Traditionally, the whole piece to be decorated is covered in a series of identical, or similar, mosaic-like panels cut from the end of a made-up "log."

This log is formed from ½in (1mm) or ⅟₁₆in (1.5mm) square lines, glued together to produce something like a stick of rock with an identical design running the whole length. Different-colored woods are used to produce the patterns, and ebony, boxwood, walnut, pear, and rosewood are all commonly used. Here, boxwood, padauk, and dyed veneer lines have been chosen. The black-and-red squares used are formed by taking ⅟₁₆in (1.5mm) slices off the edge of a laminated sheet of red-and-black veneers.

The basic method of producing a "log" is described here, but you will see that by making a log that is more and more complex and by using a combination of different logs, extremely intricate and impressive designs can be gradually built up.

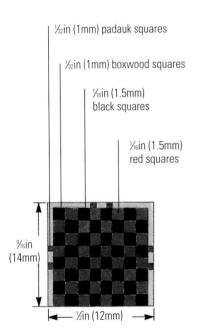

½in (1mm) padauk squares

⅟₃₂in (1mm) boxwood squares

⅟₁₆in (1.5mm) black squares

⅟₁₆in (1.5mm) red squares

⁹⁄₁₆in (14mm)

½in (12mm)

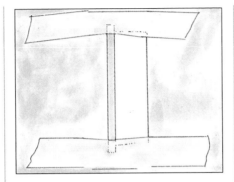

1 Stick a piece of waxed paper, 1in x 3¼in (25mm x 80mm), to a setting-up board and tape a piece of ⅛in (3mm) square boxwood or similar down the left side as shown.

2 Cut 40 x ⅟₁₆in (1.5mm) square strips, 20 each of black and red, 2¾in (70mm) long from triple veneer "sandwiches." Put a red piece against the left-hand stop and brush 10 percent diluted PVA glue along its right-hand edge. Repeat for ten pieces, alternately black and red.

LEFT: Plan to show the arrangement of squares for the tunbridgeware log demonstrated here. Note that the outer boxwood squares go around three sides only.

3 Place a piece of the boxwood square down the right-hand edge and tape it firmly in place. Repeat these steps until you have four identical pieces. Repeat to produce the two pieces of boxwood and padauk the same length and cut all pieces in two.

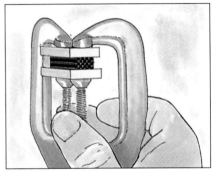

4 Glue and clamp four of the red/black pieces together, making sure that they are perfectly lined up at both ends. Protect the surfaces with scrap and repeat for the other four pieces. When both are dry, glue and clamp them together to produce one block.

5 When this block is dry, plane the four edges flush and square. Do this as little as possible, otherwise you will be visibly reducing the dimensions of the outer layers of squares and spoiling the geometric effect.

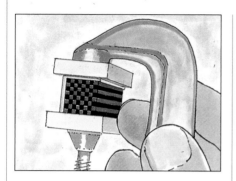

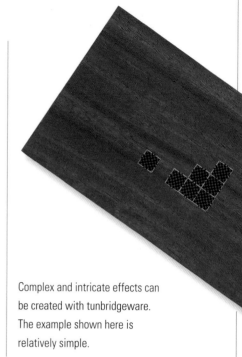

6 Now, one by one, glue in place three of the four prepared boxwood and padauk pieces, these should be a little overwide. Glue the first one in place with ½in (1mm) of boxwood overhanging one long edge. The second pieces should butt against this, and so on.

7 When dry, trim the edges flush and cut ⅟₁₆in (2mm) slivers off the end of the completed log. Here, some of the pieces have been combined and inlaid to form a geometric design.

Complex and intricate effects can be created with tunbridgeware. The example shown here is relatively simple.

Parquetry

Parquetry is the traditional technique of using repeated geometric veneer shapes to produce an overall pattern. Sometimes this is achieved by using different veneers, but more often, as here, the same wood with the grain running in different directions is used. Here, you are shown how to produce a classic parquetry design.

Ash is a good wood to use because it has a very visible grain, and the contrast between the two grain directions shows up well. Oak would do equally well, or, if you wanted a darker effect, rosewood or any wood with a good, streaky figure would be suitable.

Choose your own dimensions, but you will need to make a metal template for cutting the strips. You can use ply instead, but it is not as good in this application because it is too soft. The easiest solution initially is to use something that you already have: a steel rule is ideal. The basic technique can be used to produce a wide range of pleasing effects, but give careful thought to planning exactly what you want. Take your time and make readable plans.

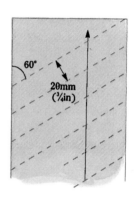

The arrow indicates the direction of the grain; the dotted lines show where the cuts should be made. Work carefully and precisely.

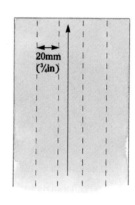

The technique relies for its effect on subtle changes in the direction of the grain. Ash, which was used here, is particularly well-suited to the process.

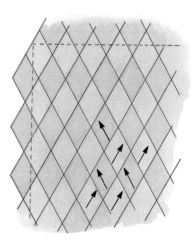

The diagonal cuts made at an angle of 60 degrees to the grain, as indicated by the dotted lines, must be just as precise.

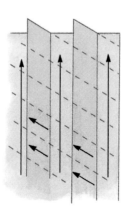

Make a careful plan before you begin, remembering that symmetry is all-important. Use a steel rule or some other hard, straight edge for cutting.

WOOD CARVING

Wood carving is an activity that spans the globe and the centuries. It embraces a huge range of applications, from the creation of everyday objects and decorative patterns, to architectural features and abstract sculptures. It can be an art or a craft—and is often both.

Getting started

The practical part of designing may be no more than a sketch, or it may be a sketch model, or it may involve carefully-measured plans—sometimes all three. This preparatory work helps you to visualize the object and give you the necessary information to start carving, so you only need to do what the piece seems to demand and what you think is most useful.

Once you have chosen your subject, completed your research and made some preliminary sketches, it is helpful to make a drawing or drawings (actual-size, if possible, or accurately to scale). For some objects, a single view is enough, but the more three-dimensional the piece, the more necessary it is to draw a number of views to get an all-around image. For certain objects, it is useful to design like an architect and draw up plans and elevations.

Squaring up

It may not always be practical to draw your design to size, or you may change your mind about its proportions. A photocopier can help you enlarge or reduce it, but grids can be more useful. For example, to increase an existing design to four times its present size, you could draw a grid of ¼in (6.5mm) squares over the design and then make a grid of 1in (25mm) squares on a clean sheet of paper for the target size, numbering the squares in each case. This will allow you to enlarge the drawing accurately, a square at a time, as you copy it.

Attributed to Grinling Gibbons
This limewood overmantel is typical of Grinling Gibbons' ornate, delicate style.

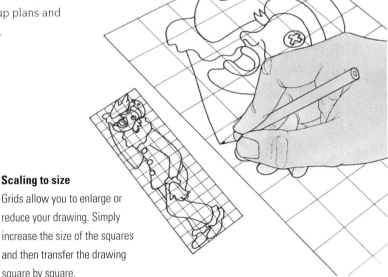

Scaling to size
Grids allow you to enlarge or reduce your drawing. Simply increase the size of the squares and then transfer the drawing square by square.

Starting points

Nature is a rich source of inspiration, but ideas for carving can spring from all kinds of unexpected places if you keep an open mind and eye. Design requires visual planning, and that is helped by any kind of drawing—even a simple doodle. Words can also aid the process, especially those that stimulate images. Carry a sketchpad or notebook around with you and get into the habit of making thumbnail sketches of buildings, machines, people, and animals, or jotting down a brief detail of any image that impresses you. Photographs can be a valuable aid to memory, and an inspiration in themselves, and illustrations in books, magazines, and newspapers often stimulate ideas. Because we want to think three-dimensionally, sketch modeling in plasticine or clay will also be useful.

Drawing is probably the greatest aid to design, not because you need drawing talent to carve wood, but because drawing can help you to understand the nature and structure of your subject. This does not, however, mean that you must draw before carving. Drawings, photographs, and clay models all have a part to play in sorting out ideas and exploring forms.

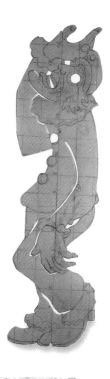

Templates

Templates can be made from paper, cardboard or specialist stonemason's material.

Using templates

A template, or silhouette of the design—sometimes with details cut through it like a stencil—can help when establishing the basic shapes on a block of wood, and later when part of the drawing has been carved away. Templates can be traced from your accurate drawings and cut from paper or cardboard. Protect them with a few coats of shellac if they are likely to get damp.

Sketch models

Some carvers are opposed to making a sketch model before carving, because, as they point out, modeling and carving are opposite processes: modeling involves addition, and carving sub-traction. Also, malleable substances like clay do not impose the disciplines of wood. The result, it is argued, will be a copy of a clay model that will lack the qualities of direct carving. There is a lot to be said for this line of thought, but it is not always easy for the layman to visualize a three-dimensional object inside a piece of wood, and a sketch model can be an enormous help in at least two ways.

First, a rough sketch model provides a way of thinking through a design, of trying out ideas and rejecting those that do not work. Second, an actual-size sketch model can be used to establish the depths and approximate shapes of

the final form. Think in terms of wood carving as you model, imagining how the shapes will carve, and leave your model as a rough sketch so that the final statement is made in the actual carving of the wood.

Plasticine and clay are the most popular modeling materials because they can be used again and again. Plasticine is suitable for small models and is relatively clean (though virtually impossible to remove if it is crushed into a carpet). Clay can be used for models of any size, but may need an internal support, such as a wire armature, for large models.

Modeling is mostly done with the fingers, but a few boxwood or steel tools are useful (see step 2 opposite), and a cheesewire is good for cutting clay and for sliding under still-soft models to remove them from the modeling board. It is always possible to improvize: for example, bits of broken hacksaw blades are helpful for scraping away and for smoothing clay. Pencils, bits of sticks, and old nail files all come in handy at times. For three-dimensional forms, it is worth having a model-ing stand with a turntable, so that you can keep viewing the model from different angles; a small table stand is good enough for most jobs.

sketch model

plotted drawing

transferred to wood

profile cut from wood

From sketch model to carving

First make a clay or plasticine sketch model, then make an outline drawing. Draw a grid over your outline. Transfer both drawing and grid to the block of wood, freehand or using carbon paper.

Making a sketch model

Although modeling is basically a process of building up forms, you can also remove material, using wire-ended tools or hacksaw blades. This makes modeling an ideal way of planning your approach to a carving and of visualizing and modifying your ideas three-dimensionally. Your aim is to arrive at an actual-sized rough sketch that will show how the forms interact and dispose themselves, and will help you to gauge the depths to which you can carve.

Choosing wood

Some woods are better for carving than others, but I believe it is worth trying any wood that is available. You may make a master-piece, but if you don't, you will almost certainly have learned something from the exercise. I am sure that many good carvings have come from wood that was not thought of as suitable and, equally, many bad carvings have emerged from perfect material.

There are numerous species of wood for carving, and the same type of tree can vary according to the conditions in which it grows. The list given here is therefore a general guide to some of the more widely available woods that carvers use. When choosing your wood, try to get it quarter-sawed and without the center. Look for an even grain and no knots. Avoid sapwood—the wood between the inner bark and the heartwood—and pieces that have sunken parts.

Right: This piece entitled "Portable Model" is carved in pear wood.

1 Draw the outline on a piece of plastic-coated or painted board. Make a bridge the depth of the proposed carving to check the depth of your model.

2 Press clay onto the board within the outline, gradually building up the forms. You can use quite large pieces of clay to start with, but these should get smaller as you get closer to the surface, so that you can press them easily into place with your thumbs and fingers.

3 One approach to this partic-ular subject would be to model the face first and then to model the leaves on the face. Spray the model occasionally with water, and cover it in plastic wrap when not in use to keep it damp and malleable.

Some woods for carving

Common name	Characteristics
AMERICAN WHITEWOOD (Liriodendron tulipifera)	This is the wood of the tulip tree. It seems to have, or have had, many names: saddletree, poplar, Virginian poplar, yellow poplar, yellow-wood, canary-wood, and canoe wood. It is fairly soft, close, and straight-grained, and has an even texture. The color varies a lot, from pale greenish-white to grayish-yellow; there have even been some which had gone a dark brown.
BASSWOOD, (Tilia)	One of the best woods to carve, with an even texture and close grain. Good for beginners and experts alike, this was the favorite wood of the marvellous German carvers of the 1400s and 1500s, such as Tilman Riemenschneider and Veit Stoss, and of Grinling Gibbons in England. Its grain is scarcely apparent, and the original pale color can darken to a pleasant light brown with a pinkish tinge. It is particularly suitable for work containing detail and texture.
BOXWOOD (Buxus sempervirens),	The box shrub or tree does not grow large, so this wood comes in small sizes only. A hard, yellow wood it is liked by experts for detailed work, but it does not carve easily.
CHESTNUT (Castanea)	Very similar to oak in appearance but without the medullary rays. Less hard than oak, it is not difficult to carve. The wood is liable to have ring shakes (cracks that follow the annular rings), so check for these when you get it.
EBONY (Diospyros)	A dense, dark or black wood, which tends to come in small sizes and is very hard to carve.
HOLLY (Ilex)	A fine-grained, white or grayish white wood, good for carving, and noted for its resemblance to ivory alongside which it is sometimes worked.
JELUTONG (Dyera costulata)	Straight-grained and fine-textured, it is known for being readily carved but uninteresting to look at, so it is usually painted. It is often used for rocking horses.
LIGNUM VITAE (Cuaiacum)	A hard and dense wood, this is usually dark brown streaked with black, but it can have much lighter brown and greenish tinges. Difficult to carve, but can be highly polished.
MAHOGANY (Swietenia)	This name covers a variety of tropical lumbers and the label is often extended to mahogany-like woods. Colors tend to be reddish brown but can encompass shades from pale-golden brown to deep red. Structure also varies: for example, Brazilian and Honduran mahogany can be good to carve and African can have difficult grain.
OAK (Quercus)	A large family with American, European, and Japanese and varieties. American oak can be pale or reddish; European oak is a pale fawn color which darkens to a pleasant brown; and Japanese oak has interesting subtleties of grain. Oak is hard, though rewarding to carve, and is not recommended for work with fine detail. Avoid the sapwood, which is loved by beetles.
PEAR (Pyrus communis)	Pale yellowish red to pinkish brown, this is a good carving wood, close-grained and moderately hard.
PINE OR YELLOW PINE (Pinus strobus)	A relatively soft yellowish wood, this carves well, but—as with all softwoods—the tools need to be very sharp and have longer bevels than those used for hardwoods.
SYCAMORE (Acer pseudoplatanus)	A white wood of the maple family, close-grained and hard, so difficult to carve. It is a popular choice for objects used for food.
WALNUT (Juglans)	Dense and dark brown, walnut carves well. Carvers tend to prefer the walnut wood that comes from Italy as well as American black walnut.

Tools and equipment

The traditional tools for wood carving have changed little over the centuries, as early pictures and carvings show. A medieval bench-end in the Provinzial Museum in Hanover, Germany portrays a monk using the round mallet still employed by wood carvers and stonemasons today, and he has some "fishtail" gouges in a rack on the wall. The bench end dates from c.1285.

Traditional mallet

The tools that every wood carver must have are chisels, gouges, and a mallet. They come in a wide range of shapes and sizes, and referring to the illustrations given overleaf, as you read, will help you become familiar with them. Some makers supply chisels and gouges without handles (which are supplied separately). The suppliers will often fit the handles for free, and it is worth taking advantage of this because fitting them can be tricky, and if you don't get one straight, you have to fit another.

Chisels and gouges

Straight chisels and gouges A gouge is a chisel with a concave blade. Straight chisels and gouges are the strongest tools, used to do the bulk of the work. Most work with the mallet is done with them. Their sides are parallel nearly as far as the shoulder and they are straight when looked at from the side.

Salmon bend, curved, long bent, and double bent All these terms describe gouges with a long, gentle curve. They are useful for carving bowls and hollow shapes where a straight gouge would start to dig in instead of flattening out as it neared the bottom. They are usually robust, and will often be used with a mallet.

Bent, front bent, spoonbit/entering chisels and gouges These gouges do not get a lot of use unless you are carving a piece with fairly small but deep hollows. Bent chisels and corner chisels are also known as grounders or background tools, reflecting their usefulness in carving a flat background, for example, behind raised relief work, and for getting into awkward corners.

A basic tool kit

Here are the tools to get you started, and you can add to these when the need arises.

Number/type	Size
1 Straight chisel	½in (13mm)
2 Corner chisel/Skew chisel	½in (13mm)
3 Gouge (straight)	¾in (20mm)
8 Gouge (straight)	½in (13mm)
9 Gouge (straight)	⅝in (16mm)
11 Veiner (straight)	⅛in (3mm)
11 Veiner (straight)	³⁄₁₆in (5mm)
39 Parting tool/V tool (straight) (about 60 degree angle)	¼in (6mm)
17 Gouge (salmon bend/long bent)	⅜in (10mm)
21 Chisel (bent)	¼in (6mm)
22 Corner chisel—right (bent)	¼in (6mm)
23 Corner chisel—left (bent)	¼in (6mm)
31 Gouge (bent)	⅜in (10mm)
65 Gouge (fishtail)	⁵⁄₁₆in (8mm)
66 Gouge (fishtail)	⅜in (10mm)

(metric equivalents are not exact and numbers may vary depending on the manufacturer)
Mallet Lignum vitae (if possible) 3in or 3½in. But try before you buy, and choose a weight that feels right.

Dog leg chisel This is stepped instead of curved. It serves a similar purpose to the grounding chisel.

Fishtail/spade chisels and gouges The working part of these tools is triangular, which makes them particularly useful for detail carving. The terms used to be sub-divided, so that the fishtail or spade tool had a small triangular end on a straight shank, the long-pod spade tool had a long, slim triangle probably reaching about halfway up the shank, and the long-spade, or allongée, gouge or chisel was triangular as far as the shoulder. The tendency now seems to be to call them all fishtail. It is worth noting that some toolmakers make all their large tools—that is, ¾in (20mm) wide and above—in

Chisels and gouges

From left: 2 long fishtail gouges, straight gouge, salmon bend gouge, straight gouge, salmon bend parting tool ("V"), fishtail "V" tool, long fishtail chisel, straight chisel No. 1, skew chisel, backbent fishtail gouge, bent fishtail gouge, 2 bent corner chisels (English numbering).

Carving tools

From top: No. 8 gouge, No. 9 gouge, salmon bend gouge, bent gouge, straight gouge, fishtail gouge, straight gouge, straight chisel, skew chisel, "V" tool, veiner (Swiss numbering).

the long-spade or full-length fishtail shape.

Sections Nearly all the tools described come in a variety of sectional shapes, and each section comes in a number of widths. Some catalogs list chisels or gouges of nine different sectional shapes, starting with ½in (1mm), through about 15 widths for each section up to 2in (50mm) wide. Each section carries a number, which applies to it however narrow or wide it might be. For example, No. 1 is a straight chisel, and a straight chisel will be No. 1 whether it is ³⁄₁₆in (5mm) or 1in (25mm) wide. You would order it as: ³⁄₁₆in (5mm) No. 1 straight chisel.

Curved sections The curved section gouges are numbered from 3 to 11. No. 3 is the flattest, nearly a chisel; No. 11 is "U"-shaped. Nos. 10 and 11 are sometimes separated from the other gouges and called Fluters (No. 10) and Veiners (No. 11). The "V"-section gouges are called parting tools or "V" tools, and there is usually a choice of different angles. One which is about 60 degrees is probably the best at first.

Mallets

Though a large proportion of carving is done with two hands on the chisel or gouge—one hand pushing hard, the other restraining and guiding—there are times when a mallet is essential. For example, in the initial stages when

roughing out it is undoubtedly quicker to remove large amounts of waste with a gouge and mallet than with just your hands and a gouge. Carvers' mallets are round and are traditionally made of beech or lignum vitae. There are now very good nylon mallets, but they tend to be too big for anything but large-scale work. Lignum vitae is excellent because its density allows the mallet to be smaller than one made of beech. It is important to choose a mallet that feels comfortable when used, so handle it before you buy it.

One of my favorite tools is the so-called dummy mallet, which has a malleable iron or lead head; this tool nestles in the hand and is very useful for making controlled cuts with gentle tapping, as in letter cutting or following around a curve. The dense metal head of this type of mallet also means it is more compact and therefore better able to work in confined areas on larger carvings. It also requires less force because of its weight, making it less tiring for prolonged use.

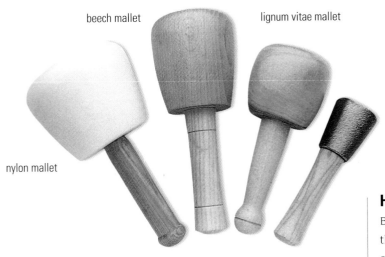

beech mallet

lignum vitae mallet

dummy mallet

nylon mallet

Holding the work

Both hands are needed for carving, so the piece being carved must be held securely. The holding device will vary according to the type of work. A length of molding, for example, might be held down fairly crudely with nails at each end. A fretted piece that is somewhat fragile can be glued to a larger board with two or three layers of newspaper in between to make removal easy when the carving is finished. The board can then be held with one or two "G" clamps. This method is also useful for securing a relief carving where you need continuous access to all parts of the piece. When there is no danger of tools striking them, you can use screws to secure backing board to it. A carver who is making a series of pieces the same size might devise a jig to hold them.

Sometimes it is possible to hold the work itself with "G" clamps or with a bench holdfast (see page 33). Woodworkers' vices are also suitable, especially the kind known as carver's chops. When placing your work directly in a clamp or vise, you may have to pad it first to prevent marking or strain— pieces of cork, leather, or soft wood can provide good protection.

An ingenious gadget is the "universal work positioner," consisting of a circular plate to which a piece of work can be fixed. The plate can then be swiveled and tilted to whatever position is required and locked there until the carver wishes to change it. This makes it easy to

Workshop safety

As with most occupations, carving can be dangerous, and it is essential to take a few sensible precautions to prevent possible accidents. If you bear in mind that to carve effectively you need very sharp tools, you will probably treat them with respect. What may be less obvious is that the dust from sawing and sanding, particularly with power tools, can be hazardous and even poisonous. For instance, all parts of the yew are reported to be poisonous, although yew is a very desirable wood for sculpture, and can be safely carved. Always bear the following points in mind.

- Have a first aid kit in the workshop.
- Your working surface must be firm.
- Make sure the piece you are carving is securely held by a device. You need both hands for carving.
- Always test the sharpness of your tools on a spare piece of wood, never with your fingers.
- Work in a good light.
- Have the floor around you reasonably clear and clean. There should be nothing to trip or slip on.
- Wear a mask and eyeshields when using power tools, and ear protectors when using noisier tools.
- Power tools come with safety instructions, and it is important to read and follow these exactly.
- If you are creating a lot of dust, try to work outside. If you have to be inside, use an extractor fan. Always wear a dust mask.
- Don't blow sawdust clear of a cavity unless you are wearing eyeshields.
- Don't neglect splinters: some people react badly to these, particularly if they come from some exotic hardwoods. Check with your doctor if you think a cut or splinter is becoming septic.
- Never carve toward yourself.
- Never carve when you are tired or unwell.
- Store your tools safely and replace them carefully as you work. If they roll off a cluttered worktop, they can damage themselves and you.
- Clear away shavings to reduce fire risk.

keep viewing the carving from different angles. In contrast, one of the simplest and most effective ways of holding a piece is the cobblers' strap. A length of webbing, a leather strap, or braided sisal is firmly attached on the far side of the bench, taken over the work and kept tightly in place by the carver's foot in a stirrup at the strap's end. This could literally be a stirrup, and the length of the strap could be adjusted at that end. Make a permanent loop and adjust the length of the strap from the fixed end. It only takes seconds to move the piece to a new position.

Improvised devices

As well as the devices you can buy to hold your work, there are others that you can adapt or improvize, including those shown here. Additional solutions are bound to suggest themselves as you go along. You should always pad work that might otherwise be under strain when clamped, for instance, and for that you could use a pencil eraser or a piece of cardboard. Alternatively, if you have cut a shape with a coping, jig, or band saw, the offcuts provide ideal packing.

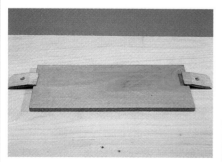

1&2   Methods for holding thin panels.

3   A modification for thicker panels. In 2 and 3 the closer the screws are to the work, the stronger the hold.

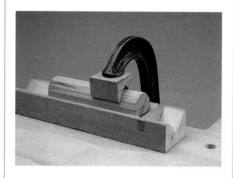

4   The "V" block to hold, for example, a cylindrical shape. Note the hardwood stop let into the 90 degree "V" groove. This allows you to plane the shape after removing the clamp and holding the block in a vise.

5&6   Alternative ways of holding balls for drilling. For 5, first make a hole the same diameter as the sphere and about three-quarters of its depth. Then saw the block in half down its length. If this does not give a tight enough fit, plane the saw-cut faces to allow more pressure to be applied in the vise.

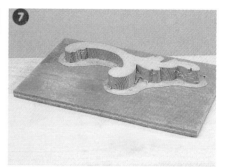

7   Delicate work glued to a board with cardboard or paper in between. The board can then be held with clamps. More robust pieces can be screwed to a board from behind. The base board can be thicker, enabling it to be held in a vise.

8   A bench hook.

9   A carver's bench screw (German pattern).

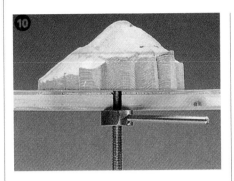

10 Cut-away view of a carvers' bench screw passing through the work surface and screwed into the base or back of the carving, with the nut tightened on the underside.

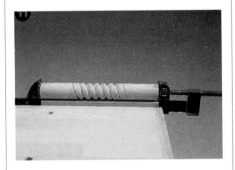

11 A bar clamp used to hold a spindle while a double spiral is being carved. Some 2in x 1in (50mm x 25mm) packing is placed on either side of the clamp beam.

12 A spare block of wood can be screwed or clamped to the bench to stop the work from rotating during carving.

13 A bench holdfast in use.

Dealing with faults

However careful you are, you may occasionally cut too deeply or break a piece off your carving. Faults can also be inherent in your material, or you may inherit them when repairing or restoring. The solution will depend on the carving, its purpose, and intended final finish.

Pieces broken off during carving can usually be glued back quite easily. Carvers in the past are reputed to have broken pieces off deliberately to gain access to awkward areas of carving; so before you replace the piece, check if you can take advantage of the accident in this way. Be careful to keep the broken edges as they were when they parted company, then they will glue back together more easily. Cutting too deeply is more difficult to remedy. Usually the only solution is to carve all-around the cut until it appears to have been what you intended from the start. Typical repairs include:

Splitting caused by drying out: Insert a wood wedge into the split, pare the ends to fit, and apply PVA glue to the sides before knocking the piece home. Trim the projections with a small hand saw, which cuts only in straight lines, leaving an uneven edge. Pare the wedge flush with a chisel.

Breakages: Make sure the clamping points are in the same plane: this may necessitate cutting a small shelf for one end of the clamp. Always dry assemble before clamping to test that the forces are in parallel. When the glue is cured, apply appropriate finish.

Repairing a split in a narrow panel: Open the split to gauge its extent. Cut a piece of oak roughly to size and insert with PVA glue. Pare using a flat chisel. Stain.

Replacement carving (for example, to a picture frame): Pare the broken stump with a wide, flat chisel. Test with a small try square. Draw a full-sized plan of the missing piece. Mark out a small block of limewood, roughly shaped with the grain running in the same direction as the stump. Draw on the profiles and glue. Carve in the back of the pendant, supporting the piece in a vise, padded if necessary. Apply finish.

Relief panel

A relief carving lies somewhere between a painting and a fully three-dimensional object. The depth of carving can vary from virtually 3D high relief, called *alto-rilievo*, through a medium depth, or *mezzo-rilievo*, and low or bas relief, known as *basso-rilievo*—to something hardly more than drawn relief called *relievo-schiacciato*.

Stage one

1 Make an actual-sized sketch model, so that you can transfer measurements easily as you carve.

2 Plane the wood, so that your drawing will show more clearly.

3 & 4 Transfer the drawing to the wood by pricking through the paper with a point, such as an awl, and pencil in the lines. Alternatively, use carbon paper. Your panel will now appear as illustrated.

Stage two

5 Before starting to carve, draw on the sides of your wood the lines of the sections of the flat background, the sloping table, and the under edge of the table.

6 Carve away the background to just above your line with a ½in (13mm) No. 6 gouge. The early stages of a carving provide the ideal opportunity to get to know your material, so try the gouge in different directions to see how the wood behaves.

Plans

Square up some paper and enlarge the drawing to actual size. You will use this to prick around or trace (stage one, steps 3 and 4).

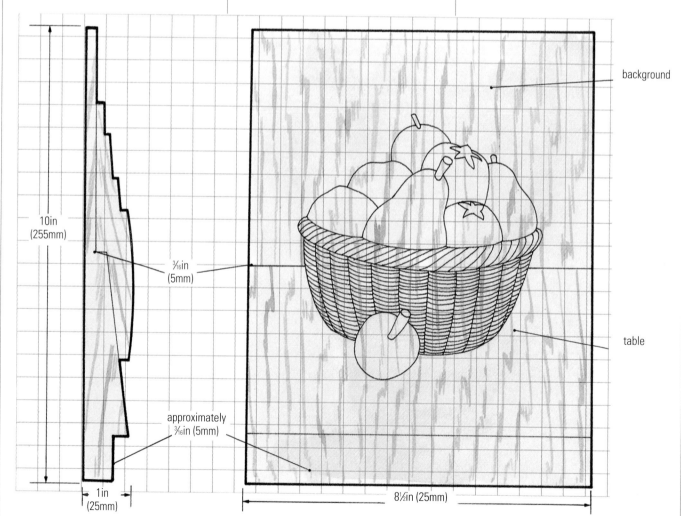

background

³⁄₁₆in (5mm)

10in (255mm)

table

approximately ³⁄₁₆in (5mm)

1in (25mm)

8½in (25mm)

First stage

The drawing (above) has been transferred to the wood (right) from the drawing that was the basis for the plasticine sketch model (below).

Stage three

7 Begin carving the fruit by taking it down in flattish steps. The model is essential for establishing the relative depths of the different pieces of fruit. Use a strongly directional light source, such as an adjustable reading lamp, to illuminate your carving, put your sketch model beside your work and compare the two.

Stage four

8 Draw the detail on the basket carefully, because when it is carved it will play an important role in expressing the form. The lower the relief, the closer it will be to a drawing.

9 & 10 Continue work on the fruit and carve the undulations of the basket.

Second stage (above left)

The profile has been set in and you can now begin to establish depth and detail.

Third stage (above right)

The basic forms have been established.

Fourth stage

The composition has been adjusted
and work has begun on the detail.

Stage five

11 Draw in the texture detail with a
pencil. This will give you a clear
impression of the finished basket, and provide
guidelines to follow when you are carving the
fine gouge cuts.

12 Replace the pencil lines with fine
gouge cuts. Keep the solid shapes
firmly in mind and take the gouge all the way
around, almost as if you were making a three-
dimensional piece.

Fifth stage

Concentration
on detail and
perspective has
given the carving
greater depth and
subtlety.

Relief panel

The subject is
reminiscent of a
still-life painting.

Stage six

13 Carve away the area beneath the
edge of the table, making a step of
about ³⁄₁₆in (5mm), to create a strong shadow.
Finish the fruit with a texture of small, shallow
gouge cuts. Make the texture on the apple in
front of the basket a little more pronounced, and
under-cut it very slightly around the edges to
create the shadow that will cause it to stand out
against the basket. You will now have
completed the panel.

Carving in the round

T he subject for your three-dimensional carving could be a human figure, or an animal. It is probably wise to limit yourself to a single form at first and make more complex compositions later. The carver of this project chose a cat as his subject. Some of the objects in other projects—such as the box and the bowl—are free-standing and three-dimensional, but the figurative carving is in relief and has, to all intents and purposes, a best viewing point.

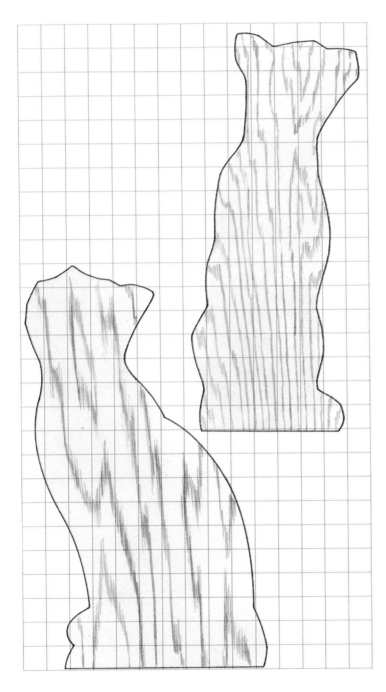

Plans

Make an orthographic projection of the front and side views using the practical method described on page 306. Cut out the two templates.

Method

Wood with a marked grain or figure could be very successful for this project, but any wood would do. Here the carver has chosen pine from a local lumberyard. The dimensions are 10½in x 6in x 3¾in (266mm x 152mm x 95mm). An extra piece is left on to secure the work in a vise. The cat will be 8in (203mm) high.

Stage one

1 Make a maquette like the one below and, when you are happy with it, use the method described on page 306 to create two templates. Draw the base line upon which the cat sits, 2½in (63mm) from the bottom edge, all around the wood.

First stage
Plasticine maquette.

Second stage
The profile drawn on the wood around the side template.

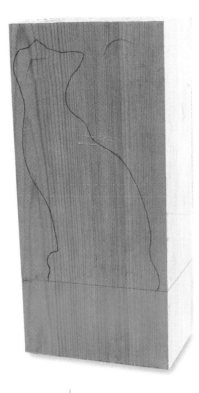

Stage two

2 Saw some large, roughly wedge-shaped pieces off the front and back, keeping outside the line, and then make frequent saw cuts in to the line to help prevent the wood from splitting.

Third stage
The profile carved straight across.

4 Draw the front profile. A stiff template will be more effective than a paper one on the uneven surface.

Stage three

3 Cut off the spare wood with chisels, straight across. Use a try square from time to time to check that you are shaving wood off the profile perpendicular to the flat side.

Stage four

5 Hatch a few lines to indicate what needs to be removed. Make saw cuts and carve away the waste wood with chisels as you did on the side profile. Alternatively, you can cut both profiles with a band saw.

Fourth stage
Cut with band saw.

Tips box

For any carving in the round project, always form the basic outline first using a band saw to make the basic shape if necessary. Next, form the overall shape and dominant features but don't start on the detail at this stage. Only once the shape is formed should you begin to add the surface detail.

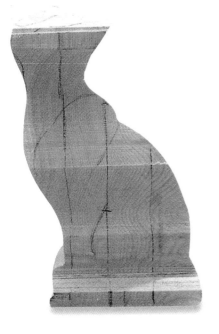

6 The sketch model will be important for general visual reference and for measurement. Draw on the larger shapes and the grid lines which will be useful for measuring. To establish measuring points, mark the maquette at significant places, such as the tops of the shoulders, with a matchstick or point. Most particularly, indicate the centerline on the model and on the wood. Constant reference to this line will help you keep the two sides even. It will also prove essential when you are taking measurements with calipers, so immediately redraw any part of it that you carve away.

Fifth stage
Compare the profile with the maquette.

Tip box

• Take photographs of your subject in different poses or from various angles to help you better understand the whole structure. Look carefully at the light and shadow created by high and low points. It often helps to have a strong directional light to one side of the subject to emphasize these points.

• It may help to mark your tools with a dot of different-colored paint on the handle of each one to help you identify them quickly and easily.

Sixth stage
The form of the cat has been revealed, but it is still very rough.

Seventh stage
Rifflers have softened the outline and removed the tool marks.

Seated cat

A smooth finish enhances the
feline appearance.

Stage five

7   Remove the corners and other bulky
areas, using a large, flat gouge, such
as a No. 3 or 4, so that you are not tempted to
think in terms of detail. Your aim is to rough out
a rather blocky looking cat with somewhat flat
planes and grades of coarseness.

8   Add the details, such as eyes and
mouth. Draw two faint guidelines to
help you: one down the center of the head and
nose, and the other at right angles to it through
the middle of the eyes. You have now reached
the point shown above.

9   Carefully carve in the details, and
carry out any final finishing.

Stage six

The cat was sanded to a very fine finish
to show up the grain, and given three
coats of clear French polish.

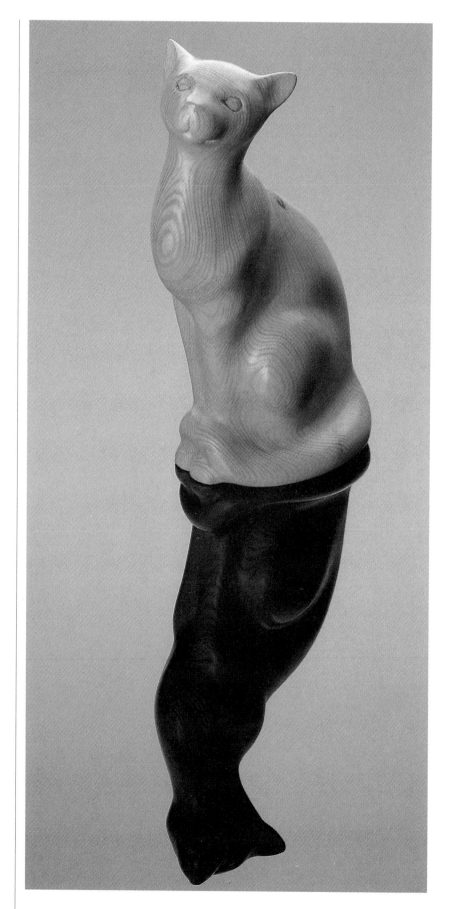

Chip carving

Chip carving is an ancient craft used for the embellishment of everyday articles from figurines and breadboards to furniture and even parts of buildings. Museums will often contain chests, cradles and other objects decorated in this way. Chip carving is a straight-forward, relatively shallow-cut technique, using few tools. Many of the patterns are based on simple geometry, but are very effective.

Chip carving consists of a series of two or three linked, angled cuts, usually made with the tip of a knife, which release a clean chip of wood and reveal a "V"-bottomed groove or a tri-faceted hole.

Only two knives are needed: a chip knife and a stab knife. You can choose these from among the knives you have available, depending on your individual taste and hand size. In the past, when sailors and shepherds would decorate objects like Welsh lovespoons to wile away the hours, pocketknives or clasp knives were commonly used.

Design considerations

It is probably a good idea to start with geometrical designs, but you certainly don't need to be limited to them. Many of the examples in museums have stylized but quite freely-drawn plants and animals as well as abstract patterns. My own feeling is that attempts to be naturalistic are not very successful, but you can study traditional motifs based upon natural forms and adopt the principles of stylization to make your own designs. In this way, it is possible to use any subject—even cars, airplanes, and buildings—as the basis of new designs. In this project, the carver has taken a design from a sixteenth-century box and has modified it only slightly. It is a good idea to make a careful drawing with ruler and compasses on paper before transferring it to the wood.

Plan

Enlarge this pattern onto paper first. Draw the concentric circles. Keep the radius of the innermost circle to construct the design within. To find the six points, walk the compasses or dividers around the circle. Use these points as centers for drawing the arcs that make the petals. By continuing the arcs outside the circle, you can find the centers for the inward curves in the bases of the triangles.

Tools and materials

- Chip knife & stab knife
- Draughtsman's pencil
- Ruler
- Compasses (screw adjustment)
- Dividers (curved surfaces)
- Try squares (right angles)
- Plastic eraser (optional)
- Fine abrasives
- Any easily carved wood (not pine)

Although the list of tools seems long, you can carry out most of the work with the straight knife and the stab knife. Progress to the other blades for more complex designs once you have mastered the basic techniques.

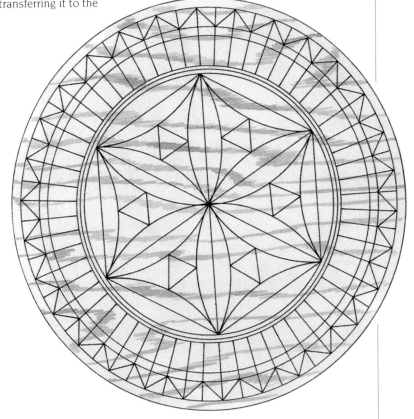

Holding

The wood is traditionally held in the carver's free hand, and rotated after each cut, presenting the next line to be carved: the knife hand is always working in the same direction and the grip doesn't need to be altered. Hold the chip knife as though you are about to spread butter —edge toward the thumb and first finger wrapped around the handle.

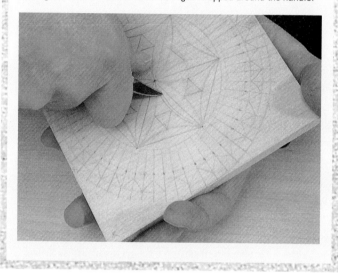

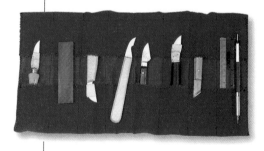

A homemade tool roll containing a selection of knives, a fine sharpening stone, ruler, and draftsman's propeling pencil. The carver's favorite chip knife is on the left.

Method

A chip knife does not need a large blade, since only the point is used, but small blades tend to be thin and liable to bend. A blade measuring 1-1½in (25-38mm), taped with masking tape to leave ⅜in (10mm) of the tip showing should work well. Flat-sided wooden handles give the best control—a round handle can twist in your grip.

The stab knife, which makes graduating perpendicular cuts, is similar to a skew chisel, and should have a straight blade 1in (25mm) long and ½in (13mm) wide, with the cutting edge sloping back at about 45 degrees from the tip. Sharpen the chip knife to give it a 10 degree bevel and the stab knife to give a 30 degree bevel.

Cutting techniques

During cutting, the thumb is always in contact with the wood and the knuckle of the first finger also rubs on the surface, aiding control of the knife in the depth and angle of cutting. Draw the tip of the knife through the surface by pressing the outside edge of your thumb—by the nail—onto the wood, and then "closing" your hand toward the thumb, taking the knife along the cutting line ¼in (6.5mm) at a time. Move the thumb forward another ¼in (6.5mm), close the hand again, and so on. Cuts usually start shallow, deepen to the middle, and get shallower again toward the end. The tip of the knife must be able to move easily through the wood. If it cuts too deeply, or if the blade is blunt, it is likely to jump or jam and may cause injury. The gap between the masked blade and your thumb should never exceed ¼in (6.5mm) so as to limit the danger if the knife does jump forward and cut you.

The stab knife is held in a dagger-type grip and is used for making two perpendicular cuts, the chip being removed by a third cut from the chip knife. Locate the knife point on the line where the cut will be deepest, then push it down and "roll" it along the line, to give a cut that graduates from deep to shallow. Repeat the action in a second cut, at about 90 degrees to the first, so that the deep parts are adjacent. Then take out the chip with the chip knife.

Practice your technique on a piece of spare wood before beginning the project. Keep the knife at an angle of about 60 degrees—any steeper makes the cut too deep and difficult to do, any shallower means the carving will look flat and lifeless. For the deeper cuts in the project pattern, you will first need to remove a small chip from the center of the shape to reduce pressure on the knife for the finishing cuts.

1 Begin with the deep-cut petal shapes. Hold the wood in your free hand and make the initial "relieving" cut to remove a small sliver before taking out the full-sized chip (above). Turn the workpiece to allow you to keep carving in the same direction as you make the next cut. The chip should pop out.

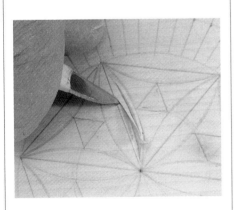

2 Make the first finishing cut close to the line.

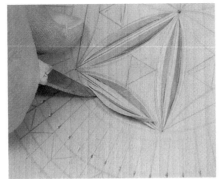

3 Carve the second finishing cut to the line and release the chip. Clear any remaining whiskers of wood from the valley bottom with some gentle tidying cuts. The five remaining similar sections would normally be carved in sequence at this stage.

4 Three knife cuts are made to release this triangular chip. Again, first remove a small chip from the middle to ease the final cuts. Notice how the wood is rotated in the hand to present the line to be cut. This ensures that consistency of depth and angle of blade are maintained.

First stage
The outer edges of one petal have been completed.

5 Begin the second series of cuts up to the line to give the finished shape.

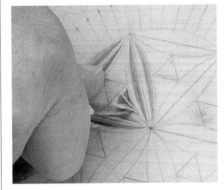

6 At the completion of the three cuts, the chip is released. The petal of your carving will now appear as shown below.

Second stage
The petal is almost complete, with the exception of the central triangle.

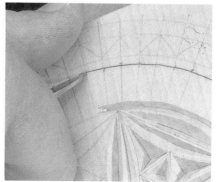

7 Carve the central triangles by the same method, taking out a small "pressure chip" and then making the three final cuts. Again, the other five sections would usually be finished to the same degree before proceeding to the next stage.

8 The circular groove is a long "V"-shaped chip. This is a shallow cut, so no pressure chip needs to be removed. In chip carving, always try to make your initial cuts away from previous juxtaposed carving to reduce the risk of raised parts of the pattern flaking off, especially on end grain.

10 Carve the radiating dovetail shapes with shorter "V" cuts. Turn the wood for the second cut, which removes the chip.

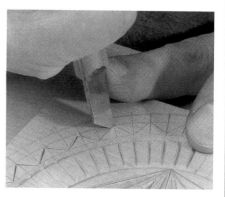

11 Stab cuts are used to set in the outer ring of "dragon's teeth" and the chip is released by a third cut from the chip knife. Set in two cuts, at about 90 degrees to each other, with the stab knife held like a dagger. Position the point and push.

Third stage (above)
The petal is now complete.

9 The chip comes out cleanly as the second cut is made on the outer "V." You should complete each circle before continuing.

Fourth stage (right)
Both circles have been started. Complete them both before moving on to the next stage.

Fifth stage
In order to demonstrate all the different cuts, one segment has been finished ahead of the others. When carving this yourself, it is better to complete each type of cut all around the circle before moving on to the next.

12   When the desired depth is reached, the knife blade is lowered forward along the line to its junction with the next line. This gives a cut that slopes gradually from nothing to the full depth at the corner. Practice on some scrap wood first.

13   When two stab cuts are complete, remove the chip using a chip knife. If the chip is too large to come out conveniently in one go, take out a small chip first. Again, the circles of both should be completed. Sand the work or use an eraser to remove pencil marks.

Coffeepot stand

Chip carving is particularly good for decorating furniture and other domestic objects, although it can also be used to decorate cabinet or door panels with symmetrical repeated patterns. If you want to use this form of decoration, keep to the same basic pattern for each room. You could also use one of the simple border patterns as a decorative motif in its own right, say, for a table edge.

Letter cutting

The basic process of carving letters in wood is extremely simple; the skill lies in doing it well. The key to good lettering is due as much to the spaces between the letters as to the letters themselves. A group of letters imperfectly cut but well arranged looks better than beautiful letters badly spaced. This is another example of the balance between art and craft, because spacing depends on the eye—not on rules.

Design considerations

A crucial consideration when planning the design of your letter carving is spacing. Because we take in words as units, it is the shape of the entire unit—or the spacing and arrangement of several units—which is important.

It is advisable to use capital letters only until you have acquired a good degree of skill and confidence. To draw and space the letters correctly all at once is difficult, so try starting with the following system. Choose a one-word inscription, such as the name of your house, and determine the shape of letters you want. Use the alphabet illustrated (pages 335-36), or look for alternative letter forms in a catalog of typefaces. Decide the height of the letters, and rule a set of parallel lines that distance apart on a sheet of paper.

Draw each letter individually until you are satisfied with it. You will find it helpful to rule in a few faint guidelines to make your letters consistent—say, one at the half-way mark, and others the width of the top and bottom horizontals of an "E"—but do not be slavish in keeping to these. Occasional lightly-ruled verticals will provide a reference for correct vertical strokes. Make yourself a rule on a piece of paper or construction paper, marking on it the full width and three-quarter, half and quarter widths of the vertical strokes. You could decide, for example, to make the full width of the vertical strokes one-eighth of the height of the letter. Once that is established and drawn on your rule, it only takes a second to check the widths of your full-width verticals, and so on.

When drawing an "O," take it a hair's breadth over the line above and below. Allow the points at the base of "M," "N," "V" and "W" just to pierce the bottom line, and those at the tops of "A" and "W" similarly to penetrate the top line. When all the letters are drawn to your satisfaction, cut the containing rectangle around each one. Draw a new pair of parallel lines on a fresh sheet of paper and arrange the letters between them until the spacing looks right. You may want to adjust some letter shapes to make them fit better with their neighbors. (For example, an "R" next to a "T" could have a longer tail than one next to an "A.") Then stick the letters down.

Now pin the design on the wall and look critically again at the spacing. Turn the paper upside down and take another look. Ask yourself if the letters make a well-balanced unit. When the design is upright, can you read the word right away? If it is incorrectly spaced, there may appear to be a break in it. If you are not satisfied and feel that slight alterations are needed, draw parallel lines on some tracing paper and trace the design, adjusting the spaces as necessary. It does not matter if these tracings are not as perfectly drawn as the original, because you can go back to your best letters when required. It is a good idea to shade in the letters, as this gives

Tools and materials

- Three straight chisels:
  No. 1, ¾in, ½in and ¼in
  (18mm, 13mm and 6mm)
- Skew chisel No. 2, ⅜in (10mm)
- Three straight gouges:
  Nos. 3, 4 and 6, all ¼in (6mm)
- Black pencil carbon
- Any hardwood with an even grain
  and color
- You will also need a straight-edge and
  try square to set out your design.

Raised letters

This diagram illustrates the difference between incized and raised letters. To carve letters in relief, the wood around them has to be removed to an even depth. It is normal to leave a slight slope on the sides to give strength to letters that would otherwise be vulnerable, especially at the ends.

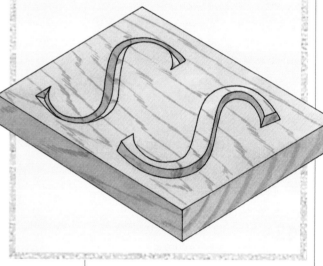

Drawing up a letter

To transfer your drawing to the wood, first draw guidelines on the piece of wood. Then, using masking tape, tape the paper to the wood with the black pencil carbon underneath. Make sure that the lines on the paper align perfectly with those on the wood. Draw lightly over your drawing with a ballpoint pen. Check each letter as you do it, to make sure that the transfer is working. When all the letters are traced, you will see that the outlines look shaky. Make minor corrections with a very soft-leaded pencil.

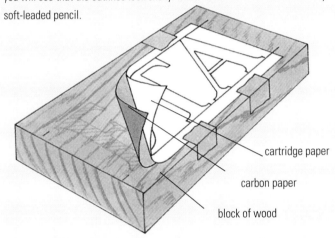

cartridge paper

carbon paper

block of wood

a clearer picture of the effect. The adjustment of spacing is a subtle and important process, so it is worth taking time over it. If you leave your design for a night, or even for a week, and return to it with a fresh eye, you will be able to see it more clearly.

Method

This project uses incized lettering and incorporates all the techniques you will need to carve any letter of the alphabet. There are two basic incizing methods known as chasing and stabbing. In chasing, the "V" section is carved with a skew chisel with an angle about 75 degrees back from the point, starting with a "V" that is narrower than the final letter and gradually enlarging it by the removal of fine shavings from alternate sides, following the line of the letter. In stabbing, a combination of chisels and gouges is used to form the letters, and the tools are driven in at an angle to form the "V" section. Many carvers stab vertically down the center of the letter before making angled cuts from each

side. Most letter cutters develop their own methods, which are often a blend of the two techniques. Here, the carver uses a stabbing technique, with chasing to finish some letters. He sharpens his tools with long bevels and slightly-curved edges. Not all letter cutters do this, but it is obviously worth trying methods that get excellent results. If you expect to do a lot of letter cutting, it is a good idea to keep some chisels and gouges especially for the purpose.

If you would like to carve raised letters, use an alphabet in which there are no very thin strokes or fine serifs. Draw the letters on the wood and cut away the spaces between them in the same way as you carved the background of the pattern on the box. Leave a slight slope on the edges of the letters, as they tend to be somewhat fragile if you cut them perpendicular to the surface.

It is possible to cut letters in any wood, but hardwoods with a close grain and an even color are the best choice. If the grain or figure is too apparent, it makes the letters difficult to read.

Breadboard
This cherry breadboard has been given an olive oil finish.

Letters and numerals

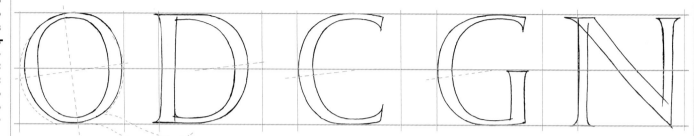

"O" ("Q") All letters should be designed in relation to "O," which is not quite circular in outline. The thinnest part is about a third of a wide stroke.

"D" ("I") The vertical wide stem forms the letter "I." Its sides are neither straight nor parallel, but curve inward slightly.

"C" and **"G"** are related to the left-hand half of "O." The tops and bottoms of each letter are only slightly curved. The vertical stem of "G" is a full, wide stroke and reaches up to the centerline.

"N" The vertical stems should be two-thirds of a wide stroke. The diagonal, a full, wide stroke, is slightly curved.

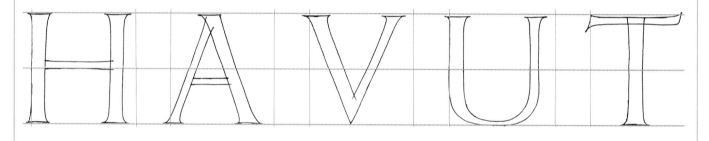

"H" The crossbar is half a wide stroke in thickness, and rests on the centerline.

"A" The left-hand oblique stroke is two-thirds of a wide stroke in thickness, while the crossbar is half a wide stroke.

"V" The same width as "A," but the diagonals are slightly curved.

"U" The same width as "A" and "V"; the right-hand stem is two-thirds of a wide stroke in thickness. Start the curve low down.

"T" The crossbar is half a wide stroke in thickness. The width of "T" can be varied to achieve even spacing and texture.

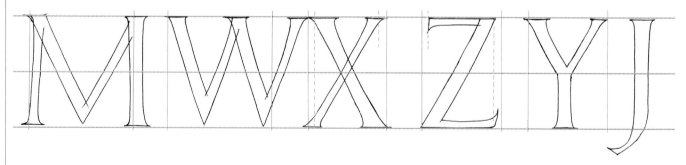

"M" Slightly wider than a square. The two outer strokes are slightly oblique and the inner strokes are slightly curved.

"W" Not a double V. All four strokes are slightly curved; narrow ones two-thirds of a wide stroke in thickness. As in "M," the triangular spaces at either side should be similar.

"X" fits into three-quarters of a square. The top of the letter is narrower, and asymmetry is generated by difference in stroke width.

"Z" The main diagonal has a slight curve; horizontals are half a wide stroke in thickness.

"Y" The junction sits on the center line. The right-hand diagonal is two-thirds of a wide stroke in thickness.

"J" The only letter that breaks out of the parallel lines. It can be difficult to use, but the shape of the tail can be changed.

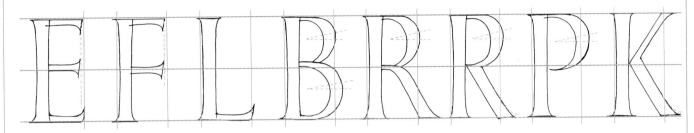

"E" Related to half a square, its horizontals are half a wide stroke in thickness, and are of slightly different lengths.

"F" Note that the central horizontal is slightly lower that that of "E."

"L" The horizontal is longer than that of "E."

"B" Each bowl has its widest point above the center of the curve. The enclosed shapes give the letter much of its character and quality.

"R" The bowl is half the height of the letter. The angle of the tail is variable to make even spacing easier. The right-hand version harmonizes better with "K" and many find it easier to carve. Lifting the foot gives "R" a gentle forward movement.

"P" The upper bowl is deeper and wider than that of "R" and "B," and its counter has a subtly different shape.

"K" The proportions relate to those of "R." The upper diagonal is two-thirds of a wide stroke in thickness, and so relates to the corresponding stroke in "Y."

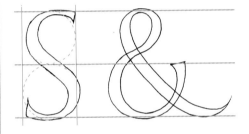

"S" is built up from two unequal circles—the upper one being the smaller—placed so that they lean forward very slightly.

"&" Built up from two circles like number "8," but with the upper circle much the smaller. The curved diagonal is a full, wide stroke.

Numerals

"1" Like "I," but with the top modified.

"2" The top and its serif relate to "C," but in reverse; horizontal is a half wide stroke in thickness with serif related to "L."

"3" Horizontal half wide stroke in thickness, with serif related to "T." Bottom serif related to "S."

"4" Diagonal two-thirds of a wide stroke in thickness; horizontal half a wide stroke with serif related to "T."

"5" Proportions similar to those of "3."

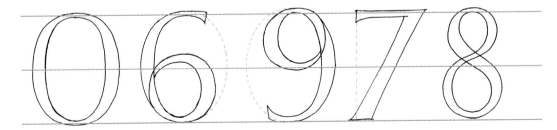

"0" Much narrower than the letter "O", and symmetrical.

"6" Left-hand side related to "O"; proportion of bowl related to "5"; serif related to "C."

"9" Related to "0," but not an upside-down "6," the bowl is much smaller.

"7" Horizontal half a wide stroke in width, with serif related to "T." Placement of the bottom serif in relation to the top one is critical.

"8" Built up from two circles like "S," but without the forward lean. Note differences in thickness between the two sides of each bowl.

Letter "I"

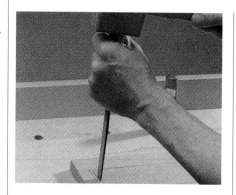

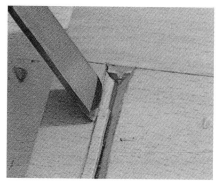

1 & 2 After drawing, score lightly down the center with a chisel. The stem is called a wide stroke. Then, using a ½in (13mm) No. 1 chisel, make a stab cut to the full depth of the letter. Carve to within half a wide stroke of the top and base—not right to the ends.

5 The bulk of the wood is removed by downward-sloping cuts, starting and ending a little short of the ends of the stem. Note how each cut overlaps the previous one so that a smooth, slightly curved surface is produced. Use a wide ¾in (20mm) No. 1 chisel.

7 Finish the stem by cutting away the small triangles of wood left at the ends. Make sure that the sides run smoothly out to the corners.

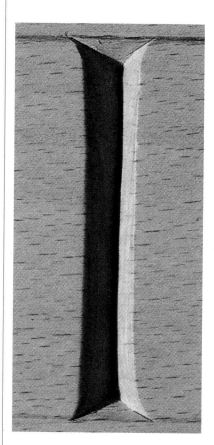

3 Make "Y"-shaped sloping cuts to the corners at the ends of the stem with a No. 2 skew chisel.

6 Use the same wide chisel without the mallet to pare away any irregularities. Notice how the edge is controlled by the fingers.

Most people can learn to cut basic lettering, but creating the more subtle shapes of letters with the correct spacing is more an art than a craft and can take many years to perfect.

4 Still using the No. 2 chisel, cut the sloping "triangles" of wood from either end of the stem.

Letter "E"

8 Start the "E" by carving a wide stem as before. Then stab in the horizontal arms. Remember, they are narrower, and therefore less deep than the main stem. Also they run along the grain, so the stab cuts must be made gently. Add little "Y"-shaped cuts into the comers at the end of each arm.

9 Cut out the end of each arm with a No. 2 skew chisel.

10 Using downward-sloping cuts, gently carve out the wood from the arms. Often a sideways slicing cut is better than trying to cut straight down. Control the blade with the fingers.

11 Smooth and finish off the arms with chasing cuts, pushing the chisel along the line of cut. Care is needed here to make sure that the cut does not run out along the grain. If it begins to do so, stop right away and carve in the reverse direction.

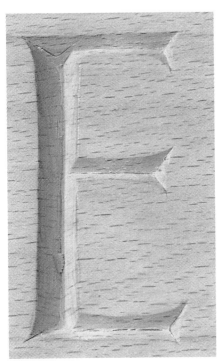

The completed letter "E". Notice particularly the angular junctions where the arms of the letter join the stem.

Letter "R"

12 Carve the wide upright stem. Then stab-cut the tail, and carve the triangles at either end. Cut away the wood from the left side of the tail first, carving downward to avoid splitting.

13 Using a No. 3 or No. 4 gouge (depending on the tightness of the curve), stab in the rounded part of the "R," known as the bowl. The gouge is held off the vertical at the start of the cut; when the cut is finished, it should be upright.

Tips box

Use a router fitted with a small diameter, straight, flute- cutter to remove the bulk of the waste wood for letter carving in relief. Texture the area around the letters with a punch – these can be made up of various patterns including small circles and diamond shapes.

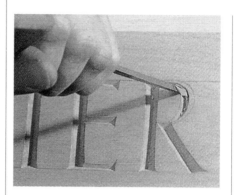

14 Carve the inside of the bowl with a ¼in (6mm) chisel. Start at the junction with the tail and cut up and around to the middle. Then carve from the top of the stem around to the middle again. Overlap the cuts for a smooth surface.

15 Use a No. 3 or No. 4 gouge to cut the outside of the bowl. Begin in the middle (at the deepest part), cutting up and around to the top of the stem.

16 Return to the middle and cut around and down to the junction with the tail. The gouge will probably leave a "scalloped" surface where the main cuts are made. This should be smoothed by delicate paring away of the ridges.

The combination of straight and curved lines in this completed letter "R" may take many years to perfect.

Letter "G"

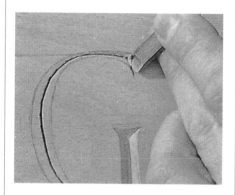

17 Stab the entire letter "G" before carving the upright wide stem. Remove the triangle of wood from the top end of the bowl.

18 Using ½in (13mm) and ¼in (6mm) No. 1 chisels, cut the inside of the bowl, starting at either end and working toward the middle.

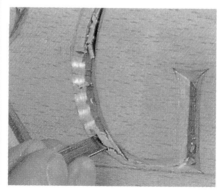

19 Cut the outside of the bowl with a No. 3 gouge. The "scallops" produced by the gouge will later be smoothed by paring.

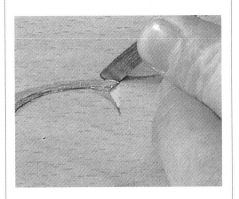

20 When most of the outside of the bowl has been roughly cut, carve the top of the "G" from the end, moving left to the start of the curve. This has to be done delicately with a No. 3 gouge. The ridges can then be pared away to finish the letter.

21 Begin by stabbing the whole letter. Be especially careful at the acute angle junctions, stab them as gently as possible.

Letter "M"

22 Cut both wide stems, but stop a little short of the "V"-junction in the middle. Then carve the right side of the narrow left-hand stroke. Begin at the junction, using a wide chisel and making sure that it overlaps the junction completely to achieve a clean cut.

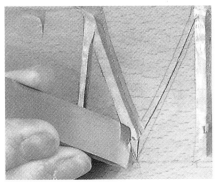

23 When the left-hand narrow stroke is complete, cut the left side of the central "V"-junction with the same chisel.

24 Begin the left side of the angled narrow stroke at its bottom junction. Again, ensure that the chisel completely covers the junction.

25 Finish the letter by cutting away the right-hand side of the central "V"-junction.

Notice particularly the forms of the acute-angled junctions in this completed letter "M."

Letter "S"

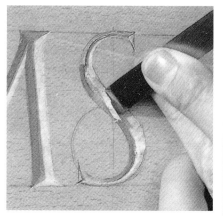

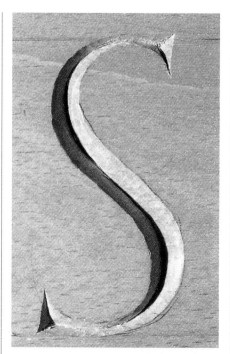

26   Stab the whole letter, including the "Y"-cuts at the ends.

27   Carve the inside curves by starting at their outermost points. Make the short cuts out to the corners, then work in and around each curve. Stop when the chisel is cutting across the grain (above).

29   As you reach the straight central part, change from a gouge to a straight chisel. Continue along the center portion to join the inside curve cut earlier.

30   Cut away the triangles of wood at the two ends.

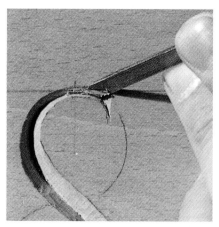

28   Begin cutting the outside curves across the grain, and work in toward the central part of the letter.

Choose a straight-forward design when you first begin carving—basic designs can produce just as pleasing a result as more complex ones.

31   Carve the remaining outside curves, beginning across the grain and working out to the top and bottom of each curve. Finally, cut, moving left from the top corner, and right from the bottom corner, to form the narrow parts of the letter and then complete it.

RIGHT: The technique of letter carving can be used to transform even the simplest articles.0

Sample alphabets

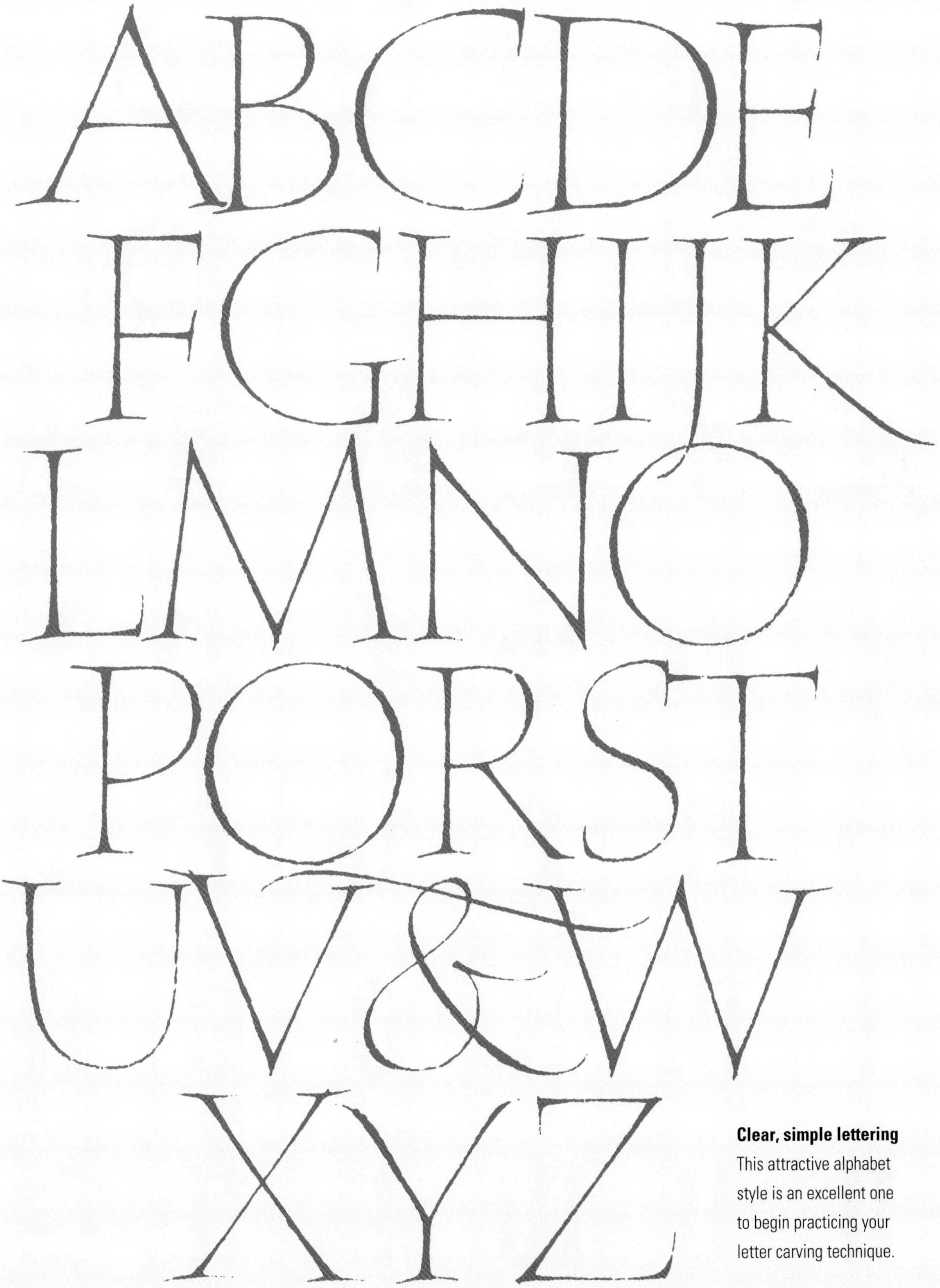
ABCDE
FGHIJK
LMNO
PQRST
UV&W
XYZ

Clear, simple lettering
This attractive alphabet style is an excellent one to begin practicing your letter carving technique.

Decorative lettering

Once you have gained some experience, more elaborate letter shapes may be tackled. Photocopy these letters, enlarging them, if necessary, to the required size.

ADVANCED FINISHING

Stippling

Stippling (sometimes referred to as sponging) is probably the simplest of paint effects to produce on wood, fiberboard, and walls. By far the best substrate for stippling is MDF, which is smooth and takes finishes perfectly.

The background color is a matter of choice, so experiment with pastel and darker colors. To mix the color, blend artists' oil paints with household undercoat or eggshell paint. Apply the background color with a flat brush. Leave it to dry, then sand with fine sandpaper.

For the stipple itself, use latex paint, which is the easiest to apply. Pour it into a shallow container and mix with other latex colors, keeping in mind the shade of the undercoat. Matching colors, only distinguished by a slight difference in shade, may be most suitable—but startling results can be achieved with contrasting colors.

Alternatively, you can use scumbles or glaze instead of water-based paint. Scumbles are sold off the shelf, ready-mixed with color, or you can make your own; glaze can be mixed with artists' oil colors, gold size, mineral spirit and driers. Mix the colors to suit, and apply with a pad. Both glaze and scumbles take longer to dry than latex paint.

Whichever method you choose, once you are certain that the paint is dry, seal the surface with a coat of flat or gloss varnish applied with a flat brush. Polyurethane or oil varnish will alter the color of the paint. A water-based varnish is a much better option. It will dry faster and the surface will not "yellow" as much as a polyurethane finish. Wash brushes out in water.

Making a scumble for stippling

To make a scumble, you need artists' color (sold in a tube), gold size, turpentine, or mineral spirit, and linseed oil. You will also need a spatula and a container.

Select the color you want to use, and place a small quantity in the container. There is, of course, no reason why more than one color cannot be mixed together. A rough guide to the proportions required is one part color to one part turpentine, two parts linseed oil and two parts gold size.

Creating a stipple finish

1 Prepare the surface—in this case MDF—with primer and an undercoat, making sure to apply them evenly.

2 Once the undercoat is dry, apply a thin coat of glaze or scumble, using a flat brush. Lay it on the surface, keeping it wet, and do not brush it around. Do not allow to dry. You can now buy plenty of specialist paint effect tools from hardware stores and paint merchants, which can be used to distribute the scumble in different ways over the base coat. Look out for serated rollers and bunched cloth rollers which produce a heavily-textured random pattern. Most of these tools work best when used on small areas of interest, instead of over a wall or whole piece of furniture.

Tips box

- Practice on scrap board and test effects before stippling.
- Do not apply the stipple too wet.
- Dab the stipple on gently. Do not use too much pressure.
- Make sure scumble or glaze is completely dry before varnishing.
- Vary the way you dab the stipple for a random effect.
- Try different materials for stippling—almost anything will do.

Adding interest

The wall above the basin unit has been
stippled with a gray glaze. Note how
the surface is more varied and
interesting than a painted plain gray
wall. You can also use the paint effects
described so far to transform a boring
floor covering. Hardware stores sell a
range of paint colors especially for lino
and vinyl floors. Roller or brush on a
base coat and leave to dry overnight.
Add a scumble glaze top coat and
protect the finished effect with at least
two coats of flooring grade varnish. You
can do the same with concrete and
wood floors. Create a more finished
look by adding a border in a contrasting
color, following the outline of the room.

3 Hold the stipple brush firmly, and dab
over the surface. Try not to go over
one area more often than the others. Continue
until the whole surface has been stippled. There
is always enough working time to touch up
areas that have been missed. Make sure you
complete one entire area or piece of furniture
without taking a break. If you are working on a
large piece of furniture or wall, divide the work
into complete sections.

Graining

Before attempting to reproduce the grain of any wood, take a good look at the natural wood—compare it with other woods, to identify its distinguishing characteristics, and try to memorize its grain pattern and color. You will notice, for example, that the medullary rays of oak are unique (their appearance depends on the way the wood has been milled); and that mahogany has a distinctive range of red, brown, and pink shades.

When graining, it may also help to have a piece of the relevant wood available, to act as a guide.

Graining is done with scumbles. You can buy these in a range of wood colors, ready-mixed with pigments, gold size, mineral spirit, and driers.

Oak graining

After smoothing the surface and sealing the wood with shellac sanding sealer, use a flat brush to lay down the background color. For oak, the undercoat should be beige. Leave the undercoat to dry, then sand it lightly with fine sandpaper.

Tips box

• Remember when testing scumble colors that the idea is to move wet coats around, combining the various colors, in order to produce the grain pattern.

• Test on scrap materials.

• Take good care of specialist brushes —they are expensive.

• Most standard scumbles will need tinting with pigments.

Creating a simple open-grain finish

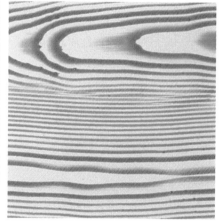

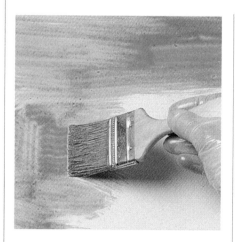

1 After smoothing the surface and sealing the wood with shellac sanding sealer, apply the colored scumble using a flat brush, laying the finish on evenly over an undercoat. Using long, straight strokes, cover the full length of the piece.

3 This open-grained effect is designed to imitate pine and other softwoods. Notice how the grain pattern widens and narrows, and contours are produced. Increase the depth of graining with other colors. Once dry, protect the surface with varnish, or stain it.

2 Use a comb to etch an open-grain pattern into the colored scumble. Draw the comb across the surface, tipping and rolling it from end to end. Remember that the grain does not always run straight, and has shakes and knots. By rocking the comb from side to side, wider patterns are produced.

Next, lay down some oak-colored scumble with a flat brush, using a badger brush to take out the brush marks. Draw a steel graining comb across the surface, making lines in the scumble. Continue right across the surface, making sure each stroke is in line with the preceding one. Wipe the comb clean after each stroke.

Take the comb and draw it across the lines at angles of about 30 degrees. Use a softener or badger brush to blend the lines in so they match the natural look of wood. Add more figuring with an artists' brush. Make the dark strokes with an artists' brush, softening afterward. This produces the straight grain of oak.

To create fake medullary rays, prepare the surface in the same way, and draw the steel comb over the oak scumble. Soften the effect, then cake a graining brush (a long, broad-headed, stiff-bristled brush), and, using a dabbing action, follow the grain, with the graining brush laid on its back. This reproduces the flecked appearance of the grain. Traditionally, medullary rays are simulated with the thumbnail, covered with cloth. Alternatively, use the back of a comb wrapped in a cloth. Once the finish is satisfactory, leave to dry and then apply flat or gloss varnish.

Mahogany graining

After preparing the surface as above, apply a pink-beige undercoat. Sand when dry, then apply the mahogany scumble with a flat brush, using a curling action to produce the appearance of mahogany figure. Soften the brush marks, then brush with a darker scumble, softening the two coats together.

For straight-grain mahogany, apply the scumble with straight strokes of a flat brush, dabbing the grain with the tip of the brush and blending with a badger.

Highlight the grain pattern by dragging a Vandyke water stain across the surface.

Glaze graining
Here, a gray-toned paint glaze was brushed on freely. The cross-grains were then scraped out of the wet glaze with a pencil wrapped in a cloth.

Creating a simple close-grain finish

1 Having applied an undercoat and let it dry, apply the scumble as you would for a simple open-grain effect, with long, straight strokes. Make sure the scumble is applied evenly.

2 Work the scumble with a graining brush to create the tight, straight grain. Hold the brush loosely, and use a beating action along the panel, lengthwise, to produce flecks in the grain.

Marbled effects

The most obvious reason for creating a marbled effect is the desire to imitate real marble, and, in great period houses, there are often outstanding examples of marbling that are difficult to distinguish from the real thing. Today's materials, available off the shelf, are refinements of those used through the ages, but they are more stable and more consistent.

Preparing the surface

Prepare the substrate, filling the grain if necessary. Apply a flat undercoat paint, either acrylic or oil, usually white or pastel. Leave the undercoat to dry, then sand with fine sandpaper.

Working with glaze

The next stage is to apply a glaze, for manipulation while still wet. At this point the colored glazes are not meant to stick to the undercoat, so wipe the surface with linseed oil. You can buy glaze in either a colored or a clear form. Clear glaze needs to be mixed with colored oils or pigments, which are supplied in tubes by art suppliers, ready for use. Mix the colors in a shallow container, always using plenty of white. Mix the glaze in equal proportions with gold size and mineral spirit. Apply a thin layer to the surface, using a flat brush.

Add more glaze layers while the previous coat of glaze is still wet. Use thin layers with subtle colors, gradually merging the layers together. This can be repeated until the required effect has been achieved. Make sure the edges are treated in the same manner, to make the piece look like solid marble.

The veins and streaks are applied with an artists' brush, or a feather. Hold the brush between finger and thumb, and move across the surface, oscillating the brush and making irregular strokes. This will form graduated streaks in the glaze, giving a natural effect. Soften streaks with a badger brush, blending the glazes.

1 Using a flat brush, first apply the undercoat as a background color—it does not need to be white, any color can be used—to suit the marbling effect desired. When the undercoat is dry, sand it flat to make sure that the surface is as even as is possible.

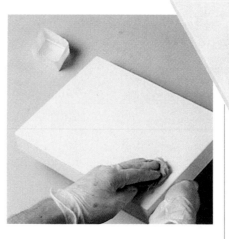

2 Wipe linseed oil over the surface, using a piece of rag, before applying the glaze. This allows the color to float on the surface, so that it can be manipulated before it dries.

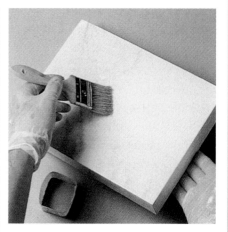

3 Apply the glaze with a flat brush, laying it on using straight strokes along the length of the piece. Make sure the glaze is applied evenly, leaving as few brush marks as possible.

4 Once the glaze has been applied, stipple the surface with a sponge. Use gentle dabs of the sponge, without taking too much paint from the surface. This softens the effect of the glaze, giving it a mottled look, as well as removing any brush marks.

A selection of different marble finishes

1 Sky-blue background, red ocher and black glaze

2 Off-white and pink background, red oxide, and yellow and red glaze

3 Off-white background, raw sienna, and yellow ocher glaze

4 White background, black, and white glaze

5 Black background, gold glaze

6 Dark-green background, white scumble glaze

5 Soften the effect produced by the sponge with a badger brush. Lightly brush the stippled glaze, blending it in with the background color.

6 Use an artists' brush to work in the veins of the marble. Draw across the surface, manipulating the veins by rolling the brush between thumb and finger. Try to produce a random pattern of veins, imitating the natural feel of marble.

7 Soften the veins—again with the badger brush—to blend into the overall marble effect.

8 Varnish the finished piece, to protect it from wear and tear. Whatever finish you choose, it's essential to protect your work with some sort of sealer coat. Make sure the paint has completely dried before sealing. An acrylic varnish is usually the best option for protecting a piece of furniture or wall from abrasion. Brush on two light coats instead of one heavy coat to avoid "sagging," and only dip around one third of the brush into the varnish.

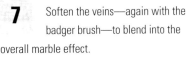

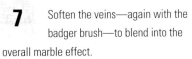

Rag rolling

A traditional way of creating a mottled paint effect on furniture, paneling and walls is to roll the surface with rags before the finish dries. There are any number of techniques used to achieve this decorative effect—from literally rolling cloth across the surface, to dabbing the substrate with a rag or other closely-knitted cloth.

From a furnituremaker's point of view, MDF is the best substrate on which to work. Other materials need filling with plaster of Paris.

Apply an undercoat and sand lightly to achieve a flat surface. You can now buy purpose-made MDF primer that seals the surface and forms an ideal painting surface. Use a fine-textured 4in (100mm) wide roller to spread the primer over the surface. Acrylic paint dries well, but oil-based paints give stronger adhesion. White or pastel eggshell is probably the best base over the undercoat, and can be mixed with artists' oil colors.

When choosing the material for rag rolling, select paints that are compatible with those applied as a base - for example, oil on oil or water on water. Alternatively, mix up paints with glaze and oil colors. The glaze flows more easily, as it contains linseed—but, because of the oil content, take care when drying rags, which can heat up and combust.

Applying the glaze

Thinly apply the wet coat to the surface. It is important to work fast while the paint is still wet, otherwise it will be difficult to manipulate.

Apply the rag rolling with a piece of cotton cloth rolled around some dowels. Alternatively, you can simply roll up the cloth, making sure that the outside is uneven in order to produce the mottled effect. Roller in diagonal overlapping stripes rather than straight up and down the surface to give a more subtle effect.

Tips box

Never leave rags containing linseed oil rolled up, as they can spontaneously combust, especially in warm weather or a hot workshop. Wash out in soapy water or leave overnight in a container of water and mild detergent. Lay them flat to dry.

Creating a rag rolled finish

1 Coat the surface with colored glaze, using a flat brush, and laying the glaze onto the piece, instead of brushing it around. Cover the surface evenly. You are going to move the material around, so do not work so slowly that it dries. You will have approximately 20 minutes (longer with some oil-based paints) to create the paint effect before the surface begins to dry.

2 Any material can be used for rag rolling, including cotton cloth, polyethylene or, as in this case, a paper towel. Larger hardware stores now sell special rag-rolling applicators. Try to use a cloth that will not leave strands of thread on the surface or it will spoil the finished effect.

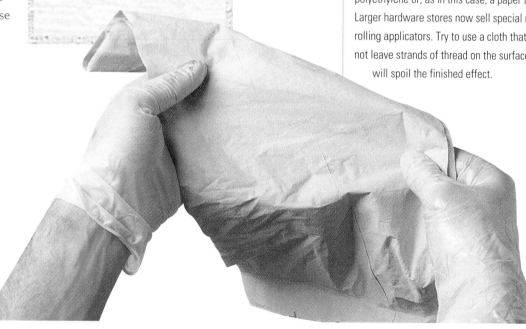

3 Roll the paper or cloth into a long roll. It is important that it is not rolled too tightly, and that the surface remains uneven. Different effects can be produced by changing the tightness of the roll, and it is worth experimenting.

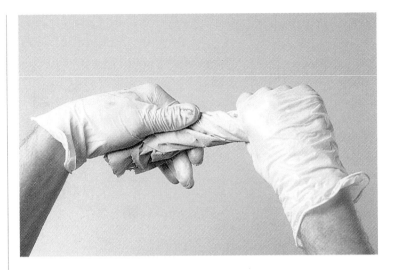

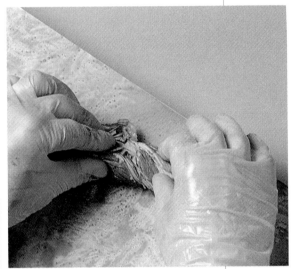

4 Hold the "rag" in both hands, and roll it across the wet surface, to produce a mottled effect. Use a badger brush to soften the effect, and leave to dry before applying more glazes.

5 Wipe off a border, if required, around the rag rolled area while the final glaze is still damp. Use a clean cloth dampened with mineral spirit. When the glaze has dried thoroughly, apply a coat of gloss or flat varnish to protect it. Keep in mind that polyurethane or oil varnish will alter the color of the paint.

Rag rolled paneling

The paneling behind and around the bath has been rag rolled. Notice how the effect has been extended up onto the walls. The straight lines are achieved by removing any excess finish—using a piece of cloth dampened with mineral spirit—following a light pencil line.

Ebonizing

The rarity and expense of ebony as a natural wood has made ebonizing a popular imitative finish, especially on reproduction Regency furniture such as chairs and side tables, and as a substitute for black Chinese lacquer. Today, ebonizing has become synonymous with a uniform finish, with no graining, except for the pores, showing through.

With ebonizing, the slightest imperfection is magnified, so prepare the surface assiduously (fingers are often the best judge of preparation), and take extra care throughout the finishing process. The aim is to a achieve a high-gloss, jet-black finish with no imperfections beneath the highly-polished surface.

Application

Traditionally, a nigrosine water stain is used for staining the wood. Nigrosine water stain is available by mail order from finish suppliers.

Once the stain has dried, apply white or blond polish, mixed with black alcohol stain, using a polishing pad (as used for French polish).

To give depth to the finish, apply a final coat of white or blond polish, using a few drops of linseed oil as lubrication. Once the finish looks full enough, remove the oil with denatured alcohol in the polishing pad to produce a deep gloss. Leave to dry for at least a day, then lightly sieve a small amount of pumice powder over the entire surface and burnish with a soft cloth. Be careful to rub any of the powder out of moldings or tight corners where it can collect and spoil the finished effect.

Ebonizing a small chest

1 Ebony is a very dense wood, with very little grain. It is therefore essential that any piece to be ebonized is prepared thoroughly, with all the holes and pores filled in and sanded flat.

Drying time

- Water stains take 40 minutes to dry.
- Leave the first coat of polish to dry for 20 minutes.
- Topcoats take eight hours to dry.
- The finishing polish takes five hours to dry.
- Keep the project in a dust-free atmosphere or under cover until the last coat is completely dry.

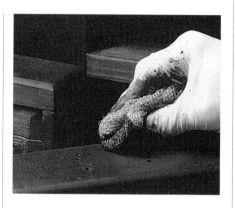

2 Stain the prepared piece with a nigrosine water stain, or a black alcohol stain. Apply the stain wet, and rub well into the grain until an even effect is achieved.

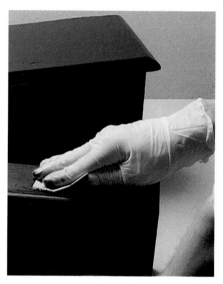

3 Once dry, you will probably still be able to see and feel the open pores of the wood's surface. These have to be filled flush with the surface to create the high-gloss ebonized effect. Lightly sand the surface to remove any specks of dust and wipe the surface with a tack cloth to remove all loose particles. Next, apply black grain filler to fill any open pores. Wipe the filler across the surface with a piece of burlap. Clean off any surplus grain filler and leave to dry. Turn the burlap pad frequently to expose a fresh surface and rub fairly hard to push the filler deep into the grain pores.

Crackle finishes

Crackle finishes are used for two very distinct reasons. The first is to age a piece, simulating the cracking of finish over the years. Alternatively, an interesting decorative effect can be created with contrasting colors. This is sometimes used for imitating leather. In both cases, a coat of crackle glaze (a clear glaze available from finishing suppliers) is applied to the piece. As the glaze dries, surface tensions are produced, causing the finish to craze. It is possible to apply this finish by spraying, but the technique and materials used are different.

Apply a coat of oil varnish. Leave until tacky, then apply the glaze to the surface with a flat brush—laying it on the surface without working it at all, as the cracking will appear at once. To highlight the effect, once the glaze is dry, rub paste wax into the cracks using a soft cloth, then lightly burnish the surface.

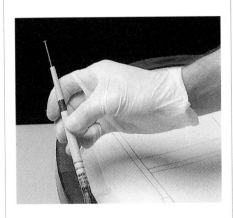

2 When the varnish is tacky, apply a coat of crackle glaze. This is usually supplied ready for use. The size of the pattern produced depends on how much glaze is applied. A thicker coat results in a wider crackle. As with the varnish, lay on the glaze, allowing it to flow freely.

3 As the glaze dries it cracks, producing the distinctive pattern. This can be enhanced by rubbing the cracks with dyes or pigmented wax, which can be made to contrast or complement the undercoat color.

4 Once the filler has dried, lightly sand and wipe clean. It is now time to start applying the black polish. Use a black alcohol stain dissolved in white shellac polish. Use 10 parts of polish to one part of stain. Load the polishing pad with the black polish, and apply as if French polishing (see page 219). When the build of black polish is completely dry, cut it back with 320 silicon-carbide self-lubricating sandpaper. The surface must look satin as well as flat. To produce greater depth to the ebonized surface, apply white polish. Load the polishing rubber with white polish and build up the surface as if French polishing, until a full gloss finish has been achieved. For a satin finish, rub the piece with fine 000-grade steel wool and wax polish.

5 What was once pine is now ebony. It is at this stage that you realize that any blemishes will show the piece for what it really is.

1 After preparing the surface and marking off any areas that do not need to be cracked, apply a coat of oil varnish. Do this with a flat brush, laying it on so that there are no brush marks.

Drying time

- Let shellac sealer dry for 30 minutes.
- Glaze takes about 30 minutes to dry, but always allow longer.
- Leave crackle glaze to dry for 60 minutes.

Distressing

Distressing—also known as antiquing or faking—is used to "age" contemporary furniture or new components of antique pieces. The simplest guide is to look at furniture of the relevant period and try to imitate the markings.

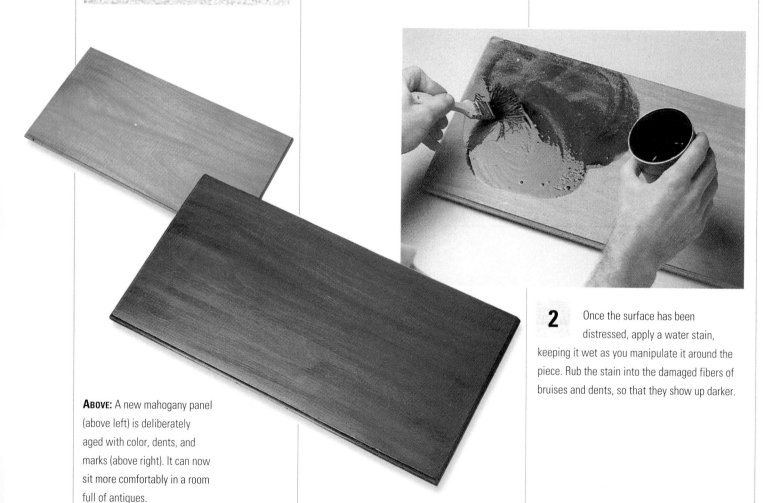

Drying time

- Water stain takes about 40 minutes to dry.

- Allow 30 minutes for shellac sealer to dry.

1 Use a bag of nuts and bolts to make bruises and dents on the surface. The contents need to be heavy enough to do some damage. Make sure you move the bag around in a random motion.

2 Once the surface has been distressed, apply a water stain, keeping it wet as you manipulate it around the piece. Rub the stain into the damaged fibers of bruises and dents, so that they show up darker.

ABOVE: A new mahogany panel (above left) is deliberately aged with color, dents, and marks (above right). It can now sit more comfortably in a room full of antiques.

Corner cabinet with distressed finish

A corner cabinet, made from recycled materials, is a fine example of how marks and dents can give an aged appearance.

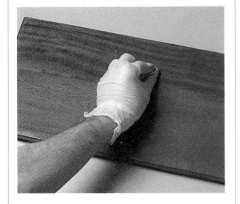

3 When the stain has dried, seal the surface with a shellac sealer. Wipe the sealer across the surface with a soft cloth using straight strokes along the grain. The idea is to seal in the stain and not to build up a finish. Make sure that the coat of sealer is applied evenly.

4 Many old pieces have ring marks from alcohol on glasses—or hot water marks under cups and bowls. To imitate these marks, fill a metal container with hot water and wet the bottom. Leave this on the surface for five to ten minutes to make a dark ring.

5 Stain is not sufficient to give the piece a color that reproduces the effects of aging. Mix alcohol stains and pigments with French polish in a container, and apply with a brush. Cover the whole surface liberally with color, and rub into the wood to produce a darker finish.

6 After the color has dried, apply a coat of transparent polish, using the polishing pad. Work up a build until a finish just short of full grain has been produced. Start with a circular pattern, moving across across the surface. End with straight strokes following the grain. Finish by applying a coat of dark-colored paste wax to enhance the aged appearance.

Advanced Techniques

Rubbed finishes

A rubbed finish is used to simulate the effects of age on a piece of furniture or paneling. This is achieved by rubbing stain selectively on different areas to produce the highlights and dark patches of wear. The technique is most commonly used on oak reproduction furniture, particularly reproduction Jacobean items, but it can be used on other woods, too.

Start by preparing the surface in the normal way—though, since the aim is to achieve an antique feel, it will look more convincing if you leave some of the blemishes and bruises.

Stain the piece using Vandyke crystals mixed with water, to create a dark color.

Once the stain has dried, sand lightly to remove any roughness. Then overstain, using a dark oil dye. Work the stain into the grain, but leave corners and moldings unwiped, so that they are darker than the rest. Leave to dry before starting the rubbing.

Make a pad of 000 steel wool, small enough to fit in your hand. Work on the highlights until the dark stain has been rubbed off, then continue rubbing until the patchy effect has been subtly blended in, and there are no obvious lines remaining between the light and dark areas.

Use a dark garnet polish for finishing the rubbed effect. Apply at first with a soft cloth, then leave to dry. Sand, using fine abrasive paper (about 320 grit), then dust off and continue to apply polish with a pad. Shade in any parts that show up too distinctively, using an alcohol color with small amounts of pigment— applied with either a soft cloth or a brush.

1 Prepare the stool to produce a smooth surface, then apply color. In this case a dark water stain (Vandyke) is used. It penetrates well, and can be worked into corners and crevices to give a darker color. Rub the stain into the moldings.

2 Once the stool has been stained, wipe off the surplus and leave to dry. Then sand lightly and overstain using dark oil dye. Note the darker areas on legs and corners.

3 When the piece is dry, rub off the stain with fine 000 steel wool or flexible abrasive (as shown here). Start from the center of a rail or panel, and work toward the corners. Rub off more stain in the center than in the corners, blending gradually toward them. Use alcohol dyes, mixed with French polish and applied with a brush to enhance the rubbed effect. A dark oil dye will help the contrast, but make sure the color blends in. Use a dark garnet polish for finishing the rubbed effect.

4 Give the finished stool a coat of white polish, working up to a semi-full gloss finish. Then wax polish the piece.

Tips box

- Do not make sharp lines—the rubbed effect must blend in subtly.
- Use the technique sparingly for the best effect.
- On tabletops, try to suggest areas of heavy wear around serving places by rubbing away more of the color in these areas.
- Chair rails at the front of the frame are subject to a great deal of wear and tear, shown by a much lighter area than the surrounding woodwork.

Liming

Liming is used on open-grained woods (most commonly oak). A liming paste is worked into the pores of the wood to fill the grain. When the surface is fully finished, liming enhances the grain pattern by emphasizing the pores and leaving a contrasting color.

1 Open up the grain to take the liming paste by rubbing the surface with a stiff wire brush, using straight strokes along the grain. After opening the grain, stain the piece with any color. It is best not to use oil dye, as this can cause patchiness at a later stage. Leave the stain to dry.

2 Seal the stain with a pale or white polish, to make sure that the liming paste does not dry patchy. Leave to dry, preferably overnight as it is important that the stain or polish has sufficient time to properly harden before you attempt the next stage of the process.

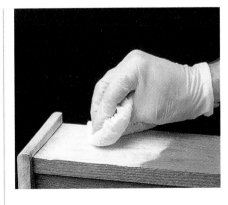

3 Smooth the sealed surface with a flexible abrasive, or use fine 320-grade sandpaper. Liming paste is a combination of wax and white pigments, and is supplied ready mixed. If desired, other colors can be added to the paste before it is applied to the piece. Apply the paste with a cloth, before rubbing it into the pores using a piece of burlap. Work across the grain.

4 Before the paste dries, wipe off any excess with burlap, again working across the grain. Make sure the grain is filled evenly and that not too much is wiped off. Leave the paste to dry overnight, then burnish the surface with a soft cloth. Apply a coat of white or pale polish, but seal the paste.

Gilding

Gilding is the art of decorating with gold leaf. It is found mainly on fancy moldings, especially those surrounding elaborate picture and mirror frames.

Traditional gilding was laid on gesso, a kind of pigmented plaster. The gesso was built up into shapes and forms and the gold was laid on top.

Today, it is comparatively simple to touch up damaged gilding, thanks to the large number of gold paints and pastes that are usually mixed with an oil- or wax-based binding. You can even get gilding sticks that work bit like a wax crayon. Of course, few of these touch-up materials contain real gold, but, if you want to go the whole hog, you can always use gold leaf. Paints and pastes are usually rubbed or brushed on, though some types demand that the surface be primed with size before application.

Using transfer leaf

1 Coat the surface where the repair is to be made with red-oxide primer, and sand very smooth. Brush a thin coat of gold size over the primed area, and set aside.

3 Use a clean camel-hair brush to pat the gold leaf down against the sticky size. Use fragments of leaf to fill any gaps in the coverage.

2 Transfer leaf is gold leaf on a wax-paper backing. Half an hour after sizing, the gilding can be done. Press the leaf gently onto the still-tacky surface.

4 Burnish gently with a pad of cotton wool until the leaf adheres completely to the surface beneath. Dip the wool into a little spirit to remove smears.

SPRAY FINISHES

Finishing can be completely carried out by hand methods, but there may be occasions when you wish to apply paint, stain, varnish, or lacquer with a spray gun. Once you have mastered the technique, spraying gives a perfectly even finish. The two main spraying methods are: air spraying (the finishing liquid is atomized with compressed air) and airless spraying (the finish is compressed to atomize it and no compressed air is needed).

BELOW: When spraying, always use smooth, steady sweeps of the gun parallel to the surface.

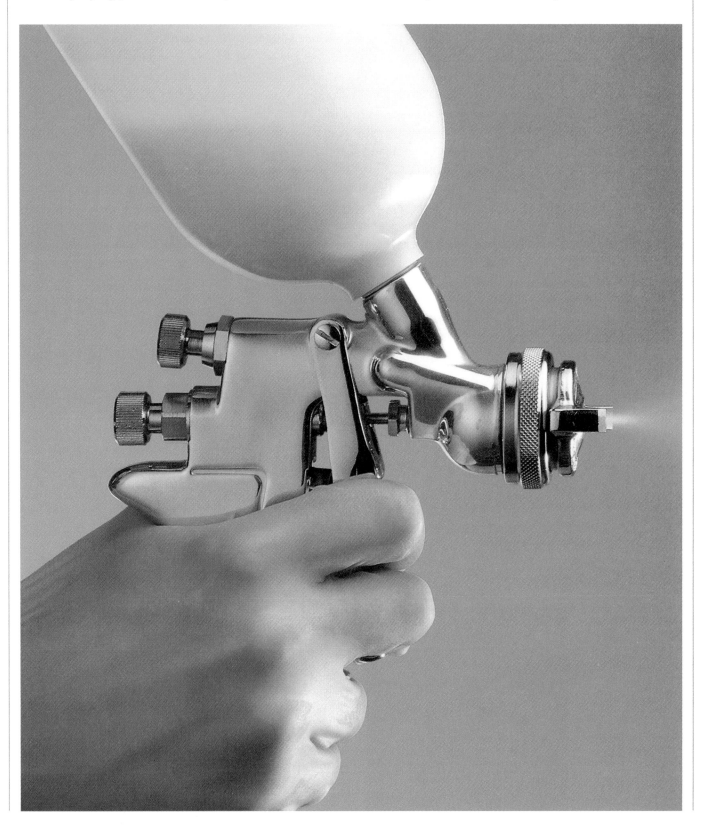

Types of spray guns

The principal feature that distinguishes the various types of spray guns is the way the finish is held and then passed to the nozzle for atomizing with compressed air. There are basically only three options—and unless bulk spraying with a pressure-feed gun is required, the choice is really limited to gravity-feed and suction-feed guns. For small jobs such as stenciling, the range can be extended to aerosols, but they are rarely used by professional finishers—except for touching up damaged spray finishes on site.

Convenience, economy, and the types of finishes to be used are the criteria to consider when choosing a spray gun. For the small workshop, gravity-feed guns are normally the most convenient. They are easy to handle, economical (as small quantities can be mixed for short jobs), and suitable for most finishes.

Suction-feed guns are less convenient, as the underslung reservoir makes them unwieldy. However, they only need small quantities of finish at a time, and they are the most popular option when using heavy pigmented finishes for spraying cars and other metallic surfaces.

All of these guns (possibly with the exception of aerosols) produce the smooth finish associated with spraying, so long as they are maintained properly, and the materials and workpiece are thoroughly prepared. Aerosols are more difficult to use, because they cannot be adjusted and the material is not atomized as consistently.

Gravity-feed guns

Most woodworkers wanting to fit up their workshop for spraying are likely to buy a gravity-feed spray system. The suction variety tends to be used for spraying metal with colored paints. Gravity guns are simple and easy to use. The finish is mixed and stored in a cup that screws on to the top of the gun. The cup takes just over a pint, which is ample for spraying both sides of a 6ft (2m) long tabletop with one coat of finish.

It is important not to run out of material midway through spraying a large surface such as a tabletop. Spray finishes dry within minutes and the gun must be kept on the move all the time, so trying to spray a surface in stages can result in a patchy finish. There are few wood-finishing operations that will use up a full cup for one coat—but always err on the side of generosity when measuring finish, to make sure that you do not run out at a critical moment. Equally, do not overfill the cup on a gravity-feed gun, as it can then spill finish onto the piece as you spray, leaving conspicuous droplets that take time to flatten with sandpaper.

When assembling the spray gun, make sure that the small plastic filter at the bottom of the cup is in place, to stop dirt from getting into the gun and blocking the nozzle. In use, the finish flows down into the gun and out of the nozzle. There the finish is atomized by air blown through small holes (called atomizing holes) in the air cap, which surrounds the nozzle, and through the horn holes that stand proud on each side of the air cap.

With the compressor working, the gun is constantly ready, but the compressed air will only flow when the trigger is squeezed. Squeezing the trigger opens the air valve and draws the needle away from the nozzle to let the finish out. However, the initial pressure on the trigger opens the air valve only a little, without allowing the finish to flow, thus ensuring that material does not drip out of the gun onto the workpiece without being atomized.

Spraying is a technique that does require some practice to master the correct techniques for a really smooth finish. If you plan to use a spray finish for future projects, it is worth making up a spraying booth to mask the surrounding workshop and provide a clean area for working. The booth doesn't need to be anything more than a few manmade boards hinged together and draped with polythylene. Always make sure you are properly protected with a respirator mask that is intended for use with spray finishes.

Tips box

- Always select a good quality spray gun. Buy the best one you can afford.
- Try out the gun to see how it feels.
- Always clean out after use, making sure that the holes are not blocked.
- Lubricate all parts with an all-purpose oil.

LEFT: A shaded or sunburst finish is extremely useful for items such as guitars or dashboards, where wooden surfaces need to blend in with plastic and metal.

A GRAVITY-FEED GUN
This gun is probably the best piece of equipment
for anyone taking up spray finishing.

Cup: The cup stores the
finish and screws into
the top of the gun.

Spread adjuster:
This regulates the
quantity of air
flowing out of the
horn holes in the cap,
so changing the
shape of the fan.

Air flow adjuster:
This is adjusted to suit
the material being
sprayed—higher for
thicker materials,
lower for thin
materials.

Needle adjuster:
The needle restricts
the amount of fluid
flowing out of the gun.

Air cap: Air is
blown through small
holes in the air cap,
atomizing the finish.

Handle: This is for
gripping the gun.

Trigger: Squeezing
the trigger opens the
air valve and draws a
needle away from
the nozzle to release
the fluid.

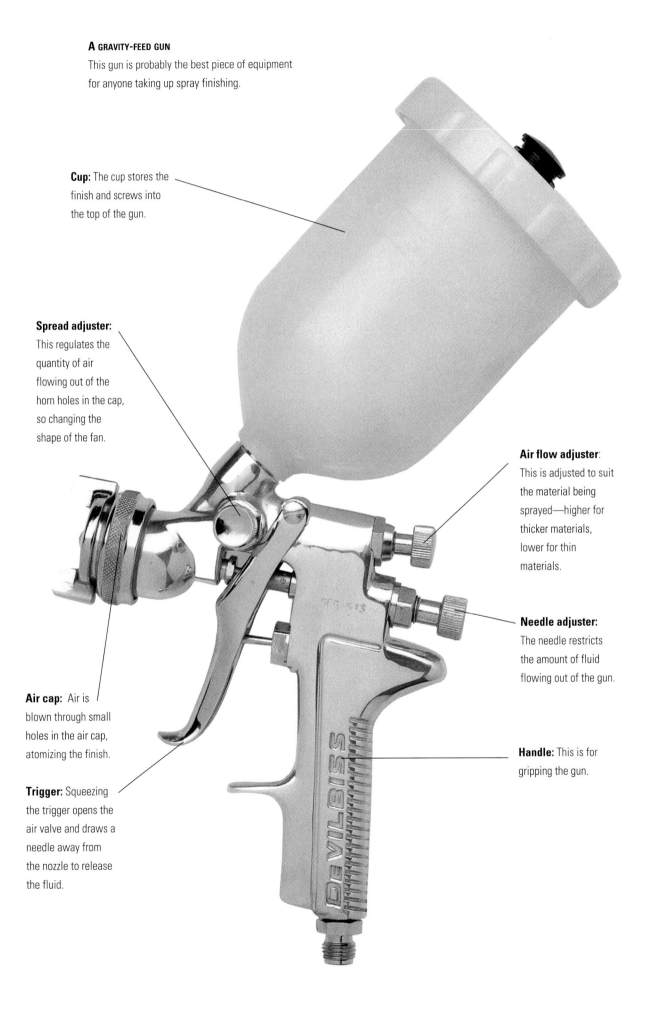

Other types of spray guns

You don't have to make a big investment in professional spray equipment to get started in spray finishing. You can use a basic electric sprayer or even an aerosol, although the finish will not be as consistent.

RIGHT: Electric spray pump—this is very useful for finishes that are near the correct viscosity, since over thinning can affect some finishes.

electric motor

pump

trigger

feed tube

pressurized container

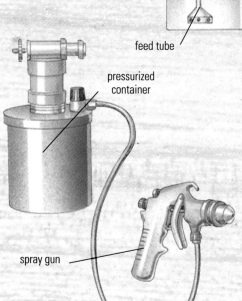

spray gun

LEFT: Airless spray gun—here the finish is pressurized and forced out of the nozzle in an atomized form. This system is limited to large equipment for bulk or industrial use, but there are some adaptations for smaller users.

lacquer feed line

RIGHT: Glass jar aerosol—this allows you to spray whatever finish you wish. It is necessary to use the fluid at the correct viscosity.

Suction-feed guns

Suction-feed spray guns are broadly similar to gravity-feed types, but the finish is siphoned up from a cup slung below the gun. The nozzle of a suction-fed gun protrudes farther through the air cap than on gravity-feed or pressure-feed guns. As the air rushes out through the air cap, a vacuum is formed that sucks up the finish from the reservoir. Adjustments are much the same as on the other guns, though the set-up of nozzle, needle, and air cap is different.

One advantage of suction guns is that the reservoir can be larger than on a gravity gun. You therefore do not have to refill it as frequently, which saves time. It also helps when mixing the finish. Since the cup holds that much more, mixing up in another container may be unnecessary. However, the size of the cup, and the fact that it is often made of metal (instead of plastic as for gravity-feed guns), does make the gun heavy. Also, if you lose concentration, the cup tends to hit the surface and mark the finish.

Another advantage is that you can mix the finish in the cup before attaching it to the gun (whereas on a gravity gun the cup has to be screwed in place before it can be filled, which is less convenient). When fitting the cup to the gun, make sure the filter at the bottom of the tube is in place.

When you look at a suction gun, you will notice that the tube that picks up the finish from the cup is bent. This is a design feature. When the gun is tipped forward, as often happens while spraying, the tube needs to point toward the front of the cup, to make sure that it sucks up finish and not air. If air is sucked up, then the finish is likely to be uneven.

Spray finishing is no longer confined to trade workshops. You can now buy all-in-one packages of a budget spray gun, connectors, and a mini compressor to get you started, and these systems can provide perfectly good results for almost any woodworking task.

A SUCTION-FEED SPRAY GUN
This type of gun is recommended for spraying heavy pigmented finishes.

Spread adjuster:
This regulates the quantity of air flowing out of the horn holes in the cap and so changes the shape of the fan.

Needle adjuster:
The needle restricts the amount of fluid flowing out of the gun.

Air cap: Air is blown through small holes in the air cap, atomizing the finish.

Trigger: Squeezing the trigger opens the air valve and draws a needle away from the nozzle to release the fluid.

Handle: This is for gripping the gun.

Air-flow adjuster:
This is adjusted to suit the material being sprayed—higher for thicker materials, lower for thin materials.

Cup: The cup stores the finish and is carried below the gun.

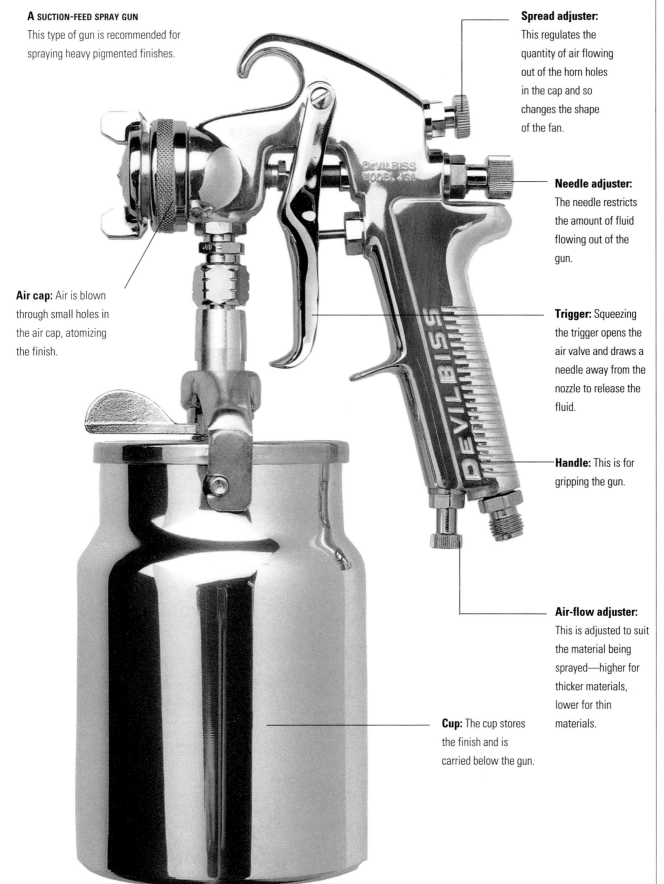

Using a spray gun

Modern finishes are popular not only for their qualities of resistance, but also because they can be applied consistently at an economic rate. A professional spray finisher will say that a consistent finish is the most important characteristic of a job done well. Some practice is needed in order to fully understand the formula for a fine finish, and to learn the hand-to-eye coordination required when working with a spray gun. Even so, you will be surprised how easy and quick it is to get started—and you will soon appreciate the potential of a spraying system.

The important variables to experiment with are the fluid, spread, and air-supply adjustments on the gun and air regulator, and the viscosity of the finish being used. There is no benefit to be gained from high air pressure, as high pressure makes the air and atomized finish bounce back onto the finisher—so keep the pressure as low as possible, without allowing globules of finish to form. About 130lb psi is sufficient for most finishes. If the flow of fluid is too fast, you will be unable to keep up, and the finish will start to run. Always use two or more thin applications, instead of one thick coat.

The distance between the gun and the surface, along with the smoothness of the sweep as you are spraying, is critical for the finish. This is where the skill of the finisher really shows. Generally, unless the manufacturer of the finish recommends otherwise, spray with the gun about 8in (20cm) from the surface. Too near will result in runs; too far will spread the finish too wide.

Adjusting a spray gun (left)
Adjust the needle travel to alter the flow of the material from the gun.

Cleaning a gun

- Clean all parts of the gun with thinners, paying special attention to the holes in the air cap and nozzle. It is not necessary to remove the nozzle, but take off the air cap and clean it thoroughly.

- Use a brush to clean the inside of the gun, and make sure that all holes are clear.

- Do not leave the gun to soak in thinners overnight, as the packing may shrink and dirty solvent can block vital air passages. After cleaning, reassemble the gun and oil all moving parts.

ABOVE: Unscrew the knurled knob to allow more material out of the gun and tighten to restrict the flow.

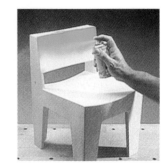

A children's chair is an ideal project to practice your paint-spraying techniques.

RIGHT: Test the flow of material through the gun and keep adjusting the needle stop until the required flow is achieved. Spray a piece of scrap as a test. If the coat is heavy and runs, too much material is being used. If the surface does not look wet, not enough lacquer is passing from the nozzle.

Safety precautions

- When spraying, always wear goggles and a mask or, if possible, a respirator.

- Wear protective gloves when working with acid catalysts.

- Wear overalls at all times.

- If you do accidentally get any paint on your skin or in your eyes, wash it off immediately and seek medical advice if any irritation occurs.

Keeping the spray consistent

Consistent spraying is accomplished with smooth, steady sweeps of the gun—parallel to the surface. When learning to spray, there is an almost irresistible tendency to keep the wrist firm, as if putting in golf. When putting, the arms form an arc, with the hands farther from the ground at the beginning and end of each stroke than at the moment when the club hits the ball. So, if you keep your wrist rigid when spraying, the part of the work closest to you will receive a thick coat of finish (often with runs), whereas the areas farthest away from you will be more thinly coated.

The trick is to flex your wrist as your arm moves. Try not to move your body unless absolutely necessary. If you do move your body, it will upset the consistency of the sweep—so keep your body still and move only your arms. The aim is to keep the spray gun parallel with the surface all the time. Flex your wrist as if ironing a pair of pants, or painting a door.

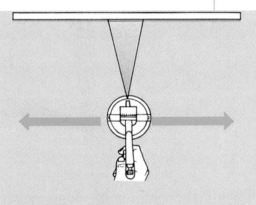

SPRAYING METHODS
Correct: Always keep the spraying path parallel with the workpiece.

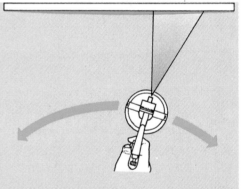

Incorrect: Swinging the gun produces uneven coverage of the piece.

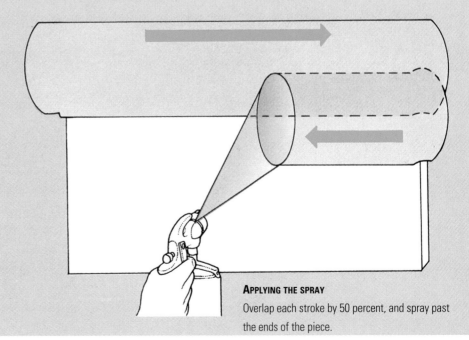

APPLYING THE SPRAY
Overlap each stroke by 50 percent, and spray past the ends of the piece.

Types of spray finishes

Preparing surfaces for spraying

When it comes to preparing the surface for spraying, the usual rules for producing a smooth, blemish-free surface apply.

Use shellac or two-part wood fillers where appropriate (the latter are recommended for larger repairs). Paste-wood fillers should be used for a full-grain finish. It can be used between coats of lacquer finish to fill dents that have been missed during preparation.

Oil dyes should not be used for staining pieces that are to be sprayed. Catalyzed finishes in particular are likely to react with these stains, changing the color of the wood radically. A dark oak, for example, may suddenly turn rose red.

Water and alcohol stains can be used under spray finishes, though before applying a water stain, remember to raise the grain by wetting the wood, then sanding it flat. Water-based NGR stains and alcohol stains can be sprayed on, though the results are unlikely to be superior to application by hand.

Sealing and color matching

Most woods will need to be sealed before the first spray coat. The type of sealer varies from finish to finish, and can be determined by the wood type. Once the first spray coat has been applied, some color matching may be necessary. In all cases, this can be done using alcohol dyes, either mixed into lacquer and sprayed onto the workpiece, or simply rubbed on. The alcohol base will bite into all spray finishes, even acid catalyst.

Alternatively, use dyes specially prepared for use with lacquer. They are powerful—so use them in small quantities. Apply more

Stripping a chair for spraying

1 The gloss finish on this chair needs to be stripped before preparing to spray. It is quicker to strip with chemicals than to try to cut back the old finish using sandpaper.

than one color to obtain the right match, spraying on and leaving to dry for about five minutes. Dyes are the most suitable option for shading and are best used after the first sealer coat.

How many coats?

Depending on the effect or protection required, one or two coats of finish will be enough. It varies from one piece to another.

An average-sized kitchen-tabletop will need about 1½ pints (850ml) for spraying both sides with one coat of finish, while a chair will need about 1¼ pints (700ml).

Spray finishes dry quickly (within 20 minutes), but take longer to cure. It is important to apply the second coat as soon as possible after the first—once the surface is touch dry, and has been lightly sanded (de-nibbed)—so that it can bite in before the curing process starts.

Tips box

- Do not use shellac finishes with a spray gun, as they tend to cobweb.

- Several light coats are always better than one heavy one.

2   Always wear protective gloves, overalls, and goggles when working with chemical strippers. Decant a little stripper at a time into a can. Ventilate the workshop, or work outside.

3   Using a flat brush, lay the stripper onto the surface, keeping it wet as it is applied. Do not brush it around—this will only speed up evaporation, and reduce the effectiveness of the stripper.

4   Use a paint scraper to test to see if the old finish is ready to be scraped off. Always scrape with the grain.

5   Use a bunch of coarse steel wool to rub off any of the finish that is left on the surface. Always wear heavy gloves when working with this grade of steel wool, because it is very sharp, and do not try to tear it from the roll—instead, cut it with shears, or a pair of old scissors.

6   Apply another coat of stripper, and rub off waste with more coarse steel wool, using a stick or spatula to remove finish from nooks and crannies. Do not use a metal point—it is likely to scratch the wood. Check the manufacturer's instructions to see if the stripper needs to be neutralized. Follow their directions for doing so.

LEFT: The finished chair, ready for sanding through the grades with garnet paper, from coarse to fine.

Staining with a spray gun

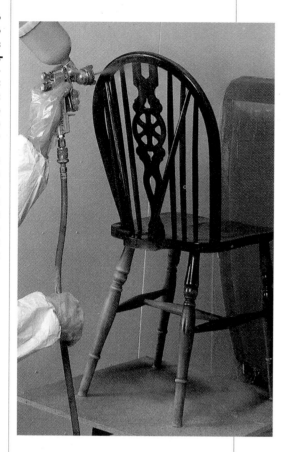

1 Alcohol stains can be sprayed, though rubbing stain in by hand is likely to produce a superior result. Use a gravity-feed spray gun to apply the stain. This type of gun is the easiest to handle around the chair. Regulate the pressure at 25lb psi, and apply a wet, even coat. Work from the inside of the legs out. Then stain the edges and the underneath of the seat before starting work on the top. The idea is to stain the most visible areas last.

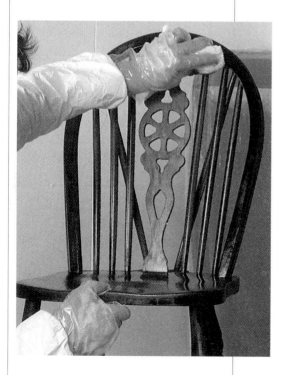

2 As with any staining mix, it is important to use an even layer of color, or the result will be patchy. Wipe off any surplus stain, especially around frame joints, using a clean cloth. Work until an even color has been achieved and leave to dry.

Acid catalyst finishes

The main drawback to acid catalyst finishes is that they have to be mixed with a catalyst, which adds to the setting-up time. The catalyst needs to be handled carefully, wearing protective gloves. Acid catalyst finishes have been in use for about 40 years, and are supplied with either a melamine-formaldehyde or urea-formaldehyde base in flat or gloss. Their great advantage is that they are hard-wearing, and are therefore especially popular for table- and countertops.

When spraying acid catalyst, try not to apply it as wet and thick as you would other finishes. Turn down the flow rate slightly, and sweep a little faster with the gun. Always use two coats of acid catalyst. The proportion of catalyst to base varies from manufacturer to manufacturer. However, adding more catalyst than recommended does not speed up the curing time, and will produce a brittle finish. It is also more likely to react with stains. If you use too little catalyst, the finish will not cure at all. Always follow the instructions provided with the finish.

Because acid catalyst has a high solid content, it may be necessary to thin it with thinners recommended for acid catalyst finishes. This helps produce a more flowing coat.

An acid catalyst finish takes 30 minutes to one and a half hours to dry, depending on the room temperature, and can be recoated as soon as it is touch dry. The hardness of the coating increases over a period of about seven days; the harder the lacquer the easier it is to burnish. Therefore, wait at least 24 hours before burnishing. If the article you are finishing is a table, use place mats for the first seven days and wipe off any water spills immediately.

Drying times

- Most spray finishes are dry within 20 minutes, though some take hours or days to cure fully.

- Acid catalyst dries in 30 to 90 mins and can be given more coats as soon as it feels dry to the touch.

- Undercoat spray finishes usually take around an hour to dry.

Staining with a spray gun

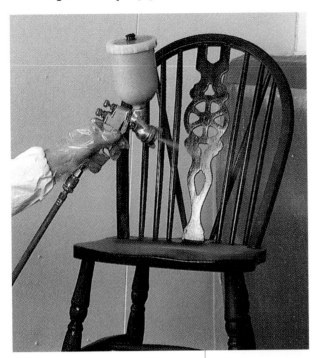

1 Use a gravity-feed spray gun to apply the sealer. Set the pressure at 25lb psi. Apply an even coat, making sure that all areas are covered. Again, work from the least visible toward the most conspicuous parts. Do not apply too heavy a coat—this is only meant to be a sealing application.

2 Leave the sealer to dry for about 20 minutes at 63° (F17°C). The surface is then slightly rough and will need smoothing. Use fine 320 grit self-lubricating silicon-carbide sandpaper, always following the grain and being careful not to break through the sealer and stain. Be especially gentle on the corners, and hold the paper flat in the hand, with the two middle fingers pressing it down onto the surface.

Pros and cons of acid catalyst finishes

Pros
- Acid catalyst finishes are hard-wearing.
- They are resistant to abrasions, and to some acids and alkalis.
- They dry clear, without yellowing.

Cons
- Acid catalyst finishes are slow to cure, and are vulnerable to wet heat.

Pros and cons of paint finishes

Pros
- Paint finishes are available in a range of colors.
- They will mask discoloration in wood.
- They can be used for special effects.

Cons
- Pigmented finishes dry more slowly than clear lacquers.
- They exaggerate woodworking and spraying defects, and are sensitive to dust.
- Faultless preparation is required.
- Before spraying with them, your gun needs to be cleaned very thoroughly.

Paint finishes

Nitrocellulose lacquer and acid catalyst finishes are available in paint form for special effects, such as splatter, and also for simple painted surfaces.

Waterborne finishes

With most spray finishes, the solid element is carried from the gun to the surface by a petroleum-based solvent, which then evaporates. In some cases, the solvent comprises as much as 70 percent of the finish. It therefore made sense to try to discover a solvent that was inexpensive and environmentally harmless. The answer—water!

Unlike most spray finishes, waterborne finishes do not liven up the surface, and, although they are available in gloss form if required, they have a flatter, more natural appearance than other lacquers. As a result, they are a common choice for Scandinavian-style pine products. You can buy waterborne finishes in either one-part or two-part form. In the latter type, a cross-linker is used as the hardener. Follow the manufacturer's instructions for mixing this catalyst with the bulk of the finish.

If staining is needed, use water or NGR stains (not oil dyes). Before applying water stains, raise the grain and then sand.

A waterborne sealer should be used prior to spraying. Before applying the sealer, dampen the surface to raise the grain, then let it dry, and sand it lightly. Do not use a grain filler when working with waterborne finishes, as adhesion is not always satisfactory. After sealing, do any color matching that may be needed, using alcohol dyes.

When spraying, turn the fluid rate down. Most solvents evaporate to some degree between the gun and the surface, but this is not the case with waterborne finishes—so try to use thin coats and keep the viscosity up, in order to avoid runs.

Waterborne finishes are not compatible with other spray finishes. The gun and other equipment must therefore be absolutely clean before use, otherwise the finish is likely to foam. The final coat can be left as it is, or rubbed with 000 steel wool and wax. Rub in the direction of the grain, with even strokes, to produce a satin finish.

Pros and cons of waterborne finishes

Pros
- Waterborne finishes do not harm the environment.
- They do not constitute a fire hazard.

Cons
- Waterborne finishes are still comparatively expensive.
- They are difficult to use, as they tend to sag or run.
- They are sensitive to cold, and are easily contaminated by other finishes.
- Grain filler cannot be used with them.

Staining color and lacquer

1 Once the sealer has dried, lightly sand the chair and then wipe off any dust. There will be parts of the chair, particularly the highlights, that need to be touched up with color. Turn the pressure right down to 15lb psi for touching up (right).

2 Picking out the lighter areas, gradually build up an even color. Do not try to use too much color in one pass. Work from front to back, finishing with the back slats. The back usually needs more color than any other part of the chair. Unlike any other spraying operation, touching up the color may require more spray in some areas than others (above).

3 After the final application of color, apply gloss lacquer. Turn the pressure up to 25lb psi, and plan your route around the chair. Start inside the legs, moving on to the slats, and finishing with the seat. Always spray the most important surfaces last (above).

LEFT: The finished chair has an even glow.

Splatter finishes

Splatter finishes are among the easiest creative spray effects to produce. By hand, surfaces can be splattered with a toothbrush, creating an irregular speckled pattern. The same results can be achieved in the spraying shop, by adjusting the air pressure, fluttering the trigger, and altering the distance between gun and surface.

Pastel colors are normally best for the background, with brighter splattering on top. There are no strict rules to follow, and you may find other color combinations suit the situation better. Choose colors that complement each other.

Any type of paint or pigmented finishes, which are available from finishing suppliers, can be used for the base coat and for splattering. Make sure the surface is thoroughly prepared. Apply one layer of undercoat and then the required base, using fine sandpaper between coats.

Fill the spray gun cup with splatter finish mixed to the same viscosity as the base coat. Turn down the air pressure at the air regulator, until it is just sufficient to atomize the finish (test this on some scrap wood). By pulling back the trigger further, more material will flow to the nozzle, creating a thicker splatter pattern. The closer the gun is to the surface, the bigger the speckles will be, as the particles of finish break up in the air.

Shading

While either suction or gravity-feed guns can be used for a splattered finish, the latter are best for shading, as they are much easier to manipulate when trying to replicate the aged look produced by rubbing. Though it may take time to develop the skills necessary for accurate shading (especially, creating darker areas in corners and recesses), you will find that gradual shading of a panel from the center out is just as easy by hand.

Stain the piece using a water or alcohol stain. Stain to the color required

Applying a splatter finish

1 Turn down the air pressure at the air regulator until it is just sufficient to atomize the finish (left). Test the effects of this on a piece of scrap, or the side of the spray booth. The finish must not be mixed too thinly, otherwise it will continue to atomize without forming the characteristic splatter globules.

2 Patchiness is not always a disadvantage when splattering. If you want an even splatter, keep the gun moving all the time. Vary the distance of the gun from the work surface to alter the size of the splatter globules. The closer the gun is to the piece, the larger the blobs of finish (right).

for the lightest areas. Seal this with a shellac sealer, then sand gently with 320 grit silicon-carbide paper and dust off.

Use spray tints for the shading. Mix to a color about half a shade darker than the original stain. The trick is to use a tint that is not too dark, otherwise it becomes very difficult to produce gradual shading from light to dark. The aim is to avoid any sharp definition between shaded and unshaded areas. Darken those areas that are most likely to collect dust with age, building up the color in recesses and internal corners with coats of spray tint. Finish with a flat nitrocellulose lacquer.

3 The finished panel shows fine blue speckles on a white background. Light colors are best for the background, but there are no limitations to the number, size, and color of the splatter marks (above).

Advanced Techniques

Sunburst effects

You may be excused for mistaking sunburst for shading. The effect is similar, though sunburst is used for decoration as opposed to reproduction and restoration. It is popular on guitars, car dashboards, and wooden surfaces that have to blend in with plastic and metal.

Staining color and lacquer

2 Apply the base stain, using a spraying or spirit stain. Choose a color that is lighter than the finished color required. Keep the coat as even as possible. If you have a choice of spray guns, use a gravity-feed type for this operation (below).

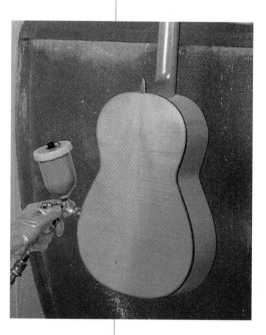

1 Guitars and dashboards are the most common objects for a sunburst, or shaded finish. Make sure the surface is flat and smooth before starting the spraying operation, removing any blemishes where necessary. Use fine, self-lubricating silicon-carbide abrasive paper for the final sanding. Always sand with the grain, holding the paper flat in the hand.

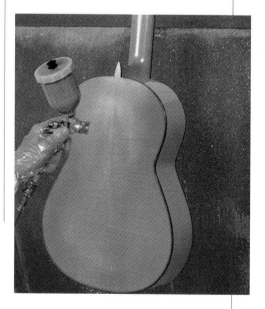

3 Start applying the darker shading spray, gradually building up the color from the outer edges of the guitar. The principle of producing the brightest areas in the center of panels is true for the majority of pieces (left).

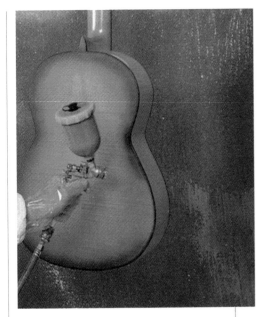

4 Build up the shading, blending it with the lighter areas. Although the aim is to produce a darker ring around the edges, it is important that there is no obvious line between dark and light. Build up the shading slowly, instead of applying a single, heavy coat (above).

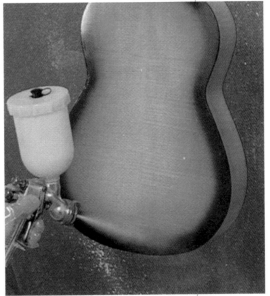

5 Protect the sunburst effect with two even coats of clear lacquer (left). De-nib between applications. Dashboards are often sprayed with a high-gloss finish, but it is equally appropriate to use satin or matt lacquers. In this example, the sunburst finish has been used as decoration, but it can also be used to imitate the rubbed quality of older pieces.

Hammered finish

A hammered finish is produced by two spraying applications. The first coat is a lacquer based on an aluminum paste, to give the metallic content. Once this has been applied, on a thoroughly prepared surface, leave for 5 to 10 minutes, then apply a splattered coat of ethyl acetate (the appropriate solvent) at low pressure, to break up the aluminum and create the hammered look.

The lower the pressure—for example, 5-10lb psi—the wider the hammered pattern will be. Higher pressure—about 10-15lb psi—produces a tighter effect. Use the air regulator to control the levels of pressure.

Crackle finish

A sprayed crackle finish is produced in much the same way as by hand, the effect depending largely on the

Before and after hammered finish
An oval panel before and after spraying with a hammered finish, which in this case imitates pewter. The effect is produced by a combination of two spray applications: the second coat is sprayed on when the first is still tacky.

heaviness of the coat. A thick wet application results in a wider pattern. The resins in the crackle are described as 'underbound'. This means that there is not a sufficient solid content to cover the surface—so, as the solvents evaporate, the solids are drawn together, forming a crazed pattern.

After preparing the surface, spray or brush on an undercoat, and flatten with fine sandpaper, ready for the base coat. This background color will be seen through the cracks of the pattern, so you need to work out in advance what colors are compatible. Mix small quantities of the base and crackle to test the colors.

Leave the base coat for about an hour, or until dry, before applying the crackle. Add spray tints to the crackle to produce the desired color.

Before spraying, turn down the air pressure to about 15lb psi. The cracks form almost immediately, as the crackle hits the surface and the solvents

evaporate. The background color breaks through the cracks. As with hand-applied crackle glaze, the heavier and wetter the coat, the bigger the pattern. Vary the size to suit the piece. A large tabletop will need a 2in (5cm) crackle pattern, while rails and small items need a pattern no more than 1in (25mm) wide.

Finally, spray the crackle with either a gloss or flat nitrocellulose lacquer, then leave it to dry for about 10 to 15 minutes.

Before and after crackle finish

This old shelf unit (above) has been sprayed with a crackle finish to give it more color and a feeling of age (left). This particular crackle effect was produced using a white background color oversprayed with blue crackle glaze and a matt cellulose coat.

PAINTING AND STENCILING

Painting and stenciling have been popular forms of furniture decoration for hundreds of years. Using simple repeat stencil patterns doesn't require any artistic skill and is an ideal way to transform an old or plain piece of furniture. If you want a more individual finish, try using the patterns given in this chapter to create your own design.

BELOW: Stenciling effects can be applied in a variety of ways: here, the natural wood grain shows through the bright patterning.

Tools and materials

The basic materials and equipment needed to complete the projects featured in this book are detailed below. All are readily available either from art materials suppliers or paint stores.

Paints

WATER-BASED PAINTS: For general-purpose decorating, water-based paints come in four basic finishes: flat (matt), satin, semi-gloss, and high gloss (enamel). The flat finish has a completely matt finish when dry and remains absorbent to further coats of paint; always use a flat finish for crackle glazing. The satin finish has a low sheen. It is not absorbent when dry and is therefore water-resistant and washable. Some manufacturers offer an eggshell finish, which looks flat head-on but when viewed at an angle, has a light sheen. Semi-gloss has a higher sheen than satin or eggshell and is somewhat more durable; it's ideal where frequent washing is required. High gloss or enamel is intended as an alternative to oil-based paint. It's designed for use in high-traffic areas that need frequent washing, or on items that will be subject to a lot of wear and tear.

ARTISTS' ACRYLICS: Artists' acrylics are available from art materials suppliers. They tend to be more expensive than the decorating water-based paints, but are worth using for motif and detail work and for certain strong, rich pigments.

Tints

ARTISTS' ACRYLICS: These can also be used as tints for mixing with varnishes and glazes. In addition, there are special acrylic tints designed for glaze work and wood graining.

UNIVERSAL TINTING COLOURS: These are available from some paint stores and hardware stores. Sold in tubes, these are inexpensive and can be mixed with both water- and oil-based products.

Solvents

MINERAL SPIRIT: This is the solvent for all oil-based products. Used to thin oil-based paints and varnishes and to clean any tools used.

DENATURED ALCOHOL: This is a solvent and thinner for French polish and pigments used for French polishing.

DISHWASHING LIQUID/DETERGENT:
Household detergent can be used with acrylic glazes the way mineral spirit is used with oil-based glazes. The detergent will get rid of drying glaze that has gone wrong and can be dropped onto a glaze to eat into it where desired.

Tapes

MASKING TAPE is the most commonly used tape to mask out areas when applying paint to other areas of your design. Always rub the edges well into the surface to avoid having the paint bleed in under the masked area, and paint away from the edge of the tape and not into it, to prevent any smudging or bleeding.
LOW-TACK TAPE is also available and is useful for complex designs which require a lot of quick masking and remasking.
LOW-TACK SPRAY is used in graphics projects. It is an excellent light spray

glue for fixing tracings and stencils in place while painting or drawing in your design.

Papers

TRACING PAPER is a transparent paper that allows the artist to see through to an underlying design. By drawing the design onto the tracing paper, the image can be reproduced and reversed if desired.
SANDPAPER: There are different grades of sandpaper, from very coarse, which is ideal for keying old, thick layers of paint or varnish, to very fine, suitable for finishing touches to subtle distressing.
STENCILING PAPER AND ACETATE PAPER:
Stenciling paper is a tough, water-resistant paper. It is easy to cut with a small, sharp blade or craft knife and stays firm after repeated use due to its waxy coating. Acetate paper is also used

for stenciling, but is transparent and therefore useful for lining up intricate repeat motifs.
CARBON PAPER: This can be used under tracing paper to give a carbon copy of the traced design.

1   Stenciling paper
2   Household detergent
3   Eraser
4   Artists' acrylics
5   Carbon paper
6   Low-tack spray
7   Low-tack tape
8   Sharp blade for stencil cutting
9   Tracing paper
10 Mineral spirit
11 Acetate paper
12 Measuring tape
13 Sandpaper
14 Masking tape
15 Compass for marking out designs

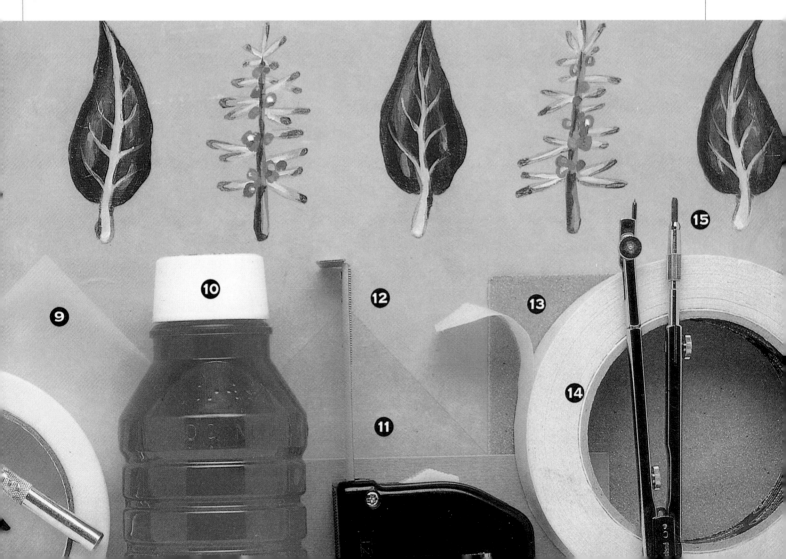

Technical tips

The projects in this book have, as far as possible, been executed using acrylic, water-based products because they dry faster and do not need environmentally unfriendly thinners and solvents.

What to do before you start your decorative work

Before starting any decorative work on a piece of furniture, some preparation will be necessary, whether the item has been worked on before or not.

Dealing with existing paint

If there is any paint on the piece, it will be important to determine what type of paint it is. If it is an oil-based paint and the new decoration is to be water-based acrylic, it will be very important to break up the hard, impermeable surface of the oil-based paints and to give the surface a key, that is, a surface that the acrylic paint can adhere to. Total stripping of the oil-based paint will not always be necessary, unless there are so many old layers of paint that the piece has lost some of its molding detail. In most cases, a light sanding will be enough. If the decorative work is to be achieved with more oil-based paints, then existing layers of oil- or water-based paints will not be a problem, neither will application of acrylics on existing acrylic surfaces. In other words, oil paint will adhere to oil- or water-based existing coats, but acrylic will only adhere to existing acrylic.

To determine which type of paint has been used on an old, secondhand piece, paint a small area with an acrylic paint and leave to dry. If, when dry, the acrylic paint is easy to scrape or peel off, then the existing paint is an oil-based finish. If, however, the acrylic paint adheres well and can only be removed by sanding, then the existing paint will most likely be a water-based paint.

Dealing with raw, untreated surfaces

Even if the chosen piece of furniture is unpainted, it is still important to ensure that the surface is clean and dust free and to smooth any rough edges with sandpaper. Furniture that is made from real wood, that is, not pressed wood (also called fiberboard or particleboard) or plywood, can be scrubbed with mineral spirit to open up the wood grain. To do this, pour some mineral spirit onto the raw wood and scrub in the direction of the grain with a wire brush. After this treatment, it will be important to clean off the mineral spirit with warm, soapy water if the decorative work is to be executed in acrylics. MDF is a perfect medium for painted furniture projects. The surface is smooth and only needs a primer coat to seal the surface before the paint finish is applied.

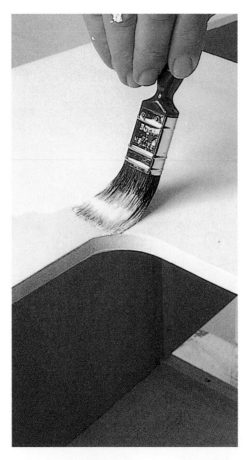

Determine whether an existing coat of paint is oil- or water-based before applying a fresh coat.

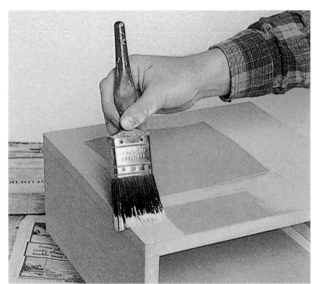

Apply a priming coat to seal the wood and to help obtain an even topcoat.

Creating a new look

All kinds of choices can be made for changing features on a piece of furniture, such as changing existing handles or adding moldings, and extra beading. These changes can make a modern flat-pack piece of furniture look much more like an older style of furniture. If you decide to alter these features, make sure the replacements are all in the same style – Victorian, Gustavian, etc. Texture and interest can also be added to the surface by using a chisel and nails to distress the piece to give an authentic weathered look. Make random scratches and dents in the surface of the project, focusing on areas of heavy wear such as around drawer handles and feet.

Priming and base coats

Oil-based paints have separate undercoat paints that are thinner than their oil-based topcoats and easier to apply. They not only seal the surface to prevent the topcoats from sinking into the wood and drying dull and patchy, but also help to obtain an even topcoat which should only require one application. Acrylic, water-based paints do not require a separate undercoat, watered down, they will act as their own undercoat and primer. This first coat will sink into the wood and seal the surface.

Once dry, this first coat can be followed by a coat of the same paint undiluted. If the furniture has a good, smooth, existing coat of paint, then again determine whether it is oil- or water-based. If it is water-based, then an immediate change of color can be made with an oil-based or water-based paint. If the existing coat is oil-based, then only a further coat of oil-based paint can be immediately applied without first keying the surface.

Another way of distressing is to wipe off streaks of paint before they are dry.

Methods for distressing paint

There are various ways of distressing, or achieving a distressed look, with paint, some of which are utilized on projects contained in this book.

SANDING: After priming with the undiluted acrylic paint and applying a solid base coat of the same color, add further coats of contrasting shades of acrylic paint and, when dry, sand areas and edges to give an excellent multi-tone distressed background to further motif work. Don't sand away too much of the finish to leave large bare patches – the effect should be quite subtle. Feather the sanded areas so the contrast between paint and raw wood is gradual.

WIPING: Apply primer coat and base coat in acrylic paint then, in a contrasting shade, apply another coat of acrylic paint in sections, brushing the paint on in the direction of the wood grain—across the top, down the sides. Before the paint is dry, wipe off streaks of paint to expose the underlying color. This effect gives a strong distressed, dragged look.

WATER ON OIL: This distressing technique breaks all the rules mentioned about not putting acrylic paint over oil. Apply an oil-based primer and a base coat of semi-gloss oil-based paint, allowing each to dry. Now apply a coat of acrylic paint. Be generous with the paint and work in the direction of the wood grain so that the paint dries in ridges of dragged paint. Allow to dry, and wipe away areas of the thinner acrylic paint with a cloth soaked in denatured alcohol. The denatured alcohol will only remove areas of acrylic paint, the oil-based base coat will remain intact. Because of the rule of not putting acrylic on top of an oil-based paint, this method will need protecting with a couple of coats of a good oil-based varnish.

STRIPPING: Existing old layers of paint can be stripped and sanded in desired areas for a genuine distressed look. Also experiment with blobs of beeswax in chosen areas on old layers of acrylic paint. Allow the beeswax to sit on the paint for at least ten minutes and then remove with a cloth. The beeswax will have eaten through the layers of paint.

After applying contrasting layers of paint, sand areas and edges for a distressed look.

LIMING: Liming wax is a white oil-based wax that is applied to wood with a good grain. Open up the wood grain with mineral spirit and a wire-brush. The liming wax can be applied to the raw, scrubbed wood or a coat of wood stain or acrylic paint can be applied as a base coat. Wood stains are available in oil-based or acrylic form. If an oil-based wood stain is used, then cleaning the wood with warm water and detergent will not be necessary, but if using water-based wood stain or paint, the mineral spirit will need to be cleaned off. Acrylic base colors which work very well under liming wax are terracotta, blue, green, and black. Once the base coat is dry, apply a layer of liming wax with a brush, work it well into the grain of the wood, wait about five minutes, and then remove any excess with a soft cloth. The result is a white grain to a wood or colored background.

DRY BRUSHING: This is an effective technique to use on furniture with carved detail or moldings. Once a base coat of acrylic paint has been applied and allowed to dry, a lighter tone or white acrylic paint thickened with whiting (a fine white chalk) is used to highlight the molding detail. Dry brushing is achieved by having very little paint on the brush, and using a small flat fitch catch the edges of any detail with the thick, dry, lighter shade.

Glazes and acrylic washes

GLAZES: Oil- and water-based glazes are available. The oil-based glaze has to be mixed with some oil-based undercoat paint to help the glaze set and to keep it from yellowing with age. It must also be diluted with mineral spirit to obtain easy and even application. Mix up the glaze as directed by the manufacturer. The glaze can be tinted by adding a little artists' oil color or universal tinting colors. Water-based glazes come ready mixed and are colored with artists' acrylic, acrylic tints, or universal tinting colors. Experiment with the amount of dilution necessary for the chosen effect by slowly adding water.

ACRYLIC WASHES are thin layers of acrylic paint that have been diluted. There is no set recipe to what degree washes should be diluted; simply experiment until you achieve the desired effect. Acrylic glaze can also be added to an acrylic wash to give the wash a glazelike transparency and extra drying time. When acrylic glaze is added to an acrylic paint, the paint becomes glazelike and can be softened with a softening brush.

Finishing touches

VARNISHING: Oil- and water-based varnishes are available in all the finishes – matt, semi-gloss, and gloss. Varnishes not only protect all the underlying artwork, but also even out the finish. The choice of finish, including whether or not to tint the varnish, is made after all the decorative work is completed. For example, the design may benefit from a yellow tint to add warmth and age. This can be achieved by adding some oil color to an oil-based varnish or a little acrylic to a water-based varnish. Varnishing will always protect your work and is highly recommended for items that will be in constant use and prone to wear and tear. Varnish will protect furniture from sunlight and fading, water marks, condensation, and peeling and chipping. Varnish any item in contact with kitchens, children, or pets, twice, for good measure. It is always a good idea to check the effect of a varnish on a test area first. Oil-based varnishes can have a yellow tint to them, so if no yellowing is desired (remember yellow varnish can make underlying blues look green), check that the varnish is clear or extra pale. Water-based varnishes have been known to dry misty or milky sometimes – this can be due to the climate – so varnish the piece in a well ventilated, dry room.

POLISHING: Another way of sealing and protecting your work is by using French enamel or shellac. Shellacs are available in various tones from blond shellac which is almost clear, to rich golden shellacs such as button polish which is used for French polishing. Shellac will give the piece a lacquered look and the darker, richer shellacs will add age and warmth. Many marbling artists use shellac to bring out the depth and colors in oil-based marbling. To obtain an even coating of shellac, pour the shellac onto the surface of the furniture where possible and spread with a soft brush.

An aged mottled polish can be achieved by splattering the shellac with a little denatured alcohol, which will eat into the shellac and create mottled rings.

WAXING: Waxing is also a way of protecting decorative work. A dark, warm wax for woods such as walnut can be diluted with a little mineral spirit and brushed into any wood grain, joins, chips, and crevices, and after five minutes, wiped with a soft cloth. This layer of wax will protect and again give the piece more age and character, and is particularly effective when worked into any molding or carved detail. Dark, rich brown shoe polish can also be used for the same result.

ANTIQUING: Antiquing fluids create the same umber film over decorative work and can be used instead of a wax, but will need a coat of varnish over the top afterward.

BLOOMING: A bloom describes a milky film over underlying work. A bloom can be applied over acrylic artwork by mixing a cream acrylic paint with some water to produce a wash. This is brushed over the entire piece and worked in with a soft cloth until all the brush marks have disappeared and a smooth film of cream is left. This bloom will soften the underlying artwork and give the piece a faded look.

Antiquing fluids add a mellow tone but do not protect, so brush on a coat of varnish afterward.

Squaring up and enlarging designs and motifs

Reference for designs and motifs can be taken from anywhere. Design and motif ideas are not usually the right size to trace and place immediately onto the piece of furniture, so some enlarging to the correct scale will often be necessary. One way is to make a color copy made of the design and enlarge it on a copying machine. Many copiers have a percentage enlargement button that allows you to make fairly precise sizings of an original plan. Sometimes the ratio is easier to work out by squaring up the reference. By squaring up the design, any size can be decided on.

LEFT: You can use a copy machine or squared paper to enlarge a design.

Measure the area intended for the painted design on the furniture and the area of the original. Divide the two areas into the same number of squares; it does not matter what size the squares are on each of the two areas as long as they both have the same number, across and down. Either pencil in the grid of squares over the original, or place a piece of tracing paper over the design and draw the grid onto this. Chalk can be used to draw the grid on the furniture. Number the squares from one to however many squares along the top and bottom and up the sides of the grid, making sure that both grids are numbered identically. The grid will give a reference for enlarging the same design by following square by square on the original onto the larger squares on the chosen area on the furniture. This is painstaking work but does give an accurate enlargement of a motif. With a little experience, you may be able to draw simpler motifs freehand and use your designs simply as a handy reference to check the proportions.

Advanced Techniques

Stenciling

The beauty of stenciling is that it allows anyone, from a complete novice to the most creative and experienced artist, to enhance the simplest of finishes with elaborate and attractive decoration.

American settlers decorated their homes with stenciling, and the effect became a measure of status. The patterns, which were usually done on a pale background, were taken from pictures or drawn and cut freehand. Today, patterns for stenciling can be bought ready-made from craft shops, and, if you do not wish to draw them yourself, you can use a photocopier to enlarge or reduce images for tracing.

Cutting a stencil

Almost any material can be used for the stencil, but clear acetate is best. It allows the paint or finish to be wiped off easily. Acetate can be difficult to cut, as it has a tendency to split, but, being clear, it can be used for direct tracing.

Make sure there is at least a 2in (50mm) border around the pattern, for support. Large motifs may need a wider border. Also, keep in mind that you may want to use the edges as a reference when you are applying the finish. Position the decoration in the center, and trim the edges later.

Use a razorsharp knife or craft knife for cutting the shapes. It is best to use a sheet of glass as a cutting board (pad the edges with masking tape) or special self-healing rubberized board. This prevents the board blade from being deflected by old cut marks, which can happen on cutting boards made from other materials. Only the point of the knife is used for cutting the stencil. It can be sharpened by grinding the back of the blade to create a new tip. Start with simple designs, without cutting out large areas of the stencil. If too much rigidity is lost, you will find it difficult to manage the stencil while applying the finish. As the patterns become more complex, bridges will be needed to keep the stencil stiff. Cut these bridges as thin as possible, because the unpainted areas will need to be touched up after stenciling.

Multi-colored patterns are produced by using a number of stencils. The important thing is to make sure all the stencils are compatible. You can do so by punching holes in the corners of each stencil, then line the holes up with marks on the original drawing or tracing. The holes can also be used as references when applying the finish.

ABOVE: These simple two-color patterns brighten up surfaces by following the line of the staircase and by picking out the drawer fronts on the chest.

Making a stencil

1 Draw out the motifs for the design on tracing paper, using a soft, dark pencil.

2 Transfer the motifs to acetate film and go over them to mark the outlines clearly.

3 With a fine, sharp craft knife, cut carefully around the outlines.

4 Place the stencil firmly on the surface and fill the shape with color using a stenciling brush.

Applying the finish

The groundwork for stenciling can be any color or material – but for walls a flat undercoat or eggshell is best, though latex paint works well. The advantage of water-based paints is that they dry fast: although that does not matter for the background, it is vital when coloring the stencil shapes. Stencils are generally applied on a light or pastel background, but there is no reason why the pattern should not be picked out in bright colors against a darker background. On wooden objects, seal the piece first with flat varnish (gloss has less key) or a sanding sealer.

The position of the pattern is important, so try it out first, marking off reference lines along the edges with chalk. This can easily be wiped off later – but you must remember to do so, as a coat of varnish would seal the lines in forever. Do not start applying the stencil before the background is completely dry; similarly, never add more stencil colors until the previous one is dry. The best way of applying the paint is with a special stenciling brush. These are not expensive and have short, stiff bristles shaped a bit like those of a shaving brush. Use the stenciling brush with a dabbing action, as if stippling. First, though, you need to attach the stencil to the workpiece, making sure that it fits as snugly against the surface as possible. Any gaps will allow the paint to creep, producing a poorly-defined and untidy finish. When applying the paint, have an instrument such as a paint scraper ready for pressing down the stencil in place with your spare hand.

Mix the color to suit, using artists' colors in an oil paint or glaze. Mix sufficient paint or glaze to complete the job, as it will be difficult to reproduce the exact color later. Do not make the paint too thin, or it will run. Decant a small quantity of the finish onto a palette of some sort (glass works well). This helps to keep the amount of paint on the brush to a minimum, and also reduces the chance of paint creep.

After painting the pattern, leave the stencil in place for at least 30 seconds and then remove vertically in one action. This may need some practice. Wipe off any excess from the stencil, using mineral spirit, before applying more paint. This is why acetate is so good. When creating a repetitive pattern, make sure that the stencil does not disturb the previous motif as you move on. Sometimes the stencil will have to overlap, in which case wait until the paint is dry, and in the meantime work on another area. It is important to have marked out the position of each pattern with chalk before starting. Try to keep the spacings and borders regular.

Wait until the pattern is dry before applying another layer or a protective coat of gloss or flat varnish. One effect worth trying is to apply a single coat of flat varnish over two coats of gloss. This softens the glossiness a little. Use polyurethane for a tough coating for floors, but make sure before application that it doesn't react with the colors.

Advanced Techniques

Stenciling a chest of drawers using a ready-cut stencil

1 Painted furniture is a common recipient for stenciling, though natural wood can also provide an excellent background for subtle patterns and colors. Make sure the painted piece is thoroughly prepared before application, using an undercoat as a base. The undercoat does not have to be white – pastel colors are the best alternative.

LEFT: Craft shops sell a large range of designs to suit any room in the home.

2 For these small patterns on a painted surface, use artists' colors mixed in shallow dishes. Test the color on white paper. Position the stencil and tape it down firmly. Apply the color by dabbing with a stencil brush. Press down hard on the stencil, and do not use too much paint, to ensure that none of the material creeps under the stencil. Sharp lines are essential.

3 Once the first color has started to dry, remove the stencil. Try to avoid dragging the color—it will be difficult to touch up. Leave the motif to dry.

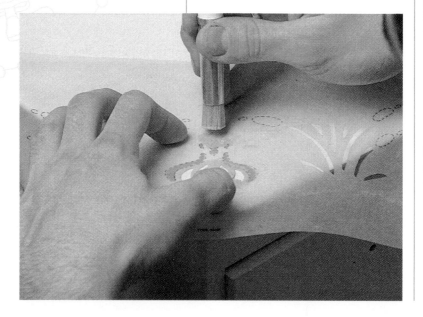

4 Apply a second color by dabbing with the stencil brush.

5 Select the next motif to be applied, and mix up a suitable color. Make sure that the colors match, and that enough is mixed to complete the stenciling – mixed colors are difficult to repeat.

7 Use a simple, repetitive pattern to join up the more detailed shapes. This livens up the piece without making it too fussy. Try to follow the shape of the piece being stenciled; highlight edges, corners, door panels, and drawers.

8 Stenciling is particularly effective for brightening up a nursery, bathroom, or kitchen. Any combination of colors can be used, but always make sure each application is dry before attempting the next, and keep the stencil clean at all times.

6 Three colors have now been applied, and the pattern is taking shape. Notice how the stalks of the flowers are a dark color, and the emphasis is given to the flowers or seed pods, which are brighter.

Motif library

The motif outlines shown here provide an easy way of reproducing some of the more detailed designs in this book. You can either simply trace around them, or copy them in any size you require.

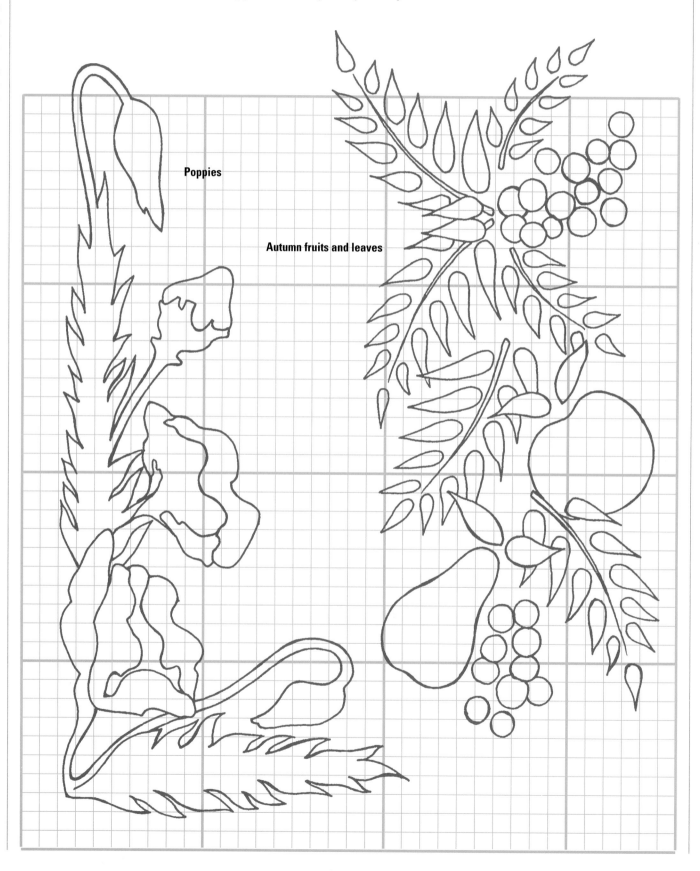

Poppies

Autumn fruits and leaves

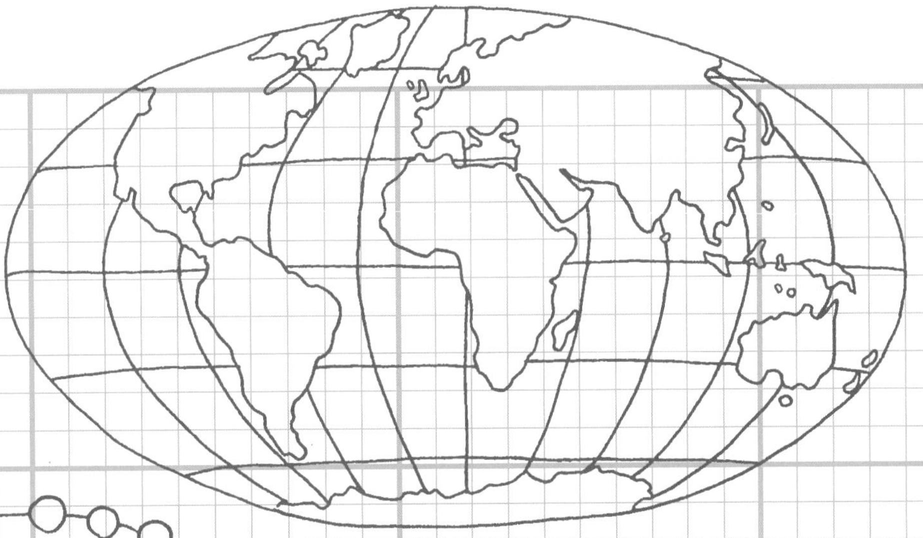

Map of the world

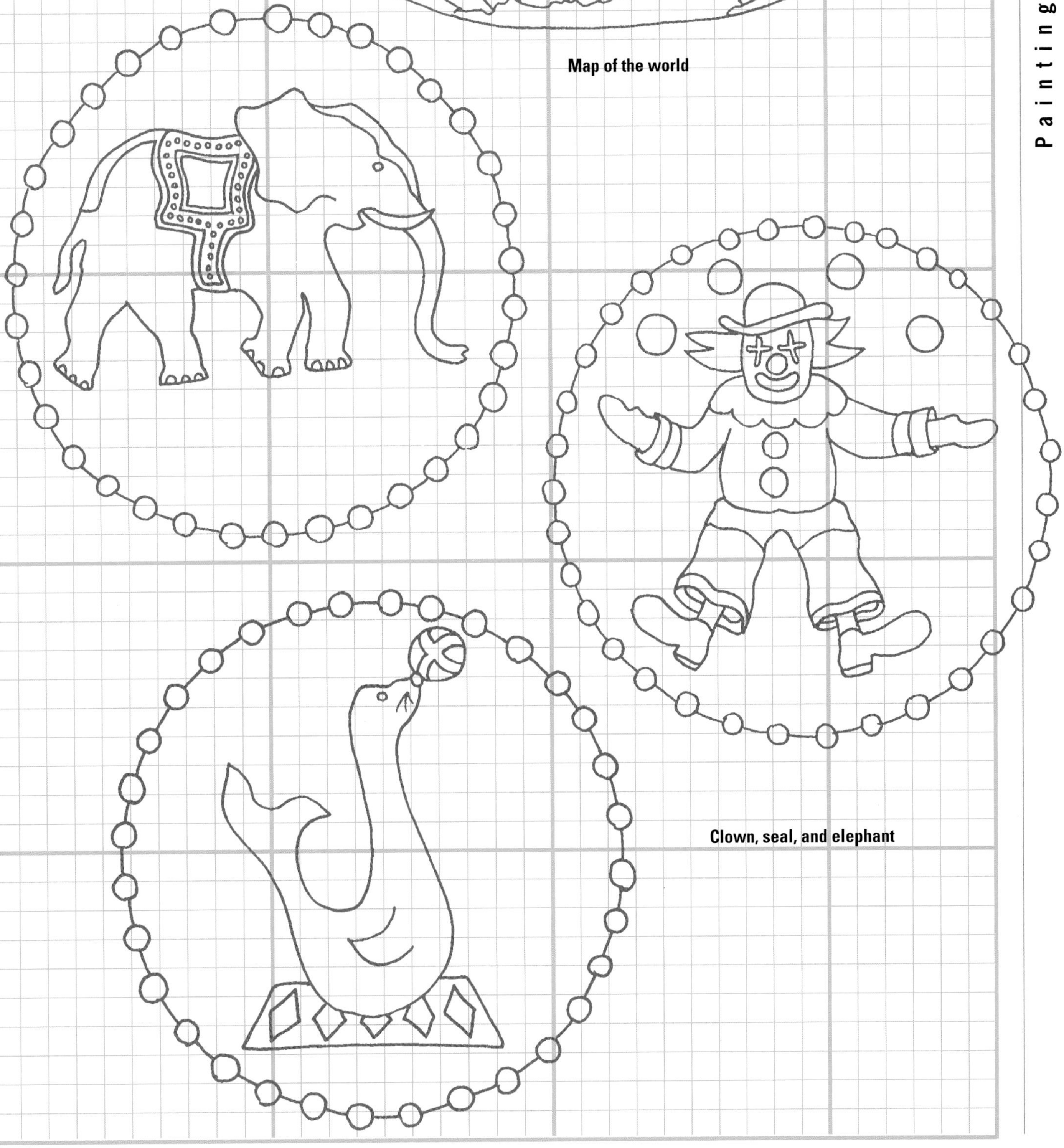

Clown, seal, and elephant

Roses and rose leaves

Ivy leaves

Bunch of grapes

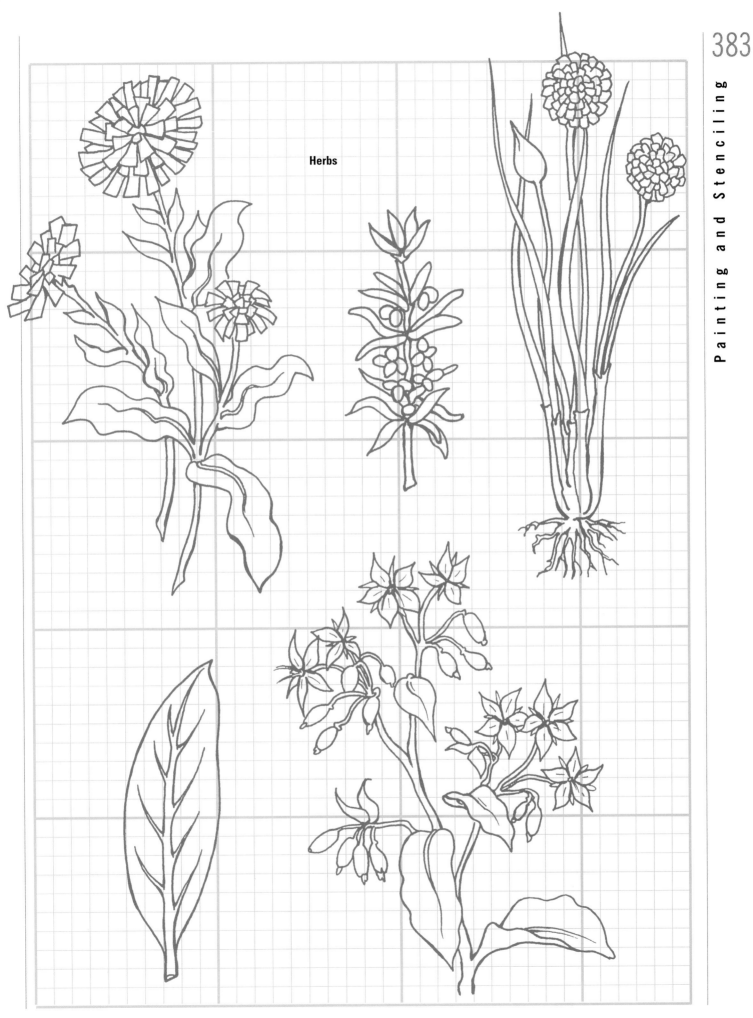

Herbs

Design gallery

LEFT: This is a fine example of repetitive stenciling. The floorboards have been given a thin wash. The larger pattern has been stenciled in a darker shade and the smaller stencil is picked out in a more contrasting white. Notice how the faults and holes in the floorboards complement the repetition of the stencil, softening its effect.

ABOVE: Before stenciling, this shelf unit was rag-rolled to give the background a rustic feel. The eye is drawn toward the two painted plant pots, but notice how the repetitive patterns above the shelves and along the leading edges balance the design.

LEFT: This Art and Crafts style motif was copied from an original design by Charles F. Annesley Voysey (1857-1905). The rubbed-back two-color paint finish and the blistered paint technique on the panels give the piece an aged look.

ABOVE: This sideboard has been painted, though some of the wood's grain has been allowed to show through. The effect is enhanced by the light patterns on the rails and end panel.

STAINS PALETTE

Applying a finish to wood both changes its color and protects the surface from dirt, heat and spilled liquids. Here we look at eight different woods and show the effects of different manufactured stains; the same eight woods are treated to further treatments based on colored dyes and erosion techniques; showing how the woods react to treatments especially tailored for each of them—these special treatments are more complex and should be attempted only when a good degree of confidence has been achieved.

NOTE: Get fit before you begin: fast repeat arm and hand exercises are essential.

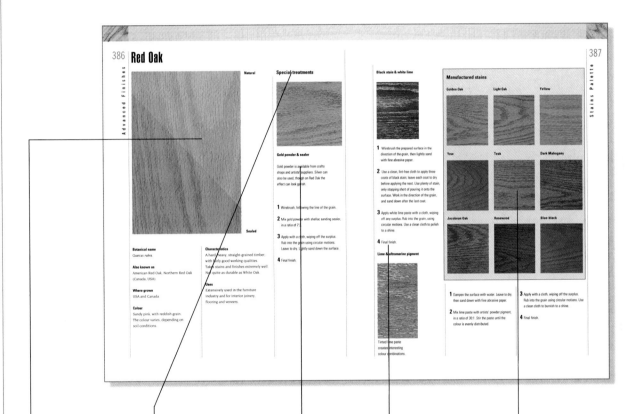

Planed lumber in its untreated state and (right) the same sample after sealing and waxing.

Special treatments
Finishing treatments, tailored to each of the nine woods.

Recipes
Step-by-step recipes for you to follow to create the different effects.

Final finish
Each of the samples has been given the same final finish; two coats of white French polish, sanded between coats and buffed with a clear polish.

Manufactured stains
These are commercial stains, ranging from the lightest to the darkest to give you a feel for the possibilities. Generic names, not trade names, have been used to describe the colors they represent.

Always apply a thinned coat of stain first; you can always increase the density, but never reduce it without removing the surface of the wood.

Red Oak

Natural

Sealed

Special treatments

Gold powder & sealer

Gold powder is available from crafts shops and artists' suppliers. Silver can also be used, though on Red Oak the effect can look garish.

1 Wirebrush, following the line of the grain.

2 Mix gold powder with shellac sanding sealer, in a ratio of 7:3.

3 Apply with a cloth, wiping off the surplus. Rub into the grain using circular motions. Leave to dry. Lightly sand down the surface.

4 Final finish.

Botanical name
Quercus rubra.

Also known as
American Red Oak, Northern Red Oak (Canada, US).

Where grown
US and Canada.

Color
Sandy pink, with reddish grain. The color varies, depending on soil conditions.

Characteristics
A hard, heavy, straight-grained lumber, with fairly good working qualities. Takes stains and finishes extremely well. Not quite as durable as White Oak.

Uses
Extensively used in the furniture industry and for interior joinery, flooring, and veneers.

Black stain & white lime

1 Wirebrush the prepared surface in the direction of the grain, then lightly sand with fine, abrasive paper.

2 Use a clean, lint-free cloth to apply three coats of black stain; leave each coat to dry before applying the next. Use plenty of stain, only stopping short of pouring it onto the surface. Work in the direction of the grain, and sand down after the last coat.

3 Apply white lime paste with a cloth, wiping off any surplus. Rub into the grain, using circular motions. Use a clean cloth to polish to a shine.

4 Final finish.

Lime & ultramarine pigment

Tinted lime paste creates interesting color combinations.

Manufactured stains

Golden Oak

Light Oak

Yellow

Yew

Teak

Dark Mahogany

Jacobean Oak

Rosewood

Blue-black

1 Dampen the surface with water. Leave to dry, then sand down with fine, abrasive paper.

2 Mix lime paste with artists' powder pigment, in a ratio of 30:1. Stir the paste until the color is evenly distributed.

3 Apply with a cloth, wiping off the surplus. Rub into the grain using circular motions. Use a clean cloth to burnish to a shine.

4 Final finish.

English Oak

Natural

Sealed

Special treatments

Wire brushing & thinned latex

The latex is thinned to lighten the color, give better penetration and allow you to more easily wipe off any surplus paint. Any color latex can be used to suit the job.

1 Wirebrush in the direction of the grain, then sand lightly.

2 Thin latex paint with water, in a ratio of 50:50.

3 Use a clean, lint-free cloth to apply the paint, then wipe off any surplus.

4 Rub the paint into the grain, using circular motions. Leave to dry, then sand.

5 Final finish.

Botanical name

Quercus robur.

Also known as

Pedunculate Oak; French, Polish Oak, etc., according to country of origin.

Where grown

Europe (including UK), the Middle East, and North Africa.

Color

Generally a pale, sandy brown with mid-brown grain fleck, similar to White Oak. Heartwood is darker than sapwood.

Characteristics

An extremely hard, strong, durable wood (the hardness increases with age). The grain is generally straight, but can be quirky. When quarter-sawed, English Oak has a spectacular silver grain. Stains and clear finishes give excellent results. The burr (burl) wood, produced by abnormal growths, is particularly decorative. Acids present in oak corrode ferrous-metal fittings.

Uses

Cabinetwork, furniture, paneling, boat building, church fittings and coffins. Whisky casks are often made from oak, because of the tannic acid in the wood.

Gold powder & sealer

The fairly tight grain in this example resulted in less gold powder being taken up. The result is less dramatic than other, more open-grained examples.

1 Wirebrush following the line of the grain.

2 Mix gold powder with shellac sanding sealer, in a ratio of 7:3. Stir in the gold powder until it is evenly distributed throughout the sealer.

3 Apply with a cloth, wiping off the surplus. Rub into the grain using circular motions. Use a clean cloth to burnish to a shine.

4 Final finish.

Stain & tinted lime paste

Manufactured stains

Golden Oak

Light Oak

Yellow

Yew

Teak

Dark Mahogany

Jacobean Oak

Rosewood

Blue-black

1 Dampen the surface with water. Leave to dry, then sand down with fine, abrasive paper.

2 Use a clean, lint-free cloth to apply green stain. Use plenty of stain, only stopping short of pouring it onto the surface. Work in the direction of the grain. Lightly sand down.

3 Mix lime paste with artists' powder pigment, in a ratio of 30:1.

4 Apply the paste with a cloth, wiping off the surplus. Rub into the grain, using circular motions. Use a clean cloth to burnish to a shine.

5 Final finish.

Rock Maple

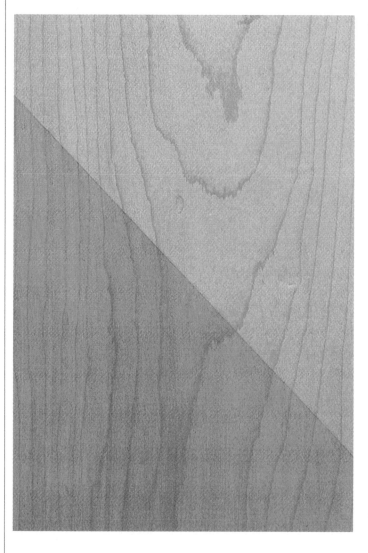

Natural

Sealed

Botanical name

Acer saccharum.

Also known as

Hard Maple, Sugar Maple; White Maple (US).

Where grown

Canada and US.

Color

Very pale, with a pinkish tinge and pinky gray grain. The heartwood is purple brown (similar to walnut).

Characteristics

A very hard, strong, even-textured wood, with good bending properties. The attractive grain sometimes has a curving or wavy pattern. Since it is difficult to work, a reduced cutting angle is often necessary, especially on curvy or wavy grain. To avoid uneven staining, you may need to pre-seal the surface with French polish, then layer the stain between coats.

Uses

Because it is smooth and hard-wearing, Rock Maple is used for flooring and butcher's blocks. It is also an excellent wood for furniture and turning. Maple veneers with a distinctive bird's-eye pattern are highly prized.

Special treatments

Red fabric dye

Rock Maple is a tricky wood to stain without the result looking patchy. Because of its variable absorbency, be very careful to sand down thoroughly before applying the dye.

1 Apply undiluted liquid fabric dye, using a clean, lint-free cloth. Stain the piece thoroughly, then wipe off any surplus dye.

2 Rub into the grain, using circular motions. Leave to dry.

3 Apply more coats, depending on the depth of color you want to achieve. Sand down after applying the last coat.

4 Final finish.

Green fabric dye

Bright colors can look very effective on this pale wood. Three coats of fabric dye were used on this sample.

1 Apply undiluted liquid fabric dye, using a clean, lint-free cloth. Stain the piece thoroughly, then wipe off any surplus.

2 Rub into the grain, using circular motions. Leave to dry, then sand down. Apply more coats, depending on the depth of color required.

3 Final finish.

Rhubarb leaves

Manufactured stains

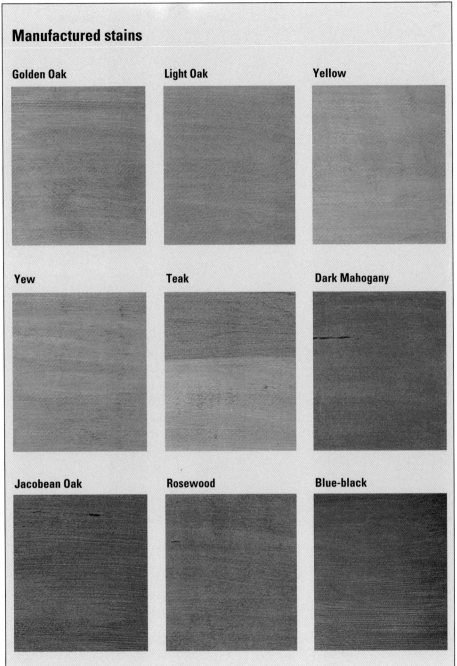

Golden Oak

Light Oak

Yellow

Yew

Teak

Dark Mahogany

Jacobean Oak

Rosewood

Blue-black

The rhubarb imparts a very pale color change. Rhubarb leaves are toxic when eaten; don't store the mulch in food containers, and always throw away the pulp after use.

1 Process rhubarb leaves in a food processor, reducing them to a pulp. Wash and dry the processor thoroughly after use.

2 Lay the pulp thickly on the surface of the wood and leave for 24 hours.

3 Wash off with lots of water. Leave to dry, then sand down.

4 Final finish.

American Walnut

Natural

Sealed

Special treatments

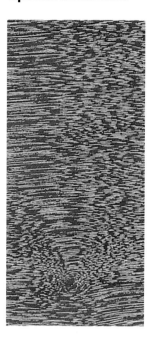

Wire brushing & white lime

Compare the sample above with the one on the left. The wire brush has opened the grain, resulting in more lime penetrating the surface.

1 Wirebrush following the direction of the grain.

2 Use a clean, lint-free cloth to apply lime paste, being careful to cover the surface. Wipe off any surplus.

3 Rub into the grain, using circular motions. Try to keep the pressure even. Use a clean cloth to burnish to a shine.

4 Final finish.

Botanical name

Juglans nigra.

Also known as

Black Walnut (UK, US), Canaletto, Black Hickory Nut, Canadian Walnut, Walnut Tree, Black American Walnut, Virginia Walnut (UK).

Where grown

US and Canada.

Color

An unusual purplish gray and mid-brown, with evenly-flecked grain.

Characteristics

American Walnut is mostly straight-grained, with occasional wavy figuring. A very hard and durable wood, it works cleanly and has exceptionally good bending qualities. The wood shrinks very little in use. Burr (burl), butt and curl walnut veneers are particularly attractive; butt veneers are cut from the stump of the tree, curl veneers from the fork of the trunk.

Uses

High-quality cabinetwork and furniture, turning and carving, gun stocks, clock cases, and musical instruments.

White lime

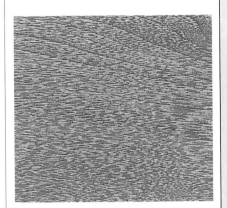

1 Damp the surface with water. Leave the wood to dry, then sand down lightly, using fine, abrasive paper.

2 Use a clean, lint-free cloth to apply the lime paste, being careful to cover the surface. Wipe off any surplus.

3 Rub into the grain, using circular motions. Use a clean cloth to burnish to a shine.

4 Final finish.

Iron filings & zinc chloride

This naturally dark wood can be darkened even more by the application of iron filings and zinc chloride. The result is a rich, dense effect.

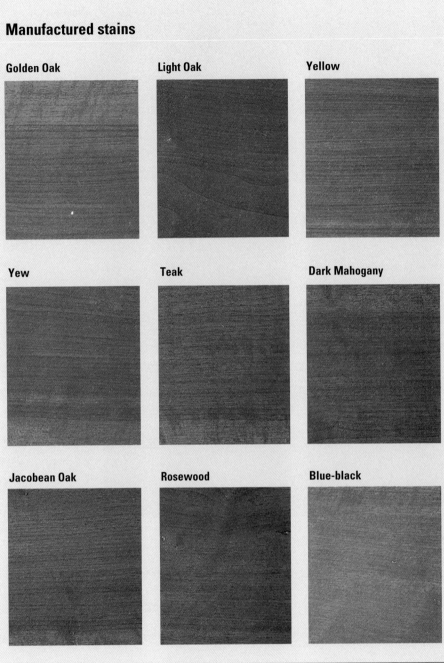

Manufactured stains

Golden Oak

Light Oak

Yellow

Yew

Teak

Dark Mahogany

Jacobean Oak

Rosewood

Blue-black

1 Pour on enough zinc chloride to cover the surface, and dab it around with a clean, lint-free cloth.

2 Randomly scatter iron filings onto the surface. Leave for 24 hours.

3 Wash off with lots water. Leave to dry, then sand down.

4 Final finish.

American Cherry

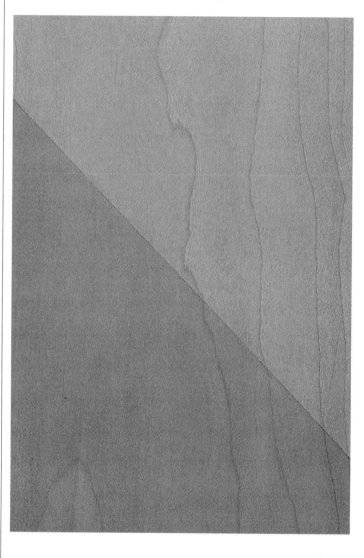

Natural

Sealed

Special treatments

Ink

When dry, writing ink leaves a beautiful metallic sheen on the wood's surface. The blue color left by ink is rich and dense.

1 Apply undiluted ink, using a clean, lint-free cloth. Stain the piece thoroughly, then wipe off any surplus.

2 Rub into the grain using circular motions. Leave to dry then sand down. Apply more coats, depending on the depth of the color required.

3 Final finish.

Botanical name
Prunus serotina.

Also known as
Wild Cherry, Whisky Cherry, Black Cherry (Canada, US), Cabinet Cherry (US).

Where grown
Amongst deciduous forests in Canada and the US.

Color
Has an attractive pinkish tinge with darker grain. The heartwood is a deeper red or reddish brown. Gum pockets are dark brown.

Characteristics
A fine, smooth-grained wood of medium strength. The grain is straight, with occasional attractive figuring and small gum pockets. Cherry is easy to work, bends well, and is an excellent wood for turning. It stains and polishes well.

Uses
High-class joinery and interior fittings, furniture, patternmaking, turning, and musical instruments.

Fabric dye

Bright colors can look very effective on this pale wood. Three coats of fabric dye were used on this sample.

1 Apply undiluted liquid fabric dye, using a clean, lint-free cloth. Stain the piece thoroughly, then wipe off any surplus.

2 Rub into the grain, using circular motions. Leave to dry, then sand down. Apply more coats, depending on the depth of color required.

3 Final finish.

Zinc chloride

American Cherry can be made to resemble walnut by applying zinc chloride. The longer you leave the zinc chloride, the more definite the blackish-brown color will be.

Manufactured stains

Golden Oak

Light Oak

Yellow

Yew

Teak

Dark Mahogany

Jacobean Oak

Rosewood

Blue-black

1 Damp the surface with water. Leave to dry, then sand down with fine, abrasive paper.

2 Pour on enough zinc chloride to cover the surface. Using a dabbing action, move the zinc chloride around with a clean, lint-free cloth.

3 Wash off with lots water. Leave to dry, then sand down.

4 Final finish.

White Ash

Natural

Sealed

Special treatments

Wire brushing & white lime

Liming can be used on any raised-grained wood.

1 Wirebrush with the grain, then sand lightly.

2 Use a clean, lint-free cloth to apply lime paste being careful to cover the surface. Wipe off any surplus.

3 Rub into the grain using circular motions. Use a clean cloth to polish to a shine.

4 Final finish.

Botanical name
Fraxinus americana.

Also known as
American Ash, American White Ash, Canadian Ash (UK).

Where grown
US and Canada.

Color
Fairly yellow, with a pronounced darker grain that is sometimes grayish or slightly pinky red.

Characteristics
Although of medium weight, ash is a surprisingly strong, tough, elastic wood, with excellent shock-resistance. The grain pattern is similar to oak, but without oak's silver grain. Ash stains and polishes to a handsome finish. It has excellent bending qualities, providing that the wood is knot-free.

Uses
Tool handles, sports equipment (including billiard cues), and agricultural implements. Historically, used for making carts, shafts, and wheels.

Rhubarb leaves

Rhubarb leaves are toxic, so wash and dry the food processor thoroughly after use.

1 Process rhubarb leaves in a food processor, reducing them to a pulp.

2 Lay the pulp thickly on the surface and leave for 24 hours.

3 Wash off with lots water. Leave the piece to dry then sand down.

4 Final finish.

Burning, wire brushing & lime

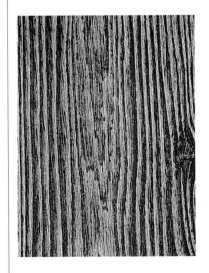

Take the recommended safety precautions when using a blowtorch.

Manufactured stains

Golden Oak

Light Oak

Yellow

Yew

Teak

Dark Mahogany

Jacobean Oak

Rosewood

Blue-black

1 Burn the surface with a blowtorch until the wood blackens. Leave to cool.

2 Wirebrush following the line of the grain, then wipe down with a damp cloth to remove char dust.

3 Apply one coat of seal, then sand down.

4 Use a clean cloth to apply lime paste, being careful to cover the surface. Wipe off any surplus.

5 Rub into the grain using circular motions, then polish to a shine.

6 Final finish.

White Pine

Natural

Sealed

Special treatments

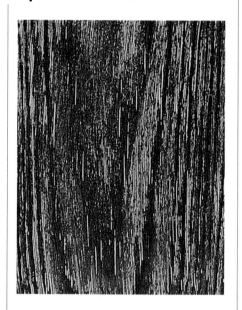

Burning & liming

1 Use a blowtorch to blacken the surface. Leave until the wood has cooled.

2 Wirebrush, following the grain, to remove charred wood, then wipe down with a damp cloth.

3 Seal with shellac sanding sealer, then sand lightly.

4 Use a clean, lint-free cloth to apply lime paste, being careful to cover the surface. Wipe off any surplus.

5 Rub into the grain, using circular motions. Use a clean cloth to burnish to a shine.

6 Final finish.

Botanical name
Pinus strobus.

Also known as
Yellow Pine (Canada, US), Eastern White Pine, Northern White Pine, Northern Pine (US), Quebec Pine, Soft Pine, Weymouth Pine (UK).

Where grown
Canada and US.

Color
Pale yellow, with yellow to brown grain.

Characteristics
The heartwood is soft but has an even texture and a very straight grain. White Pine is exceptionally easy to work and takes finishes extremely well, but is not a good wood for steam bending. It is subject to very little movement in use.

Uses
Guitars and organ pipes (because of its resonance), furniture, joinery, and construction work. It is an excellent wood for patternmaking, carving and turning.

Fabric dye

1 Apply undiluted liquid fabric dye, using a clean, lint-free cloth. Stain the piece thoroughly, then wipe off any surplus.

2 Rub into the grain, using circular motions. Leave to dry, then sand down. Apply more coats, depending on the depth of the color required.

4 Final finish.

Wire brushing, lime & ultramarine pigment

Heavy wire brushing gives a characteristic aged finish to softwoods.

Manufactured stains

Golden Oak

Light Oak

Yellow

Yew

Teak

Dark Mahogany

Jacobean Oak

Rosewood

Blue-black

1 Wirebrush the prepared surface in the direction of the grain, then lightly sand down the surface with fine, abrasive paper.

2 Mix lime paste with artists' powder pigment, in a ratio of 30:1. Stir the paste until the color is evenly distributed.

3 Apply with a cloth, wiping off the surplus. Rub into the grain using circular motions. Use a clean cloth to burnish to a shine.

4 Final finish.

Inlaid stained veneers

LEFT: Although the construction of this box is complex, the clever use of small areas of inlaid color is a strong factor in the design, as are the black edge bandings that emphasize the geometric design.

ABOVE: A detail of the pyramid box (shown left), showing the darker-colored drawer pulls.

Inlaying dyed veneers gives a bold architectural feeling to these pieces by Nicholas Pryke. Pure silver inlay has then been added to this intricate pattern. The designer has used commercially-produced veneers, which are available with colored or natural finishes. All Pryke's pieces are meticulously constructed and extremely detailed in their graphic imagery.

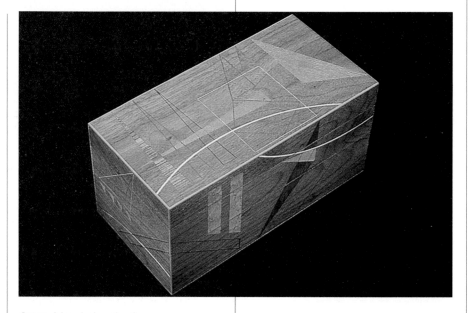

ABOVE: A jewelry box showing a very fine use of English walnut with natural inlaid wood and dyed veneers. The pure silver inlay gives a rich quality to the work.

ADVANCED PROJECTS

| # Desk

ABOVE: Advanced furniture construction can actually be broken down into a series of simpler stages that are then put together to create the finished, complex article.

This desk brings together a number of the techniques you have learned and practiced in earlier projects.

Making this project demonstrates how a complicated furniture construction is broken down into a series of simpler components—frames, carcases, drawers, and framed panels. Each component is made separately, then combined in stages into the completed desk.

Choosing wood

With the experience gained on earlier projects, you should be able to choose any quality hardwood that is available and that fits in with your decor.

Cutting list

No.		Sawed	
1		TOP	
2 long	rails	3ft 2in x 2¼in x 1¼in	(939mm x 56mm x 31mm)
2 short	rails	1ft 10in x 2¼in x 1¼in	(555mm x 56mm x 31mm)
1 sheet		3ft x 1ft 8in x ½in	(914mm x 505mm x 12mm)
plywood or MDF			
2		SIDE FRAMES	
4 legs		2ft 6in x 1¾in x 1¼in	(455mm x 45mm x 31mm)
4 legs		1ft 9in x 2½in x 1¼in	(530mm x 62mm x 31mm)
1		REAR FRAME	
2 long	rails	3ft x 2¼in x 1¼in	(914mm x 56mm x 31mm)
2 short	rails	1ft 8in x 1¾in x 1¼in	(505mm x 45mm x 31mm)
1 sheet		2ft 9in x 1ft 4in x ⅜in	(835mm x 405mm x 9mm)
plywood or MDF			
1		DRAWER FRAME	
4 cross	rails	3ft x 3 at 2¼in	(914mm x 3 at 56mm)
		1 at 3¼in x 1in	(1 at 81mm x 25mm)
3 side	rails	1ft 8in x 5½in x 1in	(405mm x 137mm x 25mm)
8 drawer	runners	1ft 8in x 1½in x 1in	(505mm x 37mm x 25mm)
2		DRAWERS	
2 drawer	fronts	1ft 5in x 5½in x 1¼in	(430mm x 137mm x 31mm)
4 drawer	sides	1ft 7in x 4in x ¾in	(480mm x 100mm x 20mm)
2 drawer	backs	1ft 5in x 3in x ⅝in	(430mm x 75mm x 16mm)
2 drawer	bottoms	1ft 5in x 12in x ¼in	(430mm x 305mm x 6mm)
plywood or MDF			

Plans

These drawings show the elevations and sections, with an exploded perspective view of the finished piece.

Scale 1:10

Vertical facing

Exploded diagram

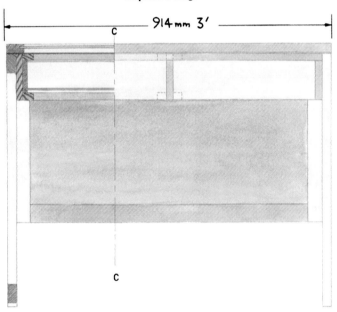

914mm 3'

C

C

Front elevation with part section on C-C

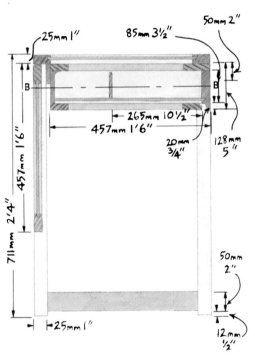

25mm 1"   85mm 3½"   50mm 2"

B   B

265mm 10½"

457mm 1'6"

20mm 3/4"

128mm 5"

711mm 2'4"   457mm 1'6"

50mm 2"

25mm 1"   12mm ½"

Sectional end elevation through A-A

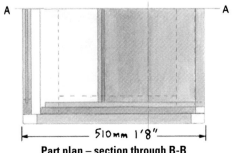

A   A

510mm 1'8"

Part plan – section through B-B

Buying wood

1 Most of the solid wood is bought sawed at 1¼in (30mm) to finish at 1in (25mm). The drawer unit and drawers use 1in (25mm) or ¾in (20mm) to finish at ¾in (20mm) and ⅝in (16mm). You also need three pieces of plywood or MDF.

2 Mark and saw out all components. Then plane them and leave slightly over length.

3 The project is designed in the form of a set of components, so the process for each one is described in order.

Side frames—make two

4 Mark mortise and tenon joints on the four legs and four rails. The rails should have shoulders all around and the top rails a haunch.

Tips box

• It is often worth fitting a sheet of thin plywood over the top of a hardwood workbench to protect the surface from glue and stains at the assembly stage of a project.

• Lightly sand the bench top before starting a new project—it reduces the chances of a stray piece of debris bruising the new lumber.

• You may be able to use up a lot of thin off-cuts from previous projects in this type of carcase construction. Just make sure the visible areas are all matched in colour and grain.

5 Cut and fit the joints. Assemble the frames dry, check that they are both the same size and that they are square and flat. Disassemble and sand all the components (above).

6 Reassemble, glue, and clamp. Afterward, give a sanding and a coat of finish.

Surface finish—top and rear frame

7 These finishes should be considered before you make up the panels, and at the same time since they will be seen together.

Linoleum was used for the prototype, since it gives a pleasant writing surface. If you wish to save time, you can buy plywood or MDF that is pre-veneered. You could also apply your own veneer, using plastic laminate, or paint the surface. Whichever you choose, the finish should be applied before either panel is inserted into the frame.

Rear frame—make one

8 This is a frame and panel construction and is fitted to the front of the desk between the legs to form a closed front to the desk. The board is covered in the same material as the top. The board will be screwed into the legs at the final assembly stage, so there are external joints to make—just the meeting corner joints. Mark the vertical stiles and the horizontal rails for the frame and cut the groove on the inside faces that will take the panel. Use a router with a straight cutter to make the groove. With such narrow strips, the easiest way is to mount your router in a router table and pass the workpieces over the cutter to form the recess.

9 Mark and cut all mortise and tenon joints. Remember that the haunches will fill the groove.

10 Assemble the frame dry and mark the plywood panel to be a snug fit in the frame. Cut and fit the panel.

14 Begin to apply the four frame pieces to the panel. Care is needed, since the frame corners will be mitered and you are building this frame around the panel. Cut the miter on the long sides and dry clamp them to the board. Then fit the short ends so that the frame is tight around the panel and the four miters are a good fit.

11 Disassemble the dry frame, check that the panel fits and everything is square and flat. Glue and clamp it together. When the glue has cured, sand and apply final finish.

15 Glue and clamp the frame to the panel. After the glue has cured, sand and finish the frame. Set the top aside with the side frames and the rear frame.

13 Mark the four pieces for the frame edging, and cut the grooves around the inside edges. Mark the panel precisely to its final size, and cut the rebate around all four edges.

Drawer frame—make one

16 Mark all components. The two side pieces have the cross rails attached to them. The upper front cross rail is wider than the other three since the drawer front sits underneath flush with its edge. Use up your off-cut hardwood strips in the back of the carcase and in the central partition between the drawers. This area will not be seen from either side of the desk.

Top—make one

12 Cut the frame material to slightly over the finished size. The panel has a rebate cut around the edges to fit into grooves in the frame. The frame is only 1⅛in (30mm) thick for this project, so make sure the router is set up accurately and machine the groove in one operation so all the parts match up exactly. You can use MDF or plywood for the top—MDF tends to be more stable.

19 Instead of seeing end grain on the front of the side rails, add a small edge banding at the front (above).

17 Due to the grain direction on the sides, it is not a good practise to dovetail these four rails, so the four corners are notched (above).

20 In the center of the desk frame, a small vertical partition runs from front to back, to separate the two drawers. The drawer runners are fixed to this partition, so it is essential to position it exactly between the two drawer positions. It is notched to the front and back rails, and screwed in place like the ends. This frame is not difficult to make, but it is essential to lay it out very precisely so that the places where the drawers will run are square and parallel. Double check all your measurements before fixing.

Tips box

- Lightly sand the bench top before starting a new project—it reduces the chances of a stray piece of debris bruising the new wood.
- Take care clamping up the frame pieces to the top as the miters can easily slip out of position. You could use a fabric band clamp to tighten all the corners at the same time.
- Wipe any excess glue as soon as it seeps out of the joints to reduce the possibility of staining.

18 The cross rails are screwed and glued in place. Countersink the screw holes so the screws are buried just below the surface of the wood. Always make a clearance hole so that the screws do not split the thin wood frame as you assemble the joint.

21 Add the drawer runners, eight in all. These are attached by screws in between the four long cross rails and provide a surface on which the drawers slide and run. This component can now be sanded and finished.

Drawers—make two

22 These are made in a similar way to previous drawers. Notice that the drawer sides are the complete depth of the drawer frame, but the back is located in one-third from the back edge. Drawers should only be pulled out two-thirds of their possible length; if you pull them right out, they and their contents can end up on the floor.

Tips box

- If you don't want to use a recess for the handle, use a conventional metal fixing in the center of each drawer. Remember that this should not protrude too far or it may be awkward to sit at the desk comfortably. Simple rounded or square steel drawer pulls would work well.

- Whatever finishing material you choose for the top, make sure it is properly sealed against ink, stains, and general wear and tear.

23 Plane the drawer sides to be a smooth-running fit. Make sure that the back fits the opening precisely. Fit the front. Make grooves in the sides and the front to take the plywood bottom. Gauge the thickness of the side on the ends of the back and front. Make twin through tenons between the back and sides and half-blind dovetails between the front and the sides.

24 Assemble the drawers and fit them in the frame. They should now run smoothly in the drawer frame.

25 Form the drawer handles from routed grooves underneath the drawer fronts, or by cutting spaces in the lower front rail.

Overall assembly

26 Attach the side frames to the end of the drawer frame and the end of the rear frame. The desk can be assembled permanently using dowels, biscuits, or tongues, or by screwing the side frames to the desk frame and rear frame. The prototype was screwed. The advantage of using screws is that if you customize the desk to make it larger, it is much easier to transport the components and assemble them in the room.

27 Screw the side frames at the top from the inside of the drawer frame.

28 The easiest way to screw the rear frame in position is from the outside of the side frames into the end of the drawer frame and the end of the rear frame. The screw heads are then visible in the side frames. Recess the screw heads into a hole and plug that hole if you wish to hide the screws. However, many woodworkers find Posidrive or Allen-head screws are visually quite acceptable.

30 The finished desk brings together earlier wood-working techniques and some new ones.

Tips box

A screwdriver is often the most efficient tool for accurate final fitting of components. It is easier to control than a powered drill/driver and can be used in cramped, awkward spaces.

29 When the basic structure has been assembled, place the top in position and attach it with screws from underneath. Complete the final finish to all components. Slide the drawers into position.

Desk design

RIGHT: With computers, the desk has become a "workstation" that must provide space for a variety of different pieces of equipment.

ABOVE: The bureau dates back to the 1600s. The sloping fall flap opens to create a writing surface and to reveal a variety of storage compartments. When open, the flap is supported by pull-out lopers.

RIGHT: A pedestal or kneehole desk takes the writing table one step further with frame and panel sides to create storage areas in one or more sides.

ABOVE: This table is a simple four-leg design, enriched by curves on the legs and rails. The contrast between the woods is particularly effective.

ABOVE: The roll-top desk became popular in the US in the 1800s. The sliding door (tambor) is made of wooden slats glued to a canvas backing. This flexibility allows the tambor to slide around curves.

ABOVE: Brass stays provide an alternative means of supporting the fall flap. The internal storage is set back slightly to allow for the movement of the stay.

ABOVE: The sculptural form of this "clam"-style top and the shapes of the pedestal complement each other. This desk is approached from three sides, one for writing (upper surface), one for typing (lower surface), and a third for access to the storage drawers.

| # Chest of drawers

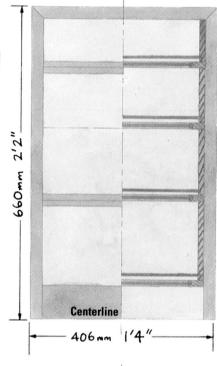

Centerline

← 406mm 1'4" →

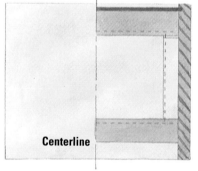

Centerline

Sectional halfplan (drawers removed)

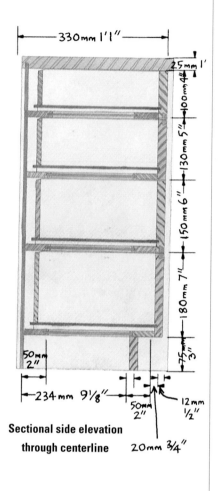

← 330mm 1'1" →

25mm 1"

100mm 4"

130mm 5"

150mm 6"

180mm 7"

75mm 3"

50mm 2"

← 234mm 9⅛" →

50mm 2"

12mm ½"

Sectional side elevation through centerline 20mm ¾"

Scale 1:8

This cabinet contains four drawers, each of a different depth. The drawers are opened by finger grooves positioned so that they form a distinctive design feature across the cabinet front. Classic fine furnituremaking techniques used in this chest of drawers include dovetail drawer joints, and dustboards between the drawers.

Choosing wood

If you have made the other projects in order, you will now have experience in using both solid wood and manmade board.

The prototype was made from ash. For this first project of making drawers, choose wood that is fairly easy to work. Beech is useful for the drawer sides and interior parts of the cabinet, while the drawer fronts and outside of the cabinet can be any wood of your choice.

Buying wood

1 The top and sides are made from 1¼in (30mm) wood, whereas most of the rest will come from 1in or ¾in (25mm or 20mm) wood. The back is made of plywood. Dustboards between the drawers are also made of ply and the drawers have ply bottoms.

2 Mark and cut out all components. Plane face side, face edge, width, and thickness, leaving slightly over length.

Plans

The drawings on this page and overleaf show the elevations and sections, with an exploded perspective view of the finished piece.

Cutting list: drawers

No.		Sawed	Planed
1	FRONT	1ft 3in x 4¼in x 1in	1ft 2in x 4in x ¾in
		(380mm x 105mm x 25mm)	(356mm x 100mm x 20mm)
2	SIDES	12in x 3¾in x ¾in	11in x 3½in x ½in
		(305mm x 90mm x 20mm)	(280mm x 85mm x 12mm)
1	BACK	1ft 3in x 3in x ¾in	1ft 2in x 2⅞in x ⅜in
		(380mm x 75mm x 20mm)	(356mm x 72mm x 10mm)
1	BOTTOM	1ft 2in x 11in x ¼in plywood	
		(356mm x 280mm x 6mm)	

The cutting list for the other 3 drawers is similar to drawer 1, but some parts change in width since the drawer depth increases. The widths are:

	Sawed	Planed
2nd DRAWER		
Front	5½in (140mm)	5in (130mm)
Sides	4¾in (120mm)	4½in (115mm)
Back	4in (100mm)	3⅞in (95mm)
3rd DRAWER		
Front	6½in (162mm)	6in (150mm)
Sides	5¾in (146mm)	5½in (140mm)
Back	5in (130mm)	4⅞in (122mm)
4th DRAWER		
Front	7½in (190mm)	7in (180mm)
Sides	6¾in (172mm)	6½in (162mm)
Back	6in (150mm)	5⅞in (148mm)

+ glue, finishing screws

Cutting list: body

No.		Sawed	Planed
2	SIDES	(2ft 3in x 1ft 1½in x 1¼in)	(2ft 2in x 1ft 1in x 1in)
		686mm x 343mm x 30mm	660mm x 330mm x 25mm
1	TOP	(1ft 5in x 1ft 1½in x 1¼in)	(1ft 4in x 1ft 1in x 1in)
		432mm x 343mm x 30mm	406mm x 330mm x 25mm
1	BOTTOM RAIL	1ft 5in x 3 in x 1in	1ft 4in x 2⅞in x ¾in
		(432mm x 75 mm x 25mm)	(406mm x 72mm x 20mm)
8	DRAWER CROSS RAILS	1ft 4in x 2ft 4in x ¾in	2in x ½in
		(406mm x 57mm x 20mm)	(50mm x 12mm)
8	DRAWER RUNNERS	8in x 1½in x ¾in	1½in x ½in
		(200mm x 38mm x 20mm)	(30mm x 12mm)
1	CABINET BACK	2ft 2in x 1ft 4in x ¼in plywood	
		(660mm x 406mm x 6mm)	
4	DUSTBOARDS	1ft 1in x 8in x ¼in plywood	
		(330mm x 200mm x 6mm)	

+ glue, finishing screws

**Section showing
detail of cabinet and
top drawers**

Scale ½ actual size

Exploded diagram

Joints at junction of top
and sides can be dove-
tailed as shown here, or
mitered with tongues or
biscuits as shown in the
photographs.

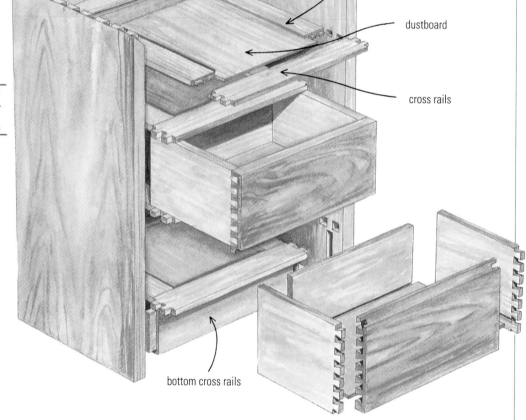

drawer runners

dustboard

cross rails

bottom cross rails

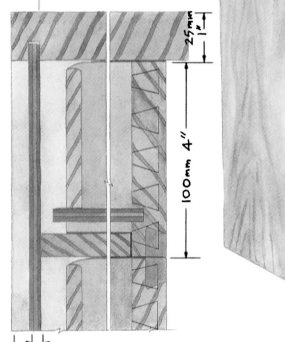

25mm 1"

100mm 4"

6mm ¼"

9mm ³/₈"

Carcase construction

3 Mark out the two sides and the top.
The carcase consists of the sides and
top, a bottom cross rail, and a back panel.

4 Make the corner joints. The wall-
hung cabinet project used secret
miter dovetail corner joints. Continue to practice
by making dovetails on the top two corners or,
miter these joints and use tongues, biscuits,
or dowels. This is an ideal project to use
tongues if you have a router.

5 It is essential to get a very good miter
at these two corners. You will
probably spend some time planing the miter and
making sure that it is a good fit at 90 degrees.

6 Rout the groove in the miter for the
tongues, or use a biscuit jointer (right).

7 Place the tongue in the groove and fit the joint dry.

9 Work the groove for the back panel in the top and the sides (above).

10 Cut and fit the ply back. Its function is to hold the cabinet square and, as is normal practise, it slides into place from the bottom and will later be attached to one of the cross rails.

11 Sand the interior, then apply a finish if required.

Drawer runners and cross rails

12 Under each drawer is a frame consisting of a runner at each side and a front and back cross rail. A ply dustboard is set within grooves cut on the inside faces of these pieces.

13 The front and back cross rails are glued in place. The runners and dustboards are slightly undersize from front to back. The runners are tenoned into the groove in the cross rails.

14 The design assumes that the sides are made from solid wood, which means that there is likely to be wood movement. To allow for expansion and contraction, the tenon on the runners is fitted tight and glued at the front, while at the back the tenon and its shoulder are cut short about ⅛in (3mm) to allow for any back-to-front movement in the cabinet.

8 Mark the bottom rail and make the joints that will hold it in place. The rail has a stub tenon fitted into mortises on the two sides.

15 Mark out the components with a sharp pencil or ballpoint pen, then carefully double check all your measurements (above).

16 Make stub tenons in the back, and front cross rails and make corresponding mortises on the inside of the cabinet. Make sure that these shoulders are the same as those on the bottom cabinet rail (above).

17 In order to fit the dustboard, work the groove on the inside edges of the cross rails as shown in the drawing.

18 Fit the carcase together dry. Make sure all the rails meet the side panels and are a snug fit in the mortises. The rails must be exactly spaced so that the drawers will sit parallel to each other. Make any adjustments if necessary and take it apart again (above).

Tips box

Use a try square to check that the rails meet the sides at an exact right angle.

19 Mark the positions of the front-to-back drawer runners on the inside of the sides. These are not tenoned into a mortise, but into the groove in the cross rails (above).

20 Run a groove for the dustboard in each runner.

21 Mark, cut, and fit four plywood dustboards.

22 Try assembling these components together. If all is well, check that these internal components are sanded and that you can glue the carcase together (above).

23 It is not usual to finish inside a cabinet where drawers are fitted, but you can apply a simple sealing coat of the chosen finish if you wish. Drawers should slide wood onto wood. You should now have a firm carcase structure in which to run the drawers.

Making drawers

24 Make and fit one drawer at a time, repeating the procedure for the other three. Plane the drawer sides so that they are an exact fit and slide in and out of the carcase with ease (above).

25 Each drawer back is not a tight fit vertically since it sits on the drawer bottom and does not extend the full depth of the drawer. It does, however, need to fit precisely across the carcase and you should be able to insert it from front to back (above).

26 Take the drawer front and fit it into its opening. It should fit exactly on the inside face from end to end, but make a bevel so that it tapers toward the outside face, which is slightly longer (above).

27 You will see from the drawing that the top drawer fits from the underside of the cabinet top to the lower face of the first drawer rail (above).

28 Once sides, back and front have been fitted, make the groove for the drawer bottom on the inside of the two sides and the front.

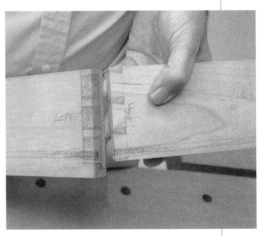

29 Mark the dovetail joints. Lap dovetails join the front to the sides (above).

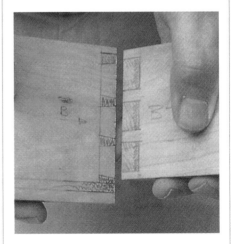

30 Through dovetails join the sides to the back (above).

31 Remember to make allowances for the handle groove that is on the lower edge of the top drawer. The groove is on the upper edge of the second drawer, the lower edge of the third drawer, and the upper edge of the bottom drawer. When assembled, the grooves make a decorative feature running across the cabinet.

32 Cut the dovetails with care. Make sure that your gauge lines are precisely the thickness of the components. This technique does not allow for major planing of the drawer sides to make sure they fit. The precise marking of the drawer back and front should mean that the drawer fits if the dovetails have been well made, with only a slight cleaning up necessary.

33 Mark the plywood bottom and cut to fit (above).

34 Slide the bottom into place. The drawer bottom is not glued in the grooves; slot it in place and insert two screws at the back, through the drawer bottom up into the drawer back. Assemble the drawer dry and check that it is a tight fit (above).

35 Add glue and assemble the drawer. When the glue has cured, it should only need a few touches of the plane to allow the drawer to run smoothly in its space.

36 Now that you have mastered drawermaking on the first drawer, follow the same procedure for the other three.

37 The cabinet back is fitted with a couple of screws through the back into the bottom back drawer rail.

38 Sand the carcase and the drawer fronts, and apply the final finish.

39 The finished chest of drawers, waxed and polished—an asset to any room.

Easy chair

This chair calls for two different shaping techniques: shaping curved rails from solid wood, and making curved slats from laminate strips. You can buy veneer for the laminate, or cut your own. The chair is comfortable as it is, but it can also have a seat cushion made of leather or fabric, filled with feathers.

Choosing the wood

The design calls for "sturdy" looking wood. Wood with too fine a grain would be less appropriate than woods like oak, ash, teak, beech, or elm. The prototype was made in cherry wood. Your choice may be affected by the material for the laminated back slats. If you buy veneer, your choice will be limited by the species available, but if you intend to cut and plane your own veneer, there will be no such limitation.

LEFT: This project provides the perfect opportunity to introduce shaping and laminating wood into your repertoire.

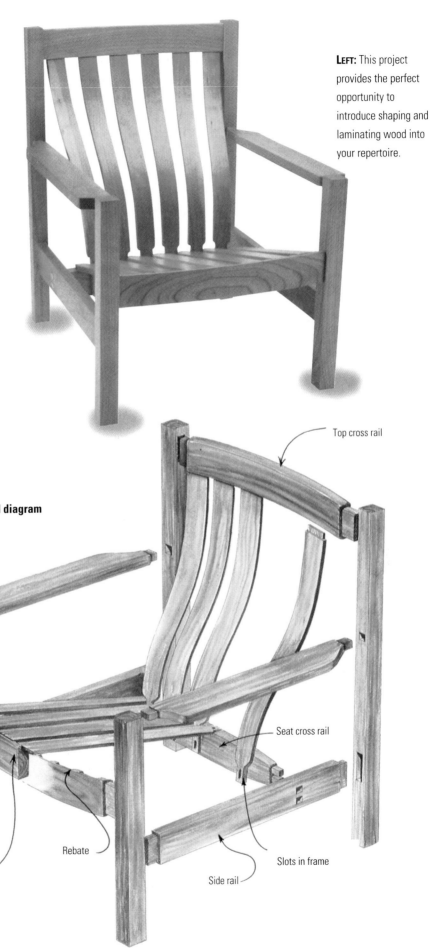

Exploded diagram

PLANS
The drawings on this page show the elevations and sections, with an exploded perspective view of the finished piece.

Top cross rail

Seat cross rail

Rebate

Front cross rail

Slots in frame

Side rail

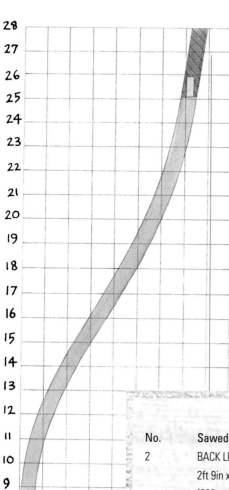

Template for the curved laminates

Enlarge this template to full size on graph or squared paper. Then transfer the outline to a piece of softwood to make the lamination former. Each square equals 1in (25mm).

Side frames

1 Prepare all wood except back slats to face side, face edge, width, and thickness.

2 Mark the lengths of the legs. Mark the positions of the mortises for the side rails, the arms, and the mortises that will take the top and front cross rails (above). All mortises into the legs are blind mortises.

Cutting list

No.	Sawed	Planed
2	BACK LEGS	
	2ft 9in x 2in x 2in	2ft 7in x 1¾in x 1¾in
	(838mm x 50mm x 50mm)	(787mm x 45mm x 45mm)
2	FRONT LEGS	
	1ft 10in x 2in x 2in	1ft 8in x 1¾in x 1¾in
	(560mm x 50mm x 50mm)	(508mm x 45mm x 45mm)
3	CURVED CROSS RAILS	
	2ft x 3in full x 2½in	1ft 10½in x 3in x 1¼in
	(610mm x 75mm full x 60mm)	(572mm x 75mm x 30mm)
2	SIDE RAILS AND 2 ARMS	
	4 at 2ft 3in x 3in full x 1¼in	2ft 2in x 3in x 1in
	(686mm x 75mm full x 30mm	660mm x 75mm x 25mm)
7	SEAT SLATS	
	1ft 9in x 2¼in x ¾in	from 1ft 8½in x 2in x ⅝in
	(533mm x 57mm x 20mm)	(521mm x 50mm x 14mm)
6	BACK SLATS	
	2ft 6in x 2in x ½in	
	(762mm x 50mm x 12mm)	

Each to be laminated from eight veneers 2ft 6in x 2in x 1⁄16in (762mm x 50mm x 1.5mm). Total of 48 required.

+ For lamination former: joinery softwood approximately 2ft 6in x 6in x 2½in (762mm x 150mm x 60mm); large sheet of paper, or graph paper, for full-sized drawing of back slats; polyethylene sheets, screws; adhesive.

3 Mark the tenons on the end of the cross rails, side rails, and the arms. The tenons on the side rail have shoulders all around. Mark the through mortises on the side rail that will accept the twin through tenons on the seat cross rail. These through mortises run with the grain for strength. The seat cross rail is set low in the side rail.

4 Check the marking and make cut lines and gauge lines where you intend to cut. Remember that you are making a matching pair of frames, right and left.

5 Cut the mortise and tenon joints for the two side frames. Also cut the mortises for the cross rails. When working through mortises, mark and cut from both sides (above).

Shape the arms

6 Each arm is set so that the inside face is in line with the inside surfaces of the legs, and the outside edge protrudes. To begin shaping the end, drill a hole to make the inner curve at the end of the arm, and saw the hole.

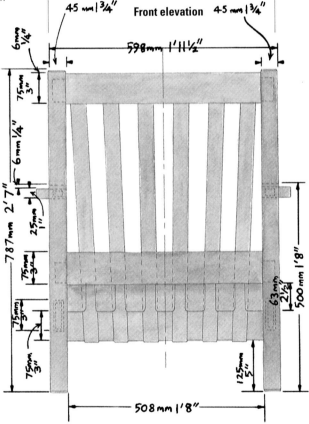

Front elevation

Sectional side elevation through centerline

Half plan

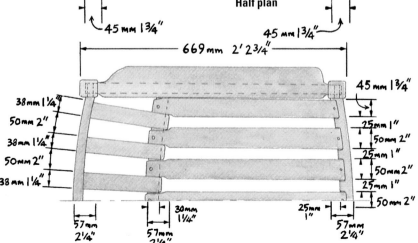

Plans

These drawings show the elevations and sections, with an exploded perspective view of the finished piece.

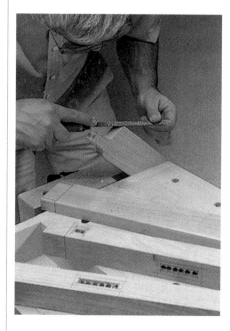

7 Finish the shape with rasps, files, and sandpaper. You can be more adventurous with this shaping if you wish (above).

Dry assembly

8 Assemble both frames dry, and check that the frames are square and out of wind, and that the joints are tight. Then disassemble, and sand the four sides of the arm and side rail, as well as the two inside surfaces of each leg.

Glue, clamp, and finish

9 Glue up both frames, clamp, and remove excess glue. When the glue has cured, remove from the clamps, and apply a coat of finish, making sure that you mask the faces of the joints where the cross rails will be fitted.

Three cross rails

10 These rails should be planed all round, but will be oversized on thickness to allow for cutting the curves on the front and back. Mark the rails to length, both sides and tenon lengths.

11 Mark the curves with a pencil. It is enough to bend a steel rule between the two end points and the center mark. It helps to have someone else to hold the rule on the center mark, and pencil the line (above).

12 Trim the ends of all three rails to the overall rail thickness, and pencil-mark the tenons (above).

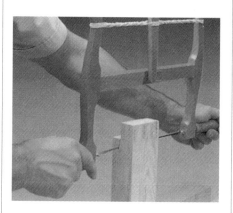

13 Saw the curve. If you only have hand tools, use a bowsaw or a coping saw (this is a slow process). Alternatively, use a power jigsaw or a band saw (above).

14 The three rails have a planed surface top and bottom, square ends marked ready for the tenons, and a sawed curve on the outside and inside faces. The curved surfaces must now be completed. Clean up the outside curve with a plane, except at the ends near the tenons, which will have to be pared. Smooth the inside curve with a spokeshave.

Mark and cut joints in the curved rails

15 The top cross rail has a simple tenon on each end that fits into the mortise on the top of the back legs. Mark the mortises on the underside of this rail to accept the six back slats. Mark, check, and cut these joints.

16 The front cross rail has two simple tenons that fit into the front leg. Mark and cut the tenons now. Later, this rail will need a bevel at the top edge, which is best marked when the whole frame is assembled dry. It will also need to have recesses cut to receive the seat slats, but this should be done after the slats have been located into their fanned position.

17 The seat cross rail has twin through tenons that fit into the side rails. The shoulders on these tenons are longer than on the other two rails. The underside of this rail sits partly below the side rail and the tenons are made near the top of the seat cross rail to allow for this. Mark and cut these tenons.

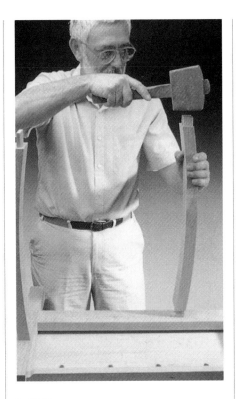

18 Fit all the above joints, number or letter them, sand the rails, and assemble the whole frame dry.

19 With a ruler placed between the seat cross rail, and the front cross rail, measure how much bevel is needed on the front rail. Mark with a pencil, remove the front cross rail, and work the bevel with a plane. Reassemble.

Laminated back slats

20 Make the former from a scrap piece of wood. Enlarge the drawing of the back slats to full size. Do this with graph paper, or by making a grid of squares and plotting the points where the lines of the curve cross. Transfer this shape to the center of the former, and cut the shape with a bowsaw, jigsaw, or handsaw. Clean up the faces.

Constructional veneers

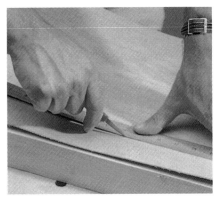

21 If you purchase the veneers, aim for a thickness of between $\frac{1}{16}$in (1.5mm) and $\frac{1}{8}$in (3mm). The number you need for each laminated slat will depend on this thickness, since the slat will have a finished thickness of $\frac{1}{2}$in (12mm). Each veneer strip should be 2ft 9in x 2¼in (838mm x 57mm) wide. Cut the strips with a craft knife against a steel ruler.

22 Alternatively, if you have the machines, you can make your own veneers. Plane a piece of wood 2ft 9in (838mm) long, 2¼in (57mm) thick, and a convenient width. Cut a strip off the side planed face 2¼in x ⅛in (57mm x 3mm) plus. Reface the sawed side on the piece, and cut another strip. Repeat refacing and cutting until you have the number of strips needed. They will have one face and two edges planed, and one face sawed. Use the thickness planer to plane the strips to ⅛in (3mm) thickness. Make a baseboard to support the thin strips safely.

Tips box

- Make sure the constructional veneers are reasonably straight-grained with no obvious faults such as knots or splits. Faults may weaken the finished lamination.

- You may need more than two clamps to apply even pressure to the mold sides when you glue up the pieces.

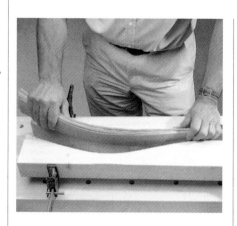

23 If your veneers are ⅛in (3mm) thick, you need four to make each slat. Try these dry in the former to check that, when clamped, they are pressed closely together, and, if necessary, adapt the mold faces.

Apply glue to the veneers

24 The glue needs to be capable of holding laminates, so either use urea formaldehyde, or one of the stronger, formulated PVA adhesives. Apply the glue to all internal surfaces, not the two outer ones, and make sure coverage by using a glue roller.

Tips box

• Spread the glue evenly over the veneer surfaces. The adhesive must be spread to the edges of each piece to make a strong bond.

Laminates in jig

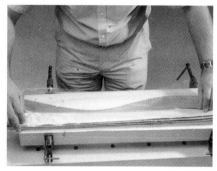

25 Wrap the glued bundle of laminates in waxed paper, so that they do not stick to the mold when the glue squeezes out.

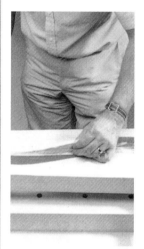

26 Place the bundle in the mold, and tighten the bar clamps. Try to make sure that the veneers stay in line. The less neat the package, the more you will have to trim off, and the result might not be wide enough for your needs (above).

27 To make sure an even pressure, you will need five clamps—three on the underside, and two placed on the top of the former after the first squeeze (right).

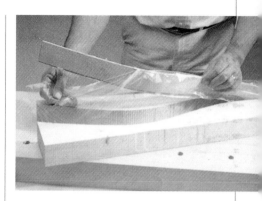

28 When the glue has cured (make sure you allow enough time for this), remove the piece from the former. This is a process that you could do each evening during the week, since it is only possible to make one laminate at a time in the one former, and it should cure overnight.

29 Plane one of the laminate edges, using the former as a support (above).

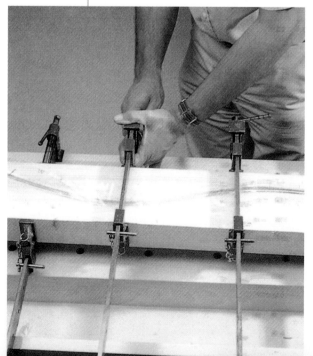

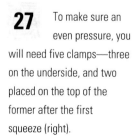

30 Alternatively, hold the laminate in the vise.

31 Gauge the laminate strip to width.

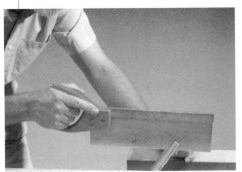

32 Saw the gauged line, and plane the last edge. The laminate is now ready for fitting into the frame. Be careful not to bruise the sides of the laminate once it is planed to the exact dimensions. The pieces can be easily damaged, so always pad the faces of clamp jaws with a scrap of softwood or cardboard.

Fitting back slats into the frame

33 Make the tenons on the top of the back slats to fit into the mortises cut in the underside of the top crossrail (step 15). Mark the top shoulder line of each tenon from the former. If you do not make sure that the line is marked on each slat in the correct place at the correct end, the curves will not line up when assembled. Clamp the slats together to mark the tenons. Cut the tenons. The shoulder lines are not yet at the correct angle, you will mark and cut this when you place each slat in its fanned position on the chair frame.

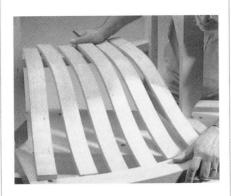

34 Push the tenoned slats into the mortises on the top rail. It is essential to make sure all the tenoned slats are fitted fully into the mortised top rail. If you make the mortises in the rail with a router and straight cutter, either square the corners with a chisel or round over the tenons to fit.

35 Mark the centerline on the seat cross rail.

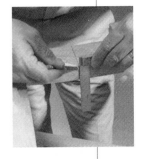

36 Make the two center back slats, and place them in their fanned position on the seat cross rail. When you are happy with this position, mark it with a pencil and hold the slats in place with two "G" clamps.

37 Now mark each tenon shoulder line at the top of the slat with a marking knife. Remove each slat from the frame, trim the tenon shoulder accurately to the cut line. The two slats can now be pushed home into the tenons.

38 The bottoms of the slats are narrowed when they are screwed to the seat cross rail. This is to allow the seat slats to fit between them, and mark the waisting on it as well.

39 To get the curved edge on the narrowed part, start with a drilled hole, then saw, and finish the curve with a spokeshave.

40 Drill screw holes. If you cut slots for the screws instead of holes, they will allow for any slight movement when sitting in the chair, and will relieve the top tenons of any stress.

41 Continue fitting the rest of the back slats: mark the position on the seat cross rail, and mark and cut the tenon shoulders. Fit the tenons, narrow the ends of the slats, drill screw slots, and screw in place. Notice the mortise and tenons are not yet glued.

Fit seat slats

42 Take the center slat, and narrow it where it will be screwed to the seat cross rail. Narrow the other slats and place in the fan position. Mark the recesses for them on the front rail.

43 Remove the rail again from the frame and cut the recesses. T be done either by hand with saw and ch with a router.

44 Replace the front rail in the frame, and, finally, fit the seat slats. You will find that, due to the curvature of the seat and front rails, the rear of the slats will not sit flat. Cut the angle to allow each slat to fit. Drill the hole and insert the screw.

45 Mark the length of the slat, and trim, if necessary, to make sure that it fits snugly into the recess on the front rail. Drill the front hole and screw the slat into place. Repeat steps 42 to 45 with the other slats.

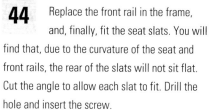

Final assembly

46 Remove all screws, slats, etc., and sand all components (but do not remove your identification numbering).

49 Mask the tenons on the top of the back slats, and sand and finish all the slats.

50 Fit the back slats, applying glue and light clamping pressure to pull the mortises and tenons together. Screw the slats at the bottom, then remove the clamps before screwing the seat slats into place.

51 Finally, check the finish. Apply a coat of wax polish if required.

47 Assemble the main seat frame, apply glue to the joints on the three cross rails, and clamp the frame. Remember to check for squareness and remove surplus glue.

48 When the glue has cured, remove the clamps, and sand. Finish the frame, but mask the mortises on the top rail.

Finishes

A variety of possible final finishes are available. Depending on the setting, you might choose to apply a simple sealant to protect and preserve the wood, or to use a transparent stain to alter the color of the wood but maintain the wood-grain effect, or even to paint or decorate the chairs to match or contrast with other pieces of furniture or the surrounding decor.

52 The finished easy chair is elegant and comfortable.

Outdoor playhouse

This sturdy and spacious playhouse is specifically designed for use in the yard. By reducing the scale, younger children may use the playhouse inside the home. This design overcomes the problems of construction, and makes the door and window openings simple to make and easy to understand. All of the parts are cut from standard-sized manufactured board, in this case exterior grade plywood, which is used for both its structural and decorative properties. You will see from the drawings how to arrange the cutting of each component: base, four sides, veranda pieces, and roof panels

Cutting the shapes

1 Mark out the ply for the two long and two short sides, and follow the illustrations opposite to see how to make the door and window openings. Making doors and windows is normally quite a complex woodworking operation, but this method is very simple and ensures that the openings will fit when finished. The illustrations detail the making of a glazed window, but you will use this basic principle to make the doors too. Start by marking out the window position on the ply. Mark the window panes and the frame.

2 Now drill a hole large enough to receive the blade of the jigsaw.

Cutting list

Part.	No	Length	Width	Thickness
From exterior-quality plywood if for outdoors, in standard 8ft x 4ft (2.4m x 1.2m) sheets, ½in (12mm) thick				
Floor	1			
Long sides	2			
Gable ends	2	See drawings for cutting final size		
Roof panels	2	See drawings for cutting final size		
From offcuts of gable ends and roof panels				
Porch ends	2			
Capping pieces	2			
From preservative-treated sawed wood				
Bearers	9	4ft (1.2m)	6in (150mm)	2in (50mm)

+ Four hinges, screws, glue, nails, abrasive paper, bitumen felt, color stain, clear varnish

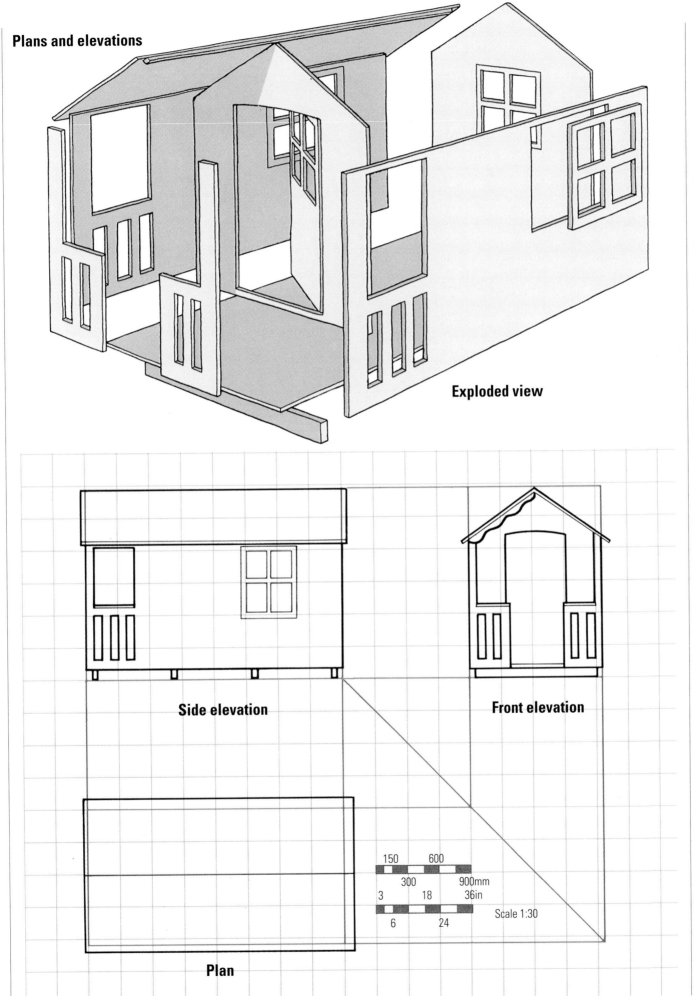

Exploded view

Side elevation

Front elevation

150   600

300   900mm

3   18   36in

Scale 1:30

6   24

Plan

3 Cut out the areas that will be glazed. When you have cut out the required number of panes, prepare to partly cut along the line that will separate the frame and the wall. For larger glazed areas, clamp a straight-edge or batten parallel with the cut line and offset by the distance from the tool's blade to the edge of its sole plate. Use this as a guide to make a straight cut.

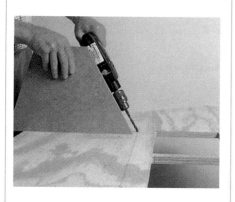

4 You will need to drill an angled hole, so make a simple 30 degree jig to guide the drill. Use a piece of thick MDF and ask a helper to check that the drill bit is following the correct angle by looking along the side of the jig.

Tips box

- You can save money by making the playhouse out of chipboard, although the finish will not be as smooth. Whatever the material you choose, seal all the surfaces with at least two coats of an exterior preservative. Repeat the preservative treatment every two or three years to extend the life of the boards.

- Most larger hardware stores will be able to deliver all the bulk materials to you for a small extra charge.

5 Set the jigsaw to an angle of 30 degrees when making the cut. It is essential that you only cut one side of the frame, since the principles of construction behind this design depend on fitting the hinges in position at this stage. This method makes sure that the window or door will fit its aperture exactly.

The hinges

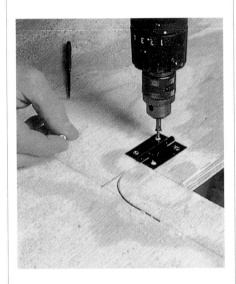

9 In this project, the frames were colored. To avoid the risk of accidentally staining adjacent parts, remove the window frame from the wall, noting carefully with letters or numbers which window goes where. Apply the finish, first by brush and then with a cloth.

6 The next stage is to fit the hinges. Drill a small pilot hole for the screws. It is important to place the hinge carefully on the line that you have cut with the jigsaw, so that the knuckle (the part around which the hinge opens) is exactly over the line and in line with the cut. Only insert a couple of screws to hold the hinge until you are sure that the correct position has been achieved.

7 Screw the two hinges in place over the cut line and then cut the other three sides of the frame with the jigsaw. Make sure that the cut is angled the same way on the three sides as the hinge side, and that the angle is from the outside toward the center of the frame, so that the frame will "sit" into the wall from the outside where it is hinged. When the complete cut has been made, all around the window or door, the frame will open easily.

8 A similar procedure is used for the door. Again, make sure to cut the hinged side first and fix the hinges before cutting the other three sides to create the door.

Glazing the windows

10 This design uses rigid plastic sheet for the glazing. The plastic is safer than glass and is easily fitted using woodworking tools. First cut the plastic sheet to fit in position. Fix in place with screws, countersink the plastic sheet to receive the screw head, and then screw it in place. It is better to do this before applying the sealing mastic between the plastic and the frame.

11 Remove all the screws, and apply mastic to the outside frame and to the montins.

12 Now put the plastic sheet back in place over the window frame.

13 Make temporary marks to make sure that the sheet is relocated in exactly the same position—edge to edge—as it was when first screwed in place. Replace all the screws, then turn the sheet over and carefully remove any excess mastic that may have squeezed out.

14 Fit knobs to the windows and doors, so they can be opened easily. There is a wide range of ready-made knobs available.

15 You will also need to cut out the openings as shown on the porch end to create the large, unglazed open "windows" of the veranda, and the slatted railing effect beneath them. Also cut the capping pieces, stain them to match the windows, and, when dry, check for fit. These pieces will reduce the amount of water that can penetrate the board, as well as add strength to these vulnerable exterior pieces.

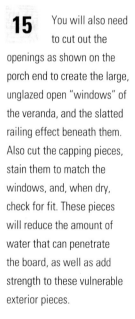

Tips box

• You can buy clear plastic sheet in various sizes from larger hardware stores. Cut the sheet with either a sharp craft knife or a jigsaw blade made for cutting plastic.

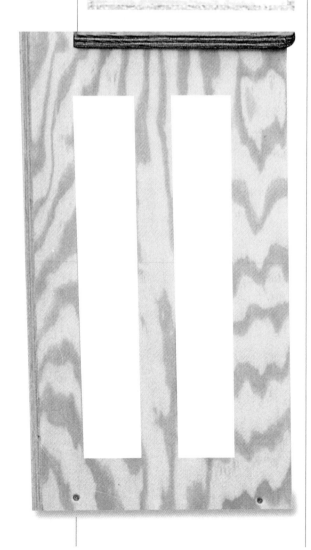

Assembling the house

17 The next step is to attach the rear end and one long side onto the base. Use locating pegs to position these pieces, or screw battens into the corners where the panels meet (left).

18 Fit the end with the door in position, then position the other long side to complete the sides. Now fit both the front cutout pieces of the veranda in place, and secure the capping pieces on top of the railings (below).

16 Lay the base in position in the yard (above). If you used plywood, support it on wood bearers that have been treated against rot. These do not need to be planed, they can be sawed wood, and the ply should be fitted to them with screws. Where you locate the playhouse will depend on the ground conditions, but it is a good idea to make sure that the bearers do not sit directly on the grass or dirt. You can either remove any grass and topsoil and cover the area underneath with gravel, or place the bearers on brick or stone slabs with a moisture-proof membrane in between for longer life.

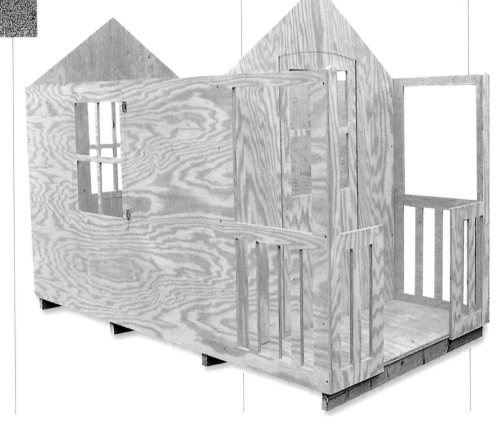

Advanced Projects

19 Finish the assembly by attaching the two roof panels. Cut out the shaped barge boards and fix on the veranda end.

20 Finally, to make the roof waterproof, nail the bitumen felt over the roof and eaves. The house is now ready for its new occupants to take up residence.

Tips box

- It's simple to make a variation on the playhouse idea using the same techniques and materials. Change the front to make a gas station, or alter the side to form a store window.

- Just by changing the colors of the playhouse exterior, you can transform the entire look. Try making the windows in an arched or round shape to add interest.

- Site the playhouse on the patio or preservative-treated wood rather than directly onto the ground.

21 Add some garden furniture, and perhaps a few home comforts so your children can play safely and cosily in this great hideaway for hours. If you want to have more exterior details, add small jalousies, made from rectangles of plywood screwed to each side of the windows. You could also fix small plywood window boxes to the sides and around the veranda.

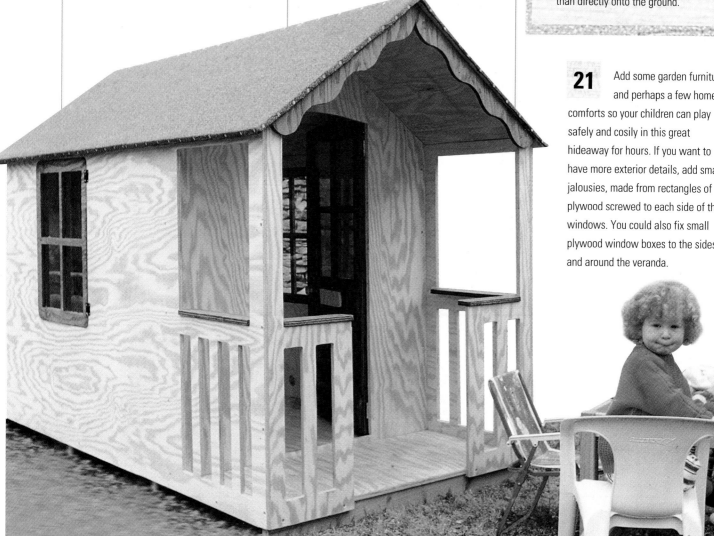

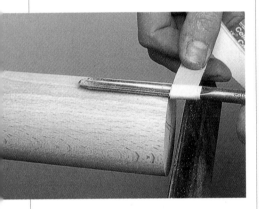

Small turned scoop

From a tiny salt scoop to a large one for animal feeds, the method of turning varies little. The bowl is shaped like a goblet, with the opening slightly narrower than the body, instead of straight-sided, and with a handle in place of the stem.

1 Prepare and mount the blank in the chuck. Measure off 2½in (65mm) on your spindle gouge or ½in (12mm) drill held in a Jacobs chuck, and mark the depth with a piece of masking tape.

2 Line up the point of the gouge with the center of the blank and plunge it in, withdrawing the tool regularly to clear the shavings, until you reach the tape. Drilling this hole takes away any later uncertainty as to the depth of the bowl.

3 Start hollowing the bowl with a fingernail-ground spindle gouge laid on its side, making small cuts in an arc from the center out toward the rim.

4 Open out and deepen the bowl, keeping the eventual goblet shape in mind as you proceed.

5 As you get deeper into the bowl, you may need to use a scraper, which has a stiffer shank and will flex less while cutting.

Tool and material list

Fingernail-ground spindle gouge

½in (12mm) drill bit

Parting tool

Scraper

Hardwood

(for example, beech, sycamore,

maple, or birch);

dimensions 2¾in x 2¾in x 6in

(70mm x 70mm x 150mm)

Fast-speed lathe

Liquid paraffin

6 Refine the internal shape, eliminating any ridges and hollows, and aim to leave a smooth, full curve.

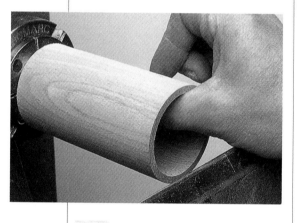

7 Stop the lathe and check the shape and depth of the bowl until you are happy with it. Touch gives you a much better representation of the shape than the eye can. When it feels right, sand the inside to as good a finish as you would on the outside.

8 Measure the depth of the bowl and transfer it to the outside. Resist the temptation to add a bit, as this only makes it more difficult to keep track of the bowl's depth and therefore achieve an even wall thickness.

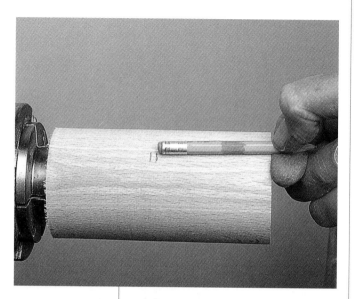

9 Part in at the headstock side of the first line to about two-thirds of the overall diameter or until the sound begins to change. Go too far, and you will end up with a miniature lampshade.

10 Shape the outside of the bowl to match the internal curve, using your spindle gouge and aiming for an eventual wall thickness of about ⅛in (3mm).

11 Create a bead where the handle meets the bowl. If everything has gone as planned, this should be about the same diameter that you finished the parting cut.

12 The handle should be kept simple but still flowed through the bowl so that it looks as though it belongs, and not as if it has been tacked on afterward.

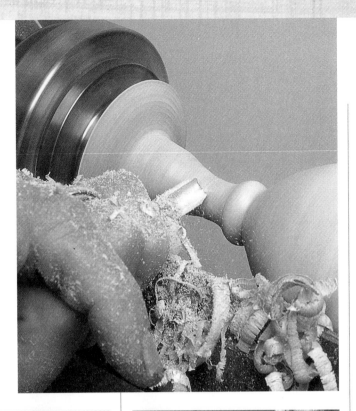

16 Final shaping can be done on a belt sander or, as here, a drum sander mounted on the lathe. Hand-sand sharp edges left by the drum.

13 After sanding, round off the end of the handle so that it has a comfortable grip and part it off with the skew chisel. Hold the bowl loosely with your left hand to stop it from hitting the tool rest as it comes free.

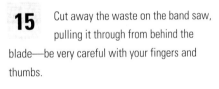

15 Cut away the waste on the band saw, pulling it through from behind the blade—be very careful with your fingers and thumbs.

17 Give the scoop a coat of food-safe liquid paraffin.

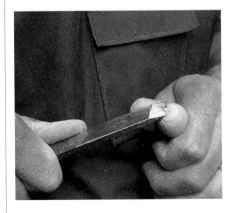

14 Pare away any waste, and hand-sand the end to remove any tooling marks.

Tips box

Take special care when using a sanding attachment on your lathe. Wear a respirator mask, as very fine dust particles are produced. Keep the scoop constantly moving to reduce the chances of making flat areas on the surface.

Nursery furniture

This nursery furniture is an ideal opportunity to explore the possibilities of working with manmade board using hand power tools. The construction is straightforward, the joints can be tongued and grooved using a router, or you can use a biscuit jointer. The decorative possibilities are limited only by your imagination. Simple nursery or children's furniture can be an ideal opportunity to experiment with paint effects. Bright stencil patterns can look great on this type of project, but always use paints that are safe to use on children's furniture—this should be on the labeling.

Choosing material

MDF has been used here because it is so simple to finish, however, plywood or chipboard would do equally well.

With this project, the "cutting list" is in the form of a drawn layout instead of a set of components so that you can reduce waste. Follow the layout of the pieces carefully so that you can cut each piece out without overlapping the adjacent pieces.

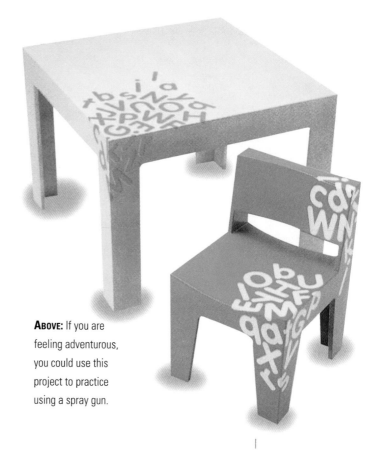

ABOVE: If you are feeling adventurous, you could use this project to practice using a spray gun.

Plans

The drawings on this page show the elevations and sections, along with an exploded perspective view of the finished piece.

Exploded diagram

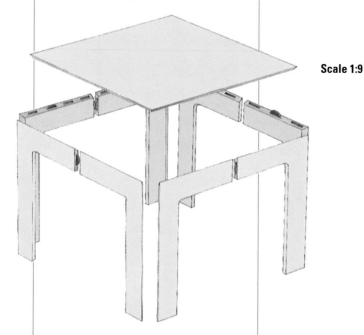

Scale 1:9

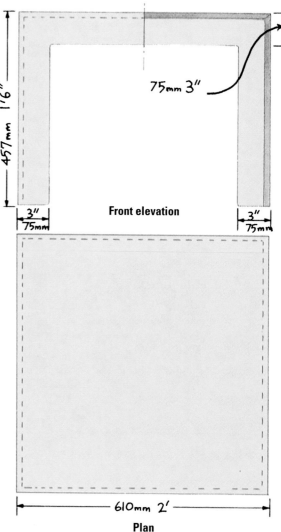

75mm 3"

457mm 1'6"

3" 75mm

Front elevation

3" 75mm

610mm 2'

Plan

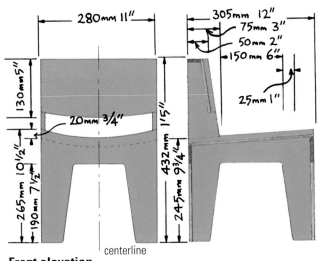

Front elevation

centerline

**Sectional side elevation
through centerline**

Exploded diagram

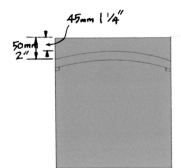

Plan

Making the table

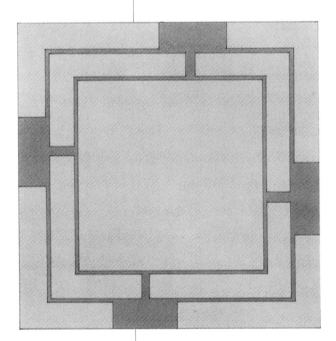

1 Follow the diagram to mark out components on the board. The board is cut in order to utilize the material as economically as possible (above).

2 The legs are grouped around the tabletop. You will need either a coping saw or a power jigsaw to cut the "L"-shaped pieces for the legs. If you decide to use a jigsaw, choose a medium-grade woodcutting blade and use the scroll action to increase the cutting speed. Clean up any rough edges with a sanding block, but be careful not to round over the cut edges. Use the block flat onto the sanding surfaces (above).

Jointing the legs

3 The eight "L"-shaped pieces are mitered together in pairs to form four leg-and-rail corner components. To fit these to the top, you can either miter the top and the tops of the corner components, or set the legs directly under the top. The project is described using miters all around for a neater finish. Use filler to hide any small gaps or cracks around the miters.

Cutting miters

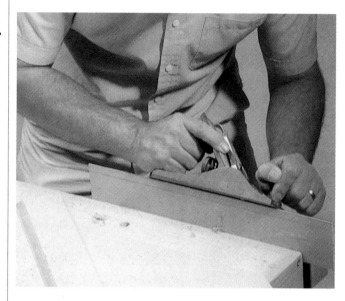 

4 Plane a 45-degree miter all around the tabletop, and also around the outer edges of the eight "L"-shaped leg components. Alternatively, cut the miters using a router. Cutting with a router set in a router table will produce a very accurate result, but you will need an angled cutter that is wide enough to cut across the MDF board in one pass.

Making the joints

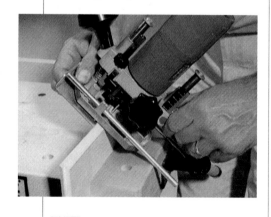

5 Set the router with a small cutter (³⁄₁₆in/4.5mm) and cut grooves for the tongues along the mitered surfaces. You will need to cut tongues from a piece of plywood of the same thickness as the grooves. Set the router up with its fence set to guide the cutter along the top edge of the top. Be sure to hold the tool steady as it cuts.

6 Alternatively, use a biscuit jointer to make short grooves for biscuits. Each section should be firmly secured to the bench with clamps before you start to cut the slots for the biscuits.

7 Assemble the four corner joints using two "L"-shaped pieces per corner. Note that the long lengths form the legs and the short lengths fit to the top. Use masking tape to hold the joints together. Make sure that the corners are square and let the glue cure before working on them more (right).

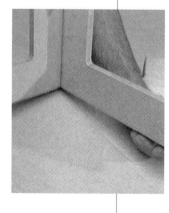

8 Take two leg assemblies and glue them to the top on opposite corners. The geometry of the joint should mean that everything will be square when these joints are glued and clamped home. Again, let the adhesive cure before going on to the next stage (above).

9 With the first legs in position, fit the final pair. Not only will you be jointing legs to the top, but you will be jointing the rail between each leg section. Glue these last two leg components in position, and when the glue has cured, your table structure should be finished and very strong.

10 The corners of the table are very sharp, however, and you will need to plane the outside edges. For small children, a larger rounded edge may be preferable—this is a chance to use the router with a rounding-over or other specially shaped cutter.

Chair

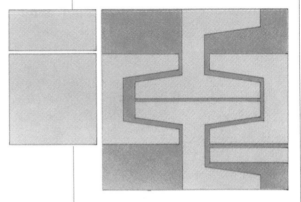

11 Now sand the table all over in preparation for the sealing coat. MDF needs slightly less sealing than either chipboard or plywood, but any manmade board needs one or more sealing coats before applying the finished color coat. Sand down between each coat to get rid of any small imperfections and brush or wipe away any sanding dust (above).

12 Apply the finishing coat or coats in the color you have chosen. Next, apply any decorative effects you have. This project used a "falling letters" design, but you will no doubt think of a variety of ways of adding interest. There is now a wide range of safe non-toxic and bright paints suitable for all sorts of children's furniture.

13 Mark out components on the board as shown in the diagram above. Two thicknesses of board are specified—⅜in (9mm) for the main and ⅛in (3mm) or 3⁄16in (5mm) for the seat and back. If you are making more than one chair, you will probably be able to use the material more economically.

14 Cut the components from the board, using a jigsaw.

15 Plane all components to the required shape with your bench plane. It is easiest to work all the edges square at this stage. Pay attention to the sloping angle on the inside. Use a pencil guideline on the inside of each leg component to guide you by forming an accurate parallel bevel.

16 Work the miters on the four corners of the main sections. Stop the miter on the back leg above the seat at the position shown and also at the top corner where the top rail fits.

17 Cut rebates for the seat and the back rest.

18 Make tongues and grooves or biscuit joints.

19 Assemble the frame dry, adjust, and check. If all is well, glue the frame, the two sides, the back and front, and the top rail and let the glue cure.

20 If you have used thin material for the seat and back, it will bend to the curve easily. When making the prototype ¼in (6mm) MDF was used and the seat and back shapes had to be pre-curved before fitting. If you need to do this, clamp the pieces in a rough jig, after cutting the seat and back very slightly oversized.

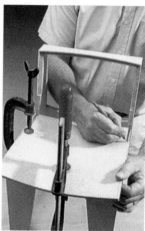

21 You will then need to fit the seat in position and it is a tricky piece of measuring to get it to fit precisely. The seat fits in the rebates on all four sides except at the rear where it is cut away to fit inside the side frames.

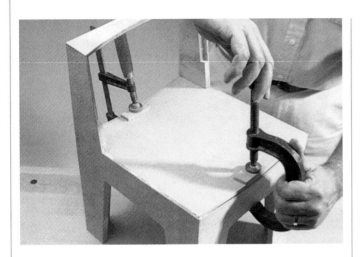

22 When the seat fits, dry, glue, and clamp in position.

23 The same, but slightly easier procedure, applies for the back rest. Fit and glue in position.

24 Now, as with the table, sand off sharp edges or use a router with a rounding-over cutter.

25 Finish the chair using the same procedures that were used for the table. Use filler if necessary, sand all over, apply sealing coats, and the finishing coat.

26 The finished table and chair is decorated here with a "falling letters" design.

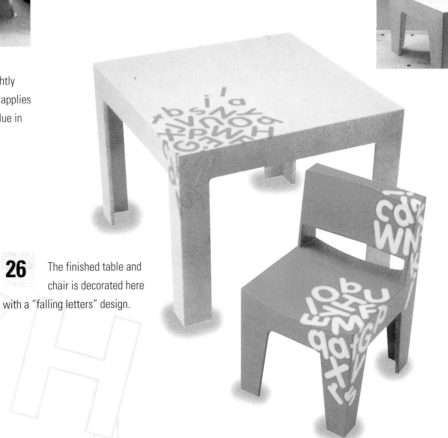

Oval box

This delightful oval box was not designed with any particular function in mind. It was inspired, in part at least, by the style of traditional hatboxes, and it could be used to store small perfume or pill bottles, essential oils or jewelry. The initial oval template can be made in a number of ways. It can be derived from something you already own, such as a small mirror or box, or it can be traced from something similar. Artists' materials and art supply stores stock elliptical templates in a wide variety of sizes. If you want to work from basics, draw one-quarter of the shape using a French curve of the kind usually available from any office supply store, and duplicate it for the four curved segments that make up the body of the box. The construction is very simple, although the making process takes patience. The four sides or segments that make up the main box need to be cut to size very accurately. They are then butt-glued to the assembled divides. The box derives strength from the base, which is glued and screwed on. The box does not need much more than a basic tool kit, although a router with rounding corner and slot cutting bits are recommended. The fine ³⁄₆₄in (1mm)-wide black/white/black inlay used in the lid decoration is available from guitar and lute makers and suppliers, and is useful for a wide variety of fine woodworking applications. Alternatively, you could make your own version from the many individual bandings available or even band saw out pieces from some scrap wood. The box is very much in the Shaker style, although not made with the original materials, or with the continuous wrap around technique, so it should not be spoiled with too much decoration.

Tool list

⅛in (3mm) slot cutter or to suit decorative inlay

⅛in (3mm) radius ovolo cutter with guide pin/bearing

Hollow plane (optional)

Curved scraper

Oval template—a rectangle of thin sheet brass with an oval 2in x 1¼in (5mm x 30mm) cut out of it

Long and short axes must be marked

A ³⁄₆₄in (1mm)-wide scraper made from a piece of hacksaw blade or similar material for use with the above

Strong rubber bands

You will also need a selection of basic hand tools (see pages 50-54)

Materials

Blue-dyed veneer 10in x 6in (250mm x 150mm)

Horse-chestnut or holly veneer 2in x 1¾in (50mm x 40mm)

Red-dyed veneer 2in x ⅜in (50mm x 10mm)

⅛in (3mm) decorative inlay, as plan, 4ft (1.3m) long

³⁄₆₄in (1mm) black/white/black inlay, 5½in (135mm) long

½in (12mm) brass piano hinge 4¼in (105mm) long

10 screws to fit above, brass, countersunk

4 x ⅜in (9mm) brass pins or 3in (75mm) of ¹⁄₁₆in (1.6mm) brass rod

¹⁄₁₆in (1.6mm) birch plywood or similar, 6½in x 10in(160mm x 240mm) for templates

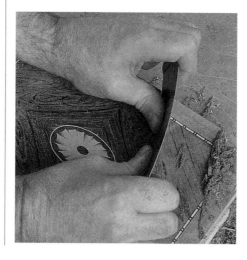

LEFT: A curved scraper being used to produce an excellent surface on this rectangular inlaid box.

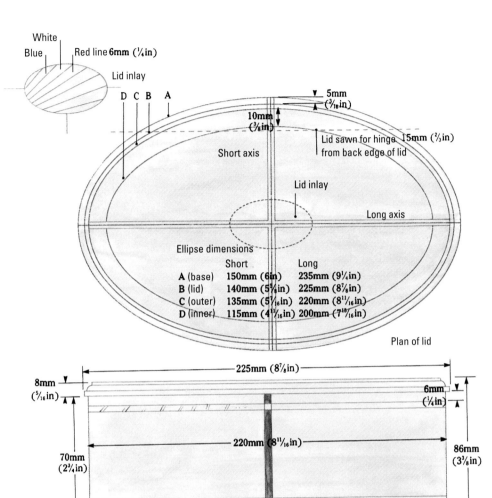

White
Blue
Red line **6mm** (¼in)
Lid inlay

D C B A

5mm
(³⁄₁₆in)

10mm
(³⁄₈in)

Short axis

Lid sawn for hinge 15mm (²⁄₃in)
from back edge of lid

Lid inlay

Long axis

Ellipse dimensions

	Short	Long
A (base)	150mm (6in)	235mm (9¼in)
B (lid)	140mm (5⅝in)	225mm (8⅞in)
C (outer)	135mm (5⁵⁄₁₆in)	220mm (8¹¹⁄₁₆in)
D (inner)	115mm (4¹¹⁄₁₆in)	200mm (7¹³⁄₁₆in)

Plan of lid

225mm (8⁷⁄₈in)

8mm
(⁵⁄₁₆in)

6mm
(¼in)

220mm (8¹¹⁄₁₆in)

70mm
(2¾in)

86mm
(3⅜in)

8mm
(⁵⁄₁₆in)

Side elevation

235mm (9¼in)

Drawing the plan

The template for this box can be made using an artists' elliptical template, an oval object, such as a mirror or dish, or made from scratch by drawing one-quarter of the ellipse using a French curve and then duplicating it for the other three segments.

Cutting list

SIDES (figured maple 1 off)
3in x 3in x 10in (75mm x 75mm x 250mm)

LID AND BASE (figured maple 4 off)
3³⁄₁₆in x ⁵⁄₁₆in x 10in (80mm x 8mm x 250mm)

LONG DIVIDER (birch plywood 1 off)
*2¾in x ⅛in x *8½in (*70mm x 3mm x *216mm)

SHORT DIVIDER (birch plywood 1 off)
*2¾in x ⅛in x *5¼in (*70mm x 3mm x *131mm)

Sides cut from 3in x 3in x 10in
(75mm x 75mm x 250mm) length

*Allowance for waste

1 First, prepare the wood for the lid and base. Joint the pieces for the base and lid, and plane and sand them even, marking the lines dividing the length and width as shown on the plan.

Making the templates

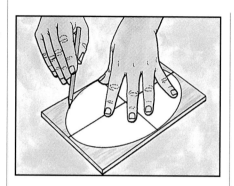

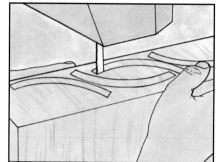

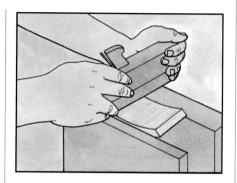

2 Make an oval template from ⅟₁₆in (1.5mm) birch plywood, clearly marking the long and short axes. Mark around this on the pieces for the base. Set a marking gauge to ³⁄₁₆in (5mm) and mark around the template, reducing it to this size. Mark around this onto the lid piece.

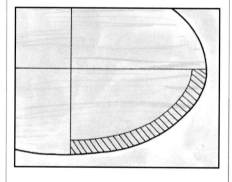

3 Set the marking gauge to ³⁄₃₂in (2.5mm). Mark around the template again and reduce it to this size. Set the marking gauge to ³⁄₈in (10mm) and mark around one quarter of the remaining template. Cut out this section. Remove ⅟₁₆in (2mm) from each end of this piece.

4 Mark out the four pieces for the "sides" or segments forming the body of the box, using the template, and cut them out on the band saw. This will be quite a deep cut for most small workshop band saws, so work slowly in order to give the blade plenty of time to clear the waste.

5 Smooth the inside faces of these pieces using a hollow plane, curved scraper, and sandpaper. Hollow planes may be difficult to achieve, but with patience you can achieve the same result with a carving gouge. Coat the inside faces with thinned sanding sealer.

Below: The four segments of the box, along with the top and bottom before shaping up. The side pieces are cut from a piece of figured maple. They are cut out with a band saw and smoothed to exact shape with a hollow plane. The lid and base are also made from figured maple. There are several ways of making the true oval shape needed for the top and bottom sections, but a French curve is probably the easiest for the novice to master.

Making the dividers

6 Veneer the pieces of ⅛in (3mm) birch plywood on both sides with the blue-dyed veneer. When they are dry, trim the pieces square to 8½in x 2¾in (218mm x 68m) or 5in x 2¾in (130mm x 68mm).

7 Lip each piece on one long and both short sides with strips of ebony ⅛in x ³⁄₁₆in (3mm x 5mm) cut from the prepared piece. When dry, plane these bandings flush and lightly sand, being careful not to get ebony dust on the blue veneer.

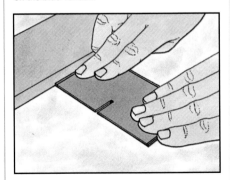

8 Cut ⁵⁄₃₂in (4mm) housing slots halfway along each of the pieces, one from the top (lipped edge) and one from the bottom. Make each slightly more than half the width. Seal and sand. Install with the ebony edge banding uppermost.

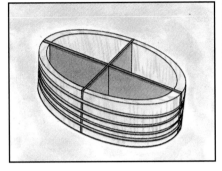

9 Sand the inside faces of the four side segments smooth and wax them. This is best to do now while they are easy to get at. Set up the pieces as shown in the plan and hold them together with strong rubber bands.

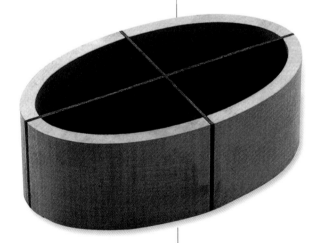

The assembled box with the dividers showing through the sides to give dramatic visual effect.

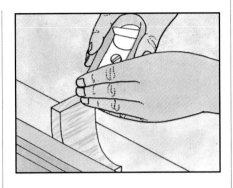

10 If the pieces have been accurately cut, the joints should fit snugly. Carefully plane anything that is not perfectly square. Then take apart and repeat the whole operation with glue. When dry, plane and sand the outer surfaces flat and even.

Installing the inlay

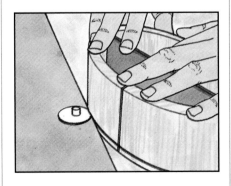

11 Cut a groove for the decorative inlay strips with a ⅛in (3mm) slot cutter as shown. Glue the strips in place, making sure they are the correct length. When dry, scrape flush, then sand and seal.

Shaping lid and base

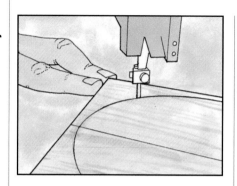

12 Carefully cut the lid and base to shape on the band saw and smooth them exactly to size. The disc sander is an excellent tool to use for doing this.

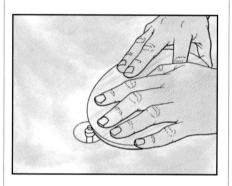

13 Form an ovolo around the top edge of the base and lid using a ⅛in (3mm) ovolo cutter with guide pin/bearing. Do this with at least three cuts, increasing the height of the bit each time. The final cut must remove only the smallest amount of material. This prevents scorching.

Tips box

Forming the decorative edge around the base and lid requires care, because the wood can easily be scorched or worked unevenly if the wood is not fed over the cutter at an even rate. Keep the wood moving all the time and press firmly down on the router table.

14 Make a template in ⅟₁₆in (1.5mm) birch plywood, 2in (50mm) long, tapering from ¼in (7mm) to ⅛in (3mm). Cut around this to produce four pieces each of blue and white veneer. Also cut seven strips of red veneer ⅟₁₆in (1mm) wide and 2in (50mm) long.

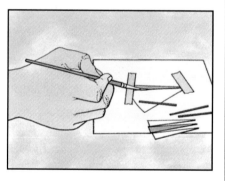

15 Tape waxed paper to a small, flat board and secure one tapered piece along one edge by taping its extreme ends. Brush a little 15 percent-diluted white glue along its edge, place a strip of red edge up next to it, brush on a little glue and repeat, taping each piece.

16 Cover with a piece of paper, some carpet underlay, and another small board, then clamp up. Repeat with the other tapered pieces and join the two halves in the same way. When dry, cut out your oval using the prepared brass template.

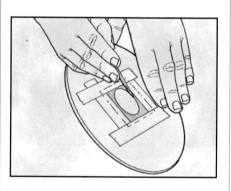

17 Tape the oval template to the lid, making sure you line up the long and short axes. Cut around the inside of the template with a craft knife, angling the blade slightly to produce a slightly smaller oval. Remove the wood in this area to a depth of ⅟₆₄in (0.5mm). This angled cut technique should make sure that the prepared black-and-white inlay will fit perfectly, once the oval motif has been fixed and scraped back to the required dimension.

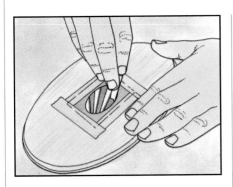

18 Glue the oval motif into this recess, sanding as necessary; it does not need to fit perfectly. When it is dry, tape the template in position again and work around the inside edge with the prepared scraper to produce a neat groove for the black/white/black inlay.

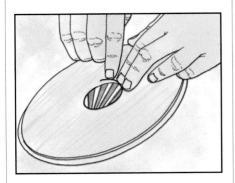

19 Dip the inlay in hot water for a few seconds to make it more flexible, and then secure it around a block the size of the required oval. When it is dry and has taken on the required shape, it can be glued into the groove. When dry, trim to length, glue, and scrape flush.

Tips box

Specialist wood suppliers or hardware stores stock lengths of piano hinge to use on the lid. This is usually sold in around 1 yard (1 meter) lengths, so keep the spare piece for possible future projects.

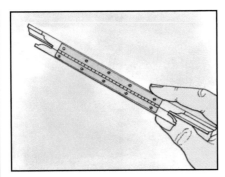

20 Using a band saw and fence cut the lid into two ⅗₈in (15mm) from the back edge by taping it to a board with its edge parallel to the lid's long axis. Prepare a piece of fine piano hinge and fit with an incomplete rebate on the back edge of the lid, half the thickness of the closed hinge.

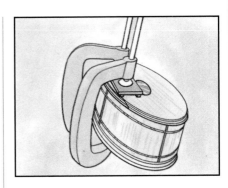

21 Smooth and wax all external surfaces, and glue and screw in the base. Glue the back edge of the lid. Pin using four ¾in (9mm) brass pins (cut off heads) or pieces of ⅟₁₆in (1.5mm) brass rod. Space rods to enter between the hinge screws.

22 The finished box—the ovolo molding on the lid and base—gives a pleasing decorative finish. The brass hinge line is almost lost in the similarly-colored maple lid. You can use the inside dividers to separate items of jewelry or sewing odds and ends.

Box gallery

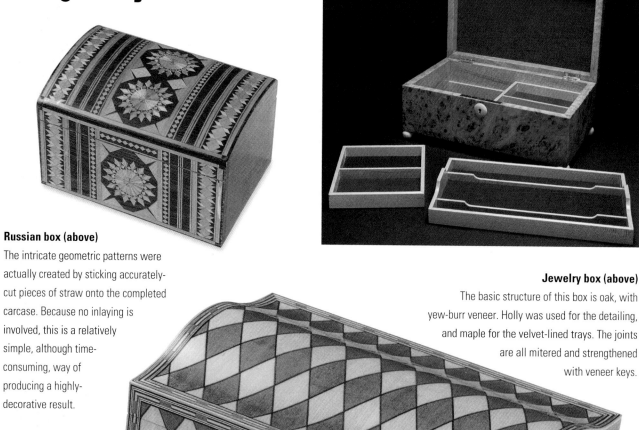

Russian box (above)

The intricate geometric patterns were actually created by sticking accurately-cut pieces of straw onto the completed carcase. Because no inlaying is involved, this is a relatively simple, although time-consuming, way of producing a highly-decorative result.

Jewelry box (above)

The basic structure of this box is oak, with yew-burr veneer. Holly was used for the detailing, and maple for the velvet-lined trays. The joints are all mitered and strengthened with veneer keys.

Card index box (below)

This sleekly-designed box is constructed from olive ash and has secret dovetails. The contrasting detail lines and inlays are in bog oak, and the lids are hinged with bog oak pegs .

Jewelry box (above)

The unusual shape of this jewelry box is emphasized by the geometric, parquetry-style decoration. The lid and front are bordered by a multi-colored, decorative line, made from dyed veneers. The lid opens to reveal a dark-green, silk-and-velvet-lined interior with two ebony trays.

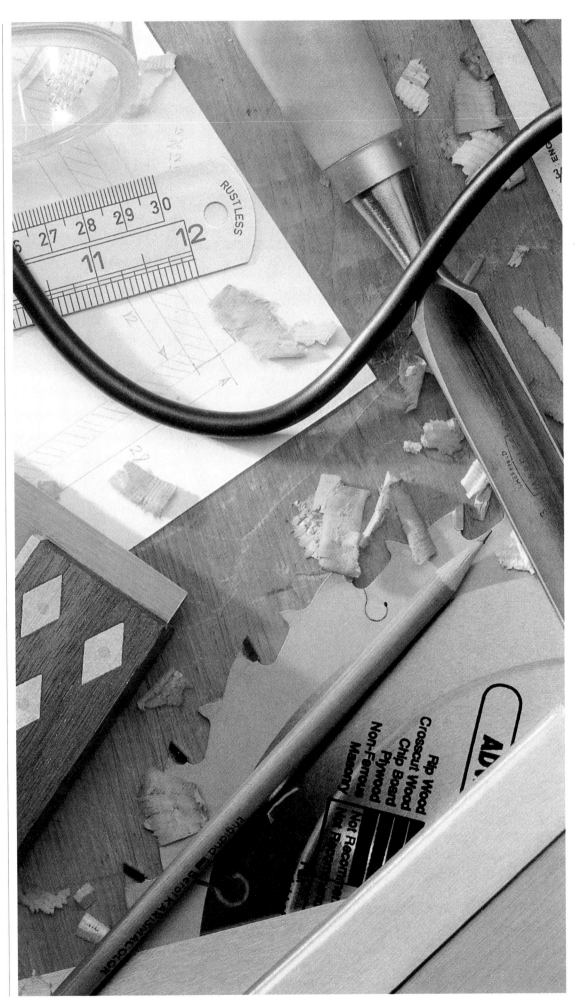

FURNITURE REPAIR

REPAIRING SOLID WOOD

Isolating weak points

Faults in furniture can be divided into two groups: structural and superficial. In pieces of furniture composed mainly of frames, such as chairs and tables, the most common faults include loose joints, broken legs, broken rails, damaged corners, and missing parts, such as decorative molding.

Chairs

Chairs suffer a greater variety of problems than any other piece of furniture, simply because they are open to more abuse—people stand on them and often tilt them onto their back legs.

The weak points are inevitably the joints that hold the legs to the seat— if these become loose, the chair will wobble. It is worth remembering that most traditionally-made chairs are held together by glue alone, and in most cases this glue is brittle and inflexible. In other words, if the glue cracks, there is little that can be done to help stability other than dismantling the chair and rebuilding it using fresh adhesive.

Arms and spindles on certain types of chairs are also vulnerable, and again the best way of curing weak joints is to strip them down, clean them up, and reassemble them. Luckily, the joints on most chairs are straightforward and are fairly easy to strip down.

Tables

Generally speaking, tables are more susceptible to superficial faults than to structural ones—the legs tend to get kicked and scratched and the top is liable to get things dropped or spilled on it.

Superficial repairs to tables can demand a great deal of skill and, especially, patience. Perhaps one of the most difficult and frustrating things to tackle is getting rid of heat rings made by hot pans being placed on the table.

Weak points to look for—chairs

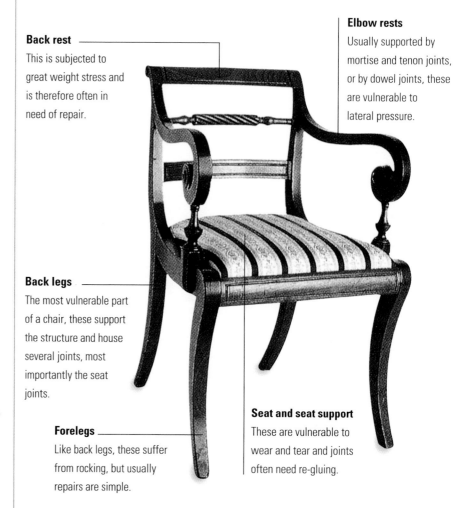

Back rest
This is subjected to great weight stress and is therefore often in need of repair.

Elbow rests
Usually supported by mortise and tenon joints, or by dowel joints, these are vulnerable to lateral pressure.

Back legs
The most vulnerable part of a chair, these support the structure and house several joints, most importantly the seat joints.

Forelegs
Like back legs, these suffer from rocking, but usually repairs are simple.

Seat and seat support
These are vulnerable to wear and tear and joints often need re-gluing.

There is a lot to be said for the old maxim "prevention is better than cure." Once you have restored a table, protect its surface—especially from hot pans and pots.

The joints found in tables can be surprisingly complicated—for example, mortise and tenon joints are often cross-dowelled for extra strength. If they come loose, these joints can be difficult to repair.

Chests and cabinets

A cabinet is essentially a box into which either drawers or doors are fitted. It is with cabinets that the skilled workmanship of the craftsman is most often to be found. The joints tend to be complicated and are therefore difficult to strip down. On the other hand, they are less likely to have come apart in the first place! Never take a cabinet apart completely unless it is absolutely necessary: it usually requires a certain amount of force to separate glued parts, and this can make matters worse, rather than better.

Cabinets and chests are often veneered and frequently have decorative moldings. Of all the repairs that you are likely to have to make on a cabinet, these are the most common. However, broken hinges and damaged drawer-runners are also frequently encountered.

Weak points to look for—tables

Surface
Susceptible to knocks and
spills—superficial repairs.

Splayed legs
These are always
vulnerable—cosmetic
repairs may be needed.

Top leg joints
These should be strong:
they become weakened
through use.

Delicate joints
Joints may succumb to
temperature changes and
become fragile.

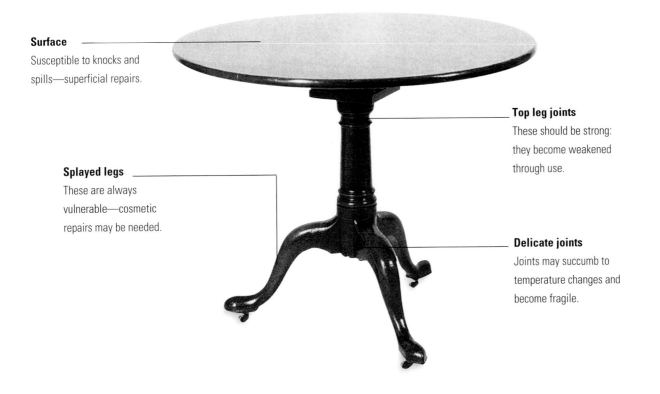

Weak points to look for—cabinets

Stains
These can be a problem
on work tables; subtle
remedies are called for.

Corner joints
These are often subjected
to strain and may need
strengthening.

Superficial
Scratches and dents
are often found.

Legs and supports
These are subject to
scuffing—cosmetic
treatment is required.

Tackling woodworm and rot

Woodworm and rot are the bane of many households. Although woodworm is found in many homes, thankfully it can be easily treated and the tell-tale holes covered up. Dry rot, however, is not so easily dealt with, and drastic measures are usually called for.

Woodworm

You are unlikely ever to see a living woodworm (or common furniture beetle), because these creatures are dull brown in color and only about ⅛in (3mm) long. The eggs are laid in summer in small cracks in the woodwork or in existing woodworm holes. The grubs hatch after six weeks or so and spend the next year or two eating their way through the wood. They then pupate, tunnel their way to the surface, and fly away as adults to start the cycle all over again.

Attacks are usually on the backs of furniture or under framing; pieces should be checked periodically for any sign of the fine dust that betrays worm activity. If you spot any symptoms of woodworm, take action immediately. Run a vacuum cleaner over the surface to remove dust from the holes, then inject each hole with woodworm-killer. Swab the surface liberally with the fluid, taking all the pre-cautions advised by the manufacturer.

If you detect woodworm in upholstered pieces of furniture, you may find that you have to remove the upholstery from the affected area before you can treat the infected wood.

Treating woodworm

1 Treat outbreaks of woodworm infestation with a proprietary woodworm fluid. Flood each hole separately, using the nozzle on the can as a guide. Aerosols are available for this. Always wear protective gloves for safety.

2 As a preventative measure, wipe the fluid over the rest of the piece of furniture—this will deter adult beetles from laying eggs in cracks or holes.

Preventing woodworm infestation and dry rot

There are several things you can do to prevent woodworm attacks.

- Treat any new wood additions, such as moldings or spindles, with a proprietary woodworm fluid before you fix them in place. Once the fluid has dried, the wood can be stained and polished in the usual way.

- If you do not want to paint a piece of furniture, you can buy special waxes that contain an insecticide. These polishes are an effective deterrent against woodworm but, to get the maximum benefit, you need to apply them regularly.

- Dry rot flourishes only in damp conditions, so if you are storing pieces of furniture, make sure the place is dry. Do not be tempted to wrap furniture up in plastic sheeting—this will cause the wood to sweat.

Dry rot

Dry rot is a fungus that breaks up wood into crumbling cubes. Contrary to its name, it thrives in damp conditions. It has a very distinctive fungal smell and can travel like wildfire through any other wood nearby. Furniture that is kept in a damp cellar can be contaminated.

Dry rot is not often found in free-standing furniture, but, when it does appear, it must be dealt with immediately. Affected wood must be cut out and burned. Sound wood should be treated with one of the proprietary preservatives recommended for the purpose. These chemicals are necessarily highly toxic and so great care should be taken when using them. Always read the instructions carefully and carry them out fully. If you are at all unsure about the correct use of these products, take the furniture to a specialist furniture restorer to treat the wood for you.

Cosmetic repairs to woodworm damage

1 Woodworm holes can be filled with an ordinary PVA adhesive. This can be easily applied using a syringe.

2 Inject the adhesive into the woodworm holes. Wipe off any excess with a damp rag, and then leave the glue to dry hard; this should take only an hour or two.

3 When the adhesive has set, rub stopping compound over the holes to disguise and camouflage them. Use a circular motion with the cloth pad to force the mixture deep into the holes so that it will not come out as you polish.

4 When the stopping compound has dried, polish the furniture to blend in the marks and seal the repaired area. If you want extra protection, use a special insecticidal polish. Inject all the visible holes, paying special attention to the underside of the piece, and leave in a well-ventilated area. Follow all the manufacturer's safety instructions.

BELOW: The existence of only a few worm holes in the surface does not mean that the damage is minimal—the inside may be badly affected. Replace seriously-damaged parts with new wood.

Superficial repairs: solid wood

Wooden furniture can be damaged in hundreds of different ways, but some are more common than others. Dents, splits, scratches, burns, and stains are possibly the most common superficial repairs. When dealing with such a repair, it is easy to think that just because it is superficial it will be easy to tackle. Unfortunately, this is seldom the case. Above all else, be prepared to take time making a superficial repair.

Splits

Very slight splits can be cleaned out and re-glued, but if the split is much more than a hairline crack, this treatment will not work—the pressure exerted by the wood will open up the wound again. If the split is wide, it should be filled with a sliver of shaped, matching wood. Use PVA adhesive—which is relatively flexible—when making such a repair. When you clamp up a split, be sure not to over-tighten the clamps—if you do, the pressure may cause one face to rise above the other.

Dents

The longer a dent has existed in a piece of wood, the harder it is to lift it. Dents in softwoods are the easiest to repair; large dents in hardwoods are the most difficult, and can even prove impossible. Dents caused physically—for example, by dropping something onto a table top —are tricky to deal with because fibers in the wood have been broken. A scar of some kind will almost always be left.

Dents caused by hot implements can usually be leveled. A hot pan placed on a table will cause moisture in the wood to evaporate. This will leave a dent, but the moisture can always be put back in again.

Steaming dents

1 Clean up around the dent before you start any treatment.

2 Place a droplet of water over the dent and allow it to settle.

3 Apply the tip of a soldering iron or a heated screwdriver to the bubble of water.

4 When the water has been absorbed and the dent levelled, apply wax.

Scratches

Shallow scratches and scuffs that penetrate the surface of the wood are best filled with wax. You can buy colored wax-sticks that can be matched to the color of the wood. Melt the wax into the scratch using a cigarette lighter or a match and scrape it level while the wax is still soft. Buff over the repair when the wax has set hard.

Deep scratches and nicks can also be filled with wax, but they should be tinted back to the surface color—that is, the color of the wood—before they are leveled. Wood stains that are guaranteed to be mixable with wax can be used to tint the wax itself—always follow the manufacturer's advice.

Burns

Burns can range from a light scorching to deep charring. Scorches can be removed by rubbing over the surface with fine (0000 gauge) steel wool and methanol. You can use a fine-grade nylon abrasive pad on oak so that no steel fibers enter the grain and stain the wood. Once you have done this, apply polish.

Deep charring has to be scraped out. The best weapon to use is a round-ended knife that is not too sharp. After scraping out the worst of the damage, smooth the dent down with fine abrasive paper. Fill the resulting depression with shellac. You can buy shellac in sticks (just like wax).

When you melt shellac into a dent, use a smokeless flame; smoke can discolor shellac. Polish the repair as soon as the shellac has set. You may need to use some fine-grade wet and dry abrasive paper to smooth the shellac surface.

Stains

Ring marks left by water or alcohol on the bottom of glasses can often be removed by buffing firmly with wax polish. If this does not work, try wiping over the mark with a cloth dampened with methanol: this often does the trick. If these methods fail, use a light abrasive. Cigarette ash mixed with linseed oil is almost always guaranteed to work. If even this fails, use a burnishing paste, such as the type used to refinish dull car paintwork, and gently work away until the stain disappears. Finish off with a polish that contains wax.

Certain stains, like ink stains, demand special treatment—bleaching. A table that has been well polished should be impenetrable to ink, but bare wood is always vulnerable.

Bleaching out stains

1 Apply diluted bleach to the end of a dowel or match stick curled with cotton balls.

2 Wearing protective gloves, dab the bleach over the stain in a circular motion.

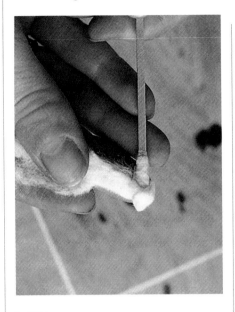

3 Give the bleach time to neutralize the stain, about half an hour is the minimum time you should allow, otherwise the bleach may not have time to react completely with the stain. Regularly check the area to see that it is doing its job and add more bleach if required.

4 Once the bleach has done its work, touch up the woodwork and finish with polish. The stain should be almost invisible, although you may still need to use some wood coloring to blend the batches in with the surrounding surface. Brush a little denatured alcohol over the area to see what the repair will look like when it is polished. The alcohol will soon evaporate so that you can continue with the finishing.

Chemical stripping

The removal of old finishes can be a laborious task, but it must be carried out properly if subsequent finishing is to be a success. It is essential to clean any evidence of previous decoration or protection from the grain, otherwise, it will show up later—and all the effort of stripping and finishing will have been wasted.

Using cabinet scrapers or sanders is an alternative to chemical stripping, but is much more time-consuming and unlikely to produce a better result. In addition, sanding or scraping removes the patina that certain woods—such as mahogany—acquire on aging. Sanding will also not remove the residue of finish from open-grained woods. It is often better to use a solvent paint remover.

Abrasives may also be used for stripping, but they can cut through the fibers of the wood, and there is always a chance of an uneven finish—with some areas sanded back more deeply than others. Another alternative is to take the piece to a stripping shop that has a caustic dipping tank. Unfortunately, caustic strippers often loosen joints in furniture and doors.

When doing the work yourself, the choice of stripper is determined by the workpiece and the original finish. It is, of course, easy to distinguish paint from wax, but other finishes are more difficult to identify. The best way to test a finish is to try a solvent on an inconspicuous part of the piece, for example, inside the rails on a chair.

Stripping old finishes

1 Always wear gloves, goggles, and protective clothing when working with chemical strippers. Be careful when opening cans of stripper—pressure can build up and force the liquid to spurt into your eyes.

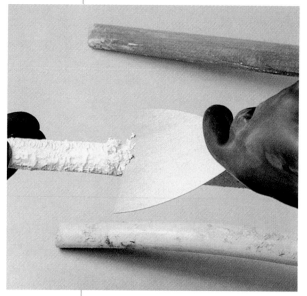

2 Test with a scraper to see if the finish has dissolved and is ready for scraping. Do not try to scrape the surface too soon—the job will be easier if you wait for the stripper to take effect fully. Use a paint scraper to remove the waste, working along the grain. The old finish is soaked in stripper, so roll it up in newspaper and make sure it is carefully discarded out of harm's way.

3 After cleaning the surface with a scraper, apply another coat of stripper, wait a few minutes and then rub off, using coarse steel wool (3 or 4 grade). Steel wool is very sharp, so use a pair of old scissors to cut it, and always wear protective gloves. Rub the remaining finish away.

Solvent strippers

Solvent strippers are supplied ready mixed. They contain methylene chloride—with some wax to stop them from evaporating—and are used to remove French polish, lacquer, oil and wax. To apply, simply lay the stripper on the surface, using a flat brush. Do not move the stripper around once it is positioned on the workpiece, as this is likely to speed up evaporation.

Leave the stripper to soak into the finish, keeping the surface wet. You will then be able to remove the finish with a paint or cabinet scraper. Always scrape in the direction of the grain (if the direction is not obvious, remove a small area of finish from an inconspicuous part

ABOVE: Stripping can reveal many problems formerly concealed under years of paint. Some of the joints may be loose, and the piece may need some filling.

to check which way the grain runs). It may be necessary to apply several coats of stripper before the bulk of the old coating is removed.

Unless a manufacturer specifically states that a product needs neutralizing, it is usually good enough to wipe the surface with a rag dipped in mineral spirits. This does not raise the grain. Be warned that solvent strippers in paste-form sometimes contain caustic soda, and will cause many woods to darken.

Fillers are used for filling larger indentations in wood, in much the same way as plaster fillers are used for repairing dents and cracks in plasterwork. The main difference is that fillers have to match the color of the piece, and require an elastic nature to cope with the movement of wood. It is best to avoid using fillers, if at all possible, because a good match is always difficult to achieve. However, for cracks, knots, and deep scratches, there is often no alternative.

Select the best filler for the situation. When choosing a filler, it is important to keep in mind the type of finish you intend to use on the piece. While shellac sticks are suitable for any finish, plastic wood (in either two-part or one-part form) is a difficult material to match. If you intend to use a stain to do so, make sure it is compatible. The instructions will say whether it is oil- or water-based.

As a general rule, use shellac sticks under traditional finishes, and two-part fillers under modern spray finishes. Only use wax fillers for small chips—and then only while polishing, or with a wax or oil finish. Plastic wood is most commonly used under varnishes. Although some fillers will take a stain once dry, a more successful technique is to mix pigment with the filler before applying.

Shellac sticks

Shellac sticks are sold in a variety of colors to suit a range of woods, and are a concentrated form of the shellac used for French polishing.

Plastic wood

This is a common filler, available from most hardware and paint stores. It comes in a can or tube, and is made in a range of colors. Plastic wood dries out quickly, so remember to replace the lid immediately after use.

Plastic wood does not always adhere effectively, so make sure any faults are clean and free from dust. Apply with a knife or chisel, pressing the filler well into the cavity. Plastic wood has a tendency to shrink, so leave it a little thick to dry. It may even be necessary to use more than one application; for large holes, fill gradually.

Tips box

A quick and cheap filler can be made by mixing glue with sawdust to match the workpiece. Mix PVA adhesive with the appropriate sawdust on a piece of cardboard. Add the sawdust to the glue, until it has a thick but workable consistency for large holes. Make sure the glue is thoroughly mixed in for a good bond.

Two-part fillers

Two-part fillers are harder versions of plastic wood. A catalyst or hardener reacts with the filler to create a very strong repair. They can be matched using stains and pigments. Achieving an exact match can be difficult, however, so they are better used for structural repairs (especially on particle board) than for filling conspicuous faults.

Wax sticks

Manufacturers of wax finishes also make sticks for small repairs. These are colored and designed for use either on surfaces to be waxed or on pieces already polished. Clear beeswax may be good enough in many circumstances, especially when the hole is small. However, wax must not be used under modern finishes. Use wax sticks like shellac sticks, warming the wax with a soldering iron. Push the wax into the holes or chips with a small filling knife, then scrape off any excess with a chisel or scraper once it has hardened.

Filling with wood filler

1 Hold a soldering iron just above the surface of the piece, and press the shellac stick against it so that it melts and drops into the fault like sealing wax. Build up the filler gradually.

2 Leave the filler to set for about five minutes. Once set, it may be necessary to level it with a small chisel. Do not try to take too much filler off at a time—it is brittle and likely to break up if too much pressure is applied.

Pigments

A selection of nine pigment colors should be enough to allow you to create most color matches.

3 Use coarse sandpaper for final leveling. On flat surfaces, sand with a sanding block, but on moldings, just fold some 100 garnet paper and delicately work with the corners. Do not over-sand, or you will create a hollow. When it is smooth, finish with fine sandpaper.

Short glossary of terms

Neutralize: To make chemically neutral (neither acidic nor alkaline).

Thinner: Solvent used to thin finishes.

Cut back: Rubbing a finish with fine, abrasive paper until the finish is flat and smooth.

Shellac: A resin secreted by the lac beetle which is only soluble in alcohol or an alkaline solution of water. When dissolved in alcohol, it is known as French polish.

Carnauba wax: Hard wax with a high melting point used for floor polishes. A mixture of beeswax and carnauba wax is used in turning.

Preparing wooden surfaces for polish

Stripping varnish and paint

Avoid taking an old piece of furniture to a firm that specializes in stripping. Such firms invariably dip entire pieces of furniture into caustic baths, a process that leaves the wood looking dead and lifeless. Stripping furniture yourself is time-consuming, but it is well worth the effort.

Chemical paint-strippers are readily available from hardware stores. Always treat them with respect: wear rubber gloves when handling them and use them only in a well-ventilated room. In addition to the stripper, you will need a scraper. For delicate or valuable furniture, do not use a steel scraper: it may gouge out chunks of wood. You would be better off using a homemade wooden or plastic scraper.

To lay the stripper on, use an old, but clean, paintbrush. To clean paint out of awkward corners, try using a sharpened dowel. Steel wool and turpentine are useful for cleaning the grain after stripping.

Turned pieces and moldings are best treated with stripping paste. This is spread thickly over the piece and can remove several layers of paint in one application. It is, however, expensive to use on large areas.

Stripping wax and polish

French polish can be removed with methanol and steel wool. The residue can be mopped up with paper towels.

Wax can usually be removed with turpentine and fine steel wool—as you get down to the wood surface, work with the grain.

Stripping varnish

1 Lay the workpiece on several layers of old newspaper and apply the chemical stripper with a paintbrush. Be sure to wear protective gloves.

2 Leave the stripper for 15 minutes or so to do its work. The varnish should start to blister and separate from the wood.

3 Scrape off the old finish and stripper with an improvized wooden tool. If necessary, apply more coats of stripper to get rid of all the old varnish.

4 Clean the grain of the stripped piece of wood with a pad of fine steel wool and neutralize the residue with turpentine.

Dismantling tables and chairs

Dismantling furniture is not something to take lightly. There is one golden rule that applies to both beginner and expert: do not dismantle a piece of valued furniture unless it is absolutely necessary. If you are left with no choice because the piece you are dealing with is a mess, but you see some future in it, examine it carefully before you start work. Above all, look out for nails and screws. These are often carefully hidden and disguised behind layers of varnish or polish—if you start dismantling and have overlooked a nail fixing, the workpiece may end up ruined beyond repair.

Dismantling a table

In many ways, dismantling a table is the most difficult of any task. This is largely because the bits and pieces are large and therefore difficult to handle.

Before you start, label each piece with tape, noting that "Piece A" joints onto "Piece B," etc. If you do not carry out this basic procedure, you will find yourself in chaos at the end of the day.

Once you have removed all the fixing devices, such as the nails and the screws, you may find that it is not easy to pry the various sections apart. Some pieces may be "fox-wedged," meaning that they were intended never to be taken apart. In such cases, you will have little option but to use a fine saw.

Try knocking the joints apart with a rubber mallet before you resort to more vicious tactics. Before hitting the piece of furniture with a mallet, protect the vulnerable wood with an off-cut of soft wood.

Dismantling a table

1 Before dismantling a table or any other piece of furniture, label all the corresponding parts.

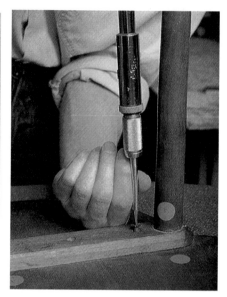

2 Carefully remove all visible nails and screws before you start dismembering the workpiece.

Using solvents

Some glues (or adhesives, as they are more correctly called) respond to solvents. In other words, if you apply an appropriate solvent, the glue may dissolve or melt, making it easier to separate a joint. Traditional glues are invariably animal-based, and so are soluble in water. If you stumble across an old joint that will not come apart, try applying water. If this does not work, try steam. Alternatively, use a wallpaper steam stripper directed over the joint. Be careful, and wear rubber gloves to protect your hands. Be sure not to wound the wood or melt the surrounding finish—let the wood dry for at least a day to allow the moisture to evaporate.

Modern glues are trickier than their traditional counterparts. Many change their initial character after they have set. However, acetone, turpentine, and methanol are all worth trying if you want to soften a stubborn adhesive. Sometimes you may be able to loosen a white PVA glue by soaking the joint in boiling water.

3 You may have to resort to the use of a mallet in order to separate pieces. If so, protect the piece from heavy blows by using an off-cut of wood.

Dismantling a chair

1 Rickety chairs are invariably weak at the front. Remove blocks so that the joints themselves can be approached.

2 Most loose joints will pull apart with a straight tug. If need be, place the chair on a bench and look for nails and screws.

3 Once you have separated a joint, clean up the parts. In this photograph, the dowels of the joint are being scraped with a chisel.

4 Once all the pieces have been freed from residue, glue, and dirt, they can be reglued and clamped together.

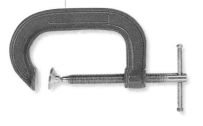

Dismantling a chair

Taking apart a chair is much like dismantling a table. One of the gentlest ways of separating pieces is to use a bar clamp in reverse; in other words, put the butts outward and turn the lever to push apart. If you use a bar clamp in this way, you may find that you have enough scope to insert the necessary blobs of glue to cure the defect. Clamp together with the bar clamp and leave overnight to dry. If you really want to go ahead and separate all the pieces, be sure to label them first. When separating pieces of furniture, the important thing to remember is the piece itself. It is much too easy to get carried away and strike a piece too hard. Use a soft-faced mallet or protect the frame with a piece of softwood scrap wood as you work. Look very carefully at the area around the joint, as chair joints have often been repaired at some time in the past with nails or screws. These may stop the joint from coming apart. Remove with pincers or by drilling if necessary. Always respect old furniture and how it was put together. If you are tackling an old piece, keep in mind that it may have been constructed traditionally. In other words, modern dismantling methods may not be appropriate.

Drawer repairs

Drawers suffer wear and damage over time simply because they are constantly being opened and closed. Loose joints are easily repaired by taking the drawer apart, cleaning out the old adhesive, and regluing the bits and pieces. As when repairing any other type of furniture, it is better to leave sound joints alone and to tackle only the weak ones. Most drawer fronts are held to the sides with dovetail joints, which can be hard to separate. If necessary, tap the sides away with a wooden mallet.

In old drawers, the bottom is generally made of thin boards glued together edge to edge. Sometimes these boards split, either because they cannot take a load or because they have shrunk. Replacing drawer bottoms is not always easy, because they are usually set into grooves in the sides. In other words, you will have to dismantle the whole drawer in order to fit a new bottom.

Drawer stops are often dislodged by the drawer being dragged over them. This is inevitable if the drawer runners have slipped or have become distorted. If a drawer is snagging on its stops, repair the damage as soon as possible— if the drawer is allowed to slide across the stops, its bottom may get broken and this will be difficult to put right.

Drawer knobs are sometimes easily pulled off. Whatever you do, do not resort to wrapping scrolls of newspaper around the shaft of the knob. This will most likely enlarge the hole and in the long run make the problem worse. A better solution is to refix the shaft in place with a gap-filling adhesive. If the hole is still too big, try adding a little sawdust to the adhesive and use it like a filler. If you lose a knob, you will be very lucky to find a matching replacement. One way around this problem of finding a match is to fit a handle so that the backplate covers the hole. If you decide on this method, fill the hole with standard doweling before you fix the handle in place.

Repairing a broken drawer

1 If the side of a drawer has been damaged, you will have to fit a replacement. First, dismantle the drawer and clean up the joints. Ease apart the drawer parts with the help of hot water or steam to melt the old animal glue. Be careful not to force the pieces apart until the glue has dissolved or the dovetail pins may break. Use a beveled-edge chisel to pare away any fragments of old glue and set aside.

2 Saw a new piece of wood to the correct width and mark the positions of the joints by holding it against the drawer front. Use a sharp pencil or, better yet, a marking knife to transfer the dimensions of the original drawer piece on to the new wood. You may need to clamp the two pieces together to keep the pieces aligned as you mark the wood.

3 Mark the dovetail shapes onto the new side panel and start cutting them out. The best tool to use for this is a coping saw. Always saw just to the inside of the marked line – the final shaping and paring is done with a bevelled-edged chisel afterwards.

4 Shape the joint housings with a sharp chisel. You should be able to do this by hand; i.e. without resorting to a mallet.

5 You may have to narrow the depth of the joints. Do this using a tenon saw, with the workpiece gripped in a vise.

6 Cut out the waste wood, again using a tenon saw. Be careful not to overdo the sawing.

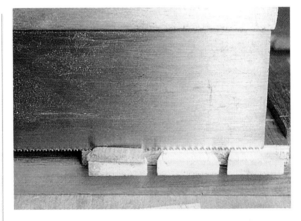

Curing drawers that stick

Drawers usually stick because the runners have become loose or weak. Remove the drawer and check the state of the runners. If they have sagged, refix them firmly in place. Drawers sometimes stick because they were badly made in the first place and the runners are too shallow. In such cases, remove the runners and replace them with new ones.

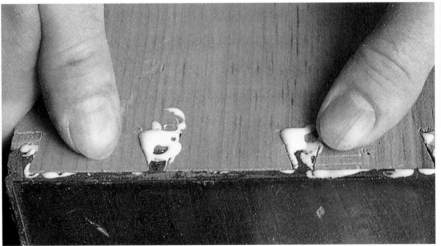

7 When you are satisfied with the shapes of the cut-outs, reassemble the drawer, using PVA adhesive.

Restoring corners/frame repairs

Frames serve a very practical role in furniture because they hold panels in place. They usually have strong mortise and tenon joints to hold them together. The joints have to be strong in order to take the strain if the wood warps. However, in old pieces of furniture, these joints sometimes separate because they can no longer withstand the pressure. Repairing frame joints is simple, in theory, but, in practice, the clamping can be difficult.

It is also quite common for the tenon in a frame joint to break, especially if the frame receives a certain amount of wear and tear. If the tenon snaps, you will have little option but to fit a fake one.

Corners on chairs, tables, and chests are very vulnerable to bumps and grazes. Repairing a broken or damaged corner on an old piece of furniture is a difficult task, and represents one of the areas where the restorer's skill has to match the cabinetmaker's. To make a decent repair to a corner, you will have to buy a wood that matches the piece of furniture. When you buy the wood, make sure that it is seasoned, and obviously do your best to match color and quality.

Repairing a broken frame

1 A broken tenon is a common reason for a frame failing.

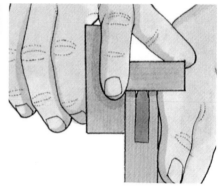

2 Before cutting a fake tenon, measure the width of the mortise.

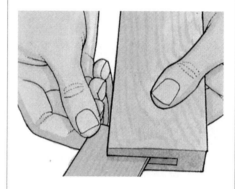

3 Cut a slot in the end of the rail and glue in a matching piece of wood to create a fake tenon.

4 Reassemble the joint, using PVA adhesive. Clamp the joint until it sets.

Repairing a damaged corner

Plane down the damaged corner so that you end up with two flat faces. Check that the planed faces are perfectly flat and even.

1 Lay a matching section of wood over the repair and mark around it. Plane one edge of the new section flat and stick it in place.

2 When the glue has set, cut off the excess wood with a tenon saw.

Repairs to panels

Panels in old furniture are usually made up of a series of boards joined together. In tabletops and the large, flat components of articles of cabinet furniture, such as sideboards and dressers, the boards are usually thick enough to allow for a joint of some kind. Feathered joints and tongue-and-groove joints are the ones most commonly used. A feather is a thin strip of wood that fits into grooves cut into the edges of the boards.

Thin panels, such as those found in cabinet doors and the bottoms of drawers, are usually simply butted and glued together.

Panels of all kinds are particularly vulnerable to climatic changes. They are likely to warp or even split. Heating systems are especially bad for furniture.

A split along a joint in a panel should be comparatively easy to repair, but of course you will have to remove the panel from its frame. Some panels may be held in place by strips of beading. Gently lever off the beading in order to remove the panel. After removing the panel, clean up the joint as much as possible, insert more glue, and then clamp the assembly together. Bar clamps are frequently the best option, but be sure to protect the wood from the jaws. The easiest way of doing this is to insert off-cuts of wood.

If a split does not run along a joint, the remedy is not quite so simple. You will need to insert a dowel to strengthen the join.

Making dowel inserts

If you want to use a dowel in the repair of a split panel, you will be unlikely to find ready-made doweling that matches the wood. Do not worry! Making your own dowels is straight-forward. Of course, you will have to obtain a piece of wood that matches the color and quality of the panel, but this should not be too difficult, because many suppliers have off-cuts of exotic lumber.

1 Drill a hole of the appropriate diameter through a stout piece of metal. Then hammer your sliver of wood through the hole. This seemingly crude method in fact produces perfectly-rounded dowels.

2 Scribe two lines down the side of the dowel using the pin on a marking gauge. These grooves will allow excess adhesive to escape when you use the dowel in the repair.

3 Drill into the edge of the panel through a protective off-cut of wood—the hole should go straight down the middle of the crack. Use the tape on the drill bit as a depth guide.

4 Smear PVA adhesive over the dowel before tapping it into the hole. Excess adhesive should ooze out via the grooves in the dowel.

5 When the adhesive has set, level the end of the dowel flush with the edge of the panel, using a sharp chisel.

Repairing broken chair legs

Of all the articles of furniture, chairs suffer from the most abuse. It is hardly surprising, therefore, that they are often in need of repairing. Back legs of chairs often break at the point where the seat rails join them. Luckily, such breaks are simple to repair. However, if the seat rails break, the chair may have to be dismantled, the damaged section cut out, and a new piece spliced in. This is tricky and requires some skill, because new joints may have to be cut.

Repairs to back legs

Most breaks in back legs occur because the chair has been tilted backward by its occupant. This places undue strain on the wood, which invariably splits along the grain. These breaks are easy to repair because the pieces can simply be glued back together again.

The type of adhesive you use is very important. PVA adhesive is probably your best option, because it is both strong and cheap. However, if the chair is to be sited in a damp room—such as a bathroom or kitchen—consider using a waterproof adhesive instead.

Much of the skill involved in repairing a broken leg lies in the clamping—sometimes special blocks have to be made to ensure an even pressure all around. It is important to clamp from the sides, as well as front to back, so that the joints stay in alignment. Always go through a dry run of the assembly first to avoid messy problems later.

Repairs to front legs

Front legs of chairs usually break immediately below the seat rail joint. Such breaks can be repaired using a sturdy dowel, but this may mean dismantling the chair to some extent. If you have to insert a dowel to link the two broken pieces together, the hardest part of the job is aligning the holes; you will probably have to make a special jig.

Repairing a wobbly joint

1 Dismantle the joint and scrape off old adhesive with a sharp chisel.

2 Cut down the length of tenon. This is a tricky operation, so take your time.

Repairing a split back leg

1 Splits follow the grain of the wood and are comparatively easy to repair. Cut a shallow wedge from an off-cut of wood and insert it into the spilt to open it up.

2 Using a knife blade or a fine piece of plastic, smear PVA adhesive into the split.

3 Wipe off excess adhesive with a damp rag and clamp the pieces together. If necessary, shape a block of wood to the profile of the leg so that the pressure is spread evenly.

3 Cut a fine wedge from a suitable off-cut of wood.

4 Smear PVA adhesive over the wedge and force it into the cut in the tenon.

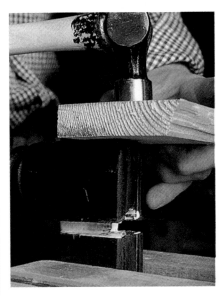

5 Reassemble the joint after spreading glue over the mating parts.

Replacing skirtings and rails

Skirtings are often missing from chests, and there is seldom any indication of the height or style of the original. Unfortunately, there is no way of knowing what the missing part looked like. In such cases, all you can do is try to match the type and color of the wood and to make an educated guess by studying pieces of a similar age and design.

The front corners of skirtings are usually mitered, whereas the back ones tend to be simply butted together. This is because most pieces of furniture that carry skirtings are designed to be pushed up against a wall.

Many skirtings are shaped along the bottom. If you want to fit a new, shaped skirting, have a look at a few designs before you start cutting out any wood. To shape the wood, use a jigsaw or a coping saw. Skirtings are sometimes nailed or screwed in place, but, thanks to modern adhesives, this is no longer really necessary.

Replacing missing rails

A missing or broken rail is not easy to replace, and you need several skills to make an effective repair. The problem is made more difficult if the replacement has to be curved. If you have a piece of furniture that has some antique value, always consult a professional as new sections of wood or repair work may devalue the piece. Some curved parts can be steamed into shape, but this is a highly technical procedure demanding special equipment: steaming and bending wood is usually beyond the scope of the amateur woodworker. Even the method illustrated here requires a certain amount of experience and skill. Only tackle repair jobs that you feel confident of completing.

Making a curved armrest

1 Clamp the piece of wood you want to shape to the sound arm and draw out the profile. Here, a new wood blank has been band sawed to the approximate overall size and clamped firmly to the arm rest ready for the transferred shape markings.

Hiding gaps in skirting

You may find that when you fit a new skirting in place there are gaps left along the top. One simple and very effective way of overcoming this is to fix lengths of molding along the top. Stain the molding to match the color of the wood before you add varnish or polish.

Hardware stores and wood merchants usually stock a large range of small molding profiles in lengths up to about 6 feet (2 meters) which you can use as a covering strip.

2 Use a bow saw to cut out the shape. Always keep to the waste side of the cutting line. You may be able to speed up the cutting by using a band saw or even an electric jigsaw, but make sure the blade does not deflect and cut through the line on the reverse side of the wood. Offer the roughly-shaped arm up to the chair, and mark off the size and position of the back joint.

3 Cut the back joint to fit, then pencil in the positions of the other joints.

4 Use an auger bit of the appropriate diameter to drill out the holes. Be careful not to drill too far, or the auger point will penetrate the back of the wood. Use a piece of tape around the bit to show the exact drilling depth you require.

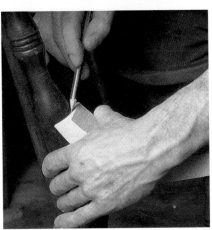

5 Position the arm on the chair once again and scribe out the profile.

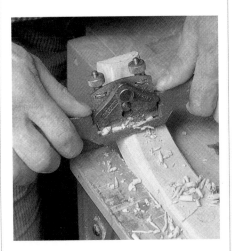

6 Shape the arm using a spokeshave. Check frequently that you are carving the right shape.

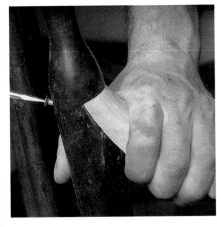

7 Screw the arm in place from behind. Add glue to the join for extra strength.

8 The finished repair. All that has to be done now is to stain and polish the arm. However, before final finishing, you may wish to lightly distress the new part to blend in with the original woodwork. Use a nail and small hammer to add light scratches and small dents to the upper surface and the armrest sides—concentrate on areas that would normally be exposed to wear and tear.

Restoring a dresser

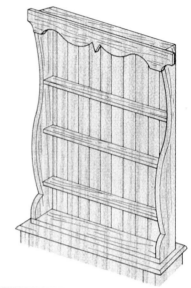

It may seem surprising, but you often come across large pieces of furniture that have pieces missing, like in the example illustrated here, where the top of a dresser has disappeared. In order to restore the dresser to its original design, a new top has to be built. Obviously, a job of this size is no small undertaking—but it is immensely satisfying in the long run.

Before you embark on a large restoration job, it is well worth doing some basic research to determine the shape, design, and size of the piece you intend to build. You could visit a library, but a few visits to some furniture shops would be equally rewarding.

Smaller replacement jobs, like making a new chair seat, can often be made satisfactorily using bits and pieces taken from old furniture that is beyond repair. The advantage of doing this is that you can be certain that the wood will be well

seasoned. Of course, it may not be easy to match grain, color, and texture perfectly, but this is something you have to live with.

Building or rebuilding substantial pieces of furniture takes time, and it also often needs extra equipment and space. It is also useful to have a friend to help you work and position the pieces accurately.

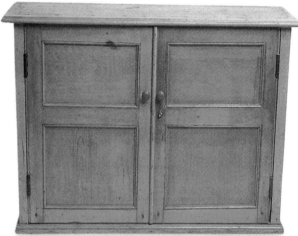

Making a new top for a dresser

1 Use new pine wood for a job of this kind. Plane down the edges of the side panels first (right). This would be the perfect opportunity to make use of reclaimed pine to match the base. You don't have to find broken pieces of furniture to salvage the lumber —reclaimed floor boards or even tongue and groove wall panels can all be cleaned up and re-sawed to the size you need. Make sure that there are no nails, or screws, buried in the wood, before cutting or planing.

2 Cut out the waste wood from the rebates with a sharp chisel. Use a wide bladed beveled-edge chisel to pare away the waste wood from the bottom of the rebate. Be careful not to cut too deeply or the corner joint will be weakened (left).

3 For cutting long rebates, like those in the side panels, use an electric router. An electric jigsaw makes light work of cutting out shapes.

4 Having shaped one side panel, use it as a template for marking the other.

BELOW: The base cupboard was all that was left of the dresser, but it provided enough clues for a designer to draw up plans for a suitable top section.

5 Before tightening the clamps, check that the frame is square by measuring the diagonals.

6 Use oval nails to consolidate the joints—these nails are less likely to split the wood (left).

7 The finished dresser mounted on top of its cupboard (right).

REPAIRING VENEERS

Re-laying whole pieces of veneer is simple when compared to laying patches in the middle of a piece of furniture. For a start, the cutting has to be accurate, and it is also important that the colors and types of veneers match up perfectly. Obviously enough, small patches can be disguised, but large repairs cannot. The greatest test of a furniture restorer's ability is whether he or she can match large pieces of veneer, not just for color and texture, but also for level and tightness of bond.

It may seem obvious enough to most people, but many of us forget the importance of matching veneers. To many, mahogany automatically matches mahogany, but this is in fact rarely true. To continue with mahogany as an example, there are many species of this particular tree—some grow in Africa, others in South America. Most old mahogany furniture was created from the African species, but most modern mahogany comes from South America. It is hardly surprising, therefore, that the two species do not necessarily match up when they are paired.

The moral of all this is: check the color, quality, and thickness of a veneer before you start placing it on a valued piece of furniture. And always remember to align the grain before you stick it into place.

Replacing veneer

When you buy sheets of veneer you will probably be surprised, and possibly disappointed, that they are not flat, shiny, complete pieces of wood. Far from it—you will most probably receive something resembling an over-grown potato chip.

To flatten a potato-chip veneer, brush it over with warm water and "squeeze" it between two sheets of damp, warm plywood (use clamps to hold the sheets of plywood together). Leave the veneer overnight and it should be flat by the morning.

Once flattened, veneer should be used as quickly as possible—otherwise it will return to its original shape. If a sheet of veneer starts to resemble a potato chip once more, treat it again with the method described above.

If you try to cut untreated veneer it will almost certainly shatter—do not forget that it is not only thin but also extremely brittle.

Modern veneering methods

1 Prepare the surface thoroughly before laying the veneer. Use abrasive paper to get rid of lumps and bumps.

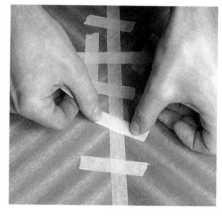

2 If you are laying several sheets of veneer, or plan a mosaic effect, tape the sheets together (masking tape is best) before laying.

3 Spread adhesive over the surface and roll it into an even coating. Wipe away any excess adhesive. This thin layer of glue will begin to dry quickly, so have all the components and veneers at hand and work quickly to achieve a good bond.

4 Use a soft roller to get the pieces flat. If you do not have a roller, a cloth will do. Start in the middle and work out. Here, the matched veneers are tightly butted together with no signs of air bubbles or chipping along the joint edges.

Insetting a small veneer

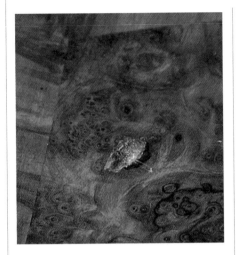

1 Mark out the area of a damaged veneer, preferably with a piece of chalk.

2 Cut out the damaged piece with a sharp chisel or knife.

3 Lift the damaged veneer with a chisel or knife blade.

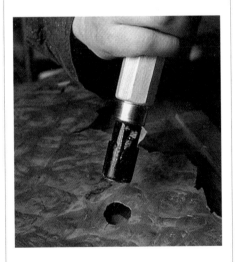

4 Make a template of the cut-out and transfer this to the new veneer.

When you cut veneer, always use a sharp knife. A handyman's knife is a good option, but a craft knife is even better. You can buy craft knives and packets of replaceable blades from most art stores.

When cutting sheets of veneer, be sure that you do so on a flat, yet receptive, surface. The kitchen table is often ideal . . . but this is not usually a good idea!

5 Prepare the surface with animal glue, filling up any dents or holes.

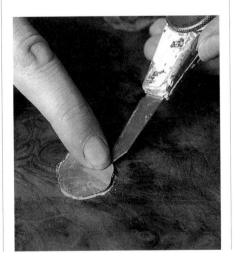

6 Firm the new section in place, squeezing out glue as you go. Wipe off any excess glue and leave to dry. The new insert can now be gently sanded to be perfectly flush with the surrounding wood. Seal and polish to complete the repair.

Buying specialist tools

Although it is possible to make your own inlay tools—a scratchstock, for example—they can also be bought. Your best bet is to hunt around in the specialist press for ads. If you reply to an advertisement, be sure to log the name of the paper or magazine it appeared in —all too often, people get disappointed because an apparently reputable company that advertized has subsequently gone out of business.

Restoring decorative veneers

"Marquetry," "parquetry," "lines," "inlays" and "strings"—all of these are semi-technical words that refer to decorative veneers (see Glossary pages 505-6). Of course, the sophisticated professional knows these terms off pat: these techniques are found only in high-quality work. To the veneering craftsman they can be the dream, the ultimate test of craft. So if you are considering repairing such work, do not go into it half-heartedly.

If you want to replace an entire design, either because you do not like it (hesitate before you act!), or because it has been damaged out of all recognition, you may be able to find "standard works" to fit. These are obtainable from certain suppliers and organizations, which often advertize in the specialized press.

If you want to create or repair from scratch, respect the woods you deal with.

Matching shapes

Presented with a panel that is partly damaged, first consider its construction. Some panels are made up of strings that form outlines and details; other panels contain whole sections of colored wood that build up a mosaic. Needless to say, it is easier to replace a section of whole wood than it is to cut minuscule sections to fit.

If you have a piece of inlaid work that has "risen," first determine the extent of the damage—it may go beyond the obvious—and, second, consider its shape and color. In nearly every case, you will find an appropriate string or edge at which the damage ends—this perimeter should form the edge of your repairs. Lift up the damaged pieces (using hot water to melt the adhesive, if necessary). Make a template of the damaged area; anchored tracing paper and a soft-leaded pencil are your best options.

Setting a string

1 Set your scratchstock (essentially a scraping tool with a guiding edge) to the appropriate depth for the string.

2 If you are laying a new string, choose the correct width of scratchstock tool. Also, calculate the length of string required for the job.

3 Use the grinding edge to ensure that the groove is parallel to the edge of the job. Apply the adhesive with a dowel or off-cut of wood.

4 Position the string in the groove and smooth it down with a hard, flat tool.

Using stringing

Strings are essentially narrow inlays set into solid wood. You can easily buy decorative strings that have designs stained into them, and you can also get plain strings. Of course, the ultimate option is to make your own strings, in which case you should consider the type of wood (beech is a common option because it is relatively pliable), the thickness of the string (too thin and it becomes brittle; too thick and it becomes unwieldy), and the color of the wood. If you are replacing a complete string, you have a wide choice of designs and colors; if you have to match a string, then you must be careful.

Laying motifs

Laying motifs—or, re-laying motifs if you are truly restoring—can cause problems. Motifs are often special—not necessarily

Cutting a template and laying a motif

1 Cut out a paper template of the damaged area and use it to shape the veneer. Tape down the veneer before cutting it.

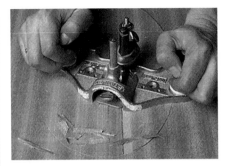

2 If you are cutting a new veneer, use a router to form the base. If you are restoring, clean with abrasive paper.

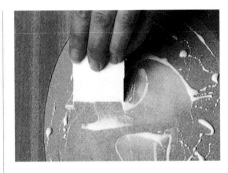

3 Paste adhesive onto the back of the new inlay. Use a sawtooth spreader to get even coverage and so avoid awkward lumps.

4 Set the inlay in place, smooth it down, and tape it securely.

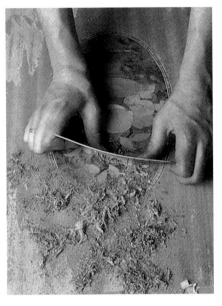

5 The finished inlay should lie flush with the surface of the base. Use a curved metal scraper to take off most of the excess veneer.

6 Finish with fine abrasive and then polish.

---

to you, but most probably to the person who laid them or to the person who commissioned them in the first place. For this reason, motifs of any kind should be respected. It is true that many motifs that have been perceived to be truly ugly have wound up in auction rooms, only to get a great deal of cash. As far as restoration is concerned, motifs should be treated in much the same way as any other inlay

repair—but adhere to the original design if possible.

Metal inlays

Metal inlays have a tendency to spring out of their grooves because the wood surrounding them expands and they cannot. If you find an inlay that has sprung, first remove it from the piece of furniture, probably using a screwdriver. Next, attempt to straighten it

(easier said than done—go gently!). Once you have straightened the piece, check how much waste there is—do this with precision, preferably from direct measurement. File down the bad parts of the metal and resort to a saw only in extreme cases.

While repairs to these types of inlay can be attempted by the amateur, it is a specialized process that is best left to experienced professionals.

Superficial repairs: veneered work

Veneering is the art of gluing thin sheets of expensive, and possibly exotic, wood, onto a base of cheaper wood or, alternatively, a manmade board. Because veneers are thin and glued, they are vulnerable to damage.

Blistered veneer

Blisters can appear on veneer for several reasons. It may be that the fixing glue has weakened over the years, with the consequence that the wood has risen up; or it may be that a hot object has been placed on the veneer, thereby causing the base glue to melt and so giving the veneer freedom to move. However, the most likely cause is that the veneer and the basework have contracted in different ways, making the veneer—the thinnest of skins—warp, buckle, and blister.

Curing blistered veneer is surprisingly basic in principle—all you have to do is smooth the skin and introduce an adhesive strong enough to hold it down.

Cracked and dented veneer

Dents in veneer can be treated in much the same way as similar wounds to solid wood—that is, they can be steamed. However, if you steam veneer, you always run the risk of melting the glue beneath, and this can cause more problems.

A crack along a veneered surface can be reduced by heating it with an iron to soften the glue beneath. Once the glue has been softened, the veneer itself can be stretched to bridge the gap. The best tool for this is a special veneering hammer.

Patching veneered corners

Veneer is easily broken at corners, especially on drawer fronts. Almost always, a jagged edge is left behind. The only satisfactory way to tackle this type of problem is to shape a new piece of

Dealing with blistered veneer

1 Blisters on old veneer can often be suppressed by applying heat from an iron.

2 Modify a syringe in order to insert PVA adhesive. Airholes are essential.

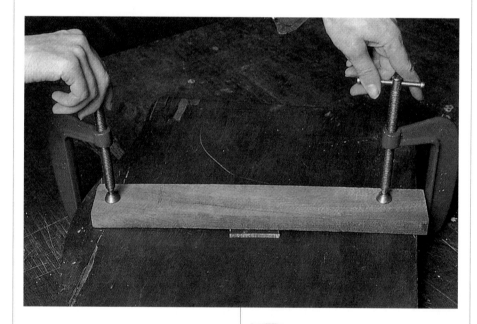

veneer to fit. Trace an outline of the damaged piece onto a sheet of paper. Transfer this shape onto a sheet of matching veneer, cut it out, and glue it into place.

One thing to remember is that the surfaces of the basework and veneer should both be completely clean and free from dust.

3 Hold down the blister with an arrangement of clamps, making sure to protect the wood from the clamp edges with pieces of wood. If necessary, straddle distances with battens. This will allow you to exert firm pressure on exactly the right spot to force the blister back into the surface. Use newspaper to stop excess glue from sticking the wood block to the veneer blister.

Stripping old veneer

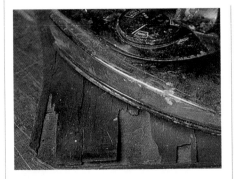

1 In severe cases, damaged veneer cannot be restored and has to be stripped off. Use an iron to soften old animal glue. A little water on the surface sometimes helps.

2 As the glue softens, slide a palette knife or chisel blade underneath the veneer.

3 Strip off the old veneer and carefully clean up the residue of old glue with hot water.

Laying new veneer

1 Stretch out the new piece of veneer and tape it down flat.

2 Make a template of the area to be covered and transfer this to the sheet of veneer.

3 Brush a coat of thin animal glue over the surface of the panel.

4 Lay the sheet of prepared veneer over the panel and smooth it out with an iron.

5 Use a veneer hammer (or other soft hammer) to beat the veneer smooth. Start in the center of the repair and work toward the edges to get rid of excess adhesive.

Laminating

1 Some curved parts can be made by gluing up plywood under pressure. Spread PVA adhesive evenly over the sheets that are to be stuck together.

2 Use a collection of clamps to make the curve. Be aware that the plywood will spring open slightly when it is released. Use a clamp at each end of the curved piece of plywood and at least one central clamp to hold the curve across the center of the block formers. Apply equal pressure at each end of the jig and leave overnight for the adhesive to set fully.

3 Bend the plywood over small blocks of wood. The size and position of the blocks will determine the radius of the curve. You may need to shape the tops of the blocks for more extreme curves to stop the blocks from moving. Slip pieces of newspaper between the blocks and the curved plywood to stop excess glue from fixing the parts together. When dry, release the clamps and clean up the edges of the curved piece with a plane before sanding.

Repairs to chipboard

Chipboard is not a particularly strong material and it can suffer severely from superficial damage. Because it is so easy to scratch, dent and break, chipboard is often covered with a veneer or laminate of some kind. Plastic laminates are tough and are usually stuck to the surface with contact adhesive. If a laminate lifts from the surface of the chipboard, it can usually be stuck back down again, provided that both surfaces are dry and clean.

Melamine is a common facing for chipboard. It is paper impregnated with a synthetic resin and is not very durable. If a sheet of melamine-faced chipboard gets severely damaged, it is often cheaper and quicker to replace it with a new sheet.

Repairs to chipboard are difficult and rarely invisible; large areas of damage are best resolved with the complete replacement of the damaged areas.

Superficial repairs to a chipboard sheet

The easiest way to repair a dent or hole in a sheet of chipboard is to use a filler. Use a two-part epoxy filler, which is both strong and durable. Clean up the dent or hole as much as possible and make sure that it is dry and free from grease.

Alternatively, you may be able to recover the whole area with an adhesive-backed vinyl covering. Clean the surface with a cloth moistened with a little mineral spirit to remove any dirt or grease from the chipboard facing material. Spread the vinyl covering over the old facing and smooth down before trimming to size.

Superficial repairs using epoxy filler

1 Mix up the two parts of the filler on an off-cut. Mix the filler in the quantities recommended by the manufacturer. The filler should take on a uniform color with no streaks. Take care to mix the resin and the hardener solutions thoroughly or the filler may not set properly. Use an old knife or piece of scrap dowel.

2 Spread the filler over the damaged area, using a flexible knife. This should be pliable enough to force the filler to the bottom of the repair so that it will be firmly fixed. When the filler is hard, sand it smooth and tint it with paint to match the chipboard finish.

Touching up scratches

- Scratches on veneered chipboard can usually be hidden by applying wax polish. Even tiny scratches may have picked up some dirt, so you should use warm water and detergent to clean over the scratched area. Leave the surface to dry.

- If wax fails, try rubbing a stick of pure beeswax over the area; this will fill the scratches, and make them barely visible.

Repairing a damaged edge

1   The edges of chipboard are notoriously vulnerable. The best remedy for a damaged edge is to cut out the damaged area and insert a new piece.

2   Mark out the piece you want to remove and drill access holes at the corners. Cut out the section with a tenon saw or an electric jigsaw.

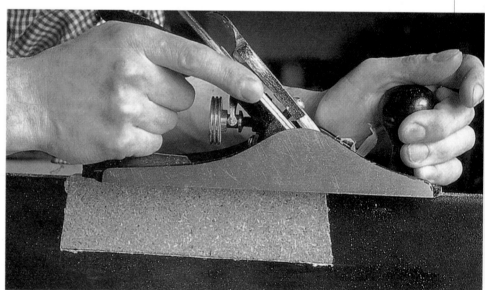

3   Cut a new section to fit, and glue it in place with PVA adhesive. To match up the surfaces, lay a flat block of wood over the repair and tap sharply with a hammer.

4   When the adhesive has set, chamfer the edges of the repair with a plane. To complete the repair, either lay on a sheet of laminate, or stain the insert.

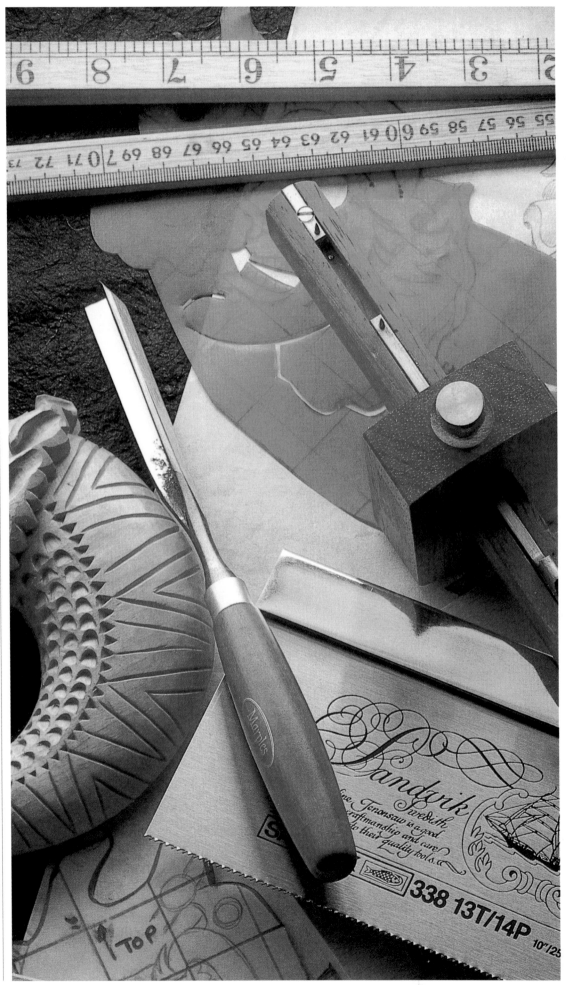

CORRECTING MISTAKES

Marking and laying out

Just about every woodworker you are likely to meet will, sooner or later, come up with the musty old woodworking adage "measure twice and cut once." It gets old hearing the same piece of workshop folklore repeated over and over, but, then again, it is absolutely right. The fact of the matter is that a huge number of mistakes can be avoided or remedied at the measuring and marking-out stage, before you even get down to cutting the wood.

Avoiding confusion

Because many mistakes have to do with mixing up the various faces of the wood, it follows that it is a good idea to identify the various parts with pencil marks. The method shown here—with marks and numbers—not only identifies the face side and face edge of a small panel, it shows the order of edge planing. The idea is that if you start by taking off the back edge corners with a chisel, and then plane the edges in the numbered sequence, you will avoid corner splitting.

Having achieved and identified the face edge, chisel off the back corners and then plane the edges in the numbered sequence.

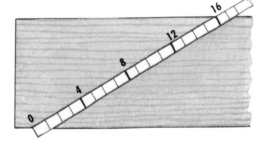

1 Set the ruler across the board and mark off four equal divisions.

2 Run parallel lines through the marked-off points.

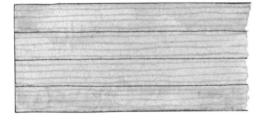

All being equal

When raw beginners to woodwork are faced with the challenge of how to divide an odd width board into a number of equal widths, they often make the mistake of trying to solve the mind-bending problem with a calculator and/or long-division arithmetic. Let's take it that your board is of a non-standard measurement—say somewhere between 2in to 15in (5cm to 38cm) wide—and you want to divide it into four equal widths. The wonderfully easy solution is to set a ruler or yardstick at a sloping angle across the board so that 0 is on one edge and 16in (40cm) is on the other. Mark it off at 4in, 8in, and 12in (10cm, 20cm, and 30cm), and then run parallel lines along the board. Easy, isn't it?

Cut lines

A classic mistake is to make a cut on the wrong side of a drawn line, so that the resulting joint is a bad fit. The best procedure is to lay out the shape of the joint first with a knife, ruler, and square. Next, check the measurements and the position of the joint against your working drawings. Then, shade in the areas that need to be cut away, and, finally, make a point of running the line of cut to the waste side of the drawn line—meaning on the shaded area. Make sure that the saw kerf is entirely in the waste wood, otherwise the thickness of the saw blade will be added to your measurements.

Unsquare square

It is plain to see that if your try square is at fault, then all your laying out is going to be less than perfect. To test that the square is really set to a right angle, first set it down on a length of straight-edged lumber so that the stock is butted hard up against the edge. Then draw a line along the steel edge. This done, flip the square over, keeping it butted to the same edge, and run a second line over the first. If you can't get the two lines to match up, then you need to get yourself another square. If you have a choice, go for an adjustable engineer's square.

1 Set the square against the stock and draw a line.

2 Flip the square over and attempt to draw a second line over the first.

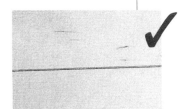

Point of reference

A frequent mistake made when marking-out a joint with the square and mortise gauge is forgetting to always limit your point of reference to the prepared good face and good edge. This potentially disastrous mistake can very easily be avoided, by simply making sure that you pencil-label the face side and face edge as soon as they have been achieved. Always make these face and edge marks clearly on the planed surfaces. It may help to use a pencil to mark the waste areas of a joint or board to make it clear which areas are to be removed.

Knife-cut accuracy

When you are running marks across a board, it is very easy to make a mistake simply by marking the line with a fat pencil. The problem is that if you cut to the waste side of a thick, blurred pencil line, then your measurements could be out by $\frac{1}{16}$in (1mm) or more. And, of course, if you mark-out all your stock with the same thick pencil, then the mistake will be compounded. The best procedure is to check and double-check the measurement requirements and then to accurately and delicately score the line with a knife. Get rid of that blunt pencil!

Sawing

Repeat accuracy

Mistakes often occur when two or more pieces have to be identically marked. What usually happens is that small inaccuracies creep in at both ends of all pieces, with the result that all lengths and joints are a poor match. To avoid this mistake, simply clamp the members together and square the marks across. For even closer accuracy when hand-sawing, you can set the blade down on the mark and then slide the square so that it is hard up against the blade.

For sawing precision, use a knife to score the line of cut.

Handsaw jams

If you want to avoid the very annoying problem of handsaw jams and slips, and/or it is essential that the ends of your workpiece be sawed perfectly square. It can be a good idea to run the marking knife or chisel at a sloping angle hard up against the waste side of the try square, so as to cut a channel in which the saw can run. This will also help to eliminate tear-out and is especially useful when cutting joinery.

1 Clamp all the members together so that the joint shoulders are aligned.

Board too short

One of the most bothersome blunders is to design a project to suit a limited number of carefully-selected boards, and then to find that one or other of the boards is easily wide enough but ever so slightly short. The good news is that you can save the work simply by slicing the board from corner to corner, so that you have two triangles. Then slide the two halves along so as to increase the length, being careful to match grain as best you can. Finally, glue the sliced halves back together.

1 Saw across the diagonals. Use a fine-toothed saw to avoid taking too much wood away in the saw kerf.

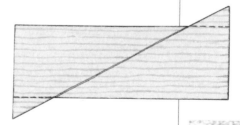

2 For super accuracy, set the knife point down at one end of the mark and slide the square up to the blade. Use a razorsharp craft or marking knife for cutting and regularly replace or re-hone the blade.

2 Realign the two pieces to achieve a greater length. Try to match up the grain of the wood once it is realigned.

Tips box

Of course, this extension method will always make a noticeable joint line that will spoil a board to be used on a very visible area of your project. In this case, check if you can alter the planned size or use a replacement board.

Board too narrow

If you find that one of your carefully-selected boards has plenty of length but is a little too narrow, you can saw it across the corners and offset and butt-glue the two halves in much the same way as described in the previous tip. Only this time, of course, you slide the boards along in the other direction so as to increase the width and decrease the length. If the board is to be used in a situation where strength is critical, reinforce the butt-glued joint with dowels or biscuits.

Wood shortages

If you make the classic mistake of optimistically estimating your matched stock and then find at the end of the day that you just don't have enough wood, then you may be able to make up what you need by splitting and laminating. The technique is very quick and easy. All you do is re-saw the board (through its thickness), glue common stock to your special wood and then plane down to the required thickness. This technique is especially useful when the back is hidden from view—as with tabletops, aprons, skirtings, plinths, and the like.

1 Use the band saw to slice the choice wood down into thick "veneers."

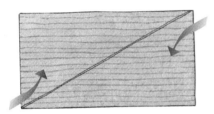

1 Saw across the diagonals. Again use a fine-toothed blade to give a clean, accurate cut—you may need to plane the cut surfaces of both boards to give a neat, close joint.

2 Glue the choice wood at either side of the common stock.

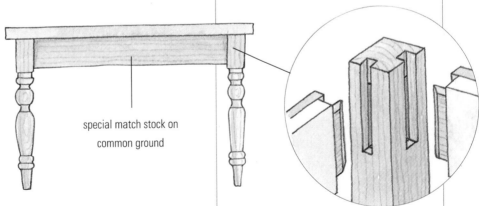

special match stock on common ground

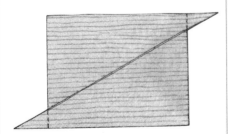

2 Realign the two pieces to achieve a greater width. Once you have made up the correct width, mark the board positions and add dowels or biscuits to reinforce the diagonal joint.

3 In this instance, you need only have the matched stock on the face that is in view on the finished project. Grain matching is less important for carcase work or on the back or interior of the project.

Tips box

Although laminating sections of matched board to make up the size required is fine for some projects, make sure the strength of a piece, such as a table rail or chair leg isn't compromised.

Short legs

If you make the mistake of sawing the legs on a table slightly too short, you will be faced with the problem of how to add a length to the legs without making a total mess of the design. The best solution is not to try to hide joints with paint or a splice—it is rarely successful—but instead to side-step the fact that a mistake was ever made by making sure that the added shoes, or castors, or turned buns, or blocks, or whatever, are made into a positive design feature. Use dynamic shape and wood color to draw the eye away from the seams.

Planing

Dirt damage

Dirt and planes are a really bad mix. What happens is that heavy boards are often repeatedly dropped on their ends when they are transported from the mill to the lumber yard, and the yard to the workshop. That means that the end grain is compacted with dirt. And, of course, when the wood gets to be planed in your shop, the dirt not only makes a mess of all the cutting edges, it also scratches the wood.

The best quick-fix is to routinely saw off a 1in (25mm) thick slice from the dirty ends before the stock is ever brought into the workshop.

ABOVE: It is often possible to add a section to the bottom of a leg that has been cut too short.

Saw off the plank end before you start machining.

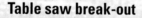

Table saw break-out

Crosscutting wood on table saws will normally result in slight splintering—known as break-out—on the underside. The problem is more acute when cutting veneered boards and plywood. Break-out can be avoided by inserting a sheet of hardboard underneath the workpiece and cutting through both layers at the same time. The hardboard supports the vulnerable cross-grain edge and contains the break-out. Splintering and break-out can also be reduced by choosing the right blade for the type of board you are cutting. A multi-purpose blade tends to do nothing very well. Invest in the right blade—look at the packaging to find which is the correct one.

remove dirt and paint

Board butting

A very common mistake, when jointing the edge of a long board that is going to be crosscut in half and then glued together edge-to-edge to make a wider board, is to finish up with an edge that is canted over at an angle. If this happens, don't go to all the trouble of jointing the edge again. Turn one or other of the boards around so that the angled edges butt together to cancel out the error.

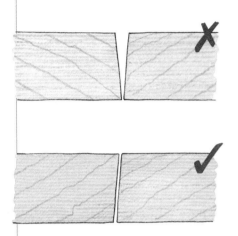

End grain split

If the wood begins to split off when you are planing end grain (for example, on a panel), you will have to first make a repair and then change your technique. The repair is simple enough; all you do is ease epoxy into the split, as already described, and clamp up. When the glue is set, pack out the end of the run with a block of scrap wood, clamp the block firmly in place and then plane as before. If the workpiece is small, then you could use a block plane.

1 If you plane across end grain, you risk splitting off the wood.

2 A sacrificial waster clamped hard up against the workpiece takes the brunt of the split-off.

Tear-out plugs

If, when you are jointing the edge of a length of wild-grained stock, a section lifts and tears, then the best remedy is to fit a boat-shaped plug—sometimes called a diamond "dutchman." The procedure is to remove the edge tear-out by making two angled saw cuts, cut a plug from matching stock, and then glue and clamp, and plane to a good finish. The secret of success is to use a fine-bladed saw and to be very careful that the two angled cuts meet without crossing—otherwise there will be a gap in the center of the repaired wood. Match the grain of the plug and glue in place. The new section should be at least a fraction oversized. When the adhesive is fully dry, use a small block plane to trim off the excess lumber and form a smooth blended edge to the repair. You can now joint up the boards with little evidence of the damaged edge.

Match the grain of the plug and glue in place.

Hand plane snipe

Many beginners to hand planing find that they repeatedly finish up with boards that are "sniped" or thinner at start and finish. This problem or mistake is easily corrected simply by pushing down on the knob at the forward end of the plane at the beginning of the stroke, and pushing down on the handle at the back end of the plane at the end of the stroke.

Work in long, even strokes and shift the weight progressively from the front to the back of the plane as you work. Or, put another way, imagine that you are trying to plane a hollow, and adjust your pressure and stroke accordingly. You should also have a comfortable stance so that you aren't overstretching to reach the far end of the board you are planing.

Warping and winding

If you are presented with a short board or panel that has warped or twisted along its length, then you will have to figure out a way of removing the wind. If the problem is with a small board – say the side of a cabinet—then the easiest solution is to use a hand plane to reduce the high corners. After using a couple of winding sticks to determine the severity of the wind and the position of the high spots, work the plane diagonally across the wood—from high spot to high spot—until the front face of the board is true.

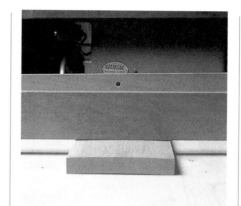

1 Sight across the winding sticks. If they are slightly off-parallel—as shown—then the surface is dipped.

2 Plane off the high spots and then rerun the sighting procedure.

Two-way planing

If you are a beginner to hand planing and have made the mistake of trying to through-plane a piece of wood that has a wild changing grain, then you will probably be presented with a board that has an area of torn grain.

The sure fix is first to set the plane blade so that it takes the finest of skimming cuts. Clarify how the grain runs and then make good by first planing in one direction and then the other.

Working diagonally across areas of wild grain introduces a shearing action instead of trying to plane directly along the board. You may still have to use a cabinet scraper to smooth the areas of wild grain. The minute raised burr (burl) on the scraper edge is capable of taking off wafer-thin shavings.

Plane tear-outs

If your typical metal hand plane digs into the board you are planing, there are several possible solutions. The simplest and most likely problem is that you have the blade or plane iron adjusted for too much depth of cut. If that's not the case, check that the chip-breaker, the part screwed to the back of the plane iron, is as close to the cutting edge as possible, and that there is no daylight between them when you look through from the side. If your plane has a lateral adjustment, make sure it is set so that the blade is perfectly parallel with the sole of the plane. A third possibility is that the frog, the triangular cast-iron part that the plane iron and chip-breaker assembly rests on, is set too far back. Move it forward so it fully supports the plane iron and so that the mouth of the plane is as small as possible.

1 The blade is set too far back – not enough depth.

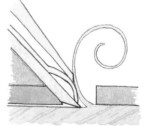

2 The blade is set too far forward—too much depth.

3 Sight along the plane and set the blade bevel parallel with the sole.

Routing

Disguise beads

If you have made a botched joint at some point along the line—say a really bad glued joint that is in full view—then you might be able to conceal the mistake by routing a decorative bead. Depending on the character of the workpiece, you might go for a mock tongue-and-groove bead, or a simple "V" groove reveal. Of course, if the bad joint is structurally important to the piece, disguising won't be enough.

1 This ragged joint is an ugly sight. The end grain forms a ragged edge that would be exaggerated if filler was used to fill the gap. The solution is to use a router and fence to clean up the line.

2 The "V" groove draws the eye away from the bad fit and finish. Use a router fitted with an edge profile cutter to hide similar problems.

Disguise banding

To disguise a badly-glued and clamped seam, a shallow groove can be routed to fit a length of decorative inlay banding. Keeping in mind that bandings vary in width and thickness, it is always a good idea to search out the banding before you start routing the groove.

1 A badly-glued and clamped seam will spoil the appearance of any project. Another method of disguising the problem is to add a decorative inlay along the joint line.

2 Rout a trench to fit a strip of inlay banding. You only need a shallow groove—slightly shallower than the thickness of the decorative inlay. Use a small ¼in (6mm) router and straight cutter for this part of the repair.

3 Glue the inlay in the trench and strap it in place with masking tape. Leave to dry completely and scrape or sand the finished joint until the decorative inlay is flush with the surrounding wood.

Right: Bandings are available in a variety of widths and thicknesses. Always choose your banding before you begin routing so that you can match it to the nearest size of straight cutter needed to make the groove. You could also use a scratchstock with a straight cutter to make the inlay recess adjacent to an edge.

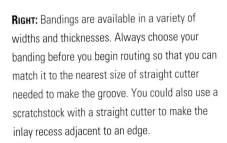

Panel tear-out

A very dangerous mistake made when routing is to swing your body around the router to the extent that you suddenly find yourself pulling instead of pushing. If this happens, the router bit invariably snags into end grain and does damage to one side of the panel. If you have made such a mistake, the best way of repairing it is first to saw off the damaged side of the panel and plane back to a straight, true edge. Then glue on an extra strip to make up the width, and finally rerun the router.

Follower bearings should be regularly checked for wear.

2 An ugly router "bite" needs fixing.

1 Be warned—if you find yourself pulling instead of pushing, then you are heading for trouble.

3 Saw off the damage, glue on a strip to make up the loss, and then take another run with the router.

Ragged edge

If you have made the mistake of trying to butt-joint two boards end to end, or you have a sawed end on a carcase—meaning one that runs out at the edge of the frame—you will almost certainly be presented with an unpleasant, ragged edge. If this is the case, then it can be made good by routing a chamfer, or a reveal, or a "V" groove that runs across the torn fibers.

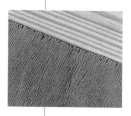

1 An unpleasant ragged edge needs fixing.

2 A "V" groove routed across the torn fibers is a good way of making an ugly mistake into a feature!

Jig mistake

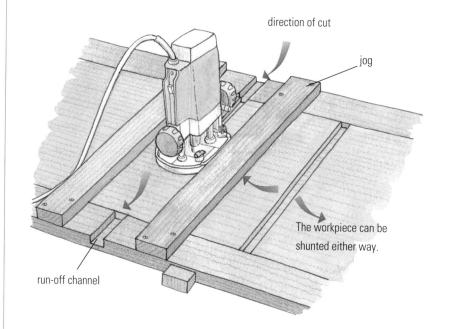

direction of cut

jog

run-off channel

The workpiece can be shunted either way.

Many router mistakes have to do with the jig being badly designed and/or inadequate. When designing a jig, it is best to have guide rails at both sides—to fit the base of the router. You will see that such an arrangement nicely counteracts the clockwise spin of the bit.

Cutting and fixing joints

Profile mess-up

The scenario: you are a beginner, and you have run a router profile around the edge of a panel, and it looks terrible—generally thin, mean, and ragged. The question is—what do you do? The answer is that you can't lose if you fit a larger bit in the router and run a second, more generous profile over the first.

A classic router error.

Make good by running a more generous profile run over the mistake.

Loose joints

If you have made the miscalculation of cutting a joint too loose, then a quick repair is to pack the joint out with shavings. First, cut a number of wedges from shavings—with the grain running along the length of the shaving. Then, one at a time, dip the shavings in PVA glue and tap them home into the sloppy joint. Finally, trim back with a sharp knife and sand or scrape down to a good finish.

1 Assess the size of the mistake—how big are the gaps?

2 Cut four thin wedges or shims to fit the gaps.

3 Dip the shims in glue and gently tap them home.

4 When the glue is dry, plane down to a good finish.

Jig run-out

A lot of mistakes have to do with sloppy practices. For example, many beginners to routing make the classic blunder of making contact with the workpiece before switching on the power or switching off the power before breaking contact. The best way of problem solving—especially when you are ploughing grooves and cutting housing channels—is to make a jig that completely frames the workpiece. In use, the router is switched on, lowered into the jig, run across the workpiece and into the other side of the jig, and then switched off and lifted out. Used in this way, the jig instead of the workpiece, bears the brunt of your switch-on blunders.

Loose dovetail

If you have cut a dovetail to the wrong side of a drawn line, the joint will be loose by the thickness of the drawn line—say about ⅟₁₆in (1mm) on both sides. The remedy is to glue strips of veneer to both sides of the tail, and then to trim to a tight fit and reglue.

1 Make up the thickness by gluing strips of veneer to the sides of the tails.

2 Glue and fit, and trim to a good finish.

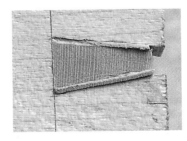

Laminated tenon

A frequent error when making rails is to reach the assembly stage—with the mortise-and-tenon joints all beautifully cut to a perfect fit—only to find that you have made the stupid mistake of cutting one or other of the rails about ½in (10mm) too short. If this happens, you can fix it by taking three lengths of thinner stock and laminating a three-layer extension to fit the tenon. If you choose your wood with care, and plane back to a good finish, then you will achieve a good, strong joint that will be almost invisible.

1 Cut three identical lengths of stock to fit the joint.

2 Glue and clamp the pieces in place.

3 When dry, plane the extension down to a good finish.

Stump tenon

A common mishap is to be cutting a delicate tenon and then to find that the wood has a hidden cavity or a twist in the grain that causes the tenon to break off, leaving you with a crisp shoulder and a ragged stump. If this happens, then the best thing to do is to trim the break back flush with the shoulder and cut a mortise in the end of the rail. Finally, cut and trim a loose tenon to fit both mortise holes, and glue it in place. Make sure that the loose tenon isn't too long.

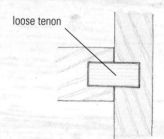

loose tenon

Glue the loose tenon in place and clamp up.

Diagonal wedge

A good way of fixing a badly-cut, through-mortise-and-tenon joint—meaning a joint that is so loose and sloppy that it just won't hold together—is to use a diagonal wedge. Let's say that there is an all-around gap of about ¹⁄₁₆in (1mm). The procedure is to run a saw cut from corner-to-corner down the length of the tenon and trim a thin hardwood wedge to fit. Next, spread glue over both faces of the wedge and drive it in place in the diagonal kerf. Drive the wedge in until the spreading tenon fills the mortise.

1 Mark across the diagonal and cut a slot.

3 Trim the wedge to a good fit-and-finish.

2 Tap a glued wedge down into the slot.

Foxtail wedge

If you have cut a loose-fitting blind tenon, the problem is how to fix it. You could pack the tenon out with veneers, but the best tried-and-true technique is to use a clever little device called a foxtail wedge. First, cut a wide wedge kerf down the length of the tenon, then a short fat wedge to fit, and finally glue and clamp. If you do it correctly, the fat end of the wedge will be driven hard up against the blind mortise, with the effect that the tenon spreads and holds.

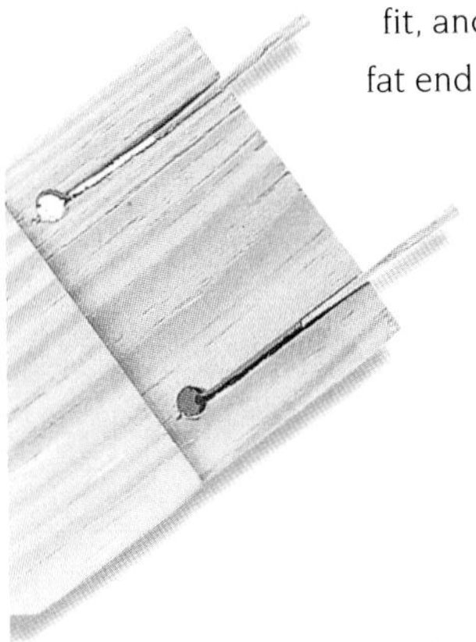

wedges

A double foxtail wedge

Double-wedge

If your through-mortise-and-tenon joint is tight across the cheeks but loose across the ends—so that the tenon slides lengthwise—the best repair is to double-wedge. This is easily achieved by cutting a matched pair of wedges, then gluing and driving them in place at both ends of the tenon.

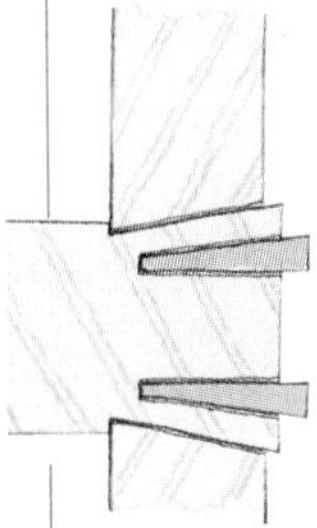

A beautiful double-wedged tenon.

Broken tenon

Picture this: you have cut and worked all the rails for a piece of furniture, and all the joinery is beautifully cut. Then, right at the last moment, one of the tenons crumbles and disintegrates. What is to be done? The answer is first to cut the damaged stub of the tenon back to the level of the shoulders. Then scribe the width of the tenon around to the underside of the rail. Saw and pare out the waste so that you are left with an angled bridle slot, and then cut and glue a wedge-tenon stub into the slot. If you have done it right, the repair will only be visible on the underside of the rail.

1 Cut the damage back to the shoulder and make two saw cuts—to match the tenon.

2 Pare out the angled bridle slot.

BELOW: Detail of the underside of the joint. From the top, the repair is invisible.

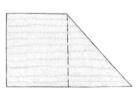

Cut the loose tenon to push-fit in the mortise.

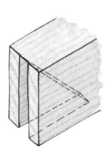

Bridle mortise slot

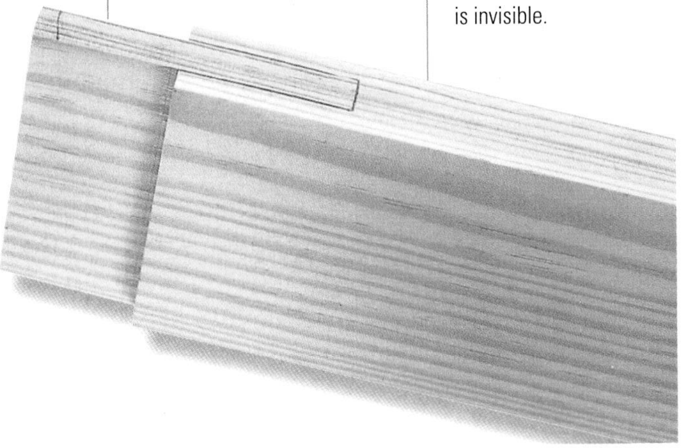

Basic lathe work

Gouge slip

The situation: the turning is three-quarters finished, and you accidentally let the gouge slip. Now there is a huge gash in the side of your otherwise beautifully-turned spindle. The response is not to rip the workpiece off the lathe and stamp on it. Just cut out the damage with two saw cuts, cut a matched wedge to fit, clean up mating faces, and then glue it in place with superglue. Finally, you can trim away the bulk of the patch with a knife and then turn it down to a good finish. It is best if all these procedures are done while the workpiece is still on the lathe.

1 A typical gouge slip.

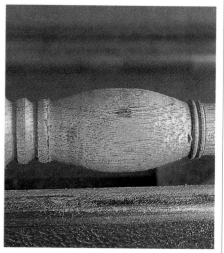

2 The repair is almost invisible.

Hidden cavity

It often happens in woodturning that the workpiece suddenly reveals an unexpected cavity. A quick fix is to plane the turning down to a level finish, glue and clamp a generous lump of well-matched wood to the level face—so that the run of the grain is perfectly aligned—and then turn the repair down to match the profile.

Broken spindle

If you make the almost routine mistake of snapping off a delicate spindle while it is being turned, the easiest repair is first to cut the spindle back to the nearest bead. Then drill, glue and dowel-fix a new length of wood to the sawed face. Finally, resume turning. If you have done it right, and the joint occurs in a valley or reveal, it will be almost invisible.

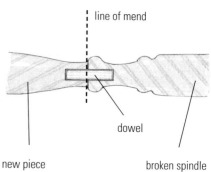

1 Use a small plane to level off the problem area.

2 Glue and clamp a piece of matched wood on the level face.

All taped up

A delicate spindle that starts to split at one or both ends while it is being turned can be rescued. All you do is wind back the tailstock slightly to release the tension, ease as much superglue as you can into the end cracks, strap the ends up with a dozen or so turns of masking tape, and then wind back the tailstock and continue turning. It is important to use a thin consistency of glue that will move by capillary action through the thin break. Hold pieces together firmly while the glue is drying.

line of mend

dowel

new piece

broken spindle

Make the repair at the bead line.

Stubby legs

Of all woodturning blunders, designing and making a table, dresser, or cupboard that is a little too short in the legs must surely come high in the "most stupid mistakes" list. That said, the mistake can easily be fixed by turning either a nice set of hardwood cups, or ball feet, or spigotted extensions in a contrasting wood. The secret of success is not to try to hide the additions, but instead to make them a positive feature.

Chuck registration

For swift and easy realignment, number the chuck jaws and the dents on the workpiece.

Although a four-jaw chuck is one of the best ways of making sure that the workpiece is held securely, if you do need to remove the workpiece for drilling or whatever, then it is not so easy to recenter. Consequently the workpiece is set slightly off-center and the turning is less than perfect. The problem of misalignment can be prevented simply by numbering the four jaws, and numbering the corresponding four dents on the workpiece made by the jaws before you remove the workpiece.

Bulging drawers

If you are building a drawer with glued slips under the base—instead of grooves—and you find at the assembly stage that the sides of the drawers bulge or bow, then a quick fix is to exchange the drawer sides, so that the bow occurs on the inside of the drawer. If you do this, the bowed sides will be pushed apart by the drawer base.

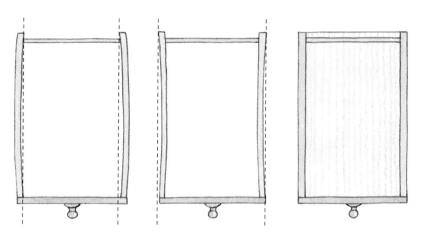

1 Drawer sides bulging out.

2 Change the drawer sides over so that they bulge in.

3 The drawer base will force the sides into alignment.

Block plane

If you find that your last-minute planing and cleaning up frequently results in wood splitting off—as when cleaning up the corners of a dovetail joint—chances are you are making the mistake of using a plane that has a high-angled cutter. The recipe for success in this situation is simply to use a block plane. Although this solution might on the face of it seem too easy, the fact is that the design of the block plane—the set of the blade—is such that there is less tendency for the grain to break off. For better results, use a special low-angle block plane that has the blade set even shallower.

Get yourself a small block plane—the size and low blade angle make it ideal for quality cuts.

Tear-outs

Tear-out is one of the most common and one of the most annoying of all woodworking mistakes. A blade is too dull, or you are trying to hurry a job that won't be rushed, or you twist a saw, and before you know it, one of the component parts is torn. The great news is that all such small rips, splits, and tears can easily be repaired with superglue. Just dribble the glue into the tear, strap up with a clamp or tape, wait a few minutes, and then go back to work. Don't leave the tear to gather dirt, dust, and dirt—it must be repaired immediately.

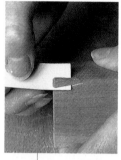

1 Use a strip of paper to ease glue into the tear-out.

2 Strap up the repair with tape—until the glue is set.

Noisy drawers

Fitting drawers is always something of a problem. Either they are too tight, or too loose, or warped across the corners, and so on. If you have a real problem drawer, one that is loose, noisy, a little bit twisted, and with slightly warped sides, you can go a long way to putting it right by simply cutting a bottom that is perfectly square and slightly too tight. What happens is that when the oversized bottom is gently eased into place, it tends to pull the drawer tight and true.

Glue and shavings

Huge glue squeeze-out is a nuisance in the workshop and a general all-round mistake. You should use only as much glue as is necessary for good bonding. That means little squeeze-out. But if you do make a big mess, it is a good idea to mop up the excess glue with shavings. For example, if you have glued up a stack of slabs to make a blank for turning a bowl, and you intend to clamp the whole thing in the jaws of the vise, then you could spread shavings on the floor under the vise to catch the glue ooze.

Dry-run clamping

A frequent woodworking complaint goes something like, "The project was fine until I came to gluing up." The primary mistakes that most beginners make when they come to gluing are: they try to do everything in a rush; they fail to spread a thin layer of glue on all mating surfaces; and, worst of all, they simply aren't organized. Okay, so there's no denying that you do need to have the correct tools and materials for the job, but that said, you should always have one or more dry-run sessions before you ever touch the glue. It is most important that everything is close at hand, and you know the assembly sequence.

Determine the working area, the type and condition of the clamps, the type of glue, and the number of wooden pads—all before you start smearing on the glue.

Pieces of cork floor tile make excellent padding between clamp heads and vulnerable wood.

Animal glue

A frequent mistake made when using hot animal glue is to be so generous that the glue collects in the corners and holes. The difficulty is how to remove the hard build-up without swamping the frame in hot water. The solution is to heat up an old chisel and then to hold the chisel on the glue in such a way that when the hot chisel starts to melt the glue, the liquid runs down the shaft. This can be a tricky process if you can't angle the chisel in a confined space. You may have to wait until the glue is fully hardened and then use the chisel blade as a scraper to remove the excess.

Dribbling glue

If you are using white glue and you are so generous with the glue that it runs in a huge dribble down the front of your project, never be tempted to wipe it off with a cloth. Leave it until the glue becomes rubbery—about 15 to 30 minutes. Then you can gently peel off the excess with the help of a chisel. Even if the glue hardens, it is much easier to chisel off a bead of rock-hard glue that is sitting on the surface than it is to sand off glue that has been smeared into the pores.

1 Don't be tempted to wipe the glue off with a cloth.

2 Wait until the glue dribble is transparent and rubbery, then pare it off with a chisel.

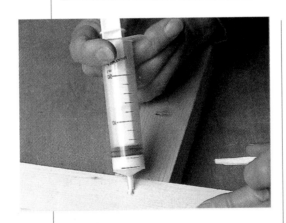

1 Use a syringe to flood the loose joint with glue.

2 Drive in the dowel to force the glue into all parts of the joint cavity.

Dry joints

If, after you have glued up and removed the cramps, you discover that one or other of the joints is loose and dry, run a small diameter hole down through the joint – in one side and out the other – and inject as much glue as you can into the joint. Finally, while the glue is still runny, drive dowels into the holes to pump the glue into the very heart of the joint.

Cleaning leather and cloth

Most people think that old leather on a chair needs replacing, but brittle and stained old leather can be easily cleaned with saddle soap. This is readily available from hardware and riding stores. Old cloth can be revived using a fabric shampoo. When applying the shampoo try to keep the cloth as dry as possible; pat rather than rub the surface and then use the chisel blade as scraper to remove any excess.

Fittings, fixtures, and hardware

Screw dowels

A common mistake made by beginners is to butt joint and screw two members to make a right-angled frame and then to find that the screws won't hold in the end grain. The problem is, of course, that by the time the joint fails, it has usually been covered or built in at the back and front. The quick fix is to draw out the screws, drill and dowel at right angles across the line of the screw holes, and then to replace the screws so that they run through the sides of the dowels. For best results, use the largest diameter dowels and smear them with glue before driving them home.

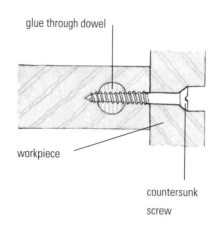

glue through dowel

workpiece

countersunk screw

Arrange the dowel so that the screw runs across the grain.

Drive the screw through the joint and on into the dowel.

Deep-set hinge

A frequent blunder when instaling hinges is to cut the hinge mortises too deep. Then the door either fails to close or threatens to tear the stile. If this is the problem, then insert one or more strips of cardboard or veneer packing to fit the hinge mortise until the door closes to a good tight fit.

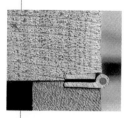

A well-set hinge.

Use strips of cardboard to pack out an overly deep hinge mortise.

Bigger hinge

If you cut a recess too big for your hinge—too long and too wide—sometimes a quick fix is simply to buy a bigger hinge and recut the recess to fit. This time around, don't make the same mistake. Alternatively, patch the recess and start again.

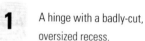

1 A hinge with a badly-cut, oversized recess.

2 Select a hinge that is bigger than the incorrect recess and then recut it to the correct size.

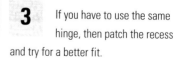

3 If you have to use the same hinge, then patch the recess and try for a better fit.

Wedged knobs

If you have a drawer with oversized knob holes but don't much like the idea of the glue and twine, you can saw a slot in the tenon. Once you set the knob in place, tap a glued wedge into the slot from the inside of the drawer. Once the glue dries, cut the wedge back flush with the drawer. If you think you might want to change the knobs at a later date, then skip the glue and the trimming.

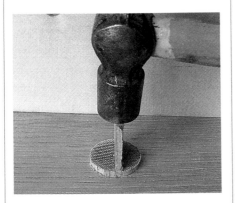

1 Arrange the knob so that the slot runs across the drawer front grain, and tap the glued wedge home.

2 Plane the tenon back flush with the inside face of the drawer.

Wider spade holes

If you have to redrill, for example, a ½in (10mm) diameter hole with a 1in (25mm) spade bit, the difficulty is that the larger bit may wander because it doesn't have anything to center on. The neatest solution is to cut a length of dowel to slide nicely into the ½in (10mm) hole, and then center the large-sized bit on the plug.

1 Cut a dowel to fit the hole.

2 Center the larger bit on the plug and redrill.

Loose knobs

A nasty little mistake when making and fitting traditional turned wooden knobs to drawers—meaning knobs with round tenons designed to be glued into holes—is to oversize the hole in the drawer front so the knob tenon is too loose. If this is the case, the simplest solution is to dip the tenon in glue, wind thin twine around the glued tenon until it is a bit too big for the drawer hole, and then push and twist the whole piece into place.

Broken screws

If you have made the frustrating mistake of twisting the head off a screw—and it is an easy mistake to make if you are using brass screws without pilot holes—don't worry. All you need to do is cut a short length of the smallest possible diameter steel tube that will fit over the screw. Then file a few cuts across one end of the tube, and use the tube like a miniature hole saw to run a drilled hole down around the screw. This done, you can twist out the core with the broken screw, glue and plug the hole with matching wood, and then rescrew—but this time, drill a pilot hole for the screw.

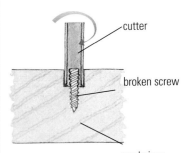

cutter

broken screw

workpiece

Use of pair of pliers to remove the core and the damaged screw.

Veneers and inlay

Veneer miter

Thin veneers are a great way of covering up mistakes. Let's say that you have made a picture frame with four horrible miters, and the design is such that a ¹⁄₁₆in (1mm) thickness isn't going to be noticed. All you do is cut four strips of veneer and cross them over at the corner. Then run a steel rule across the intersection and use a sharp knife to cut through both strips at once. Remove the waste and then stick down as described in the following tips.

1 Arrange the two strips so that they intersect at right angles.

2 Slice across the diagonal.

Edge tear-up

You have veneered a panel, say the side of a cabinet, and you make a clumsy move that results in the edge getting torn. The quick fix is to first take a piece of nicely-matched veneer and tape it in place over the damaged area so that the grain is aligned. Then cut through the double layer and down to the base board or substrate. Use a sharp chisel to pare the substrate to a smooth finish. Next apply coated cement and set in the veneer patch.

Cut through the double layer to achieve a perfectly-sized patch.

Blistering veneer

It sometimes happens that a small air pocket gets trapped under veneer, with the result that there is a bump or blister. The best way to solve this problem is first to use a craft knife to slit the blister along the line of the grain. If you have used PVA or animal glue, you can reglue with a hot iron. If, however, the veneer was originally stuck down with urea-formaldehyde glue, then squeeze superglue into the slit and apply pressure with a waxed block.

1 Carefully slit the blister along the line of the grain.

2 Use a sliver of paper to introduce thermo-reactive glue into the heart of the blister.

3 Use a hot iron to fix.

Tips box

Often a curved edge of a table or cabinet will show signs of damage as the veneer that has been curved around the profile loosens or is knocked and chipped. When you replace the curved veneer, you may need to make a shaped wood former, which follows the curve on the edge and can be clamped over the veneer to keep it in place as it dries.

Lift and patch

A nasty problem that occasionally crops up when veneering is that a loose knot in the groundwork crumbles and rises, with the result that there is a solid bump under the veneer. If this happens, you have to either scrap the whole job or lift and repair. The remedy is to cut a patch as already described—one that is larger than the bump. Then use the chisel to cut out the damaged substrate and make a diamond-shaped recess. Glue and plug the recess. When the glue is dry, trim the plug down to a good finish, and finally fit the veneer patch with contact cement.

Edge lift

Beginners often over-clamp and/or over-sand the edges of veneered work, with the result that the edge lifts and is at risk of breaking off. If this is your problem, set the tabletop or other veneered workpiece on its edge on a pad of scrap carpet so that the edge lift is facing up. Then use the blade of a craft knife to work as much PVA glue as possible down between the veneer and the substrate. When you are sure that the glue has run deeply into the pocket, wipe away any excess, and clamp up with blocks and "G" clamps. Be sure to place wax paper between the blocks and the workpiece.

1 Use a craft knife and a piece of foil to ease the glue down the cavity.

2 Place wet wax paper between the workpiece and the blocks, and the clamp.

Total lift

A frequent mistake made by beginners who use heat-activated glues is that they overheat and overwork the veneer to the point that it needs to be lifted and re-attached. If this is the case, the safest procedure is to cover the whole sheet of veneer with edge-to-edge strips of masking tape, and then carefully ease the whole layer up with a hot iron and hot scraper. You will need help—one person to be ironing and lifting, and the other person to be working the warm scraper underneath the veneer. When you come to re-attach the veneer, start from one side, all the while making sure that the glue is melting, and that stuck-down areas are free from air pockets.

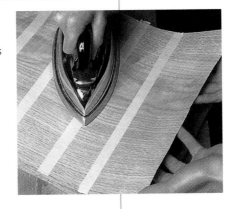

1 Reinforce the problem veneer with straps of masking tape running across the grain.

2 Melt the glue while a friend gently eases and lifts the veneer.

Panel warp

A mistake made by some beginners to veneering is that they veneer only one side of their work. Because the veneered side reacts differently to seasonal changes in moisture and humidity, and especially if the substrate is a thin board, then it usually warps. If this happens, the quick fix is to balance the stress by veneering the other side of the board. Suppliers sell inexpensive veneers for this purpose.

Mahogany is commonly used for balancing.

Pine—a more sustainable wood—is also suitable for balancing.

Cracks and hollows

If, after you have completed a piece of marquetry or parquetry, you find that there are little hollows between neighboring veneers, then the chances are that you have made the mistake of using a water-based contact adhesive. If this is the case, you can fill the cracks with a mix of veneer sawdust and PVA glue.

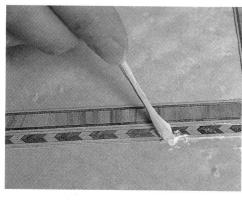

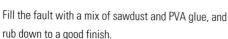

Fill the fault with a mix of sawdust and PVA glue, and rub down to a good finish.

Warped stock

What do you do if you have spent good money on a piece of expensive veneer and then find that it starts to warp and buckle? The answer is, having first repeatedly dampened, pressed and dried the veneer—between boards and under weights—brush the "glue" face of the veneer with wallpaper sizing, sandwich it between sheets of wax paper, and press it under weighted boards until it is dry. This will usually leave the veneer as flat as a pancake and ready to use.

1 Saturate the warped veneer with water and brush on a coat of wallpaper sizing—on the face to be glued.

2 Set the veneer between sheets of wax paper.

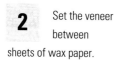

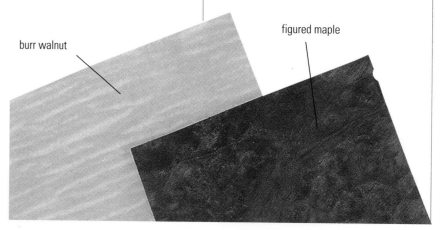

burr walnut

figured maple

Cuts and scratches

If you slip with your knife to the extent that some small part of the veneer is scratched across the grain, you will be left with a mark that needs attention before it fills up with dirt and dust. The remedy is first to dribble a few drops of water on the cut. Then take the finest knife and scratch in line with the grain and across the cut. Do this on both sides of the cut so as to raise and fluff up the grain and conceal the damage.

1 What a mistake to make!

2 Dampen the scratch and gently tease the fibers with the point of the knife.

3 Tease in the direction of the grain until the scratch vanishes from view.

3 Sandwich the whole thing between boards and press with a heavy weight.

Finishing, assembly, and showing

Of all the woodworking stages, the culmination of assembly, laying on coats of varnish and oil, and generally adjusting everything to a fine fit and finish is both the most exciting and the most nerve-racking. At last the project is finished and on show—the character of the wood, your designing and construction skills—everything is on view. And of course, because you are exhausted and excited, this is where you are going to make some really basic mistakes. But not to worry, just take it nice and easy, and stay with the following tips.

A classic example of varnish bloom.

Blooming blush

If you have made the mistake of brushing on varnish or lacquer on a day when the humidity is too high, your workpiece may develop a condition known as blush or bloom: the varnish will look white and cloudy. The secret is not to panic, but instead to wait a day or two and see what happens. If you are lucky, the blush will disappear on its own. If you are not so lucky, give the workpiece a swift sanding with the finest garnet paper and lay on another thin coat of varnish or lacquer. Follow the finish manufacturer's recommendations for temperature and humidity during application.

Burn-in sticks

Wax filler sticks, called burn-in sticks, are a bit like children's crayons. They are a great quick-fix product for filling in all those dents and scratches that sometimes happen when the piece of furniture is transported. For very minor repairs, you just choose a color to match your finish, then rub the wax stick into the small scratch or hole, and finally polish the repair to a good finish. If the hole is more than about ⅛in (2mm) deep, it's best to apply the burn-in stick according to the manufacturer's directions, with a hot knife.

1 Use a hot knife or soldering iron to puddle the dent with colored wax.

2 Rub the repair down with fine-grade garnet paper.

3 Continue rubbing down until you achieve a good finish.

Falling forward

If you have made the classic mistake of designing and building a tall cabinet or bookcase that falls forward when the upper doors are opened, a good tip is to take a shaving or two off the bottom back edge. Then the whole piece will lean slightly back against the wall.

Fuzzy grain

Some woods are very difficult to bring to a good, smooth finish. No matter how hard you try, the grain raises and generally goes fuzzy. The best procedure for achieving a smooth finish is to lay on a glue sizing mix to seal the surface and raise the grain. Let it dry before using a cabinet scraper to skim off the raised grain. Resist the temptation to use sandpaper—a scraper does the job better.

1 Brush size on the fuzzy surface and leave it to dry.

2 Use a scraper to cut the grain nibs down to a good finish.

Dented varnish

Although at first sight a dent in beautiful, clear varnish finish can look to be a huge mistake, it can easily be removed by adding more coats of the same varnish. All you need to do is touch in a dab of varnish and let it dry, then touch in another dab and let it dry, and so on, until the dent has been filled up. Don't be tempted to fill the dent by pouring the varnish—if you do, it will pucker.

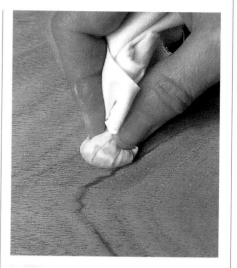

1 Dab a small amount of varnish into the dent.

2 Repeat until the dent has been filled up.

3 Rub the dry varnish down with fine-grade garnet paper.

4 Use metal polish to cut the repair down to a polished finish.

Burn marks

Though a cigarette burn is one of those really annoying mistakes that shouldn't be allowed to happen, the truth is that cigarette burns are common. The simple repair is not to try to remove the burn mark with sandpaper, but instead to scrape the burn out with a cabinet scraper. Run the scraper diagonally across the grain—first one way and then the other—and then finish up by scraping parallel to the grain.

1 Run the scraper diagonally across the grain.

2 Work the whole area—in all directions—until the burn mark has been cut back.

Varnish bubbles

Although you can't do much about bubbles that have dried in a coat of varnish—other than to scrape off the varnish and start again—you can make sure that you don't make the same mistake the next time around. The best procedure is only to brush on thin coats of varnish, and to always let one coat dry before you attempt to apply another.

Scrape the varnish off and start again.

GLOSSARY

Aluminum oxide

A long-life grit for abrasive wheels and papers.

Awl

A type of marking tool.

Back (or tenon) saw

Used for small work on the benchtop.

Banding

Thin, narrow strips of different-colored woods made up in patterns and inlaid into grooves cut in cabinet work as a decorative feature.

Batten

Square strips of wood of varying size.

Beading

A semi-circular cut in a molding.

Bench stop

A wood insert, passed through the bench top close to the left-hand end, against which wood can be held when planing.

Bevel

A tool used for setting off angles, as in dovetailing.

Biscuit

A thin, flat, oval of compressed beech that is inserted between two pieces of wood into mating saw kerfs made by a biscuit or plate joining machine.

Book matched

A board sliced in half through its thickness, and then joined together so that the back of the top section mirrors the top of the bottom section, like the page of a book. This match can also be made with consecutive sheets of veneer sliced from the same tree.

Building up

The stage in French polishing when the polish is applied to give depth to the finish.

Bull nose plane

A plane for cutting close into a corner. The cutter is very close to the front of the plane.

Burr

An excrescence found on many trees, usually formed around an injury to the trunk. Valued for veneers. Also known as burl.

Calipers

Both outside and inside —used for measuring curved work.

Carcase

The main body or frame of a piece of cabinet work.

Carver's screw

A screw turned into the base of a carving, passed through the bench and screwed down with a wing nut to hold the carving securely.

Caul

A metal plate used in veneering. It is warmed and applied to the veneer to keep it in position while the glue is setting.

Chamfering

Cutting a square edge equally on both sides of a piece of wood to form a bevel.

Cheek

The face of a tenon, center lap or end lap, the long-grain walls of a mortise, or the long-grain mating surfaces of dovetails and their pins or box pin joint fingers.

Chip carving

Shallow carving in straight lines and geometric forms.

Clamp

A tool that holds pieces of wood or other items together.

Compass plane

Sometimes called a circular plane, it has a flexible sole that can be set for convex or concave cutting.

Cove

A concave cut.

Cupping

A drying defect where one side of the board shrinks across the grain more than the other, causing the board to curl in on itself like a trough.

Cut back

Rubbing a finish with fine, abrasive paper until the finish is flat and smooth.

Dado

A groove or housing made across the grain.

Dowel

A round pin or peg used in jointing.

End grain

Lumber grain that shows when a piece is cut transversely.

Fad

A pear-shaped piece of wadding used to apply French polish to nooks and crannies and as the core of a polishing rubber.

Fence

A part of a tool designed to limit movement, as in the fence of the plow plane.

Fillet

A strip of wood added to the work as either a guide or a support.

Flat (or spade) bit

Designed for use in the electric drills.

Forstner bit

An auger bit that runs on its periphery, used exclusively for boring shallow, flat-bottomed holes.

French polish

Shellac and denatured alcohol mixed to produce a polish, which is also supplied as garnet, white, pale, button, and transparent polish.

Gesso

A pigmented plaster that can be formed into a molding, as in a picture frame.

Green wood

Unseasoned or newly felled lumber that has not been dried.

Haunch

A secondary shoulder cut into the edge of a tenon.

Glossary

Heartwood
The center of a log that has stopped growing, and is usually darker and harder than the outer layer of sapwood.

Holdfast
A clamping device, dropped through a hole in the benchtop and used to secure wood for carving and other work.

Honing guide
A device to hold chisels and plane cutters at a constant angle during sharpening on an oilstone.

Housing
A milled cut, usually a rebate, dado, or groove, but sometimes a pocket, which encloses all or part of a mating piece.

Inlay
A form of decoration where pieces of wood and other materials are set into a base of wood and left flush.

Kerf
The visible path or subtracted wood left by a sawblade.

MDF (Medium Density Fiberboard)
Fiberboard, similar to chipboard, but denser. Made from wood dust bonded by a resin.

Marquetry
The art of combining veneers of different colors and figurings to produce pictures.

PVA (poly-vinyl acetate)
A general-purpose, water-based wood adhesive.

Parquetry
A geometric pattern constructed from inlaid pieces of wood, often of different textures and colors. Parquetry is most frequently employed in flooring.

Pass
The single movement of a plane along a piece of lumber or the movement of a piece of lumber through a machine.

Pigments
Colors that do not dissolve, but are suspended in a medium to produce opaque colors. Mixed with paints, scumbles, and glazes.

Pilot hole
A small drilled hole, used as a guide and pressure relief for screw insertion, or to locate additional drilling work like countersinking and counterboring.

Rebate
A square recess along the edge of a piece of wood. Also known as a rabbet.

Ripping
Sawing down the length of a board, with the grain.

Router
A hand or machine tool used to make a variety of cuts.

Rubber
A pad, made from cotton wadding and covered with cotton sheet, used to apply French polish.

Saw set
A pincerlike tool for setting saw teeth.

Scraper
Used in the hand to finish after planing.

Scratch stock
A small tool used to cut shallow recesses for inlaying.

Scribe
To make layout lines or index marks using a knife or awl.

Scumbles
A semi-transparent stain for application over an opaque base of paint.

Shellac resin
A resin secreted by the lac beetle that is only soluble in alcohol or an alkaline solution of water. When dissolved in alcohol it is known as French polish.

Silicon carbide grit
Used on wet-and-dry abrasive papers. The paper and glue are waterproof, permitting the paper to be used wet.

Skew chisel
For planing wood between lathe centers, squaring, beading, curving, and tapering.

Spindle gouge
Round-nosed gouge for coving in spindle work on the lathe.

Spokeshave
A cutting tool with two handles used for small curved work. It has a similar action to the plane.

Stile
The vertical component of a frame.

Story pole
A layout stick that holds the actual-sized project in section view. Also known as a gauge rod.

Tail vise
A vise at the end of a bench that uses dogs to clamp boards for planing, etc.

Template
A piece of thin, rigid material that has been accurately cut to facilitate the repeated, precise marking out of a shape. Also known as a templet.

Tongue
A thin sliver or wood glued into a slot sawed horizontally across a mitre to strengthen the joint. Also known as a spline.

Twisting
A drying defect in wood that causes it to twist so the faces at each end of the board are in a different plane.

Veiner
A tiny, deep "U"-shaped gouge used in texturing and veining.

White polish
Hydrocarbon solvent used to thin oil stains, scumbles, gold size, and glazes.

Yankee screwdriver
A screwdriver having a spiral ratchet for easy screwing.

INDEX

Picture credits

The material in this book previously appeared in the following titles:

Basic Woodworking Techniques; The Carpenter's Companion; The Complete Guide to Woodworking; The Encyclopedia of Joint Making; The Encyclopedia of Wood; 100 Keys to Woodshop Safety; Mastering Hand Tool Techniques; 100 Keys to Preventing and Fixing Woodworking Mistakes; How to Restore and Repair Furniture; The Craft of Woodcarving; The Complete Guide to Wood Finishes; Woodworking School; The Woodworker's Solution Book; The Woodworker's Pocket Palette; The Book of Boxes; The Encyclopedia of Woodworking Techniques; Two Books in One: Woodturning; The Art & Craft of Making Children's Furniture; Painted Wooden Furniture. p43, 93: © Groupe Eyrolles

Acknowledgments

Quantum Publishing would like to thank the following people and organizations for their assistance in the production of this book:

Caroline Hunt for proofreading, Heather McCarry for DTP design, Dawn Butcher for the index, Coyote Editorial and Language Service for Americanization; and The Woodworker magazine for providing images of electric planers (p.112) and the Workbench project (pp.251-256).